Readings in American Government

EIGHTH EDITION

Mary P. Nichols
David K. Nichols
Baylor University

Kendall Hunt
publishing company

MARY P. NICHOLS teaches political theory at Baylor University.

DAVID K. NICHOLS teaches in American politics in the department of political science at Baylor University.

Cover images courtesy of Corel and © 2004 PhotoDisc, Inc.

Kendall Hunt
publishing company

www.kendallhunt.com
Sent all inquiries to:
4050 Westmark Drive
Dubuque, IA 52004-1840

Contents

Chapter I

The Founding and the Principles of Government

The Declaration of Independence states the principles of equality and freedom which provide the basis for an American public philosophy. American politics has revolved around interpretation and applications of those principles. Abraham Lincoln provides a classic statement of the meaning of the Declaration when he argues against the institution of slavery. The equality of rights proclaimed by the Declaration, he argues, was meant to function as a goal or standard for Americans to revere and to seek to approximate in their politics.

The equal rights that legitimate governments protect, according to the Declaration, include the rights to life, liberty, and the pursuit of happiness. Men are equal in their possession of freedom. But when equality is interpreted to mean an equal right to rule, or democratic government, a conflict between equality and freedom might result. The Lincoln-Douglas exchange reveals the danger in deriving an unqualified majority rule from the principle of equality. Douglas, supporting state sovereignty on the question of slavery, argues that slavery should be permitted in a state if a majority of its people desire it. In contrast to Douglas, Lincoln maintains that no majority can legislate slavery because that institution deprives men of their inalienable rights. There are some things that are not open to majority decision. It is necessary to limit majority rule by the ends of government stated in the Declaration.

Martin Diamond argues that the Declaration actually leaves open the possibility that other forms of government besides democracy may be legitimate. The principle of equality in the Declaration, according to Diamond, demands only that governments protect the inalienable rights of men and that they be based on the consent of the governed. Majority rule is only one way to achieve the legitimate end of government. While the Declaration established both the legitimate end and foundation of government, it is the Constitution, Diamond argues, that institutes a democracy, although one that tries to check majority rule in order to safeguard the end of government—security of rights.

The Founders, then, tried to establish a government that would combine the ends given in the Declaration with majority rule. Alternate means to these ends, the Virginia and the New Jersey Plans, were presented at the Constitutional Convention. The Virginia Plan assumes that only a strong

1

national government would protect liberty, while the New Jersey Plan reflects a concern that a strong national government operating over a large territory would eventually destroy liberty and prevent the people from governing themselves. This small republic argument is stated by the Anti-Federalist Centinel: a republic is possible only in a small territory, since only a despotism could hold a large country together. Madison, one of the authors of the Virginia Plan, gives his answer to the partisans of the small republic in his account to Jefferson of what happened at the Convention. He says that those who oppose a strong national government fearing that its distance from the people would lead to tyranny forget that majorities too can be tyrannical. They trust majorities, says Madison, because they assume that the local population is homogeneous in character, with no conflicts of interest among the parts.

Indeed, for Madison, the way to prevent majority tyranny is to establish a large republic with a flourishing commerce. Since commerce over a large territory produces many different interests, especially those based on different kinds of property, no one interest could form a majority of the whole. Majorities would be composed of a large number of smaller groups which would have to moderate their demands in order to form majorities. A tyrannical majority would therefore be less likely. Separation of powers, checks and balances, and bicameralism are institutional arrangements that work together with the extended sphere of the large republic to protect liberty. As in the formation of majorities by coalition, interest will counteract interest, in a system that necessitates compromise and mutual accommodation.

John Adams, like Madison, sought to prevent despotism and preserve liberty by the working of self-interest. And in this regard, bicameralism is a crucial part of Adam's theory of government. For Adams, however, the Senate was to represent the wealthy class of citizens, and the House to represent the poor; and since the concurrence of both was necessary to pass laws, neither class could oppress the other. Adams is perhaps too optimistic about the ability of such simple means to achieve the desired end of accommodating rich and poor to each other, and he fails to see, as did Madison, that the people of a large commercial republic would form groups not so much on the basis of the amount of property as on the kind of property they own. Indeed, Madison thought that the large commercial republic would overcome divisions between rich and poor—precisely what Adams sought to institutionalize. Because Madison understood that the two houses of Congress would not represent different classes, he sought to ensure their dissimilarity by institutional means.

Hamilton too is well aware of the benefits of economic self-interest, but attempts to elevate its operation in government above the mean or petty. At the Constitutional Convention he proposed life tenure for Senators in order to give the office sufficient power and prestige to interest the best citizens. He doubted that a shorter term "would induce the sacrifices of private affairs, which an acceptance of public trust would require, so as to ensure the services of the best citizens." He had written earlier that the best legislator would consider it "not more the duty, than the privilege of his office, to do good to mankind; from this commanding eminence, he would look down on any mean or interested pursuit." Intrigue for personal aggrandizement, Hamilton thought, would be inconsistent with the legislator's "dignity of pride" and "delicacy of honor."

Hamilton gives a higher tone to the notion of a commercial republic, as he did to the self-interest of a legislator. In Federalist 11, he shows how union will bring commercial prosperity. United, America could establish a navy to protect her ships, set the terms for foreign trade, "make herself the admiration and envy of the world"; divided into separate states she would suffer "poverty and disgrace." The economic strength derived from union is a condition for political strength, but should the states remain separate, Europe could confine them to merely "passive commerce" and thereby be able to "prescribe the conditions of [their] political existence." The country's ability to command respect depends on its strength. Our neutrality will be respected, Hamilton writes, only when it is defended by an adequate power; a country "despicable in its weakness" forfeits even the privilege of being neutral. While Madison favors union because it provides the large size necessary to moderate the conflict of the parts, Hamilton favors union because it overcomes the debilitating and petty conflict of the parts.

Hamilton's argument for a standing army suggests that in a commercial republic men are preoccupied by their private affairs, pursuing their own economic gain. It is for this reason we cannot rely on a militia, whose members would not wish to leave their occupations and families in peacetime. But why would such private men take delight, as Hamilton does, in America as the "admiration and envy of the world"? Would such men be the material out of which Hamilton could forge America's strength? Must not there be something more than commercialism to make Hamilton's splendid commercial republic? Tocqueville explains how men in times of equality have a passion for physical well-being, or a desire to satisfy even the least wants of the body. Men continually seek greater wealth and fear economic ruin. As Tocqueville describes him, the American is not someone who would look down on anything from "a commanding eminence." Although Hamilton thought that properly promoted commercial activity would be "the wings" enabling America to "soar to dangerous greatness," Tocqueville thought that commercial activity in times of equality produces only mediocrity.

Furthermore, although the commercial man Tocqueville describes would be a good member of the groups of which Madison hoped majorities would be formed, he might not be a good citizen of a republican or self-governing community. The Anti-Federalists, somewhat more than the Federalists, were concerned with the good character of the citizenry. When the Centinel asks how the happiness of the community can come from "jarring adverse interests," he is not asking about the efficacy of coalition majorities and checks and balances, but about the quality of life in a republic where such expedients set the tone of life. The alternative he suggests is not the aristocratic society described by Tocqueville, where only a few can attain a lofty greatness, nor Hamilton's complex, industrious society infused with pride. Rather, Centinel longs for a simple society of citizens whose liberties are preserved by their own participation in a government close to them and simple enough for them to understand. Checks and balances are not needed to prevent majority tyranny, for the people are virtuous and there are no great disparities in wealth.

The Anti-Federalists and Hamilton both have reservations against the low character of the commercial republic. Hamilton attempted to elevate the commercial spirit to great heights, and endow Americans with strength of character and breadth of vision. The Anti-Federalists, in contrast, emphasized simple or unchecked democracy, virtue in the citizens, and public spiritedness as the best means to preserve republican liberty. These reservations against the commercial republic have continued to this day in various forms, for each represent legitimate, if conflicting, aspirations. Indeed, the American regime itself is constituted by a tension or dialogue between the commercial republic and the reservations against it.

Jefferson shares with the Anti-Federalists a concern with republican liberty. He desired to divide the country into wards or "small republics" where every citizen transacted in person the public business. Because each man participated in political affairs, he would be ready to fight for his liberties and serve in the militia of his ward.

One does not have to go as far as organizing the country into wards, however, to obtain some of the benefits that the Anti-Federalists saw attached to small republics. American federalism itself institutionalizes local self-government and thus necessitates the involvement of the people in governing themselves. Federalism is a way of combining some of the advantages of a small republic with those of a national commercial republic. Federalist 39 and *McCulloch v. Maryland* present the argument for a strong national government that nevertheless maintains a sphere for independent state action.

Tocqueville shows why the community and local government that the Anti-Federalists desired is all the more important where the principle of equality prevails. Equal social conditions, Tocqueville argues, isolate or alienate men, whereas local governments serve to bring men together into communities, converting self-interested individuals into citizens who consider the interests of others as well as their own.

Robert Putnam observes a decline in Americans' participation in organizations such as bowling leagues. He sees this as a sign of the alienating effects of liberal individualism as described by Tocqueville. Without the lessons in social organization learned through participation in such groups, Putnam fears that democracy cannot function. But how can participation be encouraged?

William A. Schambra argues that we need to create a contemporary vision for government and society based upon the idea of a "new citizenship." The goal of this new citizenship according to Schambra is "the reconstruction of civil society, the return of America to the self-governing republic described by Alexis de Tocqueville and envisioned by the Founding Fathers." This "new citizenship" stands in contrast to the idea of national community created by progressive thinkers such as Herbert Croly and Walter Lippman, and championed by politicians from Theodore Roosevelt to Lyndon Johnson, Jimmy Carter, and Bill Clinton. This Progressive idea sought to attain at the national level the kind of community Anti-Federalists desired, with its public spirited sacrifice and egalitarianism. By combining the Anti-Federalist view of community with the nationalism of the Federalists, the progressives sought an easy resolution of these two strands of American political thought. But Schambra points out that the idea of national community is not only based on unreasonable expectations of human nature, but also undermines the local governments and civic associations, where public spiritedness is actually nurtured. It is not enough, Schambra concludes, for conservatives to preach against the evils of an ever-expanding national government based upon the national community ideal, they must also develop a positive message of citizenship that shows that they too "care enough about the whole."

1

Thomas Jefferson

The Declaration of Independence (1776)

When in the Course of human events, it becomes necessary for one people to dissolve the political bands which have connected them with another, and to assume among the powers of the earth, the separate and equal station to which the Laws of Nature and of Nature's God entitle them, a decent respect to the opinions of mankind requires that they should declare the causes which impel them to the separation. We hold these truths to be self-evident, that all men are created equal, that they are endowed by their Creator with certain unalienable Rights, that among these are Life, Liberty and the pursuit of Happiness. That to secure these rights, Governments are instituted among Men, deriving their just powers from the consent of the governed, That whenever any Form of Government becomes destructive to these ends it is the Right of the People to alter or to abolish it, and to institute new Government, laying its foundation on such principles and organizing its powers in such form, as to them shall seem most likely to effect their Safety and Happiness. Prudence, indeed, will dictate that Governments long established should not be changed for light and transient causes; and accordingly all experience hath shewn, that mankind are more disposed to suffer, while evils are sufferable, than to right themselves by abolishing the forms to which they are accustomed. But when a long train of abuses and usurpations, pursuing invariably the same Object evinces a design to reduce them under absolute Despotism, it is their right, it is their duty, to throw off such Government, and to provide new Guards for their future security. Such has been the patient sufferance of these Colonies; and such is now the necessity which constrains them to alter their former Systems of Government. The history of the present King of Great Britain is a history of repeated injuries and usurpations, all having in direct object the establishment of an absolute

The text reprinted here is from *The Papers of Thomas Jefferson*, edited by Julian P. Boyd (Princeton: Princeton University Press, 1950–). This is the text of the parchment copy of the Declaration (now in the National Archives) which was signed on August 2, 1776. It is generally accepted as the most authentic of various copies.

Tyranny over these States. To prove this, let Facts be submitted to a candid world. He has refused his Assent to Laws, the most wholesome and necessary for the public good. He has forbidden his Governors to pass Laws of immediate and pressing importance, unless suspended in their operation till his Assent should be obtained; and when so suspended, he has utterly neglected to attend to them. He has refused to pass other Laws for the accommodation of large districts of people, unless those people would relinquish the right of Representation in the Legislature, a right inestimable to them and formidable to tyrants only. He has called together legislative bodies at places unusual, uncomfortable, and distant from the depository of their public Records, for the sole purpose of fatiguing them into compliance with his measures. He has dissolved Representative Houses repeatedly, for opposing with manly firmness his invasions on the rights of the people. He has refused for a long time, after dissolutions, to cause others to be elected; whereby the Legislative powers, incapable of Annihilation, have returned to the People at large for their exercise; the State remaining in the mean time exposed to all the dangers of invasion from without, and convulsions within. He has endeavoured to prevent the population of these States; for that purpose obstructing the Laws for Naturalization of Foreigners; refusing to pass others to encourage their migrations hither, and raising the conditions of new Appropriations of Lands. He has obstructed the Administration of Justice, by refusing his Assent to Laws for establishing Judiciary powers. He has made Judges dependent on his Will alone, for the tenure of their offices, and the amount and payment of their salaries. He has erected a multitude of New Offices, and sent hither swarms of Officers to harrass our people, and eat out their substance. He has kept among us, in times of peace, standing Armies without the Consent of our legislatures. He has affected to render the Military independent of and superior to the Civil power. He has combined with others to subject us to a jurisdiction foreign to our constitution, and unacknowledged by our laws; giving his Assent to their Acts of pretended Legislation: For Quartering large bodies of armed troops among us: For protecting them, by a mock Trial, from punishment for any Murders which they should commit on the Inhabitants of these States: For cutting off our Trade with all parts of the world: For imposing Taxes on us without our Consent: For depriving us in many cases of the benefits of Trial by Jury: For transporting us beyond Seas to be tried for pretended offences: For abolishing the free System of English Laws in a neighbouring Province, establishing therein an Arbitrary government, and enlarging its Boundaries so as to render it at once an example and fit instrument for introducing the same absolute rule into these Colonies: For taking away our Charters, abolishing our most valuable Laws, and altering fundamentally the Forms of our Governments: For suspending our own Legislatures, and declaring themselves invested with power to legislate for us in all cases whatsoever. He has abdicated Government here, by declaring us out of his Protection and waging War against us. He has plundered our seas, ravaged our Coasts, burnt our towns, and destroyed the Lives of our people. He is at this time transporting large Armies of foreign Mercenaries to compleat the works of death, desolation and tyranny, already begun with circumstances of Cruelty & perfidy scarcely paralleled in the most barbarous ages, and totally unworthy the Head of a civilized nation. He has constrained our fellow Citizens taken Captive on the high Seas to bear Arms against their Country, to become the executioners of their friends and Brethren, or to fall themselves by their Hands. He has excited domestic insurrections amongst us, and has endeavoured to bring on the inhabitants of our frontiers, the merciless Indian Savages, whose known rule of warfare, is an undistinguished destruction of all ages, sexes and conditions. In every stage of these Oppressions We have Petitioned for Redress in the most humble terms: Our repeated Petitions have been answered only by repeated injury. A Prince, whose character is thus marked by every act which may define a Tyrant, is unfit to be the ruler of a free people. Nor have We been wanting in attentions to our Brittish brethren. We have warned them from time to time of attempts by their legislature to extend an unwarrantable jurisdiction over us. We have reminded them of the circumstances of our emigration and settlement here. We have appealed to their native justice and magnanimity, and we have conjured them by the ties of our common kindred to disavow these usurpations, which, would inevitably interrupt our connections and correspondence. They too have been deaf to the voice of Justice and of consanguinity. We must, therefore, acquiesce in the necessity, which denounces our Separation, and hold them, as we hold the rest of mankind, Enemies in War, in Peace Friends.

We, therefore, the Representatives of the United States of America, in General Congress, Assembled, appealing to the Supreme Judge of the world for the rectitude of our intentions, do, in the Name, and by Authority of the good People of these Colonies, solemnly publish and declare, That these United Colonies are, and of Right ought to be Free and Independent States; that they are Absolved from all Allegiance to the British Crown, and that all political connection between them and the State of Great Britain, is and ought to be totally dissolved; and that as Free and Independent States, they have full Power to levy War, conclude Peace, contract Alliances, establish Commerce, and to do all other Acts and Things which Independent States may of right do. And for the support of this Declaration, with a firm reliance on the protection of divine Providence, we mutually pledge to each other our Lives, our Fortunes and our sacred Honor.

2

Abraham Lincoln

The Meaning of the Declaration of Independence (1857)

. . . Chief Justice Taney, in his opinion in the Dred Scott case, admits that the language of the Declaration is broad enough to include the whole human family, but he and Judge Douglas argue that the authors of that instrument did not intend to include negroes, by the fact that they did not at once, actually place them on an equality with the whites. Now this grave argument comes to just nothing at all, by the other fact, that they did not at once, *or ever afterwards*, actually place all white people on an equality with one or another. And this is the staple argument of both the Chief Justice and the Senator, for doing this obvious violence to the plain unmistakable language of the Declaration. I think the authors of that notable instrument intended to include all men, but they did not intend to declare all men equal in all respects. They did not mean to say all were equal in color, size, intellect, moral developments, or social capacity. They defined with tolerable distinctness, in what respects they did consider all men created equal—equal in "certain inalienable rights, among which are life, liberty, and the pursuit of happiness." This they said, and this meant. They did not mean to assert the obvious untruth, that all were then actually enjoying that equality, nor yet, that they were about to confer it immediately upon them. In fact they had no power to confer such a boon. They meant simply to declare the *right*, so that the *enforcement* of it might follow as fast as circumstances should permit. They meant to set up a standard maxim for free society, which should be familiar to all, and revered by all; constantly looked to, constantly labored for, and even though never perfectly attained, constantly approximated, and thereby constantly spreading and deepening its influence, and augmenting the happiness and value of life to all people of all colors everywhere. The assertion that "all men are created equal" was of no practical use in effecting our separation from Great Britain; and it was

From Speech at Springfield, Illinois, June 26, 1857, in *The Collected Works of Abraham Lincoln*, Vol. II, Rutgers University Press, 1953.

placed in the Declaration, not for that, but for future use. Its authors meant it to be, thank God, it is now proving itself, a stumbling block to those who in after times might seek to turn a free people back into the hateful paths of despotism. They knew the proneness of prosperity to breed tyrants, and they meant when such should re-appear in this fair land and commence their vocation they should find left for them at least one hard nut to crack.

I have now briefly expressed my view of the *meaning and objects* of that part of the Declaration of Independence which declares that "all men are created equal."

Now let us hear Judge Douglas' view of the same subject, as I find it in the printed report of his late speech. Here it is:

"No man can vindicate the character, motives and conduct of the signers of the Declaration of Independence, except upon the hypothesis that they referred to the white race alone, and not to the African, when they declared all men to have been created equal—that they were speaking of British subjects on this continent being equal to British subjects born and residing in Great Britain—that they were entitled to the same inalienable rights, and among them were enumerated life, liberty, and the pursuit of happiness. The Declaration was adopted for the purpose of justifying the colonists in the eyes of the civilized world in withdrawing their allegiance from the British crown, and dissolving their connection with the mother country."

My good friends, read that carefully over some leisure hour, and ponder well upon it—see what a mere wreck—mangled ruin—it makes of our once glorious Declaration.

"They were speaking of British subjects on this continent being equal to British subjects born and residing in Great Britain!" Why, according to this, not only negroes but white people outside of Great Britain and America are not spoken of in that instrument. The English, Irish, and Scotch, along with white Americans, were included to be sure, but the French, Germans, and other white people of the world are all gone to pot along with the Judge's inferior races.

I had thought the Declaration promised something better than the condition of British subjects; but no, it only meant that we should be *equal* to them in their own oppressed and *unequal* condition. According to that, it gave no promise that having kicked off the King and Lords of Great Britain, we should not at once be saddled with a King and Lords of our own.

I had thought the Declaration contemplated the progressive improvement in the condition of all men everywhere; but no, it merely "was adopted for the purpose of justifying the colonists in the eyes of the civilized world in withdrawing their allegiance from the British crown, and dissolving their connection with the mother country." Why, that object having been effected some eighty years ago, the Declaration is of no practical use now—mere rubbish—old wadding left to rot on the battle-field after the victory is won.

I understand you are preparing to celebrate the "Fourth," tomorrow week. What for? The doings of that day had no reference to the present; and quite half of you are not even descendants of those who were referred to at that day. But I suppose you will celebrate; and will even go so far as to read the Declaration. Suppose after you read it once in the old fashioned way, you read it once more with Judge Douglas' version. It will then run thus: "We hold these truths to be self-evident that all British subjects who were on this continent eighty-one years ago, were created equal to all British subjects born and *then* residing in Great Britain."

And now I appeal to all—to Democrats as well as others,—are you really willing that the Declaration shall be thus frittered away?—thus left no more at most, than an interesting memorial of the dead past? thus shorn of its vitality, and practical value; and left without the *germ* or even the *suggestion* of the individual rights of man in it? . . .

3

Stephen A. Douglas and Abraham Lincoln

Exchange on State Sovereignty and the Problem of Majority Rule (1858)

SENATOR DOUGLAS' SPEECH

LADIES AND GENTLEMEN: It is now nearly four months since the canvass between Mr. Lincoln and myself commenced. On the 16th of June the Republican Convention assembled at Springfield and nominated Mr. Lincoln as their candidate for the U.S. Senate, and he, on that occasion, delivered a speech in which he laid down what he understood to be the Republican creed and the platform on which he proposed to stand during the contest. The principal points in that speech of Mr. Lincoln's were: First, that this government could not endure permanently divided into free and slave States, as our fathers made it; that they must all become free or all become

From the Lincoln-Douglas Debates, Oct. 15, 1858, in *The Collected Works of Abraham Lincoln*, Vol. III, Rutgers University Press, 1953.

slave; all become one thing or all become the other, otherwise this Union could not continue to exist. I give you his opinions almost in the identical language he used. His second proposition was a crusade against the Supreme Court of the United States because of the Dred Scott decision; urging as an especial reason for his opposition to that decision that it deprived the negroes of the rights and benefits of that clause in the Constitution of the United States which guarantees to the citizens of each State, all the rights, privileges, and immunities of the citizens of the several States. . . . In that Chicago speech [of July 11] he even went further than he had before, and uttered sentiments in regard to the negro being on an equality with the white man. (That's so.) He adopted in support of this position the argument which Lovejoy and Codding, and other Abolition lecturers had made familiar in the northern and central portions of the State, to wit: that the Declaration of Independence having declared all men free and equal, by Divine law, also that negro equality was an inalienable right, of which they could not be deprived. He insisted, in that speech, that the Declaration of Independence included the negro in the clause asserting that all men were created equal, and went so far as to say that if one man was allowed to take the position, that it did not include the negro, others might take the position that it did not include other men. He said that all these distinctions between this man and that man, this race and the other race, must be discarded, and we must all stand by the Declaration of Independence, declaring that all men were created equal. . . .

I took up Mr. Lincoln's . . . propositions in my several speeches, analyzed them, and pointed out what I believed to be the radical errors contained in them. First, in regard to his doctrine that this government was in violation of the law of God which says, that a house divided against itself cannot stand, I repudiated it as a slander upon the immortal framers of our constitution. I then said, have often repeated, and now again assert, that in my opinion this government can endure forever, (good) divided into free and slave States as our fathers made it,—each State having the right to prohibit, abolish or sustain slavery just as it pleases. ("Good," "right," and cheers.) This government was made upon the great basis of the sovereignty of the States, the right of each State to regulate its own domestic institutions to suit itself, and that right was conferred with understanding and expectation that inasmuch as each locality had separate interests, each locality must have different and distinct local and domestic institutions, corresponding to its wants and interests. Our fathers knew when they made the government, that the laws and institutions which were well adapted to the green mountains of Vermont, were unsuited to the rice plantations of South Carolina. They knew then, as well as we know now, that the laws and institutions which would be well adapted to the beautiful prairies of Illinois would not be suited to the mining regions of California. They knew that in a Republic as broad as this, having such a variety of soil, climate and interest, there must necessarily be a corresponding variety of local laws—the policy and institutions of each State adapted to its condition and wants. For this reason this Union was established on the right of each State to do as it pleased on the question of slavery, and every other question; and the various States were not allowed to complain of, much less interfere, with the policy of their neighbors. ("That's good doctrine," "that's the doctrine," and cheers.)

Suppose the doctrine advocated by Mr. Lincoln and the abolitionists of this day had prevailed when the Constitution was made, what would have been the result? Imagine for a moment that Mr. Lincoln had been a member of the convention that framed the Constitution of the United States, and that when its members were about to sign that wonderful document, he had arisen in that convention as he did at Springfield this summer, and addressing himself to the President, had said "a house divided against itself cannot stand: (laughter) this government divided into free and slave States cannot endure, they must all be free or all be slave, they must all be one thing or all be the other, otherwise, it is a violation of the law of God, and cannot continue to exist;"—suppose Mr. Lincoln had convinced that body of sages, that that doctrine was sound. What would have been the result? Remember that the Union was then composed of thirteen States, twelve of which were slaveholding and one free. Do you think that the one free State would have outvoted the twelve slaveholding States, and thus have secured the abolition of slavery? (No, no.) On the other hand, would not the twelve slaveholding States have outvoted the one free State, and thus have fastened slavery, by a Constitutional provision, on every foot of the American Republic forever? You see that if this abolition doctrine of Mr. Lincoln had prevailed when the government was made, it would have established slavery as a permanent institution, in all the States whether they wanted it or not, and the question for us to determine in Illinois now as one of the free States is, whether or not we are willing, having become the majority section, to enforce a doctrine on the minority, which we would have resisted with our heart's blood had it been attempted on us when we were in a minority. ("We never will," "good, good," and cheers.) How has the South lost her power as the majority section in this Union, and how have the free States gained it, except under the operation of that principle which declares the right of the people of each State and each territory to form and regulate their domestic institutions in their own way. It was under that principle that slavery was abolished in New Hampshire, Rhode Island, Connecticut, New York, New Jersey, and Pennsylvania; it was under that principle that one half of the slaveholding States became free; it was under that principle that the number of free States increased until from being one out of twelve States, we have grown to be the majority of States of the whole Union, with the power to control the House of Representatives and Senate, and the power, consequently, to elect a President by Northern votes without the aid of a Southern State. Having obtained this power under the operation of that great principle, are you now prepared to abandon the principle and declare that merely because we have the power you will wage a war against the Southern States and their institutions until you force them to abolish slavery everywhere. (No, never, and great applause.) . . .

I hold that there is no power on earth, under our system of government, which has the right to force a constitution upon an unwilling people. (That's so.) Suppose there had been a majority of ten to one in favor of slavery in Kansas, and suppose there had been an abolition President, and an abolition administration, and by some means the abolitionists succeeded in forcing an abolition constitution on those slaveholding people, would the people of the South have submitted to that act for one instant. (No, no.) Well, if you of the South would not have submitted to it a day, how can you, as fair, honorable, and honest men insist on putting a slave constitution on a people who desire a free State. ("That's so," and cheers.) Your safety and ours depend upon both of us acting in good faith, and living up to that great principle which asserts the right of every people to form and regulate their domestic institutions to suit themselves, subject only to the Constitution of the United States. ("That's the doctrine," and immense applause.) . . .

I hold that it is a violation of the fundamental principles of this government to throw the weight of federal power into the scale, either in favor of the free or the slave States. Equality among all the States of this Union is a fundamental principle in our political system. We have no more right to throw the weight of the federal government into the scale in favor of the slaveholding than the free States, and last of all should our friends in the South consent for a moment that Congress should withhold its powers either way when they know that there is a majority against them in both Houses of Congress. . . .

The whole South are rallying to the support of the doctrine that if the people of a Territory want slavery they have a right to have it, and if they do not want it that no power on earth can force it upon them. I hold that there is no principle on earth more sacred to all the friends of freedom than that which says that no institution, no law, no constitution, should be forced on an unwilling people contrary to their wishes. . . . I say to you that there is but one hope, one safety for this country, and that is to stand immovably by that principle which declares the right of each State and each territory to decide these questions for themselves. (Hear him, hear him.) This government was founded on that principle, and must be administered in the same sense in which it was founded.

But the Abolition party really think that under the Declaration of independence the negro is equal to the white man, and that negro equality is an inalienable right conferred by the Almighty, and hence, that all human laws in violation of it are null and void. With such men it is no use for me to argue. I hold that the signers of the Declaration of Independence had no reference to negroes at all when they declared all men to be created equal. They did not mean negro, nor the savage Indians, nor the Fejee Islanders, nor any other barbarous race. They were speaking of white men. ("It's so," "it's so," and cheers.) They alluded to men of European birth and European descent—to white men, and to none others, when they declared that doctrine. ("That's the truth.") I hold that this government was established on the white basis. It was established by white men for the benefit of white men and their posterity forever, and should be administered by white men, and none others. But it does not follow, by any means, that merely because the negro is not a citizen, and merely because he is not our equal, that, therefore, he should be a slave. On the contrary, it does follow, that we ought to extend to the negro race, and to all other dependent races all the rights, all the privileges, and all the immunities which they can exercise consistently with the safety of society. Humanity requires that we should give them all these privileges; christianity commands that we should extend those privileges to them. The question then arises what are those privileges, and what is the nature and extent of them. My answer is that that is a question which each State must answer for itself. We in Illinois have decided it for ourselves. We tried slavery, kept it up for twelve years, and finding that it was not profitable we abolished it for that reason, and became a free State. We adopted in its stead the policy that a negro in this State shall not be a slave and shall not be a citizen. We have a right to adopt that policy. For my part I think it is a wise and sound policy for us. You in Missouri must judge for yourselves whether it is a wise policy for you. If you choose to follow our example, very good; if you reject it, still well, it is your business, not ours. So with Kentucky. Let Kentucky adopt a policy to suit herself. If we do not like it we will keep away from it, and if she does not like ours let her stay at home, mind her own business and let us alone. If the people of all the States will act on that great principle, and each State mind its own business, attend to its own affairs, take care of its own negroes and not meddle with its neighbors, then there will be peace between the North and the South, and East and the West, throughout the whole Union. (Cheers.) Why can we not thus have peace? Why should we thus allow a sectional party to agitate this country, to array the North against the South, and convert us into enemies instead of friends, merely that a few ambitious men may ride into power on a sectional hobby? How long is it since these ambitious Northern men wished for a sectional organization? Did any one of them dream of a sectional party as long as the North was the weaker section and the South the stronger? Then all were opposed to sectional parties; but the moment the North obtained the majority in the House and Senate by the admission of California, and could elect a President without the aid of Southern votes, that moment ambitious Northern men formed a scheme to excite the North against the South, and make the people be governed in their votes by geographical lines, thinking that the North, being the stronger section, would outvote the South, and consequently they, the leaders, would ride into office on a sectional hobby. I am told that my hour is out. It was very short.

MR. LINCOLN'S REPLY

. . . I have stated upon former occasions, and I may as well state again, what I understand to be the real issue in this controversy between Judge Douglas and myself. On the point of my wanting to make war between the free and the slave States, there has been no issue between us. So, too, when he assumes that I am in favor of introducing a perfect social and political equality between the white and black races. These are false issues, upon which Judge Douglas has tried to force the controversy. There is no foundation in truth for the charge that I maintain either of these propositions. The real issue in this controversy—the one pressing upon every mind—is the sentiment on the part of one class that looks upon the institution of slavery *as a wrong*, and of another class that *does not* look upon it as a wrong. The sentiment that contemplates the institution of slavery in this country as a wrong is the sentiment of the Republican party. It is the sentiment around which all their actions—all their arguments circle—from which all their propositions radiate. They look upon it as being a moral, social and political wrong; and while they contemplate it as such, they nevertheless have due regard for its actual existence among us, and the difficulties of getting rid of it in any satisfactory way and to all the constitutional obligations thrown about it. Yet having a due regard for these, they desire a policy in regard to it that looks to its not creating any more danger. They insist that it should as far as may be, *be treated* as a wrong, and one of the methods of treating it as a wrong is to *make provision that it shall grow no larger*. (Loud applause.) They also desire a policy that looks to a peaceful end of slavery at sometime, as being wrong. These are the views they entertain in regard to it as I understand them; and all their sentiments—all their arguments and propositions are brought within this range. I have said and I repeat it here, that if there be a man amongst us who does not think that the institution of slavery is wrong in any one of the aspects of which I have spoken, he is misplaced and ought not to be with us. And if there be a man amongst us who is so impatient of it as a wrong as to disregard its actual presence among us and the difficulty of getting rid of it suddenly in a satisfactory way, and to disregard the constitutional obligations thrown about it, that man is misplaced if he is on our platform. We disclaim sympathy with him in practical action. He is not placed properly with us.

On this subject of treating it as a wrong, and limiting its spread, let me say a word. Has any thing ever threatened the existence of this Union save and except this very institution of Slavery? What is it that we hold most dear amongst us? Our own liberty and prosperity. What has ever threatened our liberty and prosperity save and except this institution of Slavery? If this is true, how do you propose to improve the condition of things by enlarging Slavery—by spreading it out and making it bigger? You may have a wen or a cancer upon your person and not be able to cut it out lest you bleed to death; but surely it is no way to cure it, to engraft it and spread it over your whole body. That is no proper way of treating what you regard a wrong. You see this peaceful way of dealing with it as a wrong—restricting the spread of it, and not allowing it to go into new countries where it has not already existed. That is the peaceful way, the old-fashioned way, the way in which the fathers themselves set us the example.

On the other hand, I have said there is a sentiment which treats it as *not* being wrong. That is the Democratic sentiment of this day. I do not mean to say that every man who stands within that range positively asserts that it is right. That class will include all who positively assert that it is right, and all who like Judge Douglas treat it as indifferent and do not say it is either right or wrong. These two classes of men fall within the general class of those who do not look upon it as a wrong. And if there be among you anybody who supposes that he as a Democrat, can consider himself "as much opposed to slavery as anybody," I would like to reason with him. You never treat it as a wrong. What other thing that you consider as a wrong, do you deal with as you deal with that? Perhaps you *say* it is wrong, *but your leader never does, and you quarrel with anybody who says it is wrong.* Although you pretend to say so yourself you can find no fit place to deal with it as a wrong. You must not say anything about it in the free States, *because it is not here.* You must not say anything about it in the slave States, *because it is there.* You must not say anything about it in the pulpit, because that is religion and has nothing to do with it. You must not say anything about it in politics, *because that will disturb the security of "my place."* (Shouts of laughter and cheers.) There is no place to talk about it as being a wrong, although you say yourself it *is* a wrong. But finally you will screw yourself up to the belief that if the people of the slave States should adopt a system of gradual emancipation on the slavery question, you would be in favor of it. You would be in favor of it. You say that is getting it in the right place, and you would be glad to see it succeed. But you are deceiving yourself. You all know that Frank Blair and Gratz Brown, down there in St. Louis, undertook to introduce that system in Missouri. They fought as valiantly as they could for the system of gradual emancipation which you pretend you would be glad to see succeed. Now I will bring you to the test. After a hard fight they were beaten, and when the news came over here you threw up your hats *and hurrahed for Democracy.* (Great applause and laughter.) More than that, take all the argument made in favor of the system you have proposed, and it carefully excludes the idea that there is anything wrong in the institution of slavery. The arguments to sustain that policy carefully excluded it. Even here to-day you heard Judge Douglas quarrel with me because I uttered a wish that it might sometime come to an end. Although Henry Clay could say he wished every slave in the United States was in the country of his ancestors, I am denounced by those pretending to respect Henry Clay for uttering a wish that it might sometime, in some peaceful way, come to an end. The Democratic policy in regard to that institution will not tolerate the merest breath, the slightest hint, of the least degree of wrong about it. Try it by some of Judge Douglas' arguments. He says he "don't care whether it is voted up or voted down" in the Territories. I do not care myself in dealing with that expression, whether it is intended to be expressive of his individual sentiments on the subject, or only of the national policy he desires to have established. It is alike valuable for my purpose. Any man can say that who does not see anything wrong in slavery, but no man can logically say it who does see a wrong in it; because no man can logically say he don't care whether a wrong is voted up or voted down. He may say he don't care whether an indifferent thing is voted up or down, but he must logically have a choice between a right thing and a wrong thing. He contends that whatever community wants slaves has a right to have them. So they have if it is not a wrong. But if it is a wrong, he cannot say people have a right to do wrong. He says that upon the score of equality, slaves should be allowed to go in a new Territory, like other property. This is strictly logical if there is no difference between it and other property. If it and other property are equal, his argument is entirely logical. But if you insist that one is wrong and the other right, there is no use to institute a comparison between right and wrong. You may turn over everything in the Democratic policy from beginning to end, whether in the shape it takes on the statute book, in the shape it takes in the Dred Scott decision, in the shape it takes in conversation or the shape it takes in short maxim-like arguments—it everywhere carefully excludes the idea that there is anything wrong in it. . . .

4

Martin Diamond

The Revolution of Sober Expectations (1975)

. . . What wants understanding is precisely how our institutions of government sprang from the principle of the Declaration of Independence. How
and to what extent were they generated by the Declaration of Independence?
And what more had to be added actually to frame those institutions? . . .

We must read the Declaration closely to free ourselves from two centuries of obscuring usage. We have transformed the Declaration in our minds
by reading the phrase "consent of the governed" as meaning rule by majorities, that is, democratic government. Indeed we think of the Declaration as
our great democratic document, as the clarion call to and the guide to our
democratic nature. But the Declaration does *not* say that consent is the
means by which government is to operate. Rather, it says that consent is
necessary only to institute the government, that is, to establish it.

The people need not, then, *establish* a government which *operates* by means
of their consent. In fact, the Declaration says that they may organize government on "such principles" as they choose, and they may choose "any form of
government" they deem appropriate to secure their rights. That is, the Declaration was not prescribing any particular form of government at all, but rather
was following John Locke's contract theory, which taught the right of the people, in seeking to secure their liberties, to establish *any* form of government.
And by any form of government the Declaration emphatically includes—as any
literate eighteenth century reader would have understood—not only the democratic form of government but also aristocratic and monarchical government as
well. That is why, for example, the Declaration has to submit facts to a "candid
world" to prove the British king guilty of a "long train of abuses." Tom Paine,
by way of contrast, could dispose of King George more simply. Paine deemed

From Diamond, "The Revolution of Sober Expectations," in *America's Continuing
Revolution: An Act of Conservation*, published by American Enterprise Institute, 1975.
Reprinted by permission.

George III unfit to rule simply because he was a *king* and kingly rule was illegitimate as such. The fact that George was a "Royal Brute" was only frosting on the cake; for Paine his being royal was sufficient warrant for deposing him. But the Declaration, on the contrary, is obliged to prove that George was indeed a brute. That is, the Declaration holds George III "unfit to be the ruler of a free people" not because he was a king, but because he was a *tyrannical* king. Had the British monarchy continued to secure to the colonists their rights, as it had prior to the long train of abuses, the colonists would not have been entitled to rebel. It was only the fact, according to the Declaration, that George had become a tyrannical king that supplied the warrant for revolution.

Thus the Declaration, strictly speaking, is neutral on the question of forms of government: *any* form is legitimate provided it secures equal freedom and is instituted by popular consent. . . .

It is to the constitution that we must ultimately turn as the completion of the American Revolution. As to those democratic institutions, the Declaration says no more than this: If you choose the democratic form of government, rather than the aristocratic or monarchic or any mixture thereof, it must be a democratic government which secures to all people their unalienable rights. But how to do that? The Declaration is silent. . . .

What was truly revolutionary in the American Revolution and its Declaration of Independence was that liberty, civil liberty—the doctrine of certain unalienable rights—was made the end of government. Not, as had been the case for millennia, whatever end power haphazardly imposed upon government; nor any longer the familiar variety of ends—not virtue, not piety, not privilege or wealth, not merely protection, and not empire and dominion; but now deliberately the principle of liberty. . . .

While modern followers of Edmund Burke may warn of the dangers of devotion to abstract principles, they cannot blink aside the revolutionary American devotion to precisely such an abstract principle. The American truth was undeniably as abstract as, say, Robespierre's tyrannizing truth or Lenin's tyrannizing truth. And yet there is indeed something moderate and nonutopian in the American devotion to liberty which warrants Burkean celebration. Whence then the difference? Wherein was the American Revolution one of sober expectations while the Jacobin and Leninist were revolutions of unbridled expectations? The answer lies not in degrees of devotion to abstractness, but in the substantive nature of the principle each was abstractly devoted to. It is one thing to be abstractly devoted to the Reign of Virtue or to unlimited equality in all respects or to mass fraternity or to classless society or to the transformation of the human condition itself, and quite another to be devoted to the abstract principle of civil liberty. Civil liberty as a goal constrains its followers to moderation, legality, and rootedness in regular institutions. Moreover, moderate civil liberty does not require terror and tyranny for its fulfillment.

Liberty is an abstract principle capable of achievement; Jacobin or Leninist equality or mass fraternity are not. Moderate civil liberty is a possible dream, utopian equality and fraternity are impossible dreams. And the recent popular song to the contrary notwithstanding, the political pursuit of impossible dreams leads to terror and tyranny in the vain effort to actualize what cannot be. . . .

[S]obriety also lies in the Founding Fathers' coolheaded and cautious acceptance of democracy. Perhaps not a single American voice was raised in unqualified, doctrinaire praise of democracy. On the contrary, there was universal recognition of the problematic character of democracy, a concern for its weaknesses and a fear of its dangers. The debate in American life during the founding decade gradually became a debate over how to create a decent democratic regime. Contrary to our too complacent modern perspective regarding democracy, which assumes that a government cannot be decent unless democratic, our Founding Fathers more skeptically, sensibly, and soberly, were concerned how to make this new government *decent even though democratic*. All the American revolutionaries, whether they were partisans of the theory that democratic republics had to be small or agrarian or only loosely confederated in order to remain free, or whether they retained the traditional idea that democracy had to be counterbalanced by nobility or wealth, or whether they subscribed to the large-republic theory implicit in the new Constitution—all the American revolutionaries knew that democracy was a problem in need of constant solution, in constant need of moderation, in constant need of institutions and measures to mitigate its defects and guard against its dangers. . . .

The half-revolution begun in 1776 reached its completion only when the peculiar American posture toward democracy received its definitive form in the framing and ratification of the Constitution a decade later. . . . [I]n contemplating that convention we would find the answer to our earlier question: how did our institutions spring from the Declaration and what had to be added to bring those institutions into being? They sprang on the one hand from the love of free government inspired by the *noble sentiments* of Jefferson's Declaration, and on the other hand from the theoretic *wisdom* of James Madison whose sober clarity regarding democracy gave the shape and thrust to our unique democratic form of government and way of life. . . .

5

Centinel

The Small Republic Argument (1787)

. . . The late Convention have submitted to your consideration a plan of a new federal government. The subject is highly interesting to your future welfare. Whether it be calculated to promote the great ends of civil society, viz., the happiness and prosperity of the community, it behoves you well to consider, uninfluenced by the authority of names. Instead of that frenzy of enthusiasm, that has actuated the citizens of Philadelphia, in their approbation of the proposed plan, before it was possible that it could be the result of a rational investigation into its principles, it ought to be dispassionately and deliberately examined on its own intrinsic merit, the only criterion of your patronage. If ever free and unbiased discussion was proper or necessary, it is on such an occasion. All the blessings of liberty and the dearest privileges of freemen are now at stake and dependent on your present conduct. . . .

The late revolution having effaced in a great measure all former habits, and the present institutions are so recent, that there exists not that great reluctance to innovation, so remarkable in old communities, and which accords with reason, for the most comprehensive mind cannot foresee the full operation of material changes on civil polity. . . .

I am fearful that the principles of government inculcated in Mr. Adams' treatise, and enforced in the numerous essays and paragraphs in the newspapers, have misled some well designing members of the late Convention. . . . He asserts that the administrators of every government, will ever be actuated by views of private interest and ambition, to the prejudice of the public good; that therefore the only effectual method to secure the rights of the people and promote their welfare, is to create an opposition of interests. . . .

Suppose a government could be formed and supported on such principles, would it answer the great purposes of civil society? If the administrators

From "Centinel I" (believed to have been written by Samual Bryan), in *Pennsylvania and the Federal Constitution 1787–1788*, ed. John Bach McMaster and Frederick D. Stone, The Historical Society of Pennsylvania, 1888.

of every government are actuated by views of private interest and ambition, how is the welfare and happiness of the community to be the result of such jarring adverse interests?

Therefore, as different orders in government will not produce the good of the whole, we must recur to other principles. I believe it will be found that the form of government, which holds those entrusted with power in the greatest responsibility to their constituents, the best calculated for freemen. A republican, or free government, can only exist where the body of the people are virtuous, and where property is pretty equally divided. In such a government the people are the sovereign and their sense or opinion is the criterion of every public measure; for when this ceases to be the case, the nature of the government is changed, and an aristocracy, monarchy or despotism will rise on its ruin. The highest responsibility is to be attained in a simple structure of government, for the great body of the people never steadily attend to the operations of government, and for want of due information are liable to be imposed on. If you complicate the plan by various orders, the people will be perplexed and divided in their sentiments about the source of abuses or misconduct; some will impute it to the senate, others to the house of representatives, and so on, that the interposition of the people may be rendered imperfect or perhaps wholly abortive. But if, imitating the constitution of Pennsylvania, you vest all the legislative power in one body of men (separating the executive and judicial) elected for a short period, and necessarily excluded by rotation from permanency, and guarded from precipitancy and surprise by delays imposed on its proceedings, you will create the most perfect responsibility; for then, whenever the people feel a grievance, they cannot mistake the authors, and will apply the remedy with certainty and effect, discarding them at the next election. This tie of responsibility will obviate all the dangers apprehended from a single legislature, and will the best secure the rights of the people. . . .

[I]f the United States are to be melted down into one empire, it becomes you to consider whether such a government, however constructed, would be eligible in so extended a territory; and whether it would be practicable, consistent with freedom? It is the opinion of the greatest writers, that a very extensive country cannot be governed on democratical principles, on any other plan than a confederation of a number of small republics, possessing all the powers of internal government, but united in the management of their foreign and general concerns.

It would not be difficult to prove, that anything short of despotism could not bind so great a country under one government; and that whatever plan you might, at the first setting out, establish, it would issue in a despotism.

If one general government could be instituted and maintained on principles of freedom, it would not be so competent to attend to the various local concerns and wants, of every particular district, as well as the peculiar governments, who are nearer the scene, and possessed of superior means of information; besides, if the business of the *whole* union is to be managed by one government, there would not be time. Do we not already see, that the inhabitants in a number of larger States, who are remote from the seat of government, are loudly complaining of the inconveniences and disadvantages they are subjected to on this account, and that, to enjoy the comforts of local government, they are separating into smaller divisions? . . .

6

Selections from the Records
of the Federal Convention of 1787

A. THE VIRGINIA PLAN

Mr. Randolph (then) opened the main business. He expressed his regret, that it should fall to him, rather than those, who were of longer standing in life and political experience, to open the great subject of their mission. But, as the convention had originated from Virginia, and his colleagues supposed, that some proposition was expected from them, they had imposed this task on him.

He then commented on the difficulty of the crisis, and the necessity of preventing the fulfillment of the prophecies of the American downfall. . . .

1. In speaking of the defects of the confederation he professed a high respect for its authors, and considered them as having done all that patriots could do, in the then infancy of the science, of constitutions, & of confederacies,—when the inefficiency of requisitions was unknown—no commercial discord had arisen among any states—no rebellion had appeared as in Mass.—foreign debts had not become urgent—the havoc of paper money had not been foreseen—treaties had not been violated—and perhaps nothing better could be obtained from the jealousy of the states with regard to their sovereignty.

From *Records of the Federal Convention of 1787*, ed. Max Farrand.

He then proceeded to enumerate the defects: 1. that the confederation produced no security against foreign invasion; congress not being permitted to prevent a war nor to support it by their own authority—Of this he cited many examples; most of which tended to show, that they could not cause infractions of treaties or of the law of nations, to be punished: that particular states might by their conduct provoke war without control; and that neither militia nor draughts being fit for defense on such occasions, enlistments only could be successful, and these could not be executed without money.

2. that the federal government could not check the quarrels between states, nor a rebellion in any not having constitutional power nor did it have means to interpose according to the exigency.

3. that there were many advantages, which the U.S. might acquire, which were not attainable under the confederation—such as a productive impost—counteraction of the commercial regulations of other nations—pushing of commerce. . . .

4. that the federal government could not defend itself against the encroachments from the states.

5. that it was not even paramount to the state constitutions, ratified as it was in many of the states.

6. He next reviewed the danger of our situation, appealed to the sense of the best friends of the U.S.—the prospect of anarchy from the laxity of government everywhere; and to other considerations.

7. He then proceeded to the remedy; the basis of which he said, must be the republican principle.

He proposed as conformable to his ideas the following resolutions, which he explained one by one.

Resolutions proposed by Mr. Randolph in Convention. May 29, 1787.

1. Resolved that the articles of Confederation ought to be so corrected & enlarged as to accomplish the objects proposed by their institution; namely, "common defense, security of liberty and general welfare."

2. Resd. therefore that the rights of suffrage in the National Legislature ought to be proportioned to the quotas of contribution, or to the number of free inhabitants, as the one or the other rule may seem best in different cases.

3. Resd. that the National Legislature ought to consist of two branches.

4. Resd. that the members of the first branch of the National Legislature ought to be elected by the people of the several States every _____ for the term of _____; to be of the age of _____ years at least, to receive liberal stipends by which they may be compensated for the devotion

of their time to public service; to be ineligible to any office established by a particular State, or under the authority of the United States, except those peculiarly belonging to the functions of the first branch, during the term of service, and for the space of _____ after its expiration; to be incapable of re-election for the space of _____ after the expiration of their term of service, and to be subject to recall.

5. Resd. that the members of the second branch of the National Legislature ought to be elected by those of the first, out of a proper number of persons nominated by the individual Legislatures, to be of the age of _____ years at least; to hold their offices for a term sufficient to ensure their independency, to receive liberal stipends, by which they may be compensated for the devotion of their time to public service; and to be ineligible to any office established by a particular State, or under the authority of the United States, except those peculiarly belonging to the functions of the second branch, during the term of service, and for the space of _____ after the expiration thereof.

6. Resd. that each branch ought to possess the right of originating Acts; that the National Legislature ought to be impowered to enjoy the Legislative Rights vested in Congress by the Confederation & moreover to legislate in all cases to which the separate States are incompetent, or in which the harmony of the United States may be interrupted by the exercise of individual Legislation; to negative all laws passed by the several States, contravening in the opinion of the National Legislature the articles of Union; and to call forth the force of the Union against any member of the Union failing to fulfill its duty under the articles thereof.

7. Resd. that a National Executive be instituted; to be chosen by the National Legislature for the term of _____ years, to receive punctually at stated times, a fixed compensation for the services rendered, in which no increase or diminution shall be made so as to affect the Magistracy, existing at the time of increase or diminution, and to be ineligible a second time; and that besides a general authority to execute the National laws, it ought to enjoy the Executive rights vested in Congress by the Confederation.

8. Resd. that the Executive and a convenient number of the National Judiciary, ought to compose a council of revision with authority to examine every act of the National Legislature before it shall operate, & every act of a particular Legislature before a Negative thereon shall be final; and that the dissent of the said Council shall amount to a rejection, unless the Act of the National Legislature be again passed, or that of a particular Legislature be again negatived by _____ of the members of each branch.

9. Resd. that a National Judiciary be established. . . .

10. Resd. that a Republican Government & the territory of each State, except in the instance of a voluntary junction of Government & territory, ought to be guaranteed by the United States to each State. . . .

11. Resd. that the Legislative Executive & Judiciary powers within the several States ought to be bound by oath to support the articles of Union.

12. Resd. that the amendments which shall be offered to the Confederation, by the Convention ought at a proper time, or times, after the approbation of Congress to be submitted to an assembly or assemblies of Representatives, recommended by the several Legislatures to be expressly chosen by the people, to consider & decide thereon.

B. The New Jersey Plan

Mr. Patterson, laid before the Convention the plan which he said several of the deputations wished to be substituted in place of that proposed by Mr. Randolph. . . .

The propositions from N. Jersey moved by Mr. Patterson were in the words following.

1. Resd. that the articles of Confederation ought to be so revised, corrected & enlarged, as to render the federal Constitution adequate to the exigencies of Government, & the preservation of the Union.

2. Resd. that in addition to the powers vested in the U. States in Congress, by the present existing articles of Confederation, they be authorized to pass acts for raising a revenue by levying a duty or duties on all goods or merchandizes of foreign growth or manufacture, imported into any part of the U. States, by stamps on paper, vellum or parchment and by a postage on all letters or packages passing through the general post-office, to be applied to such federal purposes as they shall deem proper & expedient; to make rules & regulations for the collection thereof; and the same from time to time, to alter & amend in such manner as they shall think proper: to pass Acts for the regulation of trade & commerce as well with foreign nations as with each other provided that all punishments, fines, forfeitures & penalties to be incurred for contravening such acts rules and regulations shall be adjudged by the Common law Judiciaries of the State in which any offense contrary to the true intent & meaning of such Acts rules & regulations shall have been committed or perpetrated, with liberty of commencing in the first instance all suits & prosecutions for that purpose in the superior common law Judiciary in such State, subject nevertheless, for the correction of all errors, both in law & fact in rendering judgment, to an appeal to the Judiciary of the U. States. . . .

3. Resd. that the U. States in Congress be authorized to elect a federal Executive to consist of _____ persons, to continue in office for the term of _____ years, to receive punctually at stated times a fixed compensation for their services, in which no increase or diminution shall be made so as to affect the persons composing the Executive at the time of such

increase or diminution, to be paid out of the federal treasury; to be incapable of holding any other office or appointment during their time of service and for _____ years thereafter; to be ineligible a second time, & removable by Congress on application by a majority of the Executives of the several States; that the Executives besides their general authority to execute the federal acts ought to appoint all federal officers not otherwise provided for, & to direct all military operations; provided that none of the persons composing the federal Executive shall on any occasion take command of any troops, so as personally to conduct any enterprise as General, or in other capacity.

4. Resd. that a federal Judiciary be established. . . .

5. Resd. that all Acts of the U. States in Congress made by virtue & in pursuance of the powers hereby & by the articles of confederation vested in them, and all Treaties made & ratified under the authority of the U. States shall be the supreme law of the respective States so far forth as those Acts or Treaties shall relate to the said States or their Citizens, and that the Judiciary of the several States shall be bound thereby in their decisions, any thing in the respective laws of the Individual States to the contrary notwithstanding; and that if any State, or any body of men in any State, shall oppose or prevent the carrying into execution such acts or treaties, the federal Executive shall be authorized to call forth the power of the Confederated States, or so much thereof as may be necessary to enforce and compel an obedience to such Acts, or an observance of such Treaties. . . .

C. Alexander Hamilton: Proposal for a New Government

The extent of the Country to be governed, discouraged him. The expense of a general Govt. was also formidable; unless there were such a diminution of expense on the side of the State Govts. as the case would admit. If they were extinguished, he was persuaded that great economy might be obtained by substituting a general Govt. He did not mean however to shock the public opinion by proposing such a measure. On the other hand he saw no *other* necessity for declining it. They are not necessary for any of the great purposes of commerce, revenue, or agriculture. Subordinate authorities he was aware would be necessary. There must be district tribunals: corporations for local purposes. But cui bono, the vast & expensive apparatus now appertaining to the States. The only difficulty of a serious nature which occurred to him, was that of drawing representatives from the extremes to the center of the community. What inducements can be offered that will suffice? The moderate wages for the 1st. branch, would only be a bait to little demagogues. Three dollars or thereabouts he supposed would be the utmost. The Senate he feared from a similar cause, would be filled by certain undertakers who wish for particular offices under the Govt. This view of the subject almost led him to despair that a Republican Govt. could be established over so great an extent. He was sensible at the same time that it would be unwise to propose one of any other form. In his private opinion he had no scruple in declaring, supported as he was by the opinions of so many of the wise & good, that the British Govt. was the best in the world: and that he doubted much whether any thing short of it would do in America. He hoped gentlemen of different opinions would bear with him in this, and begged them to recollect the change of opinion on this subject which had taken place and was still going on. It was once thought that the power of Congress was amply sufficient to secure the end of their institution. The error was now seen by every one. The members most tenacious of republicanism, he observed, were as loud as any in declaiming against the vices of democracy. This progress of the public mind led him to anticipate the time, when others as well as himself would join in the praise bestowed by Mr. Neckar on the British Constitution, namely, that it is the only Govt. in the world "which unites public strength with individual security."—In every community where industry is encouraged, there will be a division of it into the few & the many. Hence separate interests will arise. There will be debtors & creditors &c. Give all power to the many, they will oppress the few. Give all power to the few they will oppress the many. Both therefore ought to have power, that each may defend itself against the other. To the want of this check we owe our paper money—installment laws &c. To the proper adjustment of it the British owe the excellence of their Constitution. Their house of Lords is a most noble institution. Having nothing to hope for by a change, and a sufficient interest by means of their property, in being faithful to the national interest, they form a permanent barrier against every pernicious innovation, whether attempted on the part of the Crown or of the Commons. No temporary Senate will have firmness enough to answer the purpose. . . Gentlemen differ in their opinions concerning the necessary checks, from the different estimates they form of the human passions. They suppose seven years a sufficient period to give the Senate an adequate firmness, from not duly considering the amazing violence & turbulence of the democratic spirit. When a great object of Govt. is pursued, which seizes the popular passions, they spread like wild fire, and become irresistable. He appealed to the gentlemen from the N. England States whether experience had not there verified the remark. As to the Executive, it seemed to be admitted that no good one could be established on republican principles. Was not this giving up the merits of the question; for can there be a good govt. without a good Executive. The English model was the only good one on this subject. The hereditary interest of the King was so interwoven with that of the nation, and his personal emoluments so great, that he was placed above the danger of being corrupted from abroad—and at the same time was both sufficiently independent and sufficiently controlled, to answer the purpose of the institution at home. One of the weak sides of Republics was their being liable to foreign influence & corruption. Men of little character, acquiring great power become easily the tools of intermedling neighbors. Sweden was a striking instance. The French & English had each their parties during the late Revolution which was effected by the predominant influence of the former. What is the inference from all these observations? That we ought to go as far in order to attain stability and permanency, as republican principles will admit. Let one branch of the Legislature hold their places for life or at least during good-behavior. Let the Executive also be for life. He appealed to the feelings of the members present whether a term of seven years, would induce the sacrifices of private affairs which an acceptance of public trust would require, so as to ensure the services of the best citizens. On this plan we should have in the Senate a permanent will, a weighty interest, which would answer essential purposes. But is this a Republican Govt. it will be asked? Yes, if all the Magistrates are appointed, and vacancies are filled, by the people, or a process of election originating with the people. He was sensible that an Executive constituted as he proposed would have in fact but little of the power and independence that might be necessary. On the other plan of appointing him for 7 years, he thought the Executive ought to have but little power. He would be ambitious, with the means of making creatures; and as the object of his ambition would be to *prolong* his power, it is probable that in case of a war, he would avail himself of the emergency, to evade or refuse a degradation from his place. An Executive for life has not this motive for forgetting his fidelity, and will therefore be a safer depositary of power. It will be objected probably, that such an executive will be an *elective Monarch*, and will give birth to the tumults which characterize that form of Govt. He would reply that *Monarch* is an indefinite term. It marks not either the degree or duration of power. If this Executive Magistrate would be a monarch for life— the other proposed by the Report from the Committee of the whole, would be a monarch for seven years. The circumstance of being elective was also applicable to both. It had been observed by judicious writers that elective monarchies would be the best if they could be guarded against the *tumults* excited by the ambition and intrigues of competitors. . . .

7

James Madison

The Work of the Constitutional Convention (1787)

To Thomas Jefferson

Dear Sir:

You will herewith receive the result of the convention, which continued its session till the 17th of September. . . .

It appeared to be the sincere and unanimous wish of the convention to cherish and preserve the union of the states. No proposition was made, no suggestion was thrown out, in favor of a partition of the empire into two or more confederacies.

It was generally agreed that the objects of the Union could not be secured by any system founded on the principle of a confederation of sovereign states. A *voluntary* observance of the federal law by all the members could never be hoped for. A *compulsive* one could evidently never be reduced to practice, and if it could, involved equal calamities to the innocent & the guilty, the necessity of a military force both obnoxious & dangerous, and in general a scene resembling much more a civil war than the administration of a regular government.

Hence was embraced the alternative of a government which instead of operating, on the states, should operate without their intervention on the individuals composing them; and hence the change in the principle and proportion of representation.

This ground-work being laid, the great objects which presented themselves were (1) to unite a proper energy in the Executive, and a proper stability in the Legislative departments, with the essential characters of Republican Government. (2) to draw a line of demarkation which would give to the General Government every power requisite for general purposes, and leave to the States every power which might be most beneficially administered by them. (3) to provide for the different interests of different parts of the Union. (4) to adjust the clashing pretensions of the large and small States. Each of

From *The Writings of James Madison*, Oct. 24, 1787, Vol. V, G. P. Putnam's Sons, 1904.

these objects was pregnant with difficulties. The whole of them together formed a task more difficult than can be well conceived by those who were not concerned in the execution of it. Adding to these considerations the natural diversity of human opinions on all new and complicated subjects, it is impossible to consider the degree of concord which ultimately prevailed as less than a miracle.

The first of these objects, as respects the Executive, was peculiarly embarrassing. On the question whether it should consist of a single person, or a plurality of co-ordinate members, on the mode of appointment, on the duration in office, on the degree of power, on the re-eligibility, tedious and reiterated discussions took place. The plurality of co-ordinate members had finally but few advocates. Governor Randolph was at the head of them. The modes of appointment proposed were various, as by the people at large—by electors chosen by the people—by the Executives of the States—by the Congress, some preferring a joint ballot of the two Houses—some a separate concurrent ballot, allowing to each a negative on the other house—some, a nomination of several candidates by one House, out of whom a choice should be made by the other. Several other modifications were started. The expedient at length adopted seemed to give pretty general satisfaction to the members. As to the duration in office, a few would have preferred a tenure during good behavior—a considerable number would have done so in case an easy & effectual removal by impeachment could be settled. It was much agitated whether a long term, seven years for example, with a subsequent & perpetual ineligibility, or a short term with a capacity to be re-elected, should be fixed. In favor of the first opinion were urged the danger of a gradual degeneracy of re-elections from time to time, into first a life and then a hereditary tenure, and the favorable effect of an incapacity to be reappointed on the independent exercise of the Executive authority. On the other side it was contended that the prospect of necessary degradation would discourage the most dignified characters from aspiring to the office, would take away the principal motive to the faithful discharge of its duties—the hope of being rewarded with a reappointment would stimulate ambition to violent efforts for holding over the Constitutional term—and instead of producing an independent administration, and a firmer defense of the constitutional rights of the department, would render the officer more indifferent to the importance of a place which he would soon be obliged to quit forever, and more ready to yield to the encroachments of the Legislature of which he might again be a member. The questions concerning the degree of power turned chiefly on the appointment to offices, and the control on the Legislature. An absolute appointment to all offices—to some offices—to no offices, formed the scale of opinions on the first point. On the second, some contended for an absolute negative, as the only possible mean of reducing to practice the theory of a free Government which forbids a mixture of the Legislative & Executive powers. Others would be content with a revisionary power, to be overruled by three fourths of both Houses. It was warmly urged that the judiciary department should be associated in the revision. The idea of some was that a separate revision should be given to the two departments—that if either objected two thirds, if both, three fourths, should be necessary to overrule.

In forming the Senate, the great anchor of the Government, the questions as they came within the first object, turned mostly on the mode of appointment, and the duration of it. The different modes proposed were (1) by the House of Representatives, (2) by the Executive. (3) by electors chosen by the people for the purpose. (4) by the State Legislature. On the point of duration, the propositions descended from good behavior to four years, through the intermediate terms of nine, seven, six, & five years. The election of the other branch was first determined to be triennial, and afterwards reduced to biennial.

The second object, the due partition of power between the General & local Governments, was perhaps of all, the most nice and difficult. A few contended for an entire abolition of the States; some for indefinite power of Legislation in the Congress, with a negative on the laws of the States; some for such a power without a negative; some for a limited power of legislation, with such a negative; the majority finally for a limited power without the negative. The question with regard to the negative underwent repeated discussions, and was finally rejected by a bare majority. As I formerly intimated to you my opinion in favor of this ingredient, I will take this occasion of explaining myself on the subject. Such a check on the States appears to me necessary (1) to prevent encroachments on the General authority, (2) to prevent instability and injustice in the legislation of the States.

1. Without such a check in the whole over the parts, our system involves the evil of imperia in imperio. If a complete supremacy somewhere is not necessary in every Society, a controlling power at least is so, by which the general authority may be defended against encroachments of the subordinate authorities, and by which the latter may be restrained from encroachments on each other. If the supremacy of the British Parliament is not necessary as has been contended, for the harmony of that Empire; it is evident I think that without the royal negative or some equivalent control, the unity of the system would be destroyed. The want of some such provision seems to have been mortal to the ancient Confederacies, and to be the disease of the modern. Of the Lycian confederacy little is known. That of the Amphyctions is well known to have been rendered of little use whilst it lasted, and in the end to have been destroyed, by the predominance of the local over the federal authority. . . . The case of the United Netherlands is in point. The authority of a Stadtholder, the influence of a Standing Army, the common interest in the conquered possessions, the pressure of surrounding danger, the guarantee of foreign powers, are not sufficient to

secure the authority and interest of the generality against the anti-federal tendency of the provincial sovereignties. . . . Still more to the purpose is our own
experience both during the war and since the peace. Encroachments of the
States on the general authority, sacrifices of national to local interests, interfer-
ences of the measures of different States, form a great part of the history of our
political system. It may be said that the new Constitution is founded on different principles, and will have a different operation. I admit the difference to be
material. It presents the aspect rather of a feudal system of republics, if such a
phrase may be used, than of a Confederacy of independent States. And what
has been the progress and event of the feudal Constitutions? In all of them a
continual struggle between the head and the inferior members, until a final victory has been gained in some instances by one, in others, by the other of them.
In one respect indeed there is a remarkable variance between the two cases. In
the feudal system the sovereign, though limited, was independent; and having
no particular sympathy of interests with the Great Barons, his ambition had as
full play as theirs in the mutual projects of usurpation. In the American Constitution the general authority will be derived entirely from the subordinate
authorities. The Senate will represent the States in their political capacity; the
other House will represent the people of the States in their individual capacity.
The former will be accountable to their constituents at moderate, the latter at
short periods. The President also derives his appointment from the States, and
is periodically accountable to them. This dependence of the General on the
local authorities, seems effectually to guard the latter against any dangerous
encroachments of the former; whilst the latter, within their respective limits,
will be continually sensible of the abridgement of their power, and be stimulated by ambition to resume the surrendered portion of it. We find the representatives of Counties and Corporations in the Legislatures of the States, much
more disposed to sacrifice the aggregate interest, and even authority, to the
local views of their constituents, than the latter to the former. I mean not by
these remarks to insinuate that an esprit de corps will not exist in the National
Government or that opportunities may not occur of extending its jurisdiction
in some points. I mean only that the danger of encroachments is much greater
from the other side, and that the impossibility of dividing powers of legislation,
in such a manner, as to be free from different constructions by different interests, or even from ambiguity in the judgment of the impartial, requires some
such expedient as I contend for. Many illustrations might be given of this
impossibility. . . . The line of distinction between the power of regulating
trade and that of drawing revenue from it, which was once considered the barrier of our liberties, was found on fair discussion, to be absolutely
undefinable. . . . Even the boundaries between the Executive, Legislative, &
Judiciary powers, though in general so strongly marked in themselves, consist in
many instances of mere shades of difference. It may be said that the Judicial
authority, under our new system will keep the States within their proper limits,

and supply the place of a negative on their laws. The answer is, that it is more convenient to prevent the passage of a law than to declare it void after it is passed; that this will be particularly the case, where the law aggrieves individuals, who may be unable to support an appeal against a State to the supreme Judiciary; that a State which would violate the Legislative rights of the Union, would not be very ready to obey a Judicial decree in support of them, and that a recurrence to force, which, in the event of disobedience would be necessary, is an evil which the new Constitution meant to exclude as far as possible.

2. A constitutional negative on the laws of the States seems equally necessary to secure individuals against encroachments on their rights. The mutability of the laws of the States is found to be a serious evil. The injustice of them has been so frequent and so flagrant as to alarm the most steadfast friends of Republicanism. I am persuaded I do not err in saying that the evils issuing from these sources contributed more to that uneasiness which produced the Convention, and prepared the Public mind for a general reform, than those which accrued to our national character and interest from the inadequacy of the Confederation to its immediate objects. A reform therefore which does not make provision for private rights, must be materially defective. The restraints against paper emissions, and violations of contracts are not sufficient. Supposing them to be effectual as far as they go, they are short of the mark. Injustice may be effected by such an infinitude of legislative expedients, that where the disposition exists it can only be controlled by some provision which reaches all cases whatsoever. The partial provision made, supposes the disposition which will evade it. It may be asked how private rights will be more secure under the Guardianship of the General Government than under the State Governments, since they are both founded on the republican principle which refers the ultimate decision to the will of the majority, and are distinguished rather by the extent within which they will operate, than by any material difference in their structure. A full discussion of this question would, if I mistake not, unfold the true Principles of Republican Government, and prove in contradiction to the concurrent opinions of the theoretical writers that this form of Government, in order to effect its purposes, must operate not within a small but an extensive sphere. I will state some of the ideas which have occurred to me on the subject. Those who contend for a simple Democracy, or a pure republic, actuated by the sense of the majority, and operating within narrow limits, assume or suppose a case which is altogether fictitious. They found their reasoning on the idea, that the people composing the Society, enjoy not only an equality of political rights; but that they have all precisely the same interests, and the same feelings in every respect. Were this in reality the case, their reasoning would be conclusive. The interest of the majority would be that of the minority also; the decisions could only turn on mere opinion concerning the good of the whole, of which the major voice would be the safest criterion; and within a small sphere, this

voice could be most easily collected, and the public affairs most accurately managed. We know however that no society ever did or can consist of so homogeneous a mass of Citizens. In the savage state indeed, an approach is made towards it; but in that state little or no Government is necessary. In all civilized societies, distinctions are various and unavoidable. A distinction of property results from that very protection which a free Government gives to unequal faculties of acquiring it. There will be rich and poor; creditors and debtors; a landed interest, a monied interest, a mercantile interest, a manu-facturing interest. These classes may again be subdivided according to the different productions of different situations & soils, & according to different branches of commerce and of manufactures. In addition to these natural dis-tinctions, artificial ones will be founded, on accidental differences in politi-cal, religious, or other opinions, or an attachment to the persons of leading individuals. However erroneous or ridiculous these grounds of dissention and faction may appear to the enlightened Statesman or the benevolent philoso-pher, the bulk of mankind who are neither Statesmen nor Philosophers, will continue to view them in a different light. It remains then to be enquired whether a majority having any common interest, or feeling any common pas-sion, will find sufficient motives to restrain them from oppressing the minor-ity. An individual is never allowed to be a judge or even a witness in his own cause. If two individuals are under the bias of interest or enmity against a third, the rights of the latter could never be safely referred to the majority of the three. Will two thousand individuals be less apt to oppress one thousand, or two hundred thousand one hundred thousand? Three motives only can restrain in such cases: (1) a prudent regard to private or partial good, as essentially involved in the general and permanent good of the Whole. This ought no doubt to be sufficient of itself. Experience however shows that it has little effect on individuals, and perhaps still less on a collection of indi-viduals, and least of all on a majority with the public authority in their hands. If the former are ready to forget that honesty is the best policy; the last do more. They often proceed on the converse of the maxim, that whatever is politic is honest. (2) respect for character. This motive is not found sufficient to restrain individuals from injustice. And loses its efficacy in proportion to the number which is to divide the pain or the blame. Besides as it has reference to public opinion, which is that of the majority, the standard is fixed by those whose conduct is to be measured by it. (3) Religion. The inefficacy of this restraint on individuals is well known. The conduct of every popular Assembly, acting on oath, the strongest of religious ties, shows that individuals join without remorse in acts against which their consciences would revolt, if proposed to them separately in their closets. When indeed Religion is kindled into enthusiasm, its force like that of other passions is increased by the sympathy of a multitude. But enthusiasm is only a temporary state of Religion, and whilst it lasts will hardly be seen with pleasure at the helm. Even in its coolest state, it has been much oftener a motive to oppression than a restraint from it. If then there must be different interests and parties in society; and a majority when united by a common interest or passion cannot be restrained from oppressing the minority, what remedy can be found in a republican Government, where the majority must ultimately decide, but that of giving such an extent to its sphere, that no common interest or passion will be likely to unite a majority of the whole number in an unjust pursuit. In a large Society, the people are broken into so many interests and parties, that a common sentiment is less likely to be felt, and the requisite concert less likely to be formed, by a majority of the whole. The same security seems requisite for the civil as for the religious rights of individuals. If the same sect form a majority and have the power, other sects will be sure to be depressed. Divide et impera, the reprobated axiom of tyranny, is under certain qualifications, the only policy, by which a republic can be administered on just principles. It must be observed however that this doctrine can only hold within a sphere of a mean extent. As in too small a sphere oppressive combinations may be too easily formed against the weaker party; so in too extensive a one, a defensive concert may be rendered too difficult against the oppression of those entrusted with the administration. The great desideratum in Government is, so to modify the sovereignty as that it may be sufficiently neutral between different parts of the Society to control one part from invading the rights of another, and at the same time sufficiently controlled itself, from setting up an interest adverse to that of the entire Society. In absolute monarchies, the Prince may be tolerably neutral towards different classes of his subjects but may sacrifice the happiness of all to his personal ambition or avarice. In small republics, the sovereign will is controlled from such a sacrifice of the entire Society, but is not sufficiently neutral towards the parts composing it. In the extended Republic of the United States, the General Government would hold a pretty even balance between the parties of particular States, and be at the same time sufficiently restrained by its dependence on the community, from betraying its general interests.

Begging pardon for this immoderate digression I return to the third object above mentioned, the adjustments of the different interests of different parts of the Continent. Some contended for an unlimited power over trade including exports as well as imports, and over slaves as well as other imports; some for such a power, provided the concurrence of two thirds of both Houses were required; Some for such a qualification of the power, with an exemption of exports and slaves, others for an exemption of exports only. The result is seen in the Constitution. S. Carolina & Georgia were inflexible on the point of the slaves.

The remaining object created more embarrassment, and a greater alarm for the issue of the Convention than all the rest put together. The little States insisted on retaining their equality in both branches, unless a complete abolition of the State Governments should take place; and made an equality in the Senate a sine qua non. The large States on the other hand urged that as the new Government was to be drawn principally from the people immediately and was to operate directly on them, not on the States; and consequently as the States would lose that importance which is now proportioned to the importance of their voluntary compliances with the requisitions of Congress, it was necessary that the representation in both Houses should be in proportion to their size. It ended in the compromise which you will see, but very much to the dissatisfaction of several members from the large States. . . .

8

James Madison

Federalist 10 (1787)

Among the numerous advantages promised by a well-constructed Union, none deserves to be more accurately developed than its tendency to break and control the violence of faction. The friend of popular governments never finds himself so much alarmed for their character and fate as when he contemplates their propensity to this dangerous vice. He will not fail, therefore, to set a due value on any plan which, without violating the principles to which he is attached, provides a proper cure for it. The instability, injustice, and confusion introduced into the public councils have, in truth, been the mortal diseases under which popular governments have everywhere perished, as they continue to be the favorite and fruitful topics from which the adversaries to liberty derive their most specious declamations. The valuable improvements made by the American constitutions on the popular models, both ancient and modern, cannot certainly be too much admired; but it would be an unwarrantable partiality to contend that they have as effectually obviated the danger on this side, as was wished and expected. Complaints are everywhere heard from our most considerate and virtuous citizens; equally the friends of public and private faith and of public and personal liberty, that our governments are too unstable, that the public good is disregarded in the

From *The Federalist.*

conflicts or rival parties, and that measures are too often decided, not according to the rules of justice and the rights of the minor party, but by the superior force of an interested and overbearing majority. However anxiously we may wish that these complaints had no foundation, the evidence of known facts will not permit us to deny that they are in some degree true. It will be found, indeed, on a candid review of our situation, that some of the distresses under which we labor have been erroneously charged on the operation of our governments; but it will be found, at the same time, that other causes will not alone account for many of our heaviest misfortunes; and, particularly, for that prevailing and increasing distrust of public engagements and alarm for private rights which are echoed from one end of the continent to the other. These must be chiefly, if not wholly, effects of the unsteadiness and injustice with which a factious spirit has tainted our public administration.

By a faction I understand a number of citizens, whether amounting to a majority or minority of the whole, who are united and actuated by some common impulse of passion, or of interest, adverse to the rights of other citizens, or to the permanent and aggregate interests of the community.

There are two methods of curing the mischiefs of faction: the one, by removing its causes; the other, by controlling its effects.

There are again two methods of removing the causes of faction: the one, by destroying the liberty which is essential to its existence; the other, by giving to every citizen the same opinions, the same passions, and the same interests.

It could never be more truly said than of the first remedy that it was worse than the disease. Liberty is to faction what air is to fire, an aliment without which it instantly expires. But it could not be a less folly to abolish liberty, which is essential to political life, because it nourishes faction than it would be to wish the annihilation of air, which is essential to animal life, because it imparts to fire its destructive agency.

The second expedient is as impracticable as the first would be unwise. As long as the reason of man continues fallible, and he is at liberty to exercise it, different opinions will be formed. As long as the connection subsists between his reason and his self-love, his opinions and his passions will have a reciprocal influence on each other; and the former will be objects to which the latter will attach themselves. The diversity in the faculties of men, from which the rights of property originate, is not less an insuperable obstacle to a uniformity of interests. The protection of these faculties is the first object of government. From the protection of different and unequal faculties of acquiring property, the possession of different degrees and kinds of property immediately results; and from the influence of these on the sentiments and views of the respective proprietors ensues a division of the society into different interests and parties.

The latent causes of faction are thus sown in the nature of man; and we see them everywhere brought into different degrees of activity, according to the different circumstances of civil society. A zeal for different opinions concerning religion, concerning government, and many other points, as well of speculation as of practice; an attachment to different leaders ambitiously contending for pre-eminence and power; or to persons of other descriptions whose fortunes have been interesting to the human passions, have, in turn, divided mankind into parties, inflamed them with mutual animosity, and rendered them much more disposed to vex and oppress each other than to co-operate for their common good. So strong is this propensity of mankind to fall into mutual animosities that where no substantial occasion presents itself the most frivolous and fanciful distinctions have been sufficient to kindle their unfriendly passions and excite their most violent conflicts. But the most common and durable source of factions has been the various and unequal distribution of property. Those who hold and those who are without property have ever formed distinct interests in society. Those who are creditors, and those who are debtors, fall under a like discrimination. A landed interest, a manufacturing interest, a mercantile interest, a moneyed interest, with many lesser interests, grow up of necessity in civilized nations, and divide them into different classes, actuated by different sentiments and views. The regulation of these various and interfering interests forms the principal task of modern legislation and involves the spirit of party and faction in the necessary and ordinary operations of government.

No man is allowed to be a judge in his own cause, because his interest would certainly bias his judgment, and, not improbably, corrupt his integrity. With equal, nay with greater reason, a body of men are unfit to be both judges and parties at the same time; yet what are many of the most important acts of legislation but so many judicial determinations, not indeed concerning the rights of single persons, but concerning the rights of large bodies of citizens? And what are the different classes of legislators but advocates and parties to the causes which they determine? Is a law proposed concerning private debts? It is a question to which the creditors are parties on one side and the debtors on the other. Justice ought to hold the balance between them. Yet the parties are, and must be, themselves the judges; and the most numerous party, or in other words, the most powerful faction must be expected to prevail. Shall domestic manufacturers be encouraged, and in what degree, by restrictions on foreign manufacturers? are questions which would be differently decided by the landed and the manufacturing classes, and probably by neither with a sole regard to justice and the public good. The apportionment of taxes on the various descriptions of property is an act which seems to require the most exact impartiality; yet there is, perhaps, no legislative act in which greater opportunity and temptation are given to a predominant party to trample on the rules of justice. Every shilling with which they overburden the inferior number is a shilling saved to their own pockets.

It is in vain to say that enlightened statesmen will be able to adjust these clashing interests and render them all subservient to the public good. Enlightened statesmen will not always be at the helm. Nor, in many cases, can such an adjustment be made at all without taking into view indirect and remote considerations, which will rarely prevail over the immediate interest which one party may find in disregarding the rights of another or the good of the whole.

The inference to which we are brought is that the *causes* of faction cannot be removed and that relief is only to be sought in the means of controlling its *effects*.

If a faction consists of less than a majority, relief is supplied by the republican principle, which enables the majority to defeat its sinister views by regular vote. It may clog the administration, it may convulse the society; but it will be unable to execute and mask its violence under the forms of the Constitution. When a majority is included in a faction, the form of popular government, on the other hand, enables it to sacrifice to its ruling passion or interest both the public good and the rights of other citizens. To secure the public good and private rights against the danger of such a faction, and at the same time to preserve the spirit and the form of popular government, is then the great object to which our inquiries are directed. Let me add that it is the great desideratum by which alone this form of government can be rescued from the opprobrium under which it has so long labored and be recommended to the esteem and adoption of mankind.

By what means is this object attainable? Evidently by one of two only. Either the existence of the same passion or interest in a majority at the same time must be prevented, or the majority, having such coexistent passion or interest, must be rendered, by their number and local situation, unable to concert and carry into effect schemes of oppression. If the impulse and the opportunity be suffered to coincide, we well know that neither moral nor religious motives can be relied on as an adequate control. They are not found to be such on the injustice and violence of individuals, and lose their efficacy in proportion to the number combined together, that is, in proportion as their efficacy becomes needful.

From this view of the subject it may be concluded that a pure democracy, by which I mean a society consisting of a small number of citizens, who assemble and administer the government in person, can admit of no cure for the mischiefs of faction. A common passion or interest will, in almost every case, be felt by a majority of the whole; a communication and concert results from the form of government itself; and there is nothing to check the inducements to sacrifice the weaker party or an obnoxious individual. Hence it is that such democracies have ever been spectacles of turbulence and contention; have ever been found incompatible with personal security or the rights of property; and have in general been as short in their lives as they have been violent in their deaths. Theoretic politicians, who have patron-ized this species of government, have erroneously supposed that by reducing mankind to a perfect equality in their political rights, they would at the same time be perfectly equalized and assimilated in their possessions, their opin-ions, and their passions.

A republic, by which I mean a government in which the scheme of repre-sentation takes place, opens a different prospect and promises the cure for which we are seeking. Let us examine the points in which it varies from pure democracy, and we shall comprehend both the nature of the cure and the effi-cacy which it must derive from the Union.

The two great points of difference between a democracy and a republic are: first, the delegation of the government, in the latter, to a small number of citizens elected by the rest; secondly, the greater number of citizens and greater sphere of country over which the latter may be extended.

The effect of the first difference is, on the one hand, to refine and enlarge the public views by passing them through the medium of a chosen body of citizens, whose wisdom may best discern the true interest of their country and whose patriotism and love of justice will be least likely to sacri-fice it to temporary or partial considerations. Under such a regulation it may well happen that the public voice, pronounced by the representatives of the people, will be more consonant to the public good than if pronounced by the people themselves, convened for the purpose. On the other hand, the effect may be inverted. Men of factious tempers, of local prejudices, or of sinister designs, may, by intrigue, by corruption, or by other means, first obtain the suffrages, and then betray the interests of the people. The question resulting is, whether small or extensive republics are most favorable to the election of proper guardians of the public weal; and it is clearly decided in favor of the latter by two obvious considerations.

In the first place it is to be remarked that however small the republic may be the representatives must be raised to a certain number in order to guard against the cabals of a few; and that however large it may be they must be limited to a certain number in order to guard against the confusion of a multitude. Hence, the number of representatives in the two cases not being in proportion to that of the constituents, and being proportionally greatest in the small republic, it follows that if the proportion of fit characters be not less in the large than in the small republic, the former will present a greater option, and consequently a greater probability of a fit choice.

In the next place, as each representative will be chosen by a greater number of citizens in the large than in the small republic, it will be more dif-ficult for unworthy candidates to practice with success the vicious arts by which elections are too often carried; and the suffrages of the people being more free, will be more likely to center on men who possess the most attrac-tive merit and the most diffusive and established characters.

It must be confessed that in this, as in most other cases, there is a mean, on both sides of which inconveniencies will be found to lie. By enlarging too much the number of electors, you render the representative too little acquainted with all their local circumstances and lesser interest; as by reducing it too much, you render him unduly attached to these, and too little fit to comprehend and pursue great and national objects. The federal Constitution forms a happy combination in this respect; the great and aggregate interests being referred to the national, the local and particular to the State legislatures.

The other point of difference is the greater number of citizens and extent of territory which may be brought within the compass of republican than of democratic government; and it is this circumstance principally which renders factious combinations less to be dreaded in the former than in the latter. The smaller the society, the fewer probably will be the distinct parties and interests composing it; the fewer the distinct parties and interests, the more frequently will a majority be found of the same party; and the smaller the number of individuals composing a majority, and the smaller the compass within which they are placed, the more easily will they concert and execute their plans of oppression. Extend the sphere and you take in a greater variety of parties and interests; you make it less probable that a majority of the whole will have a common motive to invade the rights of other citizens; or if such a common motive exists, it will be more difficult for all who feel it to discover their own strength and to act in unison with each other. Besides other impediments, it may be remarked that, where there is a consciousness of unjust or dishonorable purposes, communication is always checked by distrust in proportion to the number whose concurrence is necessary.

Hence, it clearly appears that the same advantage which a republic has over a democracy in controlling the effects of faction is enjoyed by a large over a small republic—is enjoyed by the Union over the States composing it. Does this advantage consist in the substitution of representatives whose enlightened views and virtuous sentiments render them superior to local prejudices and to schemes of injustice? It will not be denied that the representation of the Union will be most likely to possess these requisite endowments. Does it consist in the greater security afforded by a greater variety of parties, against the event of any one party being able to outnumber and oppress the rest? In an equal degree does the increased variety of parties comprised within the Union increase this security. Does it, in fine, consist in the greater obstacles opposed to the concert and accomplishment of the secret wishes of an unjust and interested majority? Here again the extent of the Union gives it the most palpable advantage.

The influence of factious leaders may kindle a flame within their particular States but will be unable to spread a general conflagration through the other States. A religious sect may degenerate into a political faction in a part of the

Confederacy; but the variety of sects dispersed over the entire face of it must secure the national councils against any danger from that source. A rage for paper money, for an abolition of debts, for an equal division of property, or for any other improper or wicked project, will be less apt to pervade the whole body of the Union than a particular member of it, in the same proportion as such a malady is more likely to taint a particular county or district than an entire State.

In the extent and proper structure of the Union, therefore, we behold a republican remedy for the diseases most incident to republican government. And according to the degree of pleasure and pride we feel in being republicans ought to be our zeal in cherishing the spirit and supporting the character of federalists.

9

James Madison

Federalist 51 (1788)

To what expedient, then, shall we finally resort, for maintaining in practice the necessary partition of power among the several departments as laid down in the Constitution? The only answer that can be given is that as all these exterior provisions are found to be inadequate the defect must be supplied, by so contriving the interior structure of the government as that its several constituent parts may, by their mutual relations, be the means of keeping each other in their proper places. Without presuming to undertake a full development of this important idea I will hazard a few general observations which may perhaps place it in a clearer light, and enable us to form a more correct judgment of the principles and structure of the government planned by the convention.

In order to lay a due foundation for that separate and distinct exercise of the different powers of government, which to a certain extent is admitted on all hands to be essential to the preservation of liberty, it is evident that each department should have a will of its own; and consequently should be so constituted that the members of each should have as little

From *The Federalist*.

agency as possible in the appointment of the members of the others. Were this principle rigorously adhered to, it would require that all the appointments for the supreme executive, legislative, and judiciary magistracies should be drawn from the same fountain of authority, the people, through channels having no communication whatever with one another. Perhaps such a plan of constructing the several departments would be less difficult in practice than it may in contemplation appear. Some difficulties, however, and some additional expense would attend the execution of it. Some deviations, therefore, from the principle must be admitted. In the constitution of the judiciary department in particular, it might be inexpedient to insist rigorously on the principle: first, because peculiar qualifications being essential in the members, the primary consideration ought to be to select that mode of choice which best secures these qualifications; second, because the permanent tenure by which the appointments are held in that department must soon destroy all sense of dependence on the authority conferring them.

It is equally evident that the members of each department should be as little dependent as possible on those of the others for the emoluments annexed to their offices. Were the executive magistrate, or the judges, not independent of the legislature in this particular, their independence in every other would be merely nominal.

But the great security against a gradual concentration of the several powers in the same department consists in giving to those who administer each department the necessary constitutional means and personal motives to resist encroachments of the others. The provision for defense must in this, as in all other cases, be made commensurate to the danger of attack. Ambition must be made to counteract ambition. The interest of the man must be connected with the constitutional rights of the place. It may be a reflection on human nature that such devices should be necessary to control the abuses of government. But what is government itself but the greatest of all reflections on human nature? If men were angels, no government would be necessary. If angels were to govern men, neither external nor internal controls on government would be necessary. In framing a government which is to be administered by men over men, the great difficulty lies in this: you must first enable the government to control the governed; and in the next place oblige it to control itself. A dependence on the people is, no doubt, the primary control on the government; but experience has taught mankind the necessity of auxiliary precautions.

This policy of supplying, by opposite and rival interests, the defect of better motives, might be traced through the whole system of human affairs, private as well as public. We see it particularly displayed in all the subordinate distributions of power, where the constant aim is to divide and arrange the several offices in such a manner as that each may be a check on the other—that the private interest of every individual may be a sentinel over the public rights.

These inventions of prudence cannot be less requisite in the distribution of the supreme powers of the State.

But it is not possible to give to each department an equal power of self-defense. In republican government, the legislative authority necessarily predominates. The remedy for this inconveniency is to divide the legislature into different branches; and to render them, by different modes of election and different principles of action, as little connected with each other as the nature of their common functions and their common dependence on the society will admit. It may even be necessary to guard against dangerous encroachments by still further precautions. As the weight of the legislative authority requires that it should be thus divided, the weakness of the executive may require, on the other hand, that it should be fortified. An absolute negative on the legislature appears, at first view, to be the natural defense with which the executive magistrate should be armed. But perhaps it would be neither altogether safe nor alone sufficient. On ordinary occasions it might not be exerted with the requisite firmness, and on extraordinary occasions it might be perfidiously abused. May not this defect of an absolute negative be supplied by some qualified connection between this weaker department and the weaker branch of the stronger department, by which the latter may be led to support the constitutional rights of the former, without being too much detached from the rights of its own department?

If the principles on which these observations are founded be just, as I persuade myself they are, and they be applied as a criterion to the several State constitutions, and to the federal Constitution, it will be found that if the latter does not perfectly correspond with them, the former are infinitely less able to bear such a test.

There are, moreover, two considerations particularly applicable to the federal system of America, which place that system in a very interesting point of view.

First. In a single republic, all the power surrendered by the people is submitted to the administration of a single government; and the usurpations are guarded against by a division of the government into distinct and separate departments. In the compound republic of America, the power surrendered by the people is first divided between two distinct governments, and then the portion allotted to each subdivided among distinct and separate departments. Hence a double security arises to the rights of the people. The different governments will control each other, at the same time that each will be controlled by itself.

Second. It is of great importance in a republic not only to guard the society against the oppression of its rulers, but to guard one part of the society against the injustice of the other part. Different interests necessarily exist in different classes of citizens. If a majority be united by a common interest, the rights of the minority will be insecure. There are but two methods of providing against this evil: the one by creating a will in the community independent of the majority—that is, of the society itself; the other, by comprehending in the society so many separate descriptions of citizens as will render an unjust combination of a majority of the whole very improbable, if not impracticable. The first method prevails in all governments possessing an hereditary or self-appointed authority. This, at best, is but a precarious security; because a power independent of the society may as well espouse the unjust views of the major as the rightful interests of the minor party, and may possibly be turned against both parties. The second method will be exemplified in the federal republic of the United States. Whilst all authority in it will be derived from and dependent on the society, the society itself will be broken into so many parts, interests, and classes of citizens, that the rights of individuals, or of the minority, will be in little danger from interested combinations of the majority. In a free government the security for civil rights must be the same as that for religious rights. It consists in the one case in the multiplicity of interests, and in the other in the multiplicity of sects. The degree of security in both cases will depend on the number of interests and sects; and this may be presumed to depend on the extent of country and number of people comprehended under the same government. This view of the subject must particularly recommend a proper federal system to all the sincere and considerate friends of republican government, since it shows that in exact proportion as the territory of the Union may be formed into more circumscribed Confederacies, or States, oppressive combinations of a majority will be facilitated; the best security, under the republican forms, for the rights of every class of citizen, will be diminished; and consequently the stability and independence of some member of the government, the only other security, must be proportionally increased. Justice is the end of government. It is the end of civil society. It ever has been and ever will be pursued until it be obtained, or until liberty be lost in the pursuit. In a society under the forms of which the stronger faction can readily unite and oppress the weaker, anarchy may as truly be said to reign as in a state of nature, where the weaker individual is not secured against the violence of the stronger; and as, in the latter state, even the stronger individuals are prompted, by the uncertainty of their condition, to submit to a government which may protect the weak as well as themselves; so, in the former state, will the more powerful factions or parties be gradually induced, by a like motive, to wish for a government which will protect all parties, the weaker as well as the more powerful. It can be little doubted that if the State of Rhode Island was separated from the Confederacy and left to itself, the insecurity of rights under the popular form of government within such narrow limits would be displayed by such reiterated oppressions of factious majorities that some power altogether independent of the people would soon be called for by the voice of the very factions whose misrule had proved the necessity of it. In the extended republic of the United States, and among the great variety of interests, parties, and sects which it embraces, a coalition of a majority of the whole society could seldom take place on any other principles than those of justice and the general good; whilst there being thus less danger to a minor from the will of a major party, there must be less pretext, also, to provide for the security of the former, by introducing into the government a will not dependent on the latter, or, in other words, a will independent of the society itself. It is no less certain than it is important, notwithstanding the contrary opinions which have been entertained, that the larger the society, provided it lie within a practicable sphere, the more duly capable it will be of self-government. And happily for the *republican cause*, the practicable sphere may be carried to a very great extent by a judicious modification and mixture of the *federal principle*.

10

John Adams

The Role of the Rich and the Poor in the Legislature (1787)

. . . There can be no free government without a democratical branch in the constitution. . . .

The rich, the well-born, and the able, acquire an influence among the people that will soon be too much for simple honesty and plain sense, in a house of representatives. The most illustrious of them must, therefore, be separated from the mass, and placed by themselves in a senate; this is, to all honest and useful intents, an ostracism. A member of a senate, of immense wealth, the most respected birth, and transcendent abilities, has no influence in the nation, in comparison of what he would have in a single representative assembly. When a senate exists, the most powerful man in the state may be safely admitted into the house of representatives, because the people have it in their power to remove him into the senate as soon as his influence becomes dangerous. The senate becomes the great object of ambition; and the richest and the most sagacious wish to merit an advancement to it by services to the public in the house. When he has obtained the object of his wishes, you may still hope for the benefits of his exertions, without dreading his passions; for the executive power being in other hands, he has lost much

From A *Defense of the Constitutions of the Government of the United States*, in *The Life and Work of John Adams*, Vol. IV and Vol. VI, Little, Brown, and Co., 1851.

of his influence with the people, and can govern very few votes more than his own among the senators. . . .

〰〰〰

Marchamont Nedham lays it down as a fundamental principle and an undeniable rule, "that the people, (that is, such as shall be successively chosen to represent the people), are the best keepers of their own liberties, and that for many reasons. First, because they never think of usurping over other men's rights, but mind which way to preserve their own." . . .

Would Mr. Nedham be responsible that, if all were to be decided by a vote of the majority, the eight or nine millions who have no property, would not think of usurping over the rights of the one or two millions who have? Property is surely a right of mankind as really as liberty. Perhaps, at first, prejudice, habit, shame or fear, principle or religion, would restrain the poor from attacking the rich, and the idle from usurping on the industrious; but the time would not be long before courage and enterprise would come, and pretexts be invented by degrees, to countenance the majority in dividing all the property among them, or at least, in sharing it equally with its present possessors. Debts would be abolished first; taxes laid heavy on the rich, and not at all on the others; and at last a downright equal division of every thing be demanded, and voted. What would be the consequence of this? The idle, the vicious, the intemperate, would rush into the utmost extravagance of debauchery, sell and spend all their share, and then demand a new division of those who purchased from them. The moment the idea is admitted into society, that property is not as sacred as the laws of God, and that there is not a force of law and public justice to protect it, anarchy and tyranny commence. . . .

Though we allow benevolence and generous affections to exist in the human breast, yet every moral theorist will admit the selfish passions in the generality of men to be the strongest. There are few who love the public better than themselves, though all may have some affection for the public. . . .

The only remedy is to take away the power, controlling the selfish avidity of the governor, by the senate and house; of the senate, by the governor and house; and of the house, by the governor and senate. Of all possible forms of government, a sovereignty in one assembly, successively chosen by the people, is perhaps the best calculated to facilitate the gratification of self-love, and the pursuit of the private interest of a few individuals; a few eminent conspicuous characters will be continued in their seats in the sovereign assembly, from one election to another, whatever changes are made in the seats around them, by superior art, address, and opulence, by more splendid birth, reputations, and connections, they will be able to intrigue with the people and their leaders, out of doors, until they worm out most of their opposers, and introduce their friends; to this end, they will bestow all offices, contracts, privileges in commerce, and other emoluments, on the latter and their connections, and throw every vexation and disappointment in the way of the former, until they establish such a system of hopes and fears throughout the state, as shall enable them to carry a majority in every fresh election of the house. The judges will be appointed by them and their party, and of consequence, will be obsequious enough to their inclinations. . . .

It is agreed that "the end of all government is the good and ease of the people, in a secure enjoyment of their rights, without oppression;" but it must be remembered, that the rich are *people* as well as the poor; that they have rights as well as others; that they have as clear and as *sacred* a right to their large property as others have to theirs which is smaller; that oppression to them is as possible and as wicked as to others; that stealing, robbing, cheating, are the same crimes and sins, whether committed against them or others. The rich, therefore, ought to have an effectual barrier in the constitution against being robbed, plundered, and murdered, as well as the poor; and this can never be without an independent senate. The poor should have a bulwark against the same dangers and oppressions; and this can never be without a house of representatives of the people. But neither the rich nor the poor can be defended by their respective guardians in the constitution, without an executive power, vested with a negative, equal to either, to hold the balance even between them, and decide when they cannot agree. If it is asked, When will this negative be used? it may be answered, Perhaps never. The known existence of it will prevent all occasion to exercise it; but if it has not a being, the want of it will be felt every day. . . .

11

Alexander Hamilton

On the Character of the Legislator (1778)

. . . The station of a member of Congress is the most illustrious and important of any I am able to conceive. He is to be regarded not only as a legislator, but as the founder of an empire. A man of virtue and ability, dignified with so precious a trust, would rejoice that fortune had given him birth at a time, and

From Hamilton, "Publius Letter, III." Nov. 16, 1779, in *The Papers of Alexander Hamilton*, Vol. I, Columbia University Press, 1969.

placed him in circumstances so favourable for promoting human happiness. He would esteem it not more the duty, than the privilege and ornament of his office, to do good to mankind; from this commanding eminence, he would look down with contempt upon every mean or interested pursuit.

To form useful alliances abroad—to establish a wise government at home—to improve the internal resources, and finances of the nation would be the generous objects of his care. He would not allow his attention to be diverted from these to intrigue for personal connections, to confirm his own influence; nor would be able to reconcile it, either to the delicacy of his honour, or to the dignity of his pride, to confound in the same person the representative of the Commonwealth, and the little member of a trading company. Anxious for the permanent power and prosperity of the State, he would labour to perpetuate the union and harmony of the several parts. He would not meanly court a temporary importance, by patronizing the narrow views of local interest, or by encouraging dissensions either among the people or in Congress. In council, or debate, he would discover the candor of a statesman, zealous for truth, and the integrity of a patriot studious of the public welfare; not the cavilling petulance of an attorney, contending for the triumph of an opinion, nor the perverse duplicity of a partisan, devoted to the service of a cabal. Despising the affectation of superior wisdom, he would prove the extent of his capacity, by foreseeing evils, and contriving expedients to prevent or remedy them. He would not expose the weak sides of the State, to find an opportunity of displaying his own discernment, by magnifying the follies and mistakes of others. In his transactions with individuals, whether foreigners or countrymen, his conduct would be guided by the sincerity of a man, and the politeness of a gentleman, not by the temporising flexibility of a courtier, nor the fawning complaisance of a sycophant. . . .

12

Alexander Hamilton

Federalist 11 (1787)

The importance of the Union, in a commercial light, is one of those points about which there is least room to entertain a difference of opinion. . . .

From *The Federalist.*

There are appearances to authorize a supposition that the adventurous spirit, which distinguishes the commercial character of America, has already excited uneasy sensations in several of the maritime powers of Europe. . . . Those of them which have colonies in America look forward to what this country is capable of becoming, with painful solicitude. . . . Impressions of this kind will naturally indicate the policy of fostering divisions among us, and of depriving us, as far as possible, of an ACTIVE COMMERCE in our own bottoms. This would answer the threefold purpose of preventing our interference in their navigation, of monopolizing the profits of our trade, and of clipping the wings by which we might soar to a dangerous greatness. Did not prudence forbid the detail, it would not be difficult to trace, by facts, the workings of this policy to the cabinets of ministers.

If we continue united, we may counteract a policy so unfriendly to our prosperity in a variety of ways. By prohibitory regulations, extending, at the same time, throughout the States, we may oblige foreign countries to bid against each other, for the privileges of our markets. . . .

A further resource for influencing the conduct of European nations towards us, in this respect, would arise from the establishment of a federal navy. There can be no doubt that the continuance of the Union under an efficient government, would put it in our power, at a period not very distant, to create a navy which, if it could not vie with those of the great maritime powers, would at least be of respectable weight if thrown into the scale of either of two contending parties. This would be more peculiarly the case in relation to operations in the West Indies. A few ships of the line, sent opportunely to the reinforcement of either side, would often be sufficient to decide the fate of a campaign, on the event of which interests of the greatest magnitude were suspended. Our position is, in this respect, a most commanding one. And if to this consideration we add that of the usefulness of supplies from this country, in the prosecution of military operations in the West Indies, it will readily be perceived that a situation so favorable would enable us to bargain with great advantage for commercial privileges. A price would be set not only upon our friendship, but upon our neutrality. By a steady adherence to the Union, we may hope, erelong, to become the arbiter of Europe in America, and to be able to incline the balance of European competitions in this part of the world as our interest may dictate.

But in the reverse of this eligible situation, we shall discover that the rivalships of the parts would make them checks upon each other, and would frustrate all the tempting advantages which nature has kindly placed within our reach. In a state so insignificant our commerce would be a prey to the wanton intermeddlings of all nations at war with each other; who, having nothing to fear from us, would with little scruple or remorse supply their wants by depredations on our property as often as it fell in their way. The rights of neutrality will only be respected when they are defended by an adequate power. A nation, despicable by its weakness, forfeits even the privilege of being neutral.

Under a vigorous national government, the natural strength and resources of the country, directed to a common interest, would baffle all the combinations of European jealousy to restrain our growth. This situation would even take away the motive to such combinations, by inducing an impracticability of success. An active commerce, an extensive navigation, and a flourishing marine would then be the offspring of moral and physical necessity. We might defy the little arts of the little politicians to control or vary the irresistible and unchangeable course of nature.

But in a state of disunion, these combinations might exist and might operate with success. It would be in the power of the maritime nations, availing themselves of our universal impotence, to prescribe the conditions of our political existence; and as they have a common interest in being our carriers, and still more in preventing our becoming theirs, they would in all probability combine to embarrass our navigation in such a manner as would in effect destroy it, and confine us to a PASSIVE COMMERCE. We should then be compelled to content ourselves with the first price of our commodities, and to see the profits of our trade snatched from us to enrich our enemies and persecutors. That unequalled spirit of enterprise, which signalizes the genius of the American merchants and navigators, and which is in itself an inexhaustible mine of national wealth, would be stifled and lost, and poverty and disgrace would overspread a country which, with wisdom, might make herself the admiration and envy of the world. . . .

An unrestrained intercourse between the States themselves will advance the trade of each by an interchange of their respective productions, not only for the supply of reciprocal wants at home, but for exportation to foreign markets. The veins of commerce in every part will be replenished, and will acquire additional motion and vigor from a free circulation of the commodities of every part. Commercial enterprise will have much greater scope, from the diversity in the productions of different States. When the staple of one fails from a bad harvest or unproductive crop, it can call to its aid the staple of another. The variety, not less than the value, of products for exportation contributes to the activity of foreign commerce. It can be conducted upon much better terms with a large number of materials of a given value than with a small number of materials of the same value; arising from the competitions of trade and from the fluctuations of markets. Particular articles may be in great demand at certain periods, and unsalable at others; but if there be a variety of articles, it can scarcely happen that they should all be at one time in the latter predicament, and on this account the operations of the merchant would be less liable to any considerable obstruction or stagnation. . . .

The world may politically, as well as geographically, be divided into four parts, each having a distinct set of interests. Unhappily for the other three, Europe, by her arms and by her negotiations, by force and by fraud, has, in different degrees, extended her dominion over them all. Africa, Asia, and America, have successively felt her domination. The superiority she has long maintained has tempted her to plume herself as the Mistress of the World, and to consider the rest of mankind as created for her benefit. . . . Facts have too long supported these arrogant pretensions of the Europeans. It belongs to us to vindicate the honor of the human race, and to teach that assuming brother, moderation. Union will enable us to do it. Disunion will add another victim to his triumphs. Let Americans disdain to be the instruments of European greatness! Let the thirteen States, bound together in a strict and indissoluble Union, concur in erecting one great American system, superior to the control of all transatlantic force or influence, and able to dictate the terms of the connection between the old and the new world!

13

Alexander Hamilton

The Military in a Commercial Republic (1787)

. . . [Opponents of the Constitution would like standing armies to be prohibited.] From a close examination it will appear that restraints upon the discretion of the legislature in respect to military establishments in time of peace, would be improper to be imposed, and if imposed, from the necessities of society, would be unlikely to be observed.

Though a wide ocean separates the United States from Europe, yet there are various considerations that warn us against an excess of confidence or security. On one side of us, and stretching far into our rear, are growing settlements subject to the dominion of Britain. On the other side, and extending to meet the British settlements, are colonies and establishments subject to the dominion of Spain. This situation and the vicinity of the West India Islands, belonging to these two powers, create between them, in respect to their American possessions and in relation to us, a common interest. . . .

From Federalist 8 and 24, in *The Federalist*.

Previous to the Revolution, and ever since the peace, there has been a constant necessity for keeping small garrisons on our Western frontier. No person can doubt that these will continue to be indispensable, if it should only be against the ravages and depredations of the Indians. These garrisons must either be furnished by occasional detachments from the militia, or by permanent corps in the pay of the government. The first is impracticable; and if practicable, would be pernicious. The militia would not long, if at all, submit to be dragged from their occupations and families to perform that most disagreeable duty in times of profound peace. And if they could be prevailed upon or compelled to do it, the increased expense of a frequent rotation of service, and the loss of labor and disconcertion of the industrious pursuits of individuals, would form conclusive objections to the scheme. It would be as burdensome and injurious to the public as ruinous to private citizens. The latter resource of permanent corps in the pay of the government amounts to a standing army in time of peace; a small one, indeed, but not the less real for being small. Here is a simple view of the subject, that shows us at once the impropriety of a constitutional interdiction of such establishments, and the necessity of leaving the matter to the discretion and prudence of the legislature. . . .

. . . The industrious habits of the people of the present day, absorbed in the pursuits of gain, and devoted to the improvements of agriculture and commerce, are incompatible with the condition of a nation of soldiers, which was the true condition of the people of those republics. The means of revenue, which have been so greatly multiplied by the increase of gold and silver and of the arts of industry, and the science of finance, which is the off-spring of modern times, concurring with the habits of nations, have produced an entire revolution in the system of war, and have rendered disciplined armies, distinct from the body of the citizens, the inseparable companions of frequent hostility. . . .

14

Alexis de Tocqueville

Equality and Commerce (1840)

In America the passion for physical well-being is not always exclusive, but it is general; and if all do not feel it in the same manner, yet it is felt by all. Carefully to satisfy all, even the least wants of the body, and to provide the little conveniences of life is uppermost in every mind. . . .

When riches are hereditarily fixed in families, there are a great number of men who enjoy the comforts of life without feeling an exclusive taste for those comforts. The heart of man is not so much caught by the undisturbed possession of anything valuable as by the desire, as yet imperfectly satisfied, of possessing it and by the incessant dread of losing it. In aristocratic communities the wealthy, never having experienced a condition different from their own, entertain no fear of changing it; the existence of such conditions hardly occurs to them. The comforts of life are not to them the end of life, but simply a way of living; they regard them as existence itself, enjoyed but scarcely thought of. As the natural and instinctive taste that all men feel for being well off is thus satisfied without trouble and without apprehension, their faculties are turned elsewhere and cling to more arduous and lofty undertakings, which excite and engross their minds.

Hence it is that in the midst of physical gratifications the members of an aristocracy often display a haughty contempt of these very enjoyments and exhibit singular powers of endurance under the privation of them. All the revolutions which have ever shaken or destroyed aristocracies have shown how easily men accustomed to superfluous luxuries can do without the necessaries of life; whereas men who have toiled to acquire a competency can hardly live after they have lost it.

If I turn my observation from the upper to the lower classes, I find analogous effects produced by opposite causes. Among a nation where aristocracy predominates in society and keeps it stationary, the people in the end get as much accustomed to poverty as the rich to their opulence. The latter bestow

From *Democracy in America* by Alexis de Tocqueville, translated by Henry Reeve, 1862, with minor changes.

no anxiety on their physical comforts because they enjoy them without an effort; the former do not think of things which they despair of obtaining and which they hardly know enough of to desire. In communities of this kind the imagination of the poor is driven to seek another world; the miseries of real life enclose it, but it escapes from their control and flies to seek its pleasures far beyond.

When, on the contrary, the distinctions of ranks are confounded together and privileges are destroyed, when hereditary property is subdivided and education and freedom widely diffused, the desire of acquiring the comforts of the world haunts the imagination of the poor, and the dread of losing them that of the rich. Many scanty fortunes spring up; those who possess them have a sufficient share of physical gratifications to conceive a taste for these pleasures, not enough to satisfy it. They never procure them without exertion, and they never indulge in them without apprehension. They are therefore always straining to pursue or to retain gratifications so delightful, so imperfect, so fugitive.

If I were to inquire what passion is most natural to men who are stimulated and circumscribed by the obscurity of their birth or the mediocrity of their fortune, I could discover none more peculiarly appropriate to their condition than this love of physical prosperity. The passion for physical comforts is essentially a passion of the middle classes; with those classes it grows and spreads, with them it preponderates. From them it mounts into the higher orders of society and descends into the mass of the people.

I never met in America with any citizen so poor as not to cast a glance of hope and envy on the enjoyments of the rich or whose imagination did not possess itself by anticipation of those good things that fate still obstinately withheld from him.

On the other hand, I never perceived among the wealthier inhabitants of the United States that proud contempt of physical gratifications which is sometimes to be met with even in the most opulent and dissolute aristocracies. Most of these wealthy persons were once poor; they have felt the sting of want; they were long a prey to adverse fortunes; and now that the victory is won, the passions which accompanied the contest have survived it; their minds are, as it were, intoxicated by the small enjoyments which they have pursued for forty years. . . .

〜〜〜〜ॐ〜〜〜

. . . It commonly happens that in the ages of privilege the practice of almost all the arts becomes a privilege, and that every profession is a separate walk, upon which it is not allowable for everyone to enter. Even when productive industry is free, the fixed character that belongs to aristocratic nations gradually segregates all the persons who practice the same art till they form a distinct class, always composed of the same families, whose members are all known to each other and among whom a public opinion of their own and a species of corporate pride soon spring up. In a class or guild of this kind each artisan has not only his fortune to make, but his reputation to preserve. He is not exclusively swayed by his own interest or even by that of his customer, but by that of the body to which he belongs; and the interest of that body is that each artisan should produce the best possible workmanship. In aristocratic ages the object of the arts is therefore to manufacture as well as possible, not with the greatest dispatch or at the lowest cost.

When, on the contrary, every profession is open to all, when a multitude of persons are constantly embracing and abandoning it, and when its several members are strangers to each other, indifferent, and from their numbers hardly seen among themselves, the social tie is destroyed, and each workman, standing alone, endeavors simply to gain the greatest quantity of money at the least possible cost. The will of the customer is then his only limit. But at the same time a corresponding revolution takes place in the customer also. In countries in which riches as well as power are concentrated and retained in the hands of a few, the use of the greater part of this world's goods belongs to a small number of individuals, who are always the same. Necessity, public opinion, or moderate desires exclude all others from the enjoyment of them. As this aristocratic class remains fixed at the pinnacle of greatness on which it stands, without diminution or increase, it is always acted upon by the same wants and affected by them in the same manner. The men of whom it is composed naturally derive from their superior and hereditary position a taste for what is extremely well made and lasting. This affects the general way of thinking of the nation in relation to the arts. It often occurs among such a people that even the peasant will rather go without the objects he covets than procure them in a state of imperfection. In aristocracies, then, the handicraftsmen work for only a limited number of very fastidious customers; the profit they hope to make depends principally on the perfection of their workmanship.

Such is no longer the case when, all privileges being abolished, ranks are intermingled and men are forever rising or sinking upon the ladder of society. Among a democratic people a number of citizens always exists whose patrimony is divided and decreasing. They have contracted, under more prosperous circumstances, certain wants, which remain after the means of satisfying such wants are gone; and they are anxiously looking out for some surreptitious method of providing for them. On the other hand, there is always in democracies a large number of men whose fortune is on the increase, but whose desires grow much faster than their fortunes, and who gloat upon the gifts of wealth in anticipation, long before they have means to command them. Such men are eager to find some short cut to these gratifications, already almost within their reach. From the combination of these two causes the result is that in democracies there is always a multitude of persons whose wants are above their means and who are very willing to take up with imperfect satisfaction rather than abandon the object of their desires.

The artisan readily understands these passions, for he himself partakes in them. In an aristocracy he would seek to sell his workmanship at a high price to the few; he now conceives that the more expeditious way of getting rich is to sell them at a low price to all. But there are only two ways of lowering the price of commodities. The first is to discover some better, shorter, and more ingenious method of producing them; the second is to manufacture a larger quantity of goods, nearly similar, but of less value. Among a democratic population all the intellectual faculties of the workman are directed to these two objects: he strives to invent methods that may enable him not only to work better, but more quickly and more cheaply; or if he cannot succeed in that, to diminish the intrinsic quality of the thing he makes, without rendering it wholly unfit for the use for which it is intended. When none but the wealthy had watches, they were almost all very good ones; few are now made that are worth much, but everybody has one in his pocket. Thus the democratic principle not only tends to direct the human mind to the useful arts, but it induces the artisan to produce with great rapidity a quantity of imperfect commodities, and the consumer to content himself with these commodities. . . .

The handicraftsmen of democratic ages not only endeavor to bring their useful productions within the reach of the whole community, but they strive to give to all their commodities attractive qualities that they do not in reality possess. In the confusion of all ranks everyone hopes to appear what he is not, and makes great exertions to succeed in this object. This sentiment, indeed, which is but too natural to the heart of man, does not originate in the democratic principle; but that principle applies it to material objects. To mimic virtue is of every age, but the hypocrisy of luxury belongs more particularly to the ages of democracy.

To satisfy these new cravings of human vanity the arts have recourse to every species of imposture. . . .

When I arrived for the first time at New York, by that part of the Atlantic Ocean which is called the Narrows, I was surprised to perceive along the shore, at some distance from the city, a considerable number of little palaces of white marble, several of which were built after the models of ancient architecture. When I went the next day to inspect more closely the building which had particularly attracted my notice, I found that its walls were of whitewashed brick, and its columns of painted wood. All the edifices that I had admired the night before were of the same kind.

The social condition and the institutions of democracy impart, moreover, certain peculiar tendencies to all the imitative arts, which it is easy to point out. They frequently withdraw them from the delineation of the soul to fix them exclusively on that of the body, and they substitute the representation of motion and sensation for that of sentiment and thought; in a word, they put the Real in the place of the Ideal.

I doubt whether Raphael studied the minute intricacies of the mechanism of the human body as thoroughly as the draftsmen of our own time. He did not attach the same importance to rigorous accuracy on this point as they do because he aspired to surpass nature. He sought to make of man something which should be superior to man and to embellish beauty's self. David and his scholars were, on the contrary, as good anatomists as they were good painters. They wonderfully depicted the models that they had before their eyes, but they rarely imagined anything beyond them; they followed nature with fidelity, while Raphael sought for something better than nature. They have left us an exact portraiture of man, but he discloses in his works a glimpse of the Divinity.

This remark as to the manner of treating a subject is no less applicable to the choice of it. The painters of the Middle Ages generally sought far above themselves, and away from their own time, for mighty subjects, which left to their imagination an unbounded range. Our painters frequently employ their talents in the exact imitation of the details of private life, which they have always before their eyes; and they are forever copying trivial objects, the originals of which are only too abundant in nature. . . .

<hr />

. . . In Europe we are wont to look upon a restless disposition, an unbounded desire of riches, and an excessive love of independence as propensities very formidable to society. Yet these are the very elements that ensure a long and peaceful duration to the republics of America. Without these unquiet passions the population would collect in certain spots and would soon be subject to wants like those of the Old World, which it is difficult to satisfy; for such is the present good fortune of the New World that the vices of its inhabitants are scarcely less favorable to society than their virtues. These circumstances exercise a great influence on the estimation in which human actions are held in the two hemispheres. The Americans frequently term what we should call cupidity a laudable industry; and they blame as faintheartedness what we consider to be the virtue of moderate desires.

In France simple tastes, orderly manners, domestic affections, and the attachment that men feel to the place of their birth are looked upon as great guarantees of the tranquility and happiness of the state. But in America nothing seems to be more prejudicial to society than these virtues. The French Canadians, who have faithfully preserved the traditions of their pristine manners, are already embarrassed for room in their small territory; and this little community, which has so recently begun to exist, will shortly be a prey to the calamities incident to old nations. In Canada the most enlightened, patriotic, and humane inhabitants make extraordinary efforts to render the people dissatisfied with those simple enjoyments which still content them. There the seductions of wealth are vaunted with as much zeal as the charms of a moderate but limited income in the Old World; and more exertions are made to excite the passions of the citizens there than to calm them elsewhere. If we listen to their eulogies, we shall hear that nothing is more praiseworthy than to exchange the pure and homely pleasures which even the poor man tastes in his own country for the dull delights of prosperity under a foreign sky; to leave the patrimonial hearth and the turf beneath which his forefathers sleep—in short, to abandon the living and the dead, in quest of fortune. . . .

In America too much knowledge cannot be diffused; for all knowledge, while it may serve him who possesses it, turns also to the advantage of those who are without it. New wants are not to be feared, since they can be satisfied without difficulty. . . .

The American republics of the present day are like companies of [merchants], formed to explore in common the wastelands of the New World and busied in a flourishing trade. The passions that agitate the Americans most deeply are not their political, but their commercial passions; or, to speak more correctly, they introduce the habits they contract in business into their political life. They love order, without which affairs do not prosper; and they set an especial value upon regular conduct, which is the foundation of a solid business. They prefer the good sense which amasses large fortunes to that enterprising spirit which frequently dissipates them; general ideas alarm their minds, which are accustomed to positive calculations; and they hold practice in more honor than theory. . . .

✥

In certain remote corners of the Old World you may still sometimes stumble upon a small district that seems to have been forgotten amid the general tumult, and to have remained stationary while everything around it was in motion. The inhabitants are, for the most part, extremely ignorant and poor; they take no part in the business of the country and are frequently oppressed by the government, yet their countenances are generally placid and their spirits light.

In America I saw the freest and most enlightened men placed in the happiest circumstances that the world affords; it seemed to me as if a cloud habitually hung upon their brow, and I thought them serious and almost sad, even in their pleasures.

The chief reason of this contrast is that the former do not think of the ills they endure, while the latter are forever brooding over advantages they do not possess. It is strange to see with what feverish ardor the Americans pursue their own welfare, and to watch the vague dread that constantly torments them lest they should not have chosen the shortest path which may lead to it.

A native of the United States clings to this world's goods as if he were certain never to die; and he is so hasty in grasping at all within his reach that one would suppose he was constantly afraid of not living long enough to enjoy them. He clutches everything, he holds nothing fast, but soon loosens his grasp to pursue fresh gratifications.

In the United States a man builds a house to spend his latter years in it, and he sells it before the roof is on; he plants a garden and lets it just as the trees are coming into bearing; he brings a field into tillage and leaves other men to gather the crops; he embraces a profession and gives it up; he settles in a place, which he soon afterwards leaves to carry his changeable longings elsewhere. If his private affairs leave him any leisure, he instantly plunges into the vortex of politics; and if at the end of a year of unremitting labor he finds he has a few days' vacation, his eager curiosity whirls him over the vast extent of the United States, and he will travel fifteen hundred miles in a few days to shake off his happiness. Death at length overtakes him, but it is before he is weary of his bootless chase of that complete felicity which is forever on the wing.

At first sight there is something surprising in this strange unrest of so many happy men, restless in the midst of abundance. The spectacle itself, however, is as old as the world; the novelty is to see a whole people furnish an exemplification of it.

Their taste for physical gratifications must be regarded as the original source of that secret disquietude which the actions of the Americans betray and of that inconstancy of which they afford fresh examples every day. He who has set his heart exclusively upon the pursuit of worldly welfare is always in a hurry, for he has but a limited time at his disposal to reach, to grasp, and to enjoy it. The recollection of the brevity of life is a constant spur to him. Besides the good things that he possesses, he every instant fancies a thousand others that death will prevent him from trying if he does not try them soon. This thought fills him with anxiety, fear, and regret and keeps his mind in ceaseless trepidation, which leads him perpetually to change his plans and his abode.

If in addition to the taste for physical well-being a social condition be superadded in which the laws and customs make no condition permanent, here is a great additional stimulant to this restlessness of temper. Men will then be seen continually to change their track for fear of missing the shortest cut to happiness.

It may readily be conceived that if men passionately bent upon physical gratifications desire eagerly, they are also easily discouraged; as their ultimate object is to enjoy, the means to reach that object must be prompt and easy or the trouble of acquiring the gratification would be greater than the gratification itself. Their prevailing frame of mind, then, is at once ardent and relaxed, violent and enervated. Death is often less dreaded than perseverance in continuous efforts to one end. . . .

. . . We must first understand what the purport of society and the aim of government is held to be. If you wish to give a certain elevation to the human mind and teach it to regard the things of this world with generous feelings, to inspire men with a scorn of mere temporal advantage, to give birth to living convictions and keep alive the spirit of honorable devotedness; if you hold it to be a good thing to refine the habits, embellish the manners, to cultivate the arts of a nation, and to promote the love of poetry, of beauty, and of renown; if you would constitute a people not unfitted to act with power upon all other nations, nor unprepared for those high enterprises which, whatever be the results of its efforts, will leave a name forever famous in time; if you believe such to be the principal object of society, you must avoid the government of democracy, which would be a very uncertain guide to the end you have in view.

But if you hold it to be expedient to divert the moral and intellectual activity of man to the production of comfort and the acquirement of the necessities of life; if a clear understanding be more profitable to man than genius; if your object be not to stimulate the virtues of heroism, but to create the habits of peace; if you had rather witness vices than crimes, and are content to meet with fewer noble deeds, provided offenses be diminished in the same proportion; if, instead of living in the midst of a brilliant state of society, you are contented to have prosperity around you; if, in short, you are of the opinion that the principal object of a government is not to confer the greatest possible share of power and glory upon the body of the nation, but to ensure the greatest degree of enjoyment and the least degree of misery to each of the individuals who compose it—if such be your desires, you can have no surer means of satisfying them, than by equalizing the conditions of men and establishing democratic institutions. . . .

15

Thomas Jefferson

On Citizenship (1824, 1816, 1814)

. . . My own State . . . is now proposing to call a convention for amendment. Among other improvements, I hope they will adopt the subdivision of our counties into wards. The former may be estimated at an average of twenty-four miles square; the latter should be about six miles square each, and would answer to the hundreds of your Saxon Alfred. In each of these might be: 1st. an elementary school; 2nd. a company of militia with its officers; 3rd. a justice of the peace and constable; 4th. each ward should take care of their own poor; 5th. their own roads; 6th. their own police; 7th. elect within themselves one or more jurors to attend the courts of justice; and, 8th. give in at their Folkhouse their votes for all functionaries reserved to their election. Each ward would thus be a small republic within itself, and every man in the State would thus become an acting member of the common government, transacting in person a great portion of its rights and duties, subordinate indeed, yet important, and entirely within his competence. The wit of man cannot devise a more solid basis for a free, durable, and well administered republic.

. . . If it is believed that these elementary schools will be better managed by the governor and council, the commissioners of the literary fund, or any other general authority of the government, than by the parents within each ward, it is a belief against all experience. Try the principle one step further and amend the bill so as to commit to the governor and council the management of all our farms, our mills, and merchants' stores. No, my friend, the way to have good and safe government is not to trust it all to one but to divide it among the many, distributing to everyone exactly the functions he is competent to. Let the national government be entrusted with the defense of the nation and its foreign and federal relations; the State governments with the civil rights, laws, police, and administration of what concerns the

From *The Writings of Thomas Jefferson,* Vol. VII and VI, Taylor and Maury, 1854.

State generally; the counties with the local concerns of the counties, and each ward direct the interests within itself. It is by dividing and subdividing these republics from the great national one down through all its subordinations until it ends in the administration of every man's farm by himself, by placing under everyone what his own eye may superintend, that all will be done for the best. What has destroyed liberty and the rights of man in every government which has ever existed under the sun? The generalizing and concentrating all cares and powers into one body, no matter whether of the autocrats of Russia or France, or of the aristocrats of a Venetian senate. And I do believe that if the Almighty has not decreed that man shall never be free (and it is a blasphemy to believe it), that the secret will be found to be in the making himself the depository of the powers respecting himself, so far as he is competent to them, and delegating only what is beyond his competence by a synthetical process to higher and higher orders of functionaries, so as to trust fewer and fewer powers in proportion as the trustees become more and more oligarchical. The elementary republics of the wards, the county republics, the State republics, and the republic of the Union would form a gradation of authorities, standing each on the basis of law, holding every one its delegated share of powers, and constituting truly a system of fundamental balances and checks for the government. Where every man is a sharer in the direction of his ward-republic, or of some of the higher ones, and feels that he is a participator in the government of affairs, not merely at an election one day in the year but every day; when there shall not be a man in the State who will not be a member of some one of its councils, great or small, he will let the heart be torn out of his body sooner than his power be wrested from him by a Caesar or a Bonaparte. How powerfully did we feel the energy of this organization in the case of embargo? . . .

* * *

. . . [W]e have no paupers. . . . The great mass of our population is of laborers; our rich, who can live without labor, either manual or professional, being few, and of moderate wealth. Most of the laboring class possess property, cultivate their own lands, have families, and from the demand for their labor are enabled to exact from the rich and the competent such prices as enable them to be fed abundantly, clothed above mere decency, to labor moderately and raise their families. They are not driven to the ultimate resources of dexterity and skill, because their wares will sell although not quite so nice as those of England. The wealthy, on the other hand, and those at their ease, know nothing of what the Europeans call luxury. They have only somewhat more of the comforts and decencies of life than those who furnish them. Can any condition of society be more desirable than this? . . . In England, happiness is the lot of the aristocracy only; and the proportion they bear to the laborers and paupers, you know better than I do.

Were I to guess that they are four in every hundred, then the happiness of the nation would be to its misery as one in twenty-five. In the United States it is as eight millions to zero, or as all to none. But it is said they possess the means of defense, and that we do not. How so? Are we not men? Yes; but our men are so happy at home that they will not hire themselves to be shot at for a shilling a day. Hence we can have no standing armies for defense, because we have no paupers to furnish the materials. The Greeks and Romans had no standing armies, yet they defended themselves. The Greeks by their laws, and the Romans by the spirit of their people, took care to put into the hands of their rulers no such engine of oppression as a standing army. Their system was to make every man a soldier, and oblige him to repair to the standard of his country whenever that was reared. This made them invincible; and the same remedy will make us so. In the beginning of our government we were willing to introduce the least coercion possible on the will of the citizen. Hence a system of military duty was established too indulgent to his indolence. This is the first opportunity we have had of trying it, and it has completely failed; an issue foreseen by many, and for which remedies have been proposed. That of classing the militia according to age, and allotting each age to the particular kind of service to which it was competent, was proposed to Congress in 1805, and subsequently; and, on the last trial, was lost, I believe, by a single vote only.

Had it prevailed, what has now happened would not have happened. Instead of burning our Capitol, we should have possessed theirs in Montreal and Quebec. We must now adopt it, and all will be safe.

16

James Madison

Federalist 39 (1788)

. . . The first question that offers itself is whether the general form and aspect of the government be strictly republican. It is evident that no other form would be reconcilable with the genius of the people of America; with the fundamental principles of the Revolution; or with that honorable

From *The Federalist.*

determination which animates every votary of freedom to rest all our political experiments on the capacity of mankind for self-government. If the plan of the convention, therefore, be found to depart from the republican character, its advocates must abandon it as no longer defensible. . . .

If we resort for a criterion to the different principles on which different forms of government are established, we may define a republic to be, or at least may bestow that name on, a government which derives all its powers directly or indirectly from the great body of the people, and is administered by persons holding their offices during pleasure for a limited period, or during good behavior. It is *essential* to such a government that it be derived from the great body of the society, not from an inconsiderable proportion or a favored class of it; otherwise a handful of tyrannical nobles, exercising their oppressions by a delegation of their powers, might aspire to the rank of republicans and claim for their government the honorable title of republic. It is *sufficient* for such a government that the persons administering it be appointed, either directly or indirectly, by the people; and that they hold their appointments by either of the tenures just specified; otherwise every government in the United States, as well as every other popular government that has been or can be well organized or well executed, would be degraded from the republican character. . . .

On comparing the Constitution planned by the convention with the standard here fixed, we perceived at once that it is, in the most rigid sense, comformable to it. The House of Representatives, like that of one branch at least of all the State legislatures, is elected immediately by the great body of the people. The Senate, like the present Congress and the Senate of Maryland, derives its appointment indirectly from the people. The President is indirectly derived from the choice of the people, according to the example in most of the States. Even the judges, with all other officers of the Union, will, as in the several States, be the choice, though a remote choice, of the people themselves. The duration of the appointments is equally conformable to the republican standard and to the model of State constitutions.

Could any further proof be required of the republican complexion of this system, the most decisive one might be found in its absolute prohibition of titles of nobility, both under the federal and the State governments; and in its express guaranty of the republican form to each of the latter.

"But it was not sufficient," say the adversaries of the proposed Constitution, "for the convention to adhere to the republican form. They ought with equal care to have preserved the *federal* form, which regards the Union as a *Confederacy* of sovereign states; instead of which they have framed a national government, which regards the Union as a *consolidation* of the States." And it is asked by what authority this bold and radical innovation was undertaken. The handle which has been made of this objection requires that it should be examined with some precision.

Without inquiring into the accuracy of the distinction on which the objection is founded, it will be necessary to a just estimate of its force, first, to ascertain the real character of the government in question; secondly, to inquire how far the convention were authorized to propose such a government; and thirdly, how far the duty they owed to their country could supply any defect of regular authority.

First.—In order to ascertain the real character of the government, it may be considered in relation to the foundation on which it is to be established; to the sources from which its ordinary powers are to be drawn; to the operation of those powers; to the extent of them; and to the authority by which future changes in the government are to be introduced.

On examining the first relation, it appears, on one hand, that the Constitution is to be founded on the assent and ratification of the people of America, given by deputies elected for the special purpose; but, on the other, that this assent and ratification is to be given by the people, not as individuals composing one entire nation, but as composing the distinct and independent States to which they respectively belong.

It is to be the assent and ratification of the several States, derived from the supreme authority in each State—the authority of the people themselves. The act, therefore, establishing the Constitution will not be a *national* but a *federal act*.

That it will be a federal and not a national act, as these terms are understood by the objectors—the act of the people, as forming so many independent States, not as forming one aggregate nation—is obvious from this single consideration: that it is to result neither from the decision of a *majority* of the people of the Union, nor from that of a *majority* of the States. It must result from the *unanimous* assent of the several States that are parties to it, differing not otherwise from their ordinary assent than in its being expressed, not by the legislative authority, but by that of the people themselves. Were the people regarded in this transaction as forming one nation, the will of the majority of the whole people of the United States would bind the minority, in the same manner as the majority in each State must bind the minority; and the will of the majority must be determined either by a comparison of the individual votes, or by considering the will of the majority of the States as evidence of the will of a majority of the people of the United States. Neither of these rules has been adopted. Each State, in ratifying the Constitution, is considered as a sovereign body independent of all others, and only to be bound by its own voluntary act. In this relation, then, the new Constitution will, if established, be a *federal* and not a *national* constitution.

The next relation is to the sources from which the ordinary powers of government are to be derived. The House of Representatives will derive its powers from the people of America; and the people will be represented in the same proportion and on the same principle as they are in the legislature of a particular State. So far the government is *national*, not *federal*. The Senate, on the other hand, will derive its powers from the States as political and coequal societies; and these will be represented on the principle of equality in the Senate, as they now are in the existing Congress. So far the govern-ment is *federal,* not national. The executive power will be derived from a very compound source. The immediate election of the President is to be made by the States in their political characters. The votes allotted to them are in a compound ratio, which considers them partly as distinct and coequal societies, partly as unequal members of the same society. The eventual elec-tion, again, is to be made by that branch of the legislature which consists of the national representatives; but in this particular act they are to be thrown into the form of individual delegations from so many distinct and co-equal bodies politic. From this aspect of the government it appears to be of a mixed character, presenting at least as many *federal* as *national* features.

The difference between a federal and national government, as it relates to the *operation of the government,* is by the adversaries of the plan of the conven-tion supposed to consist in this, that in the former the powers operate on the political bodies composing the confederacy in their political capacities; in the latter, on the individual citizens composing the nation in their individual capacities. On trying the Constitution by this criterion, it falls under the *national* not the *federal* character; though perhaps not so completely as has been understood. In several cases, and particularly in the trial of controversies to which States may be parties, they must be viewed and proceeded against in their collective and political capacities only. But the operation of the govern-ment on the people in their individual capacities, in its ordinary and most essential proceedings, will, in the sense of its opponents, on the whole, desig-nate it, in this relation, a *national* government.

But if the government be national with regard to the *operation* of its powers, it changes its aspect again when we contemplate it in relation to the extent of its powers. The idea of a national government involves in it not only an authority over the individual citizens, but an indefinite supremacy over all persons and things, so far as they are objects of lawful government. Among a people consolidated into one nation, this supremacy is completely vested in the national legislature. Among communities united for particular purposes, it is vested partly in the general and partly in the municipal legisla-tures. In the former case, all local authorities are subordinate to the supreme; and may be controlled, directed, or abolished by it at pleasure. In the latter, the local or municipal authorities form distinct and independent portions of the supremacy, no more subject, within their respective spheres, to the gen-eral authority than the general authority is subject to them, within its own sphere. In this relation, then, the proposed government cannot be deemed a *national* one; since its jurisdiction extends to certain enumerated objects only, and leaves to the several States a residuary and inviolable sovereignty over all other objects. It is true that in controversies relating to the boundary between the two jurisdictions, the tribunal which is ultimately to decide is to be established under the general government. But this does not change the principle of the case. The decision is to be impartially made, according to the rules of the Constitution; and all the usual and most effectual precautions are taken to secure this impartiality. Some such tribunal is clearly essential to prevent an appeal to the sword and a dissolution of the compact; and that it ought to be established under the general rather than under the local governments, or, to speak more properly, that it could be safely established under the first alone, is a position not likely to be combated.

If we try the Constitution by its last relation to the authority by which amendments are to be made, we find it neither wholly *national* nor wholly *federal*. Were it wholly national, the supreme and ultimate authority would reside in the *majority* of the people of the Union; and this authority would be competent at all times, like that of a majority of every national society to alter or abolish its established government. Were it wholly federal, on the other hand, the concurrence of each State in the Union would be essential to every alteration that would be binding on all. The mode provided by the plan of the convention is not founded on either of these principles. In requiring more than a majority, and particularly in computing the proportion by *States*, not by *citizens*, it departs from the national and advances towards the *federal* character; in rendering the concurrence of less than the whole number of States sufficient, it loses again the *federal* and partakes of the *national* character.

The proposed Constitution, therefore, even when tested by the rules laid down by its antagonists, is, in strictness, neither a national nor a federal Constitution, but a composition of both. In its foundation it is federal, not national; in the sources from which the ordinary powers of the government are drawn, it is partly federal and partly national; in the operation of these powers, it is national, not federal; in the extent of them, again, it is federal, not national; and, finally in the authoritative mode of introducing amendments, it is neither wholly federal nor wholly national.

17

McCulloch v. Maryland (1819)

Mr. Chief Justice Marshall *delivered the opinion of the Court:**

In the case now to be determined, the defendant, a sovereign state, denies the obligation of a law enacted by the legislature of the Union, and

From *McCulloch v. Maryland*, 4 Wheat. 316 (1819).

*Citations omitted throughout the Supreme Court cases in this volume.

the plaintiff, on his part, contests the validity of an act which has been passed by the legislature of that state. The constitution of our country, in its most interesting and vital parts, is to be considered; the conflicting powers of the government of the Union and of its members, as marked in that constitution, are to be discussed; and an opinion given, which may essentially influence the great operations of the government. No tribunal can approach such a question without a deep sense of its importance, and of the awful responsibility involved in its decision. But it must be decided peacefully, or remain a source of hostile legislation, perhaps of hostility of a still more serious nature; and if it is to be so decided, by this tribunal alone can the decision be made. On the Supreme Court of the United States has the constitution of our country devolved this important duty.

The first question made in the cause is, has Congress power to incorporate a bank?

It has been truly said that this can scarcely be considered as an open question, entirely unprejudiced by the former proceedings of the nation respecting it. The principle now contested was introduced at a very early period of our history, has been recognized by many successive legislatures, and has been acted upon by the judicial department, in cases of peculiar delicacy, as a law of undoubted obligation.

It will not be denied that a bold and daring usurpation might be resisted, after an acquiescence still longer and more complete than this. But it is conceived that a doubtful question, one on which human reason may pause, and the human judgment be suspended, in the decision of which the great principles of liberty are not concerned, but the respective powers of those who are equally the representatives of the people, are to be adjusted; if not put at rest by the practice of the government, ought to receive a considerable impression from that practice. An exposition of the constitution, deliberately established by legislative acts, on the faith of which an immense property has been advanced, ought not to be lightly disregarded.

The power now contested was exercised by the first Congress elected under the present constitution. The bill for incorporating the bank of the United States did not steal upon an unsuspecting legislature, and pass unobserved. Its principle was completely understood, and was opposed with equal zeal and ability. After being resisted, first in the fair and open field of debate, and afterwards in the executive cabinet, with as much persevering talent as any measure has ever experienced, and being supported by arguments which convinced minds as pure and as intelligent as this country can boast, it became a law. The original act was permitted to expire; but a short experience of the embarrassments to which the refusal to revive it exposed the government, convinced those who were most prejudiced against the measure of its necessity and induced the passage of the present law. It would require no ordinary share of intrepidity to assert that a measure adopted under these circumstances was a bold and plain usurpation, to which the constitution gave no countenance. . . .

The government of the Union, then (whatever may be the influence of this fact on the case), is, emphatically, and truly, a government of the people. In form and in substance it emanates from them. Its powers are granted by them, and are to be exercised directly on them, and for their benefit.

This government is acknowledged by all to be one of enumerated powers. The principle, that it can exercise only the powers granted to it, would seem too apparent to have required to be enforced by all those arguments which its enlightened friends, while it was depending before the people, found it necessary to urge. That principle is now universally admitted. But the question respecting the extent of the powers actually granted, is perpetually arising, and will probably continue to arise, as long as our system shall exist.

In discussing these questions, the conflicting powers of the general and state governments must be brought into view, and the supremacy of their respective laws, when they are in opposition, must be settled.

If any one proposition could command the universal assent of mankind, we might expect it would be this—that the government of the Union, though limited in its powers, is supreme within its sphere of action. This would seem to result necessarily from its nature. It is the government of all; its powers are delegated by all; it represents all, and acts for all. Though any one state may be willing to control its operations, no state is willing to allow others to control them. The nation, on those subjects on which it can act, must necessarily bind its component parts. But this question is not left to mere reason; the people have, in express terms, decided it by saying, "this constitution, and the laws of the United States, which shall be made in pursuance thereof," "shall be the supreme law of the land," and by requiring that the members of the state legislatures, and the officers of the executive and judicial departments of the states shall take the oath of fidelity to it.

The government of the United States, then, though limited in its powers, is supreme; and its laws when made in pursuance of the constitution, form the supreme law of the land, "anything in the constitution or laws of any state to the contrary notwithstanding."

Among the enumerated powers, we do not find that of establishing a bank or creating a corporation. But there is no phrase in the instrument which, like the articles of confederation, excludes incidental or implied powers; and which requires that everything granted shall be expressly and minutely described. Even the 10th amendment, which was framed for the purpose of quieting the excessive jealousies which had been excited, omits the word "expressly," and declares only that the powers "not delegated to the United States, nor prohibited to the states, are reserved to the states or to the people;" thus leaving the question, whether the particular power which may become the subject of contest has been delegated to the one government, or prohibited to the other, to depend on a fair construction of the whole instrument. The men who drew and adopted this amendment had experienced the embarrassments, resulting from the insertion of this word in the articles of confederation, and probably omitted it to avoid those embarrassments. A constitution, to contain an accurate detail of all the subdivisions of which its great powers will admit, and of all the means by which they may be carried into execution, would partake of a prolixity of a legal code, and could scarcely be embraced by the human mind. It would probably never be understood by the public. Its nature, therefore, requires, that only its great outlines should be marked, its important objects designated, and the minor ingredients which compose those objects be deduced from the nature of the objects themselves. . . . In considering this question, then, we must never forget that it is a constitution we are expounding.

Although, among the enumerated powers of government, we do not find the word "bank" or "incorporation," we find the great powers to lay and collect taxes; to borrow money; to regulate commerce; to declare and conduct a war; and to raise and support armies and navies. The sword and the purse, all the external relations, and no inconsiderable portion of the industry of the nation, are entrusted to its government. It can never be pretended that these vast powers draw after them others of inferior importance, merely because they are inferior. Such an idea can never be advanced. But it may with great reason be contended, that a government, entrusted with such ample powers, on the due execution of which the happiness and prosperity of the nation so vitally depends, must also be entrusted with ample means for their execution. The power being given, it is the interest of the nation to facilitate its execution. It can never be their interest, and cannot be presumed to have been their intention, to clog and embarrass its execution by withholding the most appropriate means. Throughout this vast republic, from the St. Croix to the Gulf of Mexico, from the Atlantic to the Pacific, revenue is to be collected and expended, armies are to be marched and supported. The exigencies of the nation may require that the treasure raised in the north shall be transported to the south, that raised in the east conveyed to the west, or that this order should be reversed. Is that construction of the constitution to be preferred which would render these operations difficult, hazardous, and expensive? Can we adopt that construction (unless the words imperiously require it) which would impute to the framers of that instrument, when granting these powers for the public good, the intention of impeding their exercise by withholding a choice of means? If, indeed, such be the mandate of the constitution, we have only to obey; but that instrument does not profess to enumerate the means by which the powers it confers may be executed; nor does it prohibit the creation of a corporation, if the existence of such a being be essential to the beneficial exercise of those powers. It is, then, the subject of fair inquiry, how far such means may be employed. . . .

The power of creating a corporation, though appertaining to sovereignty, is not, like the power of making war, or levying taxes, or of regulating commerce, a great substantive and independent power, which cannot be implied as incidental to other powers, or used as a means of executing them. It is never the end for which other powers are exercised, but a means by which other objects are accomplished. . . .

But the constitution of the United States has not left the right of Congress to employ the necessary means for the execution of the powers conferred on the government to general reasoning. To its enumeration of powers is added that of making "all laws which shall be necessary and proper, for carrying into execution the foregoing powers, and all other powers vested by this constitution, in the government of the United States, or in any department thereof."

The counsel for the State of Maryland have urged various arguments, to prove that this clause, though in terms a grant of power, is not so in effect; but is really restrictive of the general right, which might otherwise be implied of selecting means for executing the enumerated powers. . . .

[T]he argument on which most reliance is placed, is drawn from the peculiar language of this clause. Congress is not empowered by it to make all laws, which may have relation to the powers conferred on the government, but such only as may be "necessary and proper" for carrying them into execution. The word "necessary" is considered as controlling the whole sentence, and as limiting the right to pass laws for the execution of the granted powers, to such as are indispensable, and without which the power would be nugatory. That it excludes the choice of means, and leaves to Congress, in each case, that only which is most direct and simple.

Is it true that this is the sense in which the word "necessary" is always used? Does it always import an absolute physical necessity, so strong that one thing, to which another may be termed necessary, cannot exist without that other? We think it does not. If reference be had to its use, in the common affairs of the world, or in approved authors, we find that it frequently imports no more than that one thing is convenient, or useful, or essential to another. To employ the means necessary to an end, is generally understood as employing any means calculated to produce the end, and not as being confined to those single means, without which the end would be entirely unattainable. Such is the character of human language, that no word conveys to the mind, in all situations, one single definite idea; and nothing is more common than to use words in a figurative sense. Almost all compositions contain words, which, taken in their rigorous sense, would convey a meaning different from that which is obviously intended. It is essential to just construction, that many words which import something excessive should be understood in a more mitigated sense—in that sense which common usage justifies. The word "necessary" is of this description. It has not a fixed character peculiar to itself. It admits of all degree of comparison; and is often connected with other words, which increase or diminish the impression the mind receives of the urgency it imports. A thing may be necessary, very necessary, absolutely or indispensably necessary. To no mind would the same idea be conveyed by these several phrases. This comment on the word is well illustrated by the passage cited at the bar, from the 10th section of the Ist article of the constitution. It is, we think, impossible to compare the sentence which prohibits a state from laying "imposts or duties on imports or exports, except what may be absolutely necessary for executing its inspection laws," with that which authorizes Congress "to make all laws which shall be necessary and proper for carrying into execution" the powers of the general government, without feeling a conviction that the convention understood itself to change materially the meaning of the word "necessary," by prefixing the word "absolutely." This word, then, like others, is used in various senses; and, in its construction, the subject, the context, the intention of the person using them, are all to be taken into view.

Let this be done in the case under consideration. The subject is the execution of those great powers on which the welfare of a nation essentially depends. It must have been the intention of those who gave these powers, to insure, as far as human prudence could insure, their beneficial execution. This could not be done by confiding the choice of means to such narrow limits as not to leave it in the power of Congress to adopt any which might be appropriate, and which were conducive to the end. This provision is made in a constitution intended to endure for ages to come, and consequently, to be adapted to the various crises of human affairs. To have prescribed the means by which government should, in all future time, execute its powers, would have been to change entirely the character of the instrument, and give it the properties of a legal code. It would have been an unwise attempt to provide, by immutable rules, for exigencies which, if foreseen at all, must have been seen dimly, and which can be best provided for as they occur. To have declared that the best means shall not be used, but those alone without which the power given would be nugatory, would have been to deprive the legislature of the capacity to avail itself of experience, to exercise its reason, and to accommodate its legislation to circumstances. If we apply this principle of construction to any of the powers of the government, we shall find it so pernicious in its operation that we shall be compelled to discard it. . . .

Take, for example, the power "to establish post-offices and post-roads." This power is executed by the single act of making the establishment. But, from this has been inferred the power and duty of carrying the mail along the post-road, from one post-office to another. And, from this implied power, has again been inferred the right to punish those who steal letters from the post-office, or rob the mail. It may be said, with some plausibility, that the right to carry the mail, and to punish those who rob it, is not indispensably necessary to the establishment of a post-office and post-road. This right is indeed essential to the beneficial exercise of the power, but not indispensably necessary to its existence. So, of the punishment of the crimes of stealing or falsifying a record or process of a court of the United States, or of perjury in such court. To punish these offenses is certainly conducive to the due administration of justice. But courts may exist, and may decide the cause brought before them, though such crimes escape punishment. . . .

This clause, as construed by the state of Maryland, would abridge, and almost annihilate this useful and necessary right of the legislature to select its means. That this could not be intended is, we should think, had it not been already controverted, too apparent for controversy. We think so for the following reasons:

1st. The clause is placed among the powers of Congress, not among the limitations on those powers.

2nd. Its terms purport to enlarge, not to diminish the powers vested in the government. It purports to be an additional power, not a restriction on those already granted. . . .

If no other motive for its insertion can be suggested, a sufficient one is found in the desire to remove all doubts respecting the right to legislate on that vast mass of incidental powers which must be involved in the constitution, if that instrument is not a splendid bauble.

We admit, as all must admit, that the powers of the government are limited, and that its limits are not to be transcended. But we think the sound construction of the constitution must allow to the national legislature that discretion, with respect to the means by which the powers it confers are to be carried into execution, which will enable that body to perform the high duties assigned to it, in the manner most beneficial to the people. Let the end be legitimate, let it be within the scope of the constitution, and all means which are appropriate, which are plainly adapted to that end, which are not prohibited, but consist with the letter and spirit of the constitution, are constitutional. . . .

Should congress, in the execution of its powers, adopt measures which are prohibited by the constitution; or should Congress, under the pretext of executing its powers, pass laws for the accomplishment of objects not intrusted to the government; it would become the painful duty of this tribunal, should a case requiring such a decision come before it, to say, that such an act was not the law of the land. But where the law is not prohibited, and is really calculated to effect any of the objects intrusted to the government, to undertake here to inquire into the degree of its necessity, would be to pass the line which circumscribes the judicial department, and to tread on legislative ground. This court disclaims all pretensions to such a power. . . .

It being the opinion of the court that the act incorporating the bank is constitutional, and that the power of establishing a branch in the state of Maryland might be properly exercised by the bank itself, we proceed to inquire:

2. Whether the state of Maryland may, without violating the constitution, tax that branch? . . .

[The] great principle is, that the constitution, and the laws made in pursuance thereof are supreme; that they control the constitution and laws of the respective states, and cannot be controlled by them. From this, which may be almost termed an axiom, other propositions are deduced as corollaries, on the truth or error of which, and on their application to this case, the cause has been supposed to depend. These are, 1st. that a power to create implies a power to preserve. 2d. That a power to destroy, if wielded by a different hand, is hostile to, and incompatible with these powers to create and to preserve. 3d. That where this repugnancy exists, that authority which is supreme must control, not yield to that over which it is supreme. . . .

That the power of taxing [the bank] by the states may be exercised so as to destroy it, is too obvious to be denied. . . .

All subjects over which the sovereign power of a state extends, are objects of taxation; but those over which it does not extend, are, upon the soundest principles, exempt from taxation. This proposition may almost be pronounced self-evident.

The sovereignty of a state extends to everything which exists by its own authority, or is introduced by its permission; but does it extend to those means which are employed by Congress to carry into execution—powers conferred on that body by the people of the United States? We think it demonstrable that it does not. Those powers are not given by the people of a single state. They are given by the people of the United States, to a government whose laws, made in pursuance of the constitution, are declared to be supreme. . . .

If we measure the power of taxation residing in a state, by the extent of sovereignty which the people of a single state possess, and can confer on its government, we have an intelligible standard, applicable to every case to which the power may be applied. We have a principle which leaves the power of taxing the people and property of a state unimpaired; which leaves to a state the command of all its resources, and which places beyond its reach, all those powers which are conferred by the people of the United States on the government of the Union, and all those means which are given for the purpose of carrying those powers into execution. We have a principle which is safe for the states, and safe for the Union. We are relieved, as we ought to be, from clashing sovereignty; from interfering powers; from a repugnancy between a right in one government to pull down what there is an acknowledged right in another to build up; from the incompatibility of a right in one government to destroy what there is a right in another to preserve. We are not driven to the perplexing inquiry, so unfit for the judicial department, what degree of taxation is the legitimate use, and what degree may amount to the abuse of the power. . . .

We are unanimously of opinion that the law passed by the legislature of Maryland, imposing a tax on the Bank of the United States, is unconstitutional and void. . . .

18

Alexis de Tocqueville

The Purposes Served by Local Self-Government (1840)

. . . Egotism is a vice as old as the world, which does not belong to one form of society more than to another; individualism is of democratic origin, and it threatens to spread in the same ratio as the equality of conditions.

Among aristocratic nations, as families remain for centuries in the same condition, often on the same spot, all generations become, as it were, contemporaneous. A man almost always knows his forefathers and respects them; he thinks he already sees his remote descendants and he loves them. He willingly imposes duties on himself towards the former and the latter, and he will frequently sacrifice his personal gratifications to those who went before and to those who will come after him. Aristocratic institutions have, moreover, the effect of closely binding every man to several of his fellow citizens. As the classes of an aristocratic people are strongly marked and permanent, each of them is regarded by its own members as a sort of lesser country, more tangible and more cherished than the country at large. As in aristocratic communities all the citizens occupy fixed positions, one above another, the result is that each of them always sees a man above himself whose patronage is necessary to him, and below himself another man whose co-operation he may claim. Men living in aristocratic ages are therefore almost always closely attached to something placed out of their own sphere, and they are often disposed to forget themselves. It is true that in those ages the notion of human fellowship is faint and that men seldom think of sacrificing themselves for mankind; but they often sacrifice themselves

From *Democracy in America* by Alexis de Tocqueville, translated by Henry Reeve, 1862, with minor changes.

for other men. In democratic ages, on the contrary, when the duties of each individual to the race are much more clear, devoted service to any one man becomes more rare; the bond of human affection is extended, but it is relaxed.

Among democratic nations new families are constantly springing up, others are constantly falling away, and all that remain change their condition; the woof of time is every instant broken and the track of generations effaced. Those who went before are soon forgotten; of those who will come after, no one has any idea: the interest of man is confined to those in close propinquity to himself. As each class approximates to other classes and mingles with them, its members become indifferent and as strangers to one other. Aristocracy had made a chain of all the members of the community, from the peasant to the king; democracy breaks that chain and severs every link of it. . . .

Thus not only does democracy make every man forget his ancestors, but it hides his descendants and separates his contemporaries from him; it throws him back forever upon himself alone and threatens in the end to confine him entirely within the solitude of his own heart. . . .

Despotism, which is of a very timorous nature, is never more secure of continuance than when it can keep men asunder; and all its influence is commonly exerted for that purpose. . . .

Thus the vices which despotism engenders are precisely those which equality fosters. These two things mutually and perniciously complete and assist each other. Equality places men side by side, unconnected by any common tie; despotism raises barriers to keep them asunder. . . .

It is easy to see that in those same ages men stand most in need of freedom. When the members of a community are forced to attend to public affairs, they are necessarily drawn from the circle of their own interests and snatched at times from self-observation. As soon as a man begins to treat of public affairs in public, he begins to perceive that he is not so independent of his fellow men as he had at first imagined, and that in order to obtain their support he must often lend them his cooperation.

When the public is supreme, there is no man who does not feel the value of public goodwill or who does not endeavor to court it by drawing to himself the esteem and affection of those among whom he is to live. Many of the passions which congeal and keep asunder human hearts are then obliged to retire and hide below the surface. Pride must be dissembled; disdain dares not break out; egotism fears its own self. Under a free government, as most public offices are elective, the men whose elevated minds or aspiring hopes are too closely circumscribed in private life constantly feel that they cannot do without the population which surrounds them. Men learn at such times to think of their fellow men from ambitious motives; and they frequently find it, in a manner, their interest to forget themselves. . . .

The desire of being elected may lead some men for a time to violent hostility; but this same desire leads all men in the long run to support each other; and if it happens that an election accidentally severs two friends, the electoral system brings a multitude of citizens permanently together who would otherwise always have remained unknown to each other. . . .

The Americans have combated by free institutions the tendency of equality to keep men asunder, and they have subdued it. The legislators of America did not suppose that a general representation of the whole nation would suffice to ward off a disorder at once so natural to the frame of democratic society and so fatal; they also thought that it would be well to infuse political life into each portion of the territory in order to multiply to an infinite extent opportunities of acting in concert for all the members of the community and to make them constantly feel their mutual dependence on each other. The plan was a wise one. The general affairs of a country only engage the attention of leading politicians, who assemble from time to time in the same places; and as they often lose sight of each other afterwards, no lasting ties are established between them. But if the object be to have the local affairs of a district conducted by the men who reside there, the same persons are always in contact, and they are, in a manner, forced to be acquainted and to adapt themselves to one another.

It is difficult to draw a man out of his own circle to interest him in the destiny of the state, because he does not clearly understand what influence the destiny of the state can have upon his own lot. But if it is proposed to make a road cross the end of his estate, he will see at a glance that there is a connection between this small public affair and his greatest private affairs; and he will discover, without its being shown to him, the close tie that unites private to general interest. Thus far more may be done by entrusting to the citizens the administration of minor affairs than by surrendering to them the control of important ones, towards interesting them in the public welfare and convincing them that they constantly stand in need one of the other in order to provide for it. A brilliant achievement may win for you the favor of a people at one stroke; but to earn the love and respect of the population that surrounds you, a long succession of little services rendered and of obscure good deeds, a constant habit of kindness, and an established reputation for disinterestedness will be required. Local freedom, then, which leads a great number of citizens to value the affection of their neighbors and of their kindred, perpetually brings men together and forces them to help one another in spite of the propensiries that sever them. . . .

19

Robert D. Putnam

Bowling Alone: America's Declining Social Capital (1995)

Many students of the new democracies that have emerged over the past decade and a half have emphasized the importance of a strong and active civil society to the consolidation of democracy. Especially with regard to the postcommunist countries, scholars and democratic activists alike have lamented the absence or obliteration of traditions of independent civic engagement and a widespread tendency toward passive reliance on the state. To those concerned with the weakness of civil societies in the developing or postcommunist world, the advanced Western democracies and above all the United States have typically been taken as models to be emulated. There is striking evidence, however, that the vibrancy of American civil society has notably declined over the past several decades.

Ever since the publication of Alexis de Tocqueville's *Democracy in America*, the United States has played a central role in systematic studies of the links between democracy and civil society. Although this is in part because trends in American life are often regarded as harbingers of social modernization, it is also because America has traditionally been considered unusually "civic" (a reputation that, as we shall later see, has not been entirely unjustified).

When Tocqueville visited the United States in the 1830s, it was the Americans' propensity for civic association that most impressed him as the key to their unprecedented ability to make democracy work. "Americans of all ages, all stations in life, and all types of disposition," he observed, "are forever forming associations. There are not only commercial and industrial associations in which all take part, but others of a thousand different types— religious, moral, serious, futile, very general and very limited, immensely

Putnam, Robert D. Bowling Alone: America's Declining Social Capital. Journal of Democracy 6:1 (1995), 65–78. Copyright © 1995 The National Endowment for Democracy and the Johns Hopkins University Press. Its argument was amplified and to some extent modified in Robert D. Putnam's book, *Bowling Alone: The Collapse and Revival of American Community* (Simon & Schuster, 2000) Reprinted with permission of the Johns Hopkins University Press.

large and very minute. . . . Nothing, in my view, deserves more attention than the intellectual and moral associations in America."

Recently, American social scientists of a neo-Tocquevillean bent have unearthed a wide range of empirical evidence that the quality of public life and the performance of social institutions (and not only in America) are indeed powerfully influenced by norms and networks of civic engagement. Researchers in such fields as education, urban poverty, unemployment, the control of crime and drug abuse, and even health have discovered that successful outcomes are more likely in civically engaged communities. Similarly, research on the varying economic attainments of different ethnic groups in the United States has demonstrated the importance of social bonds within each group. These results are consistent with research in a wide range of settings that demonstrates the vital importance of social networks for job placement and many other economic outcomes.

Meanwhile, a seemingly unrelated body of research on the sociology of economic development has also focused attention on the role of social networks. Some of this work is situated in the developing countries, and some of it elucidates the peculiarly successful "network capitalism" of East Asia. Even in less exotic Western economies, however, researchers have discovered highly efficient, highly flexible "industrial districts" based on networks of collaboration among workers and small entrepreneurs. Far from being paleoindustrial anachronisms, these dense interpersonal and interorganizational networks undergird ultramodern industries, from the high tech of Silicon Valley to the high fashion of Benetton.

The norms and networks of civic engagement also powerfully affect the performance of representative government. That, at least, was the central conclusion of my own 20-year, quasi-experimental study of subnational governments in different regions of Italy. Although all these regional governments seemed identical on paper, their levels of effectiveness varied dramatically. Systematic inquiry showed that the quality of governance was determined by longstanding traditions of civic engagement (or its absence). Voter turnout, newspaper readership, membership in choral societies and football clubs—these were the hallmarks of a successful region. In fact, historical analysis suggested that these networks of organized reciprocity and civic solidarity, far from being an epiphenomenon of socioeconomic modernization, were a precondition for it.

No doubt the mechanisms through which civic engagement and social connectedness produce such results—better schools, faster economic development, lower crime, and more effective government—are multiple and complex. While these briefly recounted findings require further confirmation and perhaps qualification, the parallels across hundreds of empirical studies in a dozen disparate disciplines and subfields are striking. Social scientists in several fields have recently suggested a common framework for understanding these phenomena, a framework that rests on the concept of *social capital*. By analogy with notions of physical capital and human capital—tools and training that enhance individual productivity—"social capital" refers to features of social organization such as networks, norms, and social trust that facilitate coordination and cooperation for mutual benefit.

For a variety of reasons, life is easier in a community blessed with a substantial stock of social capital. In the first place, networks of civic engagement foster sturdy norms of generalized reciprocity and encourage the emergence of social trust. Such networks facilitate coordination and communication, amplify reputations, and thus allow dilemmas of collective action to be resolved. When economic and political negotiation is embedded in dense networks of social interaction, incentives for opportunism are reduced. At the same time, networks of civic engagement embody past success at collaboration, which can serve as a cultural template for future collaboration. Finally, dense networks of interaction probably broaden the participants' sense of self, developing the "I" into the "we," or (in the language of rational-choice theorists) enhancing the participants' "taste" for collective benefits.

I do not intend here to survey (much less contribute to) the development of the theory of social capital. Instead, I use the central premise of that rapidly growing body of work—that social connections and civic engagement pervasively influence our public life, as well as our private prospects—as the starting point for an empirical survey of trends in social capital in contemporary America. I concentrate here entirely on the American case, although the developments I portray may in some measure characterize many contemporary societies.

Whatever Happened to Civic Engagement?

We begin with familiar evidence on changing patterns of political participation, not least because it is immediately relevant to issues of democracy in the narrow sense. Consider the well-known decline in turnout in national elections over the last three decades. From a relative high point in the early 1960s, voter turnout had by 1990 declined by nearly a quarter; tens of millions of Americans had forsaken their parents' habitual readiness to engage in the simplest act of citizenship. Broadly similar trends also characterize participation in state and local elections.

It is not just the voting booth that has been increasingly deserted by Americans. A series of identical questions posed by the Roper Organization to national samples ten times each year over the last two decades reveals that since 1973 the number of Americans who report that "in the past year" they have "attended a public meeting on town or school affairs" has fallen by more than a third (from 22 percent in 1973 to 13 percent in 1993). Similar (or even greater) relative declines are evident in responses to questions about attending a political rally or speech, serving on a committee of some local organization, and working for a political party. By almost every measure, Americans' direct engagement in politics and government has fallen steadily and sharply over the last generation, despite the fact that average levels of education—the best individual-level predictor of political participation—have risen sharply throughout this period. Every year over the last decade or two, millions more have withdrawn from the affairs of their communities.

Not coincidentally, Americans have also disengaged psychologically from politics and government over this era. The proportion of Americans who reply that they "trust the government in Washington" only "some of the time" or "almost never" has risen steadily from 30 percent in 1966 to 75 percent in 1992.

These trends are well known, of course, and taken by themselves would seem amenable to a strictly political explanation. Perhaps the long litany of political tragedies and scandals since the 1960s (assassinations, Vietnam, Watergate, Irangate, and so on) has triggered an understandable disgust for politics and government among Americans, and that in turn has motivated their withdrawal. I do not doubt that this common interpretation has some merit, but its limitations become plain when we examine trends in civic engagement of a wider sort.

Our survey of organizational membership among Americans can usefully begin with a glance at the aggregate results of the General Social Survey, a scientifically conducted, national-sample survey that has been repeated 14 times over the last two decades. Church-related groups constitute the most common type of organization joined by Americans; they are especially popular with women. Other types of organizations frequently joined by women include school-service groups (mostly parent-teacher associations), sports groups, professional societies, and literary societies. Among men, sports clubs, labor unions, professional societies, fraternal groups, veterans' groups, and service clubs are all relatively popular.

Religious affiliation is by far the most common associational membership among Americans. Indeed, by many measures America continues to be (even more than in Tocqueville's time) an astonishingly "churched" society. For example, the United States has more houses of worship per capita than any other nation on Earth. Yet religious sentiment in America seems to be becoming somewhat less tied to institutions and more self-defined.

How have these complex crosscurrents played out over the last three or four decades in terms of Americans' engagement with organized religion? The general pattern is clear: The 1960s witnessed a significant drop in reported weekly churchgoing—from roughly 48 percent in the late 1950s to roughly 41 percent in the early 1970s. Since then, it has stagnated or (according to some surveys) declined still further. Meanwhile, data from the General Social Survey show a modest decline in membership in all "church-related groups" over the last 20 years. It would seem, then, that net participation by Americans, both in religious services and in church-related groups, has declined modestly (by perhaps a sixth) since the 1960s.

For many years, labor unions provided one of the most common organizational affiliations among American workers. . . .

The parent-teacher association (PTA) has been an especially important form of civic engagement in twentieth-century America because parental involvement in the educational process represents a particularly productive form of social capital. It is, therefore, dismaying to discover that participation in parent-teacher organizations has dropped drastically over the last generation, from more than 12 million in 1964 to barely 5 million in 1982 before recovering to approximately 7 million now.

Next, we turn to evidence on membership in (and volunteering for) civic and fraternal organizations. These data show some striking patterns. First, membership in traditional women's groups has declined more or less steadily since the mid-1960s. For example, membership in the national Federation of Women's Clubs is down by more than half (59 percent) since 1964, while membership in the League of Women Voters (LWV) is off 42 percent since 1969.

Similar reductions are apparent in the numbers of volunteers for mainline civic organizations, such as the Boy Scouts (off by 26 percent since 1970) and the Red Cross (off by 61 percent since 1970). But what about the possibility that volunteers have simply switched their loyalties to other organizations? Evidence on "regular" (as opposed to occasional or "drop-by") volunteering is available from the Labor Department's Current Population Surveys of 1974 and 1989. These estimates suggest that serious volunteering declined by roughly one-sixth over these 15 years, from 24 percent of adults in 1974 to 20 percent in 1989. The multitudes of Red Cross aides and Boy Scout troop leaders now missing in action have apparently not been offset by equal numbers of new recruits elsewhere.

Fraternal organizations have also witnessed a substantial drop in membership during the 1980s and 1990s. Membership is down significantly in such groups as the Lions (off 12 percent since 1983), the Elks (off 18 percent since 1979), the Shriners (off 27 percent since 1979), the Jaycees (off 44 percent since 1979), and the Masons (down 39 percent since 1959). In sum, after expanding steadily throughout most of this century, many major civic organizations have experienced a sudden, substantial, and nearly simultaneous decline in membership over the last decade or two.

The most whimsical yet discomfiting bit of evidence of social disengagement in contemporary America that I have discovered is this: more Americans are bowling today than ever before, but bowling in organized leagues has plummeted in the last decade or so. Between 1980 and 1993 the total number of bowlers in America increased by 10 percent, while league bowling decreased by 40 percent. (Lest this be thought a wholly trivial example, I should note that nearly 80 million Americans went bowling at least once during 1993, *nearly a third more than voted in the 1994 congressional elections* and roughly the same number as claim to attend church regularly. Even after the 1980s' plunge in league bowling, nearly 3 percent of American adults regularly bowl in leagues.) The rise of solo bowling threatens the livelihood of bowling-lane proprietors because those who bowl as members of leagues consume three times as much beer and pizza as solo bowlers, and the money in bowling is in the beer and pizza, not the balls and shoes. The broader social significance, however, lies in the social interaction and even occasionally civic conversations over beer and pizza that solo bowlers forgo. Whether or not bowling beats balloting in the eyes of most Americans, bowling teams illustrate yet another vanishing form of social capital.

COUNTERTRENDS

At this point, however, we must confront a serious counterargument. Perhaps the traditional forms of civic organization whose decay we have been tracing have been replaced by vibrant new organizations. For example, national environmental organizations (like the Sierra Club) and feminist groups (like the National Organization for Women) grew rapidly during the 1970s and 1980s and now count hundreds of thousands of dues-paying members. An even more dramatic example is the American Association of Retired Persons (AARP), which grew exponentially from 400,000 card-carrying members in 1960 to 33 million in 1993, becoming (after the Catholic Church) the largest private organization in the world. The national administrators of these organizations are among the most feared lobbyists in Washington, in large part because of their massive mailing lists of presumably loyal members.

These new mass-membership organizations are plainly of great political importance. From the point of view of social connectedness, however, they are sufficiently different from classic "secondary associations" that we need to invent a new label—perhaps "tertiary associations." For the vast majority of their members, the only act of membership consists in writing a check for dues or perhaps occasionally reading a newsletter. Few ever attend any meetings of such organizations, and most are unlikely ever (knowingly) to encounter any other member. The bond between any two members of the Sierra Club is less like the bond between any two members of a gardening club and more like the bond between any two Red Sox fans (or perhaps any two devoted Honda owners): they root for the same team and they share some of the same interests, but they are unaware of each other's existence. Their ties, in short, are to common symbols, common leaders, and perhaps common ideals, but not to one another. The theory of social capital argues that associational membership should, for example, increase social trust, but this prediction is much less straightforward with regard to membership in tertiary associations. . . .

Some able researchers have argued that the last few decades have witnessed a rapid expansion in "support groups" of various sorts. Robert Wuthnow reports that fully 40 percent of all Americans claim to be "currently involved in [a] small group that meets regularly and provides support or caring for those who participate in it." Many of these groups are religiously affiliated, but many others are not. For example, nearly 5 percent of Wuthnow's national sample claim to participate regularly in a "self-help" group, such as Alcoholics Anonymous, and nearly as many say they belong to book-discussion groups and hobby clubs.

The groups described by Wuthnow's respondents unquestionably represent an important form of social capital, and they need to be accounted for in any serious reckoning of trends in social connectedness. On the other hand, they do not typically play the same role as traditional civic associations. As Wuthnow emphasizes,

> Small groups may not be fostering community as effectively as many of their proponents would like. Some small groups merely provide occasions for individuals to focus on themselves in the presence of others. The social contract binding members together asserts only the weakest of obligations. Come if you have time. Talk if you feel like it. Respect everyone's opinion. Never criticize. Leave quietly if you become dissatisfied. . . . We can imagine that [these small groups] really substitute for families, neighborhoods, and broader community attachments that may demand lifelong commitments, when, in fact, they do not.

. . . Within all educational categories, total associational membership declined significantly between 1967 and 1993. Among the college-educated, the average number of group memberships per person fell from 2.8 to 2.0 (a 26-percent decline); among high-school graduates, the number fell from 1.8 to 1.2 (32 percent); and among those with fewer than 12 years of education, the number fell from 1.4 to 1.1 (25 percent). In other words, at *all* educational (and hence social) levels of American society, and counting *all* sorts of group memberships, *the average number of associational memberships has fallen by about a fourth over the last quarter-century.* Without controls for educational levels, the trend is not nearly so clear, but the central point is this: *more Americans than ever before are in social circumstances that foster associational involvement (higher education, middle age, and so on), but nevertheless aggregate associational membership appears to be stagnant or declining.* . . . In short, the available survey evidence confirms our earlier conclusion: American social capital in the form of civic associations has significantly eroded over the last generation.

GOOD NEIGHBORLINESS AND SOCIAL TRUST

. . . [T]he most fundamental form of social capital is the family, and the massive evidence of the loosening of bonds within the family (both extended and nuclear) is well known. This trend, of course, is quite consistent with— and may help to explain—our theme of social decapitalization.

A second aspect of informal social capital on which we happen to have reasonably reliable time-series data involves neighborliness. In each General

Social Survey since 1974 respondents have been asked, "How often do you spend a social evening with a neighbor?" The proportion of Americans who socialize with their neighbors more than once a year has slowly but steadily declined over the last two decades, from 72 percent in 1974 to 61 percent in 1993. (On the other hand, socializing with "friends who do not live in your neighborhood" appears to be on the increase, a trend that may reflect the growth of workplace-based social connections.)

Americans are also less trusting. The proportion of Americans saying that most people can be trusted fell by more than a third between 1960, when 58 percent chose that alternative, and 1993, when only 37 percent did. The same trend is apparent in all educational groups; indeed, because social trust is also correlated with education and because educational levels have risen sharply, the overall decrease in social trust is even more apparent is we control for education. . . .

Why Is U.S. Social Capital Eroding?

As we have seen, something has happened in America in the last two or three decades to diminish civic engagement and social connectedness. What could that "something" be? Here are several possible explanations, along with some initial evidence on each.

The movement of women into the labor force. Over these same two or three decades, many millions of American women have moved out of the home into paid employment. This is the primary, though not the sole, reason why the weekly working hours of the average American have increased significantly during these years. It seems highly plausible that this social revolution should have reduced the time and energy available for building social capital. For certain organizations, such as the PTA, the League of Women Voters, the Federation of Women's Clubs, and the Red Cross, this is almost certainly an important part of the story. The sharpest decline in women's civic participation seems to have come in the 1970s; membership in such "women's" organizations as these has been virtually halved since the late 1960s. By contrast, most of the decline in participation in men's organizations occurred about ten years later; the total decline to date has been approximately 25 percent for the typical organization. On the other hand, the survey data imply that the aggregate declines for men are virtually as great as those for women. It is logically possible, of course, that the male declines might represent the knock-on effect of women's liberation, as dishwashing crowded out the lodge, but time-budget studies suggest that most husbands of working wives have assumed only a minor part of the housework. In short, something besides the women's revolution seems to lie behind the erosion of social capital.

Mobility. The "re-potting" hypothesis. Numerous studies of organizational involvement have shown that residential stability and such related phenomena as homeownership are clearly associated with greater civic engagement. Mobility, like frequent re-potting of plants, tends to disrupt root systems, and it takes time for an uprooted individual to put down new roots. It seems plausible that the automobile, suburbanization, and the movement to the Sun Belt have reduced the social rootedness of the average American, but one fundamental difficulty with this hypothesis is apparent: the best evidence shows that residential stability and homeownership in America have risen modestly since 1965, and are surely higher now than during the 1950s, when civic engagement and social connectedness by our measures was definitely higher.

Other demographic transformations. A range of additional changes have transformed the American family since the 1960s—fewer marriages, more divorces, fewer children, lower real wages, and so on. Each of these changes might account for some of the slackening of civic engagement, since married, middle-class parents are generally more socially involved than other people. Moreover, the changes in scale that have swept over the American economy in these years—illustrated by the replacement of the corner grocery by the supermarket and now perhaps of the supermarket by electronic shopping at home, or the replacement of community-based enterprises by outposts of distant multinational firms—may perhaps have undermined the material and even physical basis for civic engagement.

The technological transformation of leisure. There is reason to believe that deep-seated technological trends are radically "privatizing" or "individualizing" our use of leisure time and thus disrupting many opportunities for social-capital formation. The most obvious and probably the most powerful instrument of this revolution is television. Time-budget studies in the 1960s showed that the growth in time spent watching television dwarfed all other changes in the way Americans passed their days and nights. Television has made our communities (or, rather, what we experience as our communities) wider and shallower. In the language of economics, electronic technology enables individual tastes to be satisfied more fully, but at the cost of the positive social externalities associated with more primitive forms of entertainment. The same logic applies to the replacement of vaudeville by the movies and now of movies by the VCR. The new "virtual reality" helmets that we will soon don to be entertained in total isolation are merely the latest extension of this trend. Is technology thus driving a wedge between our individual interests and our collective interests? It is a question that seems worth exploring more systematically.

What Is to Be Done?

The last refuge of a social-scientific scoundrel is to call for more research. Nevertheless, I cannot forbear from suggesting some further lines of inquiry.

- We must sort out the dimensions of social capital, which clearly is not a unidimensional concept, despite language (even in this essay) that implies the contrary. What types of organizations and networks most effectively embody—or generate—social capital, in the sense of mutual reciprocity, the resolution of dilemmas of collective action, and the broadening of social identities? In this essay I have emphasized the density of associational life. In earlier work I stressed the structure of networks, arguing that "horizontal" ties represented more productive social capital than vertical ties.

- Another set of important issues involves macrosociological crosscurrents that might intersect with the trends described here. What will be the impact, for example, of electronic networks on social capital? My hunch is that meeting in an electronic forum is not the equivalent of meeting in a bowling alley—or even in a saloon—but hard empirical research is needed. . . .

- Finally, and perhaps most urgently, we need to explore creatively how public policy impinges on (or might impinge on) social-capital formation. In some well-known instances, public policy has destroyed highly effective social networks and norms. American slum-clearance policy of the 1950s and 1960s, for example, renovated physical capital, but at a very high cost to existing social capital. The consolidation of country post offices and small school districts has promised administrative and financial efficiencies, but full-cost accounting for the effects of these policies on social capital might produce a more negative verdict. On the other hand, such past initiatives as the county agricultural-agent system, community colleges, and tax deductions for charitable contributions illustrate that government can encourage social-capital formation. Even a recent proposal in San Luis Obispo, California, to require that all new houses have front porches illustrates the power of government to influence where and how networks are formed.

The concept of "civil society" has played a central role in the recent global debate about the preconditions for democracy and democratization. In the newer democracies this phrase has properly focused attention on the need to foster a vibrant civic life in soils traditionally inhospitable to self-government. In the established democracies, ironically, growing numbers of citizens are questioning the effectiveness of their public institutions at the very moment when liberal democracy has swept the battlefield, both ideologically and geopolitically. In America, at least, there is reason to suspect that this democratic disarray may be linked to a broad and continuing erosion of civic engagement that began a quarter-century ago. High on our scholarly agenda should be the question of whether a comparable erosion of social capital may be under way in other advanced democracies, perhaps in different institutional and behavioral guises. High on America's agenda should be the question of how to reverse these adverse trends in social connectedness, thus restoring civic engagement and civic trust.

20

William A. Schambra

By the People: The Old Values of the New Citizenship (1994)

. . . That the institutions and values of civil society are deeply imperiled and desperately in need of resuscitation today is a conviction widely shared across the political spectrum. . . .

The consequences of civil society's decline are evident throughout our daily life, in soaring rates of crime, divorce, illegitimacy, neighborhood deterioration, welfare dependency, chemical addiction, suicide, and virtually every other indicator of pathology. While these symptoms are most vividly on display in the inner city, they are rapidly taking root in suburban culture as well.

In his classic, *The Quest for Community*, Robert Nisbet describes the powerful forces of modernity complicit in this civic and moral unraveling, with assaults on civil society coming both from below and from above. From below, the authority of family, church, neighborhood, and school is quietly eroded by the proliferation of individual rights, especially the right of self-expression— that is, expression of self with utter disregard for civil society. From above, civil institutions are pressured to surrender authority and function to the professional elites of the centralized, bureaucratic state. Today's Boy Scout troops, for instance, may as well turn themselves over to the federal courts for management, given the relentless legal assault on their morally rigorous organizational principles by champions of the rights of "alternative lifestyles." Caught in a pincers movement between individual rights and the central state, Nisbet notes, the intermediate associations of civil society languish.

However, it would be an error to suppose that the erosion of civil society is somehow a natural or inevitable consequence of modern progress. Rather,

From Schambra, "By the People," *Policy Review*, published by the Heritage Foundation, Summer, 1994. Reprinted by permission.

the central project of the modern progressive liberal state is to eradicate civil society, and to transfer its functions to government. It is doing so, ironically, in the name of restoring community—now understood as *national* community.

THE NATIONAL COMMUNITY

The idea of national community sprang from the minds of Herbert Croly, Walter Lippmann, John Dewey, and others at the turn of the century, and was introduced into American politics by Theodore Roosevelt's enunciation of a "new nationalism" in 1910. It is progressive liberalism's grand intellectual attempt to reconcile the centralized, bureaucratic, therapeutic state with the idea of public-spirited citizenship and community.

According to the progressive vision, various forces of modernity—industrialization, urbanization, advanced communications and transportation—had forever shattered the boundaries of America's traditional, self-contained, village-centered way of life. But those same forces—when gathered into the guiding hand of the centralized bureaucratic state—now permitted a degree of rationalized, efficient management of human affairs unimaginable in the earlier epoch of diverse local communities. In Dewey's famous formulation, it was now possible and necessary to convert the "Great Society created by steam and electricity" into the "Great Community."

Humanizing and softening the harsh, mechanistic aspects of this new national leviathan was the president, standing at the center and articulating a vision of grand, national purpose—which in turn bestowed legitimacy upon the new national state. That vision would summon citizens out of merely self-interested, materialistic pursuits, into public-spirited, civic-minded devotion to a common national idea and a unifying national state. (If this sounds far-fetched, recall Walter Mondale's insistence in the 1984 campaign that the president's preeminent task was to "make us a community and keep us a community.")

If the devotion to national purpose and state should falter, the president could reach into his quiver of national "wars" and "crises," which would serve to remind Americans of the need to pull together as one in the face of perilous conditions or threats to national integrity. Thus would Lyndon Johnson describe his program as a "war on poverty" precisely because the "military image" would "sound a call to arms which will stir people . . . to lend their talents to a massive effort to eradicate the evil." Thus would Jimmy Carter declare the "energy crisis" to be the "moral equivalent of war," which would "give us all a sense of unity and purpose again."

According to the progressives, this new idea of national community—coherent, efficient, rational, yet infused with the warm glow of purpose and belonging—was vastly preferable to the chaotic jumble of divergent civic institutions and local loyalties, which the state would now proceed to elimi-nate or absorb.

The theme of national community—an old chestnut of Democratic presidential candidates throughout this century—has already found an hon-ored place in Clinton rhetoric. The "New Covenant" speech at Georgetown University in October, 1991, laying out the larger message of the Clinton campaign, was tellingly sub-titled "Responsibility and Rebuilding the Ameri-can Community." Clinton complained that "there's a hole in our politics where a sense of common purpose used to be," and called for a "New Covenant" to "restore a sense of community to this great nation." Again and again, he has returned to this vision of a renewed national family or commu-nity, sharply posing its demands for national service and public-mindedness to the "gilded age" of the 1980s, when "greed, selfishness, irresponsibility, excess, and neglect" prevailed.

In light of this larger project, one appreciates all the more Clinton's deft deployment of Oprah-style media forms to cultivate a warm, caring, nurturing, "feel your pain," family atmosphere among a sprawling population of 250 mil-lion. That there suddenly should be a great national "crisis" in health care requiring—what else?—a massive extension of government power is a page right out of liberalism's dog-eared playbook.

Moreover, the national community ideal offers a facile, rhetorical bridge over the chasm between "new Democrat" supporters who genuinely yearn for a revitalization of civic life, and "old Democrats" who prefer the further expansion of government's reach. It permits Clinton to speak the language of civic revival, while pursuing the policy of government revival.

If the national community idea is a dead end, however, how are we to go about resuscitating civil society? . . .

FALSE STARTS

Unhappily, the past three Republican administrations have left a dismal record in this regard. . . .

After boldly calling for "an end of giantism, for a return to the human scale . . . the scale of the local fraternal lodge, the church organization, the block club, the farm bureau," President Reagan could manage little more than the "Task Force on Private Sector Initiatives." Filled with liberal foun-dation officers and well-intentioned but naive corporate CEOs, the task force quickly bogged down in pointless debates about whether or not corpo-rations should be expected to foot the bill for welfare state programs, As Reagan's ACTION director Tom Pauken put it, task force members seemed to believe the mission was to "change one set of bureaucrats for another and say we've accomplished something just because they're off the federal pay-roll." A genuine return to local citizen democracy was never on the agenda.

Likewise, after grandly proclaiming his vision of America as a "nation of communities, of thousands of ethnic, religious, social, business, labor union, neighborhood, regional, and other organizations, all of them varied, voluntary, and unique," President Bush could only come up with the "points of light" initiative, which passed out hundreds of daily awards to worthy volunteer groups, but otherwise had nothing to say about the broader transformation of public policy toward a genuine, community-oriented basis.

THE LIMITS OF PUBLIC POLICY

These false starts toward civic revival should lead us to be considerably more modest in our expectations of policy. To be sure, there are some policies that could help promote localism and civic renewal—such as offering unrestricted education vouchers, restoring family income by increasing the tax deduction for children, and toughening laws concerning child support and divorce. But most useful measures in the public policy realm involve shrinking that realm itself, by diminishing the reach of the therapeutic state and its debilitating effects on private institutions.

Even when public policy approaches the civic realm with the best of intentions, it more often than not only makes things worse. . . . Again and again—whether it's child care, foster care, adoption, homes for unwed mothers, resettlement of refugees, or disaster relief—the appearance of even well-intentioned federal assistance inevitably signals the retreat of civic institutions, and the worsening of problems they previously ameliorated.

Too often in the past, conservatives have made this essential point about the limits of public policy, concluding that "it's up to civil society" to address our social problems—and then walked away. . . .

For conservatives, "it's up to civil society" should not be the conclusion of inquiry, but the beginning. Indeed, the central questions for conservatism at this moment in its history should be: How can we *recreate* civil society where it has collapsed, retreated, or never formed? And most important, how can we do so on the terms of civil society itself—that is, relying chiefly on resources available within the private sector, rather than on the problematic instrument of public policy?

If excessive conservative optimism about the resilience of civil society is one way to evade this question, excessive pessimism is another, more popular way. Many conservatives understand civic devastation to be vast—and irreparable. A minor industry has sprung up around detailing the decline and seemingly permanent disappearance of our most important civic institutions. Some conservatives go so far as to suggest that we should in essence dig moats around the remaining Midwestern towns and Southern villages where community virtues still prevail, and let the rest of the nation stew in modernity's corrosive juices.

Leaving aside other problems with this approach, let's just say that there is little reason to be so pessimistic. After all, Tocqueville was one of the first to ponder the destruction modern forces would visit on traditional institutions—over a century and a half ago. Indeed, his purpose in writing *Democracy in America* was to warn about the impending storm of modernity—to tell us that the old, established institutions of civil society would soon be borne away by the cyclonic winds of modern individualism and the centralized state.

A Genius for Association

In America, however, he witnessed the remarkable spectacle of unrelated individuals—as he put it, "people having different languages, beliefs, opinions . . . without roots, without memories, without prejudices, without routines, without common ideas"—coming together to create wholly new forms of civil institutions, in the very teeth of the modern storm. The impulse toward association—the yearning for genuine citizenship within civil society—is not so easy to destroy, he seemed to suggest. . . .

The American genius for association is evident throughout American history. . . . Even in the midst of the community-eroding forces of modernity, other powerful impulses are compelling heretofore isolated individuals to reengage with or recreate civic institutions. Parenthood is one such potent motivation.

Time and again, individuals who have abandoned themselves to disorganized lives or passive dependence on the state are suddenly galvanized into civic activity when they become parents, and realize that their children face an identically bleak future unless they take dramatic action. The sight of their children walking to school through the litter of IV needles and the clusters of drug dealers, or the thought of their daughter growing up permanently locked in welfare dependency, is simply unbearable. They may put up with any amount of abuse in their own lives, but as parents their cry becomes "not with my children, you don't."

The central goal for such parents is the recreation of a safe, orderly, structured, neighborhood environment for their children—one in which they are physically safe, emotionally and spiritually nurtured, and intellectually and morally instructed. Parents seek to reestablish the web of institutional supports that express, reinforce, and pass on to their children the wisdom and moral discipline necessary for a fruitful life, with family, church, school, and neighborhood all reflecting certain common ethical themes. . . .

This yearning for community applies equally to the urban and suburban middle class. Many professional couples for the first time are being spurred by parenthood to begin working within churches, neighborhoods, Little League teams, and a host of other groups and institutions.

In a recent New York Times interview, sociologist Wade Clark Roof suggested this was true of baby boomer parents in particular: "In an era of enormous fragmentation, parents are expressing concern about the moral and religious socialization of their children." And so they are turning toward church and community to create an orderly moral universe. As Irving Kristol notes, in the face of "the single most important question that adults face"—how shall we raise our children?—modern parents suddenly drop the trendy project of personal liberation, and begin to focus instead on the restoration of social order.

Kristol predicts that the growing urgency of this question for millions of new parents will help fuel a major religious revival across the land. Without a doubt, churches, synagogues, and other religious institutions will play a central role in civic regeneration—particularly in the inner city. Over the years he has worked with neighborhood groups, Bob Woodson has found that at the heart of the most successful—those that genuinely change individual lives, as well as material surroundings—is an explicit call for personal spiritual transformation.

In many inner-city neighborhoods, the church is one of the only institutions of civil society left. Many congregations are taking the lead in securing better housing and improved city services, providing drug and alcohol rehabilitation, job training, and family support, and opening small business opportunities—often inspired and sustained by an unwavering spiritual commitment. . . .

While such efforts must proceed largely without "benefit" of public policy, a certain degree of political involvement will nonetheless be thrust upon "new citizenship" efforts. For bureaucratic elites will need to be evicted from regions of civil society over which they currently exercise dominion, and their furious counterassaults repelled.

Certainly the struggle over education reform at the state level suggests the outlines of a new, grassroots political activism that will emerge as the new citizenship expands. Newly energized parents are striving to reclaim authority over schools from entrenched education bureaucracies. Their primary goal is to reestablish the schools as stable, structured, demanding learning environments, reflecting—rather than subverting—the moral commitments of the family. . . .

Similar battles against government elites are underway elsewhere: Families in public housing trying to rebuild community life are confronting legal obstacles to fighting crime and becoming economically self-sufficient; entrepreneurs struggle to establish small businesses in the face of oppressive regulation. . . .

The feisty populism of the new citizenship will not be welcomed by all those traditionally found under the conservative tent. Certainly the substance, to say nothing of the style, of the new citizenship will be somewhat off-putting to the old-line, country-club Republicans, who came to dominate the upper reaches of the last administration, and who winced at the Houston Convention's foray into "family values." For them, talk about fullscale assaults on ruling cultural elites will be vaguely menacing, and earnest discussion of restoring the spiritual and moral vitality of the inner city will seem, well, vulgar. . . .

OUT OF THE IVORY TOWER

. . . Conservative commitment to civic revival will thus clearly demand far more attention to and personal involvement with *doing,* with actual experience in deploying the instruments of civil society to promote that revival. Consequently, more of us must be prepared to support those conservative activists already working at the grassroots level to restore civic vitality—through encouragement of tenant management of public housing, neighborhood economic development, private schools for inner-city children, and church-based moral reconstruction. . . .

Perhaps the most widespread form and clearest practical example of conservative civic activism today, however, is the so-called "private voucher movement." In a number of cities across the nation, philanthropic foundations and corporations have finally despaired of reforming public education from within. At the same time, many inner city parents gaze longingly at nearby church-based schools, which promise instruction in morality and character as well as academics, but whose modest tuitions put them just out of reach. Private voucher systems broker the needs and desires of all these parties: Low-income parents are given vouchers to redeem at any school of their choice, religious or nonsectarian, by reform-minded philanthropists, while value-generating educational institutions receive much-needed financial support. . . .

While these groups and movements are promoting the reconstruction of civil society, they are contributing to another sort of reconstruction as well—that of American conservatism. The public image of conservatism still remains firmly fixed where it was some 15 years ago, when Jeane Kirkpatrick explained that she was not (at the time) a Republican, because Republicans simply did not seem to "*care enough* about the whole."

When conservatives respond to pressing human needs in the inner city with arid discourses on the virtues of the free market, or cuts in the capital gains tax, or vague assurances that "it's up to civil society," we are doing little to dispel our own negative image. Small wonder that liberals still find it so easy to persuade the American people that conservatives, in President Clinton's words, represent only "greed, selfishness, irresponsibility, excess and neglect."

But if conservatives will squarely back the spontaneous uprisings of citizens around the nation against the tyrannies of the therapeutic state—if conservatives place at the center of their agenda a commitment to the reconstruction of civil society, whose institutions and values are of most benefit to the least well off—then finally we may lay to rest the charge that we do not care enough about the whole. That the task of civic reconstruction promises to be complex and difficult—that it demands so much more of us than merely dashing off charity or IRS checks to perpetuate the same failed public policies—might at last begin to change public views about who is genuinely compassionate, and who merely hides behind compassion while continuing to line their own pockets.

In short, the new citizenship implies a new conservatism—a conservatism that should be able to construct for itself a broad-based and enduring majority among the citizens of the United States.

Chapter II

Political Parties
and Elections

The Constitution provided a detailed mechanism for presidential selection, but that mechanism was transformed very early in our nation's history by the development of political parties. Parties very quickly became the major institutional force structuring electoral politics as well as an important influence on the policy debate within government. Thus, one must look beyond the Founding period to fully comprehend the contemporary character of elections and parties, but it would be a mistake to neglect the importance of Constitutional principles and mechanisms in their development and operation. For example, the operation of the electoral college described by Hamilton is very different than the Presidential selection process we see today. Hamilton thought the electoral college would allow for both popular opinion and the deliberate choice of a select body of citizens to operate in the election of the President. Popular opinion would determine the choice of electors, but electors operating in "circumstances favorable to deliberation" would choose the President.

The electoral college never operated in the way Hamilton envisioned. The selection of Washington was a foregone conclusion. By the time the election of 1796 occurred, the rise of political parties transformed independent electors into delegates pledged to vote for the nominee of their party. Lord Bryce claims that party nomination of candidates is one cause of the lack of great statesmen in the office of the Presidency.

Martin Diamond argues, however, that even though the electoral college does not operate in the way intended by the framers, it nonetheless promotes Constitutional principles. Electors may not exercise independent judgment, but the building of electoral majorities on a state by state basis creates a complex majority. Presidential candidates must build a coalition of competing interests on a state by state basis rather than appeal to a simple national majority based upon the lowest common denominator of national public opinion. A national direct popular election, according to Diamond, would undermine interest based politics and encourage the development of more principled, but less stable and more dangerous political parties.

Similarly, James W. Ceaser argues that development of political parties came to promote Constitutional principles. Under the direction of Martin Van Buren parties institutionalized the screening function for Presidential candidates that was originally to be performed by the electors. Although parties would not be likely to produce the "continental figure" intended by the Founders, Van Buren thought that they would preserve the Constitutional character of the office. Broad-based consensus parties would help to moderate popular election campaigns and to restrain the President once in office.

Ceaser goes on to explain that contemporary reforms of political parties and the electoral process are rooted in the Progressive rejection of consensus politics and of institutions designed to moderate or restrain public opinion. The Progressive conception of politics viewed elections as plebiscite in which voters choose between different political principles formulated by party leaders. Only in such a purely democratic system can the corrupting influences of self-interest be replaced by a healthy concern for the public good. But Ceaser questions whether parties that substitute principles for interests will be either healthy or viable. He fears that a politics based exclusively on principles will be potentially demagogic and dangerously divisive.

Campaign finance laws passed in the early 1970s sought to minimize corruption and the appearance of corruption in the electoral process. The case of *Buckley v. Valeo* illustrates that the state's interest in restricting campaign finance practices may come into conflict with the Constitutional protection of free speech. The case also raises the question of whether equal political influence can or should be guaranteed by the government. As Justice Burger points out in his dissent, limitations on contributions and federal campaign financing may not equalize influence but will more likely provide incumbents with an increased advantage. The attempt to limit the influence of private contributors may ultimately help to insulate incumbents from effective electoral challenges.

In 2002 the Bipartisan Campaign Reform Act (BCRA) (also known as McCain-Feingold) became law. It sought to close loopholes in the earlier legislation prohibiting the use of soft money (money raised by national state and local parties) for campaign expenditures and outlawing issue advocacy ads that mention a candidate's name within 30 days of a primary election or caucus and 60 days of a general election. *In Federal Election Commission v. Wisconsin Right to Life*, the Court argues that the interest of the state in regulating campaign finance must be balanced against free speech rights. Issue advocacy ads are an essential form of political speech and any regulation of them requires strict scrutiny. The interest of the state in regulating campaign finance may be sufficient to allow restrictions of ads that advocate the election of a particular candidate, but it is not sufficient to forbid any ad that mentions the name of a particular candidate. A free discussion of political ideas is an essential First Amendment right.

The extent to which the Constitution provides guidance for elections is the central issue in *Bush v. Gore*. The conflict between the desire to determine "voter intent" and the need to uphold formal rules and procedures is clear in the opinions of the Court. As Jeffrey Poelvoorde explains, what to many appeared as mere partisanship on the part of the Court, in fact reflected a serious examination of the complexity of competing Constitutional principles.

Finally, it is important to recognize that parties and elections are driven by more than rules and laws. They also are shaped by ideas. The ideas of the modern Republican Party laid out in a 1977 speech by Ronald Reagan emphasize the centrality of the principle of individual liberty to Republicans, and a 2006 speech by Barack Obama acccentuates the importance of the ideas of mutual regard and mutual responsibility for contemporary Democrats.

21

Alexander Hamilton

The Electoral College (1788)

The mode of appointment of the Chief Magistrate of the United States is almost the only part of the system, of any consequence, which has escaped without severe censure, or which has received the slightest mark of approbation from its opponents. The most plausible of these, who has appeared in print, has even deigned to admit that the election of the President is pretty well guarded. I venture somewhat further, and hesitate not to affirm that if the manner of it be not perfect, it is at least excellent. It unites in an eminent degree all the advantages the union of which was to be wished for.

It was desirable that the sense of the people should operate in the choice of the person to whom so important a trust was to be confided. This end will be answered by committing the right of making it, not to any preestablished body, but to men chosen by the people for the special purpose, and at the particular conjuncture.

It was equally desirable, that the immediate election should be made by men most capable of analyzing the qualities adapted to the station, and acting under circumstances favorable to deliberation, and to a judicious combination of all the reasons and inducements which were proper to govern their

From Federalist 68, in *The Federalist*.

choice. A small number of persons, selected by their fellow-citizens from the general mass, will be most likely to possess the information and discernment requisite to such complicated investigations.

It was also peculiarly desirable to afford as little opportunity as possible to tumult and disorder. This evil was not least to be dreaded in the election of a magistrate, who was to have so important an agency in the administration of the government as the President of the United States. But the precautions which have been so happily concerted in the system under consideration, promise an effectual security against this mischief. The choice of *several*, to form an intermediate body of electors, will be much less apt to convulse the community with any extraordinary or violent movements, than the choice of *one* who was himself to be the final object of the public wishes. And as the electors, chosen in each State, are to assemble and vote in the State in which they are chosen, this detached and divided situation will expose them much less to heats and ferments, which might be communicated from them to the people, than if they were all to be convened at one time, in one place.

Nothing was more to be desired than that every practicable obstacle should be opposed to cabal, intrigue, and corruption. . . . They have not made the appointment of the President to depend on any preexisting bodies of men, who might be tampered with beforehand to prostitute their votes; but they have referred it in the first instance to an immediate act of the people of America, to be exerted in the choice of persons for the temporary and sole purpose of making the appointment. And they have excluded from eligibility to this trust, all those who from situation might be suspected of too great devotion to the President in office. No senator, representative, or other person holding a place of trust or profit under the United States, can be of the numbers of the electors. Thus without corrupting the body of the people, the immediate agents in the election will at least enter upon the task free from any sinister bias. Their transient existence, and their detached situation, already taken notice of, afford a satisfactory prospect of their continuing so, to the conclusion of it. The business of corruption, when it is to embrace so considerable a number of men, requires time as well as means. Nor would it be found easy suddenly to embark them, dispersed as they would be over thirteen States, in any combinations founded upon motives, which though they could not properly be denominated corrupt, might yet be of a nature to mislead them from their duty.

Another and no less important desideratum was, that the Executive should be independent for his continuance in the office on all but the people themselves. He might otherwise be tempted to sacrifice his duty to his complaisance for those whose favor was necessary to the duration of his official consequence. This advantage will also be secured, by making his reelection to depend on a special body of representatives, deputed by the society for the single purpose of making the important choice. . . .

The process of election affords a moral certainty, that the office of President will never fall to the lot of any man who is not in an eminent degree endowed with the requisite qualifications. Talents for low intrigue, and the little arts of popularity, may alone suffice to elevate a man to the first honors in a single State; but it will require other talents, and a different kind of merit, to establish him in the esteem and confidence of the whole Union, or of so considerable a portion of it as would be necessary to make him a successful candidate for the distinguished office of President of the United States. It will not be too strong to say, that there will be a constant probability of seeing the station filled by characters preeminent for ability and virtue. And this will be thought no inconsiderable recommendation of the Constitution, by those who are able to estimate the share which the executive in every government must necessarily have in its good or ill administration. Though we cannot acquiesce in the political heresy of the poet who says:

> "For forms of government let fools contest—
> That which is best administered is best."

—yet we may safely pronounce, that the true test of a good government is its aptitude and tendency to produce a good administration. . . .

22

James Bryce

Why Great Men Are
Not Chosen Presidents (1888)

Europeans often ask, and Americans do not always explain, how it happens that this great office, the greatest in the world, unless we except the Papacy, to which any man can rise by his own merits, is not more frequently filled by great and striking men? In America, which is beyond all other countries the country of a "career open to talents," a country, moreover, in which political life is unusually keen and political ambition widely diffused, it might be

From *The American Commonwealth*, Vol. 1, Chapter 3.

expected that the highest place would always be won by a man of brilliant gifts. But since the heroes of the Revolution died out with Jefferson and Adams and Madison some sixty years ago, no person except General Grant has reached the chair whose name would have been remembered had he not been President, and no President except Abraham Lincoln has displayed rare or striking qualities in the chair. Who now knows or cares to know anything about the personality of James K. Polk or Franklin Pierce? The only thing remarkable about them is that being so commonplace they should have climbed so high.

Several reasons may be suggested for the fact, which Americans are themselves the first to admit.

One is that the proportion of first-rate ability drawn into politics is smaller in America than in most European countries. This is a phenomenon whose causes must be elucidated later: in the meantime it is enough to say that in France and Italy, where half-revolutionary conditions have made public life exciting and accessible; in Germany, where an admirably-organized civil service cultivates and develops statecraft with unusual success; in England, where many persons of wealth and leisure seek to enter the political arena, while burning questions touch the interests of all classes and make men eager observers of the combatants, the total quantity of talent devoted to parliamentary or administrative work is far larger, relatively to the population, than in America, where much of the best ability, both for thought and for action, for planning and for executing, rushes into a field which is comparatively narrow in Europe, the business of developing the material resources of the country.

Another is that the methods and habits of Congress, and indeed of political life generally, seem to give fewer opportunities for personal distinction, fewer modes in which a man may commend himself to his countrymen by eminent capacity in thought, in speech, or in administration, than is the case in the free countries of Europe.

A third reason is that eminent men make more enemies, and give those enemies more assailable points, than obscure men do. They are therefore in so far less desirable candidates. It is true that the eminent man has also made more friends, that his name is more widely known, and may be greeted with louder cheers. Other things being equal, the famous man is preferable. But other things never are equal. The famous man has probably attacked some leaders in his own party, has supplanted others, has expressed his dislike to the crotchet of some active section, has perhaps committed errors which are capable of being magnified into offences. No man stands long before the public and bears a part in great affairs without giving openings to censorious criticism. Fiercer far than the light which beats upon a throne is the light which beats upon a presidential candidate, searching out all the recesses of his past life. Hence, when the choice lies between a brilliant man and a safe man, the safe man is preferred. Party feeling, strong enough to carry in on its back a man without conspicuous positive merits, is not always strong enough to procure forgiveness for a man with positive faults.

A European finds that this phenomenon needs in its turn to be explained, for in the free countries of Europe brilliancy, be it eloquence in speech, or some striking achievement in war or administration, or the power through whatever means of somehow impressing the popular imagination, is what makes a leader triumphant. Why should it be otherwise in America? Because in America party loyalty and party organization have been hitherto so perfect that any one put forward by the party will get the full party vote if his character is good and his "record," as they call it, unstained. The safe candidate may not draw in quite so many votes from the moderate men of the other side as the brilliant one would, but he will not lose nearly so many from his own ranks. Even those who admit his mediocrity will vote straight when the moment for voting comes. Besides, the ordinary American voter does not object to mediocrity. He has a lower conception of the qualities requisite to make a statesman than those who direct public opinion in Europe have. He likes his candidate to be sensible, vigorous, and, above all, what he calls "magnetic," and does not value, because he sees no need for, originality or profundity, a fine culture or a wide knowledge. Candidates are selected to be run for nomination by knots of persons who, however expert as party tacticians, are usually commonplace men; and the choice between those selected for nomination is made by a very large body, an assembly of over eight hundred delegates from the local party organizations over the country, who are certainly no better than ordinary citizens. How this process works will be seen more fully when I come to speak of those Nominating Conventions which are so notable a feature in American politics.

It must also be remembered that the merits of a President are one thing and those of a candidate another thing. An eminent American is reported to have said to friends who wished to put him forward, "Gentlemen, let there be no mistake. I should make a good President, but a very bad candidate." Now to a party it is more important that its nominee should be a good candidate than that he should turn out a good President. A nearer danger is a greater danger. As Saladin says in *The Talisman*, "A wild cat in a chamber is more dangerous than a lion in a distant desert." It will be a misfortune to the party, as well as to the country, if the candidate elected should prove a bad President. But it is a greater misfortune to the party that it should be beaten in the impending election, for the evil of losing national patronage will have come four years sooner. "B" (so reason the leaders), "who is one of our possible candidates, may be an abler man than A, who is the other. But we have a better chance of winning with A than with B, while X, the candidate of our opponents, is anyhow no better than A. We must therefore run A." This reasoning is all the more forcible because the previous career of the possible candidates has generally made it easier to say who will succeed as a candidate than who will succeed as a President; and because the wire-pullers with whom the choice rests are better judges of the former question than of the latter.

After all, too, and this is a point much less obvious to Europeans than to Americans, a President need not be a man of brilliant intellectual gifts. Englishmen, imagining him as something like their prime minister, assume that he ought to be a dazzling orator, able to sway legislatures or multitudes, possessed also of the constructive powers that can devise a great policy or frame a comprehensive piece of legislation. They forget that the President does not sit in Congress, that he ought not to address meetings, except on ornamental and (usually) non-political occasions, that he cannot submit bills nor otherwise influence the action of the legislature. His main duties are to be prompt and firm in securing the due execution of the laws and maintaining the public peace, careful and upright in the choice of the executive officials of the country. Eloquence, whose value is apt to be overrated in all free countries, imagination, profundity of thought or extent of knowledge, are all in so far a gain to him that they make him a bigger man, and help him to gain a greater influence over the nation, an influence which, if he be a true patriot he may use for its good. But they are not necessary for the due discharge in ordinary times of the duties of his post. A man may lack them and yet make an excellent President. . . .

So far we have been considering personal merits. But in the selection of a candidate many considerations have to be regarded besides personal merits, whether they be the merits of a candidate, or of a possible President. The chief of these considerations is the amount of support which can be secured from different States or from different regions, or, as the Americans say, "sections," of the Union. State feeling and sectional feeling are powerful factors in a presidential election. The Northwest, including the States from Ohio to Dakota, is now the most populous region of the Union, and therefore counts for most in an election. It naturally conceives that its interests will be best protected by one who knows them from birth and residence. Hence *prima facie* a North-western man makes the best candidate. A large State casts a heavier vote in the election; and every State is of course more likely to be carried by one of its own children than by a stranger, because his fellow-citizens, while they feel honoured by the choice, gain also a substantial advantage, having a better prospect of such favours as the administration can bestow. Hence, *coeteris paribus*, a man from a large State is preferable as a candidate. . . . The problem is further complicated by the fact that some States are already safe for one or other party, while others are doubtful. The North-western and New England States are most of them certain to go Republican: the Southern States are (at present) all of them certain to go Democratic. It is more important to gratify a doubtful State than one you have got already; and hence, *coeteris paribus*, a candidate from a doubtful State, such as New York or Indiana, is to be preferred. . . .

"What shall we do with our ex-Presidents?" is a question often put in America, but never yet answered. The position of a past chief magistrate is not a happy one. He has been a species of sovereign at home. He is received—General Grant was—with almost royal honours abroad. His private income may be insufficient to enable him to live in ease, yet he cannot without loss of dignity, the country's dignity as well as his own, go back to practice at the bar or become partner in a mercantile firm. If he tries to enter the Senate, it may happen that there is no seat vacant for his own State, or that the majority in the State legislature is against him. It has been suggested that he might be given a seat in that chamber as an extra member; but to this plan there is the objection that it would give to the State from which he comes a third senator, and thus put other States at a disadvantage. In any case, however, it would seem only right to bestow such a pension as would relieve him from the necessity of re-entering business or a profession.

We may now answer the question from which we started. Great men are not chosen Presidents, firstly, because great men are rare in politics; secondly, because the method of choice does not bring them to the top; thirdly, because they are not, in quiet times, absolutely needed. I may observe that the Presidents, regarded historically, fall into three periods, the second inferior to the first, the third rather better than the second.

Down till the election of Andrew Jackson in 1828, all the Presidents had been statesmen in the European sense of the word, men of education, of administrative experience, of a certain largeness of view and dignity of character. All except the first two had served in the great office of secretary of state; all were well known to the nation from the part they had played. In the second period, from Jackson till the outbreak of the Civil War in 1861, the Presidents were either mere politicians, such as Van Buren, Polk, or Buchanan, or else successful soldiers, such as Harrison or Taylor, whom their party found useful as figure-heads. They were intellectual pygmies beside the real leaders of that generation—Clay, Calhoun, and Webster. A new series begins with Lincoln in 1861. He and General Grant his successor, who cover sixteen years between them, belong to the history of the world. The other less distinguished Presidents of this period contrast favourably with the Polks and Pierces of the days before the war, but they are not, like the early Presidents, the first men of the country. If we compare the eighteen Presidents who have been elected to office since 1789 with the nineteen English prime ministers of the same hundred years, there are but six of the latter, and at least eight of the former whom history calls personally insignificant, while only Washington, Jefferson, Lincoln, and Grant can claim to belong to a front rank represented in the English list by seven or possibly eight names. It would seem that the natural selection of the English parliamentary system, even as modified by the aristocratic habits of that country, has more tendency to bring the highest gifts to the highest place than the more artificial selection of America.

23

Martin Diamond

The Electoral College and the American Idea of Democracy (1977)

In 1967, a distinguished commission of the American Bar Association recommended that the Electoral College be scrapped and replaced by a nationwide popular vote for the President, with provision for a runoff election between the top two candidates in the event no candidate received at least 40 percent of the popular vote. This recommendation was passed by the House in 1969, came close to passage in the Senate in 1970, and is now once again upon us. It is this proposal that has just been endorsed by President Carter and that is being pressed upon Congress under the leadership of Senator Bayh.

The theme of this attack upon the Electoral College is well-summarized in a much-quoted sentence from the 1969 ABA Report: "The electoral college method of electing a President of the United States is archaic, undemocratic, complex, ambiguous, indirect, and dangerous." . . .

Not only is [the Electoral College] not at all archaic, [however,] but one might say that it is the very model of up-to-date constitutional flexibility. Perhaps no other feature of the Constitution has had a greater capacity for dynamic historical adaptiveness. The electors became nullities; presidential elections became dramatic national contests; the federal elements in the process became strengthened by the general-ticket practice (that is, winner-take-all); modern mass political parties developed; campaigning moved from rather rigid sectionalism to the complexities of a modern technological society—and all this occurred tranquilly and legitimately within the original constitutional framework (as modified by the Twelfth Amendment).

The Electoral College thus has experienced an immense historical evolution. But the remarkable fact is that while it now operates in historically transformed ways, in ways not at all as the Framers intended, it nonetheless still operates largely to the ends that they intended. What more could one ask of a constitutional provision?

To appreciate why the original electoral provisions proved so adaptable, we have to recollect what the original intention was. . . .

The device of independent electors as a substitute for direct popular election was hit upon for three reasons, none of which supports the thesis that the intention was fundamentally undemocratic. First, and above all, the electors were not devised as an undemocratic substitute for the popular will, but rather as a nationalizing substitute for the state legislatures. In short, the Electoral College, like so much else in the Constitution, was the product of the give-and-take and the compromises between the large and the small states, or, more precisely, between the confederalists—those who sought to retain much of the Articles of Confederation—and those who advocated a large, primarily national, republic. . . .

[T]he confederalists fought hard to have the President selected by the state legislatures or by some means that retained the primacy of the states as states. It was to fend off this confederalizing threat that the leading Framers, Madison, James Wilson, and Gouverneur Morris, hit upon the Electoral College device. . . .

Second, the system of electors also had to be devised because most of the delegates to the Convention feared, not democracy itself, but only that a straightforward national election was "impracticable" in a country as large as the United States, given the poor internal communications it then had. Many reasonably feared that, in these circumstances, the people simply could not have the national information about available candidates to make any real choice, let alone an intelligent one. And small-state partisans feared that, given this lack of information, ordinary voters would vote for favorite sons, with the result that large-state candidates would always win the presidential pluralities. How seriously concerned the Framers were with this "communications gap" is shown by the famous faulty mechanism in the original provisions (the one that made possible the Jefferson-Burr deadlock in 1801). Each elector was originally to cast two votes, but without specifying which was for President and which for Vice-President. The Constitution required that at least one of these two votes be for a non-home-state candidate, the intention being to force the people and their electors to cast at least one electoral vote for a truly "continental" figure. Clearly, then, what the Framers were seeking was not an undemocratic way to substitute elite electors for the popular will; rather, as they claimed, they were trying to find a practicable way to extract from the popular will a nonparochial choice for the President.

The third reason for the electoral scheme likewise had nothing to do with frustrating democracy, but rather with the wide variety of suffrage practices in the states. Madison dealt with this problem at the Constitutional Convention on July 19, 1787. While election by "the people was in his opinion the fittest in itself," there was a serious circumstantial difficulty. "The right of suffrage was much more diffusive in the Northern than the Southern states; and the latter could have no influence in the election on the score of the Negroes. The substitution of electors obviated this difficulty." That is, the electoral system would take care of the discrepancies between state voting population and total population of the states until, as Madison hoped and expected, slavery would be eliminated and suffrage discrepancies gradually disappeared. . . .

These were the main reasons, then, why the leading Framers settled for the electoral system instead of a national popular election, and none may fairly be characterized as undemocratic. . . .

[T]he chief contemporary attack on the Electoral College has little to do with the autonomous elector or, as is said, the "faithless elector." The autonomous elector could be amended out of existence (and without doing violence to the constitutional intention of the Electoral College), but this would not lessen the contemporary hostility to it as undemocratic. . . .

The gravamen of the "undemocratic" indictment of the Electoral College rests on the possibility that, because votes are aggregated within the states by the general-ticket system, in which the winner takes all, a loser in the national popular vote may nonetheless become President by winning a majority of the electoral votes of the states. . . . [I]t suffices to reformulate the issue and get it on its proper footing.

In fact, presidential elections are already just about as democratic as they can be. We already have one-man, one-vote—but *in the states.* Elections are as freely and democratically contested as elections can be—*but in the states.* Victory always goes democratically to the winner of the raw popular vote— *but in the states.* The label given to the proposed reform, "direct popular election," is a misnomer; the elections have already become as directly popular as they can be—*but in the states.* Despite all their democratic rhetoric, the reformers do not propose to make our presidential elections more directly democratic, they only propose to make them more directly *national,* by entirely removing the states from the electoral process. Democracy thus is not the question regarding the Electoral College, federalism is: should our presidential elections remain in part *federally* democratic, or should we make them completely *nationally* democratic?

Whatever we decide, then, democracy itself is not at stake in our decision, only the prudential question of how to channel and organize the popular will. That makes everything easier. When the question is only whether the federally democratic aspect of the Electoral College should be abandoned in order to prevent the remotely possible election of a President who had not won the national popular vote, it does not seem so hard to opt for retaining some federalism in this homogenizing, centralizing age. When federalism has already been weakened, perhaps inevitably in modern circumstances, why further weaken the federal elements in our political system by destroying the informal federal element that has historically evolved in our system of presidential elections? The crucial general-ticket system, adopted in the 1830s for reasons pertinent then, has become in our time a constitutionally unplanned but vital support for federalism. Also called the "unit rule" system, it provides that the state's entire electoral vote goes to the winner of the popular vote in the state. Resting entirely on the voluntary legislative action of each state, this informal historical development, combined with the formal constitutional provision, has generated a federal element in the Electoral College which sends a federalizing impulse throughout our whole political process. It makes the states as states dramatically and pervasively important in the whole presidential selection process, from the earliest strategies in the nominating campaign through the convention and final election. Defederalize the presidential election—which is what direct popular election boils down to—and a contrary nationalizing impulse will gradually work its way throughout the political process. The nominating process naturally takes its cues from the electing process; were the President to be elected in a single national election, the same cuing process would continue, but in reverse. . . .

Our consciences will be further eased when we note that the abhorrence of the federal aspect of the Electoral College—which causes the potential discrepancy between electoral and popular votes—cannot logically be limited to the Electoral College. It rests upon premises that necessitate abhorrence of any and all *district* forms of election. What is complained about in the Electoral College is endemic to all districted electoral systems, whether composed of states, or congressional districts, or parliamentary constituencies. If population is not exactly evenly distributed in all the districts (and it never can be), both in sheer numbers and in their political predispositions, then the possibility cannot be removed that the winner of a majority of the districts may not also be the winner of the raw popular vote. . . .

[T]he national popular-vote/district-vote discrepancy . . . can and does occur here regarding control of both the House and the Senate. Why is it not a loaded pistol to our democratic heads when control over our lawmaking bodies can fall, and has fallen, into the hands of the party that lost in the national popular vote? . . .

The House has largely escaped the "undemocratic" charge (especially now, after major reapportionment) despite the fact that its districted basis likewise creates a potential discrepancy between winning a majority of seats and winning the national popular vote for Congress. By the populistic reasoning and rhetoric that attacks the Electoral College, the House also fails the standard of national majoritarianism. But we quite ungrudgingly see the wisdom in departing from that standard in order to secure the many advantages of local districting. To indicate only a few: First, there is democratic responsiveness to local needs, interests, and opinions in general.

Americans have always believed that there is more to democracy itself than merely maximizing national majoritarianism; our idea of democracy includes responsiveness to *local* majorities as well. Further, because of our multiplicity of interests, ethnic groups, religions, and races, we have always believed in local democratic responsiveness to geographically based minorities whose interests may otherwise be utterly neglected; such minorities secure vigorous direct representation, for example, only because of the districted basis of the House of Representatives. The state-by-state responsiveness of the Electoral College is an equally legitimate form of districted, local democratic responsiveness. There is also the security to liberty that results from the districted decentralization of the political basis of the legislature; and we cherish also the multiplication of opportunities for voluntary political participation that likewise results from that districted decentralization. Finally, we cherish the guarantee that districting provides, that power in the legislature will be nationally distributed, rather than concentrated in regional majorities, as would be possible in a nondistricted election of the House. . . .

This kind of complex reasoning is the hallmark of the American idea of democracy: a taking into account of local as well as national democratic considerations and, even more importantly, blending democratic considerations with all the other things that contribute to political well-being. . . .

[I]n the next place, t]o judge fairly the charge of ambiguity . . . the Electoral College must be compared in this regard with other electoral systems and, especially, with the 40 percent plus/runoff system proposed by President Carter and Senator Bayh as its replacement. . . .

The American electorate has a fundamental tendency to divide closely, with "photo finish" elections being almost the rule rather than the exception. The Electoral College almost always announces these close election outcomes with useful amplification. In purely numerical popular votes, an election outcome might be uncertain and vulnerable to challenge; but the Electoral College replaces the numerical uncertainty with an unambiguously visible constitutional majority that sustains the legitimacy of the electoral result. If this magnifying lens is removed, the "squeaker" aspect of our presidential elections will become more visible and, probably, much more troubling. For example, the problem of error and fraud, no doubt endemic in some degree to all electoral systems, could very well be aggravated under the proposed national system, because every single precinct polling place could come under bitter scrutiny as relevant to a close and disputed national outcome. In contrast, under the Electoral College, ambiguity of outcome sufficient even to warrant challenge is infrequent and is always limited to but a few states. . . .

Not only is it extremely unlikely that the proposed replacement could match this record of unambiguity, but the 40 percent plus plurality provision could very well introduce a different and graver kind of ambiguity into our political system. This would not be uncertainty as to who is the winner, but a profounder uncertainty as to whether the winner is truly the choice of the American people. . . .

The Electoral College strongly encourages the two-party system by almost always narrowing the election to a race between the two major-party candidates. Obviously, when there are only two serious competitors, the winner usually has a majority or large plurality of the total vote cast. But, as we shall shortly see, the new system would encourage minor and maverick candidacies. This multiplication of competitors would likely reduce the winning margin to the bare 40 percent plurality requirement of the new system. If so, we would have traded in a majority—or high plurality—presidency for one in which nearly 60 percent of the people might often have voted against the incumbent. How ironic it would be if a reform demanded in the name of democracy and majority rule resulted in a permanent minority presidency! . . .

[A]ll the dangers critics claim to see in the Electoral College are entirely matters of speculation. Some have never actually occurred, and others have not occurred for nearly a century. . . .

[But t]hree dangers seem seriously to threaten under the proposed reform: weakening the two-party system, weakening party politics generally, and further imperializing the presidency.

Many have warned that the 40 percent plus/runoff system would encourage minor parties and in time undermine the two-party system. The encouragement consists in the runoff provision of the proposed reform, that is, in the possibility that minor parties will get enough votes in the first election to force a runoff. Supporters of the proposed change deny this likelihood. For example, the ABA Report argues that a third party is unlikely to get the 20 percent of the popular vote necessary to force a runoff. Perhaps so, and this has been very reassuring to supporters of the reform. But why does it have to be just "a" third party? Why cannot the runoff be forced by the combined votes of a half dozen or more minor parties that enter the first election? Indeed, they are all there waiting in the wings. The most powerful single constraint on minor-party presidential candidacies has always been the "don't throw your vote away" fear that caused their support to melt as election day approached. Norman Thomas, who knew this better than anyone, was certain that a national popular election of the kind now proposed would have immensely improved the Socialist electoral results. Now this is not to say that the Electoral College alone is what prevents ideological parties like that of the Socialists from winning elections in America. Obviously, other and more powerful factors ultimately determine that. But what the electoral machinery can determine is whether such parties remain electorally irrelevant, minuscule failures, or whether they can achieve sufficient electoral success to fragment the present two-party system. . . .

Moreover, not only ideological parties would be encouraged by the proposed change, but also minor parties and minor candidacies of all sorts. Sectional third parties would not be weakened by the 40 percent plus/runoff arrangement; they would retain their sectional appeal and pick up additional votes all over the country. The threat that dissident wings might bolt from one of the two major parties would instantly become more credible and thereby more disruptive within them; sooner or later the habit of bolting would probably take hold. Would there not also be an inducement to militant wings of ethnic, racial, and religious groups to abandon the major party framework and go it alone? And, as the recent proliferation of primary candidacies suggests, would-be "charismatics" might frequently take their case to the general electorate, given the inducements of the proposed new machinery. . . .

If runoffs become the rule as is likely, [t]here would be two winners in [the first election]; we would have created a valuable new electoral prize—a second place finish in the preliminary election. This would be a boon to the strong minor candidacies; needing now only to seem a "viable" alternative for second place, they could more easily make a plausible case to potential supporters. But, more important, there would be something to win for nearly everyone in the first, or preliminary, election. Minor party votes now shrink away as the election nears and practically disappear on election day. As is well known, this is because minor-party supporters desert their preferred candidates to vote for the "lesser evil" of the major candidates. But the proposed reform would remove the reason to do so. On the contrary, as in multiparty parliamentary systems, the voter could vote with his heart because that would in fact also be the calculating thing to do. There would be plenty of time to vote for the lesser evil in the eventual runoff election. The trial heat would be the time to help the preferred minor party show its strength. Even a modest showing would enable the minor party to participate in the frenetic bargaining inevitably incident to runoff elections. And even a modest showing would establish a claim to the newly available public financing that would simultaneously be an inducement to run and a means to strengthen one's candidacy. . . .

Most Americans agree that the two-party system is a valuable way of channelling democracy because that mode of democratic decision produces valuable qualities of moderation, consensus, and stability. It follows then that the proposed reform threatens a serious injury to the American political system.

Not only might the change weaken the two-party system, but it might well also have an enfeebling effect on party politics generally. The regular party politicians, which is to say, the state and local politicians, would become less important to presidential candidates. This tendency is already evident in the effect the presidential primaries are having; regular party machinery is becoming less important in the nominating process, and the individual apparatus of the candidates more important. The defederalizing of the presidential election seems likely to strengthen this tendency. No longer needing to carry states, the presidential candidates would find the regular politicians, who are most valuable for tipping the balance in a state, of diminishing importance for their free-wheeling search for popular votes. They probably would rely more and more on direct-mail and media experts, and on purely personal coteries, in conducting campaigns that would rely primarily on the mass media. The consequence would seem to be to disengage the presidential campaign from the party machinery and from the states and to isolate the presidency from their moderating effect. If "merchandising" the President has become an increasingly dangerous tendency, nationalizing and plebiscitizing the presidency would seem calculated only to intensify the danger.

This raises, finally, the question of the effect of the proposed reform on the presidency as an institution, that is, on the "imperial presidency." . . . The presidency has always derived great moral authority and political power from the claim that the President is the only representative of all the people. Why increase the force of that claim by magnifying the national and plebiscitary foundations of the presidency? . . .

24

James W. Ceaser

Political Parties and Presidential Ambition (1978)

According to political scientists of the last generation, party competition was an essential feature of any form of popular government. How dismayed they would be, therefore, to learn from contemporary students of American politics that our parties are "decomposing" and that our national electoral process is increasingly taking on the characteristics of nonpartisan competition. While the labels of the two traditional parties continue to exist, the institutions bearing these labels have lost many of their previous functions.

From Ceaser, "Political Parties and Presidential Ambition," *Journal of Politics*, August, 1978. Reprinted by permission of the author and the *Journal of Politics*.

Parties no longer structure the voting behavior of large numbers of citizens. They have ceased to play a major role in constraining presidential decision-making, and presidents now place little reliance on them in their efforts to generate public support for policy initiatives. Perhaps most important of all, party organizations have lost their influence in determining the outcome of presidential nominations. Under the "open" nominating process that has emerged since 1968, the races have for all practical purposes become plebi-scitory contests among the individual contenders. Candidates create large personal campaign organizations and devise their own programs and electoral strategies, very much as if they were establishing national parties of their own. These personalistic features of the nomination contests continue into the final election stage, as the parties become the extensions of the organizations of the victorious nominees.

What are the implications of this decline in the role of traditional parties for the presidential selection process and for the presidency itself? Is it a positive development, as many reformers argue, or does it pose a serious threat to moderate republican government, as many of their opponents contend? Addressing these questions today is of more than academic significance. The recent changes in the presidential selection process have resulted not primarily from forces beyond the control of political actors but from the decisions of practicing politicians in party commissions and state legislatures. . . .

The reform theory of selection on which the current open system is based was introduced to national politics at the 1968 Democratic Convention. In its original formulation, the theory attacked the legitimacy of the influence of the regular party organizations and called for "direct democracy" in the selection of presidential nominees. As the theory evolved within the official reform commissions established by the party in 1968 and 1972, the ideal of "fairness" emerged as a single most important value for the nomination process. By fairness was meant procedural regularity and the replication in the selection of delegates of the expressed candidate preferences of the participants. While the reform commissions did not expressly call for direct democracy in the form of more primaries, the emphasis reformers placed on popular participation and the individual's right to the expression of a candidate preference certainly encouraged the subsequent adoption of presidential primaries in many states.

The reform view of presidential selection should be compared with the very different perspective of the Founders and the originators of permanent party competition. For these statesmen the concern was not so much with the procedural goal of fairness as with the substantive results of how power was sought and exercised. After satisfying themselves of the compatibility of their systems with the basic requirements of popular government, they turned their attention to regulating the behavior of presidential aspirants with a view to preventing dangerous political divisions and leadership styles that might undermine the intended character of the presidency. . . .

For the Founders, a major objective in selection was to prevent the creation of factions that form around "different leaders ambitiously contending for pre-eminence and power." By their electoral institutions the Founders sought to deflect the great force of presidential ambition from its possible manifestations in demagoguery of "image" appeals and to channel it into conduct that would promote the public good. This also was the goal of Martin Van Buren and his followers in the party school of the 1820s and 1830s. They held that the nonpartisan system that emerged in 1824 encouraged the very kind of leadership appeals that the Founders wanted to avoid. Only by instituting party competition between two parties of moderate principle could leadership be circumscribed within safe limits. The answer to personal faction for Van Buren was party, though party of a different sort from that which the Founders had feared. Whatever differences exist between the views of the Founders and Van Buren—and these, as we shall see, are not insignificant—they both accepted the premise that the electoral process should be considered as an institution that controlled candidate behavior.

This premise went unchallenged until the rise of the Populist and Progressive movements at the turn of the century. According to Woodrow Wilson, the most thoughtful spokesman of the Progressive view, the selection system should be designed to elevate a dynamic leader above the political party and make the party serve his will. In Wilson's thought, party is transformed from an institution that constrains leadership to an instrument that enhances it. "Leadership," the central theme of Wilson's proposed revision of the constitutional system, could best take root in an open nominating process in which each contender presented his program directly to the people. The winners would then earn the right to "own" their parties. Wilson accordingly proposed national primaries, making it clear that contenders might appeal beyond traditional partisan followings to form new constituencies. Wilson was satisfied that the problem of dangerous leadership appeals could be avoided in an open selection process: the wisdom of the people along with the self-restraint of the leaders obviated the need for any institutional guidance.

A balance of sorts existed throughout most of this century between institutional elements representing Van Buren's theory of selection and those representing Wilsonian ideas. This system, known sometimes as the "mixed" system because of the presence of both candidate-oriented primaries and organization—dominated selection procedures, was overthrown after 1968. Although there are some differences between the Progressive and the reform views, the reformers have accepted the crucial Progressive premise about the safety of an open nominating system. . . .

The Functions of the Presidential Selection System

To facilitate discussion of the theories of the electoral process noted above, it will be helpful first to identify four major objectives or "functions" of the selection system. By the selection system here we are referring to the nomination and the final election stages, since both are part of the same general process. . . .

First, the selection system should promote the proper character of the presidential office in respect both to its powers and to the style of presidential leadership. This implies that, at least up to a certain point, the office should be thought of as the end and the selection process the means. Many today might take exception to this assumption. Two recent defenders of reform theory, John Saloma and Frederick Sontag, argue that the goal of the selection system should be increased participation, which they see as a means of building citizen virtue. Pre-reform theorists, though no less concerned about citizen virtue, looked elsewhere for its cultivation. They focused instead on more directly related issues such as the effect of the selection system on the presidency, realizing that the way in which power is sought will have a profound influence on how it is subsequently exercised. Many of the important historical debates on the role of parties in our system have centered on this issue. The Founders and John Quincy Adams opposed party competition because they thought it would compromise the president's independence, while Woodrow Wilson sought to transform parties into candidate-centered organizations in order to increase the president's power.

Second, the selection system should ensure an accession to power that is unproblematic and widely regarded as legitimate. . . . Legitimacy refers to whether the people accept the process as being in accord with their understanding of republican principles. . . . On the other hand, since the selection system can be an important "teacher" of the meaning of democracy, there is a danger in its being changed in response to an ephemeral interpretation of republican principles backed by some candidate or faction seeking a temporary advantage. This possibility is greatest in the nominating system which is outside the sphere of direct Constitutional regulation.

Third, the selection system should help promote the choice of an able executive. What transforms this concern from a meaningless expression of hope to a legitimate institutional question is the reasonable assumption, backed by comparative research into selection in various liberal democracies, that different systems affect the type of person apt to compete and succeed. A plebiscitory nomination system would seem to place a greater premium on those qualities that appeal to a mass audience, such as vigor, appearance, and the aura of sanctimony; "closed" systems will value to a greater degree those qualities esteemed by the narrower group empowered to select, for example, "keeping one's word" in the case of American politicians or trustworthiness in the case of British parliamentarians. . . .

Finally, the selection system should prevent the harmful effects of the pursuit of office by highly ambitious contenders. Almost every major politician will at one time or another fix his attention on becoming president and adjust his behavior to improve his chances of being considered. For those who enter the select circle of legitimate contenders, the tendency will be to adopt whatever strategies are legal and acceptable—and even some that are not—if they promise results. It is reasonable to assume, therefore, that the ambition of contenders, if not properly guided, can lead to strategies and appeals that threaten the public good. . . .

The problems that presidential ambition can create may be classified under two broad headings. The first is the disruption of the proper functioning of an office or institution: office-holders, using their positions to further their presidential aspirations, may perform in a way that conflicts with their intended constitutional role. . . .

The second problem, by no means exclusive of the first, is the attempt of candidates to build a popular following by the "arts of popularity"—by empty "image" appeals, by flattery, or by the exploitation of dangerous passions. The general term for such appeals is demagoguery, although one often finds the term restricted today to harsh utterances that evoke anger and fear. It is a mistake, however, to fail to recognize the demagogic character of a "soft" flattery that tells the people they can do no wrong or of seductive appeals that hide behind a veil of liberality, making promises that can never be kept or raising hopes that can never be satisfied. . . .

Institutional regulation of behavior consists in establishing certain constraints and incentives—not criminal penalities—that promote desired habits and actions and discourage unwanted behavior. The selection system, conceived in this sense, is the institution that structures the conduct of presidential aspirants and their supporters. By marking out a certain path to the presidency, it influences the behavior of the nation's leading politicians and, by their example, the style of politics in the regime as a whole. Regulation of presidential ambition is likely to work most effectively where it relies on the candidates' own strongest impulse: if matters can be arranged such that undesirable behavior will detract from the chance of success, candidates will turn "voluntarily" to other strategies. Properly channeled, ambition can be used to curb its own excesses.

The Founders

The Founders' two main objectives for presidential selection were to help secure the executive's independence from Congress and to prevent the kind of campaign that would undermine the constitutional character of the office. The first objective, which has been identified by nearly every scholar of the Founders' thought, was to be accomplished by giving the president an electoral base outside of the legislature. The second objective, which has been almost entirely overlooked in the literature on the founding, can only be understood after treating the more general question of constitutional authority and the threat posed to it by the claim to popular leadership.

One of the distinguishing features of constitutional government for the Founders was rule based on institutional authority. Office-holders, in their view, were to rest their claim to govern on the legally defined rights and prerogatives of their offices. This kind of authority was threatened by claims to rule on informal grounds, such as personal heroic standing or assertions of embodying the will of the people. The latter claim was particularly dangerous to constitutional government in a popular regime. The people were already recognized as the source of ultimate authority for the system as a whole, and it would involve but one small step for an enterprising leader to activate the principle of popular sovereignty and make it the immediate basis of political rule. . . .

The Founders' analysis of the problem of popular authority appears in *The Federalist* in the context of their discussion of the House. Here Publius warns against the danger that the House, urged on by some of its "leaders," might seek to "draw all power into its impetuous vortex." But it is crucial to observe that it is not the House itself that the Founders fear, but the claim to informal popular authority. Any institution asserting power on the basis of "its supposed influence over the people" is properly suspect on the Founders' grounds. . . .

The general name we have given to this kind of noninstitutional rule is "popular leadership." "Popular" refers to the source of the authority and "leadership" to its informal character. . . . The establishment of the Constitution, [the Founders] doubtless thought, obviated the need for leaders, as authority would henceforth rest on an institutional foundation. This foundation was also understood to protect the possibility for the exercise of statesmanship by providing the president with a margin of discretion free from the immediate constraints of public opinion. . . .

Besides serving as a claim to authority, popular leadership is a way of soliciting power. The Founders refer to it in this context as "the popular arts." Where the popular arts are employed in seeking office, the danger increases that informal authority will be claimed as the basis for governing. The popular arts accustom the people to the style of popular leadership and train aspirants to generate support and power by this means. To protect the constitutional character of the presidency, the Founders accordingly thought it essential to discourage the use of the popular arts in the selection process.

The Founders identified two basic forms of the popular arts. The first was issue arousal. From their experience with elections for state legislatures after the Revolutionary War, the Founders became deeply concerned about demagogic issue appeals directed against property and merit . . . The other form of the popular arts was the use of appeals that played upon certain passions relating to the personal qualities of the leader, what we might call today "image" appeals. Of course the Founders wanted the voters to focus on character qualifications, but they drew a distinction between character assessments based on a calm consideration of the candidates' merits and those influenced by strong emotions or flattery. . . .

The general principle the Founders followed in attempting to discourage the use of the popular arts was to make the election turn on personal reputation, not issue appeals. Personal reputation, the Founders believed, would serve as a rough approximation for merit: those who became well-known at the national level would most likely have had to earn a reputation by distinguished service to the state. The institutional means for favoring reputation over issue appeals was sought in the first instance by creating large electoral districts. . . . The Founders reasoned that since all elections pose the problem of name recognition for the candidates, persons with established reputations begin with a decided advantage. The larger the size of the district, the more difficult it becomes for one using issue arousal to overcome this advantage—an assessment that might need to be reversed today in light of modern communications and of the extended campaign which gives a greater chance to the "outsider." . . . Applied to the case of the largest possible district, a nationwide constituency, there was all the more reason to expect a safe result. . . .

The proposal for direct election failed to gain the support of most delegates at the Convention. The opposition came from a number of quarters, including some who objected on the "practical" grounds that there would not normally be persons with a sufficient national reputation to command the votes of the people in the face of competition from strong regional candidates. This opposition obliged the direct election advocates to search for another plan, and they readily shifted their support to the proposal of an election by specially chosen electors. Along with providing the same guarantee of presidential independence, this plan increased the likelihood of selecting a continental figure, as the electors would be more knowledgeable about national affairs and could practically be given two votes for the presidential contest. The system also had the advantage of allowing for a certain degree of indirectness in the choice of the president. It therefore provided further insurance that the election would turn on reputation rather than the use of the popular arts. The electors, it was thought, would be less likely than the people to be swayed by popular appeals and might even resent them, even as—to cite an analogy that is only partly apt—convention delegates who formerly had discretion resented attempts by candidates to go over their heads to the people. By making the use of the popular arts unnecessary and perhaps counterproductive, the Founders sought to close the door to direct popular appeals and induce the ablest candidates to "campaign" by establishing a record of distinguished public service that might earn them a reputation for virtue.

From a cursory reading of the one paper in *The Federalist* that is devoted to presidential selection (#68), one might receive the impression that the Founders viewed the pursuit of the presidency as a gentlemanly affair conducted among reluctant participants. Yet nothing could be further from the truth. There was a sense, of course, in which they expected that the immediate campaign would *appear* in this light, just as it was formerly the practice for aspirants to wait for their party to confer the nomination upon them. But this kind of campaign would conceal, even as it controlled, the powerful ambitions of the candidates. No more "realistic" analysis of political motivation exists in American thought than that which Hamilton provides in *The Federalist*. Hamilton begins with politicians as we find them: high-spirited, ambitious, and in some cases committed to achieving a noble fame. Hamilton's aim is . . . to make politicians serve popular government. Ambition, the dominant force that drives most major politicians, is a neutral quality that leads them to seek out the path to success. Properly channeled it can divert politicians from destructive behavior and lead them to act for the public good, even to take risks and incur momentary displeasure for the sake of long-term glory. Hamilton's understanding of virtue admits and allows for the desire for reward: it can best be described as conduct on behalf of the public, even if that conduct is undertaken for self-interested reasons. The office of the presidency was designed by the Founders to attract persons of the highest ambition or virtue, and the selection system was meant to point their ambition in the proper direction.

MARTIN VAN BUREN

Martin Van Buren began his national political career as a senator from New York in 1821, during the Era of Good Feelings. Competition between parties had ceased at the national level, and the dominant opinion in Washington was hostile to any manifestations of partisanship. . . . Van Buren quickly became the leading opponent of this view, calling immediately on his arrival at the capitol for a "resuscitation of the old Democratic Party" and later, after the election of 1824, for a renewal of two-party competition. . . .

Van Buren developed his case for parties in response to an impending crisis in the presidential selection process. His objectives were to ensure the legitimacy of the choice of the president by keeping the election from the House of Representatives and to prevent a dangerous politics of personal factionalism caused by nonpartisan competition. . . .

The advocates of a strong, independent executive at the Constitutional Convention fought the idea of selection by Congress on the grounds that it would make the president, in Morris's words, "the tool of a faction of some leading demagogue in the Legislature." They won their main point with the adoption of the system of electors, but an auxiliary election by the House, voting by states, was also included for the purpose of breaking a tie or making the choice where no candidate received the required minimum of electoral votes.

The likelihood of an election by the House increased with the adoption of the Twelfth Amendment in 1804. Designed to eliminate intrigue between the electors of the defeated party and the vice-presidential candidate of the victorious party, the amendment also made it less likely that a final decision could be made at the electoral stage by reducing the number of presidential votes of each elector from two to one while maintaining the same requirement for election. As long as the Republican Party continued to coalesce behind one candidate, the tendency of the amendment was obscured. But with the collapse of the Republican caucus in 1824, it became evident that under nonpartisan competition a House election would be the normal result. The outcome of the election of 1824 demonstrated that at the same time that it confirmed some of the worst fears about the House system—its tendency to promote confusion and intrigue and its inability to gain full public confidence.

Van Buren and his followers argued that party competition could ensure that the election was determined at the electoral stage by providing the candidates with broad national followings. If there were no continental figures in the nation, the reputations of the parties would take their place; if there were too many continental figures, the parties would limit the field. Party competition thus offered an institutional solution to a problem that the Founders had relied on chance to resolve. . . .

Van Buren's second defense of party competition was that it was the best device under existing circumstances for controlling presidential ambition. In proposing party competition to solve a problem that the Founders had wanted to solve by nonpartisanship, Van Buren was not necessarily challenging the Founders' plan, for nonpartisan competition in the 1820s bore little resemblance to what the Founders had envisioned. Direct popular appeals by the candidates had become an accepted element of the campaign, a change that resulted from the precedent of the election of 1800 and from the transformation of the elector from the discretionary trustee to a bound agent. Given this new circumstance, a different solution to the problem of controlling the popular arts was required. If popular leadership was now legitimate, the challenge was somehow to distinguish its healthy from its unhealthy expressions and to devise some institutional means to admit the former and exclude the latter.

Nonpartisan competition, according to Van Buren, was no longer an answer to this problem. On the contrary, it was the very cause of personal factionalism and dangerous leadership appeals. It allowed a large number of candidates to enter the contest without doing anything to channel the direction of their ambition. . . .

According to Van Buren . . . , party competition would prevent candidates from devising their own appeals and compel them to adhere to the safer principles on which they planned to establish the major parties. The character of leadership appeals would be controlled by institutions rather than left subject to accident and personal candidate strategies. Nominations would be made by party leaders knowledgeable about national politics and in a position to deliberate about which candidate could best maintain a delicately balanced party coalition. Issue appeals in the name of one or another of the parties would be admitted, but appeals independent of parties would be discouraged. The system would remain formally open to challenges by new parties, as two-party competition was a doctrine founded on opinion, not law. But the bias of the electoral process was against openness in the modern sense of eliminating all institutional controls designed to discourage certain kinds of appeals. It was the task of those founding the new parties to establish their credibility and enlist public support behind them on a long-term basis. Party in this respect would be made "prior" to political leadership. Leadership would not formulate new principles or create new electoral alignments but articulate the established principles and maintain existing coalitions. If this implied a loss in the dynamic character of leadership, it also promised a greater degree of safety and moderation.

Having made the theoretical case for renewed party competition, Van Buren turned to his partisan task of creating the Democratic party. . . .

While Van Buren wanted to retain the same basic electoral alignment that existed under the first party division, he sought to establish a different kind of partisanship. The contest over first principles of the regime would be replaced by a more moderate division over the scope of federal power. Parties dividing on this question could exist together without each feeling the need to destroy a seditious rival. To go along with this more restrained partisanship, Van Buren proposed a new ethic of tolerance. The original partisans, Jefferson once wrote, "cross the streets and turn their heads the other way, lest they should be obliged to touch their hats." Van Buren offered a different model. He proclaimed his pride in not being "rancorous in my party prejudices" and in maintaining friendly personal relations with many political opponents. . . .

Van Buren acknowledged that the principles of the parties would be very general, in part so that each party could accommodate a broad coalition of interests. Moreover, Van Buren recognized the need for patronage, no doubt in the belief that with a partisan division based on secondary issues, it was necessary, in order to sustain party organizations, to supplement the motivation of purpose with that of interest. . . . Although the modern "amateur" conception of party finds the slightest touch of interest unacceptable, it remains an unanswered question whether an ideal equilibrium point can be found and maintained at which the division over principle is sufficiently serious to sustain partisan organizations yet not so great as to threaten the underlying consensus in the regime.

While there is much in Van Buren's plan for party competition that is consistent with the views of the Founders, it nonetheless served to modify the regime in some very important ways. First, party competition recognized and institutionalized a more active role for the voice of the majority in determining national policy. Elections were no longer understood merely as a way of elevating a worthy individual; they were also contests between competing groups in which the victorious party could claim authority for carrying out its program.

Second, party competition implied a different conception of executive leadership. The Founders had wanted illustrious "continental figures" whose freedom from control by any electoral group would enable them to stand above the conflict of factions. By recognizing the need for parties of a broad coalitional character under an umbrella of general principle, Van Buren was required to accept a less elevated kind of leadership. His model was what we might call the "politician," one skilled at brokering among various groups. Executive leadership would have to be partisan in character, although the broad principles on which the parties stood would still leave room for considerable discretion. Many have seen a connection between Van Buren's concept of parties and the so-called "Madisonian system" of the Founders, for in both one finds encouragement for the formation of coalitional majorities. But it is also important to observe the differences. Madison intended the system of competing factions and coalitions to take place in the House and to be balanced by an executive standing above factions. Van Buren, on the other hand, extended the influence of the "Madisonian system" to the executive by introducing a coalitional concept of leadership into the choice of a president.

Finally, in emphasizing the restraint of ambition, Van Buren, in contrast to the Founders, may not have given sufficient scope to it. One finds a continual concern in Van Buren's thought with preventing the potential abuse of power, but little appreciation of its positive uses. It was the absence of a doctrine of the positive executive power, much more than the self-interested character of the parties, that troubled Woodrow Wilson.

WOODROW WILSON

The Progressives inaugurated the modern idea of presidential selection—a plebiscitory nomination race in which the candidates build their own constituencies within the electorate and in which the victorious candidate "captures" his party label. Along with this idea came a rejection of the view that the electoral process should control presidential ambition. The new purpose of the selection process was to build a base of popular support for the victorious candidate and help establish the concept of leadership as the central feature of the regime. . . .

A number of Progressive spokesmen articulated a new conception of how to attain the public good that rejected entirely the pluralist concept of adding together various interests to make a coalitional majority. The public good, in the view of these Progressives, could only be known directly and as a whole. The connection between this conception of politics and the new institutional roles for the presidency and presidential selection is most clearly formulated in the thought of Woodrow Wilson.

Wilson began with nothing less than a full-scale attack on the old basis of constitutional government. The public good, in his view, could not be realized through the operation of formal institutions working within the confines of legally delegated and separated powers. It had to be forged in a "life" relationship between a leader and the people. . . .

The most striking aspect of this concept of leadership is its informal or noninstitutional character. Wilson called for the rule of those who would lead "not by reason of legal authority, but by reason of their contact and amenability to public opinion." . . .

[W]hile Wilson sought to give great scope to executive power—more, in many respects, than Hamilton might have countenanced—he did so by draining the office of its formal constitutional authority and by transforming the premise of statesmanship from one that was understood to require a substantial degree of freedom from public opinion to one that operated entirely on the plane of public opinion. . . .

Although Wilson is known today as the father of the party government school in America, it is necessary to understand that he conceived of party in an entirely different sense than Van Buren. A party is a body of people that forms around and serves a particular leader. . . .

Wilson makes parties appear and be strong when they can assist the leader but transforms them into empty shells where they might restrict the leader's freedom. . . .

Wilson's objective, at least while a scholar, was not to delineate the principles of a new partisan division—indeed he was always vague about what programs the parties should adopt—but to alter the traditional relationship between party and leader in order to institutionalize dynamic leadership.

Every regime, it is clear, needs to be "renewed" at moments of crisis by extraordinary acts of political leadership. Given this fact, it might be said that the constraints that the Founders and Van Buren imposed on leadership were too severe. Yet one must bear in mind that they were speaking at the level of analysis of institutional structures, and institutions operating "as usual" may not be able to meet every situation or challenge. Seen from this perspective, they might not have wanted to prevent absolutely a recourse to popular leadership, but only to erect a bias against it, such that it would have to "prove" itself in the face of institutional deterrents. A bias of this kind would normally prevent the dangers of popular leadership yet still not prevent change and renewal when needed. Wilson took the opposite view and argued that a bias in favor of change in the electoral process was desirable and that under such a system leaders of high quality would continually emerge. . . .

A fundamental question is whether in opening the selection system to continual change Wilson did not also open it to dangerous or demeaning leadership appeals. . . .

MODERN REFORM

The Progressives' call for a plebiscitory selection system met with only partial success. The movement for universal state primaries got off to a promising start between 1911 and 1916, but then stalled with the decline of the Progressive movement after the First World War. In some states primary laws were repealed, while in others the party organizations were able to reassert control over the primary process. What resulted was a "mixed" system that contained elements deriving from the conflicting theories of Martin Van Buren and the Progressives. . . . Its two constituent elements continued to be reflected in two alternative nomination campaigns—the inside strategy of negotiation with party leaders and the outside strategy of direct appeals to the people. The representation of the party organization served to thwart a demagogue, while the primaries enabled a popular candidate to challenge the insularity of the power-brokers. . . .

Even before the recent reform movement, a slight shift had begun to occur in the direction of a greater reliance on the outside strategy. But it was the reforms, and in particular the increase in primaries which they prompted, that decisively established the plebiscitory character of the current system. . . .

[O]ne might well ask whether the reformers did not concede too much to the populist sentiments of the moment. . . . The reliance on "closed" nominating procedures by parties in other democratic nations seems to belie the claim that direct democracy in candidate selection is a requisite of republican legitimacy. As long as the *electoral* system remains open, meaning that the right of new parties to challenge is not denied or impaired, it would seem that the legitimacy of the system could be defended. . . .

If the plebiscitory system is not required to assure the legitimacy of the selection process, neither, it—seems, can it be justified in terms of its effects on the other three functions of presidential selection. . . . [T]here is no basis in theory and surely none in experience for concluding that a plebiscitory system guarantees candidates of greater competence or superior virtue.

As regards the prevention of the harmful effects of the campaign, a number of serious problems have already become evident. By encouraging more candidates and an earlier start of the campaign, the new system introduces considerations of electoral politics into the process of governing at a much earlier date. Campaigns inevitably tend to drain normal legal authority and force an incumbent who is re-eligible to become absorbed, in Tocqueville's words, "in the task of defending himself [rather than] ruling in the interest of the state." Moreover, the "openness" of the campaign to many contestants excites the ambitions of a large number of politicians and influences their conduct in the performance of their official duties. Observers of the Congress have already noted the effect of the new system in contributing to a decline of the Senate as a serious deliberative body. In accord with the need under the current system to build popular constituencies, Senators having presidential aspirations have been more apt to emphasize "media coverage over legislative craftmanship." . . .

The checks on presidential power in the American system have traditionally been formal as well as informal, deriving from the Constitutional system of separated powers and from the power-brokers within the parties whose support was required by candidates and incumbent presidents seeking re-election. Under the present system, however, the successful candidate "owns" his party and need not answer to specific persons who can hold him accountable. This ownership, it must be added, has come at a high price, for the decline of parties has taken away from the executive a valuable resource that could buy support from the public and from members of Congress. The president now stands directly before the bar of public opinion, and it therefore should not be surprising if presidents become more assertive in their claims to authority and more "popular" or demagogic in their methods of appeal, if only to compensate for their loss of partisan support. In light of these difficulties, it may be asked whether we should not reconsider the wisdom of the recent reforms, even if this implies resisting "the inexorable movement . . . toward direct democracy."

25

Buckley v. Valeo (1976)

Per Curiam.*

These appeals present constitutional challenges to the key provisions of the Federal Election Campaign Act of 1971, as amended in 1974. . . . The Act, summarized in broad terms, contains the following provisions: (a) individual political contributions are limited to $1,000 to any single candidate per election, with an overall annual limitation of $25,000 by any contributor; independent expenditures by individuals and groups "relative to a clearly identified candidate" are limited to $1,000 a year; campaign spending by candidates for various federal offices and spending for national conventions by political parties are subject to prescribed limits; (b) contributions and expenditures above certain threshold levels must be reported and publicly disclosed; (c) a system for public funding of Presidential campaign activities is established by Subtitle H of the Internal Revenue Code. . . .

The Act's contribution and expenditure limitations operate in an area of the most fundamental First Amendment activities. Discussion of public issues and debate on the qualifications of candidates are integral to the operation of the system of government established by our Constitution. . . . In a republic where the people are sovereign, the ability of the citizenry to make informed choices among candidates for office is essential. . . .

The interests served by the Act include restricting the voices of people and interest groups who have money to spend and reducing the overall scope of federal election campaigns. Although the Act does not focus on the ideas expressed by persons or groups subjected to its regulations, it is aimed in part

From *Buckley v. Valeo*, 424 U.S. 1 (1976).

---

*Only Justices Brennan, Stewart, and Powell joined all portions of the per curiam opinion. Included among the plaintiffs were a candidate for the Presidency of the United States, a United States Senator who is a candidate for reelection, a potential contributor, the Committee for a Constitutional Presidency—McCarthy '76, the Conservative Party of the State of New York, the Mississippi Republican Party, the Libertarian Party, the New York Civil Liberties Union, Inc., the American Conservative Union, the Conservative Victory Fund, and Human Events, Inc.

at equalizing the relative ability of all voters to affect electoral outcomes by placing a ceiling on expenditures for political expression by citizens and groups. . . .

A restriction on the amount of money a person or group can spend on political communication during a campaign necessarily reduces the quantity of expression by restricting the number of issues discussed, the depth of their exploration, and the size of the audience reached. This is because virtually every means of communicating ideas in today's mass society requires the expenditure of money. . . .

By contrast with a limitation upon expenditures for political expression, a limitation upon the amount that any one person or group may contribute to a candidate or political committee entails only a marginal restriction upon the contributor's ability to engage in free communication. A contribution serves as a general expression of support for the candidate and his views, but does not communicate the underlying basis for the support. The quantity of communication by the contributor does not increase perceptibly with the size of his contribution, since the expression rests solely on the undifferentiated, symbolic act of contributing. . . . While contributions may result in political expression if spent by a candidate or an association to present views to the voters, the transformation of contributions into political debate involves speech by someone other than the contributor.

Given the important role of contributions in financing political campaigns, contribution restrictions could have a severe impact on political dialogue if the limitations prevented candidates and political committees from amassing the resources necessary for effective advocacy. There is no indication, however, that the contribution limitations imposed by the Act would have any dramatic adverse effect on the funding of campaigns and political associations. The overall effect of the Act's contribution ceilings is merely to require candidates and political committees to raise funds from a greater number of persons and to compel people who would otherwise contribute amounts greater than the statutory limits to expend such funds on direct political expression, rather than to reduce the total amount of money potentially available to promote political expression.

The Act's contribution and expenditure limitations also impinge on protected associational freedoms. . . . [T]he Act's contribution limitations permit associations . . . to aggregate large sums of money to promote effective advocacy. By contrast, the Act's $1,000 limitation on independent expenditures "relative to a clearly identified candidate" precludes most associations from effectively amplifying the voice of their adherents, the original basis for the recognition of First Amendment protection of the freedom of association. . . .

In sum, although the Act's contribution and expenditure limitations both implicate fundamental First Amendment interests, its expediture ceilings impose significantly more severe restrictions on protected freedoms of political expression and association than do its limitations on financial contributions. . . .

It is unnecessary to look beyond the Act's primary purpose—to limit the actuality and appearance of corruption resulting from large individual financial contributions—in order to find a constitutionally sufficient justification for the $1,000 contribution limitation. . . . To the extent that large contributions are given to secure political quid pro quos from current and potential officeholders, the integrity of our system of representative democracy is undermined. . . .

Of almost equal concern as the danger of actual quid pro quo arrangements is the impact of the appearance of corruption stemming from public awareness of the opportunities for abuse inherent in a regime of large individual financial contributions. . . . Congress could legitimately conclude that the avoidance of the appearance of improper influence "is also critical [if] confidence in the system of representative Government is not to be eroded to a disastrous extent." . . .

[However, w]e find that the governmental interest in preventing corruption and the appearance of corruption is inadequate to justify 608(e) (1)'s ceiling on independent expenditures.

The parties defending § 608(e) (1) contend that it is necessary to prevent would-be contributors from avoiding the contribution limitations by the simple expedient of paying directly for media advertisements or for other portions of the candidate's campaign activities. . . . Yet such controlled or coordinated expenditures are treated as contributions rather than expenditures under the Act. . . . Unlike contributions, such independent expenditures may well provide little assistance to the candidate's campaign and indeed may prove counterproductive. The absence of prearrangement and coordination of an expenditure with the candidate or his agent not only undermines the value of the expenditure to the candidate, but also alleviates the danger that expenditures will be given as a quid pro quo for improper commitments from the candidate. . . .

It is argued, however, that the ancillary governmental interest in equalizing the relative ability of individuals and groups to influence the outcome of elections serves to justify [this limitation]. But the concept that government may restrict the speech of some elements of our society in order to enhance the relative voice of others is wholly foreign to the First Amendment, which was designed "to secure 'the widest possible dissemination of information from diverse and antagonistic sources,' " and " 'to assure unfettered interchange of ideas for the bringing about of political and social changes desired by the people.' " *New York Times v. Sullivan.* The First Amendment's protection against governmental abridgment of free expression cannot properly be made to depend on a person's financial ability to engage in public discussion. . . .

The Act also sets limits on expenditures by a candidate "from his personal funds, or the personal funds of his immediate family, in connection with his campaigns during any calander year." . . .

[These ceilings also impose] a substantial restraint on the ability of persons to engage in protected First Amendment expression. The candidate, no less than any other person, has a First Amendment right to engage in the discussion of public issues and vigorously and tirelessly to advocate his own election and the election of other candidates. . . .

The primary governmental interest served by the Act—the prevention of actual and apparent corruption of the political process—does not support the limitation on the candidate's expenditure of his own personal funds. . . . [T]he use of personal funds reduces the candidate's dependence on outside contributions and thereby counteracts the coercive pressures and attendant risks of abuse to which the Act's contribution limitations are directed.

The ancillary interest in equalizing the relative financial resources of candidates competing for elective office, therefore, provides the sole relevant rationale for Section 608(a)'s expenditure ceiling. . . . [T]he First Amendment simply cannot tolerate § 608(a)'s restriction upon the freedom of a candidate to speak without legislative limit on behalf of his own candidacy. . . .

Section 608(c) of the Act places limitations on overall campaign expenditures by candidates seeking nomination for election and election to federal office. . . .

No governmental interest that has been suggested is sufficient to justify the restriction on the quantity of political expression imposed by § 608(c)'s campaign expenditure limitations. . . . The interest in alleviating the corrupting influence of large contributions is served by the Act's contribution limitations and disclosure provisions rather than by § 608(c)'s campaign expenditure ceilings.

The interest in equalizing the financial resources of candidates competing for federal office is no more convincing a justification for restricting the scope of federal election campaigns. Given the limitation on the size of outside contributions, the financial resources available to a candidate's campaign, like the number of volunteers recruited, will normally vary with the size and intensity of the candidate's support. There is nothing invidious, improper, or unhealthy in permitting such funds to be spent to carry the candidate's message to the electorate. . . .

In sum, the [contribution limits] are constitutionally valid. These limitations along with the disclosure provisions, constitute the Act's primary weapons against the reality or appearance of improper influence stemming from the dependence of candidates on large campaign contributions. The contribution ceilings thus serve the basic governmental interest in safeguarding the integrity of the electoral process without directly impinging upon the rights of individual citizens and candidates to engage in political debate and discussion. By contrast, the First Amendment requires the invalidation of the Act's independent expenditure ceiling, its limitation on a candidate's expenditures from his own personal funds, and its ceilings on overall campaign expenditures. These provisions place substantial and direct restrictions on the ability of candidates, citizens, and associations to engage in protected political expression, restrictions that the First Amendment cannot tolerate. . . .

[The disclosure requirements of the Act] are attacked as overbroad—both in their application to minor-party and independent candidates and in their extension to contributions as small as $10 or $100. . . .

The governmental interests sought to be vindicated by the disclosure requirements . . . fall into three categories. First, disclosure provides the electorate with information "as to where political campaign money comes from and how it is spent by the candidate" in order to aid the voters in evaluating those who seek Federal office. . . .

Second, disclosure requirements deter actual corruption and avoid the appearance of corruption by exposing large contributions and expenditures to the light of publicity. . . . A public armed with information about a candidate's most generous supporters is better able to detect any postelection special favors that may be given in return. . . .

Third, and not least significant, record-keeping, reporting and disclosure requirements are an essential means of gathering the data necessary to detect violations of the contribution limitations described above.

The disclosure requirements, as a general matter, directly serve substantial governmental interests. In determining whether these interests are sufficient to justify the requirements we must look to the extent of the burden that they place on individual rights.

It is undoubtedly true that public disclosure of contributions to candidates and political parties will deter some individuals who otherwise might contribute. In some instances, disclosure may even expose contributors to harassment or retaliation. . . .

[A]ppellants primarily rely on "the clearly articulated fears of individuals, well experienced in the political process." At best they offer the testimony of several minor-party officials that one or two persons refused to make contributions because of the possibility of disclosure. On this record, the substantial public interest in disclosure identified by the legislative history of this Act outweighs the harm generally alleged. . . .

[The Court next considers public financing of Presidential campaigns.] A series of statutes for the public financing of Presidential election campaigns produced [this] scheme. . . .

A major party is defined as a party whose candidate for President in the most recent election received 25% or more of the popular vote. A minor party is defined as a party whose candidate received at least 5% but less than 25% of the vote at the most recent election. . . . Major parties are entitled to $2,000,000 to defray their national committee Presidential nominating convention expenses [and] must limit total expenditures to that amount. . . . A minor party receives a portion of the major-party entitlement determined by the ratio of the votes received by the party's candidate in the last election to the average of the votes received by the major-parties' candidates. . . . No financing is provided for [the conventions of] new parties. . . .

For expenses in the general election campaign, § 9004(a)(1) entitles each major-party candidate to $20,000,000. To be eligible for funds the candidate must pledge not to incur expenses in excess of the entitlement under § 9004(a)(1) and not to accept private contributions except to the extent that the fund is insufficient to provide the full entitlement. Minor-party candidates are also entitled to funding, again based on the ratio of the vote received by the party's candidate in the preceding election to the average of the major-party candidates. Minor-party candidates must certify that they will not incur campaign expenses in excess of the major-party entitlement and that they will accept private contributions only to the extent needed to make up the difference between that amount and the public funding grant. New-party candidates receive no money prior to the general election, but any candidate receiving 5% or more of the popular vote in the election is entitled to post-election payments according to the formula applicable to minor-party candidates. . . .

Chapter 96 establishes a third account in the Fund, the Presidential Primary Matching Payment Account. . . . The threshold eligibility requirement is that the candidate raise at least $5,000 in each of 20 States, counting only the first $250 from each person contributing to the candidate. In addition, the candidate must agree to abide by the spending limits in § 9035. Funding is provided according to a matching formula: each qualified candidate is entitled to a sum equal to the total private contributions received, disregarding contributions from any person to the extent that total contributions to the candidate by that person exceed $250. . . .

Appellants argue that as constructed public financing invidiously discriminates. . . .

In several situations concerning the electoral process, the principle has been developed that restrictions on access to the electoral process must survive exacting scrutiny. The restriction can be sustained only if it furthers a "vital" governmental interest, that is "achieved by a means that does not unfairly or unnecessarily burden either a minority party's or an individual candidate's equally important interest in the continued availability of political opportunity." . . . [T]he inability, if any, of minority-party candidates to wage effective campaigns will derive not from lack of public funding but from their inability to raise private contributions. . . . Congress enacted Subtitle H in furtherance of sufficiently important governmental interests and has not unfairly or unnecessarily burdened the political opportunity of any party or candidate.

It cannot be gainsaid that public financing as a means of eliminating the improper influence of large private contributions furthers a significant governmental interest. . . . Congress' interest in not funding hopeless candidacies with large sums of public money necessarily justifies the withholding of public assistance from candidates without significant public support. . . .

Mr. Chief Justice Burger, concurring in part and dissenting in part.

. . . Disclosure is, in principle, the salutary and constitutional remedy for most of the ills Congress was seeking to alleviate. I therefore agree fully with the broad proposition that public disclosure of contributions by individuals and by entities—particularly corporations and labor unions—is an effective means of revealing the type of political support that is sometimes coupled with expectations of special favors or rewards. . . .

Disclosure is, however, subject to First Amendment limitations which are to be defined by looking to the relevant public interests. The legitimate public interest is the elimination of the appearance and reality of corrupting influences. . . .

The Court's theory, however, goes beyond permissible limits. Under the Court's view, disclosure serves broad informational purposes, enabling the public to be fully informed on matters of acute public interest. Forced disclosure of one aspect of a citizen's political activity, under this analysis, serves the public right-to-know. This open-ended approach is the only plausible justification for the otherwise irrationally low ceilings of $10 and $100 for anonymous contributions. The burdens of these low ceilings seem to me obvious, and the Court does not try to question this. With commendable candor, the Court acknowledges:

> "It is undoubtedly true that public disclosure of contributions to candidates and political parties will deter some individuals who otherwise might contribute."

Examples come readily to mind. Rank-and-file union members or rising junior executives may now think twice before making even modest contributions to a candidate who is disfavored by the union or management hierarchy. Similarly, potential contributors may well decline to take the obvious risks entailed in making a reportable contribution to the opponent of a well-entrenched incumbent. . . .

The public right-to-know ought not be absolute when its exercise reveals private political convictions. Secrecy, like privacy, is not *per se* criminal. On the contrary, secrecy and privacy as to political preferences and convictions are fundamental in a free society. . . .

Finally, no legitimate public interest has been shown in forcing the disclosure of modest contributions that are the prime support of new, unpopular or unfashionable political causes. There is no realistic possibility that such modest donations will have a corrupting influence especially on parties that enjoy only "minor" status. Major parties would not notice them; minor parties need them. . . .

I would therefore hold unconstitutional the provisions requiring reporting of contributions of $10 or more and to make a public record of the name, address, and occupation of a contributor of $100 or more.

I agree fully with that part of the Court's opinion that holds unconstitutional the limitations the Act puts on campaign expenditures which "place substantial and direct restrictions on the ability of candidates, citizens, and associations to engage in protected political expression, restrictions that the First Amendment cannot tolerate." Yet when it approves similarly stringent limitations on contributions, the Court ignores the reasons it finds so persuasive in the context of expenditures. For me contributions and expenditures are two sides of the same First Amendment coin. . . .

Limiting contributions, as a practical matter, will limit expenditures and will put an effective ceiling on the amount of political activity and debate that the Government will permit to take place. . . .

I dissent from Part III sustaining the constitutionality of the public financing provisions of the Act.

Since the turn of this century when the idea of Government subsidies for political campaigns first was broached, there has been no lack of realization that the use of funds from the public treasury to subsidize political activity of private individuals would produce substantial and profound questions about the nature of our democratic society. . . .

The Court chooses to treat this novel public financing of political activity as simply another congressional appropriation whose validity is "necessary and proper" to Congress' power to regulate and reform elections and primaries. . . .

Senator Howard Baker remarked during the debate on this legislation:

> "I think there is something politically incestuous about the Government financing and, I believe, inevitably then regulating, the day to day procedures by which the Government is selected. I think it is extraordinarily important that the Government not control the machinery by which the public expresses the range of its desires, demands, and dissent."

[I]n my view, the inappropriateness of subsidizing, from general revenues, the actual political dialog of the people—the process which begets the Government itself—is as basic to our national tradition as the separation of church and state . . . or the separation of civilian and military authority, neither of which is explicit in the Constitution but which have developed through case by case adjudication of express provisions of the Constitution.

Recent history shows dangerous examples of systems with a close, "incestuous" relationship between "government" and "politics." . . . [T]he Court points to no basis for predicting that the historical pattern of "varying measures of control and surveillance," which usually accompany grants from

Government will not also follow in this case. . . . Up to now, this Court has scrupulously refrained, absent claims of invidious discrimination, from entering the arena of intra-party disputes concerning the seating of convention delegates. . . . But once the Government finances these national conventions by the expenditure of millions of dollars from the public treasury, we may be providing a springboard for later attempts to impose a whole range of requirements on delegate selection and convention activities. . . .

[T]he scheme approved by the Court today invidiously discriminates against minor parties. . . . [T]he present system could preclude or severely hamper access to funds before a given election by a group or an individual who might, at the time of the election, reflect the views of a major segment or even a majority of the electorate. . . .

I would also find unconstitutional the system of "matching grants" which makes a candidate's ability to amass private funds the sole criterion for eligibility for public funds. Such an arrangement can put at serious disadvantage a candidate with a potentially large, widely diffused—but poor—constituency. The ability of a candidate's supporters to help pay for his campaign cannot be equated with their willingness to cast a ballot for him.

I cannot join in the attempt to determine which parts of the Act can survive review here. The statute as it now stands is unworkable and inequitable.

I agree with the Court's holding that the Act's restrictions on expenditures made "relative to a clearly identified candidate," independent of any candidate or his committee, are unconstitutional. Paradoxically the Court upholds the limitations on individual contributions, which embrace precisely the same sort of expenditures "relative to a clearly identified candidate" if those expenditures are "authorized or requested" by the "candidate or his agents." The Act as cut back by the Court thus places intolerable pressure on the distinction between "authorized" and "unauthorized" expenditures on behalf of a candidate. . . .

Moreover, the Act—or so much as the Court leaves standing—creates significant inequities. A candidate with substantial personal resources is now given by the Court a clear advantage over his less affluent opponents, who are constrained by law in fundraising, because the Court holds that the "First Amendment cannot tolerate" any restrictions on spending. Minority parties, whose situation is difficult enough under an Act that excludes them from public funding, are prevented from accepting large single-donor contributions. At the same time the Court sustains the provision aimed at broadening the base of political support by requiring candidates to seek a greater number of small contributors, it sustains the unrealistic disclosure thresholds of $10 and $100 that I believe will deter those hoped-for small contributions. . . .

26

Federal Election Commission v. Wisconsin Right to Life, Inc. (2007)

Chief Justice Roberts announced the judgment of the Court and delivered the opinion of the Court [in part]:

Section 203 of the Bipartisan Campaign Reform Act of 2002 (BCRA) makes it a federal crime for any corporation to broadcast, shortly before an election, any communication that names a federal candidate for elected office and is targeted to the electorate. In McConnell v. *Federal Election Comm'n* (2003), this Court considered whether §203 was facially overbroad under the First Amendment because it captured within its reach not only campaign speech, or "express advocacy," but also speech about public issues more generally, or "issue advocacy," that mentions a candidate for federal office. The Court concluded that there was no overbreadth concern to the extent the speech in question was the "functional equivalent" of express campaign speech. On the other hand, the Court "assume[d]" that the interests it had found to "justify the regulation of campaign speech might not apply to the regulation of genuine issue ads." . . .

. . . We have long recognized that the distinction between campaign advocacy and issue advocacy "may often dissolve in practical application. Candidates, especially incumbents, are intimately tied to public issues involving legislative proposals and governmental actions" *Buckley* v. *Valeo* (1976). Our development of the law in this area requires us, however, to draw such a line, because we have recognized that the interests held to justify the regulation of campaign speech and its "functional equivalent" "might not apply" to the regulation of issue advocacy.

In drawing that line, the First Amendment requires us to err on the side of protecting political speech rather than suppressing it. We conclude that the speech at issue in this as-applied challenge is not the "functional equivalent" of express campaign speech. We further conclude that the interests held to justify restricting corporate campaign speech or its functional equivalent do not justify restricting issue advocacy, and accordingly we hold that BCRA §203 is unconstitutional as applied to the advertisements at issue in these cases. . . .

From *Federal Election Commission v. Wisconsin Right to Life, Inc.*, 551 U.S. 449 (2007).

BCRA significantly cut back on corporations' ability to engage in political speech. BCRA §203, at issue in these cases, makes it a crime for any labor union or incorporated entity—whether the United Steelworkers, the American Civil Liberties Union, or General Motors—to use its general treasury funds to pay for any "electioneering communication." BCRA's definition of "electioneering communication" is clear and expansive. It encompasses any broadcast, cable, or satellite communication that refers to a candidate for federal office and that is aired within 30 days of a federal primary election or 60 days of a federal general election in the jurisdiction in which that candidate is running for office.

Appellee Wisconsin Right to Life, Inc. (WRTL) . . . began broadcasting a radio advertisement entitled "Wedding." The transcript of "Wedding" reads as follows:

"'PASTOR: And who gives this woman to be married to this man?

"'BRIDE'S FATHER: Well, as father of the bride, I certainly could. But instead, I'd like to share a few tips on how to properly install drywall. Now you put the drywall up . . .

"'VOICE-OVER: Sometimes it's just not fair to delay an important decision.

"'But in Washington it's happening. A group of Senators is using the filibuster delay tactic to block federal judicial nominees from a simple "yes" or "no" vote. So qualified candidates don't get a chance to serve.

"'It's politics at work, causing gridlock and backing up some of our courts to a state of emergency.

"'Contact Senators Feingold and Kohl and tell them to oppose the filibuster.

"'Visit: BeFair.org

"'Paid for by Wisconsin Right to Life (befair.org), which is responsible for the content of this advertising and not authorized by any candidate or candidate's committee."

On the same day, WRTL aired a similar radio ad entitled "Loan." It had also invested treasury funds in producing a television ad entitled "Waiting," which is similar in substance and format to "Wedding" and "Loan."

WRTL planned on running "Wedding," "Waiting," and "Loan" throughout August 2004 and financing the ads with funds from its general treasury. It recognized, however, that as of August 15, 30 days prior to the Wisconsin primary, the ads would be illegal "electioneering communication[s]" under BCRA §203.

Believing that it nonetheless possessed a First Amendment right to broadcast these ads, WRTL filed suit against the Federal Election Commission (FEC) on July 28, 2004, seeking declaratory and injunctive relief before a three-judge District Court. WRTL alleged that BCRA's prohibition on the use of corporate treasury funds for "electioneering communication[s]" as defined in the Act is unconstitutional as applied to "Wedding," "Loan," and "Waiting," as well as any materially similar ads it might seek to run in the future. . . .

"The freedom of speech . . . guaranteed by the Constitution embraces at the least the liberty to discuss publicly and truthfully all matters of public concern without previous restraint or fear of subsequent punishment." [First Nat. Bank of Boston v.] Bellotti (1978). To safeguard this liberty, the proper standard for an as-applied challenge to BCRA §203 must be objective, focusing on the substance of the communication rather than amorphous considerations of intent and effect. It must entail minimal if any discovery, to allow parties to resolve disputes quickly without chilling speech through the threat of burdensome litigation. And it must eschew "the open-ended rough-and-tumble of factors," which "invit[es] complex argument in a trial court and a virtually inevitable appeal." Jerome B. Grubart, Inc. v. Great Lakes Dredge & Dock Co. (1995). In short, it must give the benefit of any doubt to protecting rather than stifling speech.

In light of these considerations, a court should find that an ad is the functional equivalent of express advocacy only if the ad is susceptible of no reasonable interpretation other than as an appeal to vote for or against a specific candidate. Under this test, WRTL's three ads are plainly not the functional equivalent of express advocacy. First, their content is consistent with that of a genuine issue ad: The ads focus on a legislative issue, take a position on the issue, exhort the public to adopt that position, and urge the public to contact public officials with respect to the matter. Second, their content lacks indicia of express advocacy: The ads do not mention an election, candidacy, political party, or challenger; and they do not take a position on a candidate's character, qualifications, or fitness for office.

Despite these characteristics, appellants assert that the content of WRTL's ads alone betrays their electioneering nature. Indeed, the FEC suggests that any ad covered by §203 that includes "an appeal to citizens to contact their elected representative" is the "functional equivalent" of an ad saying defeat or elect that candidate. We do not agree. To take just one example, during a blackout period the House considered the proposed Universal National Service Act. There would be no reason to regard an ad supporting or opposing that Act, and urging citizens to contact their Representative about it, as the equivalent of an ad saying vote for or against the Representative. Issue advocacy conveys information and educates. An issue ad's impact on an election, if it exists at all, will come only after the voters hear the information and choose—uninvited by the ad—to factor it into their voting decisions.

The FEC and intervenors try to turn this difference to their advantage, citing McConnell's statements "that the most effective campaign ads, like the most effective commercials for products . . . avoid the . . . magic words [expressly advocating the election of defeat of a candidate]," and that advertisers "would seldom choose to use such words even if permitted," An expert for the FEC in these cases relied on those observations to argue that WRTL's ads are especially effective electioneering ads because they are "subtl[e]," focusing on issues rather than simply exhorting the electorate to vote against Senator Feingold. Rephrased a bit, the argument perversely maintains that the less an issue ad resembles express advocacy, the more likely it is to be the functional equivalent of express advocacy. This "heads I win, tails you lose" approach cannot be correct. It would effectively eliminate First Amendment protection for genuine issue ads. . . . Under appellants' view, there can be no such thing as a genuine issue ad during the blackout period—it is simply a very effective electioneering ad. . . .

At best, appellants have shown what we have acknowledged at least since *Buckley:* that "the distinction between discussion of issues and candidates and advocacy of election or defeat of candidates may often dissolve in practical application." Under the test set forth above, that is not enough to establish that the ads can only reasonably be viewed as advocating or opposing a candidate in a federal election. "Freedom of discussion, if it would fulfill its historic function in this nation, must embrace all issues about which information is needed or appropriate to enable the members of society to cope with the exigencies of their period." Discussion of issues cannot be suppressed simply because the issues may also be pertinent in an election. Where the First Amendment is implicated, the tie goes to the speaker, not the censor. . . .

Because WRTL's ads may reasonably be interpreted as something other than as an appeal to vote for or against a specific candidate, we hold they are not the functional equivalent of express advocacy, and therefore fall outside the scope of McConnell's holding.

BCRA §203 can be constitutionally applied to WRTL's ads only if it is narrowly tailored to further a compelling interest. This Court has never recognized a compelling interest in regulating ads, like WRTL's, that are neither express advocacy nor its functional equivalent. The District Court below considered interests that might justify regulating WRTL's ads here, and found none sufficiently compelling. We reach the same conclusion. . . .

This Court has long recognized "the governmental interest in preventing corruption and the appearance of corruption" in election campaigns. This interest has been invoked as a reason for upholding *contribution limits.* As *Buckley* explained, "[t]o the extent that large contributions are given to secure a political *quid pro quo* from current and potential office holders, the integrity of our system of representative democracy is undermined." We have suggested that this interest might also justify limits on electioneering *expenditures* because it may be that, in some circumstances, "large independent expenditures pose the same dangers of actual or apparent quid pro quo arrangements as do large contributions."

McConnell arguably applied this interest—which this Court had only assumed could justify regulation of express advocacy—to ads that were the "functional equivalent" of express advocacy. But to justify regulation of WRTL's ads, this interest must be stretched yet another step to ads that are not the functional equivalent of express advocacy. Enough is enough. Issue ads like WRTL's are by no means equivalent to contributions, and the *quid-pro-quo* corruption interest cannot justify regulating them. To equate WRTL's ads with contributions is to ignore their value as political speech. . . .

Because WRTL's ads are not express advocacy or its functional equivalent, and because appellants identify no interest sufficiently compelling to justify burdening WRTL's speech, we hold that BCRA §203 is unconstitutional as applied to WRTL's "Wedding," "Loan," and "Waiting" ads.

*   *   *

These cases are about political speech. The importance of the cases to speech and debate on public policy issues is reflected in the number of diverse organizations that have joined in supporting WRTL before this Court: the American Civil Liberties Union, the National Rifle Association, the American Federation of Labor and Congress of Industrial Organizations, the Chamber of Commerce of the United States of America, Focus on the Family, the Coalition of Public Charities, the Cato Institute, and many others.

Yet, as is often the case in this Court's First Amendment opinions, we have gotten this far in the analysis without quoting the Amendment itself: "Congress shall make no law . . . abridging the freedom of speech." The Framers' actual words put these cases in proper perspective. Our jurisprudence over the past 216 years has rejected an absolutist interpretation of those words, but when it comes to drawing difficult lines in the area of pure political speech—between what is protected and what the Government may ban—it is worth recalling the language we are applying. McConnell held that express advocacy of a candidate or his opponent by a corporation shortly before an election may be prohibited, along with the functional equivalent of such express advocacy. We have no occasion to revisit that determination today. But when it comes to defining what speech qualifies as the functional equivalent of express advocacy subject to such a ban—the issue *we do* have to decide—we give the benefit of the doubt to speech, not censorship. The First Amendment's command that "Congress shall make no law . . . abridging the freedom of speech" demands at least that.

The judgment of the United States District Court for the District of Columbia is affirmed.

Justice Souter, with whom Justice Stevens, Justice Ginsburg, and Justice Breyer join, dissenting:

. . . After today, the ban on contributions by corporations and unions and the limitation on their corrosive spending when they enter the political arena are open to easy circumvention, and the possibilities for regulating corporate and union campaign money are unclear. The ban on contributions will mean nothing much, now that companies and unions can save candidates the expense of advertising directly, simply by running "issue ads" without express advocacy, or by funneling the money through an independent corporation like WRTL.

But the understanding of the voters and the Congress that this kind of corporate and union spending seriously jeopardizes the integrity of democratic government will remain. The facts are too powerful to be ignored, and further efforts at campaign finance reform will come. It is only the legal landscape that now is altered, and it may be that today's departure from precedent will drive further reexamination of the constitutional analysis: of the distinction between contributions and expenditures, or the relation between spending and speech, which have given structure to our thinking since *Buckley* itself was decided.

I cannot tell what the future will force upon us, but I respectfully dissent from this judgment today.

27

Jeffrey J. Poelvoorde

Party Politics and the Judiciary: *Bush v. Gore* and the Election of 2000 (2001)

The presidential election of 2000 was one of the closest and most controversial in memory, let alone history. Even more controversial than the partisan conflict between George Bush and Al Gore, however, was the involvement of the judiciary in the election. From the initial forays of the Florida courts into the contest up to the final decision of the United States

By permission of the author.

Supreme Court, each candidate (and his supporters) accused the other of inappropriately resorting to the judicial process. And, as the "partisans" in the election became "parties" in the various courts, they accused the judiciary itself of partiality and the exercise of illegitimate power. Although this was true of the Republicans as they criticized the decisions of the Florida Supreme Court, it was especially true of the Democrats as the United States Supreme Court put an end to court-ordered manual recounts in *Bush v. Gore*. Moreover, many journalists and academics—both liberal and conservative, during and after the election—expressed concern about the Supreme Court's action. Soon after the election prominent law professor at Harvard University, Alan M. Dershowitz, published *Supreme Injustice: How the High Court Hijacked Election 2000*. Another commentator likened the Supreme Court's decision to the now-infamous Dred Scott decision in 1857, where, in his judgment, the Court's majority under Chief Justice Taney blatantly misread constitutional history and principle in order to achieve the result it wanted. So, too, he argued, Chief Justice Rehnquist and the majority in *Bush v. Gore* would come to be tarnished by history as reckless "judicial activists"—*conservative* judicial activists, to be sure—imperiling the nation, trashing the Constitution and undermining the Supreme Court's own legitimacy and authority. And, he predicted, just as the minority in Dred Scott would be vindicated by subsequent judgment, so too would the minority on the Court in 2000 come to be seen as the ones expressing the proper understanding of the Constitution and of the role of the judiciary.

It is not so surprising or so unusual that a Supreme Court decision arouses such passion, such criticism. From the beginnings of the Republic, Supreme Court justices have been accused of subverting the Constitution or the national good to their partisan political positions. Nor is it so unusual that the Court exercises its power in such a way that the fate of the nation is involved. However, it is unusual—in fact, unprecedented—for the courts in general and the Supreme Court in particular to be so intimately involved in a presidential election, certainly to the point that the outcome *may* have turned on the Court's decision.

Given this unprecedented involvement, did the Court overreach itself? Did the nation "cede" the presidential election to the judiciary? Was the minority in *Bush v. Gore* correct in arguing that the Court should never have heard the case or that the majority was exercising raw "political" power? These pointed questions, raised in 2000 by the peculiarly close nature of the presidential contest and the manner in which our electoral system focuses attention on localities and legalities in the presidential election, are simply more dramatic versions of longer-standing and more fundamental ones that inhere in our constitutional system: What is the role of the judiciary in partisan politics? Is there a role for partisanship in constitutional interpretation?

Contrary to the critics of the Supreme Court, I shall argue that Chief Justice Rehnquist and the other members of the Court majority in *Bush v. Gore* did not constitute a judicial "junta," overriding the popular will of the American people or the normal processes of politics in order to allow their candidate to "win" the election. Its decision did allow Bush to win the presidential election, but the Courts decision was based on appeal to Constitutional principle. When the Supreme Court takes the part of the nation and the Constitution that guides it, its partisanship is not inappropriate activism but a judicial statesmanship that interprets and applies constitutional principle.

THE EVENTS OF THE ELECTION

As Election Day in November approached, the narrow advantage that George Bush maintained over Al Gore in the polls began to diminish. Support for the third-party candidate, Ralph Nader, shifted to Gore, and Bush's reputation for "integrity" (a potential electoral advantage, given Vice-President Gore's connection to the scandal-ridden Clinton administration), was tainted by revelations that he had not revealed a prior drunk-driving citation. The relatively-even partisan affiliation of the American people came to be reinforced by an ambivalence about the preferability of either of the two major candidates, leading to a near draw.

Because the Electoral College transforms a national presidential campaign into an election held and decided at the state level, as Election Night unfolded, the centrality of certain states to the election became evident. By late evening, Florida's twenty-five electoral votes became pivotal. Yet, the popular vote in Florida reflected the even division in the rest of the nation. The news media reversed themselves several times during the evening in calling the election, finally withholding judgment as Florida's electoral laws played out during the next several days. One realm of uncertainty was the large number of absentee and overseas ballots resulting from the presence of the military in Florida and the possession by many of its citizens of dual citizenship in other countries; these ballots would come to present their own controversies and court challenges. Also, charges erupted that election officials discouraged or even harassed minority voters or engaged in deliberately confusing polling practices. These charges would be amplified in the passionate claims of national activists and party leaders and would not be laid to rest for months to come.

The main drama, however, began to unfold over the punch-card machines which Florida, again, like many of the states, had and has employed for years. The machines require voters to insert a stylus and punch out perforated squares by candidates' names. The cards are read by machines that count a clearly-punched hole for a single candidate as a vote. Problems can occur when a voter does not completely punch out a square, leaving it indented (or "dimpled") or hanging by one or more corners—or punches out more than one candidate's name for a single office. Voters who do so may be untrained, incompetent, confused, hasty, undecided, ambivalent or even angry. At any rate, the machines cannot read such partial or duplicated punches as "votes." Controversy arose when it became apparent that there was an "undercount" of clearly-punched holes for the presidential candidates in comparison with the votes for other offices, especially in several counties with large numbers of registered Democrats. The actual statewide number of presidential "undervotes" in Florida was never finally ascertained, but during the controversy estimates ranged from possibly 60,000 to 170,000. In such cases, Florida law allows candidates to request a "manual" recount, either partial (within a county or in several counties) or over the entire state. The task in a manual (or visual) examination of a ballot is to see if "voter intent" can be discerned in an incompletely-punched hole, depending upon the manner and degree of the indentation. Some states have very specific legal definitions of standards for identifying the intent of the voter in these circumstances; Florida does not.

A candidate may request a manual recount of undervotes either before the election returns are certified as the law requires by local officials or the Secretary of State or after the certification of the election. The law also sets a mandatory seven-day deadline after the election for certifying election results, reserving some discretion to the Secretary of State to accept late returns. The law reflects the need to balance accuracy of the vote with timeliness or finality. Legitimacy must be grounded in a vote that reflects, as accurately as possible, the wishes of the electorate, but also in a vote that is conclusive by virtue of coming to a conclusion. By the end of election week, Vice-President Gore requested manual recounts in four of the counties with large Democratic registration and possibly large undercounts. County election officials began to comply, setting up counting committees with bi-partisan membership.

The state and federal judiciaries were pulled into the political contest in several complex paths. When Al Gore first pressed for selected manual recounts in only four counties, Bush sued in the U.S. District Court of Southern Florida to have the recounts stopped on what came to be understood as the "equal protection" argument. He claimed that for four counties to undergo recounts treated the voters in those counties differently—with more "importance"—than voters in other counties in Florida. Meanwhile, Gore fought in Florida courts first to extend the deadline for the certification of votes in order to give the counting committees time to do their work. After the Secretary of State certified the popular votes in favor of Bush in compliance with the new deadline established by the judiciary, Gore sued in Florida Circuit Court to have the election continue by continuing manual recounts and by counting votes which had been rejected by several of the county election commissions, and appealed to the Florida

Supreme Court when that lower court decision went against him. Events unfolded rapidly: On December 8, the Florida Supreme Court ruled 4–3 to continue manual recounts and to include in the final tally votes which had been rejected both by some of the counties and the Secretary of State. The tide turned again, when Bush appealed to the US Supreme Court. In a 5–4 decision, that Court voted to stop the recounts, holding that the Florida Supreme Court's intervention in the election did not meet constitutional standards and that no judicially-imposed remedy could meet the December 12 deadline for choosing presidential electors established by US statutes governing the procedures of the Electoral College. In effect, the election was over. Bush won the popular vote by the slimmest of margins—a few hundred out of six million cast in Florida, a result confirmed the next week when the Electoral College met across the nation in state capitals and awarded the Governor 271 electoral votes.

One may wonder why the partisan energies of the participants was so intense. After all, the difference between the positions of the candidates and the parties on most issues, while not identical, was not particularly great. It was this perception that generated the momentum to the two nationally visible "third party" candidacies: Ralph Nader for the Green Party and Pat Buchanan for the Reform Party. In domestic issues, both major parties advocated some version of prescription drug benefits for the elderly, education reform, Social Security reform, tax cuts, and support for the environment. The difference in foreign affairs was even harder to identify, with the exception of a Republican inclination to support anti-ballistic missile defense and a Democratic inclination to remain within the existing framework of treaty limits on weapons development. True, regarding each of these issues, the most ideological and partisan core of the parties pronounced different ways of defining and addressing them. But, on the whole, the candidates perceived that they were competing for the same "middle" of the electorate. The electorate, too, had no clear or strong partisan or candidate preference.

Some of the partisanship of the election derived from specific circumstances. Residual bitterness from the impeachment of President Clinton had left its mark on American politics. No one knows how much of a factor either Clinton's actions or the movement to impeach and remove him actually were with the voters, but those events left unquestionably soured relations between the Republican and Democratic Parties and their leadership. Given Vice-President Gore's connection with the Clinton Administration, Democrats perhaps wished to see him victorious as a sign that their party had put this issue behind it. Republicans perhaps wanted Governor Bush to win as a confirmation that the American people had, in fact, held the Democratic Party responsible for not holding President Clinton responsible.

Of course, both Gore and Bush wanted very much to win the presidency for perfectly obvious reasons. We should not forget that the American presidency is the most powerful office in the world. Even in relatively calm times, the presidency awakens ambition. Then, too, one more issue, hovering quietly but persistently in the background of partisan conflict for almost three decades, intertwined itself in the party contest in Florida: the appointment of judges to the Federal judiciary and the Supreme Court in particular. Since the heyday of the "activist" Warren Court in the 1950's and 1960's, the judiciary's broad approach to constitutional and statutory interpretation, together with much of the content of specific issues (such as abortion, religion in the public sphere, criminal procedure), had come to align itself along the "liberal" and "conservative" ideological spectrum in contemporary politics. The judicial philosophy of "activism," involving wide judicial discretion in interpreting the Constitution and an eagerness to intervene in the processes of the other branches, came to be opposed to the philosophy of "restraint," by which judges would read the Constitution and statutes "narrowly," guided by the "original intention" of their drafters. These philosophies, now roughly labeled as "liberal" and "conservative," coincided neatly with party identification especially during the bitter confirmation struggle over President Reagan's nomination of Judge Robert Bork to the Supreme Court in the 1980s.

Bush v. Gore and Judicial Politics

Accusing the judiciary of partisan politics dressed up in constitutional language is no new phenomenon. Often, this accusation goes hand-in-hand with disagreement with the Court over the principles it employs in interpreting the Constitution. When constitutional questions go to court, the particular interests and partisan positions involved must justify themselves in light of principles, such as voting rights, fairness, separation of powers, federalism, and the rule of law. "Parties" in court cases may make raw assertions of self-interest while trying to persuade the "disinterested" that their assertion has more justice to it. But that their arguments about justice are tied to self-interest does not render their claims about justice false. Nor are they merely rhetorical window-dressing to hide self-interest, but plausible (in most instances) claims generated by the inescapable clash of human beings living under law. The function of judges, after all, is to decide which "party" has a stronger claim to justice under the law. Unless a case is dismissed for some reason, *somebody* has to win it. And like the parties in the case, judges present their reasons. They cannot present their judgements as pre-existing or prejudicial preferences for either of the parties in the case. Even if they have such preferences, as judges they must resort to principles of justice, the law or the Constitution. Theirs is a difficult and delicate function in our republican form of government. They are "bridges," in a sense, between the partisanship and principles. Ultimately, all the institutions under the Constitution must do this, but judges more habitually and frequently, for they are the "umpires" whose decisions govern the rest of us as "players."

All sides sought a Constitutional basis for action. Indeed seven of the justices agreed that the procedures being used in the recounts were questionable under the equal protection clause of the Fourteenth Amendment. As the majority opinion argued: The Fourteenth Amendment to the Constitution prohibits a state from denying "equal protection of the laws" to any persons under its jurisdiction. The recount procedures mandated by the Florida Supreme Court constituted "arbitrary and disparate treatment of the members of the [Florida] electorate" and therefore violated the equal protection clause of the Constitution. Far from acting in an arbitrary manner, the majority of the Court acted to prevent arbitrary decisions that violated the equal rights of individuals. Moreover, in doing so, the Court acknowledges the rights of states: "the State legislature's power to select the manner for appointing electors is plenary"; it is only because the legislature has vested the right to vote for presidential electors in the people, that equal weight must be afforded to each vote, and equal dignity to each voter.

The famous 5–4 split occurred only on the question of the proper remedy for this constitutional violation. Two of the justices who found equal protection violations (Breyer and Souter) wished to remand the case to the Florida Supreme Court for a remedy. The remaining five believed that no such remedy was possible given time constraints imposed by existing laws and procedures. This was a significant disagreement, but hardly the sign of a Court that has rejected constitutional principle in favor of mere partisanship.

Three of the justices who concurred in the opinion of the Court (Rehnquist, Scalia and Thomas) identified additional constitutional problems. They believed that Article II of the Constitution (and federal laws in support thereof) assigned direct responsibility to the *legislature* of the state to select the means of choosing presidential electors. According to this argument, the Florida Supreme Court violated the US Constitution by altering the statutory deadlines for certification which had been set by state law. In the name of a vague notion of "voter intent" based on the Florida Constitution's embrace of the right to vote in each citizen, these justices argued, the Florida Court had "legislated" new electoral procedures, violating the Constitution's assignment of this function to the state legislature. Thus the Supreme Court's decision, denounced as unprincipled and arbitrary, protected the role of the states in the presidential electoral process as well as the role of the state legislature against the judicial activism of the Florida court. Far from arbitrary or outcomes-oriented decision making, the opinion of these justices who went beyond the Court's majority of which they formed a predominant part, recognized the principle of federalism as one that must be at times preserved by federal institutions. It also recognized the principle of judicial restraint in relation to legislative action; in fact, its decision was an activism aiming at guaranteeing restraint.

The opinions of the four dissenting justices (Stevens, Souter, Ginsburg and Breyer) varied in rationale and in tone (Justice Ginsburg even dropping the "respectfully" in the phrase that typically concludes a dissenting opinion, simply stating, "I dissent."). But each recognized that there were constitutional issues at stake. Stevens and Ginsburg found that the Florida Court had merely interpreted mildly unclear and somewhat conflicting provisions of the Florida code (a common practice of all courts when they interpret the sometimes confusing body of statute law in front of them), presuming to give a consistent application of what the Court perceived to be the "intent" of the legislature. As for the varying standards of ascertaining "voter intent" regarding the incompletely-punched ballots, the minority held that the Florida Court was fashioning an "equitable" and flexible remedy to injuries which both certain voters and Vice-President Gore had suffered—not from malice or forethought, but still "injuries." At the same time, the Florida justices were simply deferring to local agencies and standards, and as long as the methods of counting were essentially uniform, no violation of the Fourteenth Amendment had occurred. Thus the dissenting U.S. Supreme Court Justices based their arguments on the Constitutional principles of federalism and judicial restraint.

Conclusion

The Supreme Court did not elect George Bush as President, nor did the American people "lose" the election to their "judicial masters." Rather, the Court decided the terms under which the rules governing this remarkably close election were to be interpreted and applied. Most accurately, the Court decided under what terms the judicial branches of government were to step in as participants in the electoral process. That answer was, "very cautiously." Even assuming the worst—that the Florida Supreme Court was willing to interpret Florida's Constitution and laws in any way it could to benefit Al Gore and that a majority of U.S. Supreme Court was simply doing the same for George Bush—there would still be a difference between the two Supreme Courts. It is not so much that the U.S. Supreme Court intervened in order to ensure that George Bush won, but that it intervened in order to ensure that the Florida Supreme Court did not intervene in order to ensure that Al Gore won.

But we do not have to assume the worst. What could have motivated the majority of the Florida Court in its multiple decisions favoring Vice-President Gore other than a desire to see him win the election? A desire to give voters the benefit of the doubt, even against their own ignorance or incompetence?

A suspicion that election officials were not generous enough in allowing for voters' inexperience? A conviction that state statutes did not erect a procedure scrupulous enough to ensure that a maximum of even marginally legal ballots be included in the final tally? A concern to extend the enjoyments of the franchise beyond what the statutes "narrowly" define as "legal" voting? All of these are possibilities, all are reflected at times in the Florida Court's majority opinions as well as in the dissenting opinions of the U.S. Supreme Court. What is common to them all is a disposition to reshape electoral laws and procedures, even or especially during an ongoing election, to maximize the broad value of "voter intent."

But the Court's majority—and probably the majority of the Constitution's drafters and ratifiers—would have argued for a narrower constitutional discretion to act on broader constitutional grounds, including especially the Constitution's general structure as embodied in the theory of separation of powers and checks and balances and its embrace of the rule of law as the foundation of decent and stable republican government. The Court saw a threat to that structure and its principles in the behavior of a state court willing to redesign electoral procedures to fit its view of "voter intent." Aside from worrying about a court that would redesign statutes in the name of its view of "basic human liberties," the Court was worried about a republican order where the electoral rules can be shifted in the middle of an election. Sensing that electoral legitimacy in a republic is more than a matter of numbers, but of stable and predictable legal procedures, the Supreme Court acted to shore up the legal foundations of political rule. Unquestionably aware of criticism, both from inside and out, regarding the legitimacy of its decision, the majority was nevertheless willing to risk its own "short-range" legitimacy in order to preserve the larger and more fundamental legitimacy of constitutional republicanism. The issues of the presidential election 2000 demonstrate how partisanship—on both sides—shades into statesmanship.

28

Ronald Reagan

The New Republican Party (1977)

. . . Three weeks ago here in our nation's capital I told a group of conservative scholars that we are currently in the midst of a re-ordering of the political realities that have shaped our time. We know today that the principles and values that lie at the heart of conservatism are shared by the majority.

Despite what some in the press may say, we who are proud to call ourselves "conservative" are not a minority of a minority party; we are part of the great majority of Americans of both major parties and of most of the independents as well. . . .

Yes, conservatism can and does mean different things to those who call themselves conservatives.

You know, as I do, that most commentators make a distinction between [what] they call "social" conservatism and "economic" conservatism. The so-called social issues—law and order, abortion, busing, quota systems—are usually associated with blue-collar, ethnic and religious groups themselves traditionally associated with the Democratic Party. The economic issues—inflation, deficit spending and big government—are usually associated with Republican Party members and independents who concentrate their attention on economic matters.

Now I am willing to accept this view of two major kinds of conservatism—or, better still, two different conservative constituencies. But at the same time let me say that the old lines that once clearly divided these two kinds of conservatism are disappearing.

In fact, the time has come to see if it is possible to present a program of action based on political principle that can attract those interested in the so-called "social" issues and those interested in "economic" issues. In short, isn't it possible to combine the two major segments of contemporary American conservatism into one politically effective whole? . . .

Delivered on February 6, 1977 at the 4th Annual Convention of the Conservative Political Action Conference. The speech can be found at http://www.conservative.org/pressroom/reagan/reagaon1977.asp

. . . What I envision is not simply a melding together of the two branches of American conservatism into a temporary uneasy alliance, but the creation of a new, lasting majority.

This will mean compromise. But not a compromise of basic principle. What will emerge will be something new: something open and vital and dynamic, something the great conservative majority will recognize as its own, because at the heart of this undertaking is principled politics.

I have always been puzzled by the inability of some political and media types to understand exactly what is meant by adherence to political principle. All too often in the press and the television evening news it is treated as a call for "ideological purity." Whatever ideology may mean—and it seems to mean a variety of things, depending upon who is using it—it always conjures up in my mind a picture of a rigid, irrational clinging to abstract theory in the face of reality. We have to recognize that in this country "ideology" is a scare word. And for good reason. Marxist-Leninism is, to give but one example, an ideology. All the facts of the real world have to be fitted to the Procrustean bed of Marx and Lenin. If the facts don't happen to fit the ideology, the facts are chopped off and discarded.

I consider this to be the complete opposite to principled conservatism. If there is any political viewpoint in this world which is free from slavish adherence to abstraction, it is American conservatism.

When a conservative states that the free market is the best mechanism ever devised by the mind of man to meet material needs, he is merely stating what a careful examination of the real world has told him is the truth.

When a conservative says that totalitarian Communism is an absolute enemy of human freedom he is not theorizing—he is reporting the ugly reality captured so unforgettably in the writings of Alexander Solzhenitsyn.

When a conservative says it is bad for the government to spend more than it takes in, he is simply showing the same common sense that tells him to come in out of the rain. . . .

Conservatism is the antithesis of the kind of ideological fanaticism that has brought so much horror and destruction to the world. The common sense and common decency of ordinary men and women, working out their own lives in their own way—this is the heart of American conservatism today. Conservative wisdom and principles are derived from willingness to learn, not just from what is going on now, but from what has happened before. . . .

Let us lay to rest, once and for all, the myth of a small group of ideological purists trying to capture a majority. Replace it with the reality of a majority trying to assert its rights against the tyranny of powerful academics, fashionable left-revolutionaries, some economic illiterates who happen to hold elective office and the social engineers who dominate the dialogue and set the format in political and social affairs. If there is any ideological fanaticism in American political life, it is to be found among the enemies of freedom on the left or right—those who would sacrifice principle to theory, those who worship only the god of political, social and economic abstractions, ignoring the realities of everyday life. They are not conservatives.

Our first job is to get this message across to those who share most of our principles. If we allow ourselves to be portrayed as ideological shock troops without correcting this error we are doing ourselves and our cause a disservice. Wherever and whenever we can, we should gently but firmly correct our political and media friends who have been perpetuating the myth of conservatism as a narrow ideology. Whatever the word may have meant in the past, today conservatism means principles evolving from experience and a belief in change when necessary, but not just for the sake of change.

Once we have established this, the next question is: What will be the political vehicle by which the majority can assert its rights?

I have to say I cannot agree with some of my friends—perhaps including some of you here tonight—who have answered that question by saying this nation needs a new political party.

I respect that view and I know that those who have reached it have done so after long hours of study. But I believe that political success of the principles we believe in can best be achieved in the Republican Party. I believe the Republican Party can hold and should provide the political mechanism through which the goals of the majority of Americans can be achieved. For one thing, the biggest single grouping of conservatives is to be found in that party. It makes more sense to build on that grouping than to break it up and start over. Rather than a third party, we can have a new first party made up of people who share our principles. I have said before that if a formal change in name proves desirable, then so be it. But tonight, for purpose of discussion, I'm going to refer to it simply as the New Republican Party.

And let me say so there can be no mistakes as to what I mean: The New Republican Party I envision will not be, and cannot, be one limited to the country club-big business image that, for reasons both fair and unfair, it is burdened with today. The New Republican Party I am speaking about is going to have room for the man and the woman in the factories, for the farmer, for the cop on the beat and the millions of Americans who may never have thought of joining our party before, but whose interests coincide with those represented by principled Republicanism. If we are to attract more working men and women of this country, we will do so not by simply "making room" for them, but by making certain they have a say in what goes on in the party. The Democratic Party turned its back on the majority of social conservatives during the 1960s. The New Republican Party of the late '70s and '80s must welcome them, seek them out, enlist them, not only as rank-and-file members but as leaders and as candidates.

The time has come for Republicans to say to black voters: "Look, we offer principles that black Americans can, and do, support." We believe in jobs, real jobs; we believe in education that is really education; we believe in treating all Americans as individuals and not as stereotypes or voting blocs—and we believe that the long-range interest of black Americans lies in looking at what each major party has to offer, and then deciding on the merits. The Democratic Party takes the black vote for granted. Well, it's time black America and the New Republican Party move toward each other and create a situation in which no black vote can be taken for granted. . . .

I need not remind you that you can have the soundest principles in the world, but if you don't have candidates who can communicate those principles, candidates who are articulate as well as principled, you are going to lose election after election. I refuse to believe that the good Lord divided this world into Republicans who defend basic values and Democrats who win elections. We have to find tough, bright young men and women who are sick and tired of cliches and the pomposity and the mind-numbing economic idiocy of the liberals in Washington.

It is at this point, however, that we come across a question that is really the essential one: What will be the basis of this New Republican Party? To what set of values and principles can our candidates appeal? Where can Americans who want to know where we stand look for guidance? . . .

The New Republican Party can and should use the Republican platform of 1976 as the major source from which a Declaration of Principles can be created and offered to the American people.

Tonight I want to offer to you my own version of what such a declaration might look like. I make no claim to originality. This declaration I propose is relatively short, taken, for most part, word for word from the Republican platform. It concerns itself with basic principles, not with specific solutions.

We, the members of the New Republican Party, believe that the preservation and enhancement of the values that strengthen and protect individual freedom, family life, communities and neighborhoods and the liberty of our beloved nation should be at the heart of any legislative or political program presented to the American people. Toward that end, we, therefore, commit ourselves to the following propositions and offer them to each American believing that the New Republican Party, based on such principles, will serve the interest of all the American people.

We believe that liberty can be measured by how much freedom Americans have to make their own decisions, even their own mistakes. Government must step in when one's liberties impinge on one's neighbor's. Government must protect constitutional rights, deal with other governments, protect citizens from aggressors, assure equal opportunity, and be compassionate in caring for those citizens who are unable to care for themselves.

Our federal system of local-state-national government is designed to sort out on what level these actions should be taken. Those concerns of a national character—such as air and water pollution that do not respect state boundaries, or the national transportation system, or efforts to safeguard your civil liberties—must, of course, be handled on the national level.

As a general rule, however, we believe that government action should be taken first by the government that resides as close to you as possible.

We also believe that Americans, often acting through voluntary organizations, should have the opportunity to solve many of the social problems of their communities. This spirit of freely helping others is uniquely American and should be encouraged in every way by government.

Families must continue to be the foundation of our nation.

Families—not government programs—are the best way to make sure our children are properly nurtured, our elderly are cared for, our cultural and spiritual heritages are perpetuated, our laws are observed and our values are preserved.

Thus it is imperative that our government's programs, actions, officials and social welfare institutions never be allowed to jeopardize the family. We fear the government may be powerful enough to destroy our families; we know that it is not powerful enough to replace them. The New Republican Party must be committed to working always in the interest of the American family.

Every dollar spent by government is a dollar earned by individuals. Government must always ask: Are your dollars being wisely spent? Can we afford it? Is it not better for the country to leave your dollars in your pocket?

Elected officials, their appointees, and government workers are expected to perform their public acts with honesty, openness, diligence, and special integrity.

Government must work for the goal of justice and the elimination of unfair practices, but no government has yet designed a more productive economic system or one which benefits as many people as the American market system.

The beauty of our land is our legacy to our children. It must be protected by us so that they can pass it on intact to their children.

The United States must always stand for peace and liberty in the world and the rights of the individual. We must form sturdy partnerships with our allies for the preservation of freedom. We must be ever willing to negotiate differences, but equally mindful that there are American ideals that cannot be compromised. Given that there are other nations with potentially hostile design, we recognize that we can reach our goals only while maintaining a superior national defense, second to none. . . .

And just to set the record straight, let me say this about our friends who are now Republicans but who do not identify themselves as conservatives: I want the record to show that I do not view the new revitalized Republican

Party as one based on a principle of exclusion. After all, you do not get to be a majority party by searching for groups you won't associate or work with. If we truly believe in our principles, we should sit down and talk. Talk with anyone, anywhere, at any time if it means talking about the principles for the Republican Party. Conservatism is not a narrow ideology, nor is it the exclusive property of conservative activists. . . .

Our party must be the party of the individual. It must not sell out the individual to cater to the group. No greater challenge faces our society today than ensuring that each one of us can maintain his dignity and his identity in an increasingly complex, centralized society.

Extreme taxation, excessive controls, oppressive government competition with business, galloping inflation, frustrated minorities and forgotten Americans are not the products of free enterprise. They are the residue of centralized bureaucracy, of government by a self-anointed elite.

Our party must be based on the kind of leadership that grows and takes its strength from the people. Any organization is in actuality only the lengthened shadow of its members. A political party is a mechanical structure created to further a cause. The cause, not the mechanism, brings and holds the members together. And our cause must be to rediscover, reassert and reapply America's spiritual heritage to our national affairs.

Then with God's help we shall indeed be as a city upon a hill with the eyes of all people upon us.

29

Barack Obama

Take Back America (2006)

My friends, we meet here today at a time where we find ourselves at a crossroads in America's history.

It's a time where you can go to any town hall or street corner or coffee shop and hear people express the same anxiety about the future; hear them convey the same uncertainty about the direction we're headed as a country.

Delivered on June 14, 2006. The speech can be found at http://www.barackobama .com/2006/06/14/take_back_america_conference_r.php

Whether it's the war or Katrina or their health care or their jobs, you hear people say that we've finally arrived at a moment where something must change.

These are Americans who still believe in an America where anything's possible–they just don't think their leaders do. These are Americans who still dream big dreams –they just sense their leaders have forgotten how. . . .

In a century just six years old, our faith has been shaken by war and terror, disaster and despair, threats to the middle-class dream, and scandal and corruption in our government.

The sweeping changes brought by revolutions in technology have torn down walls between business and government and people and places all over the globe. And with this new world comes new risks and new dangers.

No longer can we assume that a high-school education is enough to compete for a job that could easily go to a college-educated student in Bangalore or Beijing. No more can we count on employers to provide health care and pensions and job training when their bottom-lines know no borders. Never again can we expect the oceans that surround America to keep us safe from attacks on our own soil.

The world has changed. And as a result, we've seen families work harder for less and our jobs go overseas. We've seen the cost of health care and child care and gasoline skyrocket. We've seen our children leave for Iraq and terrorists threaten to finish the job they started on 9/11.

But while the world has changed around us, too often our government has stood still. Our faith has been shaken, but the people running Washington aren't willing to make us believe again.

It's the timidity–the smallness–of our politics that's holding us back right now. The idea that some problems are just too big to handle, and if you just ignore them, sooner or later, they'll go away. . . .

Now, let me say this–I don't think that George Bush is a bad man. I think he loves his country. I don't think this administration is full of stupid people–I think there are a lot of smart folks in there. The problem isn't that their philosophy isn't working the way it's supposed to–it's that it is. It's that it's doing exactly what it's supposed to do.

The reason they don't believe government has a role in solving national problems is because they think government is the problem. That we're better off if we dismantle it–if we divvy it up into individual tax breaks, hand 'em out, and encourage everyone to go buy your own health care, your own retirement security, your own child care, their own schools, your own private security force, your own roads, their own levees . . .

It's called the Ownership Society in Washington. But in our past there has been another term for it–Social Darwinism–every man or women for him or herself.

It allows us to say to those whose health care or tuition may rise faster than they can afford–life isn't fair. It allows us to say to the child who didn't have the foresight to choose the right parents or be born in the right suburb–pick yourself up by your bootstraps. It lets us say to the guy who worked twenty or thirty years in the factory and then watched his plant move out to Mexico or China–we're sorry, but you're on your own.

It's a bracing idea. It's a tempting idea. And it's the easiest thing in the world.

But there's just one problem. It doesn't work. It ignores our history. Yes, our greatness as a nation has depended on individual initiative, on a belief in the free market. But it has also depended on our sense of mutual regard for each other, of mutual responsibility. The idea that everybody has a stake in the country, that we're all in it together and everybody's got a shot at opportunity.

Americans know this. We know that government can't solve all our problems–and we don't want it to.

But we also know that there are some things we can't do on our own. We know that there are some things we do better together.

We know that we've been called in churches and mosques, synagogues and Sunday schools to love our neighbors as ourselves; to be our brother's keeper; to be our sister's keeper. That we have individual responsibility, but we also have collective responsibility to each other.

That's what America is.

And so I am eager to have this argument not just with the President, but the entire Republican Party over what this country is about.

Because I think that this is our moment to lead.

The time for our party's identity crisis is over. Don't let anyone tell you we don't know what we stand for and don't doubt it yourselves. We know who we are. And in the end, we know that it isn't enough to just say that you've had enough.

So let it be said that we are the party of opportunity. That in a global economy that's more connected and more competitive–we are the party that will guarantee every American an affordable, world-class, top-notch, life-long education–from early childhood to high school, from college to on-the-job training.

Let it be said that we are the party of affordable, accessible health care for all Americans. The party that won't make Americans choose between a health care plan that bankrupts the government and one that bankrupts families. The party that won't just throw a few tax breaks at families who can't afford their insurance, but modernizes our health care system and gives every family a chance to buy insurance at a price they can afford.

Let it be said that we are the party of an energy independent America. The party that's not bought and paid for by the oil companies. The party that will harness homegrown, alternative fuels and spur the production of fuel-efficient, hybrid cars to break our dependence on the world's most dangerous regimes.

Let it be said that we will conduct a smart foreign policy that battles the forces of terrorism and fundamentalism wherever they may exist by matching the might of our military with the power of our diplomacy and the strength of our alliances. And when we do go to war, let us always be honest with the American people about why we are there and how we will win.

And let it be said that we are the party of open, honest government that doesn't peddle the agenda of whichever lobbyist or special interest can write the biggest check. The party who believes that in this democracy, influence and access should begin and end with the power of the ballot.

If we do all this, if we can be trusted to lead, this will not be a Democratic Agenda, it will be an American agenda. Because in the end, we may be proud Democrats, but we are prouder Americans. We're tired of being divided, tired of running into ideological walls and partisan roadblocks, tired of appeals to our worst instincts and greatest fears. . . .

We are here tonight because we believe that in this country, we have it within our power to say "yes" to those questions–to forge our own destiny–to begin the world anew.

Ladies and gentlemen, this is our time.

Our time to make a mark on history.

Our time to write a new chapter in the American story.

Our time to leave our children a country that is freer and kinder, more prosperous and more just than the place we grew up.

And then someday, someday, if our kids get the chance to stand where we are and look back at the beginning of the 21st century, they can say that this was the time when America renewed its purpose.

They can say that this was the time when America found its way.

They can say that this was the time when America learned to dream again.

Chapter III

Congress and the Separation of Powers

The questions that must animate any inquiry into the character and operation of Congress are: first, does the Constitutional and extra-Constitutional structure of Congress allow it to perform its law-making and representative functions in the best possible way; and, second, how does the Congress fit into the larger framework of the separation of powers?

The authors of *The Federalist* thought that the Senate and the House would be different in character because of their different structures. The members of the House would be more dependent on their constituents and therefore more attentive to their constituents' interests. Senators, on the other hand, would have more freedom than members of the House to promote the long-term interests of the nation. Characterized by knowledge, foresight, and stability, this institution would provide a unifying sense of national character, helping to connect the particular laws to the principles and purposes of the nation. Given this complex character of Congress, legislation would emerge, in the best case, as a compromise among the particular interests of the parts, in light of a long-range conception of the good of the whole.

From *The Federalist*'s description of Congressmen, particularly Senators, it is clear that members were expected to rely on their own individual judgment rather than merely reflect the immediate interests and opinions of their constituents. Furthermore, *The Federalist* seems aware of a possible conflict between the good of the parts, which the members of Congress represent, and the good of the whole nation. Nonetheless, there is no recommendation that one good be pursued to the exclusion of the other.

Woodrow Wilson proposed major reforms of American government in an attempt to eliminate self-interested politics from the system established by the Founders. Political leaders, he thought, should aim at the common good rather than private or particular goods. To promote this goal, Wilson called for the establishment of Cabinet or parliamentary government as well as the development of ideological political parties. Ideological parties would offer the electorate a choice between coherent programs based on different views of the public good. The leaders in a parliamentary system would have the power to enact the program chosen by the voters. Thus, parliamentary government would overcome the deadlock caused by the separation of powers and the decentralized Congressional committee system.

William F. Connelly, however, argues that Congress and Congressmen continue to operate as the Founders intended and that is for the good. Connelly shows that the Founders intended to create a tension between pluralist coalition building and coherent principled policy-making, between representation of individual constituencies and representation of the national interest, between the Congressman's self-interest and the interest of his or her constituency, and between principles and self-interest more broadly understood. Congressional critics and Congressional reformers have often failed to appreciate the complex character of Congress and have consequently misdiagnosed its problems and promoted inappropriate prescriptions for reform.

Connelly draws a strong parallel between Wilson's idea of Congressional government and the ideas of Speaker Newt Gingrich in the 1990s. Connelly claims that, following Wilson, Gingrich failed to see the limits of Congressional government in the context of our Constitutional system. Gingrich overestimated the potential for a Speaker of the House of Representatives to form a government.

Another popular reform proposal of the 1990s was that of term limits. By limiting the number of terms members of Congress could serve it was thought that the hold of special interests would be broken and we could return to an ideal of citizen legislators. Although this proposal failed to gain sufficient support at the national level, several states tried to impose term limits on their Congressional delegations by limiting access to the ballot by incumbents. Although conservative dissenters found this to be a legitimate exercise of the powers of the states in our federal system, the majority of the Court determined that the qualifications for members were established by the Constitution, and that the states had no authority to alter or amend the Constitutional requirements for national office.

Morris Fiorina contends that the self-interest of individual members is far more important than particular institutional arrangements in determining the behavior of Congress. The desire for re-election leads members to ignore national policy issues in favor of pork barrel legislation and constituent services. Taking a stand on policy creates enemies as well as friends, whereas pork and constituent services are pure profit in terms of voter support. Members of Congress spend little time deliberating about issues because it is not in their self-interest to do so.

Joseph M. Bessette argues that Fiorina underestimates the role of deliberation in Congress. According to Bessette at least some members see the possibility that they can best represent their own interests and those of their constituents by engaging their colleagues in a search for common ground. Congress has succeeded in developing national policies because leaders have understood the value of genuine deliberation.

What is the role of Congressional deliberation in area of foreign policy?

The authors of the War Powers Act said they only wanted to insure that the collective judgment of Congress and the President would apply to the use of the armed forces of the United States. But the War Powers Act was clearly based on the premise that even in foreign policy Congress should establish policy. The President is to carry out Congressional policy, not to act independently. Independent executive action was thought to be inconsistent with the rule of law and the primacy of Congress in the law-making process.

The Act has proved ineffective in restraining Presidential initiatives involving the armed forces, in part because of the Supreme Court's decision in the case of *INS v. Chadha* (1983). One of the provisions of the War Powers Act stated that Congress could at any time by concurrent resolution order the immediate withdrawal of troops from hostilities. In *Chadha*, however, the Court declared that Congress violated the Constitutional separation of powers if it unilaterally vetoed an executive action or decision. Both the majority opinion by Chief Justice Burger and the concurring opinion by Justice Powell point to the limits of Congressional power as defined by the Constitution. Justice Burger defends the Constitutional role of the President in the legislative process and Justice Powell explains the Constitutional restrictions on the right of the legislature to alter the legal status of particular individuals.

The Constitution does not create a government based on the notion of legislative supremacy. Instead it establishes co-equal branches of government each with independent discretionary authority.

30

Alexander Hamilton and James Madison

On Congress (1788)

A representative of the United States must be of the age of twenty-five years; must have been seven years a citizen of the United States; must, at the time of his election, be an inhabitant of the State he is to represent; and, during the time of his service, must be in no office under the United States. Under these reasonable limitations, the door of this part of the federal government is open to merit of every description, whether native or adoptive, whether young or old, and without regard to poverty or wealth, or to any particular profession or religious faith. . . .

As it is essential to liberty that the government in general should have a common interest with the people, so it is particularly essential that the branch of it under consideration should have an immediate dependence on, and an intimate sympathy with, the people. Frequent elections are unquestionably the only policy by which this dependence and sympathy can be effectually secured. . . .

[It has been objected that] the House of Representatives is not sufficiently numerous for the reception of all the different classes of citizens in order to combine the interests and feelings of every part of the community, and to produce a true sympathy between the representative body and its constituents. . . .

The idea of an actual representation of all classes of the people by persons of each class is altogether visionary. Unless it were expressly provided in the Constitution that each different occupation should send one or more members, the thing would never take place in practice. Mechanics and manufacturers will always be inclined, with few exceptions, to give their votes to merchants in preference to persons of their own professions or trades. Those discerning citizens are well aware that the mechanic and manufacturing arts furnish the materials of mercantile enterprise and industry. Many of them, indeed, are immediately connected with the operations of commerce. They know that the merchant is their natural patron and friend; and they are aware

From Federalists 35, 52, 55, 57, 62, and 63, in *The Federalist.*

that however great the confidence they may justly feel in their own good sense, their interests can be more effectually promoted by the merchant than by themselves. They are sensible that their habits in life have not been such as to give them those acquired endowments, without which in a deliberative assembly the greatest natural abilities are for the most part useless; and that the influence and weight and superior acquirements of the merchants render them more equal to a contest with any spirit which might happen to infuse itself into the public councils, unfriendly to the manufacturing and trading interests. These considerations and many others that might be mentioned prove, and experience confirms it, that artisans and manufacturers will commonly be disposed to bestow their votes upon merchants and those whom they recommend. We must therefore consider merchants as the natural representatives of all these classes of the community.

With regard to the learned professions, little need be observed; they truly form no distinct interest in society, and according to their situation and talents, will be indiscriminately the objects of the confidence and choice of each other and of other parts of the community.

Nothing remains but the landed interest; and this in a political view, and particularly in relation to taxes, I take to be perfectly united from the wealthiest landlord to the poorest tenant. No tax can be laid on land which will not affect the proprietor of millions of acres as well as the proprietor of a single acre. Every landholder will therefore have a common interest to keep the taxes on land as low as possible; and common interest may always be reckoned upon as the surest bond of sympathy. But if we even could suppose a distinction of interest between the opulent landholder and the middling farmer, what reason is there to conclude that the first would stand a better chance of being deputed to the national legislature than the last?. . .

It is said to be necessary that all classes of citizens should have some of their own number in the representative body in order that their feelings and interests may be the better understood and attended to. But we have seen that this will never happen under any arrangement that leaves the votes of the people free. Where this is the case, the representative body, with too few exceptions to have any influence on the spirit of the government, will be composed of landholders, merchants, and men of the learned professions. But where is the danger that the interests and feelings of the different classes of citizens will not be understood or attended to by these three descriptions of men? Will not the landholder know and feel whatever will promote or injure the interest of landed property? And will he not, from his own interest in that species of property, be sufficiently prone to resist every attempt to prejudice or encumber it? Will not the merchant understand and be disposed to cultivate, as far as may be proper, the interests of the mechanic and manufacturing arts to which his commerce is so nearly allied? Will not the man of the learned profession, who will feel a neutrality to the rivalships between the different branches of industry, be likely to prove an impartial arbiter between them, ready to promote either, so far as it shall appear to him conducive to the general interests of the society?. . .

[Furthermore,] a certain number [of members of the House] at least seems to be necessary to secure the benefits of free consultation and discussion, and to guard against too easy a combination for improper purposes; as, on the other hand, the number ought at most to be kept within a certain limit, in order to avoid the confusion and intemperance of a multitude. In all very numerous assemblies, of whatever character composed, passion never fails to wrest the sceptre from reason. . . .

The number of which this branch of the legislature is to consist, at the outset of the government, will be sixty-five. Within three years a census is to be taken, when the number may be augmented to one for every thirty thousand inhabitants; and within every successive period of ten years the census is to be renewed, and augmentations may continue to be made under the above limitation. It will not be thought an extravagant conjecture that the first census will, at the rate of one for every thirty thousand, raise the number of representatives to at least one hundred. . . . At the expiration of twenty-five years, according to the computed rate of increase, the number of representatives will amount to two hundred; and of fifty years, to four hundred. This is a number which, I presume, will put an end to all fears arising from the smallness of the body. . . .

[Moreover, the members of the House] will enter into the public service under circumstances which cannot fail to produce a temporary affection at least to their constituents. . . .

[T]hose ties which bind the representative to his constituents are strengthened by motives of a more selfish nature. His pride and vanity attach him to a form of government which favors his pretensions and gives him a share in its honors and distinctions. . . .

All these securities, however, would be found very insufficient without the restraint of frequent elections. Hence . . . the House of Representatives is so constituted as to support in the members an habitual recollection of their dependence on the people. Before the sentiments impressed on their minds by the mode of their elevation can be effaced by the exercise of power, they will be compelled to anticipate the moment when their power is to cease, when their exercise of it is to be reviewed, and when they must descend to the level from which they were raised; there forever to remain unless a faithful discharge of their trust shall have established their title to a renewal of it. . . .

Such will be the relation between the House of Representatives and their constituents. Duty, gratitude, interest, ambition itself, are the chords by which they will be bound to fidelity and sympathy with the great mass of the people. . . .

I must be permitted to add [one observation on the constitution of the House of Representatives.] It is, that in all legislative assemblies the greater the number composing them may be, the fewer will be the men who will in fact direct their proceedings. In the first place, the more numerous an assembly may be, of whatever characters composed, the greater is known to be the ascendancy of passion over reason. In the next place, the larger the number, the greater will be the proportion of members of limited information and of weak capacities. Now, it is precisely on characters of this description that the eloquence and address of the few are known to act with all their force. In the ancient republics, where the whole body of the people assembled in person, a single orator, or an artful statesman, was generally seen to rule with as complete a sway as if a sceptre had been placed in his single hand. On the same principle, the more multitudinous a representative assembly may be rendered, the more it will partake of the infirmities incident to collective meetings of the people. Ignorance will be the dupe of cunning, and passion the slave of sophistry and declamation. The people can never err more than in supposing that by multiplying their representatives beyond a certain limit, they strengthen the barrier against the government of a few. Experience will forever admonish them that, on the contrary, *after securing a sufficient number for the purposes of safety, of local information, and of diffusive sympathy with the whole society*, they will counteract their own views by every addition to their representatives. The countenance of the government may become more democratic, but the soul that animates it will be more oligarchic. The machine will be enlarged, but the fewer, and often the more secret, will be the springs by which its motions are directed. . . .

I. The qualifications proposed for senators, as distinguished from those of representatives, consist in a more advanced age and a longer period of citizenship. A senator must be thirty years of age at least; as a representative must be twenty-five. And the former must have been a citizen nine years; as seven years are required for the latter. The propriety of these distinctions is explained by the nature of the senatorial trust, which, requiring greater extent of information and stability of character, requires at the same time that the senator should have reached a period of life most likely to supply these advantages; and which, participating immediately in transactions with foreign nations, ought to be exercised by none who are not thoroughly weaned from the prepossessions and habits incident to foreign birth and education. The term of nine years appears to be a prudent mediocrity between a total exclusion of adopted citizens, whose merits and talents may claim a share in the public confidence, and an indiscriminate and hasty admission of them, which might create a channel for foreign influence on the national councils.

II. It is equally unnecessary to dilate on the appointment of senators by the State legislatures. Among the various modes which might have been devised for constituting this branch of the government, that which has been proposed by the convention is probably the most congenial with the public opinion. It is recommended by the double advantage of favoring a select appointment, and of giving to the State governments such an agency in the formation of the federal government as must secure the authority of the former, and may form a convenient link between the two systems.

III. The equality of representation in the Senate is another point, which, being evidently the result of compromise between the opposite pretensions of the large and the small States, does not call for much discussion. If indeed it be right, that among a people thoroughly incorporated into one nation, every district ought to have a *proportional* share in the government, and that among independent and sovereign States, bound together by a simple league, the parties, however unequal in size, ought to have an equal share in the common councils, it does not appear to be without some reason that in a compound republic, partaking both of the national and federal character, the government ought to be founded on a mixture of the principles of proportional and equal representation. . . .

IV. The number of senators, and the duration of their appointment, come next to be considered. In order to form an accurate judgment on both these points, it will be proper to inquire into the purposes which are to be answered by a senate; and in order to ascertain these, it will be necessary to review the inconveniences which a republic must suffer from the want of such an institution.

First. It is a misfortune incident to republican government, though in a less degree than to other governments, that those who administer it may forget their obligations to their constituents, and prove unfaithful to their important trust. In this point of view, a senate, as a second branch of the legislative assembly, distinct from, and dividing the power with, a first, must be in all cases a salutary check on the government. It doubles the security to the people, by requiring the concurrence of two distinct bodies in schemes of usurpation or perfidy, where the ambition or corruption of one would otherwise be sufficient. . . . I will barely remark, that as the improbability of sinister combinations will be in proportion to the dissimilarity in the genius of the two bodies, it must be politic to distinguish them from each other by every circumstance which will consist with a due harmony in all proper measures, and with the genuine principles of republican government.

Secondly. The necessity of a senate is not less indicated by the propensity of all single and numerous assemblies to yield to the impulse of sudden and violent passions, and to be seduced by factious leaders into intemperate and pernicious resolutions. . . . All that need be remarked is, that a body which is to correct this infirmity ought itself to be free from it, and consequently ought to be less numerous. It ought, moreover, to possess great firmness, and consequently ought to hold its authority by a tenure of considerable duration.

Thirdly. Another defect to be supplied by a senate lies in a want of due acquaintance with the objects and principles of legislation. It is not possible that an assembly of men called for the most part from pursuits of a private nature, continued in appointment for a short time, and led by no permanent motive to devote the intervals of public occupation to a study of the laws, the affairs, and the comprehensive interests of their country, should, if left wholly to themselves, escape a variety of important errors in the exercise of their legislative trust. It may be affirmed, on the best grounds, that no small share of the present embarrassments of America is to be charged on the blunders of our governments; and that these have proceeded from the heads rather than the hearts of most of the authors of them. What indeed are all the repealing, explaining, and amending laws, which fill and disgrace our voluminous codes, but so many monuments of deficient wisdom; so many impeachments exhibited by each succeeding against each preceding session; so many admonitions to the people, of the value of those aids which may be expected from a well-constituted senate?. . .

Fourthly. The mutability in the public councils arising from a rapid succession of new members, however qualified they may be, points out, in the strongest manner, the necessity of some stable institution in the government. Every new election in the States is found to change one half of the representatives. From this change of men must proceed a change of opinions; and from a change of opinions, a change of measures. But a continual change even of good measures is inconsistent with every rule of prudence and every prospect of success. . . .

In the first place, it forfeits the respect and confidence of other nations, and all the advantages connected with national character. An individual who is observed to be inconstant to his plans, or perhaps to carry on his affairs without any plan at all, is marked at once, by all prudent people, as a speedy victim to his own unsteadiness and folly. His more friendly neighbors may pity him, but all will decline to connect their fortunes with his; and not a few will seize the opportunity of making their fortunes out of his. . . .

The internal effects of a mutable policy are still more calamitous. It poisons the blessing of liberty itself. It will be of little avail to the people, that the laws are made by men of their own choice, if the laws be so voluminous that they cannot be read, or so incoherent that they cannot be understood; if they be repealed or revised before they are promulgated, or undergo such incessant changes that no man, who knows what the law is to-day, can guess what it will be to-morrow. Law is defined to be a rule of action; but how can that be a rule, which is little known, and less fixed?

Another effect of public instability is the unreasonable advantage it gives to the sagacious, the enterprising, and the moneyed few over the industrious and uninformed mass of the people. Every new regulation concerning commerce or revenue, or in any manner affecting the value of the different species of property, presents a new harvest to those who watch the change, and can trace its consequences; a harvest, reared not by themselves, but by the toils and cares of the great body of their fellow-citizens. . . .

In another point of view, great injury results from an unstable government. The want of confidence in the public councils damps every useful undertaking, the success and profit of which may depend on a continuance of existing arrangements. What prudent merchant will hazard his fortunes in any new branch of commerce when he knows not but that his plans may be rendered unlawful before they can be executed? What farmer or manufacturer will lay himself out for the encouragement given to any particular cultivation or establishment, when he can have no assurance that his preparatory labors and advances will not render him a victim to an inconstant government? In a word, no great improvement or laudable enterprise can go forward which requires the auspices of a steady system of national policy.

But the most deplorable effect of all is that diminution of attachment and reverence which steals into the hearts of the people, towards a political system which betrays so many marks of infirmity, and disappoints so many of their flattering hopes. No government, any more than an individual, will long be respected without being truly respectable; nor be truly respectable, without possessing a certain portion of order and stability.

[A fifth] desideratum, illustrating the utility of a senate, is the want of a due sense of national character. Without a select and stable member of the government, the esteem of foreign powers will not only be forfeited by an unenlightened and variable policy, proceeding from the causes already mentioned, but the national councils will not possess that sensibility to the opinion of the world, which is perhaps not less necessary in order to merit, than it is to obtain, its respect and confidence.

An attention to the judgment of other nations is important to every government for two reasons: the one is, that, independently of the merits of any particular plan or measure, it is desirable, on various accounts, that it should appear to other nations as the offspring of a wise and honorable policy; the second is, that in doubtful cases, particularly where the national councils may be warped by some strong passion or momentary interest, the presumed or known opinion of the impartial world may be the best guide that can be followed. What has not America lost by her want of character with foreign nations; and how many errors and follies would she not have avoided, if the justice and propriety of her measures had, in every instance, been previously tried by the light in which they would probably appear to the unbiased part of mankind?

Yet however requisite a sense of national character may be, it is evident that it can never be sufficiently possessed by a numerous and changeable body. It can only be found in a number so small that a sensible degree of the praise and blame of public measures may be the portion of each individual; or in an assembly so durably invested with public trust, that the pride and consequence of its members may be sensibly incorporated with the reputation and prosperity of the community. . . .

I add, as a *sixth* defect, the want, in some important cases, of a due responsibility in the government to the people, arising from that frequency of elections which in other cases produces this responsibility. This remark will, perhaps, appear not only new, but paradoxical. . . .

Responsibility, in order to be reasonable, must be limited to objects within the power of the responsible party, and in order to be effectual, must relate to operations of that power, of which a ready and proper judgment can be formed by the constituents. The objects of government may be divided into two general classes: the one depending on measures which have singly an immediate and sensible operation; the other depending on a succession of well-chosen and well-connected measures, which have a gradual and perhaps unobserved operation.

The importance of the latter description to the collective and permanent welfare of every country, needs no explanation. And yet it is evident that an assembly elected for so short a term as to be unable to provide more than one or two links in a chain of measures, on which the general welfare may essentially depend, ought not to be answerable for the final result, any more than a steward or tenant, engaged for one year, could be justly made to answer for places or improvements which could not be accomplished in less than half a dozen years. Nor is it possible for the people to estimate the *share* of influence which their annual assemblies may respectively have on events resulting from the mixed transactions of several years. It is sufficiently difficult to preserve a personal responsibility in the members of a *numerous* body, for such acts of the body as have an immediate, detached, and palpable operation on its constituents.

The proper remedy for this defect must be an additional body in the legislative department, which, having sufficient permanency to provide for such objects as require a continued attention, and a train of measures, may be justly and effectually answerable for the attainment of those objects.

Thus far I have considered the circumstances which point out the necessity of a well-constructed Senate only as they relate to the representatives of the people. To a people as little blinded by prejudice or corrupted by flattery as those whom I address, I shall not scruple to add, that such an institution may be sometimes necessary as a defence to the people against their own temporary errors and delusions. As the cool and deliberate sense of the community ought, in all governments, and actually will in all free governments ultimately prevail over the views of its rulers; so there are particular moments in public affairs when the people, stimulated by some irregular passion, or some illicit advantage, or misled by the artful misrepresentations of interested men, may call for measures which they themselves will afterwards be the most ready to lament and condemn. In these critical moments, how salutary will be the interference of some temperate and respectable body of citizens, in order to check the misguided career, and to suspend the blow meditated by the people against themselves, until reason, justice, and truth can regain their authority over the public mind?. . .

31

Woodrow Wilson

The Need for Cabinet Government in the United States (1879, 1908, 1889)

. . . At its highest development, *representative* government is that form which best enables a free people to govern themselves. The main object of a representative assembly, therefore, should be the discussion of public business. They should legislate as if in the presence of the whole country, because they come under the closest scrutiny and fullest criticism of all the representatives of the country speaking in open and free debate. . . .

Nothing can be more obvious than the fact that the very life of free, popular institutions is dependent upon their breathing the bracing air of thorough, exhaustive, and open discussions, or that select Congressional committees, whose proceedings must from their very nature be secret, are, as means of legislation, dangerous and unwholesome. . . .

Our Government is practically carried on by irresponsible committees. Too few Americans take the trouble to inform themselves as to the methods

From Wilson, "Cabinet Government in the United States," *International Review*, VII (August 1879); *Constitutional Government in the United States*, Columbia University Press, 1908; "An Address on the Nature of Democracy," in *The Papers of Woodrow Wilson*, ed. by Arthur S. Link, Vol. 6, Copyright © 1969 by Princeton University Press. Reprinted by permission of Princeton University Press.

of Congressional management; and, as a consequence, not many have perceived that almost *absolute* power has fallen into the hands of men whose irresponsibility prevents the regulation of their conduct by the people from whom they derive their authority. . . .

Unless the rules of the House be suspended by a special two-thirds vote, every bill introduced must be referred, without debate, to the proper Standing Committee, with whom rests the privilege of embodying it, or any part of it, in their reports, or of rejecting it altogether. The House very seldom takes any direct action upon any measures introduced by individual members; its votes and discussions are almost entirely confined to committee reports and committee dictation. The whole attitude of business depends upon forty-seven Standing Committees. . . .

This is certainly a phase of representative government peculiar to ourselves. And yet its development was most natural and apparently necessary. It is hardly possible for a body of several hundred men, without official or authoritative leaders, to determine upon any line of action without interminable wrangling and delays injurious to the interests under their care. Left to their own resources, they would be as helpless as any other mass meeting. Without leaders having authority to guide their deliberations and give a definite direction to the movement of legislation; and, moreover, with none of that sense of responsibility which constantly rests upon those whose duty it is to work out to a successful issue the policies which they themselves originate, yet with full power to dictate policies which others must carry into execution,—a recognition of the need of some sort of leadership, and of a division of labor, led to the formation of these Standing Committees, to which are intrusted the shaping of the national policy in the several departments of administration, as well as the prerogatives of the initiative in legislation and leadership in debate. When theoretically viewed, this is an ingenious and apparently harmless device, but one which, in practice, subverts that most fundamental of all the principles of a free State,—the right of the people to a potential voice in their own government. Great measures of legislation are discussed and determined, not conspicuously in public session of the people's representatives, but in the unapproachable privacy of committee rooms.

But what less imperfect means of representative government can we find without stepping beyond the bounds of a true republicanism?. . .

What . . . is Cabinet government? What is the change proposed? Simply to give to the heads of the Executive departments—the members of the Cabinet—seats in Congress, with the privilege of the initiative in legislation and some part of the unbounded privileges now commanded by the Standing Committees. But the advocates of such a change—and they are now not a few—deceive themselves when they maintain that it would not necessarily involve the principle of ministerial responsibility,—that is, the resignation of the Cabinet upon the defeat of any important part of their plans. For, if Cabinet officers sit in Congress as official representatives of the Executive, this principle of responsibility must of necessity come sooner or later to be recognized. Experience would soon demonstrate the practical impossibility of their holding their seats, and continuing to represent the Administration, after they had found themselves unable to gain the consent of a majority to their policy. Their functions would be peculiar. They would constitute a link between the legislative and executive branches of the general Government, and, as representatives of the Executive, must hold the right of the initiative in legislation. Otherwise their position would be an anomalous one, indeed. There would be little danger and evident propriety in extending to them the first right of introducing measures relative to the administration of the several departments; and they could possess such a right without denying the fullest privileges to other members. But, whether granted this initiative or not, the head of each department would undoubtedly find it necessary to take a decided and open stand for or against every measure bearing upon the affairs of his department, by whomsoever introduced. No highspirited man would long remain in an office in the business of which he was not permitted to pursue a policy which tallied with his own principles and convictions. If defeated by both Houses, he would naturally resign; and not many years would pass before resignation upon defeat would have become an established precedent,—and resignation upon defeat is the essence of responsible government. . . .

But, to give to the President the right to choose whomsoever he pleases as his constitutional advisers, after having constituted Cabinet officers *ex officio* members of Congress, would be to empower him to appoint a limited number of representatives, and would thus be plainly at variance with republican principles. The highest order of responsible government could, then, be established in the United States only by laying upon the President the necessity of selecting his Cabinet from among the number of representatives already chosen by the people. . . .

Under the conditions of Cabinet government . . . full and free debates are sure to take place. For what are these conditions? According as their policy stands or falls, the ministers themselves stand or fall; to the party which supports them each discussion involves a trial of strength with their opponents; upon it depends the amount of their success as a party; while to the opposition the triumph of ministerial plans means still further exclusion from office; their overthrow, accession to power. To each member of the assembly every debate offers an opportunity for placing himself, by able argument, in a position to command a place in any future Cabinet that may be formed from the ranks of his own party; each speech goes to the building up (or the tearing down) of his political fortunes. Plainly, ministers must found their policies, an opposition must found its attacks, upon well-considered principles; for in this open sifting of debate, when every feature of every measure, even to the motives which prompted it, is the subject of out-spoken discussion and keen scrutiny, no chicanery, no party craft, no questionable principles can long hide themselves. . . .

In the severe, distinct, and sharp enunciation of underlying principles, the unsparing examination and telling criticism of opposite positions, the careful, painstaking unravelling of all the issues involved, which are incident to the free discussion of questions of public policy, we see the best, the only effective, means of educating public opinion. . . .

Only a single glance is necessary to discover how utterly Committee government must fail to give effect to public opinion. In the first place, the exclusion of debate prevents the intelligent formation of opinion on the part of the nation at large; in the second place, public opinion, when once formed, finds it impossible to exercise any immediate control over the action of its representatives. There is no one in Congress to speak for the nation. Congress is a conglomeration of inharmonious elements; a collection of men representing each his neighborhood, each his local interest; an alarmingly large proportion of its legislation is "special;" all of it is at best only a limping compromise between the conflicting interests of the innumerable localities represented. There is no guiding or harmonizing power. Are the people in favor of a particular policy,—what means have they of forcing it upon the sovereign legislature at Washington? None but the most imperfect. If they return representatives who favor it (and this is the most they can do), these representatives being under no directing power will find a mutual agreement impracticable among so many, and will finally settle upon some policy which satisfies nobody, removes no difficulty, and makes little definite or valuable provision for the future. They must, indeed, be content with whatever measure the appropriate committee chances to introduce. Responsible ministries, on the other hand, form the policy of their parties; the strength of their party is at their command; the course of legislation turns upon the acceptance or rejection by the Houses of definite and consistent plans upon which they determine. . . . The question would then no longer be, What representatives shall we choose to represent our chances in this haphazard game of legislation? but, What plans of national administration shall we sanction? Would not party programmes mean something then? . . .

But, above and beyond all this, a responsible Cabinet constitutes a link between the executive and legislative departments of the Government which experience declares in the clearest tones to be absolutely necessary in a well-regulated, well-proportioned body politic. None can so well judge of the perfections or imperfections of a law as those who have to administer it. . . .

When we come to speak of the probable influence of responsible Cabinet government upon the development of statesmanship and the renewal of the now perishing growth of statesmanlike qualities, we come upon a vital interest of the whole question. Will it bring with it worthy successors of Hamilton and Webster? Will it replace a leadership of trickery and cunning device by one of ability and moral strength? . . .

Crises give birth and a new growth to statesmanship because they are peculiarly periods of action, in which talents find the widest and the freest scope. They are periods not only of action, but also of unusual opportunity for gaining leadership and a controlling and guiding influence. It is opportunity for transcendent influence, therefore, which calls into active public life a nation's greater minds,—minds which might otherwise remain absorbed in the smaller affairs of private life. And we thus come upon the principle,—a principle which will appear the more incontrovertible the more it is looked into and tested,—that governmental forms will call to the work of administration able minds and strong hearts constantly or infrequently, according as they do or do not afford them at all times an opportunity of gaining and retaining a commanding authority and an undisputed leadership in the nation's councils. Now it certainly needs no argument to prove that government by supreme committees, whose members are appointed at the caprice of an irresponsible party chief, by seniority, because of reputation gained in entirely different fields, or because of partisan shrewdness, is not favorable to a full and strong development of statesmanship. The cardinal feature of Cabinet government, on the other hand, is responsible leadership,—the leadership and authority of a small body of men who have won the foremost places in their party by a display of administrative talents, by evidence of high ability upon the floor of Congress in the stormy play of debate. . . .

It is said . . . that [Cabinet Government] would render the President a mere figure-head, with none of that stability of official tenure, or that traditional dignity, which are necessary to such figure-heads. Would the President's power be curtailed, then, if his Cabinet ministers simply took the place of the Standing Committees? Would it not rather be enlarged? He would then be in fact, and not merely in name, the head of the Government. . . .

The apparently necessary existence of a partisan Executive presents itself to many as a fatal objection to the establishment of the forms of responsible Cabinet government in this country. The President must continue to represent a political party, and must continue to be anxious to surround himself with Cabinet officers who shall always substantially agree with him on all political questions. . . . [However, i]t is not hard to believe that most presidents would find no greater inconvenience, experience no greater unpleasantness, in being at the head of a Cabinet composed of political opponents than in presiding, as they must now occasionally do, over a Cabinet of political friends who are compelled to act in all matters of importance according to the dictation of Standing Committees which are ruled by the opposite party. In the former case, the President may, by the exercise of whatever personal influence he possesses, affect the action of the Cabinet, and, through them, the action of the Houses; in the latter he is absolutely helpless. . . .

But against such a responsible system, the alarm-bell of *centralization* is again sounded, and all those who dread seeing too much authority, too complete control, placed within the reach of the central Government sternly set their faces against any such change. They deceive themselves. There could be no more despotic authority wielded under the forms of free government than our national Congress now exercises. It is a despotism which uses its power with all the caprice, all the scorn for settled policy, all the wild unrestraint which mark the methods of other tyrants as hateful to freedom.

Few of us are ready to suggest a remedy for the evils all deplore. We hope that our system is self-adjusting, and will not need our corrective interference. This is a vain hope! It is no small part of wisdom to know how long an evil ought to be tolerated, to see when the time has come for the people, from whom springs all authority, to speak its doom or prescribe its remedy. . . .

. . . It was . . . [the] theory of checks and balances, which I have called the Newtonian theory of government, that prevailed in the convention which framed the Constitution of the United States,—which prevailed over the very different theory of Hamilton, that government was not a thing which you could afford to tie up in a nice poise, as if it were to be held at an inactive equilibrium, but a thing which must every day act with straightforward and unquestionable power, with definite purpose and consistent force, choosing its policies and making good its authority, like a single organism,—the theory which would have seemed to Darwin the theory of nature itself, the nature of men as well as the nature of animal organisms. Dominated by the immediate forces and aspirations of their own day, ruled in thought and action by the great contest in which they had found themselves engaged, to hold the royal power off from arbitrary interference with their interests and their liberties, they allowed themselves to become more interested in providing checks to government than in supplying it with energy and securing to it the necessary certainty and consistency of action. . . .

The most serious success of the convention in applying Whig theory to the government they were constructing was the complete separation of Congress and the executive which they effected. The English Whigs fought for long to oust the Crown from the power and intimate influence it had had in the House of Commons through its control of members' seats and its corrupting power of patronage: they succeeded only in placing the leaders of the Commons itself in executive authority in the stead of the Crown. The real executive authority of the English government is vested in the ministers of the day, who are in effect a committee of the House of Commons, and legislature and executive work together under a common party organization. The one is only an agency of the other: the ministers act for their party in the House. The separation of parliament and the Crown which the reformers of the early part of the last century finally succeeded in effecting was not, in fact, a separation of the legislature from the executive, but only a separation of the real from the nominal executive. . . . But our constitution-makers did their work during the earlier part of the struggle, when it seemed merely a contest to offset the authority of the king with effectual checks, and long before it had become evident that the outcome would be the substitution of an executive which represented the popular house for one which did not. . . .

[The results of] this absolute application of early Whig theory to the practice of our government . . . has been that, so far as the government itself is concerned, there is but one national voice in the country, and that is the voice of the President. His isolation has quite unexpectedly been his exaltation. The House represents localities, is made up of individuals whose interest is the interest of separate and scattered constituencies, who are drawn together, indeed, under a master, the Speaker, but who are controlled by no national force except that of their party, a force outside the government rather than within it. The Senate represents in its turn regions and interests distinguished by many conflicting and contrasted purposes, united only by exterior party organization and a party spirit not generated within the chamber itself. Only the President represents the country as a whole, and the President himself is cooperatively bound to the houses only by the machinery and discipline of party, not as a person and functionary, but as a member of an outside organization which exists quite independently of the executive and legislature.

It is extraordinary the influence the early Whig theory of political dynamics has had amongst us and the far-reaching consequences which have ensued from it. It is far from being a democratic theory. It is, on the contrary, a theory whose avowed object, at any rate as applied in America, was to keep government at a sort of mechanical equipoise by means of a standing amicable contest among its several organic parts, each of which it seeks to make representative of a special interest in the nation. It is particularly intended to prevent the will of the people as a whole from having at any moment an unobstructed sweep and ascendency. And yet in every step we have taken with the intention of making our governments more democratic, we have punctiliously kept to Whig mechanics. . . .

[Our government] can be solidified and drawn to system only by the external authority of party, an organization outside the government and independent of it. Not being drawn together by any system provided in our constitutions, being laid apart, on the contrary, in a sort of jealous dispersion and analysis by Whig theory enacted into law, it has been necessary to keep the several parts of the government in some kind of workable combination by outside pressure, by the closely knit imperative discipline of party, a body that has no constitutional cleavages and is free to tie itself into legislative and executive functions alike by its systematic control of the *personnel* of all branches of the government. . . .

But with us, who affect never to allow party majorities to get in complete control of governmental machinery if we can prevent it by constitutional obstacles, party programs are made up outside legislative chambers, by conventions constituted under the direction of independent politicians,—politicians, I mean, who are, at any rate in respect of that function, independent of the responsibilities of office and of public action; and these independent conventions, not charged with the responsibility of carrying out their programs, actually outline the policy of administrations and dictate the action of Congress, the irresponsible dictating to the responsible, and so, it may be, destroying the very responsibility itself. . . .

The satisfactions of power must be very great to attract so many men of unusual gifts to attempt the hazardous and little honored business of party management. We have made it necessary that we should have "bosses" and that they and their lieutenants should assign offices by appointment, but it is a very difficult and precarious business which they undertake. . . . [T]he people look askance at [this business] and often with a sudden disgust turn upon it. . . . [These occasional outbursts of discontent] come when the people happen to realize that under existing party machinery they have virtually no control at all over nominations for office, and that, having no real control over the choice of candidates, they are cut off from exercising real representative self-government,—that they have been solemnly taking part in a farce. . . .

[Y]et at the best the control which party exercises over government is uncertain. There can be, whether for the voter or for the managing politician himself, little more than a presumption that what party managers propose and promise will be done, for the separation of authority between the several organs of government itself still stands in the way. . . .

The principle of change, if change there is to be, should spring out of this question: Have we had enough of the literal translation of Whig theory into practice, into constitutions? Are we ready to make our legislatures and our executives our real bodies politic, instead of our parties? If we are, we must think less of checks and balances and more of coordinated power, less of separation of functions and more of the synthesis of action. If we are, we must decrease the number and complexity of the things the voter is called upon to do; concentrate his attention upon a few men whom he can make responsible, a few objects upon which he can easily center his purpose; make parties his instruments and not his masters by an utter simplification of the things he is expected to look to. . . .

. . . [F]or us who stand in the dusty, matter-of-fact world of to-day there is even a touch of pathos in recollections of the ardour for democratic liberty that filled the air of Europe and America a century ago with such quickening influences. We may even catch ourselves regretting that the inoculations of experience have closed our systems against the infections of hopeful revolution. . . .

It is common to say, in explanation of our regret that that dawn and youth of democracy's day is past; that our principles are cooler now and more circumspect, with the coolness and circumspection of advanced years. It seems to some that as our sinews have hardened our enthusiasms have become tamer and more decorous: that as experience has grown idealism has declined.

But to speak thus is to speak with old self-deception as to the character of our politics. If we are suffering disappointment, it is the disappointment of an awakening: we were dreaming. For we never had any business harkening to Rousseau or consorting with Europe in revolutionary sentiment. Our Government, founded one hundred years ago, was no type of an experiment in advanced democracy, as we allowed Europe and even ourselves to suppose; it was simply an adaptation of English constitutional government. If we suffered Europe to study our institutions as instances in point touching experimentation in politics *she was the more deceived*. If we began the *first* century of our national existence under a similar impression ourselves, there is the greater reason why we should start out upon a *new* century of national life with accurate conceptions about our place in history. It is my modest purpose tonight to make such contribution as I may to this end. I shall, therefore, ask you to note:

(1) That there are certain influences astir in this century which make for democracy the world over, and that these influences owe their origin in part to the radical thought of the last century; but that it was not such forces that made us democratic, nor are we responsible for them.

(2) That, so far from owing our governments to these general influences, we began, not by carrying out any theory, but by simply carrying out a history, inventing nothing, only establishing a specialized species of English government. That we founded, not Democracy, but Constitutional government, in America.

(3) That the government which we set up thus in a quite normal manner has nevertheless *changed greatly* under our hands by reason both of growth and of the operation of the general democratic forces,—the European or rather world-wide democratic forces, of which I have spoken; and

(4) That the very *size* to which our governmental organism has attained, and more particularly this new connection of its character and destiny with the character and destiny of the common democratic forces of the age of steam and electricity have created new *problems of organization* which it behooves us to meet. . . .

First, then, for the forces which are bringing in democratic temper and method the world over. . . . They are freedom of thought and the diffusion of enlightenment among the people. Steam and electricity have cooperated with systematic popular education to accomplish this diffusion. The progress of popular education and the progress of democracy have been inseparable. The publication of their great *Encyclopedia* by Diderot and his associates in France in the last century was the sure sign of the change that was setting in. Learning was turning its face away from the studious few to the curious many. The intellectual movement of the modern time was emerging from the narrow courses of scholastic thought and beginning to *spread itself abroad* over the extended, if shallow, levels of the common mind. . . .

Organized popular education is, after all, however, only one of the quickening influences which have been producing the general enlightenment which is everywhere becoming the promise of general liberty: or, rather, it is only part of a great whole vastly larger than itself. Schools are but separated seedbeds in which only the staple thoughts of the steady and stay-at-home people are prepared and nursed. Not much of the world, after all, goes to school in the school-house. But through the mighty influences of commerce and the press *the world itself has become a school*. The air is alive with the multitudinous voices of information. . . .

Looked at in the large, the newspaper press is a type of democracy, bringing all men without distinction under comment made by any man without distinction; every topic reduced to a common standard of news; everything noted and argued about by everybody. . . .

In the newspapers, it is true, there is but little concerted between the writers; little but piece-meal opinion is created by their comment and argument; there is no common voice amidst their counsellings. But the *aggregate* voice thunders with tremendous volume; and that aggregate voice is 'public opinion.' Popular education and cheap printing and travel vastly thicken the ranks of thinkers everywhere that their influence is felt, and by rousing the multitude to take *knowledge* of the affairs of government directly prepare the time when the multitude will, so far as possible, take *charge* of the affairs of government,—the time when, to repeat Carlyle's phrase, democracy will become palpably extant.

But, mighty as such forces are,—democratic as they are,—no one can fail to see that they are inadequate to *produce of themselves* such a government as ours. There is little in them of *constructive* efficacy. They could not of themselves build any government at all. They are critical, analytical, questioning, quizzing forces;—but not architectural, not powers that devise and build. The influences of popular education, of the press, of travel, of commerce, of the innumerable agencies which nowadays send knowledge and thought in quick pulsations through every part and member of society, do not necessarily mold men for effective endeavour. They may only confuse and paralyze the mind with their myriad stinging lashes of excitement. They may only strengthen the impression that 'the world's a stage,' and that no one need do more than sit and look on through his ready glass, the newspaper. They overwhelm one with impressions, but do they give stalwartness to his manhood; do they make his hand any steadier on the plow, or his purpose any clearer with reference to the duties of the moment? They stream light about him, it may be, but do they clear his vision? Is he better able to see because they give him countless things to look at? Is he better able to judge because they fill him with a delusive sense of knowing everything—? Activity of mind is not necessarily strength of mind. It may manifest itself in mere dumb show; it may run into jigs as well as into strenuous work at noble tasks. A man's farm does not yield its fruit the more abundantly in its season because he reads the world's news in the papers. A merchant's shipments do not multiply because he studies history. Banking is none the less hazardous to the banker's capital or taxing to his powers because the best writing of the best essayists is to be bought cheap.

Having thus expanded my first point by exhibiting the general forces of that democracy which we recognize as belonging to the age and to the world at large, rather than exclusively or even characteristically to ourselves, I now ask you to turn to view by contrast our origins in politics.

How different were the forces back of us! Nothing establishes the republican state save trained capacity for self-government, practical aptitude for public affairs, habitual soberness and temperateness of united action. When we look back to the moderate sagacity and steadfast, self-contained habit in self-government of the men to whom we owe the establishment of our institutions in the United States we are at once made aware that there is no communion between their democracy and the radical thought and restless spirit called by that name in Europe. . . . Democracy in America and in the English colonies, has had, almost from the first, a truly organic growth. There was nothing revolutionary in its movements: it had not to overthrow other polities; it had only to organize itself. . . .

Our democracy, plainly, was not a body of doctrine: it was a stage of development. Our democratic state was not a piece of developed theory, but a piece of developed habit. It was not created by mere aspirations or by new faith; it was built up by slow custom. . . .

Governments such as ours are founded upon discussion and government by discussion comes as late in political as scientific thought in intellectual development. It is a habit of state life created by long-established circumstance, and possible for a nation only in the adult age of its political life. The people which successfully maintains it must have gone through a period of political training which shall have prepared it by gradual steps of acquired privilege for assuming the entire control of its affairs. Long and slowly widening experience in local self-direction must have prepared them for national self-direction. . . .

So much for my second main point, as to the origins of our institutions in constitutional precedents rather than in democratic precepts. It is my object to consider, in the third place, the changes which have been or may be wrought in our institutions by means of the influences of the age, of our own growth as a political organism, and of our adulterated populations. . . .

[T]he forces peculiar to the new civilization of our day, and not only these but also the restless forces of European democratic thought and anarchic turbulence brought to us in such alarming masses by immigration, have deeply affected and may deeply modify the forms and habits of our politics.

All *vital* governments,—and by vital governments I mean those which have life *in their outlying members*, as well as life in their heads,—all systems in which self-government indeed *lives* and retains its self-possession must be governments *by neighbours*, by peoples homogeneous . . . characterized within by the existence of easy neighborly knowledge of each other among their members. Not foreseeing steam and electricity or the diffusions of news and knowledge which we have witnessed, our fathers were right in thinking it impossible for the government which they had founded to spread without strain or break over the whole of the continent. Were not California now as near neighbor to the Atlantic states as Massachusetts once was to New York, national self-government on our present scale would assuredly hardly be possible or conceivable even. Modern science, scarcely less than our pliancy and steadiness in political habit, may be said to have created the United States of to-day. . . .

I wish to give full weight to these great advantages of our big and strenuous and yet familiar way of conducting affairs; but I wish at the same time to make very plain the influences which are pointing towards threatening changes in our politics—changes which threaten loss of organic wholeness and soundness in carrying on an efficient and honest government. The union of strength with bigness depends upon the maintenance of *character*, and it is just the character of the nation which is being most deeply affected and modified by the enormous immigration which year after year pours into the country from Europe: our own temperate blood, schooled to self-possession and to the measured conduct of self-government is receiving a constant infusion and yearly experiencing a partial corruption of foreign blood: our own equable habits have been crossed with the feverish habits of the restless old world. . . .

What was true of our early circumstances is not true of our present. We are not now simply carrying out under normal conditions the principles and habits of English constitutional history. Our tasks of construction are not done: we have, not simply to conduct but also to preserve and freshly adjust our government. Europe has sent her habits to us; and she has sent also her political philosophy,—that philosophy which has never been purged by the cold bath of practical politics. The communion which we did not have at first with her heated and mistaken ambitions, with her radical speculative habit in politics, with her readiness to experiment in forms of government, we may possibly have to suffer now that we are receiving her populations. Not only printing and steam and electricity have gotten hold of us to expand our English civilization, but also those general, and yet to us alien, forces of democracy of which I have spoken; and these are apt to tell disastrously upon our Saxon habits in government. . . .

I am now to speak of the *new problems* which have been prepared for our solution by reason of our growth and of the effects of immigration, and which may require as much political capacity for their proper solution as any that faced the architects of our government.

These problems are chiefly problems of organization and leadership. Were the nation homogeneous, were it composed simply of later generations of the same stock by which our institutions were planted, few adjustments of the old machinery of our politics would, perhaps, be necessary to meet the exigencies of growth. But every added element of variety, particularly every added element of foreign variety, complicates even the simpler questions of politics. The dangers attending that variety which is heterogeneity in so vast an organism as ours are of course the dangers of *disintegration*, nothing less: and it is unwise to think these dangers remote and merely contingent because they are not as yet pressing. We are conscious of oneness as a nation, of vitality, of strength, of progress; but are we often conscious of common thought in the concrete things of national policy? Does not our legislation, rather, wear the features of a vast conglomerate? Are we conscious of any national leadership: are we not, rather, dimly conscious of being pulled in a score of directions by a score of crossing influences and contending forces?

This vast and miscellaneous democracy of ours must be led: its giant faculties must be schooled and directed. Leadership cannot belong to the multitude: masses of men cannot be self-directed. Neither can groups of communities. We speak of the sovereignty of the people, but that sovereignty, we know very well, is of a peculiar sort, quite unlike the sovereignty of a king or of a small easily concerting group of confident men. It is judicial merely, not creative. It passes judgment or gives sanction, but it cannot direct or suggest. It furnishes standards, not policies. Questions of government are infinitely complex questions, and no multitude can of themselves form clear-cut, comprehensive, consistent conclusions touching them. And yet without such conclusions, without single and prompt purposes, government cannot be carried on. Neither legislation nor administration can be done at the ballot-box. The people can only accept the governing act of representatives. But the size of the modern democracy necessitates the exercise of persuasive power by dominant minds in the shaping of popular judgments in a very different way from that in which it was exercised in former times. . . . [All self-governing nations of to-day] are not a single audience within sound of an orator's voice; but a thousand audiences. Their actions do not spring from a single thrill of feeling, but from slow conclusions following upon much talk. The talk must slowly percolate through the whole mass. It cannot be sent through them straight like the pulse which is stirred by the call of a trumpet. A score of platforms in every neighborhood must ring with the insistent voice of controversy; and for a few hundreds who hear what is said by the public speakers, many thousands must read of the matter in the newspapers, discuss it interjectionally at the breakfast table, desultorily in the street-cars, laconically on the streets, dogmatically at dinner. And all this with a certain advantage, of course. Through so many stages of consideration passion cannot possibly hold out. *It gets chilled by over-exposure.* It finds the modern popular state organized for giving and hearing counsel in such a way that those who give it must be careful that it is such counsel as will *wear well,* and those who hear it handle and examine it enough to test its wearing qualities to the utmost.

All this, however, when looked at from another point of view, but illustrates an infinite difficulty of achieving *energy and organization.* There is a certain peril almost of disintegration attending such phenomena.

Everyone now knows familiarly enough how we accomplished the wide aggregations of self-government characteristic of the modern time, how we have articulated governments as vast and yet as whole as continents like our own. The instrumentality has been *representation,* of which the ancient world knew nothing, and lacking which it always lacked national integration. . . .

But not until recently have we been able to see the full effects of thus sending men to legislate for us at capitals distant the breadth of a continent. It makes the leaders of our politics many of them mere names to our consciousness instead of real persons, whom we have seen and heard, and whom we know. We have to accept rumors concerning them, we have to know them through the variously coloured accounts of others: we can seldom test our impressions of their sincerity by standing with them face to face. . . .

Our separation from our leaders is the greater peril because democratic government more than any other needs organization in order to escape disintegration, and it can have organization only by full knowledge of its leaders and full confidence in them. Just because it is a vast body to be persuaded it must know its persuaders: in order to be effective it must always have choice of men who are *impersonated policies.* Just because none but the finest mental batteries, with pure metals and unadulterated acids, can send a current through so huge and yet so rare a medium as democratic opinion, it is the more necessary to look to the excellence of these instrumentalities. There is no permanent place in democratic leadership except for him who 'hath clean hands and a pure heart'. If other men come temporarily into power among us, it is because we cut our leadership up into so many little parts and do not subject any one man to the purifying influences of centered responsibility. Never before was consistent leadership so necessary; never before was it necessary to concert measures over so vast areas, to adjust laws to so many interests, to make a compact and intelligible unit out of so many fractions, to maintain a central and dominant force where there are so many forces. . . .

Though we be the most law-abiding and law-directed nation in the world, law has not yet attained to such efficacy among us as to frame or adjust or administer *itself.* It may restrain but it cannot lead us: and I believe that unless we concentrate legislative leadership, leadership, i.e., in progressive policy, unless we give leave to our nationality and practice to it *by such* concentration, we shall sooner or later suffer something like national paralysis in the face of emergencies. We have no one in Congress who stands for the nation. Each man stands but for his part of the nation,—and so management and combination, which may be effected in the dark, are given the place that should be held by centered and responsible leadership, which would of necessity work in the focus of the national gaze. . . .

I believe that the only way in which we can preserve our nationality in its integrity and its old-time originative force in the face of growth and imported change is by *concentrating* it, by putting leaders forward vested with abundant authority in the conception and execution of policy. There is plenty of the old vitality in our national character to tell, if you will but give it leave. Give it leave and it will the more impress and mold those who come to us from abroad. I believe that we have not made enough of leadership.

"A people is but the attempt of many
To rise to the completer life of one;
And those who live as models for the mass
Are singly of more value than they all."

We shall not again have a true national life until we compact it by such legislative leadership as other nations have. But, once thus compacted and embodied, our nationality is safe. An accute English historical scholar has said that "the Americans of the United States are a nation because they once obeyed a king": we shall remain a nation only by obeying leaders. . . .

32

William F. Connelly, Jr.

In Defense of Congress (1995)

In *Mr. Smith Goes to Washington* Jimmy Stewart pits his idealism against a Senate institution corrupted by party bosses, self-serving politicians and a cynical press. In this morality play, the pure-hearted, populist, good government reformer finally wins out over the Senate agents of selfish special

By permission of the author.

interests, thus simultaneously reaffirming our faith in American political principles and our disdain for the institutions which embody those ideals. This classic competition is a mainstay of American political culture. This gap between our ideals and our institutions, according to Samuel Huntington, leads to a "disharmony" at the core of American politics. This dissonance is at once our defect and our virtue. Congress lives this conflict every day; Congress is this conflict.

Mr. Smith reflects the conventional wisdom on Congress. All too often, we begin with the facile assumption that members of Congress are venal, selfish, corrupt pawns of special interest groups, and that consequently, Congress, as an institution, is oriented to the status quo. . . .

The self-interested model of political behavior may be a useful starting point in understanding Congress, but by itself, this perspective cannot explain the enormous complexity of the policy process. For starters, a desire for reelection forces congressmen to be attentive to the needs of others, namely, voters. Moreover, elections create incentives for members to reach out to as many different individuals and groups as possible. Finally, while attentiveness to constituents' interests may be analytically distinct from a concern for good public policy, in practice the two are often linked. . . .

At a minimum, members are constantly confronted with a conflict between their parochial re-election or constituency interests and Congress' collective responsibility to the nation. Combining these goals is often a challenge for Congress and its members. Indeed, every congressman is both a lawmaker for the nation and a representative for a part of that nation, consequently members are regularly torn between their "homestyle" and "hillstyle."

In order to understand Congress, however, we must look at the impact of the institution on the behavior of congressmen as well as the political environment in which Congress operates.

INSTITUTIONAL ANALYSIS

Institutional analysis argues, according to Christopher J. Deering, that Congress is more than the sum of its parts, and that Congress, as an institution, has a life of its own. The Founders understood that institutions can affect the behavior of men, as they structured our institutions so as to curb the selfish tendencies of men and promote public interests. They tried to pit ambition against ambition and, perhaps more importantly, promote institutional loyalty and a sense of institutional responsibility.

Politicians elected to Congress, for example, naturally will be inclined to defend the institutional prerogatives of Congress against the President. Similarly, Senators will be quick to defend the Senate against encroachments by the House, and vice versa. As parties and committees came to play a role in Congress, members of political parties fought for their party's interest, and members of congressional committees tried to protect the institutional prerogatives of their committee. In each instance, members' "self-interests" are redefined, and they, in effect, adopt new constituencies apart from the original constituency that elected them to Congress. Members are constantly confronted with the dilemma of serving different, overlapping, and often conflicting constituencies, and are thus forced to choose between conflicting loyalties. Moreover, by virtue of their participation and involvement with these different institutions, members gain a stake in the success of each, learning what Tocqueville called "the art of associating." Members learn to identify with the institution, and a sense of "team play" or esprit de corp develops.

The Founders hoped for more from their constitutional institutions than ambition checking ambition, or a channeling of the competition among the "various and interfering interests." They wanted their institutional structures to promote deliberation, to enable the peoples' representatives to "refine and enlarge the public view." . . .

In Congress, whether on the Senate floor or in House committees, persuasion matters. In *The Senate Nobody Knows*, Bernard Asbell reports former Maine Senator Edmund Muskie's argument that in Congress knowledge is power: "People have all sorts of conspiratorial theories on what constitutes power in the Senate. . . . But real power up there comes from doing your work and knowing what you're talking about. Power is the ability to change someone's mind." . . .

Key organizational characteristics of Congress—the role of bicameralism, House and Senate rules and procedures, and congressional parties and committees—all are in some fashion a function of constitutional structure and influence the activity of congressmen. We shall consider them in turn.

Bicameralism One of the most important constitutional principles governing the behavior of Congress is bicameralism, which divides the legislature into the House and Senate. In order to counter the dominance of the legislature, the Founders, according to *The Federalist*, sought to "divide the legislature into different branches; and to render them, by different modes of election and different principles of action, as little connected with each other as the nature of their common functions and their common dependence on the society will admit."

The House and Senate are very different. The old joke about the Capitol Hill tourists who, after seeing the House and Senate, ask: "Okay, now where is Congress?" is very much on point. Upon closer inspection, new observers of congressional behavior are frequently amazed at how different the two chambers are in practice. Indeed, it is almost difficult to think of them as one institution after examining more carefully the operating principles of the House and Senate. Perhaps the most convincing evidence of the extraordinary difference between the two is the distrust and even hostility between the chambers, even when they are both controlled by the same party. Following unwritten norms, for example, members of each chamber refrain from even mentioning directly "the other chamber" in floor debate. This behavioral norm is a direct function of the constitutional principle of bicameralism.

Although the Founders saw bicameralism as a means of limiting legislative power relative to the executive branch, they also saw it as a way to strengthen the legislative function. In principle, a legislature should represent and deliberate. Two chambers chosen "by different modes of election" can better represent, albeit in different ways, the needs of their constituents. Furthermore, two chambers motivated by "different principles of action" will inevitably clash. House and Senate conflict and competition will just as inevitably augment the twin virtues or functions of any democratic legislature, namely public deliberation and consensus building.

The institutional conflict bicameralism invites has long been seen as a roadblock to policy change. Bicameralism contributes to the proliferation of what are frequently called "multiple veto points" in the legislative process, the implication being that this makes it easier to slow or halt the progress of legislation. Those same points in the legislative process, including committee and subcommittee consideration in each house, however, can also be seen as "multiple access points" inviting the added energy of policy entrepreneurs inside and outside of Congress. Bicameralism has the potential to make the legislative process more dynamic. . . .

Moreover, while bicameralism divides the legislative power, it also focuses that power through a division of labor of sorts. The "advise and consent" clauses of the Constitution grant the Senate a special role in the area of foreign policy through its role in confirming executive nominations and ratifying treaties. Consequently, the Senate Foreign Relations Committee is generally recognized as being more prestigious than the House International Relations Committee. Similarly, the Constitution's "originating" clause, requiring all tax measures to originate in the House, historically has given the House Ways and Means Committee an advantage over the Senate Finance Committee in setting tax policy. The "specialization" these clauses engender are examples of the Constitution focusing power at the same time as it divides power. Again, bicameralism can strengthen as well as weaken Congress. The specialization of the House and Senate in the legislative process can be seen in broader terms. The enormous difference between the operating principles (or what Madison called "different principles of action") of the two chambers flows from their constitutionally distinct "modes of election." Differences in the rules and procedures of the House and Senate derive, in the first instance, from the Constitution. For example, due to two year terms, smaller districts and a 435 person body, House members generally are closer to their constituents and less familiar with one another. The 100 persons in the Senate, drawn from fifty statewide districts for six year terms, are noted for a greater distance from constituents and greater familiarity with one another.

Rules and Procedures The more partisan House thrives on conflict, whereas the Senate operates on the principles of comity and consensus. The House is governed by majority rule and the Senate by a time consuming concern for individual members' rights. Ironically, given its much larger size, the House is more efficient than the more deliberative Senate. The House is more efficient because of its detailed and elaborate rules; in the Senate, informal, yet painstaking, negotiations between the Majority and Minority Leaders determine floor scheduling of legislation. House members tend to be issue specialists and House Committees are reputed to be the "workshops" of Congress. Senators more often are generalists, more dependent on their larger staffs, and inclined to be less deferential to committee legislation on the floor. The Senate, as witness *Mr. Smith Goes to Washington,* is famous for its tradition of "unlimited debate," the filibuster, and the lack of a germaneness rule for floor amendments. Generally speaking, committees are more important in the House, and floor action more important in the Senate.

The differences between the House and Senate are exemplified by the way bills come to the floor. The powerful House Rules Committee, clearly an arm of the Speaker and majority party, acts as a gatekeeper in deciding which bills reach the floor with a "rule" or special order governing floor amendments and length of debate. Party leaders in the Senate, on the other hand, carefully hammer out "unanimous consent agreements" establishing ground rules for floor consideration of legislation in often lengthy negotiations. Because of its constant and literal attention to the principle of unanimous consent, it is surprising that the Senate is able to function at all, given that any member can object at virtually any time to a motion to proceed. In light of the range of ideologies and interests, and the panoply of issues debated on the floor, it is impressive that the Senate is able to act at all.

The different "principles of action" or functions of the House and Senate ultimately reflect differing expressions of democracy, referred to by political scientists as "adversary democracy" and "unitary democracy." While each chamber partakes of both forms of democracy, the characteristics of the former are more commonly found in the House and those of the latter in the Senate. According to Ross K. Baker, adversary democracy is "the faithful representation of the various interests of their states and districts by Senators and House members and the practice of bargaining among members for benefits and protections for those constituencies. Unitary democracy, in contrast, involves the establishment of a consensus among legislators on what is the common or national interest." Bicameralism enables Congress simultaneously to exhibit the character of both a pluralist democracy and a consensual democracy. Congress balances the desire to be responsive to its larger environment with need to act responsibly in the public interest.

Political Parties and Committees in Congress Congress organizes itself for business by party and by committee. The two principles of organization conflict, thus augmenting "complex majority rule." Parties and committees are both more important in the House than in the Senate.

Party leadership in Congress is weak relative to parliamentary systems of government. Congressional leaders generally have less control over members' elections, and due to our separation of powers, constituents have relatively more control over members' elections, thus making congressmen more responsive to voters than to leaders. Moreover, Senate leadership is weaker than House leadership. The leader's "right to recognition" provides a case in point. The Speaker of the House, a constitutional officer, has the active right to recognize who on the House Floor gets to speak next. The Senate Majority leader, who at best is *primus inter pares* in the Senate, has a passive right to be recognized first whenever he stands up on the floor of the Senate.

Given the relative weakness of congressional party leadership, scholars have questioned whether there is real party leadership in our decentralized national legislature. Clearly Congress is not the President, and executive style leadership does not exist on the Hill. Nevertheless, leadership does exist depending on the timing and the issue. As a general rule, the more nationally salient an issue becomes, the more likely party leaders will get involved. . . . Given the separation of powers and the nature of congressional elections, Congress is clearly not Parliament, but neither is it the local school board. Congress must address both local and national interests. Congress must be responsive and responsible.

At least since Woodrow Wilson, congressional reformers have criticized the strength of standing committees as well as the lack of strong party leadership. Wilson's lament that "congressional government is committee government" focuses on the seeming tendency of the committee system to augment the fragmentation and disintegration of the policy process. Reformers' incessant demands to style Congress after the British (but not the Italian!) Parliament, ignore the contributions the committee system makes to increasing policy-making coherence.

Committees sprang up naturally in the early decades of the Republic. They enabled Congress to cope with its own growth in numbers and workload, as well as increasing demands on the federal government. The division of labor allows Congress to concentrate expertise, to address more systematically a constantly growing array of issues, and to exercise oversight of executive agencies more effectively. Following the committee reforms of the 1970's which "opened up" committees and weakened the role of committee chairmen, scholars are beginning to reassess the contribution of strong committees to policy coherence. . . .

Environmental Analysis

As should be evident by now, discussing the internal organization of Congress—committees, parties and bicameralism—makes little sense without taking into consideration the larger system or environment within which the institution operates. Elements in the environment of Congress include voters and constituents, public opinion, the media, interest groups, executive agencies, states, and the President. For our purposes here, we shall focus on interest groups and the President.

Interest Groups If interest groups and lobbyists did not exist, Congress would have to invent them. The relationship is symbiotic, with lobbying groups of all stripes acting as virtual service bureaus in providing Congress with information. The caricature of lobbyists as wining, dining and bribing congressmen is misleading. As Bernard Asbell points out, "more than ninety-nine percent of lobbying effort is spent . . . [on] trying to persuade minds through facts and reason; some of it performed extremely well, some with comic incompetence." Moreover, there is a built in quality control in the lobbying process. All lobbyists speak from a known perspective, compete with many others arguing different positions, and need to maintain their reputation for telling the truth if they wish to be heard another day. . . .

The President Congress and the President need each other. They are like two halves of a whole; neither is a complete policy making process unto itself. Consequently policymaking is neither tidy nor especially efficient. Yet each brings its peculiar virtues to the relationship. The executive can act with energy, secrecy, dispatch and direction. Congress is deliberate. Congress is very good at talking, at second guessing the executive and equivocating. Congress is good at watching the executive, at providing oversight. It is a very open institution with few secrets. Congress is responsive to the multiplicity of interests and opinions in the nation; it is a good incubator for new ideas, including ones often borrowed by Presidents. In sum, Congress is creative chaos, but a chaos that on occasion can respond to the discipline of Presidents, public opinion or crises. The separation of powers makes Congress more open to its environment.

The Separation of Powers

The suggestion that the separation of powers prevents things from being done fails to recognize the differentiation of roles or functions at the heart of this central constitutional principle. Like bicameralism, the separation of powers does not merely limit the abuse of power, it also provides for the effective use of power. Congress is a powerful national legislature because of the institutional independence afforded by the separation of powers. Congress never fully surrenders to the executive its responsibility. The institutional independence or separation of Congress from the executive means that as a legislature it has more affirmative responsibility than its parliamentary counterpart. This institutional separation, in turn, allows Congress to more effectively exercise its legislative functions of deliberation and representation. Congress is more democratically responsive given its independence from the executive. Members are better able to represent the particular needs of their constituents, and the frequency of elections requires that they do so. Unlike a parliament, Congress cannot force consensus. If, for example, a general consensus on how to solve the budget deficit is lacking, Congress cannot create such a consensus. In this sense, Congress is more responsive to the whole as well as the parts. But at the same time Congress is designed to be more responsive, it also has more independent policy responsibility.

The functional separation of powers means that the two "political branches" can compete while they complement each other. Like the competition between the two houses of Congress, that between the president and Congress introduces more energy into the policy process. The competition also invites a more open and public deliberation between the branches, which in turn invites greater policy responsiveness. . . .

33

William F. Connelly, Jr.

Congressional Government and Separation of Powers (2000)

. . . Our parties are, to put it mildly, muddled coalitions of factions infighting over substance and style. James Madison's Constitution is one reason. Unlike the British parliamentary system in which the majority party forms the government, while the minority party plays loyal opposition, our constitutional system, with its separation of powers, federalism and bicameralism, provides no clear demarcation between government and opposition. In 1994 the GOP finally succeeded in becoming more the party of government by winning the House after 40 years in the minority.

While becoming *more* the party of government, the House GOP was, of course, not simply the party of government since, at a minimum, Bill Clinton was in the White House. Still, House Republicans became victims of their own electoral success. As Richard Fenno notes in *Learning to Govern*, these long time insurgents had trouble making the transition to governing. They were loath to surrender the politics of confrontation and embrace the politics of accommodation. Speaker Gingrich, a successful wartime *consigliere*, seemed not to appreciate that managing the peace required different leadership skills.

For the House GOP, however, was the war really over? As the majority party in the House, were they really simply the party of government? Conventional wisdom has it that the Gingrich-led House Republican revolution faltered because they failed to make the transition from opposition to governing. After forty years as the "permanent minority" they naturally were slow to embrace compromise. . . . The institution of Congress needs and invites different leadership styles; both confrontation and accommodation are normal and necessary, depending on the issue and the time. As one former Gingrich staffer noted, "Maybe a certain style of Speaker fits a certain age." . . .

Finding a leader who can balance both halves of the equation is not easy. Gingrich may not have been tempermentally suited for such a balancing act especially given his penchant for personalizing political differences (something even allies like Vin Weber criticized). Recently Gingich seemed to acknowledge his own limitations in speculating that Dick Cheney might have been a more appropriate speaker. "I think that if Dick Cheney would have stayed in the House, I would have been his chief planner . . . and I would have never run for leadership." Gingrich elaborated, "I think Cheney might well have led us to a majority. He would have done it with his own style, but probably his style with my planning. I thought we were a very good team." In retrospect, Gingrich now recognizes the need for balance.

Congressional party leaders need the skills of both compromise and confrontation; they remain at all times part of the government and part of the opposition. Successful congressional leadership requires balance; comity and partisan competition are both virtues. Gingrich erred by coupling his instinctive tendency to overplay the politics of opposition with the presumption that he was the head of a parliamentary system. His critics sometimes err in assuming that legislative majority party leaders should simply play the politics of governing while abjuring partisanship. But ours is a separation of powers, not a parliamentary, system.

PARTISANS AND POLITICAL SCIENTISTS

Some partisans demonize Gingrich as if he is the sole cause of the heightened House partisanship and "politics of personal destruction" in the 1980s and 1990s. On the other hand, some political scientists diminish his individual impact by arguing that congressional leaders are mere creatures of their institutional context. Such partisans and political scientists cannot both be right. One is reminded of Tocqueville's famous observation that scholars always find "general causes" while politicians attribute everything to "particular incidents." "It is to be presumed," Tocqueville concludes, "that both are equally deceived." Still, there may be an element of truth to each perspective. Perhaps individuals matter even though individuals are, in part, limited by their institutional context. Perhaps, too, it is time to move beyond the simple, albeit useful, "institutional context and leadership style" dichotomy.

Clearly, Newt Gingrich made a difference, even if he has been banished to his own metaphorical Elba. House Republicans generally credit him with leading them out of their "permanent minority" wilderness. This probably overstates the case; however, Gingrich did mold what Cooper and Brady call "institutional context" by, for example, his long term GOPAC recruitment efforts and by inspiring greater House GOP policy consensus with the Contract with America. While constrained by the limits of the consensus he helped engineer, Gingrich and the House Republicans accomplished significant policy innovations, including welfare reform and a balanced budget. They also accomplished important institutional reforms. House Republicans privatized non-legislative services in the House, adopted time cap floor procedures fairer to the minority, and altered the balance between party and committee leaders, thus accelerating what Richard Cohen calls the "crack up of committees" begun under the Democrats. The latter change includes cutting the number of committees, realigning jurisdictions, effectively revoking the "subcommittee bill of rights," using task forces to qualify committee fiefdoms, and term limiting committee chairs. House Republicans' willingness to continue term limiting committee chairs provides a useful measure of their commitment to governing differently than Democrats.

Ron Peters argues that "Gingrich's goal was to fundamentally change the character of the House as a legislative institution" with an experiment in party government. Yet, Gingrich's experiment in congressional party government fell short. Why?

Certainly institutional context defined as the party-in-government and the party-in-the electorate constrains leaders. Naturally, party sentiment constrains legislative leaders, including whether their party has tapped a large enough consensus in the electorate to be the majority. But institutional context can also usefully include constitutional structure and the institutional constraints of the separation of powers. *Indeed, constitutional structure mediates the influence and the coherence of the party in the electorate and the party in government.* The separation of powers affects both the electoral and the governing ambitions of the two parties.

In the 1990s, the separation of powers limited and advanced the electoral ambitions of both parties. Adopting a "losing to win" strategy, exemplified by the 1990 budget battle, House Republicans lost the White House in 1992 in order to win the House in 1994. In turn, the 1994 House GOP majority enabled Clinton to triangulate his way to his 1996 re-election. By 1998, the country seemed comfortable with divided government limiting both Gingrich and Clinton.

The separation of powers, of course, also limits and enables the governing ambitions of the two parties. Winning a House majority empowered Gingrich, though Senate and presidential ambitions were able to counteract his ambition. Madison's "different modes of election and different principles of action" for the House, Senate and Presidency clearly limited the House Republican revolution. In *Lessons Learned the Hard Way*, Gingrich acknowledges gaining a vivid lesson in constitutional constraints, beginning with "the Senate as the cooling saucer" and extending to the presidency. "Even if you pass something through both the House and the Senate, there is that presidential pen. How could we have forgotten that?" Good question.

Speaker Gingrich's political downfall may be rooted in an intellectual error. He failed to take constitutional structure seriously because he believed "institutions are what leaders make them to be." Unfortunately for Gingrich, constitutional institutions are not so malleable. He failed to recognize that neither pure congressional government nor pure party government is altogether possible in our constitutional system; he fundamentally misunderstood Madison's separation of powers. Like Woodrow Wilson, Newt Gingrich failed to take the Constitution seriously.

Professorial Politicians

Newt Gingrich once called himself "the most seriously professorial politician since Woodrow Wilson," inviting comparison between these two intellectuals cum politicians. Gingrich is clearly an intellectual heir to Wilson; indeed, Wilson's 1885 *Congressional Government* reads like a field manual for Gingrich's mid-1990s experiment in congressional party government.

Both the Woodrow Wilson of *Congressional Government* and Speaker Gingrich were legislative supremacists who saw the House as the heart of Congress and the president as an administrator. Both favored responsible "party government" and abhorred decentralized "committee government" in Congress. Both favored an open politics of ideas, principles and "grand partisanship," and both were critical of a pluralist politics of interest group bargaining, lobbying and log rolling. Both may have in theory exaggerated the role of powerful individual leaders, tending to assume that individual leaders matter more than institutions. Both had limited appreciation for constitutional forms. Both thought it possible to amend the Constitution by their actions and precedents. Both also believed that the public needs conspicuous leaders to understand Congress. Hence both appealed to the public beyond congressional politics as usual (e.g. Gingrich's use of the web and his nationally televised post-Contract address and Wilson's barnstorming national tour as president to promote the League of Nations). Both men proposed Contract-like party platforms to promote party accountability. In theory and practice Wilson and Gingrich both explored the limits and possibilities of congressional party government.

As part of their exploration into the potential for party government, Wilson and Gingrich examined the role of ideas in politics. Not surprisingly perhaps for professorial politicians, both men conflated statesmanship and rhetoric. In fact, Wilson offered a profound and clearly articulated theory of political leadership-as-education. Drawing on his British Parliamentary ideal, Wilson saw party government as promoting serious public deliberation to educate public opinion. Parties should provide voters a choice not an echo. Legislative leadership, he insisted, is government by discussion, advocacy and persuasion. For Wilson, the key function of Congress was to educate public opinion by means of deliberation; indeed, for him the informing function of Congress is paramount to the oversight and even legislative functions.

As Speaker, Gingrich seemed to take his cue from *Congressional Government*. Professor Gingrich reveled in his role of Speaker as Educator, exploiting the "bully pulpit" of the speakership as an opportunity to teach. Gingrich is known more for his didactic manner than for his interest in legislative detail. Wilson in theory and Gingrich in practice explored the outer limits of the Speaker as educator.

Yet both professors as politicians learned hard lessons. Wilson and Gingrich in theory discounted the role of institutions in limiting leaders, but both in practice learned the power of constitutional structure. As President and Speaker respectively they learned that institutions matter and the Constitution counts. Their institutional responsibilities broadened their perspectives and gave each a practical education in the limits and possibilities of party government. Heirs to Wilson's thought can learn from Gingrich's experience. Today professors and politicians both would do well to learn from Wilson and Gingrich.

Congressional or Presidential Government?

In 1885 Professor Wilson looked at our constitutional system and saw *Congressional Government*. By 1908 and *Constitutional Government* Wilson began to dream of the possibilities of presidential government. Ironically, as President, Wilson began once again to have second (or third?) thoughts. How could so brilliant a professor and politician look at the same constitutional system and at different times see both congressional and presidential government? Perhaps it is because both the President and the Congress are powerful within our constitutional system. The separation of powers is more than checks and balances. It limits and empowers the President and Congress depending on the individuals, issues, and institutional time involved.

Gingrich has also had second thoughts. Like Wilson, he began by seeing Congress as the center of our political system, yet he too learned that the presidency is powerful. Perhaps these two professors and politicians met their match in another intellectual and politician, James Madison, whose "combining mind" taught them the limits and possibilities of his separation of powers.

To their credit, both Wilson and Gingrich correctly identified a weakness of Madisonian pluralism, namely a tendency to augment the role of competing interests or factions. Both Wilson and Gingrich also explored the role of ideas and parties in our constitutional system. Both exploited the potential in our constitutional system for promoting and enabling a politics of ideas and a politics of grand partisanship.

Because both committee and party leadership are powerful (albeit often at different times), Congress as an institution encompasses both a pluralist politics of compromising interests and a principled party politics of competing ideas. Neither pluralism, nor party government completely captures the dynamic character of Congress as an institution. Each captures half the whole.

More than a century later, Woodrow Wilson's *Congressional Government* is still worth reading precisely because it provides a serious examination of the role of ideas, public deliberation, and party in American politics. Similarly, Newt Gingrich's thoughts and experience remain noteworthy. One hundred years from now, scholars will still be talking about the Gingrich speakership in much the same way that we talk today about Czars Reed and Cannon. The enduring legacy of Newt Gingrich for Congress, political parties and political science will be his exploration in theory and practice of the limits of congressional party government. Ultimately, Gingrich recognized that powerful speakers are possible within the context of our separation of powers system. Gingrich learned the limits of insurgency and the possibilities of governing, the limitations of "revolution" in an institutional structure inclined toward incrementalism, and the potential for change and policy innovation even under conditions of divided government. The experience of the Gingrich speakership can teach us that both individuals and institutions matter, both confrontation over ideas and compromise over interests are necessary.

34

U.S. Term Limits, Inc. v. Thornton (1995)

Justice Stevens delivered the opinion of the Court.

. . . Today's cases present a challenge to an amendment to the Arkansas State Constitution that prohibits the name of an otherwise eligible candidate for Congress from appearing on the general election ballot if that candidate has already served three terms in the House of Representatives or two terms in the Senate. The Arkansas Supreme Court held that the amendment violates the Federal Constitution. We agree with that holding. Such a state imposed restriction is contrary to the "fundamental principle of our representative democracy," embodied in the Constitution, that "the people should choose whom they please to govern them." *Powell v. McCormack.* Allowing individual States to adopt their own qualifications for congressional service would be inconsistent with the Framers' vision of a uniform

From *U.S. Term Limits, Inc. v. Thornton*, 514 U.S. 779 (1995)

National Legislature representing the people of the United States. If the qualifications set forth in the text of the Constitution are to be changed, that text must be amended.

[T]he constitutionality of Amendment 73 depends critically on the resolution of two distinct issues. The first is whether the Constitution forbids States from adding to or altering the qualifications specifically enumerated in the Constitution. The second is, if the Constitution does so forbid, whether the fact that Amendment 73 is formulated as a ballot access restriction rather than as an outright disqualification is of constitutional significance. Our resolution of these issues draws upon our prior resolution of a related but distinct issue: whether Congress has the power to add to or alter the qualifications of its Members.

. . . In November 1966, Adam Clayton Powell, Jr., was elected from a District in New York to serve in the United States House of Representatives for the 90th Congress. Allegations that he had engaged in serious misconduct while serving as a committee chairman during the 89th Congress led to the appointment of a Select Committee to determine his eligibility to take his seat. That Committee found that Powell met the age, citizenship, and residency requirements set forth in Art. I, §2, cl. 2. The Committee also found, however, that Powell had wrongfully diverted House funds for the use of others and himself and had made false reports on expenditures of foreign currency. Based on those findings, the House after debate adopted House Resolution 278, excluding Powell from membership in the House, and declared his seat vacant. Powell and several voters of the District from which he had been elected filed suit seeking a declaratory judgment that the House Resolution was invalid because Art. I, §2, cl. 2, sets forth the exclusive qualifications for House membership. We ultimately accepted that contention, concluding that the House of Representatives has no "authority to *exclude* any person, duly elected by his constituents, who meets all the requirements for membership expressly prescribed in the Constitution." In reaching that conclusion, we undertook a detailed historical review to determine the intent of the Framers. Though recognizing that the Constitutional Convention debates themselves were inconclusive, we determined that the "relevant historical materials" reveal that Congress has no power to alter the qualifications in the text of the Constitution.

. . . Our conclusion that States lack the power to impose qualifications vindicates the same "fundamental principle of our representative democracy" that we recognized in *Powell*, namely that "the people should choose whom they please to govern them."

As we noted earlier, the *Powell* Court recognized that an egalitarian ideal—that election to the National Legislature should be open to all people of merit—provided a critical foundation for the Constitutional structure. This egalitarian theme echoes throughout the constitutional debates. In The Federalist No. 57, for example, Madison wrote:

> "Who are to be the objects of popular choice? Every citizen whose merit may recommend him to the esteem and confidence of his country. No qualification of wealth, of birth, of religious faith, or of civil profession is permitted to fetter the judgment or disappoint the inclination of the people."

Similarly, hoping to persuade voters in New York that the Constitution should be ratified, John Stevens, Jr., wrote: "[N]o Government, that has ever yet existed in the world, affords so ample a field, to individuals of all ranks, for the display of political talents and abilities. . . . No man who has real merit, let his situation be what it will, need despair." And Timothy Pickering noted that, "while several of the state constitutions prescribe certain degrees of property as indispensable qualifications for offices, this which is proposed for the U. S. throws the door wide open for the entrance of *every man* who enjoys the confidence of his fellow citizens." Additional qualifications pose the same obstacle to open elections whatever their source. The egalitarian ideal, so valued by the Framers, is thus compromised to the same degree by additional qualifications imposed by States as by those imposed by Congress.

Similarly, we believe that state imposed qualifications, as much as congressionally imposed qualifications, would undermine the second critical idea recognized in *Powell:* that an aspect of sovereignty is the right of the people to vote for whom they wish. Again, the source of the qualification is of little moment in assessing the qualification's restrictive impact.

Finally, state imposed restrictions, unlike the congressionally imposed restrictions at issue in *Powell,* violate a third idea central to this basic principle: that the right to choose representatives belongs not to the States, but to the people. From the start, the Framers recognized that the "great and radical vice" of the Articles of Confederation was "the principle of LEGISLATION for STATES or GOVERNMENTS, in their CORPORATE or COLLECTIVE CAPACITIES, and as contradistinguished from the INDIVIDUALS of whom they consist." Thus the Framers, in perhaps their most important contribution, conceived of a Federal Government directly responsible to the people, possessed of direct power over the people, and chosen directly, not by States, but by the people. The Framers implemented this ideal most clearly in the provision, extant from the beginning of the Republic, that calls for the Members of the House of Representatives to be "chosen every second Year by the People of the several States." Art. I, §2, cl. 1. Following the adoption of the 17th Amendment in 1913, this ideal was extended to elections for the Senate. The Congress of the United States, therefore, is not a confederation of nations in which separate sovereigns are represented by appointed delegates, but is instead a body composed of representatives of the people. . . .

Petitioners argue that, even if States may not add qualifications, Amendment 73 is constitutional because it is not such a qualification, and because Amendment 73 is a permissible exercise of state power to regulate the "Times, Places and Manner of Holding Elections." We reject these contentions.

. . . As we have often noted, "[c]onstitutional rights would be of little value if they could be . . . indirectly denied." *Harman v. Forssenius.* The Constitution "nullifies sophisticated as well as simple minded modes" of infringing on Constitutional protections. In our view, Amendment 73 is an indirect attempt to accomplish what the Constitution prohibits Arkansas from accomplishing directly. As the plurality opinion of the Arkansas Supreme Court recognized, Amendment 73 is an "effort to dress eligibility to stand for Congress in ballot access clothing," because the "intent and the effect of Amendment 73 are to disqualify congressional incumbents from further service." . . . Indeed, it cannot be seriously contended that the intent behind Amendment 73 is other than to prevent the election of incumbents. The preamble of Amendment 73 states explicitly: "[T]he people of Arkansas . . . herein limit the terms of elected officials." Sections 1 and 2 create absolute limits on the number of terms that may be served. There is no hint that §3 was intended to have any other purpose.

. . . Moreover, petitioners' broad construction of the Elections Clause is fundamentally inconsistent with the Framers' view of that Clause. The Framers intended the Elections Clause to grant States authority to create procedural regulations, not to provide States with license to exclude classes of candidates from federal office. During the Convention debates, for example, Madison illustrated the procedural focus of the Elections Clause by noting that it covered "[w]hether the electors should vote by ballot or vivâ voce, should assemble at this place or that place; should be divided into districts or all meet at one place, sh[oul]d all vote for all the representatives; or all in a district vote for a number allotted to the district." Similarly, during the ratification debates, proponents of the Constitution noted: "[T]he power over the manner only enables them to determine how these electors shall elect—whether by ballot, or by vote, or by any other way." Hamilton made a similar point in The Federalist No. 60, in which he defended the Constitution's grant to Congress of the power to override state regulations. Hamilton expressly distinguished the broad power to set qualifications from the limited authority under the Elections Clause, noting that

"there is no method of securing to the rich the preference apprehended but by prescribing qualifications of property either for those who may elect or be elected. But this forms no part of the power to be conferred upon the national government. Its authority would be expressly restricted to the regulation of the *times*, the *places*, and the *manner* of elections."

As Hamilton's statement suggests, the Framers understood the Elections Clause as a grant of authority to issue procedural regulations, and not as a source of power to dictate electoral outcomes, to favor or disfavor a class of candidates, or to evade important constitutional restraints.

. . . We do not understand the dissent to contest our primary thesis, namely that if the qualifications for Congress are fixed in the Constitution, then a State passed measure with the avowed purpose of imposing indirectly such an additional qualification violates the Constitution. The dissent, instead, raises two objections, challenging the assertion that the Arkansas amendment has the likely effect of creating a qualification, and suggesting that the true intent of Amendment 73 was not to evade the Qualifications Clause but rather to simply "level the playing field". Neither of these objections has merit.

As to the first, it is simply irrelevant to our holding today. As we note, our prior cases strongly suggest that write in candidates will have only a slim chance of success, and the Arkansas plurality agreed. However, we expressly do not rest on this Court's prior observations regarding write in candidates. Instead, we hold that a state amendment is unconstitutional when it has the likely effect of handicapping a class of candidates and has the sole purpose of creating additional qualifications indirectly. Thus, the dissent's discussion of the evidence concerning the possibility that a popular incumbent will win a write in election is simply beside the point.

As to the second argument, we find wholly unpersuasive the dissent's suggestion that Amendment 73 was designed merely to "level the playing field." As we have noted, it is obvious that the sole purpose of Amendment 73 was to limit the terms of elected officials, both State and federal, and that Amendment 73, therefore, may not stand.

The merits of term limits, or "rotation," have been the subject of debate since the formation of our Constitution, when the Framers unanimously rejected a proposal to add such limits to the Constitution. The cogent arguments on both sides of the question that were articulated during the process of ratification largely retain their force today. Over half the States have adopted measures that impose such limits on some offices either directly or indirectly, and the Nation as a whole, notably by constitutional amendment, has imposed a limit on the number of terms that the President may serve. Term limits, like any other qualification for office, unquestionably restrict the ability of voters to vote for whom they wish. On the other hand, such limits may provide for the infusion of fresh ideas and new perspectives, and may decrease the likelihood that representatives will lose touch with their constituents. It is not our province to resolve this longstanding debate.

We are, however, firmly convinced that allowing the several States to adopt term limits for congressional service would effect a fundamental change in the constitutional framework. Any such change must come not by legislation adopted either by Congress or by an individual State, but rather—as have other important changes in the electoral process—through the Amendment procedures set forth in Article V. The Framers decided that the qualifications for service in the Congress of the United States be fixed in the Constitution and be uniform throughout the Nation. That decision reflects the Framers' understanding that Members of Congress are chosen by separate constituencies, but that they become, when elected, servants of the people of the United States. They are not merely delegates appointed by separate, sovereign States; they occupy offices that are integral and essential components of a single National Government. In the absence of a properly passed constitutional amendment, allowing individual States to craft their own qualifications for Congress would thus erode the structure envisioned by the Framers, a structure that was designed, in the words of the Preamble to our Constitution, to form a "more perfect Union."

Justice Thomas with whom the Chief Justice, O'Connor and Scalia join, dissent.

Nothing in the Constitution deprives the people of each State of the power to prescribe eligibility requirements for the candidates who seek to represent them in Congress. The Constitution is simply silent on this question. And where the Constitution is silent, it raises no bar to action by the States or the people.

Because the majority fundamentally misunderstands the notion of "reserved" powers, I start with some first principles. Contrary to the majority's suggestion, the people of the States need not point to any affirmative grant of power in the Constitution in order to prescribe qualifications for their representatives in Congress, or to authorize their elected state legislators to do so.

Our system of government rests on one overriding principle: all power stems from the consent of the people. To phrase the principle in this way, however, is to be imprecise about something important to the notion of "reserved" powers. The ultimate source of the Constitution's authority is the consent of the people of each individual State, not the consent of the undifferentiated people of the Nation as a whole.

The ratification procedure erected by Article VII makes this point clear. The Constitution took effect once it had been ratified by the people gathered in convention in nine different States. But the Constitution went into effect only "between the States so ratifying the same," it did not bind the people of North Carolina until they had accepted it. In Madison's words, the popular consent upon which the Constitution's authority rests was "given by the people, not as individuals composing one entire nation, but as composing the distinct and independent States to which they respectively belong."

When they adopted the Federal Constitution, of course, the people of each State surrendered some of their authority to the United States (and hence to entities accountable to the people of other States as well as to themselves). They affirmatively deprived their States of certain powers, and they affirmatively conferred certain powers upon the Federal Government. Because the people of the several States are the only true source of power, however, the Federal Government enjoys no authority beyond what the Constitution confers: the Federal Government's powers are limited and enumerated. In the words of Justice Black, "[t]he United States is entirely a creature of the Constitution. Its power and authority have no other source." *Reid v. Covert.*

In each State, the remainder of the people's powers—"[t]he powers not delegated to the United States by the Constitution, nor prohibited by it to the States," Amdt.10—are either delegated to the state government or retained by the people. The Federal Constitution does not specify which of these two possibilities obtains; it is up to the various state constitutions to declare which powers the people of each State have delegated to their state government. As far as the Federal Constitution is concerned, then, the States can exercise all powers that the Constitution does not withhold from them. The Federal Government and the States thus face different default rules: where the Constitution is silent about the exercise of a particular power—that is, where the Constitution does not speak either expressly or by necessary implication—the Federal Government lacks that power and the States enjoy it.

These basic principles are enshrined in the Tenth Amendment, which declares that all powers neither delegated to the Federal Government nor prohibited to the States "are reserved to the States respectively, or to the people." With this careful last phrase, the Amendment avoids taking any position on the division of power between the state governments and the people of the States: it is up to the people of each State to determine which "reserved" powers their state government may exercise. But the Amendment does make clear that powers reside at the state level except where the Constitution removes them from that level. All powers that the Constitution neither delegates to the Federal Government nor prohibits to the States are controlled by the people of each State.

To be sure, when the Tenth Amendment uses the phrase "the people," it does not specify whether it is referring to the people of each State or the people of the Nation as a whole. But the latter interpretation would make the Amendment pointless: there would have been no reason to provide that where the Constitution is silent about whether a particular power resides at the state level, it might or might not do so. In addition, it would make no sense to speak of powers as being reserved to the undifferentiated.people of the Nation as a whole, because the Constitution does not contemplate that those people will either exercise power or delegate it. The Constitution simply does not recognize any mechanism for action by the undifferentiated people of the Nation. Thus, the amendment provision of Article V calls for amendments to be ratified not by a convention of the national people, but by conventions of the people in each State or by the state legislatures elected by those people. Likewise, the Constitution calls for Members of Congress to be chosen State by State, rather than in nationwide elections. Even the selection of the President—surely the most national of national figures—is accomplished by an electoral college made up of delegates chosen by the various States, and candidates can lose a Presidential election despite winning a majority of the votes cast in the Nation as a whole.

In short, the notion of popular sovereignty that undergirds the Constitution does not erase state boundaries, but rather tracks them. The people of each State obviously did trust their fate to the people of the several States when they consented to the Constitution; not only did they empower the governmental institutions of the United States, but they also agreed to be bound by constitutional amendments that they themselves refused to ratify. See Art. V (providing that proposed amendments shall take effect upon ratification by three quarters of the States). At the same time, however, the people of each State retained their separate political identities. As Chief Justice Marshall put it, "[n]o political dreamer was ever wild enough to think of breaking down the lines which separate the States, and of compounding the American people into one common mass." *McCulloch v. Maryland*

Any ambiguity in the Tenth Amendment's use of the phrase "the people" is cleared up by the body of the Constitution itself. Article I begins by providing that the Congress of the United States enjoys "[a]ll legislative Powers herein granted," §1, and goes on to give a careful enumeration of Congress' powers, §8. It then concludes by enumerating certain powers that are *prohibited* to the States. The import of this structure is the same as the import of the Tenth Amendment: if we are to invalidate Arkansas' Amendment 73, we must point to something in the Federal Constitution that deprives the people of Arkansas of the power to enact such measures.

The majority disagrees that it bears this burden. But its arguments are unpersuasive.

. . . The majority's essential logic is that the state governments could not "reserve" any powers that they did not control at the time the Constitution was drafted. But it was not the state governments that were doing the reserving. The Constitution derives its authority instead from the consent of *the people* of the States. Given the fundamental principle that all governmental powers stem from the people of the States, it would simply be incoherent to assert that the people of the States could not reserve any powers that they had not previously controlled.

. . . I take it to be established, then, that the people of Arkansas do enjoy "reserved" powers over the selection of their representatives in Congress. Purporting to exercise those reserved powers, they have agreed among themselves that the candidates covered by §3 of Amendment 73—those whom they have already elected to three or more terms in the House of Representatives or to two or more terms in the Senate—should not be eligible to appear on the ballot for reelection, but should nonetheless be returned to Congress if enough voters are sufficiently enthusiastic about their candidacy to write in their names. Whatever one might think of the wisdom of this arrangement, we may not override the decision of the people of Arkansas unless something in the Federal Constitution deprives them of the power to enact such measures.

The majority settles on "the Qualifications Clauses" as the constitutional provisions that Amendment 73 violates. Because I do not read those provisions to impose any unstated prohibitions on the States, it is unnecessary for me to decide whether the majority is correct to identify Arkansas' ballot access restriction with laws fixing true term limits or otherwise prescribing "qualifications" for congressional office. . . .

In addition to its arguments about democratic principles, the majority asserts that more specific historical evidence supports its view that the Framers did not intend to permit supplementation of the Qualifications Clauses. But when one focuses on the distinction between congressional power to add qualifications for congressional office and the power of the people or their state legislatures to add such qualifications, one realizes that this assertion has little basis.

In particular, the detail with which the majority recites the historical evidence set forth in *Powell v. McCormack* should not obscure the fact that this evidence has no bearing on the question now before the Court. As the majority ultimately concedes, it does not establish "the Framers' intent that the qualifications in the Constitution be fixed and exclusive," it shows only that the Framers did not intend Congress to be able to enact qualifications laws. If anything, the solidity of the evidence supporting *Powell*'s view that Congress lacks the power to supplement the constitutional disqualifications merely highlights the weakness of the majority's evidence that the States and the people of the States also lack this power.

. . . No matter how narrowly construed . . . today's decision reads the Qualifications Clauses to impose substantial implicit prohibitions on the States and the people of the States. I would not draw such an expansive negative inference from the fact that the Constitution requires Members of Congress to be a certain age, to be inhabitants of the States that they represent, and to have been United States citizens for a specified period. Rather, I would read the Qualifications Clauses to do no more than what they say.

35

Morris P. Fiorina

The Rise of the Washington Establishment (1989)

I assume that most people most of the time act in their own self-interest. This is not to say that human beings seek only to amass tangible wealth but rather to say that human beings seek to achieve their own ends—tangible and intangible—rather than the ends of their fellow men. I do not condemn such behavior nor do I condone it (although I rather sympathize with Thoreau's comment that "if I knew for a certainty that a man was coming to my house with the conscious design of doing me good, I should run for my life"). I only claim that political and economic theories which presume self-interested behavior will prove to be more widely applicable than those which build on more altruistic assumptions.

What does the axiom imply when used in the specific context of this book, a context peopled by congressmen, bureaucrats, and voters? I assume that the primary goal of the typical congressman is reelection. Over and above the salary plus "perks" and outside money, the office of congressman carries with it prestige, excitement, and power. It is a seat in the cockpit of government. But in order to retain the status, excitement, and power (not to mention more tangible things) of office, the congressman must win reelection every two years. Even those congressmen genuinely concerned with good public policy must achieve reelection in order to continue their work. Whether narrowly self-serving or more publicly oriented, the individual congressman finds reelection to be at least a necessary condition for the achievement of his goals.

Moreover, there is a kind of natural selection process at work in the electoral arena. On average, those congressmen who are not primarily interested in reelection will not achieve reelection as often as those who are interested. We, the people, help to weed out congressmen whose primary motivation is not reelection. We admire politicians who courageously adopt the aloof role of the disinterested statesman, but we vote for those politicians who follow our wishes and do us favors.

What about the bureaucrats? A specification of their goals is somewhat more controversial—those who speak of appointed officials as public servants obviously take a more benign view than those who speak of them as bureaucrats. The literature provides ample justification for asserting that most bureaucrats wish to protect and nurture their agencies. The typical bureaucrat can be expected to seek to expand his agency in terms of personnel, budget, and mission. One's status in Washington (again, not to mention more tangible things) is roughly proportional to the importance of the operation one oversees. And the sheer size of the operation is taken to be a measure of importance. As with congressmen, the specified goals apply even to those bureaucrats who genuinely believe in their agency's mission. If they believe in the efficacy of their programs, they naturally wish to expand them and add new ones. All of this requires more money and more people. The genuinely committed bureaucrat is just as likely to seek to expand his agency as the proverbial empire-builder.

And what of the third element in the equation, us? What do we, the voters who support the Washington system, strive for? Each of us wishes to receive a maximum of benefits from government for the minimum cost. This goal suggests maximum government efficiency, on the one hand, but it also suggests mutual exploitation on the other. Each of us favors an arrangement in which our fellow citizens pay for our benefits.

With these brief descriptions of the cast of characters in hand, let us proceed.

What should we expect from a legislative body composed of individuals whose first priority is their continued tenure in office? We should expect, first, that the normal activities of its members are those calculated to enhance their chances of reelection. And we should expect, second, that the members would devise and maintain institutional arrangements which facilitate their electoral activities.

For most of the twentieth century, congressmen have engaged in a mix of three kinds of activities: lawmaking, pork barreling, and casework. Congress is first and foremost a lawmaking body, at least according to constitutional theory. In every postwar session Congress "considers" thousands of bills and resolutions, many hundreds of which are brought to a record vote (over 500 in each chamber in the 93d Congress). Naturally the critical consideration in taking a position for the record is the maximization of approval in the home district. If the district is unaffected by and unconcerned with the matter at hand, the congressman may then take into account the general welfare of the country. (This sounds cynical, but remember that "profiles in courage" are sufficiently rare that their occurrence inspires books and articles.) Abetted by political scientists of the pluralist school, politicians have propounded an ideology which maintains that the good of the country on any given issue is simply what is best for a majority of congressional districts.

This ideology provides a philosophical justification for what congressmen do while acting in their own self-interest.

A second activity favored by congressmen consists of efforts to bring home the bacon to their districts. Many popular articles have been written about the pork barrel, a term originally applied to rivers and harbors legislation but now generalized to cover all manner of federal largesse. Congressmen consider new dams, federal buildings, sewage treatment plants, urban renewal projects, etc. as sweet plums to be plucked. Federal projects are highly visible, their economic impact is easily detected by constituents, and sometimes they even produce something of value to the district. The average constituent may have some trouble translating his congressman's vote on some civil rights issue into a change in his personal welfare. But the workers hired and supplies purchased in connection with a big federal project provide benefits that are widely appreciated. The historical importance congressmen attach to the pork barrel is reflected in the rules of the House. That body accords certain classes of legislation "privileged" status: they may come directly to the floor without passing through the Rules Committee, a traditional graveyard for legislation. What kinds of legislation are privileged? Taxing and spending bills, for one: the government's power to raise and spend money must be kept relatively unfettered. But in addition, the omnibus rivers and harbors bills of the Public Works Committee and public lands bills from the Interior Committee share privileged status. The House will allow a civil rights or defense procurement or environmental bill to languish in the Rules Committee, but it takes special precautions to insure that nothing slows down the approval of dams and irrigation projects.

A third major activity takes up perhaps as much time as the other two combined. Traditionally, constituents appeal to their Congressman for myriad favors and services. Sometimes only information is needed, but often constituents request that their congressman intervene in the internal workings of federal agencies to affect a decision in a favorable way, to reverse an adverse decision, or simply to speed up the glacial bureaucratic process. On the basis of extensive personal interviews with congressmen, Charles Clapp writes:

> Denied a favorable ruling by the bureaucracy on a matter of direct concern to him, puzzled or irked by delays in obtaining a decision, confused by the administrative maze through which he is directed to proceed, or ignorant of whom to write, a constituent may turn to his congressman for help. These letters offer great potential for political benefit to the congressman since they affect the constituent personally. If the legislator can be of assistance, he may gain a firm ally; if he is indifferent, he may even lose votes.

Actually congressmen are in an almost unique position in our system, a position shared only with high-level members of the executive branch. Congressmen possess the power to expedite and influence bureaucratic decisions. This capability flows directly from congressional control over what bureaucrats value most: higher budgets and new program authorizations. In a very real sense each congressman is a monopoly supplier of bureaucratic unsticking services for his district.

Every year the federal budget passes through the appropriations committees of Congress. Generally these committees make perfunctory cuts. . . . Deep and serious cuts are made occasionally, and the threat of such cuts keeps most agencies attentive to congressional wishes. . . . Moreover, the bureaucracy must keep coming back to Congress to have its old programs reauthorized and new ones added. Again, most such decisions are perfunctory, but exceptions are sufficiently frequent that bureaucrats do not forget the basis of their agencies' existence. . . . The bureaucracy needs congressional approval in order to survive, let alone expand. Thus, when a congressman calls about some minor bureaucratic decision or regulation, the bureaucracy considers his accommodation a small price to pay for the goodwill its cooperation will produce, particularly if he has any connection to the substantive committee or the appropriations subcommittee to which it reports.

From the standpoint of capturing voters, the congressman's lawmaking activities differ in two important respects from his pork-barrel and casework activities. First, programmatic actions are inherently controversial. Unless his district is homogeneous, a congressman will find his district divided on many major issues. Thus when he casts a vote, introduces a piece of non-trivial legislation, or makes a speech with policy content he will displease some elements of his district. Some constituents may applaud the congressman's civil rights record, but others believe integration is going too fast. Some support foreign aid, while others believe it's money poured down a rathole. Some advocate economic equality, others stew over welfare cheaters. On such policy matters the congressman can expect to make friends as well as enemies. Presumably he will behave so as to maximize the excess of the former over the latter, but nevertheless a policy stand will generally make some enemies.

In contrast, the pork barrel and casework are relatively less controversial. New federal projects bring jobs, shiny new facilities, and general economic prosperity, or so people believe. Snipping ribbons at the dedication of a new post office or dam is a much more pleasant pursuit than disposing of a constitutional amendment on abortion. Republicans and Democrats, conservatives and liberals, all generally prefer a richer district to a poorer one. Of course, in recent years the river damming and stream-bed straightening activities of the Army Corps of Engineers have aroused some opposition among environmentalists. Congressmen happily reacted by absorbing the opposition and adding environmentalism to the pork barrel: water treatment plants are currently a hot congressional item.

Casework is even less controversial. Some poor, aggrieved constituent becomes enmeshed in the tentacles of an evil bureaucracy and calls upon Congressman St. George to do battle with the dragon. . . .

In sum, when considering the benefits of his programmatic activities, the congressman must tote up gains and losses to arrive at a net profit. Pork barreling and casework, however, are basically pure profit.

A second way in which programmatic activities differ from casework and the pork barrel is the difficulty of assigning responsibility to the former as compared with the latter. No congressman can seriously claim that he is responsible for the 1964 Civil Rights Act, the ABM, or the 1972 Revenue Sharing Act. Most constituents do have some vague notion that their congressman is only one of hundreds and their senator one of an even hundred. Even committee chairmen have a difficult time claiming credit for a piece of major legislation, let alone a rank-and-file congressman. Ah, but casework, and the pork barrel. In dealing with the bureaucracy, the congressman is not merely one vote of 435. Rather, he is a nonpartisan power, someone whose phone calls snap an office to attention. He is not kept on hold. The constituent who receives aid believes that his congressman and his congressman alone got results. Similarly, congressmen find it easy to claim credit for federal projects awarded their districts. The congressman may have instigated the proposal for the project in the first place, issued regular progress reports, and ultimately announced the award through his office. Maybe he can't claim credit for the 1965 Voting Rights Act, but he can take credit for Littletown's spanking new sewage treatment plant.

Overall then, programmatic activities are dangerous (controversial), on the one hand, and programmatic accomplishments are difficult to claim credit for, on the other. While less exciting, casework and pork barreling are both safe and profitable. For a reelection-oriented congressman the choice is obvious.

The key to the rise of the Washington establishment (and the vanishing marginals) is the following observation: *the growth of an activist federal government has stimulated a change in the mix of congressional activities.* Specifically, a lesser proportion of congressional effort is now going into programmatic activities and a greater proportion into pork-barrel and casework activities. As a result, today's congressmen make relatively fewer enemies and relatively more friends among the people of their districts.

To elaborate, a basic fact of life in twentieth-century America is the growth of the federal role and its attendant bureaucracy. . . .

As the years have passed, more and more citizens and groups have found themselves dealing with the federal bureaucracy. They may be seeking positive actions—eligibility for various benefits and awards of government grants. Or they may be seeking relief from the costs imposed by bureaucratic regulations—on working conditions, racial and sexual quotas, market restrictions, and numerous other subjects. While not malevolent, bureaucracies make mistakes, both of commissions and omission, and normal attempts at redress often meet with unresponsiveness and inflexibility and sometimes seeming incorrigibility. Whatever the problem, the citizen's congressman is a source of succor. The greater the scope of government activity, the greater the demand for his services. . . .

I seriously doubt that congressmen resist their gradual transformation from national legislators to errand boy-ombudsmen. As we have noted, casework is all profit. Congressmen have buried proposals to relieve the casework burden by establishing a national ombudsman or Congressman Reuss's proposed Administrative Counsel of the Congress. One of the congressmen interviewed by Clapp stated:

> Before I came to Washington I used to think that it might be nice if the individual states had administrative arms here that would take care of necessary liaison between citizens and the national government. But a congressman running for reelection is interested in building fences by providing personal services. The system is set to reelect incumbents regardless of party, and incumbents wouldn't dream of giving any of this service function away to any subagency. As an elected member I feel the same way.

In fact, it is probable that at least some congressmen deliberately stimulate the demand for their bureaucratic fixit services. (See the exhibit at the end of this chapter). Recall that the new Republican in district A travels about his district saying:

> I'm your man in Washington. What are your problems? How can I help you?

And in district B, did the demand for the congressman's services rise so much between 1962 and 1964 that a "regiment" of constituency staff became necessary? Or, having access to the regiment, did the new Democrat stimulate the demand to which he would apply his regiment?

In addition to greatly increased casework, let us not forget that the growth of the federal role has also greatly expanded the federal pork barrel. The creative pork barreler need not limit himself to dams and post offices—rather old-fashioned interests. Today, creative congressmen can cadge LEAA money for the local police, urban renewal and housing money for local politicians, educational program grants for the local education bureaucracy. And there are sewage treatment plants, worker training and retraining programs, health services, and programs for the elderly. The pork barrel is full to overflowing. The conscientious congressman can stimulate applications for federal assistance (the sheer number of programs makes it difficult for local officials to stay current with the possibilities), put in a good word during consideration, and announce favorable decisions amid great fanfare.

In sum, everyday decisions by a large and growing federal bureaucracy bestow significant tangible benefits and impose significant tangible costs. Congressmen can affect these decisions. Ergo, the more decisions the bureaucracy has the opportunity to make, the more opportunities there are for the congressman to build up credits.

The nature of the Washington system is now quite clear. Congressmen (typically the majority Democrats) earn electoral credits by establishing various federal programs (the minority Republicans typically earn credits by fighting the good fight). The legislation is drafted in very general terms, so some agency, existing or newly established, must translate a vague policy mandate into a functioning program, a process that necessitates the promulgation of numerous rules and regulations and, incidentally, the trampling of numerous toes. At the next stage, aggrieved and/or hopeful constituents petition their congressman to intervene in the complex (or at least obscure) decision processes of the bureaucracy. The cycle closes when the congressman lends a sympathetic ear, piously denounces the evils of bureaucracy, intervenes in the latter's decisions, and rides a grateful electorate to ever more impressive electoral showings. Congressmen take credit coming and going. They are the alpha and the omega.

The popular frustration with the permanent government in Washington is partly justified, but to a considerable degree it is misplaced resentment. *Congress is the linchpin of the Washington establishment.* . . . Congress does not just react to big government—it creates it. All of Washington prospers. More and more bureaucrats promulgate more and more regulations and dispense more and more money. Fewer and fewer congressmen suffer electoral defeat. Elements of the electorate benefit from government programs, and all of the electorate is eligible for ombudsman services. But the general, long-term welfare of the United States is no more than an incidental by-product of the system.

36

Joseph M. Bessette

Deliberation Defended (1994)

The deliberation that lies at the core of the kind of democracy established by the American constitutional system can be defined most simply as *reasoning on the merits of public policy*. As commonly and traditionally understood, deliberation is a reasoning process in which the participants seriously consider substantive information and arguments and seek to decide individually and to persuade each other as to what constitutes good public policy. Thus, deliberation includes a variety of activities often called "problem solving" or "analytic": the investigation and identification of social, economic, or governmental problems; the evaluation of current policies or programs; the consideration of various and competing proposals; and the formulation of legislative or administrative remedies. In any genuine deliberative process the participants must be open to the facts, arguments, and proposals that come to their attention and must share a general willingness to learn from their colleagues and others.

So defined, the proximate aim of a deliberative process is the conferral of some public good or benefit. Such a benefit need not necessarily be national in scope (such as a healthy economy or a sound national defense); it may instead be a locally oriented good (such as a flood control project or a new highway), a good directed toward a broad class of citizens (as with civil rights laws or labor legislation), or even transnational in its reach (such as foreign aid). Thus, the existence of deliberation does not turn on the distinction between local and national interests. An over-riding desire to serve one's local constituents does not in itself close a legislator to the persuasive effects of information and arguments, although such a legislator will respond to different kinds of appeals than one who seeks to promote national interests. This is true even if the desire to confer local benefits results directly from self-interested calculations, such as the representative's desire to be reelected; for the legislator who seeks singlemindedly to be reelected may well find that in some situations this goal requires him to give real consideration to the merits of legislative proposals designed to benefit his constituents. . . .

Although legislators may deliberate about local, or partial, interests as well as those of a national dimension, there remains a relationship between the likelihood and nature of deliberation in Congress and the scope of the public benefits that legislators seek to confer. Consider, for example, legislators who deliberate about how to promote the well-being of specific interests. If such legislators see their job essentially in terms of doing good for external groups, they will be inclined to accept the groups' determination as to how this should be done; for who knows the groups' interests better than they do. The narrower and more specific the group (wheat farmers, auto workers, coal miners, etc.) the less difference of opinion or conflict there will be and therefore the less need for such a legislator to consider different arguments or to reason about alternative proposals. However, as the scope of the legislator's concerns widens, to encompass more or broader interests, the more difficult it will become to defer to the interests themselves for guidance. A variety of differing and often conflicting opinions will highlight the complexity of the issues at stake and place a greater obligation on the lawmaker to exercise some independent judgment. For the legislator who seeks to promote the national interests, personal deliberation will be essential; insofar as other legislators share the same goal, collective deliberation will be pervasive.

Personal deliberation by individual legislators does not require that others in the lawmaking body share the same goals. A member of the House, for example, could deliberate in a serious way about how the federal government could solve a transportation problem within his or her district even if no other House members shared the same concern. Collective deliberation, however, necessarily requires some sharing of goals, purposes, or values. If legislators are to reason together about the merits of public policy, there must be some common ground for the arguments and appeals essential to deliberation. Whether the shared goal is quite specific and well defined (e.g., a national health insurance plan along the British model) or much broader and even somewhat vague (e.g., a healthy economy or a sound national defense), it will provide the basis for legislators, who may have little else in common, to share information and to reason and argue together about public policy.

Although the geographically based representation of the American system of government has a tendency to elevate localized interests and needs over broad programmatic concerns, district and state representation also provides a solid basis for the sharing of goals within Congress. Similar kinds of constituencies are likely to have common interests and needs and therefore similar desires or expectations for national policy. Inner-city residents throughout the nation are likely to have similar desires regarding social welfare policy. Farmers from the Midwest, South, and West are likely to agree on the need for price supports. Blue-collar workers in threatened industries across the country are likely to desire high tariffs or other protectionist measures. Those elected to Congress to represent these kinds of constituents will soon discover that many of their colleagues represent similar electorates and thus share many of the same policy goals. In some cases such like-minded legislators institutionalize and promote their shared policy interests through an informal caucus which helps them to share information and ideas and to coordinate policy efforts.

In describing what deliberation is, it is important to clarify what it is not; for policy deliberation is not just any kind of reasoning involved in the policy process. . . . [P]olicy deliberation necessarily involves reasoning about the substantive benefits of public policy, reasoning about some *public* good—some good external to the decisionmakers themselves. "Reasoning on the merits" of public policy means reasoning about how public policy can benefit the broader society or some significant portion thereof. Thus, there is a sharp analytical distinction between deliberation and merely self-interested calculations (however complex the relationship between these two in practice). Similarly, deliberation does not include reasoning about legislative tactics, such as drafting a bill to facilitate its referral to a sympathetic committee or determining how to use the rules of the House or Senate to greatest advantage during the legislative process.

Although a deliberative process is per se rational or analytical, the values or dispositions that the participants bring to bear on the determination of good public policy may reflect a host of diverse influences: general upbringing, parental values, personal experiences, the views of friends and acquaintances, influential teachers, partisan attachments, social class, economic status, etc. Thus, it is not surprising that different individuals often reach opposed conclusions about the merits of policy proposals even when exposed to the same information and arguments. Such disagreement is not in itself evidence of the absence of deliberation.

Deliberation, as defined here, may take a variety of forms. It may be a largely consensual process in which like-minded individuals work together to fashion the details of a policy they all desire; or it may involve deep-seated conflicts over fundamental issues or principles. It may result in unanimity of view, where no votes are necessary; or it may reveal sharp disagreements that require formal voting to determine the majority view. It may range from private reflection in the quiet of an office or study to an emotionally charged exchange on the floor of the House or Senate. It may take the form of open and public discussions preserved in official records or of private exchanges hidden from public view. It may involve direct discussions among elected officials themselves or, perhaps more frequently, conversations among their staff. It may be limited to those who hold formal positions in the government, either elective or appointive; or it may include the ideas and opinions of interest groups, trade associations, national organizations, or the scholarly community. . . .

[B]argaining and reelection theories are the two great pillars that support the widespread contemporary view that Congress is not a deliberative institution (at least in any fundamental sense) and, by implication, that American democracy is not a deliberative democracy. . . .

We must be careful how we frame the issue. . . .

[T]he issue here is not whether the members of Congress pursue reelection but rather whether the reelection incentive squeezes out deliberative activities in a way that undermines, or even destroys, Congress's character as a deliberative institution. This could occur in two ways. First, reelection-oriented activities could so consume the time and resources of the member that nothing is left for serious reasoning about public policy. Second, the reelection incentive could intrude upon formal legislative activities in such a way as to distort otherwise deliberative behavior. For example, the committee member who single-mindedly plays to the cameras during some hearing on a controversial matter because it is good politics has allowed his private interests to overcome his deliberative responsibilities.

While it is certainly possible for the reelection incentive to undermine deliberation in these two ways, it is not necessary. The fact that the members of Congress do certain things to promote their reelection is hardly proof that they do not do other things to reach reasoned judgments about the merits of public policy. Indeed, those who designed the American Congress saw no necessary incompatibility between the reelection incentive and deliberation. The framers believed not only that the legislator's desire to return to Congress would not disable him from engaging in genuine deliberation about national laws, but also that the reelection incentive was the vital link between deliberations in Congress and popular interests and attitudes. Indeed, to argue that the system of public accountability in the modern Congress makes genuine deliberation impossible is virtually the equivalent of saying that deliberation and democracy, as presently constituted in the United States, are incompatible.

It follows, then, that in assessing Congress as a deliberative institution the issue is not so much whether the reelection incentive is a powerful motive in influencing congressional behavior, but rather whether and to what degree legislators in the U.S. Congress embrace and act upon the independent desire to promote good public policy, the end for which deliberation is the means. How much evidence do we have that the ambitious and reelection-seeking members of Congress actually care about and work to promote good public policy?. . .

. . . A theory of legislative behavior that posits only the low motive of reelection cannot even provide the vocabulary to describe and explain serious lawmaking. . . . [H]ow can the reelection incentive explain why any legislator would choose substance over symbols, hard work over posturing, or responsibility over popularity? And, most incongruous of all, why would any legislator moved primarily by the reelection incentive ever take any political risks for the sake of substantive policy goals?

Conversely, a full understanding and appreciation of the high art of lawmaking allows the low arts of mere self-seeking to reveal themselves fully for what they are. Could it even be said that it is only some sense of what constitutes serious lawmaking that makes it possible to understand fully the nature of the lower self-seeking arts (what Hamilton called "the little arts of popularity")? Consider "posturing," for example. . . . Lawmakers and those who observe and study lawmakers have little difficulty identifying posturing when they see it; but surely this is because in the back of their minds they possess a rather clear picture or model of what posturing is not: reasoned argument and effort at genuine persuasion. Posturing can be understood fully only in contrast to this thing which it is not, in contrast to something higher than itself.

What, then, are the principal characteristics of those who engage in serious lawmaking in the United States Congress? . . .

- Serious lawmakers are not satisfied simply to serve in Congress and enjoy its many perks. They want to make a difference, to accomplish something of importance, to make the nation (and perhaps the world) a better place through their governing activities. They believe that there is a public interest, that it is knowable, and that their efforts in Congress can help to achieve it.

- By virtue of their office (membership in the House or Senate, committee and subcommittee chairmanships, leadership positions, etc.) they feel a sense of responsibility to something beyond their personal advantage, a duty to larger ends. It is the accomplishment of these larger ends that is the source of their deepest political satisfaction.

- They seek to earn the respect of their colleagues and of those outside Congress through their deliberative efforts and their substantive achievements. They want to be known as effective legislators. The respect they so earn from their colleagues is a principal source of their power in Congress.

- They develop substantive expertise in the areas under their jurisdiction through careful and thorough analysis, engaging in the hard work necessary to master a subject. Open to facts and arguments, they are willing to learn from others.

- They seek to influence others on legislative matters principally through reasoned persuasion. Although they recognize that raw political bargaining may be necessary to build majorities, their decided preference is to influence through facts and arguments, not through bargains.

- They try to protect the opportunities for responsible lawmaking from the consequences of unrestrained publicity seeking. They have little respect for "legislators" who seek only popularity and reelection.

- Although they wish and seek reelection to Congress, they are, nonetheless, willing to take some political risks for the sake of good public policy.

It would be an understatement to say that these kinds of characteristics are not well accounted for by the reigning self-interest theories of Congress or of American government more generally. Moreover, the point here is not that the 535 members of the House and Senate fall neatly into two categories: the merely ambitious who pursue only narrow self-interest and the high-minded who strive for the public good. Rather these represent something like the extremes of a continuum, from the low to the high, between which the various members of Congress can be found. . . . [S]ome members of the U.S. Congress, perhaps especially the leaders within the institution, look more like.the serious lawmaker described by these characteristics than like the mere self-seeker we have come to view as the norm. If, as those who created the U.S. Congress believed, the serious lawmaker is nothing less than essential to the success of American democracy, then we ought to have a very great interest indeed in assessing the status and activities of such legislators in the contemporary Congress: How many members of the institution behave like serious lawmakers and has this changed over time? What electoral conditions promote the election of the serious-minded, public-spirited legislator as opposed to the mere self-seeking politician? How much influence do serious lawmakers have in the two branches? What are the forces that affect their lawmaking behavior? And what procedural or structural reforms, if any, would enhance the prospects of serious lawmaking in Congress? . . .

In addition to the evidence that serious lawmakers are more prevalent within Congress than modern theories acknowledge, there is also reason for believing that they have a greater impact on policymaking than their mere numbers (and relative proportion of the membership) might suggest. One reason is that because the serious lawmaker undertakes the kind of substantive legislative work that does not interest the mere self-seeker, he will *ipso facto* influence the details of policy in a way that the self-seeker rarely will. After all, the legislator dominated by the reelection incentive has "only a modest interest in what goes into bills or what their passage accomplishes." He knows that "in a large class of undertakings the electoral payment is for positions rather than for effects." The second reason is that the serious lawmaker may be more prevalent among institutional leaders than among the membership generally. In part this is because the members of Congress may select as their leaders those with a reputation for legislative skill and seriousness of purpose. In addition, for formal leadership positions within committees and subcommittees, where selection is virtually automatic, the office itself may foster a sense of responsibility to ends larger than mere private advantage.

This latter point is one of the conclusions of Martha Derthick and Paul Quirk in their study of the deregulation movement of the Carter and Reagan years. . . . [A]s they say about congressional leaders in particular:

> To the extent that a congressman finds or places himself in [a position of leadership on an issue] . . ., two related conditions follow, both of them likely to affect his response: his actions will be more consequential to the outcome; and because they will be more consequential, they will also be more widely observed. Leaders on an issue will be more prone to act on their conception of the public interest, because it is more irresponsible for those in a position of power to do otherwise.

It follows that even a handful of serious, responsible lawmakers in key positions within Congress may have a more consequential effect on the substance of public policy than a much larger number of mere self-seeking politicians who can pursue and achieve private advantage through non-legislative means.

37

War Powers Resolution (1973)

Resolved by the Senate and House of Representatives of the United States of America in Congress assembled, That:

Section 1. This joint resolution may be cited as the "War Powers Resolution."

Sec. 2. (a) It is the purpose of this joint resolution to fulfill the intent of the framers of the Constitution of the United States and insure that the collective judgment of both the Congress and the President will apply to the introduction of United States Armed Forces into hostilities, or into situations where imminent involvement in hostilities is clearly indicated by the circumstances, and to the continued use of such forces in hostilities or in such situations.

(b) Under article 1, section 8, of the Constitution, it is specifically provided that the Congress shall have the power to make all laws necessary and proper for carrying into execution, not only its own powers but also all other powers vested by the Constitution in the Government of the United States, or in any department or officer thereof.

(c) The constitutional powers of the President as Commander-in-Chief to introduce United States Armed Forces into hostilities, or into situations where imminent involvement in hostilities is clearly indicated by the circumstances, are exercised only pursuant to (1) a declaration of war, (2) specific statutory authorization, or (3) a national emergency created by attack upon the United States, its territories or possessions, or its armed forces.

Sec. 3. The President in every possible instance shall consult with Congress before introducing United States Armed Forces into hostilities or into situations where imminent involvement in hostilities is clearly indicated by the circumstances, and after every such introduction shall consult regularly with the Congress until United States Armed Forces are no longer engaged in hostilities or have been removed from such situations.

Sec. 4. (a) In the absence of a declaration of war, in any case in which United States Armed Forces are introduced—

From War Powers Resolution, 87 Stat. 555 (1973).

(1) into hostilities or into situations where imminent involvement in hostilities is clearly indicated by the circumstances;

(2) into the territory, airspace or waters of a foreign nation, while equipped for combat, except for deployments which relate solely to supply, replacement, repair, or training of such forces; or

(3) in numbers which substantially enlarge United States Armed Forces equipped for combat already located in a foreign nation; the President shall submit within 48 hours to the Speaker of the House of Representatives and to the President pro tempore of the Senate a report, in writing, setting forth—

(A) the circumstances necessitating the introduction of United States Armed Forces;

(B) the constitutional and legislative authority under which such introduction took place; and

(C) the estimated scope and duration of the hostilities or involvement.

(b) The President shall provide such other information as the Congress may request in the fulfillment of its constitutional responsibilities with respect to committing the Nation to war and to the use of United States Armed Forces abroad. . . .

Sec. 5. (a) Each report submitted pursuant to section 4(a) (1) shall be . . . referred to the Committee on Foreign Affairs of the House of Representatives and to the Committee on Foreign Relations of the Senate for appropriate action. If, when the report is transmitted, the Congress has adjourned sine die or has adjourned for any period in excess of three calendar days, the Speaker of the House of Representatives and the President pro tempore of the Senate, if they deem it advisable (or if petitioned by at least 30 percent of the membership of their respective Houses) shall jointly request the President to convene Congress in order that it may consider the report and take appropriate action pursuant to this section.

(b) Within sixty calendar days after a report is submitted or is required to be submitted pursuant to section 4 (a) (1), whichever is earlier, the President shall terminate any use of United States Armed Forces with respect to which such report was submitted (or required to be submitted), unless the Congress (1) has declared war or has enacted a specific authorization for such use of United States Armed Forces, (2) has extended by law such sixty-day period, or (3) is physically unable to meet as a result of an armed attack upon the United States. Such sixty-day period shall be extended for not more than an additional thirty days if the President determines and certifies to the Congress in writing that unavoidable military necessity respecting the safety of United States Armed Forces requires the continued use of such armed forces in the course of bringing about a prompt removal of such forces.

(c) Notwithstanding subsection (b), at any time that United States Armed Forces are engaged in hostilities outside the territory of the United States, its possessions and territories without a declaration of war or specific statutory authorization, such forces shall be removed by the President if the Congress so directs by concurrent resolution. . . .

Sec. 8. . . . (d) Nothing in this joint resolution—

(1) is intended to alter the constitutional authority of the Congress or of the President, or the provisions of existing treaties; or

(2) shall be construed as granting any authority to the President with respect to the introduction of United States Armed Forces into hostilities or into situations wherein involvement in hostilities is clearly indicated by the circumstances which authority he would not have had in the absence of this joint resolution. . . .

[Passed over presidential veto Nov. 7, 1973.]

38

INS v. Chadha (1983)

Chief Justice Burger delivered the opinion of the Court:

Chadha is an East Indian who was born in Kenya and holds a British passport. He was lawfully admitted to the United States in 1966 on a nonimmigrant student visa. His visa expired on June 30, 1972. On October 11, 1973, the District Director of the Immigration and Naturalization Service ordered Chadha to show cause why he should not be deported for having "remained in the United States for a longer time than permitted." Pursuant to § 242(b) of the Immigration and Nationality Act, a deportation hearing was held before an Immigration Judge on January 11, 1974. Chadha conceded that he was deportable for overstaying his visa, and the hearing was adjourned to enable him to file an application for suspension of deportation under § 244(a)(1) of the Act. Section 244(a)(1), at the time in question, provided:

> As hereinafter prescribed in this section, the Attorney General may, in his discretion, suspend deportation and adjust the status to that of an alien lawfully admitted for permanent residence, in the case of an alien who applies to the Attorney General for suspension of

From *INS v. Chadha*, 462 U.S. 919 (1983).

deportation and is deportable under any law of the United States . . .; has been physically present in the United States for a continuous period of not less than seven years immediately preceding the date of such application, and proves that during all of such period he was and is a person of good moral character; and is a person whose deportation would, in the opinion of the Attorney General, result in extreme hardship to the alien or to his spouse, parent, or child, who is a citizen of the United States or an alien lawfully admitted for permanent residence.

After Chadha submitted his application for suspension of deportation, the deportation hearing was resumed on February 7, 1974. On the basis of evidence adduced at the hearing, affidavits submitted with the application, and the results of a character investigation conducted by the INS, the Immigration Judge, on June 25, 1974, ordered that Chadha's deportation be suspended. The Immigration Judge found that Chadha met the requirements of § 244(a)(1): he had resided continuously in the United States for over seven years, was of good moral character, and would suffer "extreme hardship" if deported.

Pursuant to § 244(c)(1) of the Act, the Immigration Judge suspended Chadha's deportation and a report of the suspension was transmitted to Congress. Section 244(c)(1) provides:

> . . . If the deportation of any alien is suspended under the provisions of this subsection, a complete and detailed statement of the facts and pertinent provisions of law in the case shall be reported to the Congress with the reasons for such suspension. Such reports shall be submitted on the first day of each calendar month in which Congress is in session.

Once the Attorney General's recommendation for suspension of Chadha's deportation was conveyed to Congress, Congress had the power under § 244(c)(2) of the Act, to veto the Attorney General's determination that Chadha should not be deported. Section 244(c)(2) provides:

> . . . if during the session of the Congress at which a case [that recommends suspending the deportation of an alien] is reported, or prior to the close of the session of the Congress next following the session at which a case is reported, either the Senate or the House of Representatives passes a resolution stating in substance that it does not favor the suspension of such deportation, the Attorney General shall thereupon deport such alien or authorize the alien's voluntary departure at his own expense under the order of deportation in the manner provided by law. If, within the time above specified, neither the Senate nor the House of Representatives shall pass such a resolution, the Attorney General shall cancel deportation proceedings.

. . . On December 12, 1975, Representative Eilberg, Chairman of the Judiciary Subcommittee on Immigration, Citizenship, and International Law, introduced a resolution opposing "the granting of permanent residence in the United States to [six] aliens," including Chadha. . . . So far as the record before us shows, the House consideration of the resolution was based on Representative Eilberg's statement from the floor that

> [i]t was the feeling of the committee, after reviewing 340 cases, that the aliens contained in the resolution [Chadha and five others] did not meet these statutory requirements, particularly as it relates to hardship; and it is the opinion of the committee that their deportation should not be suspended.

The resolution was passed without debate or recorded vote. Since the House action was pursuant to § 244(c)(2), the resolution was not treated as an Art. I legislative act; it was not submitted to the Senate or presented to the President for his action.

After the House veto of the Attorney General's decision to allow Chadha to remain in the United States, the Immigration Judge reopened the deportation proceedings to implement the House order deporting Chadha. Chadha . . . filed a petition for review of the deportation order in the United States Court of Appeals for the Ninth Circuit. . . .

After full briefing and oral argument, the Court of Appeals held that the House was without constitutional authority to order Chadha's deportation; accordingly it directed the Attorney General "to cease and desist from taking any steps to deport this alien based upon the resolution enacted by the House of Representatives." The essence of its holding was that § 244(c)(2) violates the constitutional doctrine of separation of powers....

We turn now to the question whether action of one House of Congress under § 244(c)(2) violates strictures of the Constitution. We begin, of course, with the presumption that the challenged statute is valid. Its wisdom is not the concern of the courts; if a challenged action does not violate the Constitution, it must be sustained:

> Once the meaning of an enactment is discerned and its constitutionality determined, the judicial process comes to an end. We do not sit as a committee of review, nor are we vested with the power of veto. *TVA v. Hill* (1978).

By the same token, the fact that a given law or procedure is efficient, convenient, and useful in facilitating functions of government, standing alone, will not save it if it is contrary to the Constitution. Convenience and efficiency are not the primary objectives—or the hallmarks—of democratic government, and our inquiry is sharpened, rather than blunted, by the fact that congressional veto provisions are appearing with increasing frequency in statutes which delegate authority to executive and independent agencies:

> Since 1932, when the first veto provision was enacted into law, 295 congressional veto-type procedures have been inserted in 196 different statutes as follows: from 1932 to 1939, five statutes were affected; from 1940–49, nineteen statutes; between 1950–59, thirty-four statutes; and from 1960–69, forty-nine. From the year 1970 through 1975, at least one hundred sixty-three such provisions were included in eighty-nine laws.

Justice White undertakes to make a case for the proposition that the one-House veto is a useful "political invention," and we need not challenge that assertion. We can even concede this utilitarian argument, although the long-range political wisdom of this "invention" is arguable. It has been vigorously debated, and it is instructive to compare the views of the protagonists. But policy arguments supporting even useful "political inventions" are subject to the demands of the Constitution, which defines powers and, with respect to this subject, sets out just how those powers are to be exercised.

Explicit and unambiguous provisions of the Constitution prescribe and define the respective functions of the Congress and of the Executive in the legislative process. Since the precise terms of those familiar provisions are critical to the resolution of these cases, we set them out verbatim. Article I provides:

> All legislative Powers herein granted shall be vested in a Congress of the United States, which shall consist of a Senate *and* House of Representatives. Art. I, § 1.
>
> Every Bill which shall have passed the House of Representatives *and* the Senate, *shall*, before it becomes a law, be presented to the President of the United States. . . . Art. I, 7, cl. 2.
>
> *Every* Order, Resolution, or Vote to which the Concurrence of the Senate and House of Representatives may be necessary (except on a question of Adjournment) *shall* be presented to the President of the United States; and before the Same shall take Effect, *shall* be approved by him, or being disapproved by him, *shall* be repassed by two thirds of the Senate and House of Representatives, according to the Rules and Limitations prescribed in the Case of a Bill. Art. I, § 7, cl. 3.

These provisions of Art. I are integral parts of the constitutional design for the separation of powers. We have recently noted that

> [t]he principle of separation of powers was not simply an abstract generalization in the minds of the Framers: it was woven into the document that they drafted in Philadelphia in the summer of 1787. *Buckley v. Valeo* (1983).

The Presentment Clauses

The records of the Constitutional Convention reveal that the requirement that all legislation be presented to the President before becoming law was uniformly accepted by the Framers. Presentment to the President and the Presidential veto were considered so imperative that the draftsmen took special pains to assure that these requirements could not be circumvented. During the final debate on Art. I, § 7, cl. 2, James Madison expressed concern that it might easily be evaded by the simple expedient of calling a proposed law a "resolution" or "vote," rather than a "bill." As a consequence, Art. I, § 7, cl. 3, was added.

The decision to provide the President with a limited and qualified power to nullify proposed legislation by veto was based on the profound conviction of the Framers that the powers conferred on Congress were the powers to be most carefully circumscribed. It is beyond doubt that lawmaking was a power to be shared by both Houses and the President. In The Federalist No. 73, Hamilton focused on the President's role in making laws:

> If even no propensity had ever discovered itself in the legislative body to invade the rights of the Executive, the rules of just reasoning and theoretic propriety would of themselves teach us that the one ought not to be left to the mercy of the other, but ought to possess a constitutional and effectual power of self-defence. . . .

The President's role in the lawmaking process also reflects the Framers' careful efforts to check whatever propensity a particular Congress might have to enact oppressive, improvident, or ill-considered measures. The President's veto role in the legislative process was described later during public debate on ratification:

> It establishes a salutary check upon the legislative body, calculated to guard the community against the effects of faction, precipitancy, or of any impulse unfriendly to the public good, which may happen to influence a majority of that body. . . . The primary inducement to conferring the power in question upon the Executive is to enable him to defend himself; the secondary one is to increase the chances in favor of the community against the passing of bad laws, through haste, inadvertence, or design.

The Court also has observed that the Presentment Clauses serve the important purpose of assuring that a "national" perspective is grafted on the legislative process:

The President is a representative of the people just as the members of the Senate and of the House are, and it may be, at some times, on some subjects, that the President elected by all the people is rather more representative of them all than are the members of either body of the Legislature, whose constituencies are local and not countrywide. . . . *United States v. Myers* (1926).

Bicameralism

The bicameral requirement of Art. I, § § 1, 7, was of scarcely less concern to the Framers than was the Presidential veto, and indeed the two concepts are interdependent. By providing that no law could take effect without the concurrence of the prescribed majority of the Members of both Houses, the Framers reemphasized their belief, already remarked upon in connection with the Presentment Clauses, that legislation should not be enacted unless it has been carefully and fully considered by the Nation's elected officials. In the Constitutional Convention debates on the need for a bicameral legislature, James Wilson, later to become a Justice of this Court, commented:

> Despotism comes on mankind in different shapes, sometimes in an Executive, sometimes in a military one. Is there danger of a Legislative despotism? Theory & practice both proclaim it. If the Legislative authority be not restrained, there can be neither liberty nor stability; and it can only be restrained by dividing it within itself, into distinct and independent branches. In a single house there is no check but the inadequate one of the virtue & good sense of those who compose it.

. . . However familiar, it is useful to recall that, apart from their fear that special interests could be favored at the expense of public needs, the Framers were also concerned, although not of one mind, over the apprehensions of the smaller states. Those states feared a commonality of interest among the larger states would work to their disadvantage; representatives of the larger states, on the other hand, were skeptical of a legislature that could pass laws favoring a minority of the people. It need hardly be repeated here that the Great Compromise, under which one House was viewed as representing the people and the other the states, allayed the fears of both the large and small states.

We see therefore that the Framers were acutely conscious that the bicameral requirement and the Presentment Clauses would serve essential constitutional functions. The President's participation in the legislative process was to protect the Executive Branch from Congress and to protect the whole people from improvident laws. The division of the Congress into two distinctive bodies assures that the legislative power would be exercised only after opportunity for full study and debate in separate settings. The President's unilateral veto power, in turn, was limited by the power of two-thirds of both Houses of Congress to overrule a veto, thereby precluding final arbitrary action of one person. It emerges clearly that the prescription for legislative action in Art. I, §§ 1, 7, represents the Framers' decision that the legislative power of the Federal Government be exercised in accord with a single, finely wrought and exhaustively considered, procedure.

The Constitution sought to divide the delegated powers of the new Federal Government into three defined categories, Legislative, Executive, and Judicial, to assure, as nearly as possible, that each branch of government would confine itself to its assigned responsibility. The hydraulic pressure inherent within each of the separate Branches to exceed the outer limits of its power, even to accomplish desirable objectives, must be resisted....

Examination of the action taken here by one House pursuant to § 244(c)(2) reveals that it was essentially legislative in purpose and effect. In purporting to exercise power defined in Art. I, § 8, cl. 4, to "establish an uniform Rule of Naturalization," the House took action that had the purpose and effect of altering the legal rights, duties, and relations of persons, including the Attorney General, Executive Branch officials and Chadha, all outside the Legislative Branch. Section 244(c)(2) purports to authorize one House of Congress to require the Attorney General to deport an individual alien whose deportation otherwise would be canceled under § 244. The one-House veto operated in these cases to overrule the Attorney General and mandate Chadha's deportation; absent the House action, Chadha would remain in the United States. Congress has acted, and its action has altered Chadha's status.

The legislative character of the one-House veto in these cases is confirmed by the character of the congressional action it supplants. Neither the House of Representatives nor the Senate contends that, absent the veto provision in § 244(c)(2), either of them, or both of them acting together, could effectively require the Attorney General to deport an alien once the Attorney General, in the exercise of legislatively delegated authority, had determined the alien should remain in the United States. Without the challenged provision in § 244(c)(2), this could have been achieved, if at all, only by legislation requiring deportation. . . .

The nature of the decision implemented by the one-House veto in these cases further manifests its legislative character. After long experience with the clumsy, time-consuming private bill procedure, Congress made a deliberate choice to delegate to the Executive Branch, and specifically to the Attorney General, the authority to allow deportable aliens to remain in this country in certain specified circumstances. It is not disputed that this choice to delegate authority is precisely the kind of decision that can be implemented only in accordance with the procedures set out in Art. I. Disagreement with the Attorney General's decision on Chadha's deportation—that is, Congress' decision to deport Chadha—no less than Congress' original choice to delegate to the Attorney General the authority to make that decision, involves determinations of policy that Congress can implement in only one way; bicameral passage followed by presentment to the President. Congress must abide by its delegation of authority until that delegation is legislatively altered or revoked.

Finally, we see that, when the Framers intended to authorize either House of Congress to act alone and outside of its prescribed bicameral legislative role, they narrowly and precisely defined the procedure for such action. There are four provisions in the Constitution, explicit and unambiguous, by which one House may act alone with the unreviewable force of law, not subject to the President's veto:

  (a) The House of Representatives alone was given the power to initiate impeachments. Art. I, § 2, cl. 5;

  (b) The Senate alone was given the power to conduct trials following impeachment on charges initiated by the House, and to convict following trial. Art. I, § 3, cl. 6;

  (c) The Senate alone was given final unreviewable power to approve or to disapprove Presidential appointments. Art. II, § 2, cl. 2;

  (d) The Senate alone was given unreviewable power to ratify treaties negotiated by the President. Art. II, 2, cl. 2.

Clearly, when the Draftsmen sought to confer special powers on one House, independent of the other House, or of the President, they did so in explicit, unambiguous terms. These carefully defined exceptions from presentment and bicameralism underscore the difference between the legislative functions of Congress and other unilateral but important and binding one-House acts provided for in the Constitution. These exceptions are narrow, explicit, and separately justified; none of them authorize the action challenged here. On the contrary, they provide further support for the conclusion that congressional authority is not to be implied, and for the conclusion that the veto provided for in § 244(c)(2) is not authorized by the constitutional design of the powers of the Legislative Branch.

Since it is clear that the action by the House under § 244(c)(2) was not within any of the express constitutional exceptions authorizing one House to act alone, and equally clear that it was an exercise of legislative power, that action was subject to the standards prescribed in Art. I. The bicameral requirement, the Presentment Clauses, the President's veto, and Congress' power to override a veto were intended to erect enduring checks on each Branch and to protect the people from the improvident exercise of power by mandating certain prescribed steps. To preserve those checks, and maintain the separation of powers, the carefully defined limits on the power of each Branch must not be eroded. To accomplish what has been attempted by one House of Congress in this case requires action in conformity with the express procedures of the Constitution's prescription for legislative action: passage by a majority of both Houses and presentment to the President.

The veto authorized by § 244(c)(2) doubtless has been in many respects a convenient shortcut; the "sharing" with the Executive by Congress of its authority over aliens in this manner is, on its face, an appealing compromise. In purely practical terms, it is obviously easier for action to be taken by one House without submission to the President; but it is crystal clear from the records of the Convention, contemporaneous writings, and debates that the Framers ranked other values higher than efficiency. . . .

The choices we discern as having been made in the Constitutional Convention impose burdens on governmental processes that often seem clumsy, inefficient, even unworkable, but those hard choices were consciously made by men who had lived under a form of government that permitted arbitrary governmental acts to go unchecked. There is no support in the Constitution or decisions of this Court for the proposition that the cumbersomeness and delays often encountered in complying with explicit constitutional standards may be avoided, either by the Congress or by the President. With all the obvious flaws of delay, untidiness, and potential for abuse, we have not yet found a better way to preserve freedom than by making the exercise of power subject to the carefully crafted restraints spelled out in the Constitution.

We hold that the congressional veto provision in § 244(c)(2) is severable from the Act, and that it is unconstitutional. Accordingly, the judgment of the Court of Appeals is *Affirmed*.

Justice Powell, concurring in the judgment:
The Court's decision, based on the Presentment Clauses, Art. I, 7, cls. 2 and 3, apparently will invalidate every use of the legislative veto. The breadth of this holding gives one pause. Congress has included the veto in

literally hundreds of statutes, dating back to the 1930's. Congress clearly views this procedure as essential to controlling the delegation of power to administrative agencies. One reasonably may disagree with Congress' assessment of the veto's utility, but the respect due its judgment as a coordinate branch of Government cautions that our holding should be no more extensive than necessary to decide these cases. In my view, the cases may be decided on a narrower ground. When Congress finds that a particular person does not satisfy the statutory criteria for permanent residence in this country, it has assumed a judicial function in violation of the principle of separation of powers. Accordingly, I concur only in the judgment. . . .

The impropriety of the House's assumption of this function is confirmed by the fact that its action raises the very danger the Framers sought to avoid— the exercise of unchecked power. In deciding whether Chadha deserves to be deported, Congress is not subject to any internal constraints that prevent it from arbitrarily depriving him of the right to remain in this country. Unlike the judiciary or an administrative agency, Congress is not bound by established substantive rules. Nor is it subject to the procedural safeguards, such as the right to counsel and a hearing before an impartial tribunal, that are present when a court or an agency adjudicates individual rights. The only effective constraint on Congress' power is political, but Congress is most accountable politically when it prescribes rules of general applicability. When it decides rights of specific persons, those rights are subject to "the tyranny of a shifting majority." . . .

Justice White, dissenting:

Today the Court not only invalidates § 244(c)(2) of the Immigration and Nationality Act, but also sounds the death knell for nearly 200 other statutory provisions in which Congress has reserved a "legislative veto." For this reason, the Court's decision is of surpassing importance. And it is for this reason that the Court would have been well advised to decide the cases, if possible, on the narrower grounds of separation of powers, leaving for full consideration the constitutionality of other congressional review statutes operating on such varied matters as war powers and agency rulemaking, some of which concern the independent regulatory agencies.

The prominence of the legislative veto mechanism in our contemporary political system and its importance to Congress can hardly be overstated. It has become a central means by which Congress secures the accountability of executive and independent agencies. Without the legislative veto, Congress is faced with a Hobson's choice: either to refrain from delegating the necessary authority, leaving itself with a hopeless task of writing laws with the requisite specificity to cover endless special circumstances across the entire policy landscape, or, in the alternative, to abdicate its lawmaking function to the Executive Branch and independent agencies. To choose the former leaves major national problems unresolved; to opt for the latter risks unaccountable policymaking by those not elected to fill that role. Accordingly, over the past five decades, the legislative veto has been placed in nearly 200 statutes. The device is known in every field of governmental concern: reorganization, budgets, foreign affairs, war powers, and regulation of trade, safety, energy, the environment, and the economy. . . .

If the legislative veto were as plainly unconstitutional as the Court strives to suggest, its broad ruling today would be more comprehensible. But the constitutionality of the legislative veto is anything but clear-cut. The issue divides scholars, courts, Attorneys General, and the two other branches of the National Government. If the veto devices so flagrantly disregarded the requirements of Art. I as the Court today suggests, I find it incomprehensible that Congress, whose Members are bound by oath to uphold the Constitution, would have placed these mechanisms in nearly 200 separate laws over a period of 50 years. . . .

If Congress may delegate lawmaking power to independent and Executive agencies, it is most difficult to understand Art. I as prohibiting Congress from also reserving a check on legislative power for itself. Absent the veto, the agencies receiving delegations of legislative or quasi-legislative power may issue regulations having the force of law without bicameral approval and without the President's signature. It is thus not apparent why the reservation of a veto over the exercise of that legislative power must be subject to a more exacting test. In both cases, it is enough that the initial statutory authorizations comply with the Art. I requirement. . . .

I do not suggest that all legislative vetoes are necessarily consistent with separation of powers principles. A legislative check on an inherently executive function, for example, that of initiating prosecutions, poses an entirely different question. But the legislative veto device here—and in many other settings—is far from an instance of legislative tyranny over the Executive. It is a necessary check on the unavoidably expanding power of the agencies, both Executive and independent, as they engage in exercising authority delegated by Congress.

I regret that I am in disagreement with my colleagues on the fundamental questions that these cases present. But even more I regret the destructive scope of the Court's holding. It reflects a profoundly different conception of the Constitution than that held by the courts which sanctioned the modern administrative state. Today's decision strikes down in one fell swoop provisions in more laws enacted by Congress than the Court has cumulatively invalidated in its history . . .

I must dissent.

Chapter IV

The Presidency

Alexander Hamilton says that "Energy in the executive is a leading character in the definition of good government." Hamilton understands the potential conflict between an energetic government and republican principles, but he claims that an energetic executive is essential to the defense of the nation against foreign attacks and the steady administration of the laws. The ingredients that will produce an energetic executive are a unified presidential office, a term of sufficient duration, adequate financial support, and competent powers. These ingredients would insulate the President from an undue dependence on Congress and public opinion. He would have the independent resources necessary to the energetic execution of his office.

Richard Neustadt suggests that the Constitutional powers of the President are dependent upon the office holder's powers of persuasion. Unless a President can persuade members of Congress, his own staff and cabinet officers, and the public to support his policies, his Constitutional authority will be of little use to him. James W. Ceaser, Glen E. Thurow, Jeffrey K. Tulis, and Joseph M. Bessette argue, however, that the greatest shortcoming of contemporary Presidents is their tendency to rely too much on popular persuasion and not enough on their Constitutional authority.

Ceaser *et al* argue that Presidents increasingly look not to their Constitutional office but to public opinion as a source of executive energy. They trace this development to the Progressives who saw public opinion as a more democratic and more powerful source of authority. But they think this is a dangerous trend. They contend that the reliance on popular opinion will undermine the exercise of Constitutionally created power, and will lead to an excessive reliance on popular rhetoric. The more rhetoric is seen as a source of authority, the more politicians will be tempted to make exaggerated claims in search of increased power.

In a 1960 campaign speech John F. Kennedy argues that his understanding of the Presidential office was far more important than his position on any particular policy issue. Kennedy accepts Hamilton's call for an energetic executive and criticizes those who wish to substitute rhetoric for more substantive results. But Kennedy is also willing to look to popular opinion and popular rhetoric as a source of presidential authority. He accepts Theodore Roosevelt's idea of the Presidency as a "bully pulpit." Kennedy wants the president "to summon his national constituency" and "alert the people to our dangers and our opportunities."

Early in his presidency George W. Bush used the bully pulpit to discuss the dangers and the opportunities presented to the nation by embryonic stem cell research. Not only did Bush seek to explain his policy decision on federal funding for stem cell research, but he also sought to educate the nation on the complex moral questions involved in any policy decision. He concludes that policies should reflect "both our capabilities and our conscience."

Can the Presidency become a bully pulpit without undermining the President's institutional sources of authority? Lincoln saw the potential for ambitious men to subvert the Constitution in search of extraordinary powers and honors. Lincoln's solution, however, relied to a great extent on rhetoric. Lincoln did not wish to encourage the passionate rhetoric that would fan the flames of a mob, he looked instead to a cooler, more reasonable rhetoric that would support the Constitution and the laws. Only through the persuasive powers of rhetoric could the President maintain the institutions of government created by the Constitution.

The rule of law must not only be supplemented by a judicious rhetoric, it must sometimes give way to action without specific legal authorization. When President Truman seized the steel mills during the Korean War, he claimed that such discretionary authority was implied in the executive power vested in him by the Constitution and by his constitutional duty "to take care that the laws be faithfully executed." But the Supreme Court found his action to be beyond the Constitutional authority of the President.

In other cases the Court has given the President a broad claim to discretionary authority. In *Curtiss-Wright Export Corporation v. United States* the Court distinguished the authority of the national government over domestic affairs, which is derived from the Constitution, and its authority over foreign affairs, which inheres in the concept of nationhood. The latter would exist whether or not the Constitution provided for it. Since the President represents the nation in foreign affairs, the Court's reasoning suggests that the President may exercise this virtually unlimited reservoir of extra-Constitutional authority.

The Court glossed over the fact that it is the Constitution that makes the President the representative of the nation in foreign affairs. Nonetheless, the idea of discretionary powers beyond the reach of Constitutional limitations has remained an important strain of judicial interpretation. The immediate problem in the case of *Korematsu v. U.S.* is whether distinctions based on race can ever be legitimate. But Justices Jackson and Frankfurter take the opportunity of the case to elaborate their different views of the discretionary authority of the executive. Both admit that military necessity may occasionally take precedence over the protection of individual rights. But Justice Jackson says that even if such action is absolutely necessary, we should never call it Constitutional. To do so would be to establish a dangerous precedent that would undermine the protection of rights. Frankfurter disagrees. He finds it more dangerous to place the actions of the executive outside of the Constitution in any circumstance. Whether or not there is an emergency, Frankfurter wants to retain the possibility of Constitutional restraint. He concludes that the Constitution can and should be understood to include the possibility of effective action in an emergency.

Frankfurter's argument brings to mind Lincoln's defense of his suspension of the writ of habeas corpus. Lincoln claims that in times of emergency the government must deprive citizens of liberty without due process of law; indeed, in granting power to suspend the writ of habeas corpus, the Constitution itself recognizes the necessity for doing so. According to Lincoln the Presidential office established by the Constitution permits and even demands the exercise of discretion in extraordinary situations. Statesmanship is necessary for the preservation of the Constitution and the rule of law.

Clinton v. Jones points to both the difficulty and the necessity of distinguishing between the office of the Presidency and the person who occupies that office. A unanimous Court determined that whereas a President has absolute immunity from a civil suit arising from the performance of his duties, he remains subject to the reach of civil law in cases unrelated to official conduct.

Frederick Douglass's speech on the statesmanship of Lincoln provides a fitting conclusion to the discussion of the presidency. Douglass captures the essence of Lincoln's statesmanship: Lincoln's recognition of the need for compromise, his appreciation of the virtues and limits of law, and his sense of when to follow, when to lead, and when to ignore popular opinion. Douglass also recognizes that although Lincoln had different personal interests from his own, and represented different social interests, their common belief in certain fundamental principles provided a basis for mutual respect and political action.

39

Alexander Hamilton

On the Presidency (1788)

There is an idea, which is not without its advocates, that a vigorous Executive is inconsistent with the genius of republican government. The enlightened well-wishers to this species of government must at least hope that the
supposition is destitute of foundation; since they can never admit its truth,
without at the same time admitting the condemnation of their own principles. Energy in the Executive is a leading character in the definition of good
government. It is essential to the protection of the community against
foreign attacks; it is not less essential to the steady administration of the
laws; to the protection of property against those irregular and high-handed
combinations which sometimes interrupt the ordinary course of justice; to
the security of liberty against the enterprises and assaults of ambition, of
faction, and of anarchy. . . .

A feeble execution is but another phrase for a bad execution; and a government ill executed, whatever it may be in theory, must be, in practice, a
bad government.

Taking it for granted, therefore, that all men of sense will agree in the
necessity of an energetic Executive, it will only remain to inquire, what are
the ingredients which constitute this energy? How far can they be combined
with those other ingredients which constitute safety in the republican sense?
And how far does this combination characterize the plan which has been
reported by the convention?

The ingredients which constitute energy in the Executive are, first,
unity; secondly, duration; thirdly, an adequate provision for its support;
fourthly, competent powers.

The ingredients which constitute safety in the republican sense are,
first, a due dependence on the people; secondly, a due responsibility. . . .

That unity is conducive to energy will not be disputed. Decision, activity, secrecy, and despatch will generally characterize the proceedings of one
man in a much more eminent degree than the proceedings of any greater

From Federalists 70–73, in *The Federalist.*

number; and in proportion as the number is increased, these qualities will be diminished.

This unity may be destroyed in two ways: either by vesting the power in two or more magistrates of equal dignity and authority; or by vesting it ostensibly in one man, subject, in whole or in part, to the control and cooperation of others, in the capacity of counsellors to him. . . .

Wherever two or more persons are engaged in any common enterprise or pursuit, there is always danger of difference of opinion. If it be a public trust or office, in which they are clothed with equal dignity and authority, there is peculiar danger of personal emulation and even animosity. From either, and especially from all these causes, the most bitter dissensions are apt to spring. Whenever these happen, they lessen the respectability, weaken the authority, and distract the plans and operations of those whom they divide. If they should unfortunately assail the supreme executive magistracy of a country, consisting of a plurality of persons, they might impede or frustrate the most important measures of the government, in the most critical emergencies of the state. And what is still worse, they might split the community into the most violent and irreconcilable factions, adhering differently to the different individuals who composed the magistracy. . . .

Upon the principles of a free government, inconveniences from the source just mentioned must necessarily be submitted to in the formation of the legislature; but it is unnecessary, and therefore unwise, to introduce them into the constitution of the Executive. It is here too they may be most pernicious. In the legislature, promptitude of decision is oftener an evil than a benefit. The differences of opinion, and the jarrings of parties in that department of the government, though they may sometimes obstruct salutary plans, yet often promote deliberation and circumspection, and serve to check excesses in the majority. When a resolution too is once taken, the opposition must be at an end. That resolution is a law, and resistance to it punishable. But no favorable circumstances palliate or atone for the disadvantages of dissension in the executive department. Here, they are pure and unmixed. There is no point at which they cease to operate. They serve to embarrass and weaken the execution of the plan or measure to which they relate, from the first step to the final conclusion of it. They constantly counteract those qualities in the Executive which are the most necessary ingredients in its composition,—vigor and expedition, and this without any counterbalancing good. In the conduct of war, in which the energy of the Executive is the bulwark of the national security, every thing would be to be apprehended from its plurality. . . .

But one of the weightiest objections to a plurality in the Executive, and which lies as much against the last as the first plan, is, that it tends to conceal faults and destroy responsibility. Responsibility is of two kinds—to censure and to punishment. The first is the more important of the two, especially in an elective office. Man, in public trust, will much oftener act in such a manner as to render him unworthy of being any longer trusted, than in such a manner as to make him obnoxious to legal punishment. But the multiplication of the Executive adds to the difficulty of detection in either case. It often becomes impossible, amidst mutual accusations, to determine on whom the blame or the punishment of a pernicious measure, or series of pernicious measures, ought really to fall. . . .

Duration in office has been mentioned as the second requisite to the energy of the Executive authority. This has relation to two objects: to the personal firmness of the executive magistrate, in the employment of his constitutional powers; and to the stability of the system of administration which may have been adopted under his auspices. With regard to the first, it must be evident, that the longer the duration in office, the greater will be the probability of obtaining so important an advantage. It is a general principle of human nature, that a man will be interested in whatever he possesses, in proportion to the firmness or precariousness of the tenure by which he holds it; will be less attached to what he holds by a momentary or uncertain title, than to what he enjoys by a durable or certain title; and, of course, will be willing to risk more for the sake of the one, than for the sake of the other. This remark is not less applicable to a political privilege, or honor, or trust, than to any article of ordinary property. The inference from it is, that a man acting in the capacity of chief magistrate, under a consciousness that in a very short time he must lay down his office, will be apt to feel himself too little interested in it to hazard any material censure or perplexity, from the independent exertion of his powers, or from encountering the ill-humors, however transient, which may happen to prevail, either in a considerable part of the society itself, or even in a predominant faction in the legislative body. . . .

There are some who would be inclined to regard the servile pliancy of the Executive to a prevailing current, either in the community or in the legislature, as its best recommendation. But such men entertain very crude notions, as well of the purposes for which government was instituted, as of the true means by which the public happiness may be promoted. The republican principle demands that the deliberate sense of the community should govern the conduct of those to whom they intrust the management of their affairs; but it does not require an unqualified complaisance to every sudden breeze of passion, or to every transient impulse which the people may receive from the arts of men, who flatter their prejudices to betray their interest. It is a just observation, that the people commonly *intend* the PUBLIC GOOD. This often applies to their very errors. But their good sense would despise the adulator who should pretend that they always *reason right* about the *means* of promoting it. They know from experience that they sometimes err; and the wonder is that they so seldom err as they do, beset, as they continually are, by the wiles of parasites and sycophants, by the snares of the ambitious, the avaricious, the desperate, by the artifices of men who possess their confidence more than they deserve it, and of those who seek to possess rather than to deserve it. When occasions present themselves, in which the interests of the people are at variance with their inclinations, it is the duty of the persons whom they have appointed to be the guardians of those interests, to withstand the temporary delusion, in order to give them time and opportunity for more cool and sedate reflection. Instances might be cited in which a conduct of this kind has saved the people from very fatal consequences of their own mistakes, and has procured lasting monuments of their gratitude to the men who had courage and magnanimity enough to serve them at the peril of their displeasure.

But however inclined we might be to insist upon an unbounded complaisance in the Executive to the inclinations of the people, we can with no propriety contend for a like complaisance to the humors of the legislature. The latter may sometimes stand in opposition to the former, and at other times the people may be entirely neutral. In either supposition, it is certainly desirable that the Executive should be in a situation to dare to act his own opinion with vigor and decision. . . .

It cannot be affirmed, that a duration of four years, or any other limited duration, would completely answer the end proposed; but it would contribute towards it in a degree which would have a material influence upon the spirit and character of the government. Between the commencement and termination of such a period, there would always be a considerable interval, in which the prospect of annihilation would be sufficiently remote, not to have an improper effect upon the conduct of a man imbued with a tolerable portion of fortitude; and in which he might reasonably promise himself, that there would be time enough before it arrived, to make the community sensible of the propriety of the measures he might incline to pursue. Though it be probable that, as he approached the moment when the public were, by a new election, to signify their sense of his conduct, his confidence, and with it his firmness, would decline; yet both the one and the other would derive support from the opportunities which his previous continuance in the station had afforded him, of establishing himself in the esteem and goodwill of his constituents. . . .

With a positive duration of considerable extent, I connect the circumstance of reeligibility. The first is necessary to give to the officer himself the inclination and the resolution to act his part well, and to the community time and leisure to observe the tendency of his measures, and thence to form an experimental estimate of their merits. The last is necessary to enable the people, when they see reason to approve of his conduct, to continue him in his station, in order to prolong the utility of his talents and virtues, and to secure to the government the advantage of permanency in a wise system of administration.

Nothing appears more plausible at first sight, nor more ill-founded upon close inspection than a scheme which in relation to the present point has had some respectable advocates,—I mean that of continuing the chief magistrate in office for a certain time, and then excluding him from it, either for a limited period or forever after. This exclusion, whether temporary or perpetual, would have nearly the same effects, and these effects would be for the most part rather pernicious than salutary.

One ill effect of the exclusion would be a diminution of the inducements to good behavior. There are few men who would not feel much less zeal in the discharge of a duty, when they were conscious that the advantages of the station with which it was connected must be relinquished at a determinate period, than when they were permitted to entertain a hope of *obtaining*, by *meriting*, a continuance of them. This position will not be disputed so long as it is admitted that the desire of reward is one of the strongest incentives of human conduct; or that the best security for the fidelity of mankind is to make their interest coincide with their duty. Even the love of fame, the ruling passion of the noblest minds, which would prompt a man to plan and undertake extensive and arduous enterprises for the public benefit, requiring considerable time to mature and perfect them, if he could flatter himself with the prospect of being allowed to finish what he had begun, would, on the contrary, deter him from the undertaking, when he foresaw that he must quit the scene before he could accomplish the work, and must commit that, together with his own reputation, to hands which might be unequal or unfriendly to the task. The most to be expected from the generality of men, in such a situation, is the negative merit of not doing harm, instead of the positive merit of doing good,

Another ill effect of the exclusion would be the temptation to sordid views, to peculation, and, in some instances, to usurpation. An avaricious man, who might happen to fill the office, looking forward to a time when he must at all events yield up the emoluments he enjoyed, would feel a propensity, not easy to be resisted by such a man, to make the best use of the opportunity he enjoyed while it lasted, and might not scruple to have recourse to the most corrupt expedients to make the harvest as abundant as it was transitory; though the same man, probably, with a different prospect before him, might content himself with the regular perquisites of his situation, and might even be unwilling to risk the consequences of an abuse of his opportunities. His avarice might be a guard upon his avarice. Add to this that the same man might be vain or ambitious, as well as avaricious. And if he could expect to prolong his honors by his good conduct, he might hesitate to sacrifice his appetite for them to his appetite for gain. But with the prospect before him of approaching an inevitable annihilation, his avarice would be likely to get the victory over his caution, his vanity, or his ambition.

An ambitious man, too, when he found himself seated on the summit of his country's honors, when he looked forward to the time at which he must descend from the exalted eminence forever, and reflected that no exertion of merit on his part could save him from the unwelcome reverse; such a man, in such a situation, would be much more violently tempted to embrace a favorable conjuncture for attempting the prolongation of his power, at every personal hazard, than if he had the probability of answering the same end by doing his duty.

Would it promote the peace of the community, or the stability of the government to have half a dozen men who had had credit enough to be raised to the seat of the supreme magistracy, wandering among the people like discontented ghosts, and sighing for a place which they were destined never more to possess?

A third ill effect of the exclusion would be, the depriving the community of the advantage of the experience gained by the chief magistrate in the exercise of his office. . . .

A fourth ill effect of the exclusion would be the banishing men from stations in which, in certain emergencies of the state, their presence might be of the greatest moment to the public interest or safety. . . .

The third ingredient towards constituting the vigor of the executive authority, is an adequate provision for its support. It is evident that, without proper attention to this article, the separation of the executive from the legislative department would be merely nominal and nugatory. The legislature, with a discretionary power over the salary and emoluments of the Chief Magistrate, could render him as obsequious to their will as they might think proper to make him. They might, in most cases, either reduce him by famine, or tempt him by largesses, to surrender at discretion his judgment to their inclinations. These expressions, taken in all the latitude of the terms, would no doubt convey more than is intended. There are men who could neither be distressed or won into a sacrifice of their duty, but this stern virtue is the growth of few soils; and in the main it will be found that a power over a man's support is a power over his will. If it were necessary to confirm so plain a truth by facts, examples would not be wanting. . . .

It is not easy, therefore, to commend too highly the judicious attention which has been paid to this subject in the proposed Constitution. It is there provided that "The President of the United States shall, at stated times, receive for his services a compensation *which shall neither be increased nor diminished during the period for which he shall have been elected.* . . ."

40

Richard E. Neustadt

The Power to Persuade (1990)

The limits on command suggest the structure of our government. The Constitutional Convention of 1787 is supposed to have created a government of "separated powers." It did nothing of the sort. Rather, it created a government of separated institutions *sharing* powers. "I am part of the legislative process," Eisenhower often said in 1959 as a reminder of his veto. Congress, the dispenser of authority and funds, is no less part of the administrative process. Federalism adds another set of separated institutions. The Bill of Rights adds others. Many public purposes can only be achieved by voluntary acts of private institutions; the press, for one, in Douglass Cater's phrase, is a "fourth branch of government." And with the coming of alliances abroad, the separate institutions of a London, or a Bonn, share in the making of American public policy. . . .

The separateness of institutions and the sharing of authority prescribe the terms on which a President persuades. When one man shares authority with another, but does not gain or lose his job upon the other's whim, his willingness to act upon the urging of the other turns on whether he conceives the action right for him. The essence of a President's persuasive task is to convince such men that what the White House wants of them is what they ought to do for their sake and on their authority. (Sex matters not at all; for *man* read *woman*.)

Persuasive power, thus defined, amounts to more than charm or reasoned argument. These have their uses for a President, but these are not the whole of his resources. For the individuals he would induce to do what he wants done on their own responsibility will need or fear some acts by him on his responsibility. If they share his authority, he has some share in theirs. Presidential "powers" may be inconclusive when a President commands, but always remain relevant as he persuades. The status and authority inherent in his office reinforce his logic and his charm.

Status adds something to persuasiveness; authority adds still more. When Truman urged wage changes on his secretary of commerce while the latter was administering the steel mills, he and Secretary Sawyer were not just two men reasoning with one another. Had they been so, Sawyer probably would never have agreed to act. Truman's status gave him special claims to Sawyer's loyalty or at least attention. . . . In Sawyer's case, moreover, the President possessed formal authority to intervene in many matters of concern to the secretary of commerce. These matters ranged from jurisdictional disputes among the defense agencies to legislation pending before Congress and, ultimately, to the tenure of the secretary, himself. There is nothing in the record to suggest that Truman voiced specific threats when they negotiated over wage increases. But given his formal powers and their relevance to Sawyer's other interests, it is safe to assume that Truman's very advocacy of wage action conveyed an implicit threat.

A President's authority and status give him great advantages in dealing with the men he would persuade. Each "power" is a vantage point for him in the degree that other men have use for his authority. From the veto to appointments, from publicity to budgeting, and so down a long list, the White House now controls the most encompassing array of vantage points in the American political system. With hardly an exception, those who share in governing this country are aware that at some time, in some degree, the doing of *their* jobs, the furthering of *their* ambitions, may depend upon the President of the United States. Their need for presidential action, or their fear of it, is bound to be recurrent if not actually continuous. Their need or fear is his advantage. . . .

The President's advantages are checked by the advantages of others. Continuing relationships will pull in both directions. These are relationships of mutual dependence. A President depends upon the persons whom he would persuade; he has to reckon with his need or fear of them. They too will possess status, or authority, or both, else they would be of little use to him. Their vantage points confront his own; their power tempers his.

Persuasion is a two-way street. Sawyer did not respond at once to Truman's plan for wage increases at the steel mills. On the contrary, the secretary hesitated and delayed and only acquiesced when he was satisfied that publicly he would not bear the onus of decision. Sawyer had some points of vantage all his own from which to resist presidential pressure. If he had to reckon with coercive implications in the President's "situations of strength," so had Truman to be mindful of the implications underlying Sawyer's place as a department head, as steel administrator, and as a cabinet spokesman for business. Loyalty is reciprocal. Having taken on a dirty job in the steel crisis, Sawyer had strong claims to loyal support. Besides, he had authority to do some things that the White House could ill afford. Emulating Wilson, he might have resigned in a huff (the removal power also works two ways). Or, emulating Ellis Arnall, he might have declined to sign necessary orders. Or he might have let it be known publicly that he deplored what he was told to do and protested its doing. By following any of these courses Sawyer almost surely would have strengthened the position of management, weakened the position of the White House, and embittered the union. But the whole purpose of a wage increase was to enhance White House persuasiveness in urging settlement upon union and companies alike. . . .

The power to persuade is the power to bargain. Status and authority yield bargaining advantages. But in a government of "separated institutions sharing powers," they yield them to all sides. With the array of vantage points at his disposal, a President may be far more persuasive than his logic or his charm could make him. But outcomes are not guaranteed by his advantages. There remain the counter pressures those whom he would influence can bring to bear on him from vantage points at their disposal. Command has limited utility; persuasion becomes give-and-take. It is well that the White House holds the vantage points it does. In such a business any President may need them all—and more.

II

This view of power as akin to bargaining is one we commonly accept in the sphere of congressional relations. Every textbook states and every legislative session demonstrates that save in times like the extraordinary Hundred Days of 1933 . . . a President will often be unable to obtain congressional action on his terms or even to halt action he opposes. The reverse is equally accepted: Congress often is frustrated by the President. Their formal powers are so intertwined that neither will accomplish very much, for very long, without the acquiescence of the other. . . .

The concept of real power as a give-and-take is equally familiar when applied to presidential influence outside the formal structure of the federal government. The Little Rock affair may be extreme, but Eisenhower's dealings with the governor—and with the citizens—become a case in point. Less extreme but no less pertinent is the steel seizure case with respect to union leaders, and to workers, and to company executives as well. When he deals with such people a President draws bargaining advantage from his status or authority. By virtue of their public places or their private rights they have some capability to reply in kind. . . .

Influence becomes still more a matter of give-and-take when Presidents attempt to deal with allied governments. A classic illustration is the long unhappy wrangle over Suez policy in 1956. . . . Behind the decorum of diplomacy—which was not very decorous in the Suez affair—relationships among allies are not unlike relationships among state delegations at a national convention. Power is persuasion, and persuasion becomes bargaining. The concept is familiar to everyone who watches foreign policy.

In only one sphere is the concept unfamiliar: the sphere of executive relations. Perhaps because of civics textbooks and teaching in our schools, Americans instinctively resist the view that power in this sphere resembles power in all others. Even Washington reporters, White House aides, and congressmen are not immune to the illusion that administrative agencies comprise a single structure, "the" executive branch, where presidential word is law, or ought to be. Yet, when a President seeks something from executive officials his persuasiveness is subject to the same sorts of limitations as in the case of congressmen, or governors, or national committeemen, or private citizens, or foreign governments. There are no generic differences, no differences in kind and only sometimes in degree. . . .

Like our governmental structure as a whole, the executive establishment consists of separated institutions sharing powers. The President heads one of these; cabinet officers, agency administrators, and military commanders head others. Below the departmental level, virtually independent bureau chiefs head many more. . . . [F]ederal operations spill across dividing lines on organization charts; almost every policy entangles many agencies; almost every program calls for interagency collaboration. Everything somehow involves the President. But operating agencies owe their existence least of all to one another—and only in some part to him. Each has a separate statutory base; each has its statutes to administer; each deals with a different set of subcommittees at the Capitol. Each has its own peculiar set of clients, friends, and enemies outside the formal government. Each has a different set of specialized careerists inside its own bailiwick. Our Constitution gives the President the "take-care" clause and the appointive power. Our statutes give him central budgeting and a degree of personnel control. All agency administrators are responsible to him. But they also are responsible to Congress, to their clients, to their staffs, and to themselves. In short, they have five masters. Only after all of those do they owe any loyalty to each other. . . .

[E]ven in the White House a President does not monopolize effective power. Even there persuasion is akin to bargaining. A former Roosevelt aide once wrote of cabinet officers:

> Half of a President's suggestions, which theoretically carry the weight of orders, can be safely forgotten by a Cabinet member. And if the President asks about a suggestion a second time, he can be told that it is being investigated. If he asks a third time, a wise Cabinet officer will give him at least part of what he suggests. But only occasionally, except about the most important matters, do Presidents ever get around to asking three times.

The rule applies to staff as well as to the cabinet, and certainly has been applied *by* staff in Truman's time and Eisenhower's. . . .

Any aide who demonstrates to others that he has the President's consistent confidence and a consistent part in presidential business will acquire so much business on his own account that he becomes in some sense independent of his chief. Nothing in the Constitution keeps a well-placed aide from converting status into power of his own, usable in some degree even against the President—an outcome not unknown in Truman's regime or, by all accounts, in Eisenhower's.

The more an officeholder's status and his powers stem from sources independent of the President, the stronger will be his potential pressure on the President. Department heads in general have more bargaining power than do most members of the White House staff; but bureau chiefs may have still more, and specialists at upper levels of established career services may have almost unlimited reserves of the enormous power which consists of sitting still. . . .

[A]s between a President and his "subordinates," no less than others on whom he depends, real power is reciprocal and varies markedly with organization, subject matter, personality, and situation. The mere fact that persuasion is directed at executive officials signifies no necessary easing of his way. Any new congressman of the Administration's party, especially if narrowly elected, may turn out more amenable (though less useful) to the President than any seasoned bureau chief "downtown." *The probabilities of power do not derive from the literary theory of the Constitution.*

III

There is a widely held belief in the United States that were it not for folly or for knavery, a reasonable President would need no power other than the logic of his argument. No less a personage than Eisenhower has subscribed to that belief in many a campaign speech and press-conference remark. But faulty reasoning and bad intentions do not cause all quarrels with Presidents. The best of reasoning and of intent cannot compose them all. For in the first place, what the President wants will rarely seem a trifle to the people he wants it from. And in the second place, they will be bound to judge it by the standard of their own responsibilities, not his. However logical his argument according to his lights, their judgment may not bring them to his view.

Those who share in governing this country frequently appear to act as though they were in business for themselves. So, in a real though not entire sense, they are and have to be. When Truman and MacArthur fell to quarreling, for example, the stakes were no less than the substance of American foreign policy, the risks of greater war or military stalemate, the prerogatives of Presidents and field commanders, the pride of a proconsul and his place in history. Intertwined, inevitably, were other stakes as well: political stakes for men and factions of both parties; power stakes for interest groups with which they were or wished to be affiliated. And every stake was raised by the apparent discontent in the American public mood. There is no reason to suppose that in such circumstances men of large but differing responsibilities will see all things through the same glasses. On the contrary, it is to be expected that their views of what ought to be done and what they then should do will vary with the differing perspectives their particular responsibilities evoke. Since their duties are not vested in a "team" or a "collegium" but in themselves, as individuals, one must expect that they will see things for themselves. Moreover, when they are responsible to many masters and when an event or policy turns loyalty against loyalty—a day-by-day occurrence in the nature of the case—one must assume that those who have the duties to perform will choose the terms of reconciliation. This is the essence of their personal responsibility. When their own duties pull in opposite directions, who else but they can choose what they will do?

When Truman dismissed MacArthur, the latter lost three posts: the American command in the Far East, the Allied command for the occupation of Japan, and the United Nations command in Korea. He also lost his status as the senior officer on active duty in the United States armed forces. So long as he held those positions and that status, though, he had a duty to his troops, to his profession, to himself (the last is hard for any man to disentangle from the rest). As a public figure and a focus for men's hopes he had a duty to constituents at home, and in Korea and Japan. He owed a duty also to those other constituents, the UN governments contributing to his field forces. As a patriot he had a duty to his country. As an accountable official and an expert guide he stood at the call of Congress. As a military officer he had, besides, a duty to the President, his constitutional commander. Some of these duties may have manifested themselves in terms more tangible or more direct than others. But it would be nonsense to argue that the last negated all the rest, however much it might be claimed to override them. And it makes no more sense to think that anybody but MacArthur was effectively empowered to decide how he himself would reconcile the competing demands his duties made upon him. . . .

Reasonable men, it is so often said, *ought* to be able to agree on the requirements of given situations. But when the outlook varies with the placement of each man, and the response required in his place is for each to decide, their reasoning may lead to disagreement quite as well—and quite as reasonably.

. . . Outside the executive branch the situation is the same, except that loyalty to the President may often matter *less*. . . .

The essence of a President's persuasive task, with congressmen and everybody else, is to induce them to believe that what he wants of them is what their own appraisal of their own responsibilities requires them to do in their interest, not his. Because men may differ in their views on public policy, because differences in outlook stem from differences in duty—duty to one's office, one's constituents, oneself—that task is bound to be more like collective bargaining than like a reasoned argument among philosopher kings. Overtly or implicitly, hard bargaining has characterized all illustrations offered up to now. This is the reason why: Persuasion deals in the coin of self-interest with men who have some freedom to reject what they find counterfeit.

IV

A President draws influence from bargaining advantages. But does he always need them? . . . The answer is that even then most outcomes turn on bargaining. The reason for this answer is a simple one: Most who share in governing have interests of their own beyond the realm of policy objectives. The sponsorship of policy, the form it takes, the conduct of it, and the credit for it separate their interest from the President's despite agreement on the end in view. In political government the means can matter quite as much as ends; they often matter more. And there are always differences of interest in the means.

Let me introduce a case externally the opposite of my previous examples: the European Recovery Program of 1948, the so-called Marshall Plan. This is perhaps the greatest exercise in policy agreement since the Cold War began. When the then secretary of state, George Catlett Marshall, spoke at the Harvard commencement in June 1947, he launched one of the most creative, most imaginative ventures in the history of American foreign relations. What makes this policy most notable for present purposes, however, is that it became effective upon action by the eightieth Congress, at the behest of Harry Truman, in the election year 1948.

Eight months before Marshall spoke at Harvard, the Democrats had lost control of both houses of Congress for the first time in fourteen years. Truman, whom the secretary represented, had just finished his second troubled year as President-by-succession. Truman was regarded with so little warmth in his own party that in 1946 he had been urged not to participate in the congressional campaign. At the opening of Congress in January 1947, Senator Robert A. Taft, "Mr. Republican," had somewhat the attitude of a President-elect. This was a vision widely shared in Washington, with Truman relegated thereby to the role of caretaker-on-term. Moreover, within just two weeks of Marshall's commencement address, Truman was to veto two prized accomplishments of Taft's congressional majority: the Taft-Hartley Act and tax reduction. Yet scarcely ten months later the Marshall Plan was under way on terms to satisfy its sponsors, its authorization completed, its first-year funds in sight, its administering agency in being: all managed by as thorough a display of executive-congressional cooperation as any we have seen since the Second World War. For any President at any time this would have been a great accomplishment. . . . And for a Truman, at this time, enactment of the Marshall Plan appears almost miraculous.

How was the miracle accomplished? How did a President so situated bring it off? In answer, the first thing to note is that he did not do it by himself. Truman had help of a sort no less extraordinary than the outcome. Although each stands for something more complex, the names of Marshall, Vandenberg, Patterson, Bevin, Stalin tell the story of that help.

In 1947, two years after V-J Day, General Marshall was something more than secretary of state. He was a man venerated by the President as "the greatest living American," literally an embodiment of Truman's ideals. He was honored at the Pentagon as an architect of victory. . . .

The Marshall Plan was launched by a lame-duck Administration "scheduled" to leave office in eighteen months. Marshall's program faced a congressional leadership traditionally isolationist and currently intent upon economy. European aid was viewed with envy by a Pentagon distressed and virtually disarmed through budget cuts, and by domestic agencies intent on enlarged welfare programs. It was not viewed with liking by a Treasury intent on budget surpluses. The plan had need of every asset that could be extracted from the personal position of its nominal author and from the skills of his assistants.

Without the equally remarkable position of the senior senator from Michigan, Arthur H. Vandenberg, it is hard to see how Marshall's assets could have been enough. Vandenberg was chairman of the Senate Foreign Relations Committee. Actually, he was much more than that. Twenty years a senator, he was the senior member of his party in the chamber. Assiduously cultivated by FDR and Truman, he was a chief Republican proponent of bipartisanship in foreign policy and consciously conceived himself its living symbol to his party, to the country, and abroad. Moreover, by informal but entirely operative agreement with his colleague Taft, Vandenberg held the acknowledged lead among Senate Republicans in the whole field of international affairs. This acknowledgment meant more in 1947 than it might have meant at any other time. With confidence in the advent of a Republican administration two years hence, most of the gentlemen were in a mood to be responsive and responsible. The war was over, Roosevelt dead, Truman a caretaker, theirs the trust. That the senator from Michigan saw matters in this light his diaries make clear . . . .

Help of another sort was furnished by a group of dedicated private citizens who organized one of the most effective instruments for public information seen since the Second World War: the Committee for the Marshall Plan, headed by the eminent Republicans whom FDR in 1940 had brought to the Department of War: Henry L. Stimson as honorary chairman and Robert P. Patterson as active spokesman. The remarkable array of bankers, lawyers, trade unionists, and editors, who had drawn together in defense of "internationalism" before Pearl Harbor and had joined their talents in the war itself, combined again to spark the work of this committee. Their efforts generated a great deal of vocal public support to buttress Marshall's arguments, and Vandenberg's, in Congress.

But before public support could be rallied, there had to be a purpose tangible enough, concrete enough, to provide a rallying ground. At Harvard, Marshall had voiced an idea in general terms. That this was turned into a hard program susceptible of presentation and support is due, in major part, to Ernest Bevin, the British foreign secretary. He well deserves the credit he has sometimes been assigned as, in effect, coauthor of the Marshall Plan. For Bevin seized on Marshall's Harvard speech and organized a European response with promptness and concreteness beyond the State Department's expectations. What had been virtually a trial balloon to test reactions on both sides of the Atlantic was hailed in London as an invitation to the Europeans to send Washington a bill of particulars. This they promptly organized to do, and the American Administration then organized in turn for its reception without further argument internally about the pros and cons of issuing the "invitation" in the first place. But for Bevin there might have been trouble from the secretary of the treasury and others besides. If Bevin's help was useful at that early stage, Stalin's was vital from first to last. . . .

By 1947 events, far more than governmental prescience or open action, had given a variety of publics an impression of inimical Soviet intentions (and of Europe's weakness) and a growing urge to "do something about it." Three months before Marshall spoke at Harvard, Greek-Turkish aid and promulgation of the Truman Doctrine had seemed rather to crystallize than to create a public mood and a congressional response. The Marshall planners, be it said, were poorly placed to capitalize on that mood, nor had the secretary wished to do so. Their object, indeed, was to cut across it, striking at the cause of European weakness rather than at Soviet aggressiveness, per se. A strong economy in Western Europe called, ideally, for restorative measures of continental scope. American assistance proffered in an anti-Soviet context would have been contradictory in theory and unacceptable in fact to several of the governments that Washington was anxious to assist. As Marshall, himself, saw it, the logic of his purpose forbade him to play his strongest congressional card. The Russians then proceeded to play it for him. When the Europeans met in Paris, Molotov walked out. After the Czechs had shown continued interest in American aid, a Communist coup overthrew their government while Soviet forces stood along their borders within easy reach of Prague. Molotov transformed the Marshall Plan's initial presentation; Czechoslovakia assured its final passage, which followed by a month the takeover in Prague.

Such was the help accorded Truman in obtaining action on the Marshall Plan. Considering his politically straitened circumstances he scarcely could have done with less. Conceivably some part of Moscow's contribution might have been dispensable, but not Marshall's or Vandenberg's or Bevin's or Patterson's or that of the great many other men whose work is represented by their names in my account. Their aid was not extended to the President for his own sake. He was not favored in this fashion just because they liked him personally or were spellbound by his intellect or charm. They might have been as helpful had all held him in disdain, which some of them certainly did. The Londoners who seized the ball, Vandenberg and Taft and the congressional majority, Marshall and his planners, the officials of other agencies who actively supported them or "went along," the host of influential private citizens who rallied to the cause—all these played the parts they did because they thought they had to, in their interest, given their responsibilities, not Truman's. Yet they hardly would have found it in their interest to collaborate with one another or with him had he not furnished them precisely what they needed from the White House. Truman could not do without their help, but he could not have had it without unremitting effort on his part.

The crucial thing to note about this case is that despite compatibility of views on public policy, Truman got no help he did not pay for (except Stalin's). Bevin scarcely could have seized on Marshall's words had Marshall not been plainly backed by Truman. Marshall's interest would not have comported with the exploitation of his prestige by a president who undercut him openly or subtly or even inadvertently at any point. Vandenberg, presumably, could not have backed proposals by a White House that begrudged him deference and access gratifying to his fellow partisans (and satisfying to himself). Prominent Republicans in private life would not have found it easy to promote a cause identified with Truman's claims on 1948—and neither would the prominent New Dealers then engaged in searching for a substitute.

Truman paid the price required for their services. So far as the record shows, the White House did not falter once in firm support for Marshall and the Marshall Plan. Truman backed his secretary's gamble on an invitation to all Europe. He made the plan his own in a well-timed address to the Canadians. He lost no opportunity to widen the involvements of his own official family in the cause. . . . Vandenberg expected advance consultation; he received it, step by step, in frequent meetings with the President and weekly conferences with Marshall. He asked for an effective liaison between Congress and agencies concerned; Lovett and others gave him what he wanted. When the senator decided on the need to change financing and administrative features of the legislation, Truman disregarded Budget Bureau grumbling and acquiesced with grace. . . .

Truman helped himself in still another way. Traditionally and practically, no one was placed as well as he to call public attention to the task of Congress (and its Republican leadership). Throughout the fall and winter of 1947 and on into the spring of 1948, he made repeated use of presidential "powers" to remind the country that congressional action was required. Messages, speeches, and an extra session were employed to make the point.

Here, too, he drew advantage from his place. However, in his circumstances, Truman's public advocacy might have hurt, not helped, had his words seemed directed toward the forthcoming election. Truman gained advantage for his program only as his own endorsement of it stayed on the right side of that fine line between the "caretaker" in office and the would-be candidate. . . .

V

. . . The President's own share in this accomplishment was vital. He made his contribution by exploiting his advantages. Truman, in effect, lent Marshall and the rest the perquisites and status of his office. In return they lent him their prestige and their own influence. The transfer multiplied his influence despite his limited authority in form and lack of strength politically. Without the wherewithal to make this bargain, Truman cold not have contributed to European aid.

Bargaining advantages convey no guarantees. Influence remains a two-way street. In the fortunate instance of the Marshall Plan, what Truman needed was actually in the hands of men who were prepared to "trade" with him. He personally could deliver what they wanted in return. . . . Suppose that Marshall had declined the secretaryship of state in January 1947; Truman might not have found a substitute so well equipped to furnish what he needed in the months ahead. Or suppose that Vandenburg had fallen victim to a cancer two years before he actually did. . . . And what if Truman then had seemed to the Republicans what he turned out to be in 1948, a formidable candidate for President? It is unlikely that a single one of these "supposes" would have changed the final outcome; two or three, however, might have altered it entirely. Truman was not guaranteed more power than his "powers" just because he had continuing relationships with cabinet secretaries and with senior senators. Here, as everywhere, the outcome was conditional on who they were and what he was and how each viewed events, and on their actual performance in response.

Granting that persuasion has no guarantee attached, how can a President reduce the risks of failing to persuade? How can he maximize his prospects for effectiveness by minimizing chances that his power will elude him? The Marshall Plan suggests an answer: He guards his power prospects in the course of making choices. Marshall himself, and Forrestal and Harriman, and others of the sort held office on the President's appointment. Vandenberg had vast symbolic value partly because FDR and Truman had done everything they could, since 1944, to build him up.

The Treasury Department and the Budget Bureau—which together might have jeopardized the plans these others made—were headed by officials whose prestige depended wholly on their jobs. What Truman needed from those "givers" he received, in part, because of his past choice of men and measures. What they received in turn were actions taken or withheld by him, himself. The things they needed from him mostly involved his own conduct where his current choices ruled. The President's own actions in the past had cleared the way for current bargaining. His actions in the present were his trading stock. Behind each action lay a personal choice, and these together comprised his control over the give-and-take that gained him what he wanted. In the degree that Truman, personally, affected the advantages he drew from his relationships with other men in government, his power was protected by his choices. . . .

If Presidents could count upon past choices to enhance their current influence, as Truman's choice of men had done for him, persuasion would pose fewer difficulties than it does. But Presidents can count on no such thing. Depending on the circumstances, prior choices can be as embarrassing as they were helpful in the instance of the Marshall Plan. . . .

But adequate or not, a President's own choices are the only means in his own hands of guarding his own prospects for effective influence. He can draw power from continuing relationships in the degree that he can capitalize upon the needs of others for the Presidency's status and authority. He helps himself to do so, though, by nothing save ability to recognize the preconditions and the chance advantages and to proceed accordingly in the course of the choice making that comes his way. To ask how he can guard prospective influence is thus to raise a further question: What helps him guard his power stakes in his own acts of choice?

41

James W. Ceaser, Glen E. Thurow, *Jeffrey K. Tulis, Joseph M. Bessette*

The Rise of the Rhetorical Presidency (1981)

Popular or mass rhetoric, which presidents once employed only rarely, now serves as one of their principal tools in attempting to govern the nation. Whatever doubts Americans may now entertain about the limitations of presidential leadership, they do not consider it unfitting or inappropriate for

From Ceaser, Thurow, Tulis, and Bessette, "The Rise of the Rhetorical Presidency," in *Presidential Studies Quarterly* (Spring, 1981). Reprinted by permission of *Presidential Studies Quarterly*.

presidents to attempt to "move" the public by programmatic speeches that exhort and set forth grand and ennobling views.

It was not always so. Prior to this century, popular leadership through rhetoric was suspect. Presidents rarely spoke directly to the people, preferring communications between the branches of the government. Washington seldom delivered more than one major speech per year of his administration, and that one—the Annual Address—was almost mandated by the Constitution and was addressed to Congress. Jefferson even ceased delivering the address in person, a precedent that continued until Woodrow Wilson's appearance before Congress in 1913. The spirit of these early presidents' examples was followed throughout the nineteenth century. The relatively few popular speeches that were made differed in character from today's addresses. Most were patriotic orations, some raised constitutional issues, and several spoke to the conduct of war. Very few were domestic "policy speeches" of the sort so common today, and attempts to move the nation by means of an exalted picture of a perfect ideal were almost unknown. . . .

Today, a president has an assembly line of speechwriters efficiently producing words that enable him to say something on every conceivable occasion. Unless a president is deliberately "hiding" in the White House, a week scarcely goes by without at least one major news story devoted to coverage of a radio or TV speech, an address to Congress, a speech to a convention, a press conference, a news release, or some other presidential utterance. But more important even than the quantity of popular rhetoric is the fact that presidential speech and action increasingly reflect the opinion that speaking is governing. Speeches are written to become the events to which people react no less than "real" events themselves. . . .

The excess of speech has perhaps fed a cynicism about it that is the opposite of [a] boundless faith in rhetoric. . . . Yet, despite this cynicism, it seems increasingly the case that for many who comment on and form opinions about the presidency, word rivals deed as the measure of presidential performance. The standard set for presidents has in large degree become an artifact of their own inflated rhetoric and one to which they frequently fall victim. While part of this difficulty can be blamed on the ineptness of certain presidents' rhetorical strategies, it is also the case that presidents operate in a context that gives them much less discretion over their rhetoric than one might think. The problem is thus not one simply of individual rhetorics, but is rather an institutional dilemma for the modern presidency. Beginning with the campaign, the candidates are obliged to demonstrate their leadership capacity through an ever growing number of rhetorical performances, with the potential impact of their words on future problems of governing often being the least of their concerns. The pressure to "say something" continues after the president has begun to govern. Presidents not only face the demand to explain what they have done and intend to do, but they also have come under increasing pressure to speak out on perceived crises and to minister to the moods and emotions of the populace. In the end, it may be the office of the presidency that is weakened by this form of leadership, puffed up by false expectations that bear little relationship to the practical tasks of governing and undermined by the resulting cynicism.

How did the rhetorical presidency come into existence? What are its strengths and weaknesses? Can presidents escape its burdens, and to what extent should they try to do so? These are some of the important questions that need addressing.

The rise of the rhetorical presidency has been primarily the result of three factors: (1) a modern doctrine of presidential leadership, (2) the modern mass media, and (3) the modern presidential campaign. Of these three, doctrine is probably the most important.

As strange as it may seem to us today, the framers of our Constitution looked with great suspicion on popular rhetoric. Their fear was that mass oratory, whether crudely demogogic or highly inspirational, would undermine the rational and enlightened self-interest of the citizenry which their system was designed to foster and on which it was thought to depend for its stability. The framers' well-known mistrust of "pure" democracy by an assembly—and by extension, of the kind of representative government that looked only to public opinion as its guide—was not based, as is generally supposed, on a simple doubt about the people's capacity go govern, but on a more complex case concerning the evils that would result from the interplay between the public and popular orators.

In democracies, they reasoned, political success and fame are won by those orators who most skillfully give expression to transient, often inchoate, public opinion. Governing by this means, if indeed it can be called governing, leads to constant instability as leaders compete with each other to tap the latest mood passing through the public. The paradox of government by mood is that it fosters neither democratic accountability nor statesmanly efficiency. Freed from the necessity to consult public opinion, understood as "the cool and deliberate sense of the community," popular orators would be so chained to public opinion, understood as "mood," that discretion and flexibility essential to statesmanship would be undermined.

The framers were not so impractical as to think that popular rhetoric could be entirely avoided in a republican system. But the government they designed was intended to minimize reliance on popular oratory and to establish institutions which could operate effectively without the immediate support of transient opinion. All of the powers of governing were to be given, not directly to the people, but to their representatives. These representatives would find themselves in a tripartite government in which the various tasks of governing would be clearly discernible and assigned, and in which they would be forced to deal with knowledgeable and determined men not easily impressed by facile oratory. As part of their solution, the framers were counting on the large size of the nation, which at the time erected a communication barrier that would mute the impact of national popular rhetoric, whether written or oral. Beyond this, the framers instituted a presidential selection system that was designed to preclude active campaigning by the candidates. As for the presidency itself, the framers discouraged any idea that the president should serve as a leader of the people who would stir mass opinion by rhetoric; their conception was rather that of a constitutional officer who would rely for his authority on the formal powers granted by the Constitution and on the informal authority that would flow from the office's strategic position.

These limitations on popular rhetoric did not mean, however, that presidents were expected to govern in silence. Ceremonial occasions presented a proper forum for reminding the public of the nation's basic principles; and communications to Congress, explicitly provided for by the Constitution, offered a mechanism by which the people also could be informed on matters of policy. Yet this intrabranch rhetoric, though public, was not meant to be popular. Addressed in the first instance to a body of informed representatives, it would possess a reasoned and deliberative character; and insofar as some in the public would read these speeches and state papers, they would implicitly be called on to raise their understanding to the level of characteristic deliberative speech.

Nineteenth century politics in America did not, of course, follow exactly the framer's model of an essentially nonrhetorical regime. . . . Yet the amount of nineteenth century presidential rhetoric that even loosely could be called popular is very little indeed, and the presidency remained, with some slight alterations, a constitutional office rather than the seat of popular leadership.

The Inaugural and the Annual Address (now called the State of the Union) were the principal speeches of a president given wide dissemination. The character of the Inaugural Address illustrates the general character of presidential popular speech during the period. Given on a formal occasion, it tended to follow a pattern which was set by Jefferson's First Inaugural Address in which he delivered an exposition of the principles of the Union and its republican character. . . .

Against this tradition Woodrow Wilson gave the Inaugural Address (and presidential speech generally) a new theme. Instead of showing how the policies of the incoming administration reflected the principles of our form of government, Wilson sought to articulate the unspoken desires of the people by holding out a vision of their fulfillment. Presidential speech, in Wilson's view, should articulate what is "in our hearts" and not necessarily what is in our Constitution. . . . Wilson articulated the doctrinal foundation of the rhetorical presidency and thereby provided an alternative theoretical model to that of the framers. . . .

The Wilsonian concept of the rhetorical presidency consists of two interfused elements. First, the president should employ oratory to create an active public opinion that, if necessary, will pressure Congress into accepting his program: "He [the president] has no means of compelling Congress except through public opinion." In advancing policy, deliberative, intrabranch rhetoric thus becomes secondary to popular rhetoric, and the president "speaks" to Congress not directly but through his popular addresses. Second, in order to reach and move the public, the character of the rhetoric must tap the public's feelings and articulate its wishes. Rhetoric does not instill old and established principles as much as it seeks to infuse a sense of vision into the president's particular legislative program.

> A nation is led by a man who . . . speaks, not the rumors of the street, but a new principle for a new age; a man in whose ears the voices of the nation do not sound like the accidental and discordant notes that come from the voice of a mob, but concurrent and concordant like the united voices of a chorus, whose many meanings, spoken by melodious tongues, unite in his understanding in a single meaning and reveal to him a single vision, so that he can speak what no man else knows, the common meaning of the common voice.

If the doctrine of the rhetorical presidency leaves us today with the occasional feeling that it is hollow or outworn, it is not because of a decline in its influence but because of the inevitable consequences of its ascendancy. . . .

The second factor that accounts for the rise of the rhetorical presidency is the modern mass media. The media did not create the rhetorical presidency—doctrine did—but it facilitated its development and has given to it some of its special characteristics. The mass media, meaning here primarily radio and television, must be understood first from the perspective of its technical capacities. It has given the president the means by which to communicate directly and instantaneously with a large national audience, thus tearing down the communications barrier on which the framers had relied to insulate representative institutions from direct contact with the populace. Besides increasing the size of the president's audience, the mass media have changed the mode by which he communicates with the public, replacing the written with the spoken word delivered in a dramatic visible performance. The written word formerly provided a partial screen or check against the most simplistic argumentations, as it allowed more control of the text by the reader and limited the audience to those with the most interest in politics. . . .

The influence of the mass media on presidential rhetoric is not limited to its technical capacities. The mass media have also created a new power center in American politics in the form of television news. If the technical aspect of the media has given the president an advantage or an opportunity, the existence of television news often serves as a rival or an impediment.

Journalists are filters in the communication process, deciding what portions of the president's non-televised speeches they will show and how their arguments will be interpreted. When presidents speak in public today, their most important audience is not the one they are personally addressing, but rather the public as it is reached through the brief cuts aired on the news. Speeches accordingly tend to be written so that any segment can be taken to stand by itself—as a self-contained lead. Argument gives way to aphorism.

The direct impact of the news media's interpretation of the president's words is perhaps less important for presidential rhetoric than the indirect influence that derives from the character of news itself. Television news not only carries the messages of governing officials to the people; it also selects the issues that are presented to the government for "action" of some sort. "Real" expressions of mass opinion, which in the past were sporadic, are replaced by the news media's continuous "sophisticated" analyses that serve as a surrogate audience, speaking to the government and supposedly representing to it what the people are saying and thinking. Driven by its own inner dynamic to find and sustain exciting issues and to present them in dramatic terms, the news media create—or give the impression of creating—national moods and currents of opinion which appear to call for some form of action by the government and especially by the president.

The media and the modern presidency feed on each other. The media have found in the presidency a focal point on which to concentrate their peculiarly simplistic and dramatic interpretation of events; and the presidency has found a vehicle in the media that allows it to win public attention and with that attention the reality, but more often the pretense, of enhanced power. . . .

The modern presidential campaign is the third factor that accounts for the rise of the rhetorical presidency. The roots of the modern campaign go back to Wilson and the Progressives and to many of the same ideas that helped to create the rhetorical presidency. Prior to 1912, the parties were largely responsible for conducting the campaigns, and the candidates, with few exceptions, restricted their communications to letters of acceptance of the nomination. Wilson was the first victorious presidential candidate to have engaged in a full-scale speaking tour during the campaign. In his view, it was essential that the candidates replace the parties as the main rhetorical instruments of the campaign. This change would serve not only to downgrade the influence of traditional parties but also to prepare the people for the new kind of presidency that he hoped to establish. Indeed, with Wilson the distinction between campaigning and governing is blurred, as both involve the same essential function of persuading through popular oratory.

Although Wilson himself did not campaign extensively in the preconvention period, he supported the idea of a preconvention campaign and pushed for nomination by national primaries. His ideal of a truly open presidential nomination campaign in which all candidates must take the "outside" route was not fully realized, however, until after the reforms that followed the 1968 election. Over the past three campaigns (1972, 1976 and 1980) we have seen the development of one of the most peculiarly irresponsible rhetorical processes ever devised. For a period of what is now well over a year, the various contenders have little else to offer except their rhetoric. Undisciplined by the responsibility of matching word to deed, they seek to create events out of their speeches, all the while operating under the constant media-created pressure to say something new. As their goal is to win power, and as that goal, especially in the preconvention period, is remote, candidates can easily afford to disregard the impact of their speech on the demands of governing and instead craft their rhetoric with a view merely to persuading. . . .

The presidential campaign is important for the kinds of inflated expectations it raises, but it is even more important for the effects it has on the process of governing. So formative has the campaign become of our tastes for oratory and of our conception of leadership that presidential speech and governing have come more and more to imitate the model of the campaign. . . .

The inflated expectations engendered by the rhetorical presidency have by now become a matter of serious concern among those who study the presidency. In response to this problem, a growing number of scholars have begun to argue that presidents should remove themselves from much day-to-day management of government and reserve themselves for crisis management. If this argument means only that presidents should not immerse themselves in details or spread themselves too thin, no one could quarrel with it. But if it means that the president should abandon the articulation of a broad legislative program or avoid general management of the bureaucracy at a time when the bureaucracy is becoming more and more unmanageable, then the argument is misguided. If the president does not give coherence to policy or enforce discipline on the Executive branch, who will? Certainly not Congress. The president remains our only national officer who, as Jefferson once said, "commands a view of the whole ground." A retrenched presidency that cedes much of its authority to others and merely reacts to crisis is hardly the answer to our difficulties. . . .

The roots of the rhetorical presidency extend so deeply into our political structure and national consciousness that talk of change may seem futile; and yet the evident failures of the current doctrine, together with the growing scholarly debate about the crisis of the presidency, suggest that the moment has arrived for a discussion of alternatives. It should not be forgotten that the foundations of the rhetorical presidency were deliberately laid by Woodrow Wilson and that other presidents might establish new doctrines. If a sensible reform of the institution is ever possible, the key will be found in reversing the order of President Carter's July 1979 formulation—that is, in restoring the president to his natural place as the head of government, and subordinating his awkward role of an itinerant leader of the people. But how could such change take place, and what would the contours of the office look like?

First, since the modern campaign is the source of so many of the problems of the presidency, it is evident that no reform of the office can hope to succeed without change in the selection process. The operative theoretical principle that must govern this change is that the selection process should be thought of not as an end in itself, but as a means of promoting, or at least not undermining, the character of the presidential office. Construed in practical terms, this principle translates into a call for electoral reform that would reduce the duration of the campaign, especially in the preconvention period. The elimination or dramatic reduction in the number of presidential primaries and the return of the power of selection to the parties would be helpful. This change would not eliminate the campaign, but it would reduce its public phase to a shorter period and thus focus public attention on the speechmaking that takes place after the nomination. . . .

Second, presidents should reduce the number of their speeches. As they speak less, there is at least the chance that their words will carry more weight; and if their words carry more weight, then perhaps more thought will be given to speech that can sensibly direct action. What applies to speeches applies equally to press conferences. Press conferences without cameras would probably allow for a more detailed exchange of information between the president and the press corps and avoid the pressures on the president (and the journalists) to make each news conference dramatic and newsworthy. Written messages might replace many presently oral performances, and personal television appearances would be reserved for truly important issues of public concern.

Third, it is obvious that a reduction in the quantity of rhetoric itself is not enough; its character must also change. To avoid inspirational rhetoric does not mean that the president must abandon firm principles, practical ideals or even a political party that connects this generation with the moorings of our political system. Indeed, such a rhetoric is perfectly consistent with the dignity of a head of state and the character of our political order. In respect to policy, however, presidents must recapture the capacity to address the nation's enlightened self-interest no less than its sense of idealism and the related capacity to approach Congress directly rather than through the people.

The gravest problem of the rhetorical presidency, however, goes deeper than any issue confined to presidential practice. It extends to the basic questions of how our nation can be governed. No one would deny that presidents need to hold up America's basic principles and on occasion mobilize the public to meet genuine challenges. Indeed, in a liberal system of government that frees men's acquisitive instincts and allows them to devote their energies to individual material improvement, there is room on occasion for presidents to lift up the public's vision to something beyond the clash of interests. But under the influence of the rhetorical presidency, we have seen an ever-increasing reliance on inspirational rhetoric to deal with the normal problems of politics. If there is a place for such rhetoric, it is necessary also to be aware of its danger and of the corresponding need to keep it within limits.

By itself, rhetoric does not possess the power to make citizens devote themselves selflessly to the common weal, particularly where the basic principles of society protect and encourage men's independent and private activities. The founders of our country created a complex representative governement designed to foster a knowledgeable concern for the common good in the concrete circumstances of political life that would be difficult, if not impossible, to elicit directly from a people led by orators. What the continued use of inspirational rhetoric fosters is not a simple credibility problem, but a deep tension between the publicly articulated understanding of the nature of our politics and the actual springs that move the system. No wonder, then, that some politicians, deceived by their own rhetoric, find it difficult to come to terms with the job of governing a nation of complex multiple interests. Far from reinforcing our country's principles and protecting its institutions, the rhetorical presidency leads us to neglect our principles for our hopes and to ignore the benefits and needs of our institutions for a fleeting sense of oneness with our leaders.

42

John F. Kennedy

Campaign Speech on the Presidency (1960)

The modern presidential campaign covers every issue in and out of the platform from cranberries to creation. But the public is rarely alerted to a candidate's views about the central issue on which all the rest turn. That central issue—and the point of my comments this noon—is not the farm problem or

Speech delivered to the National Press Club by John F. Kennedy on January 14, 1960.

defense or India. It is the Presidency itself. Of course a candidate's views on specific policies are important—but Theodore Roosevelt and William Howard Taft shared policy views with entirely different results in the White House. Of course it is important to elect a good man with good intentions— but Woodrow Wilson and Warren G. Harding were both good men of good intentions—so were Lincoln and Buchanan—but there is a Lincoln Room in the White House, and no Buchanan Room.

The history of this nation—its brightest and its bleakest pages—has been written largely in terms of the different views our Presidents have had of the Presidency itself. This history ought to tell us that the American people in 1960 have an imperative right to know what any man bidding for the Presidency thinks about the place he is bidding for—whether he is aware of and willing to use the powerful resources of that office—whether his model will be Taft or Roosevelt—Wilson or Harding.

Not since the days of Woodrow Wilson has any candidate spoken on the Presidency itself before the votes have been irrevocably cast. Let us hope that the 1960 campaign, in addition to discussing the familiar issues where our positions too often blur, will also talk about the Presidency itself—as an instrument for dealing with those issues—as an office with varying roles, powers, and limitations.

During the past eight years, we have seen one concept of the Presidency at work. Our needs and hopes have been eloquently stated—but the initiative and follow-through have too often been left to others. And too often his own objectives have been lost by the President's failure to override objections from within his own party, in the Congress or even in his Cabinet.

The American people in 1952 and 1956 may well have preferred this detached, limited concept of the Presidency after twenty years of fastmoving, creative presidential rule. Perhaps historians will regard this as necessarily one of those frequent periods of consolidation, a time to draw breath, to recoup our national energy. To quote the State of the Union Message: "No Congress . . . on surveying the state of the nation, has met with a more pleasing prospect than that which appears at the present time." Unfortunately this is not Mr. Eisenhower's last message to the Congress, but Calvin Coolidge's. He followed to the White House Mr. Harding, whose "sponsor" declared very frankly that the times did not demand a first-rate President. If true, the times and the man met.

But the question is what do the times—and the people—demand for the next four years in the White House?

They demand a vigorous proponent of the national interest—not a passive broker for conflicting private interests. They demand a man capable of acting as the commander in chief of the grand alliance, not merely a bookkeeper who feels that his work is done when the numbers on the balance sheet come out even. They demand that he be the head of a responsible party, not rise so far above politics as to be invisible—a man who will formu-late and fight for legislative policies, not be a casual bystander to the legisla-tive process.

Today a restricted concept of the Presidency is not enough. For beneath today's surface gloss of peace and prosperity are increasingly dangerous, unsolved, long-postponed problems—problems that will inevitably explode to the surface during the next four years of the next Administration—the growing missile gap, the rise of Communist China, the despair of the under-developed nations, the explosive situations in Berlin and in the Formosa Straits, the deterioration of NATO, the lack of an arms control agreement, and all the domestic problems of our farms, cities, and schools.

This Administration has not faced up to these and other problems. Much has been said—but I am reminded of the old Chinese proverb: "There is a great deal of noise on the stairs but nobody comes into the room." The President's State of the Union Message reminded me of the exhortation from "King Lear" that goes: "I will do such things—what they are I know not . . . but they shall be the wonders of the earth. "

In the decade that lies ahead—in the challenging, revolutionary Sixties—the American Presidency will demand more than ringing manifestoes issued from the rear of the battle. It will demand that the President place himself in the very thick of the fight, that he care passionately about the fate of the peo-ple he leads, that he be willing to serve them at the risk of incurring their momentary displeasure.

Whatever the political affiliation of our next President, whatever his views may be on all the issues and problems that rush in upon us, he must above all be the Chief Executive in every sense of the word. He must be prepared to exercise the fullest powers of his office—all that are specified and some that are not. He must master complex problems as well as receive one-page memoranda. He must originate action as well as study groups. He must reopen the channels of communication between the world of thought and the seat of power.

Ulysses Grant considered the President "a purely administrative officer." If he administered the government departments efficiently, delegated his functions smoothly, and performed his ceremonies of state with decorum and grace, no more was to be expected of him. But that is not the place the Presi-dency was meant to have in American life. The President is alone, at the top—the loneliest job there is, as Harry Truman has said. If there is destruc-tive dissension among the services, he alone can step in and straighten it out—instead of waiting for unanimity. If administrative agencies are not car-rying out their mandate—if a brushfire threatens some part of the globe—he alone can act, without waiting for the Congress. If his farm program fails, he alone deserves the blame, not his Secretary of Agriculture.

"The President is at liberty, both in law and conscience, to be as big a man as he can." So wrote Professor Woodrow Wilson. But President

Woodrow Wilson discovered that to be a big man in the White House inevitably brings cries of dictatorship. So did Lincoln and Jackson and the two Roosevelts. And so may the next occupant of that office, if he is the man the times demand. But how much better it would be, in the turbulent Sixties, to have a Roosevelt or a Wilson than to have another James Buchanan, cringing in the White House, afraid to move.

Nor can we afford a Chief Executive who is praised primarily for what he did not do, the disasters he prevented, the bills he vetoed—a President wishing his subordinates would produce more missiles or build more schools. We will need instead what the Constitution envisioned: a Chief Executive who is the vital center of action in our whole scheme of government.

This includes the legislative process as well. The President cannot afford—for the sake of the office as well as the nation—to be another Warren G. Harding, described by one backer as a man who "would, when elected, sign whatever bill the Senate sent him—and not send bills for the Senate to pass." Rather he must know when to lead the Congress, when to consult it and when he should act alone. Having served fourteen years in the Legislative Branch, I would not look with favor upon its domination by the Executive. Under our government of "power as the rival of power," to use Hamilton's phrase, Congress must not surrender its responsibilities. But neither should it dominate. However large its share in the formulation of domestic programs, it is the President alone who must make the major decisions of our foreign policy.

That is what the Constitution wisely commands. And even domestically, the President must initiate policies and devise laws to meet the needs of the nation. And he must be prepared to use all the resources of his office to insure the enactment of that legislation—even when conflict is the result. By the end of his term Theodore Roosevelt was not popular in the Congress—particularly when he criticized an amendment to the Treasury appropriation which forbade the use of Secret Service men to investigate congressmen! And the feeling was mutual, Roosevelt saying: "I do not much admire the Senate, because it is such a helpless body when efficient work is to be done." And Woodrow Wilson was even more bitter after his frustrating quarrels—asked if he might run for the Senate in 1920, he replied: "Outside of the United States, the Senate does not amount to a damn. And inside the United States, the Senate is mostly despised. They haven't had a thought down there in fifty years."

But, however bitter their farewells, the facts of the matter are that Roosevelt and Wilson did get things done—not only through their Executive powers but through the Congress as well. Calvin Coolidge, on the other hand, departed from Washington with cheers of Congress still ringing in his ears. But when his World Court bill was under fire on Capitol Hill he sent no messages, gave no encouragement to the bill's leaders and paid little or no attention to the whole proceeding—and the cause of world justice was set back. To be sure, Coolidge had held the usual White House breakfasts with congressional leaders—but they were aimed, as he himself said, at "good fellowship," not a discussion of "public business." And at his press conferences, according to press historians, where he preferred to talk about the local flower show and its exhibits, reporters who finally extracted from him a single sentence"I am against that bill"—would rush to file tongue-in-cheek dispatches, proclaiming that: "President Coolidge, in a fighting mood, today served notice on Congress that he intended to combat, with all the resources at his command, the pending bill. . . ."

But in the coming years, we will need a real fighting mood in the White House—a man who will not retreat in the face of pressure from his congressional leaders—who will not let down those supporting his views on the floor. Divided government over the past six years has only been further confused by this lack of legislative leadership. To restore it next year will help restore purpose to both the Presidency and the Congress.

The facts of the matter are that legislative leadership is not possible without party leadership, in the most political sense—and Mr. Eisenhower prefers to stay above politics (although a weekly news magazine last fall reported the startling news that "President Eisenhower is emerging as a major political figure"). When asked, early in his first term, how he liked the "game of politics," he replied with a frown that his questioner was using a derogatory phrase. "Being President," he said, "is a very great experience . . . but the word 'politics' . . . I have no great liking for that." But no President, it seems to me, can escape politics. He has not only been chosen by the nation—he has been chosen by his party. And if he insists that he is "President of all the people" and should, therefore, offend none of them—if he blurs the issues and differences between the parties—if he neglects the party machinery and avoids his party's leadership—then he has not only weakened the political party as an instrument of the democratic process—he has dealt a blow to the democratic process itself. I prefer the example of Abe Lincoln, who loved politics with the passion of a born practitioner. For example, he waited up all night in 1863 to get the crucial returns on the Ohio governorship. When the Unionist candidate was elected, Lincoln wired: "Glory to God in the highest! Ohio has saved the nation!"

But the White House is not only the center of political leadership. It must be the center of moral leadership—a "bully pulpit," as Theodore Roosevelt described it. For only the President represents the national interest. And upon him alone converge all the needs and aspirations of all parts of the country, all departments of the government, all nations of the world. It is not enough merely to represent prevailing sentiment—to follow McKinley's practice, as described by Joe Cannon, of "keeping his ear so close to the ground he got it full of grasshoppers." We will need in the Sixties a President who is willing and able to summon his national constituency to its finest hour—to alert the people to our dangers and our opportunities—to demand of them the sacrifices that will be necessary. Despite the increasing evidence of a lost national purpose and a soft national will, F.D.R.'s words in his first inaugural still ring true: "In every dark hour of our national life, a leadership of frankness and vigor has met with that understanding and support of the people themselves which is essential to victory."

Roosevelt fulfilled the role of moral leadership. So did Wilson and Lincoln, Truman and Jackson and Teddy Roosevelt. They led the people as well as the government—they fought for great ideals as well as bills. And the time has come to demand that kind of leadership again. And so, as this vital campaign begins, let us discuss the issues the next President will face— but let us also discuss the powers and tools with which he must face them. For he must endow that office with extraordinary strength and vision. He must act in the image of Abraham Lincoln summoning his wartime Cabinet to a meeting on the Emancipation Proclamation. That Cabinet had been carefully chosen to please and reflect many elements in the country. But "I have gathered you together," Lincoln said, "to hear what I have written down. I do not wish your advice about the main matter—that I have determined for myself." And later when he went to sign it after several hours of exhausting handshaking that had left his arm weak, he said to those present: "If my name goes down in history, it will be for this act. My whole soul is in it. If my hand trembles when I sign this proclamation, all who examine the document hereafter will say: 'He hesitated.' " But Lincoln's hand did not tremble. He did not hesitate. He did not equivocate. For he was the President of the United States. It is in this spirit that we must go forth in the coming months and years.

43

George W. Bush

On Stem Cell Research (2001)

Good evening. I appreciate you giving me a few minutes of your time tonight so I can discuss with you a complex and difficult issue, an issue that is one of the most profound of our time.

The issue of research involving stem cells derived from human embryos is increasingly the subject of a national debate and dinner table discussions. The issue is confronted every day in laboratories as scientists ponder the ethical ramifications of their work. It is agonized over by parents and many couples as they try to have children or to save children already born. The issue is debated within the church, with people of different faiths, even many of the same faith, coming to different conclusions.

Many people are finding that the more they know about stem cell research, the less certain they are about the right ethical and moral conclusions.

My administration must decide whether to allow federal funds, your tax dollars, to be used for scientific research on stem cells derived from human embryos.

A large number of these embryos already exist. They are the product of a process called in vitro fertilization which helps so many couples conceive children. When doctors match sperm and egg to create life outside the womb, they usually produce more embryos than are implanted in the mother. Once a couple successfully has children or if they are unsuccessful, the additional embryos remain frozen in laboratories. Some will not survive during long storage, others are destroyed. A number have been donated to science and used to create privately funded stem cell lines. And a few have been implanted in an adoptive mother and born and are today healthy children.

Based on preliminary work that has been privately funded, scientists believe further research using stem cells offers great promise that could help improve the lives of those who suffer from many terrible diseases, from juvenile diabetes to Alzheimer, from Parkinsons to spinal cord injuries. And

George W. Bush, when President of the United States, delivered these remarks to the nation on August 9, 2001. The speech can be found at http://georgewbushwhite house.archives.gov/news/releases/2001/08/20010809-2.html.

while scientists admit they are not yet certain, they believe stem cells derived from embryos have unique potential.

You should also know that stem cells can be derived from sources other than embryos: from adult cells, from umbilical cords that are discarded after babies are born, from human placentas. And many scientists feel research on these types of stem cells is also promising. Many patients suffering from a range of diseases are already being helped with treatments developed from adult stem cells.

However, most scientists, atleast today, believe that research on embryonic stem cells offers the most promise because these cells have the potential to develop in all of the tissues in the body.

Scientists further believe that rapid progress in this research will come only with federal funds. Federal dollars help attract the best and brightest scientists. They ensure new discoveries are widely shared at the largest number of research facilities, and that the research is directed toward the greatest public good.

The United States has a long and proud record of leading the world toward advances in science and medicine that improve human life, and the United States has a long and proud record of upholding the highest standards of ethics as we expand the limits of science and knowledge.

Research on embryonic stem cells raises profound ethical questions, because extracting the stem cell destroys the embryo, and thus destroys its potential for life.

Like a snowflake, each of these embryos is unique, with the unique genetic potential of an individual human being.

As I thought through this issue I kept returning to two fundamental questions. First, are these frozen embryos human life and therefore something precious to be protected? And second, if they're going to be destroyed anyway, shouldn't they be used for a greater good, for research that has the potential to save and improve other lives?

I've asked those questions and others of scientists, scholars, bio-ethicists, religious leaders, doctors, researchers, members of Congress, my Cabinet and my friends. I have read heartfelt letters from many Americans. I have given this issue a great deal of thought, prayer, and considerable reflection, and I have found widespread disagreement.

On the first issue, are these embryos human life? Well, one researcher told me he believes this five-day-old cluster of cells is not an embryo, not yet an individual but a pre-embryo. He argued that it has the potential for life, but it is not a life because it cannot develop on its own.

An ethicist dismissed that as a callous attempt at rationalization. "Make no mistake," he told me, "that cluster of cells is the same way you and I, and all the rest of us, started our lives. One goes with a heavy heart if we use these," he said, "because we are dealing with the seeds of the next generation."

And to the other crucial question—If these are going to be destroyed anyway, why not use them for good purpose?—I also found different answers.

Many are these embryos are byproducts of a process that helps create life and we should allow couples to donate them to science so they can be used for good purpose instead of wasting their potential.

Others will argue there is no such thing as excess life and the fact that a living being is going to die does not justify experimenting on it or exploiting it as a natural resource.

At its core, this issue forces us to confront fundamental questions about the beginnings of life and the ends of science. It lives at a difficult moral intersection, juxtaposing the need to protect life in all its phases with the prospect of saving and improving life in all its stages.

As the discoveries of modern science create tremendous hope, they also lay vast ethical mine fields.

As the genius of science extends the horizons of what we can do, we increasingly confront complex questions about what we should do. We have arrived at that brave new world that seemed so distant in 1932 when Alduous Huxley wrote about human beings created in test tubes in what he called a hatchery.

In recent weeks, we learned that scientists have created human embryos in test tubes solely to experiment on them. This is deeply troubling and a warning sign that should prompt all of us to think through these issues very carefully.

Embryonic stem cell research is at the leading edge of a series of moral hazards. The initial stem cell researcher was at first reluctant to begin his research, fearing it might be used for human cloning. Scientists have already cloned a sheep. Researchers are telling us the next step could be to clone human beings to create individual designer stem cells, essentially to grow another you, to be available in case you need another heart or lung or liver.

I strongly oppose human cloning, as do most Americans. We recoil at the idea of growing human beings for spare body parts or creating life for our convenience.

And while we must devote enormous energy to conquering disease, it is equally important that we pay attention to the moral concerns raised by the new frontier of human embryo stem cell research. Even the most noble ends do not justify any means.

My position on these issues is shaped by deeply held beliefs. I'm a strong supporter of science and technology, and believe they have the potential for incredible good—to improve lives, to save life, to conquer disease. Research offers hope that millions of our loved ones may be cured of a disease and rid of their suffering. I have friends whose children suffer from juvenile diabetes. Nancy Reagan has written me about President Reagan's struggle with

Alzheimer's. My own family has confronted the tragedy of childhood leukemia. And like all Americans, I have great hope for cures.

I also believe human life is a sacred gift from our creator. I worry about a culture that devalues life, and believe as your president I have an important obligation to foster and encourage respect for life in America and throughout the world.

And while we're all hopeful about the potential of this research, no one can be certain that the science will live up to the hope it has generated.

Eight years ago, scientists believed fetal tissue research offered great hope for cures and treatments, yet the progress to date has not lived up to its initial expectations. Embryonic stem cell research offers both great promise and great peril, so I have decided we must proceed with great care.

As a result of private research, more than 60 genetically diverse stem cell lines already exist. They were created from embryos that have already been destroyed, and they have the ability to regenerate themselves indefinitely, creating ongoing opportunities for research.

I have concluded that we should allow federal funds to be used for research on these existing stem cell lines, where the life-and- death decision has already been made.

Leading scientists tell me research on these 60 lines has great promise that could lead to breakthrough therapies and cures. This allows us to explore the promise and potential of stem cell research without crossing a fundamental moral line by providing taxpayer funding that would sanction or encourage further destruction of human embryos that have at least the potential for life.

I also believe that great scientific progress can be made through aggressive federal funding of research on umbilical cord, placenta, adult and animal stem cells, which do not involve the same moral dilemma. This year your government will spent $250 million on this important research.

I will also name a president's council to monitor stem cell research, to recommend appropriate guidelines and regulations and to consider all of the medical and ethical ramifications of bio-medical innovation.

This council will consist of leading scientists, doctors, ethicists, lawyers, theologians and others, and will be chaired by Dr. Leon Cass, a leading bio-medical ethicist from the University of Chicago.

This council will keep us apprised of new developments and give our nation a forum to continue to discuss and evaluate these important issues.

As we go forward, I hope we will always be guided by both intellect and heart, by both our capabilities and our conscience.

I have made this decision with great care, and I pray it is the right one.

Thank you for listening. Good night, and God bless America.

44

Abraham Lincoln

The Perpetuation of Our Political Institutions (1838)

As a subject for the remarks of the evening, *the perpetuation of our political institutions*, is selected.

In the great journal of things happening under the sun, we, the American People, find our account running, under date of the nineteenth century of the Christian era. We find ourselves in the peaceful possession, of the fairest portion of the earth, as regards extent of territory, fertility of soil, and salubrity of climate. We find ourselves under the government of a system of political institutions, conducing more essentially to the ends of civil and religious liberty, than any of which the history of former times tells us. We, when mounting the stage of existence, found ourselves the legal inheritors of these fundamental blessings. We toiled not in the acquirement or establishment of them—they are a legacy bequeathed us, by a *once* hardy, brave, and patriotic, but *now* lamented and departed race of ancestors. Their's was the task (and nobly they performed it) to possess themselves, and through themselves, us, of this goodly land; and to uprear upon its hills and its valleys, a political edifice of liberty and equal rights; 'tis ours only, to transmit these, the former, unprofaned by the foot of an invader; the latter, undecayed by the lapse of time, and untorn by usurpation—to the latest generation that fate shall permit the world to know. This task of gratitude to our fathers, justice to ourselves, duty to posterity, and love for our species in general, all imperatively require us faithfully to perform.

How, then, shall we perform it? At what point shall we expect the approach of danger? By what means shall we fortify against it? Shall we expect some transatlantic military giant, to step the Ocean, and crush us at a blow? Never! All the armies of Europe, Asia and Africa combined, with all the treasure of the earth (our own excepted) in their military chest; with a Buonaparte for a commander, could not by force, take a drink from the Ohio, or make a track on the Blue Ridge, in a trial of a thousand years.

From *The Collected Works of Abraham Lincoln*, Vol. VI, Rutgers University Press, 1953.

At what point then is the approach of danger to be expected? I answer, if it ever reach us, it must spring up amongst us. It cannot come from abroad. If destruction be our lot, we must ourselves be its author and finisher. As a nation of freemen, we must live through all time, or die by suicide.

I hope I am over wary; but if I am not, there is, even now, something of ill-omen amongst us. I mean the increasing disregard for law which pervades the country; the growing disposition to substitute the wild and furious passions, in lieu of the sober judgment of Courts; and the worse than savage mobs, for the executive ministers of justice. This disposition is awfully fearful in any community; and that it now exists in ours, though grating to our feelings to admit, it would be a violation of truth, and an insult to our intelligence, to deny. Accounts of outrages committed by mobs, form the every-day news of the times. They have pervaded the country, from New England to Louisiana;—they are neither peculiar to the eternal snows of the former, nor the burning suns of the latter;—they are not the creature of climate—neither are they confined to the slaveholding, or the nonslaveholding States. Alike, they spring up among the pleasure hunting masters of Southern slaves, and the order loving citizens of the land of steady habits. Whatever, then, their cause may be, it is common to the whole country.

It would be tedious, as well as useless, to recount the horrors of all of them. Those happening in the State of Mississippi, and at St. Louis, are, perhaps, the most dangerous in example, and revolting to humanity. In the Mississippi case, they first commenced by hanging the regular gamblers: a set of men, certainly not following for a livelihood, a very useful, or very honest occupation, but one which, so far from being forbidden by the laws, was actually licensed by an act of the Legislature, passed but a single year before. Next, negroes, suspected of conspiring to raise an insurrection, were caught up and hanged in all parts of the State: then, white men, supposed to be leagued with the negroes; and finally, strangers, from neighboring States, going thither on business, were, in many instances, subjected to the same fate. Thus went on this process of hanging, from gamblers to negroes, from negroes to white citizens, and from these to strangers; till, dead men were seen literally dangling from the boughs of trees upon every road side; and in numbers almost sufficient, to rival the native Spanish moss of the country, as a drapery of the forest.

Turn, then, to that horror-striking scene at St. Louis. A single victim was only sacrificed there. His story is very short; and is, perhaps, the most highly tragic, of any thing of its length, that has ever been witnessed in real life. A mulatto man, by the name of McIntosh, was seized in the street, dragged to the suburbs of the city, chained to a tree, and actually burned to death; and all within a single hour from the time he had been a freeman, attending to his own business, and at peace with the world.

Such are the effects of mob law; and such are the scenes, becoming more and more frequent in this land so lately famed for love of law and order; and the stories of which, have even now grown too familiar, to attract anything more, than an idle remark.

But you are, perhaps, ready to ask, "What has this to do with the perpetuation of our political institutions?" I answer, it has much to do with it. Its direct consequences are, comparatively speaking, but a small evil; and much of its danger consists, in the proneness of our minds, to regard its direct, as its only consequences. Abstractly considered, the hanging of the gamblers at Vicksburg, was of but little consequence. They constitute a portion of population, that is worse than useless in any community; and their death, if no pernicious example be set by it, is never matter of reasonable regret with any one. If they were annually swept, from the stage of existence, by the plague or small pox, honest men would, perhaps, be much profited, by the operation. Similar too, is the correct reasoning, in regard to the burning of the negro at St. Louis. He had forfeited his life, by the perpetration of an outrageous murder, upon one of the most worthy and respectable citizens of the city; and had he not died as he did, he must have died by the sentence of the law, in a very short time afterwards. As to him alone, it was as well the way it was, as it could otherwise have been. But the example in either case, was fearful. When men take it in their heads today, to hang gamblers, or burn murderers, they should recollect, that, in the confusion usually attending such transactions, they will be as likely to hang or burn some one, who is neither a gambler nor a murderer as one who is; and that, acting upon the example they set, the mob of tomorrow, may, and probably will, hang or burn some of them, by the very same mistake. And not only so; the innocent, those who have ever set their faces against violations of law in every shape, alike with the guilty, fall victims to the ravages of mob law; and thus it goes on, step by step; till all the walls erected for the defence of the persons and property of individuals, are trodden down, and disregarded. But all this even, is not the full extent of the evil. By such examples, by instances of the perpetrators of such acts going unpunished, the lawless in spirit, are encouraged to become lawless in practice; and having been used to no restraint, but dread of punishment, they thus become, absolutely unrestrained. Having ever regarded Government as their deadliest bane, they make a jubilee of the suspension of its operations; and pray for nothing so much, as its total annihilation. While, on the other hand, good men, men who love tranquility, who desire to abide by the laws, and enjoy their benefits, who would gladly spill their blood in the defence of their country; seeing their property destroyed; their families insulted, and their lives endangered; their persons injured; and seeing nothing in prospect that forebodes a change for the better; become tired of, and disgusted with, a Government that offers them no protection; and are not much averse to a change in which they imagine they have nothing to lose. Thus, then, by the operation of this mobocratic spirit, which all must admit, is now abroad in the land, the strongest bulwark of any Government, and particularly of those constituted like ours, may effectually be broken down and destroyed—I mean the *attachment* of the People. Whenever this effect shall be produced among us; whenever the vicious portion of population shall be permitted to gather in bands of hundreds and thousands, and burn churches, ravage and rob provision stores, throw printing presses into rivers, shoot editors,* and hang and burn obnoxious persons at pleasure, and with impunity; depend on it, this Government cannot last. By such things, the feelings of the best citizens will become more or less alienated from it; and thus it will be left without friends, or with too few, and those few too weak, to make their friendship effectual. At such a time and under such circumstances, men of sufficient talent and ambition will not be wanting to seize the opportunity, strike the blow, and overturn that fair fabric, which for the last half century, had been the fondest hope, of the lovers of freedom, throughout the world.

I know the American People are *much* attached to their Government;— I know they would suffer *much* for its sake;—I know they would endure evils long and patiently, before they would ever think of exchanging it for another. Yet, notwithstanding all this, if the laws be continually despised and disregarded, if their rights to be secure in their persons and property, are held by no better tenure than the caprice of a mob, the alienation of their affections from the Government is the natural consequence; and to that, sooner or later, it must come.

Here then, is one point at which danger may be expected.

The question recurs "how shall we fortify against it?" The answer is simple. Let every American, every lover of liberty, every well wisher to his posterity, swear by the blood of the Revolution, never to violate in the least particular, the laws of the country; and never to tolerate their violation by others. As the patriots of seventy-six did to the support of the Declaration of Independence, so to the support of the Constitution and Laws, let every American pledge his life, his property, and his sacred honor;—let every man remember that to violate the law, is to trample on the blood of his father, and to tear the character [charter?] of his own, and his children's liberty. Let reverence for the laws, be breathed by every American mother, to the lisping babe, that prattles on her lap—let it be taught in schools, in seminaries, and in colleges;—let it be written in Primmers, spelling books, and in Almanacs;—let it be preached from the pulpit, proclaimed in legislative halls, and enforced in courts of justice. And, in short, let it become the *political religion* of the nation; and let the old and the young, the rich and the poor, the grave and the gay, of all sexes and tongues, and colors and conditions, sacrifice unceasingly upon its altars.

While ever a state of feeling, such as this, shall universally, or even, very generally prevail throughout the nation, vain will be every effort, and fruitless every attempt, to subvert our national freedom.

When I so pressingly urge a strict observance of all the laws, let me not be understood as saying there are no bad laws, nor that grievances may not arise, for the redress of which, no legal provisions have been made. I mean to say no such thing. But I do mean to say, that, although bad laws, if they exist, should be repealed as soon as possible, still while they continue in force, for the sake of example, they should be religiously observed. So also in unprovided cases. If such arise, let proper legal provisions be made for them with the least possible delay; but, till then, let them if not too intolerable, be borne with.

There is no grievance that is a fit object of redress by mob law. In any case that arises, as for instance, the promulgation of abolitionism, one of two positions is necessarily true; that is, the thing is right within itself, and therefore deserves the protection of all law and all good citizens; or, it is wrong, and therefore proper to be prohibited by legal enactments; and in neither case, is the interposition of mob law, either necessary, justifiable, or excusable.

But, it may be asked, why suppose danger to our political institutions? Have we not preserved them for more than fifty years? And why may we not for fifty times as long?

We hope there is no *sufficient* reason. We hope all dangers may be overcome; but to conclude that no danger may ever arise, would itself be extremely dangerous. There are now, and will hereafter be, many causes, dangerous in their tendency, which have not existed heretofore; and which are not too insignificant to merit attention. That our government should have been maintained in its original form from its establishment until now, is not much to be wondered at. It had many props to support it through that period, which now are decayed, and crumbled away. Through that period, it was felt by all, to be an undecided experiment; now, it is understood to be a successful one. Then, all that sought celebrity and fame, and distinction, expected to find them in the success of that experiment. Their *all* was staked upon it:—their destiny was *inseparably* linked with it. Their ambition aspired to display before an admiring world, a practical demonstration of the truth of a proposition, which had hitherto been considered, at best no better, than problematical; namely, *the capability of a people to govern themselves.* If they succeeded, they were to be immortalized; their names were to be transferred to counties and cities, and rivers and mountains; and to be revered and sung, and toasted through all time. If they failed, they were to be called knaves and fools, and fanatics for a fleeting hour; then to sink and be forgotten. They succeeded. The experiment is successful; and thousands have won their deathless names in making it so. But the game is caught; and I believe it is true, that with the catching, end the pleasures of the chase. This field of glory is harvested, and the crop is already appropriated. But new reapers will arise, and *they*, too, will seek a field. It is to deny, what the history of the world tells us is true, to suppose that men of ambition and talents will not continue to spring up amongst us. And, when they do, they will as naturally seek the gratification of their ruling passion, as others have so done before them. The question then, is, can that gratification be found in supporting and maintaining an edifice that has been erected by others? Most certainly it cannot. Many great and good men sufficiently qualified for any task they should undertake, may ever be found, whose ambition would aspire to nothing beyond a seat in Congress, a gubernatorial or a presidential chair; *but such belong not to the family of the lion, or the tribe of the eagle*. What! think you these places would satisfy an Alexander, a Caesar, or a Napoleon? Never! Towering genius disdains a beaten path. It seeks regions hitherto unexplored. It sees *no distinction* in adding story to story, upon the monuments of fame, erected to the memory of others. It *denies* that it is glory enough to serve under any chief. It *scorns* to tread in the footsteps of *any* predecessor, however illustrious. It thirsts and burns for distinction; and, if possible, it will have it, whether at the expense of emancipating slaves, or enslaving freemen. Is it unreasonable then to expect, that some man possessed of the loftiest genius, coupled with ambition sufficient to push it to its utmost stretch, will at some time, spring up among us? And when such a one does, it will require the people to be united with each other, attached to the government and laws, and generally intelligent, to successfully frustrate his designs.

Distinction will be his paramount object; and although he would as willingly, perhaps more so, acquire it by doing good as harm; yet, that opportunity being past, and nothing left to be done in the way of building up, he would set boldly to the task of pulling down.

Here then, is a probable case, highly dangerous, and such a one as could not have well existed heretofore.

Another reason which *once was*; but which, to the same extent, is *now no more*, has done much in maintaining our institutions thus far. I mean the powerful influence which the interesting scenes of the revolution had upon the *passions* of the people as distinguished from their judgment. By this influence, the jealousy, envy, and avarice, incident to our nature, and so common to a state of peace, prosperity, and conscious strength, were, for the time, in a great measure smothered and rendered inactive; while the deep rooted principles of *hate*, and the powerful motive of *revenge*, instead of being turned against each other, were directed exclusively against the British nation. And thus, from the force of circumstances, the basest principles of our nature, were either made to lie dormant, or to become the active agents in the advancement of the noblest of causes—that of establishing and maintaining civil and religious liberty.

But this state of feeling *must fade, is fading, has faded*, with the circumstances that produced it.

I do not mean to say, that the scenes of the revolution *are now* or *ever will be* entirely forgotten; but that like every thing else, they must fade upon the memory of the world, and grow more and more dim by the lapse of time. In history, we hope, they will be read of, and recounted, so long as the bible shall be read;—but even granting that they will, their influence *cannot be* what it heretofore has been. Even then, they *cannot be* so universally known, nor so vividly felt, as they were by the generation just gone to rest. At the close of that struggle, nearly every adult male had been a participator in some of its scenes. The consequence was, that of those scenes, in the form of a husband, a father, a son or a brother, a *living history* was to be found in every family—a history bearing the indubitable testimonies of its own authenticity, in the limbs mangled, in the scars of wounds received, in the midst of the very scenes related—a history, too, that could be read and understood alike by all, the wise and the ignorant, the learned and the unlearned. But *those* histories are gone. They *can* be read no more forever. They *were* a fortress of strength; but, what invading foemen could *never do,* the silent artillery of time *has done*; the levelling of its walls. They are gone. They *were* a forest of giant oaks; but the all-resistless hurricane has swept over them, and left only, here and there, a lonely trunk, despoiled of its ver-dure, shorn of its foliage; unshading and unshaded, to murmur in a few more gentle breezes, and to combat with its mutilated limbs, a few more ruder storms, then to sink, and be no more.

They *were* pillars of the temple of liberty; and now, that they have crumbled away, that temple must fall, unless we, their descendants, supply their places with other pillars, hewn from the solid quarry of sober reason. Passion has helped us; but can do so no more. It will in future be our enemy. Reason, cold, calculating, unimpassioned reason, must furnish all the materials for our future support and defence. Let those materials be molded into *general intelligence, sound morality* and, in particular, a *reverence for the constitution and laws;* and, that we improved to the last; that we remained free to the last; that we revered his name to the last; that, during his long sleep, we permitted no hostile foot to pass over or desecrate his resting place; shall be that which to learn and last trump shall awaken our WASHINGTON.

Upon these let the proud fabric of freedom rest, as the rock of its basis; and as truly as has been said of the only greater institution, "*the gates of hell shall not prevail against it.*"

45

Youngstown Sheet and Tube Co. v. Sawyer (1952)

Justice Black *delivered the opinion of the Court:*

We are asked to decide whether the President was acting within his constitutional power when he issued an order directing the Secretary of Commerce to take possession of and operate most of the Nation's steel mills. . . .

The President's power, if any, to issue the order must stem from an act of Congress or from the Constitution itself. There is no statute that expressly authorizes the President to take possession of property as he did here. Nor is there any act of Congress to which our attention has been directed from which such a power can fairly be implied. . . .

Moreover, the use of the seizure technique to solve labor disputes in order to prevent work stoppages was not only unauthorized by any congressional enactment; prior to this controversy, Congress has refused to adopt that method of settling labor disputes. When the Taft-Hartley Act was under consideration in 1947, Congress rejected an amendment which would have authorized such governmental seizures in cases of emergency. . . .

It is clear that if the President had authority to issue the order he did, it must be found in some provisions of the Constitution. And it is not claimed that express constitutional language grants this power to the President. The contention is that presidential power should be implied from the aggregate of his powers under the Constitution. Particular reliance is placed on provisions in Article II which say that "the executive Power shall be vested in a President . . ."; that "he shall take Care that the Laws be faithfully executed"; and that he "shall be Commander in Chief of the Army and Navy of the United States."

The order cannot properly be sustained as an exercise of the President's military power as Commander in Chief of the Armed Forces. The Government attempts to do so by citing a number of cases upholding broad powers in military commanders engaged in day-to-day fighting in a theater of war. Such cases need not concern us here. Even though "theater of war" be an expanding concept, we cannot with faithfulness to our constitutional system hold that the Commander in Chief of the Armed Forces has the ultimate

From *Youngstown Sheet & Tube Co. v. Sawyer*, 343 U.S. 579 (1952).

power as such to take possession of private property in order to keep labor disputes from stopping production. This is a job for the Nation's lawmakers, not for its military authorities.

Nor can the seizure order be sustained because of the several constitutional provisions that grant executive power to the President. In the framework of our Constitution, the President's power to see that the laws are faithfully executed refutes the idea that he is to be a lawmaker. The Constitution limits his functions in the law-making process to the recommending of laws he thinks wise and the vetoing of laws he thinks bad. And the Constitution is neither silent nor equivocal about who shall make laws which the President is to execute. . . .

The President's order does not direct that a congressional policy be executed in a manner prescribed by Congress—it directs that a presidential policy be executed in a manner prescribed by the President. The preamble of the order itself, like that of many statutes, sets out reasons why the President believes certain policies should be adopted, proclaims these policies as rules of conduct to be followed, and again, like a statute, authorizes a government official to promulgate additional rules and regulations consistent with the policy proclaimed and needed to carry that policy into execution. The power of Congress to adopt such public policies as those proclaimed by the order is beyond question. It can authorize the taking of private property for public use. It can make laws regulating the relationships between employers and employees, prescribing rules designed to settle labor disputes, and fixing wages and working conditions in certain fields of our economy. . . .

The Founders of this Nation entrusted the lawmaking power to the Congress alone in both good and bad times. It would do no good to recall the historical events, the fears of power and the hopes for freedom that lay behind their choice. Such a view would but confirm our holding that this seizure order cannot stand. . . .

Chief Justice Vinson, *dissenting:*

. . . Those who suggest that this is a case involving extraordinary powers should be mindful that these are extraordinary times. A world not yet recovered from the devastation of World War II has been forced to face the threat of another and more terrifying global conflict. . . .

The steel mills were seized for a public use. The power of eminent domain, invoked in this case, is an essential attribute of sovereignty and has long been recognized as a power of the Federal Government. . . .

Admitting that the Government could seize the mills, plaintiffs claim that the implied power of eminent domain can be exercised only under an Act of Congress; under no circumstances, they say, can that power be exercised by the President unless he can point to an express provision in enabling legislation. . . .

Under this view, the President is left powerless at the very moment when the need for action may be most pressing and when no one, other than he, is immediately capable of action. Under this view, he is left powerless because a power not expressly given to Congress is nevertheless found to rest exclusively with Congress. . . .

A review of executive action demonstrates that our Presidents have on many occasions exhibited the leadership contemplated by the Framers when they made the President Commander in Chief, and imposed upon him the trust to "take Care that the Laws be faithfully executed." With or without explicit statutory authorization, Presidents have at such times dealt with national emergencies by acting promptly and resolutely to enforce legislative programs, at least to save those programs until Congress could act. Congress and the courts have responded to such executive initiative with consistent approval. . . .

Jefferson's initiative in the Louisiana Purchase, the Monroe Doctrine, and Jackson's removal of Government deposits from the Bank of the United States further serve to demonstrate by deed what the Framers described by words when they vested the whole of the executive power in the President.

Without declaration of war, President Lincoln took energetic action with the outbreak of the Civil War. He summoned troops and paid them out of the Treasury without appropriation therefor. He proclaimed a naval blockade of the Confederacy and seized ships violating that blockade. Congress, far from denying the validity of these acts, gave them express approval. The most striking action of President Lincoln was the Emancipation Proclamation, issued in aid of the successful prosecution of the Civil War, but wholly without statutory authority.

In an action furnishing a most apt precedent for this case, President Lincoln directed the seizure of rail and telegraph lines leading to Washington without statutory authority. Many months later, Congress recognized and confirmed the power of the President to seize railroads and telegraph lines and provided criminal penalties for interference with Government operation. This Act did not confer on the President any additional powers of seizure. Congress plainly rejected the view that the President's acts had been without legal sanction until ratified by the legislature. Sponsors of the bill declared that its purpose was only to confirm the power which the President already possessed. Opponents insisted a statute authorizing seizure was unnecessary and might even be construed as limiting existing Presidential powers. . . .

[The Chief Justice then cites other examples of the exercise of emergency powers by American Presidents.]

Focusing now on the situation confronting the President on the night of April 8, 1952, we cannot but conclude that the President was performing his duty under the Constitution "to take care that the laws be faithfully executed"—a duty described by President Benjamin Harrison as "the central idea of the office."

The President reported to Congress the morning after the seizure that he acted because a work stoppage in steel production would immediately imperil the safety of the Nation by preventing execution of the legislative programs for procurement of military equipment. And, while a shutdown could be averted by granting the price concessions requested by plaintiffs, granting such concessions would disrupt the price stabilization program also enacted by Congress. Rather than fail to execute either legislative program, the President acted to execute both.

Much of the argument in this case has been directed at straw men. We do not now have before us the case of a President acting solely on the basis of his own notions of the public welfare. Nor is there any question of unlimited executive power in this case. The President himself closed the door to any such claim when he sent his Message to Congress stating his purpose to abide by any action of Congress, whether approving or disapproving his seizure action. Here, the President immediately made sure that Congress was fully informed of the temporary action he had taken only to preserve the legislative programs from destruction until Congress could act.

The absence of a specific statute authorizing seizure of the steel mills as a mode of executing the laws—both the military procurement program and the anti-inflation program—has not until today been thought to prevent the President from executing the laws. Unlike an administrative commission confined to the enforcement of the statute under which it was created, or the head of a department when administering a particular statute, the President is a constitutional officer charged with taking care that a "mass of legislation" be executed. Flexibility as to mode of execution to meet critical situations is a matter of practical necessity. . . .

46

United States v. Curtiss-Wright Export Corporation (1936)

Justice Sutherland *delivered the opinion of the Court:*

On January 27, 1936, an indictment was returned in the court below, the first count of which charges that appellees, beginning with the 29th day of May, 1934, conspired to sell in the United States certain arms of war, namely, fifteen machine guns, to Bolivia, a country then engaged in armed conflict in the Chaco, in violation of the Joint Resolution of Congress approved May 28, 1934, and the provisions of a proclamation issued on the same day by the President of the United States pursuant to authority conferred by section 1 of the resolution. In pursuance of the conspiracy, the commission of certain overt acts was alleged, details of which need not be stated. The Joint Resolution follows:

> *Resolved by the Senate and House of Representatives of the United States of America in Congress assembled,* That if the President finds that the prohibition of the sale of arms and munitions of war in the United States to those countries now engaged in armed conflict in the Chaco may contribute to the reestablishment of peace between those countries, and if after consultation with the governments of other American Republics and with their cooperation, as well as that of such other governments as he may deem necessary, he makes proclamation to that effect, it shall be unlawful to sell, except under such limitations and exceptions as the President prescribes, any arms or munitions of war in any place in the United States to the countries now engaged in that armed conflict, or to any person, company, or association acting in the interest of either country, until otherwise ordered by the President or by Congress.
>
> Sec. 2. Whoever sells any arms or munitions of war in violation of section 1 shall, on conviction, be punished by a fine not exceeding $10,000 or by imprisonment not exceeding two years, or both.

The President's proclamation, after reciting the terms of the joint Resolution, declares:

> Now, therefore, I, Franklin D. Roosevelt, President of the United States of America, acting under and by virtue of the authority conferred in me by the said joint resolution of Congress, do hereby declare and proclaim that I have found that the prohibition of the sale of arms and munitions of war in the United States to those countries now engaged in armed conflict in the Chaco may contribute to the reestablishment of peace between

From *United States v. Curtiss-Wright Export Corporation,* 299 U.S. 304 (1936).

these countries, and that I have consulted with the governments of other American Republics and have been assured of the cooperation of such governments as I have deemed necessary as contemplated by the said joint resolution; and I do hereby admonish all citizens of the United States and every person to abstain from every violation of the provisions of the joint resolution above set forth, hereby made applicable to Bolivia and Paraguay, and I do hereby warn them that all violations of such provisions will be rigorously prosecuted. . . .

On November 14, 1935, this proclamation was revoked, in the following terms:

> Now, therefore, I, Franklin D. Roosevelt, President of the United States of America, do hereby declare and proclaim that I have found that the prohibition of the sale of arms and munitions of war in the United States to Bolivia or Paraguay will no longer be necessary as a contribution to the reestablishment of peace between those countries. . . .

Appellees severally demurred. . . [urging] that the Joint Resolution effects an invalid delegation of legislative power to the executive. . . .

It is contended that by the Joint Resolution the going into effect and continued operation of the resolution was conditioned (a) upon the President's judgment as to its beneficial effect upon the reestablishment of peace between the countries engaged in armed conflict in the Chaco; (b) upon the making of a proclamation, which was left to his unfettered discretion, thus constituting an attempted substitution of the President's will for that of Congress; (c) upon the making of a proclamation putting an end to the operation of the resolution, which again was left to the President's unfettered discretion; and (d) further, that the extent of its operation in particular cases was subject to limitation and exception by the President, controlled by no standard. In each of these particulars, appellees urge that Congress abdicated its essential functions and delegated them to the Executive.

Whether, if the Joint Resolution had related solely to internal affairs, it would be open to the challenge that it constituted an unlawful delegation of legislative power to the Executive, we find it unnecessary to determine. The whole aim of the resolution is to affect a situation entirely external to the United States, and falling within the category of foreign affairs. The determination which we are called to make, therefore, is whether the Joint Resolution, as applied to that situation, is vulnerable to attack under the rule that forbids a delegation of the lawmaking power. In other words, assuming (but not deciding) that the challenged delegation, if it were confined to internal affairs, would be invalid, may it nevertheless be sustained on the ground that its exclusive aim is to afford a remedy for a hurtful condition within foreign territory?

It will contribute to the elucidation of the question if we first consider the differences between the powers of the federal government in respect of foreign or external affairs and those in respect of domestic or internal affairs. That there are differences between them, and that these differences are fundamental, may not be doubted.

The two classes of powers are different, both in respect of their origin and their nature. The broad statement that the federal government can exercise no powers except those specifically enumerated in the Constitution, and such implied powers as are necessary and proper to carry into effect the enumerated powers, is categorically true only in respect of our internal affairs. In that field, the primary purpose of the Constitution was to carve from the general mass of legislative powers *then possessed by the states* such portions as it was thought desirable to vest in the federal government, leaving those not included in the enumeration still in the states. That this doctrine applies only to powers which the states had is self-evident. And since the states severally never possessed international powers, such powers could not have been carved from the mass of state powers but obviously were transmitted to the United States from some other source. During the Colonial period, those powers were possessed exclusively by and were entirely under the control of the Crown. By the Declaration of Independence, "the Representatives of the United States of America" declared the United (not the several) Colonies to be free and "independent states," and as such to have "full Power to levy War, conclude Peace, contract Alliances, establish Commerce and to do all other Acts and Things which Independent States may of right do."

As a result of the separation from Great Britain by the colonies, acting as a unit, the powers of external sovereignty passed from the Crown not to the colonies severally, but to the colonies in their collective and corporate capacity as the United States of America. Even before the Declaration, the colonies were a unit in foreign affairs, acting through a common agency— namely, the Continental Congress, composed of delegates from the thirteen colonies. That agency exercised powers of war and peace, raised an army, created a navy, and finally adopted the Declaration of Independence. Rulers come and go; governments end and forms of government change; but sovereignty survives. A political society cannot endure without a supreme will somewhere. Sovereignty is never held in suspense. When, therefore, the external sovereignty of Great Britain in respect of the colonies ceased, it immediately passed to the Union. That fact was given practical application almost at once. The treaty of peace, made on September 3, 1783, was concluded between his Brittanic Majesty and the "United States of America."

The Union existed before the Constitution, which was ordained and established among other things to form "a more perfect Union." Prior to that event, it is clear that the Union, declared by the Articles of Confederation to be "perpetual," was the sole possessor of external sovereignty, and in the Union it remained without change save in so far as the Constitution in express terms qualified its exercise. The Framers' Convention was called and exerted its powers upon the irrefutable postulate that though the states were several their people in respect of foreign affairs were one. In that convention, the entire absence of state power to deal with those affairs was thus forcefully stated by Rufus King:

> The states were not "sovereigns" in the sense contended for by some. They did not possess the peculiar features of sovereignty,—they could not make war, nor peace, nor alliances, nor treaties. Considering them as political beings, they were dumb, for they could not speak to any foreign sovereign whatever. They were deaf, for they could not hear any propositions from such sovereign. They had not even the organs or faculties of defence or offence, for they could not of themselves raise troops, or equip vessels, for war.

It results that the investment of the federal government with the powers of external sovereignty did not depend upon the affirmative grants of the Constitution. The powers to declare and wage war, to conclude peace, to make treaties, to maintain diplomatic relations with other sovereignties, if they had never been mentioned in the Constitution, would have vested in the federal government as necessary concomitants of nationality. Neither the Constitution nor the laws passed in pursuance of it have any force in foreign territory unless in respect of our own citizens; and operations of the nation in such territory must be governed by treaties, international understandings and compacts, and the principles of international law. As a member of the family of nations, the right and power of the United States in that field are equal to the right and power of the other members of the international family. Otherwise, the United States is not completely sovereign. The power to acquire territory by discovery and occupation, the power to make such international agreements as do not constitute treaties in the constitutional sense [citations omitted], none of which is expressly affirmed by the Constitution, nevertheless exist as inherently inseparable from the conception of nationality. This the court recognized, and in each of the cases cited found the warrant for its conclusions not in the provisions of the Constitution, but in the law of nations. . . .

Not only, as we have shown, is the federal power over external affairs in origin and essential character different from that over internal affairs, but participation in the exercise of the power is significantly limited. In this vast external realm, with its important, complicated, delicate and manifold problems, the President alone has the power to speak or listen as a representative of the nation. He *makes* treaties with the advice and consent of the Senate; but he alone negotiates. Into the field of negotiation the Senate cannot intrude; and Congress itself is powerless to invade it. As Marshall said in his great argument of March 7, 1800, in the House of Representatives, "The President is the sole organ of the nation in its external relations, and its sole representative with foreign nations." The Senate Committee on Foreign

Relations at a very early day in our history (February 15, 1816), reported to the Senate, among other things, as follows:

> The President is the constitutional representative of the United States with regard to foreign nations. He manages our concerns with foreign nations and must necessarily be most competent to determine when, how, and upon what subjects negotiation may be urged with the greatest prospect of success. For his conduct he is responsible to the Constitution. The committee considers this responsibility the surest pledge for the faithful discharge of his duty. They think the interference of the Senate in the direction of foreign negotiations calculated to diminish that responsibility and thereby to impair the best security for the national safety. The nature of transactions with foreign nations, moveover, requires caution and unity of design, and their success frequently depends on secrecy and dispatch.

It is important to bear in mind that we are here dealing not alone with an authority vested in the President by an exertion of legislative power, but with such an authority plus the very delicate, plenary and exclusive power of the President as the sole organ of the federal government in the field of international relations—a power which does not require as a basis for its exercise an act of Congress, but which, of course, like every other governmental power, must be exercised in subordination to the applicable provisions of the Constitution. It is quite apparent that if, in the maintenance of our international relations, embarrassment—perhaps serious embarrassment—is to be avoided and success for our aims achieved, congressional legislation which is to be made effective through negotiation and inquiry within the international field must often accord to the President a degree of discretion and freedom from statutory restriction which would not be admissible were domestic affairs alone involved. Moreover, he, not Congress, has the better opportunity of knowing the conditions which prevail in foreign countries, and especially is this true in time of war. He has his confidential sources of information. He has his agents in the form of diplomatic, consular and other officials. Secrecy in respect of information gathered by them may be highly necessary, and the premature disclosure of it productive of harmful results. Indeed, so clearly is this true that the first President refused to accede to a request to lay before the House of Representatives the instructions, correspondence and documents relating to the negotiation of the Jay Treaty—a refusal the wisdom of which was recognized by the House itself and has never since been doubted. In his reply to the request, President Washington said:

> The nature of foreign negotiations requires caution, and their success must often depend on secrecy; and even when brought to a conclusion a full disclosure of all the measures, demands, or eventual concessions which may have been proposed or contemplated would be extremely impolitic; for this might have a pernicious influence on future negotiations, or produce immediate inconveniences, perhaps danger and mischief, in relation to other powers. The necessity of such caution and secrecy was one cogent reason for vesting the power of making treaties in the President, with the advice and consent of the Senate, the

principle on which that body was formed confining it to a small number of members. To admit, then, a right in the House of Representatives to demand and to have as a matter of course all the papers respecting a negotiation with a foreign power would be to establish a dangerous precedent.

The marked difference between foreign affairs and domestic affairs in this respect is recognized by both houses of Congress in the very form of their requisitions for information from the executive departments. In the case of every department except the Department of State, the resolution *directs* the official to furnish the information. In the case of the State Department, dealing with foreign affairs, the President is *requested* to furnish the information "if not incompatible with the public interest." A statement that to furnish the information is not compatible with the public interest rarely, if ever, is questioned.

When the President is to be authorized by legislation to act in respect of a matter intended to affect a situation in foreign territory, the legislator properly bears in mind the important consideration that the form of the President's action—or, indeed, whether he shall act at all—may well depend, among other things, upon the nature of the confidential information which he has or may thereafter receive, or upon the effect which his action may have upon our foreign relations. This consideration, in connection with what we have already said on the subject, discloses the unwisdom of requiring Congress in this field of governmental power to lay down narrowly definite standards by which the President is to be governed. As this court said in *Mackenzie v. Hare*, "As a government, the United States is invested with all the attributes of sovereignty. As it has the character of nationality it has the powers of nationality, especially those which concern its relations and intercourse with other countries. *We should hesitate long before limiting or embarrassing such powers*." (Italics supplied.)

In the light of the foregoing observations, it is evident that this court should not be in haste to apply a general rule which will have the effect of condemning legislation like that under review as constituting an unlawful delegation of legislative power. The principles which justify such legislation find overwhelming support in the unbroken legislative practice which has prevailed almost from the inception of the national government to the present day.

Let us examine, in chronological order, the acts of legislation which warrant this conclusion:

The Act of June 4, 1794, authorized the President to lay, regulate and revoke embargoes. He was "authorized" whenever, in his opinion, the public safety shall so require, "to lay the embargo upon all ships and vessels in the ports of the United States, including those of foreign nations, under such regulations as the circumstances of the case may require, and to continue or revoke the same, whenever he shall think proper." A prior joint resolution of May 7, 1794, had conferred *unqualified* power on the President to grant clearances, notwithstanding an existing embargo, to ships or vessels belonging to citizens of the United States bound to any port beyond the Cape of Good Hope. . . .

[The other examples are omitted.]

Practically every volume of the United States Statutes contains one or more acts or joint resolutions of Congress authorizing action by the President in respect of subjects affecting foreign relations, which either leave the exercise of the power to his unrestricted judgment, or provide a standard far more general than that which has always been considered requisite with regard to domestic affairs. . . .

The result of holding that the joint resolution here under attack is void and unenforceable as constituting an unlawful delegation of legislative power would be to stamp this multitude of comparable acts and resolutions as likewise invalid. And while this court may not, and should not, hesitate to declare acts of Congress, however many times repeated, to be unconstitutional if beyond all rational doubt it finds them to be so, an impressive array of legislation such as we have just set forth, enacted by nearly every Congress from the beginning of our national existence to the present day, must be given unusual weight in the process of reaching a correct determination of the problem. A legislative practice such as we have here, evidenced not by only occasional instances, but marked by the movement of a steady stream for a century and a half of time, goes a long way in the direction of proving the presence of unassailable ground for the constitutionality of the practice, to be found in the origin and history of the power involved, or in its nature, or in both combined. . . .

The uniform, long-continued and undisputed legislative practice just disclosed rests upon an admissible view of the Constitution which, even if the practice found far less support in principle than we think it does, we should not feel at liberty at this late day to disturb.

We deem it unnecessary to consider, *seriatim*, the several clauses which are said to evidence the unconstitutionality of the Joint Resolution as involving an unlawful delegation of legislative power. It is enough to summarize by saying that, both upon principle and in accordance with precedent, we conclude there is sufficient warrant for the broad discretion vested in the President to determine whether the enforcement of the statute will have a beneficial effect upon the reestablishment of peace in the affected countries; whether he shall make proclamation to being the resolution into operation; whether and when the resolution shall cease to operate and to make proclamation accordingly; and to prescribe limitations and exceptions to which the enforcement of the resolution shall be subject. . . .

The judgment of the court below must be reversed. . . .

47

Korematsu v. United States (1944)

Justice Black delivered the opinion of the Court.

The petitioner, an American citizen of Japanese descent, was convicted in the federal district court for remaining in San Leandro, California, a "Military Area," contrary to Civilian Exclusion Order No. 34 of the Commanding General of the Western Command, U.S. Army, which directed that after May 9, 1942, all persons of Japanese ancestry should be excluded from that area. No question was raised as to petitioner's loyalty to the United States. The Circuit Court of Appeals affirmed, and the importance of the constitutional question involved caused us to grant certiorari.

It should be noted, to begin with, that all legal restrictions which curtail the civil rights of a single racial group are immediately suspect. That is not to say that all such restrictions are unconstitutional. It is to say that courts must subject them to the most rigid scrutiny. Pressing public necessity may sometimes justify the existence of such restrictions; racial antagonism never can.

In the instant case prosecution of the petitioner was begun by information charging violation of an Act of Congress, of March 21, 1942, which provides that "whoever shall enter, remain in, leave, or commit any act in any military area or military zone prescribed, under the authority of an Executive order of the President, by Secretary of War, or by any military commander designated by the Secretary of War, contrary to the restrictions applicable to any such area or zone or contrary to the order of the Secretary of War or any such military commander, shall, if it appears that he knew or should have known of the existence and extent of the restrictions or order and that his act was in violation thereof, be guilty of a misdemeanor and upon conviction shall be liable to a fine of not to exceed $5,000 or to imprisonment for not more than one year, or both, for each offense."

Exclusion Order No. 34, which the petitioner knowingly and admittedly violated was one of a number of military orders and proclamations, all of which were substantially based upon Executive Order No. 9066, 7 Fed. Reg. 1407. That order, issued after we were at war with Japan, declared that "the successful prosecution of the war requires every possible protection against espionage and against sabotage to national-defense material, national-defense premises, and national-defense utilities. . . .

From *Korematsu v. United States*, 323 U.S. 214 (1944).

One of the series of orders and proclamations, a curfew order, which like the exclusion order here was promulgated pursuant to Executive Order 9066, subjected all persons of Japanese ancestry in prescribed West Coast military areas to remain in their residences from 8 P.M. to 6 A.M.. As is the case with the exclusion order here, that prior curfew order was designed as a "protection against espionage and against sabotage." In *Kiyoshi Hirabayashi v. United States*, we sustained a conviction obtained for violation of the curfew order. The *Hirabayashi* conviction and this one thus rest on the same 1942 Congressional Act and the same basic executive and military orders, all of which orders were aimed at the twin dangers of espionage and sabotage. . . .

In the light of the principles we announced in the *Hirabayashi* case, we are unable to conclude that it was beyond the war power of Congress and the Executive to exclude those of Japanese ancestry from the West Coast war area at the time they did. True, exclusion from the area in which one's home is located is a far greater deprivation than constant confinement to the home from 8 P.M. to 6 A.M.. Nothing short of apprehension by the proper military authorities of the gravest imminent danger to the public safety can constitutionally justify either. But exclusion from a threatened area, no less than curfew, has a definite and close relationship to the prevention of espionage and sabotage. The military authorities, charged with the primary responsibility of defending our shores, concluded that curfew provided inadequate protection and ordered exclusion. They did so, as pointed out in our *Hirabayashi* opinion, in accordance with Congressional authority to the military to say who should, and who should not, remain in the threatened areas.

In this case the petitioner challenges the assumptions upon which we rested our conclusions in the *Hirabayashi* case. He also urges that by May 1942, when Order No. 34 was promulgated, all danger of Japanese invasion of the West Coast had disappeared. After careful consideration of these contentions we are compelled to reject them.

Here, as in the *Hirabayashi* case, "we cannot reject as unfounded the judgment of the military authorities and of Congress that there were disloyal members of that population, whose number and strength could not be precisely and quickly ascertained. We cannot say that the war-making branches of the Government did not have ground for believing that in a critical hour such persons could not readily be isolated and separately dealt with, and constituted a menace to the national defense and safety, which demanded that prompt and adequate measures be taken to guard against it."

Like curfew, exclusion of those of Japanese origin was deemed necessary because of the presence of an unascertained number of disloyal members of the group, most of whom we have no doubt were loyal to this country. It was because we could not reject the finding of the military authorities that it was impossible to bring about an immediate segregation of the disloyal from the loyal that we sustained the validity of the curfew order as applying to the whole group. In the instant case, temporary exclusion of the entire group was rested by the military on the same ground. The judgment that exclusion of the whole group was for the same reason a military imperative answers the contention that the exclusion was in the nature of group punishment based on antagonism to those of Japanese origin. That there were members of the group who retained loyalties to Japan has been confirmed by investigations made subsequent to the exclusion. Approximately five thousand American citizens of Japanese ancestry refused to swear unqualified allegiance to the United States and to renounce allegiance to the Japanese Emperor, and several thousand evacuees requested repatriation to Japan.

We uphold the exclusion order as of the time it was made and when the petitioner violated it. In doing so, we are not unmindful of the hardships imposed by it upon a large group of American citizens. But hardships are part of war, and war is an aggregation of hardships. All citizens alike, both in and out of uniform, feel the impact of war in greater or lesser measure. Citizenship has its responsibilities as well as its privileges, and in time of war the burden is always heavier. Compulsory exclusion of large groups of citizens from their homes, except under circumstances of direct emergency and peril, is inconsistent with our basic governmental institutions. But when under conditions of modern warfare our shores are threatened by hostile forces, the power to protect must be commensurate with the threatened danger.

It is argued that on May 30, 1942, the date the petitioner was charged with remaining in the prohibited area, there were conflicting orders outstanding, forbidding him both to leave the area and to remain there. Of course, a person cannot be convicted for doing the very thing which it is a crime to fail to do. But the outstanding orders here contained no such contradictory commands. . . .

It does appear, however, that on May 9, the effective date of the exclusion order, the military authorities had already determined that the evacuation should be effected by assembling together and placing under guard all those of Japanese ancestry, at central points, designated as "assembly centers," in order "to insure the orderly evacuation and resettlement of Japanese voluntarily migrating from military area No. 1 to restrict and regulate such migration." Public Proclamation No. 4, 7 Fed. Reg. 2601. And on May 19, 1942, eleven days before the time petitioner was charged with unlawfully remaining in the area, Civilian Restrictive Order No. 1, 8 Fed. Reg. 982, provided for detention of those of Japanese ancestry in assembly or relocation centers. It is now argued that the validity of the exclusion order cannot be considered apart from the orders requiring him, after departure from the area, to report and to remain in an assembly or relocation center. The contention is that we must treat these separate orders as one and inseparable; that, for this reason, if detention in the assembly or relocation center would have illegally deprived the petitioner of his liberty, the exclusion order and his conviction under it cannot stand. . . .

Since the petitioner has not been convicted of failing to report or to remain in an assembly or relocation center, we cannot in this case determine the validity of those separate provisions of the order. It is sufficient here for us to pass upon the order which petitioner violated. To do more would be to go beyond the issues raised, and to decide momentous questions not contained within the framework of the pleadings or the evidence in this case. It will be time enough to decide the serious constitutional issues which petitioner seeks to raise when an assembly or relocation order is applied or is certain to be applied to him, and we have its terms before us.

Some of the members of the Court are of the view that evacuation and detention in an Assembly Center were inseparable. After May 3, 1942, the date of Exclusion Order No. 34, Korematsu was under compulsion to leave the area not as he would choose but via an Assembly Center. The Assembly Center was conceived as a part of the machinery for group evacuation. The power to exclude includes the power to do it by force if necessary. And any forcible measure must necessarily entail some degree of detention or restraint whatever method of removal is selected. But whichever view is taken, it results in holding that the order under which petitioner was convicted was valid.

It is said that we are dealing here with the case of imprisonment of a citizen in a concentration camp solely because of his ancestry, without evidence or inquiry concerning his loyalty and good disposition towards the United States. Our task would be simple, our duty clear, were this a case involving the imprisonment of a loyal citizen in a concentration camp because of racial prejudice. Regardless of the true nature of the assembly and relocation centers—and we deem it unjustifiable to call them concentration camps with all the ugly connotations that term implies—we are dealing specifically with nothing but an exclusion order. To cast this case into outlines of racial prejudice, without reference to the real military dangers which were presented, merely confuses the issue. Korematsu was not excluded from the Military Area because of hostility to him or his race. He was excluded because we are at war with the Japanese Empire, because the properly constituted military authorities feared an invasion of our West Coast and felt constrained to take proper security measures, because they decided that the military urgency of the situation demanded that all citizens of Japanese ancestry be segregated from the West Coast temporarily, and finally, because Congress, reposing its confidence in this time of war in our military leaders—as inevitably it must—determined that they should have the power to do just this. There was evidence of disloyalty on the part of some, the military authorities considered that the need for action was great, and time was short. We cannot—by availing ourselves of the calm perspective of hindsight—now say at that time these actions were unjustified.

Affirmed.

Justice Frankfurter, concurring. . . . I join in the opinion of the Court, but should like to add a few words of my own.

The provisions of the Constitution which confer on the Congress and the President powers to enable this country to wage war are as much part of the Constitution as provisions looking to a nation at peace. And we have had recent occasion to quote approvingly the statement of former Chief Justice Hughes that the war power of the Government is "the power to wage war successfully." Therefore, the validity of action under the war power must be judged wholly in the context of war. That action is not to be stigmatized as lawless because like action in times of peace would be lawless. To talk about a military order that expresses an allowable judgment of war needs by those entrusted with the duty of conducting war as "an unconstitutional order" is to suffuse a part of the Constitution with an atmosphere of unconstitutionality. The respective spheres of action of military authorities and of judges are of course very different. But within their sphere, military authorities are no more outside the bounds of obedience to the Constitution than are judges within theirs. "The war power of the United States, like its other powers . . . is subject to applicable constitutional limitations," *Hamilton v. Kentucky Distilleries Company*. To recognize that military orders are "reasonably expedient military precautions" in time of war and yet to deny them constitutional legitimacy makes of the Constitution an instrument for dialectic subtleties not reasonably to be attributed to the hardheaded Framers, of whom a majority had had actual participation in war. If a military order such as that under review does not transcend the means appropriate for conducting war, such action by the military is as constitutional as would be any authorized action by the Interstate Commerce Commission within the limits of the constitutional power to regulate commerce. And being an exercise of the war power explicitly granted by the Constitution for safeguarding the national life by prosecuting war effectively, I find nothing in the Constitution which denies to Congress the power to enforce such a valid military order by making its violation an offense triable in the civil courts. To find that the Constitution does not forbid the military measures now complained of does not carry with it approval of that which Congress and the Executive did. That is their business, not ours.

Justice Murphy, dissenting.

This exclusion of "all persons of Japanese ancestry, both alien and non-alien," from the Pacific Coast area on a plea of military necessity in the absence of martial law ought not to be approved. Such exclusion goes over "the very brink of constitutional power" and falls into the ugly abyss of racism.

In dealing with matters relating to the prosecution and progress of a war, we must accord great respect and consideration to the judgments of the military authorities who are on the scene and who have full knowledge of the military facts. The scope of their discretion must, as a matter of necessity and common sense, be wide. And their judgments ought not to be overruled lightly by those whose training and duties ill-equip them to deal intelligently with matters, so vital to the physical security of the nation.

At the same time, however, it is essential that there be definite limits to military discretion, especially where martial law has not been declared. Individuals must not be left impoverished of their constitutional rights on a plea of military necessity that has neither substance nor support. Thus, like other claims conflicting with the asserted constitutional rights of the individual, the military claim must subject itself to the judicial process of having its reasonableness determined and its conflicts with other interests reconciled. "What are the allowable limits of military discretion, and whether or not they have been over-stepped in a particular case, are judicial questions."

The judicial test of whether the Government, on a plea of military necessity, can validly deprive an individual of any of his constitutional rights is whether the deprivation is reasonably related to a public danger that is so "immediate, imminent, and impending" as not to admit of delay and not to permit the intervention of ordinary constitutional processes to alleviate the danger. Civilian Exclusion Order No. 34, banishing from a prescribed area of the Pacific Coast "all persons of Japanese ancestry, both alien and nonalien," clearly does not meet that test. Being an obvious racial discrimination, the order deprives all those within its scope of the equal protection of the laws as guaranteed by the Fifth Amendment. It further deprives these individuals of their constitutional rights to live and work where they will, to establish a home where they choose and to move about freely. In excommunicating them without benefit of hearings, this order also deprives them of all their constitutional rights to procedural due process. Yet no reasonable relation to an "immediate, imminent, and impending" public danger is evident to support this racial restriction which is one of the most sweeping and complete deprivations of constitutional rights in the history of this nation in the absence of martial law.

It must be conceded that the military and naval situation in the spring of 1942 was such as to generate a very real fear of invasion of the Pacific Coast, accompanied by fears of sabotage and espionage in that area. The military command was therefore justified in adopting all reasonable means necessary to combat these dangers. In adjudging the military action taken in light of the then apparent dangers, we must not erect too high or too meticulous standards; it is necessary only that the action have some reasonable relation to the removal of the dangers of invasion, sabotage and espionage. But the exclusion, either temporarily or permanently, of all persons with Japanese blood in their veins has no such reasonable relation. And that relation is lacking because the exclusion order necessarily must rely for its reasonableness upon the assumption that *all* persons of Japanese ancestry may have a dangerous tendency to commit sabotage and espionage and to aid our Japanese enemy in other ways. It is difficult to believe that reason, logic or experience could be marshalled in support of such an assumption.

That this forced exclusion was the result in good measure of this erroneous assumption of racial guilt rather than bona fide military necessity is evidenced by the Commanding General's Final Report on the evacuation from the Pacific Coast area. In it he refers to all individuals of Japanese descent as "subversive," as belonging to "an enemy race" whose "racial strains are undiluted," and as constituting "over 112,000 potential enemies . . . at large today" along the Pacific Coast. In support of this blanket condemnation of all persons of Japanese descent, however, no reliable evidence is cited to show that such individuals were generally disloyal, or had generally so conducted themselves in this area as to constitute a special menace to defense installations or war industries, or had otherwise by their behavior furnished reasonable ground for their exclusion as a group.

Justification for the exclusion is sought, instead, mainly upon questionable racial and sociological grounds not within the realm of expert military judgment, supplemented by certain semi-military conclusions drawn from an unwarranted use of circumstantial evidence. Individuals of Japanese ancestry are condemned because they are said to be "a large, unassimilated, tightly knit racial group, bound to an enemy nation by strong ties of race, culture, custom and religion." They are claimed to be given to "emperor worshipping ceremonies" and to "dual citizenship." Japanese language schools and allegedly pro-Japanese organizations are cited as evidence of possible group disloyalty, together with facts as to certain persons being educated and residing at length in Japan. It is intimated that many of these individuals deliberately resided "adjacent to strategic points," thus enabling them "to carry into execution a tremendous program of sabotage on a mass scale should any considerable number of them have been inclined to do so." The need for protective custody is also asserted. The report refers without identity to "numerous incidents of violence" as well as to other admittedly unverified or cumulative incidents. From this, plus certain other events not shown to have been connected with the Japanese Americans, it is concluded that the "situation was fraught with danger to the Japanese population itself" and that the general public "was ready to take matters into its own hands." Finally, it is intimated, though not directly charged or proved, that persons of Japanese ancestry were responsible for three minor isolated shellings and bombings of the Pacific Coast area, as well as for unidentified radio transmissions and night signalling.

The main reasons relied upon by those responsible for the forced evacuation, therefore, do not prove a reasonable relation between the group characteristics of Japanese Americans and the dangers of invasion, sabotage and espionage. The reasons appear, instead, to be largely an accumulation of much of the misinformation, half-truths and insinuations that for years have been directed against Japanese Americans by people with racial and economic prejudices—the same people who have been among the foremost advocates of the evacuation. A military judgment based upon such racial and sociological considerations is not entitled to the great weight ordinarily given the judgments based upon strictly military considerations. Especially is this so when every charge relative to race, religion, culture, geographical location, and legal and economic status has been substantially discredited by independent studies made by experts in these matters.

The military necessity which is essential to the validity of the evacuation order thus resolves itself into a few intimations that certain individuals actively aided the enemy, from which it is inferred that the entire group of Japanese Americans could not be trusted to be or remain loyal to the United States. No one denies, of course, that there were some disloyal persons of Japanese descent on the Pacific Coast who did all in their power to aid their ancestral land. Similar disloyal activities have been engaged in by many persons of German, Italian and even more pioneer stock in our country. But to infer that examples of individual disloyalty prove group disloyalty and justify discriminatory action against the entire group is to deny that under our system of law individual guilt is the sole basis for deprivation of rights. Moreover, this inference, which is at the very heart of the evacuation orders, has been used in support of the abhorrent and despicable treatment of minority groups by the dictatorial tyrannies which this nation is now pledged to destroy. To give constitutional sanction to that inference in this case, however well-intentioned may have been the military command on the Pacific Coast, is to adopt one of the cruelest of the rationales used by our enemies to destroy the dignity of the individual and to encourage and open the door to discriminatory actions against other minority groups in the passions of tomorrow.

No adequate reason is given for the failure to treat these Japanese Americans on an individual basis by holding investigations and hearings to separate the loyal from the disloyal, as was done in the case of persons of German and Italian ancestry. See House Report No 2124 (77th Cong., 2d Sess.) 247-52. It is asserted merely that the loyalties of this group "were unknown and time was of the essence." Yet nearly four months elapsed after Pearl Harbor before the first exclusion order was issued; nearly eight months went by until the last order was issued; and the last of these "subversive" persons was not actually removed until almost eleven months had elapsed. Leisure and deliberation seem to have been more of the essence than speed. And the fact that conditions were not such as to warrant a declaration of martial law adds strength to the belief that the factors of time and military necessity were not as urgent as they have been represented to be.

Moreover, there was no adequate proof that the Federal Bureau of Investigation and the military and naval intelligence services did not have the espionage and sabotage situation well in hand during this long period. Nor is there any denial of the fact that not one person of Japanese ancestry was accused or convicted of espionage or sabotage after Pearl Harbor while they were still free, a fact which is some evidence of the loyalty of the vast majority of these individuals and of the effectiveness of the established methods of combatting these evils. It seems incredible that under these circumstances it would have been impossible to hold loyalty hearings for the mere 112,000 persons involved—or at least for the 70,000 American citizens—especially when a large part of this number represented children and elderly men and women. Any inconvenience that may have accompanied an attempt to conform to procedural due process cannot be said to justify violations of constitutional rights of individuals.

I dissent, therefore, from this legalization of racism. Racial discrimination in any form and in any degree has no justifiable part whatever in our democratic way of life. It is unattractive in any setting but it is utterly revolting among a free people who have embraced the principles set forth in the Constitution of the United States. All residents of this nation are kin in some way by blood or culture to a foreign land. Yet they are primarily and necessarily a part of the new and distinct civilization of the United States. They must accordingly be treated at all times as the heirs of the American experiment and as entitled to all the rights and freedoms guaranteed by the Constitution.

Justice Jackson, dissenting.

. . . [T]he "law" which this prisoner is convicted of disregarding is not found in an act of Congress, but in a military order. . . . And it is said that if the military commander had reasonable military grounds for promulgating the orders, they are constitutional and become law, and the Court is required to enforce them. There are several reasons why I cannot subscribe to this doctrine.

It would be impracticable and dangerous idealism to expect or insist that each specific military command in an area of probable operations will conform to conventional tests of constitutionality. When an area is so beset that it must be put under military control at all, the paramount consideration is that its measures be successful, rather than legal. The armed services must protect a society, not merely its Constitution. The very essence of the military job is to marshal physical force, to remove every obstacle to its effectiveness, to give it every strategic advantage. Defense measures will not, and often should not, be held within the limits that bind civil authority in peace. No court can require such a commander in such circumstances to act as a reasonable man; he may be unreasonably cautious and exacting. Perhaps he should be. But a commander in temporarily focusing the life of a community on defense is carrying out a military program; he is not making law in the sense the courts know the term. He issues orders, and they may have a certain authority as military commands, although they may be very bad as constitutional law.

But if we cannot confine military expedients by the Constitution, neither would I distort the Constitution to approve all that the military may deem expedient. That is what the Court appears to be doing, whether consciously or not. I cannot say, from any evidence before me, that the orders of General DeWitt were not reasonably expedient military precautions, nor could I say that they were. But even if they were permissible military procedures, I deny that it follows that they are constitutional. If, as the Court holds, it does follow, then we may as well say that any military order will be constitutional and have done with it.

The limitation under which courts always will labor in examining the necessity for a military order are illustrated by this case. How does the Court know that these orders have a reasonable basis in necessity? No evidence whatever on that subject has been taken by this or any other court. There is sharp controversy as to the credibility of the DeWitt report. So the Court, having no real evidence before it, has no choice but to accept General DeWitt's own unsworn, self-serving statement, untested by any cross-examination, that what he did was reasonable. And thus it will always be when courts try to look into the reasonableness of a military order.

In the very nature of things military decisions are not susceptible of intelligent judicial appraisal. They do not pretend to rest on evidence, but are made on information that often would not be admissible and on assumptions that could not be proved. Information in support of an order could not be disclosed to courts without danger that it would reach the enemy. Neither can courts act on communications made in confidence. Hence courts can never have any real alternative to accepting the mere declaration of the authority that issued the order that it was reasonably necessary from a military viewpoint.

Much is said of the danger to liberty from the Army program for deporting and detaining these citizens of Japanese extraction. But a judicial construction of the due process clause that will sustain this order is a far more subtle blow to liberty than the promulgation of the order itself. A military order, however unconstitutional, is not apt to last longer than the military emergency. Even during that period a succeeding commander may revoke it all. But once a judicial opinion rationalizes such an order to show that it conforms to the Constitution, or rather rationalizes the Constitution to show that the Constitution sanctions such an order, the Court for all time has validated the principle of racial discrimination in criminal procedure and of transplanting American citizens. The principle then lies about like a loaded weapon ready for the hand of any authority that can bring forward a plausible claim of an urgent need. Every repetition imbeds that principle more deeply in our law and thinking and expands it to new purposes. All who observe the work of courts are familiar with what Judge Cardozo described as "the tendency of a principle to expand itself to the limit of its logic." A military commander may overstep the bounds of constitutionality, and it is an incident. But if we review and approve, that passing incident becomes the doctrine of the Constitution. There it has a generative power of its own, and all that it creates will be in its own image. . . .

I should hold that a civil court cannot be made to enforce an order which violates constitutional limitations even if it is a reasonable exercise of military authority. The courts can exercise only the judicial power, can apply only law, and must abide by the Constitution, or they cease to be civil courts and become instruments of military policy.

Of course the existence of a military power resting on force, so vagrant, so centralized, so necessarily heedless of the individual, is an inherent threat to liberty. But I would not lead people to rely on this Court for a review that seems to me wholly delusive. The military reasonableness of these orders can only be determined by military superiors. If the people ever let command of the war power fall into irresponsible and unscrupulous hands, the courts wield no power equal to its restraint. The chief restraint upon those who command the physical forces of the country, in the future as in the past, must be their responsibility to the political judgments of their contemporaries and to the moral judgments of history.

My duties as justice as I see them do not require me to make a military judgment as to whether General DeWitt's evacuation and detention program was a reasonable military necessity. I do not suggest that the courts should have attempted to interfere with the Army in carrying out its task. But I do not think they may be asked to execute a military expedient that has no place in law under the Constitution. I would reverse the judgment and discharge the prisoner.

48

Abraham Lincoln

On the Suspension of the Writ of Habeas Corpus (1863)

Hon Erastus Corning and others*

Gentlemen Your letter of May 19th. inclosing the resolutions of a public meeting held at Albany, New York on the 16th of the same month, was received several days ago.

The resolutions, as I understand them, are resolvable into two propositions—first, the expression of a purpose to sustain the cause of the

From *The Collected Works of Abraham Lincoln*, Vol. VI, Rutgers University Press, 1953.

*On June 30, Corning and others replied: ". . . We have carefully considered the grounds on which your pretensions to more than regal authority are claimed to rest; and if we do not misinterpret the misty and clouded forms of expression in which those pretensions are set forth, your meaning is that while the rights of the citizen are protected by the Constitution in time of peace, they are suspended or lost in time of war, or when invasion or rebellion exist. You do not, like many others in whose minds, reason and love of regulated liberty seem to be overthrown by the excitements of the hour, attempt to base this conclusion upon a supposed military necessity existing outside of and transcending the Constitution, a military necessity behind which the Constitution intself disappears in a total eclipse. We do not find this gigantic and monstrous heresy put forth in your plea for absolute power, but we do find another equally subversive of liberty and law, and quite as certainly tending to the establishment of despotism. Your claim to have found not outside, but within the Constitution, a principle or germ of arbitrary power, which in time of war expands at once into an absolute sovereignty, wielded by one man; so that liberty perished, or is dependent on his will, his discretion or his caprice. This extraordinary doctrine, you claim to derive wholly from that clause of the Constitution, which, in case of invasion or rebellion, permits the writ of habeas corpus to be suspended. Upon this ground your whole argument is based.

"You must permit us, to say to you with all due respect, but with the earnestness demanded by the occasion, that the American people will never acquiese in this doctrine. . . ." The Robert Todd Lincoln Collection of the Papers of Abraham Lincoln, Library of Congress.

Union, to secure peace through victory, and to support the administration in every constitutional, and lawful measure to suppress the rebellion; and secondly, a declaration of censure upon the administration for supposed unconstitutional action such as the making of military arrests.

And, from the two propositions a third is deduced, which is, that the gentlemen composing the meeting are resolved on doing their part to maintain our common government and country, despite the folly or wickedness, as they may conceive, of any administration. This position is eminently patriotic, and as such, I thank the meeting, and congratulate the nation for it. My own purpose is the same; so that the meeting and myself have a common object, and can have no difference, except in the choice of means or measures, for effecting that object.

And here I ought to close this paper, and would close it, if there were no apprehension that more injurious consequences, than any merely personal to myself, might follow the censures systematically cast upon me for doing what, in my view of duty, I could not forbear. The resolutions promise to support me in every constitutional and lawful measure to suppress the rebellion; and I have not knowingly employed, nor shall knowingly employ, any other. But the meeting, by their resolutions, assert and argue, that certain military arrests and proceedings following them for which I am ultimately responsible, are unconstitutional. I think they are not. The resolutions quote from the constitution, the definition of treason; and also the limiting safeguards and guarantees therein provided for the citizen, on trials for treason, and on his being held to answer for capital or otherwise infamous crimes, and, in criminal prosecutions, his right to a speedy and public trial by an impartial jury. They proceed to resolve "That these safeguards of the rights of the citizen against the pretentions of arbitrary power, were intended more *especially* for his protection in times of civil commotion." And, apparantly, to demonstrate the proposition, the resolutions proceed "They were secured substantially to the English people, *after* years of protracted civil war, and were adopted into our constitution at the *close* of the revolution." Would not the demonstration have been better, if it could have been truly said that these safe-guards had been adopted, and applied *during* the civil wars and *during* our revolution, instead of *after* the one, and at the *close* of the other. I too am devotedly for them *after* civil war, and *before* civil war, and at all times "except when, in cases of Rebellion or Invasion, the public Safety may require" their suspension. The resolutions proceed to tell us that these safeguards "have stood the test of seventy-six years of trial, under our republican system, under circumstances which show that while they constitute the foundation of all free government, they are the elements of the enduring stability of the Republic." No one denies that they have so stood the test up to the beginning of the present rebellion if we except a certain matter at New Orleans hereafter to be mentioned; nor does anyone question that they will stand the same test much longer after the rebellion closes. But these provisions of the constitution have no application to the case we have in hand, because the arrests complained of were not made for treason—that is, not for *the* treason defined in the constitution, and upon the conviction of which, the punishment is death—; nor yet were they made to hold persons to answer for any capital, or otherwise infamous crimes; nor were the proceedings following, in any constitutional or legal sense, "criminal prosecutions." The arrests were made on totally different grounds, and the proceedings following, accorded with the grounds of the arrests. Let us consider the real case with which we are dealing, and apply to it the parts of the constitution plainly made for such cases.

Prior to my installation here it had been inculcated that any State had a lawful right to secede from the national Union; and that it would be expedient to exercise the right, whenever the devotees of the doctrine should fail to elect a President to their own liking. I was elected contrary to their liking; and accordingly, so far as it was legally possible, they had taken seven states out of the Union, had seized many of the United States' Forts, and had fired upon the United States' Flag, all before I was inaugurated; and, of course, before I had done any official act whatever. The rebellion, thus began, soon ran into the present civil war; and, in certain respects, it began on very unequal terms between the parties. The insurgents had been preparing for it more than thirty years, while the government had taken no steps to resist them. The former had carefully considered all the means which could be turned to their account. It undoubtedly was a well pondered reliance with them that in their own unrestricted effort to destroy Union, constitution, and law, all together, the government would, in great degree, be restrained by the same constitution and law, from arresting their progress. Their sympathizers pervaded all departments of the government, and nearly all communities of the people. From this material, under cover of "Liberty of speech" "Liberty of the press" and "*Habeas corpus*" they hoped to keep on foot amongst us a most efficient corps of spies, informers, suppliers, and aiders and abettors of their cause in a thousand ways. They knew that in times such as they were inaugurating, by the constitution itself, the "Habeas corpus" might be suspended; but they also knew they had friends who would make a question as to *who* was to suspend it; meanwhile their spies and others might remain at large to help on their cause. Or if, as has happened, the executive should suspend the writ, without ruinous waste of time, instances of arresting innocent persons might occur, as are always likely to occur in such cases; and then a clamor could be raised in regard to this, which might be, at least, of some service to the insurgent cause. It needed no very keen perception to discover this part of the enemies' programme, so soon as by open hostilities their machinery was fairly put in motion. Yet, thoroughly imbued with a reverence for the guaranteed rights of individuals, I was slow to adopt the strong measures, which by degrees I have been forced to regard as being within the exceptions of the constitution, and as indispensable to the public Safety. Nothing is better known to history than that courts of justice are utterly incompetent to such cases. Civil courts are organized chiefly for trials of individuals, or, at most, a few individuals acting in concert; and this in quiet times, and on charges of crimes well defined in the law. Even in times of peace, bands of horse-thieves and robbers frequently grow too numerous and powerful for the ordinary courts of justice. But what comparison, in numbers, have such bands ever borne to the insurgent sympathizers even in many of the loyal states? Again, a jury too frequently have at least one member, more ready to hang the panel than to hang the traitor. And yet again, he who dissuades one man from volunteering, or induces one soldier to desert, weakens the Union cause as much as he who kills a union soldier in battle. Yet this dissuasion, or inducement, may be so conducted as to be no defined crime of which any civil court would take cognizance.

Ours is a case of Rebellion—so called by the resolutions before me—in fact, a clear, flagrant, and gigantic case of Rebellion; and the provision of the constitution that "The privilege of the writ of Habeas Corpus shall not be suspended, unless when in cases of Rebellion or Invasion, the public Safety may require it" is *the* provision which specially applies to our present case. This provision plainly attests the understanding of those who made the constitution that ordinary courts of justice are inadequate to "cases of Rebellion"—attests their purpose that in such cases, men may be held in custody whom the courts acting on ordinary rules, would discharge. Habeas Corpus does not discharge men who are proved to be guilty of defined crime; and its suspension is allowed by the constitution on purpose that, men may be arrested and held, who cannot be proved to be guilty of defined crime, "when, in cases of Rebellion or Invasion the public Safety may require it." This is precisely our present case—a case of Rebellion, wherein the public Safety does require the suspension. Indeed, arrests by process of courts, and arrests in cases of rebellion, do not proceed altogether upon the same basis. The former is directed at the small percentage of ordinary and continuous perpetration of crime; while the latter is directed at sudden and extensive uprisings against the government, which, at most, will succeed or fail, in no great length of time. In the latter case, arrests are made, not so much for what has been done, as for what probably would be done. The latter is more for the preventive, and less for the vindictive, than the former. In such cases the purposes of men are much more easily understood, than in cases of ordinary crime. The man who stands by and says nothing, when the peril of his government is discussed, cannot be misunderstood. If not hindered, he is sure to help the enemy. Much more, if he talks ambiguously—talks for his country with "buts" and "ifs" and "ands." Of how little value the constitutional provision I have quoted will be rendered, if arrests shall never be made until defined crimes shall have been committed, may be illustrated by a few notable examples. Gen. John C. Breckenridge, Gen. Robert E. Lee, Gen. Joseph E. Johnston, Gen. John B. Magruder, Gen. William B. Preston, Gen. Simon B. Buckner, and Commodore [Franklin] Buchanan, now occupying the very highest places in the rebel war service, were all within the power of the government since the rebellion began, and were nearly as well known to be traitors then as now. Unquestionably if we had seized and held them, the insurgent cause would be much weaker. But no one of them had then committed any crime defined in the law. Every one of them if arrested would have been discharged on Habeas Corpus, were the writ allowed to operate. In view of these and similar cases, I think the time not unlikely to come when I shall be blamed for having made too few arrests rather than too many.

By the third resolution the meeting indicate their opinion that military arrests may be constitutional in localities where rebellion actually exists; but that such arrests are unconstitutional in localities where rebellion, or insurrection, does not actually exist. They insist that such arrests shall not be made "outside of the lines of necessary military occupation, and the scenes of insurrection." Inasmuch, however, as the constitution itself makes no such distinction, I am unable to believe that there is any such constitutional distinction. I concede that the class of arrests complained of, can be constitutional only when, in cases of Rebellion or Invasion, the public Safety may require them; and I insist that in such cases, they are constitutional *wherever* the public safety does require them—as well in places to which they may prevent the rebellion extending, as in those where it may be already prevailing—as well where they may restrain mischievous interference with the raising and supplying of armies, to suppress the rebellion, as where the rebellion may actually be—as well where they may restrain the enticing men out of the army, as where they would prevent mutiny in the army—equally constitutional at all places where they will conduce to the public Safety, as against the dangers of Rebellion or Invasion.

Take the particular case mentioned by the meeting. They assert in substance that Mr. Vallandigham was by a military commander, seized and tried "for no other reason than words addressed to a public meeting, in criticism of the course of the administration, and in condemnation of the military orders of that general." Now, if there be no mistake about this—if this assertion is the truth and the whole truth—if there was no other reason for the arrest, then I concede that the arrest was wrong. But the arrest, as I understand, was made for a very different reason. Mr. Vallandigham avows his hostility to the war on the part of the Union; and his arrest was made because he was laboring, with some effect, to prevent the raising of troops, to encourage desertions from the army, and to leave the rebellion without an adequate military force to suppress it. He was not arrested because he was damaging the political prospects of the administration, or the personal interests of the commanding general; but because he was damaging the army, upon the existence, and vigor of which, the life of the nation depends. He was warring upon the military; and this gave the military constitutional jurisdiction to lay hands upon him. If Mr. Vallandigham was not damaging the military power of the country, then his arrest was made on mistake of fact, which I would be glad to correct, on reasonably satisfactory evidence.

I understand the meeting, whose resolutions I am considering, to be in favor of suppressing the rebellion by military force—by armies. Long experience has shown that armies cannot be maintained unless desertion shall be punished by the severe penalty of death. The case requires, and the law and the constitution, sanction this punishment. Must I shoot a simple-minded soldier boy who deserts, while I must not touch a hair of a wiley agitator who induces him to desert? This is none the less injurious when effected by getting a father, or brother, or friend, into a public meeting, and there working upon his feelings, till he is persuaded to write the soldier boy, that he is fighting in a bad cause, for a wicked administration of a contemptible government, too weak to arrest and punish him if he shall desert. I think that in such a case, to silence the agitator, and save the boy, is not only constitutional, but, withal, a great mercy.

If I be wrong on this question of constitutional power, my error lies in believing that certain proceedings are constitutional when, in cases of rebellion or Invasion, the public Safety requires them, which would not be constitutional when, in absence of rebellion or invasion, the public Safety does not require them—in other words, that the constitution is not in its application in all respects the same, in cases of Rebellion or invasion, involving the public Safety, as it is in times of profound peace and public security. The constitution itself makes the distinction; and I can no more be persuaded that the government can constitutionally take no strong measure in time of rebellion, because it can be shown that the same could not be lawfully taken in time of peace, than I can be persuaded that a particular drug is not good medicine for a sick man, because it can be shown to not be good food for a well one. Nor am I able to appreciate the danger, apprehended by the meeting, that the American people will, by means of military arrests during the rebellion, lose the right of public discussion, the liberty of speech and the press, the law of evidence, trial by jury, and Habeas corpus, throughout the indefinite peaceful future which I trust lies before them, any more than I am able to believe that a man could contract so strong an appetite for emetics during temporary illness, as to persist in feeding upon them through the remainder of his healthful life.

In giving the resolutions that earnest consideration which you request of me, I cannot overlook the fact that the meeting speak as "Democrats." Nor can I, with full respect for their known intelligence, and the fairly presumed deliberation with which they prepared their resolutions, be permitted to suppose that this occurred by accident, or in any way other than that they preferred to designate themselves "democrats" rather than "American citizens." In this time of national peril I would have preferred to meet you upon a level one step higher than any party platform; because I am sure that from such more elevated position, we could do better battle for the country we all love, than we possibly can from those lower ones, where from the force of habit, the prejudices of the past, and selfish hopes of the future, we are sure to expend much of our ingenuity and strength, in finding fault with, and aiming blows at each other. But since you have denied me this, I will yet be thankful, for the country's sake, that not all democrats have done so. He on whose discretionary judgment Mr. Vallandigham was arrested and tried, is a democrat, having no old party affinity with me; and the judge who rejected the constitutional view expressed in these resolutions, by refusing to discharge Mr. V. on Habeas Corpus, is a democrat of better days than these, having received his judicial mantle at the hands of President Jackson. And still more, of all those democrats who are nobly exposing their lives and shedding their blood on the battle-field, I have learned that many approve the course taken with Mr. V. while I have not heard of a single one condemning it. I can not assert that there are none such. . . .

49

Clinton v. Jones (1997)

Justice Stevens delivered the opinion of the Court.

This case raises a constitutional and a prudential question concerning the Office of the President of the United States. Respondent, a private citizen, seeks to recover damages from the current occupant of that office based on actions allegedly taken before his term began. The President submits that in all but the most exceptional cases the Constitution requires federal courts to defer such litigation until his term ends and that, in any event, respect for the office warrants such a stay. Despite the force of the arguments supporting the President's submissions, we conclude that they must be rejected.

. . . Petitioner's principal submission—that "in all but the most exceptional cases," the Constitution affords the President temporary immunity

From *Clinton v. Jones,* 520 U.S. 681 (1997).

from civil damages litigation arising out of events that occurred before he took office—cannot be sustained on the basis of precedent.

Only three sitting Presidents have been defendants in civil litigation involving their actions prior to taking office. Complaints against Theodore Roosevelt and Harry Truman had been dismissed before they took office; the dismissals were affirmed after their respective inaugurations. Two companion cases arising out of an automobile accident were filed against John F. Kennedy in 1960 during the Presidential campaign. After taking office, he unsuccessfully argued that his status as Commander in Chief gave him a right to a stay under the Soldiers' and Sailors' Civil Relief Act of 1940. The motion for a stay was denied by the District Court, and the matter was settled out of court. Thus, none of those cases sheds any light on the constitutional issue before us.

The principal rationale for affording certain public servants immunity from suits for money damages arising out of their official acts is inapplicable to unofficial conduct. In cases involving prosecutors, legislators, and judges we have repeatedly explained that the immunity serves the public interest in enabling such officials to perform their designated functions effectively without fear that a particular decision may give rise to personal liability.

"As public servants, the prosecutor and the judge represent the interest of society as a whole. The conduct of their official duties may adversely affect a wide variety of different individuals, each of whom may be a potential source of future controversy. The societal interest in providing such public officials with the maximum ability to deal fearlessly and impartially with the public at large has long been recognized as an acceptable justification for official immunity. The point of immunity for such officials is to forestall an atmosphere of intimidation that would conflict with their resolve to perform their designated functions in a principled fashion." (*Nixon v. Fitzgerald*)

That rationale provided the principal basis for our holding that a former President of the United States was "entitled to absolute immunity from damages liability predicated on his official acts." . . .

This reasoning provides no support for an immunity for *unofficial* conduct. As we explained in *Fitzgerald*, "the sphere of protected action must be related closely to the immunity's justifying purposes." Because of the President's broad responsibilities, we recognized in that case an immunity from damages claims arising out of official acts extending to the "outer perimeter of his authority." But we have never suggested that the President, or any other official, has an immunity that extends beyond the scope of any action taken in an official capacity. . . .

Moreover, when defining the scope of an immunity for acts clearly taken within an official capacity, we have applied a functional approach. "Frequently our decisions have held that an official's absolute immunity should extend only to acts in performance of particular functions of his office." Hence, for example, a judge's absolute immunity does not extend to actions performed in a purely administrative capacity. As our opinions have made clear, immunities are grounded in "the nature of the function performed, not the identity of the actor who performed it." . . .

Petitioner's effort to construct an immunity from suit for unofficial acts grounded purely in the identity of his office is unsupported by precedent.

. . . Respondent, in turn, has called our attention to conflicting historical evidence. Speaking in favor of the Constitution's adoption at the Pennsylvania Convention, James Wilson—who had participated in the Philadelphia Convention at which the document was drafted—explained that, although the President "is placed [on] high," "not a single privilege is annexed to his character; far from being above the laws, he is amenable to them in his private character as a citizen, and in his public character by impeachment." This description is consistent with both the doctrine of presidential immunity as set forth in *Fitzgerald,* and rejection of the immunity claim in this case. With respect to acts taken in his "public character"—that is official acts—the President may be disciplined principally by impeachment, not by private lawsuits for damages. But he is otherwise subject to the laws for his purely private acts.

. . . Petitioner's strongest argument supporting his immunity claim is based on the text and structure of the Constitution. He does not contend that the occupant of the Office of the President is "above the law," in the sense that his conduct is entirely immune from judicial scrutiny. The President argues merely for a postponement of the judicial proceedings that will determine whether he violated any law. His argument is grounded in the character of the office that was created by Article II of the Constitution, and relies on separation of powers principles that have structured our constitutional arrangement since the founding.

As a starting premise, petitioner contends that he occupies a unique office with powers and responsibilities so vast and important that the public interest demands that he devote his undivided time and attention to his public duties. He submits that—given the nature of the office—the doctrine of separation of powers places limits on the authority of the Federal Judiciary to interfere with the Executive Branch that would be transgressed by allowing this action to proceed.

We have no dispute with the initial premise of the argument. Former presidents, from George Washington to George Bush, have consistently endorsed petitioner's characterization of the office. After serving his term, Lyndon Johnson observed: "Of all the 1,886 nights I was President, there were not many when I got to sleep before 1 or 2 A.M., and there were few mornings when I didn't wake up by 6 or 6:30." In 1967, the Twenty-fifth Amendment to the Constitution was adopted to ensure continuity in the performance of the powers and duties of the office; one of the sponsors of that Amendment stressed the importance of providing that "at all times" there be a President "who has complete control and will be able to perform" those duties. As Justice Jackson has pointed out, the Presidency concentrates executive authority "in a single head in whose choice the whole Nation has a part, making him the focus of public hopes and expectations. In drama, magnitude and finality his decisions so far overshadow any others that almost alone he fills the public eye and ear." *Youngstown Sheet & Tube Co. v. Sawyer.* We have, in short, long recognized the "unique position in the constitutional scheme" that this office occupies. Thus, while we suspect that even in our modern era there remains some truth to Chief Justice Marshall's suggestion that the duties of the Presidency are not entirely "unremitting," we accept the initial premise of the Executive's argument.

It does not follow, however, that separation of powers principles would be violated by allowing this action to proceed. The doctrine of separation of powers is concerned with the allocation of official power among the three co-equal branches of our Government. The Framers "built into the tripartite Federal Government . . . a self-executing safeguard against the encroachment or aggrandizement of one branch at the expense of the other."

. . . Of course the lines between the powers of the three branches are not always neatly defined. But in this case there is no suggestion that the Federal Judiciary is being asked to perform any function that might in some way be described as "executive." Respondent is merely asking the courts to exercise their core Article III jurisdiction to decide cases and controversies. Whatever the outcome of this case, there is no possibility that the decision will curtail the scope of the official powers of the Executive Branch. The litigation of questions that relate entirely to the unofficial conduct of the individual who happens to be the President poses no perceptible risk of misallocation of either judicial power or executive power.

Rather than arguing that the decision of the case will produce either an aggrandizement of judicial power or a narrowing of executive power, petitioner contends that—as a by-product of an otherwise traditional exercise of judicial power—burdens will be placed on the President that will hamper the performance of his official duties. We have recognized that "[e]ven when a branch does not arrogate power to itself . . . the separation-of-powers doctrine requires that a branch not impair another in the performance of its constitutional duties." As a factual matter, petitioner contends that this particular case—as well as the potential additional litigation that an affirmance of the Court of Appeals judgment might spawn—may impose an unacceptable burden on the President's time and energy, and thereby impair the effective performance of his office.

Petitioner's predictive judgment finds little support in either history or the relatively narrow compass of the issues raised in this particular case. As we have already noted, in the more than 200-year history of the Republic, only three sitting Presidents have been subjected to suits for their private actions. If the past is any indicator, it seems unlikely that a deluge of such litigation will ever engulf the Presidency. As for the case at hand, if properly managed by the District Court, it appears to us highly unlikely to occupy any substantial amount of petitioner's time.

Of greater significance, petitioner errs by presuming that interactions between the Judicial Branch and the Executive, even quite burdensome inter-actions, necessarily rise to the level of constitutionally forbidden impairment of the Executive's ability to perform its constitutionally mandated functions. . . . The fact that a federal court's exercise of its traditional Article III jurisdiction may significantly burden the time and attention of the Chief Executive is not sufficient to establish a violation of the Constitution. Two long-settled propo-sitions, first announced by Chief Justice Marshall, support that conclusion.

. . . In sum, "[i]t is settled law that the separation-of-powers doctrine does not bar every exercise of jurisdiction over the President of the United States." *Fitzgerald*. If the Judiciary may severely burden the Executive Branch by reviewing the legality of the President's official conduct, and if it may direct appropriate process to the President himself, it must follow that the federal courts have power to determine the legality of his unofficial conduct. The bur-den on the President's time and energy that is a mere by-product of such review surely cannot be considered as onerous as the direct burden imposed by judicial review and the occasional invalidation of his official actions. We therefore hold that the doctrine of separation of powers does not require fed-eral courts to stay all private actions against the President until he leaves office.

. . . [W]e are persuaded that it was an abuse of discretion for the District Court to defer the trial until after the President leaves office. Such a lengthy and categorical stay takes no account whatever of the respondent's interest in bringing the case to trial. The complaint was filed within the statutory limita-tions period—albeit near the end of that period—and delaying trial would increase the danger of prejudice resulting from the loss of evidence, including the inability of witnesses to recall specific facts, or the possible death of a party.

The decision to postpone the trial was, furthermore, premature. The proponent of a stay bears the burden of establishing its need. In this case, at the stage at which the District Court made its ruling, there was no way to assess whether a stay of trial after the completion of discovery would be war-ranted. Other than the fact that a trial may consume some of the President's time and attention, there was shown here nothing in the record to enable a judge to assess the potential harm that may ensue from scheduling the trial promptly after discovery is concluded. We think the District Court may have given undue weight to the concern that a trial might generate unrelated civil actions that could conceivably hamper the President in conducting the duties of his office. If and when that should occur, the court's discretion would permit it to manage those actions in such fashion (including deferral of trial) that interference with the President's duties would not occur. But no such impingement upon the President's conduct of his office was shown here.

We add a final comment on two matters that are discussed at length in the briefs: the risk that our decision will generate a large volume of politically motivated harassing and frivolous litigation, and the danger that national security concerns might prevent the President from explaining a legitimate need for a continuance.

We are not persuaded that either of these risks is serious. Most frivolous and vexatious litigation is terminated at the pleading stage or on summary judgment, with little if any personal involvement by the defendant. Moreover, the availability of sanctions provides a significant deterrent to litigation directed at the President in his unofficial capacity for purposes of political gain or harassment. History indicates that the likelihood that a significant number of such cases will be filed is remote. Although scheduling problems may arise, there is no reason to assume that the District Courts will be either unable to accommodate the President's needs or unfaithful to the tradition— especially in matters involving national security—of giving "the utmost deference to Presidential responsibilities." Several Presidents, including petitioner, have given testimony without jeopardizing the Nation's security. In short, we have confidence in the ability of our federal judges to deal with both of these concerns.

The Federal District Court has jurisdiction to decide this case. Like every other citizen who properly invokes that jurisdiction, respondent has a right to an orderly disposition of her claims. Accordingly, the judgment of the Court of Appeals is affirmed.

50

Frederick Douglass

Oration in Memory of Abraham Lincoln (1876)

. . . We stand today at the national center to perform something like a national act—an act which is to go into history; and we are here where every pulsation of the national heart can be heard, felt, and reciprocated. A thousand wires, fed with thought and winged with lightning, put us in instantaneous communication with the loyal and true men all over this country.

From "Oration in Memory of Abraham Lincoln," delivered at the Unveiling of the Freedmen's Monument in Memory of Abraham Lincoln, in Lincoln Park, Washington, D.C., April 14, 1876.

Few facts could better illustrate the vast and wonderful change which has taken place in our condition as a people than the fact of our assembling here for the purpose we have today. Harmless, beautiful, proper, and praiseworthy as this demonstration is, I cannot forget that no such demonstration would have been tolerated here twenty years ago. The spirit of slavery and barbarism, which still lingers to blight and destroy in some dark and distant parts of our country, would have made our assembling here the signal and excuse for opening upon us all the flood-gates of wrath and violence. That we are here in peace today is a compliment and a credit to American civilization, and a prophecy of still greater national enlightenment and progress in the future. I refer to the past not in malice, for this is no day for malice; but simply to place more distinctly in front the gratifying and glorious change which has come both to our white fellow-citizens and ourselves, and to congratulate all upon the contrast between now and then; the new dispensation of freedom with its thousand blessings to both races, and the old dispensation of slavery with its ten thousand evils to both races—white and black. . . .

[W]e are here to express, as best we may, by appropriate forms and ceremonies, our grateful sense of the vast, high, and preëminent services rendered to ourselves, to our race, to our country, and to the whole world by Abraham Lincoln.

The sentiment that brings us here to-day is one of the noblest that can stir and thrill the human heart. It has crowned and made glorious the high places of all civilized nations with the grandest and most enduring works of art, designed to illustrate the characters and perpetuate the memories of great public men. It is the sentiment which from year to year adorns with fragrant and beautiful flowers the graves of our loyal, brave, and patriotic soldiers who fell in defence of the Union and liberty. It is the sentiment of gratitude and appreciation. . . .

For the first time in the history of our people, and in the history of the whole American people, we join in this high worship, and march conspicuously in the line of this time-honored custom. First things are always interesting, and this is one of our first things. It is the first time that, in this form and manner, we have sought to do honor to an American great man, however deserving and illustrious. I commend the fact to notice; let it be told in every part of the Republic; let men of all parties and opinions hear it; let those who despise us, not less than those who respect us, know that now and here, in the spirit of liberty, loyalty, and gratitude, let it be known everywhere, and by everybody who takes an interest in human progress and in the amelioration of the condition of mankind, that . . . we, the colored people, newly emancipated and rejoicing in our blood-bought freedom, near the close of the first century in the life of this Republic, have now and here unveiled, set apart, and dedicated a monument of enduring granite and bronze, in every line, feature, and figure of which the men of this generation may read, and those of aftercoming generations may read, something of the exalted character and great works of Abraham Lincoln, the first martyr President of the United States.

Fellow-citizens, in what we have said and done today, and in what we may say and do hereafter, we disclaim everything like arrogance and assumption. We claim for ourselves no superior devotion to the character, history, and memory of the illustrious name whose monument we have here dedicated today. We fully comprehend the relation of Abraham Lincoln both to ourselves and to the white people of the United States. Truth is proper and beautiful at all times and in all places, and it is never more proper and beautiful in any case than when speaking of a great public man whose example is likely to be commended for honor and imitation long after his departure to the solemn shades, the silent continents of eternity. It must be admitted, truth compels me to admit, even here in the presence of the monument we have erected to his memory, Abraham Lincoln was not, in the fullest sense of the word, either our man or our model. In his interests, in his associations, in his habits of thought, and in his prejudices, he was a white man.

He was preëminently the white man's President, entirely devoted to the welfare of white men. He was ready and willing at any time during the first years of his administration to deny, postpone, and sacrifice the rights of humanity in the colored people to promote the welfare of the white people of this country. In all his education and feeling he was an American of the Americans. He came into the Presidential chair upon one principle alone, namely, opposition to the extension of slavery. His arguments in furtherance of this policy had their motive and mainspring in his patriotic devotion to the interests of his own race. To protect, defend, and perpetuate slavery in the states where it existed Abraham Lincoln was not less ready than any other President to draw the sword of the nation. He was ready to execute all the supposed guarantees of the United States Constitution in favor of the slave system anywhere inside the slave states. He was willing to pursue, recapture, and send back the fugitive slave to his master, and to suppress a slave rising for liberty, though his guilty master were already in arms against the Government. The race to which we belong were not the special objects of his consideration. Knowing this, I concede to you, my white fellow-citizens, a preëminence in this worship at once full and supreme. First, midst, and last, you and yours were the objects of his deepest affection and his most earnest solicitude. You are the children of Abraham Lincoln. We are at best only his step-children; children by adoption, children by forces of circumstances and necessity. . . .

Fellow-citizens, ours is no new-born zeal and devotion—merely a thing of this moment. The name of Abraham Lincoln was near and dear to our hearts in the darkest and most perilous hours of the Republic. We were no more ashamed of him when shrouded in clouds of darkness, of doubt, and defeat than when we saw him crowned with victory, honor, and glory. Our faith in him was often taxed and strained to the uttermost, but it never failed. When he tarried long in the mountain; when he strangely told us that we were the cause of the war; when he still more strangely told us that we were to leave the land in which we were born; when he refused to employ our arms in defence of the Union; when, after accepting our services as colored soldiers, he refused to retaliate our murder and torture as colored prisoners; when he told us he would save the Union if he could with slavery; when he revoked the Proclamation of Emancipation of General Fremont; when he refused to remove the popular commander of the Army of the Potomac, in the days of its inaction and defeat, who was more zealous in his efforts to protect slavery than to suppress rebellion; when we saw all this, and more, we were at times grieved, stunned, and greatly bewildered; but our hearts believed while they ached and bled. Nor was this, even at that time, a blind and unreasoning superstition. Despite the mist and haze that surrounded him; despite the tumult, the hurry, and confusion of the hour, we were able to take a comprehensive view of Abraham Lincoln, and to make reasonable allowance for the circumstances of his position. We saw him, measured him, and estimated him; not by stray utterances to injudicious and tedious delegations, who often tried his patience; not by isolated facts torn from their connection; not by any partial and imperfect glimpses, caught at inopportune moments; but by a broad survey, in the light of the stern logic of great events, and in view of that divinity which shapes our ends, rough hew them how we will, we came to the conclusion that the hour and the man of our redemption had somehow met in the person of Abraham Lincoln. It mattered little to us what language he might employ on special occasions; it mattered little to us, when we fully knew him, whether he was swift or slow in his movements; it was enough for us that Abraham Lincoln was at the head of a great movement, and was in living and earnest sympathy with that movement, which, in the nature of things, must go on until slavery should be utterly and forever abolished in the United States.

When, therefore, it shall be asked what we have to do with the memory of Abraham Lincoln, or what Abraham Lincoln had to do with us, the answer is ready, full, and complete. Though he loved Caesar less than Rome, though the Union was more to him than our freedom or our future, under his wise and beneficent rule we saw ourselves gradually lifted from the depths of slavery to the heights of liberty and manhood; under his wise and beneficent rule, and by measures approved and vigorously pressed by him, we saw that the handwriting of ages, in the form of prejudice and proscription, was rapidly fading away from the face of our whole country; under his rule, and in due time, about as soon after all as the country could tolerate the strange spectacle, we saw our brave sons and brothers laying off the rags of bondage, and being clothed all over in the blue uniforms of the soldiers of the United States; under his rule we saw two hundred thousand of our dark and dusky people responding to the call of Abraham Lincoln, and with muskets on their shoulders, and eagles on their buttons, timing their high footsteps to liberty and union under the national flag; under his rule we saw the independence of the black republic of Haiti, the special object of slaveholding aversion and horror, fully recognized, and her minister, a colored gentleman, duly received here in the city of Washington; under his rule we saw the internal slave-trade, which so long disgraced the nation, abolished, and slavery abolished in the District of Columbia; under his rule we saw for the first time the law enforced against the foreign slave trade, and the first slave-trader hanged like any other pirate or murderer; under his rule, assisted by the greatest captain of our age, and his inspiration, we saw the Confederate States, based upon the idea that our race must be slaves, and slaves forever, battered to pieces and scattered to the four winds; under his rule, and in the fullness of time, we saw Abraham Lincoln, after giving the slaveholders three months' grace in which to save their hateful slave system, penning the immortal paper, which, though special in its language, was general in its principles and effect, making slavery forever impossible in the United States. Though we waited long, we saw all this and more. . . .

I have said that President Lincoln was a white man, and shared the prejudices common to his countrymen towards the colored race. Looking back to his times and to the condition of his country, we are compelled to admit that this unfriendly feeling on his part may be safely set down as one element of his wonderful success in organizing the loyal American people for the tremendous conflict before them, and bringing them safely through that conflict. His great mission was to accomplish two things: first, to save his country from dismemberment and ruin; and, second, to free his country from the great crime of slavery. To do one or the other, or both, he must have the earnest sympathy and the powerful coöperation of his loyal fellow-countrymen. Without this primary and essential condition to success his efforts must have been vain and utterly fruitless. Had he put the abolition of slavery before the salvation of the Union, he would have inevitably driven from him a powerful class of the American people and rendered resistance to rebellion impossible. Viewed from the genuine abolition ground, Mr. Lincoln seemed tardy, cold, dull, and indifferent; but measuring him by the sentiment of his country, a sentiment he was bound as a statesman to consult, he was swift, zealous, radical, and determined.

Though Mr. Lincoln shared the prejudices of his white fellow-countrymen against the Negro, it is hardly necessary to say that in his heart of hearts he loathed and hated slavery. . . . The man who could say, "Fondly do we hope, fervently do we pray, that this mighty scourge of war shall soon pass away, yet if God wills it continue till all the wealth piled by two hundred years of bondage shall have been wasted, and each drop of blood drawn by the lash shall have been paid for by one drawn by the sword, the judgments of the Lord are true and righteous altogether," gives all needed proof of his feeling on the subject of slavery. He was willing, while the South was loyal, that it should have its pound of flesh, because he thought that it was so nominated in the bond; but farther than this no earthly power could make him go.

Fellow-citizens, whatever else in this world may be partial, unjust, and uncertain, time, time! is impartial, just, and certain in its action. In the realm of mind, as well as in the realm of matter, it is a great worker, and often works wonders. The honest and comprehensive statesman, clearly discerning the needs of his country, and earnestly endeavoring to do his whole duty, though covered and blistered with reproaches, may safely leave his course to the silent judgment of time. Few great public men have ever been the victims of fiercer denunciation than Abraham Lincoln was during his administration. He was often wounded in the house of his friends. Reproaches came thick and fast upon him from within and from without, and from opposite quarters. He was assailed by Abolitionists; he was assailed by slaveholders; he was assailed by the men who were for peace at any price; he was assailed by those who were for a more vigorous prosecution of the war; he was assailed for not making the war an abolition war; and he was bitterly assailed for making the war an abolition war.

But now behold the change: the judgment of the present hour is, that taking him for all in all, measuring the tremendous magnitude of the work before him, considering the necessary means to ends, and surveying the end from the beginning, infinite wisdom has seldom sent any man into the world better fitted for his mission than Abraham Lincoln. His birth, his training, and his natural endowments, both mental and physical, were strongly in his favor. Born and reared among the lowly, a stranger to wealth and luxury, compelled to grapple single-handed with the flintiest hardships of life, from tender youth to sturdy manhood, he grew strong in the manly and heroic qualities demanded by the great mission to which he was called by the votes of his countrymen. The hard condition of his early life, which would have depressed and broken down weaker men, only gave greater life, vigor, and buoyancy to the heroic spirit of Abraham Lincoln. He was ready for any kind and any quality of work. . . .

All day long he could split heavy rails in the woods, and half the night long he could study his English Grammar by the uncertain flare and glare of the light made by a pine-knot. He was at home on the land with his axe, with his maul, with gluts, and his wedges; and he was equally at home on water, with his oars, with his poles, with his planks, and with his boat-hooks. And whether in his flat-boat on the Mississippi River, or at the fireside of his frontier cabin, he was a man of work. A son of toil himself, he was linked in brotherly sympathy with the sons of toil in every loyal part of the Republic.

This very fact gave him tremendous power with the American people, and materially contributed not only to selecting him to the Presidency, but in sustaining his administration of the Government.

Upon his inauguration as President of the United States, an office, even when assumed under the most favorable conditions, fitted to tax and strain the largest abilities, Abraham Lincoln was met by a tremendous crisis. He was called upon not merely to administer the Government, but to decide, in the face of terrible odds, the fate of the Republic.

A formidable rebellion rose in his path before him; the Union was already practically dissolved; his country was torn and rent asunder at the center. Hostile armies were already organized against the Republic, armed with the munitions of war which the Republic had provided for its own defence. The tremendous question for him to decide was whether his country should survive the crisis and flourish, or be dismembered and perish. His predecessor in office had already decided the question in favor of national dismemberment, by denying to it the right of self-defence and self-preservation—a right which belongs to the meanest insect.

Happily for the country, happily for you and for me, the judgment of James Buchanan, the patrician, was not the judgment of Abraham Lincoln, the plebeian. He brought his strong common sense, sharpened in the school of adversity, to bear upon the question. He did not hesitate, he did not doubt, he did not falter; but at once resolved that at whatever peril, at whatever cost, the union of the States should be preserved. . . . The trust that Abraham Lincoln had in himself and in the people was surprising and grand, but it was also enlightened and well founded. He knew the American people better than they knew themselves, and his truth was based upon this knowledge.

Fellow-citizens, the fourteenth day of April, 1865, of which this is the eleventh anniversary, is now and will ever remain a memorable day in the annals of this Republic. It was on the evening of this day, while a fierce and sanguinary rebellion was in the last stages of its desolating power; while its armies were broken and scattered before the invincible armies of Grant and Sherman; while a great nation, torn and rent by war, was already beginning to raise to the skies loud anthems of joy at the dawn of peace, it was startled, amazed, and overwhelmed by the crowning crime of slavery . . . the assassination of Abraham Lincoln. It was a new crime, a pure act of malice. No purpose of the rebellion was to be served by it. It was the simple gratification of a hell-black spirit of revenge. But it has done good after all. It has filled the country with a deeper abhorrence of slavery and a deeper love for the great liberator.

Had Abraham Lincoln died from any of the numerous ills to which flesh is heir; had he reached that good old age of which his vigorous constitution and his temperate habits gave promise; had he been permitted to see the end of his great work; had the solemn curtain of death come down but gradually— we should still have been smitten with a heavy grief, and treasured his name lovingly. But dying as he did die, by the red hand of violence, killed, assassinated, taken off without warning, not because of personal hate—for no man who knew Abraham Lincoln could hate him—but because of his fidelity to union and liberty, he is doubly dear to us, and his memory will be precious forever.

Fellow-citizens, I end, as I began, with congratulations. We have done a good work for our race today. In doing honor to the memory of our friend and liberator, we have been doing highest honors to ourselves and those who come after us; we have been fastening ourselves to a name and fame imperishable and immortal; we have also been defending ourselves from a blighting scandal. When now it shall be said that the colored man is soulless, that he has no appreciation of benefits or benefactors; when the foul reproach of ingratitude is hurled at us, and it is attempted to scourge us beyond the range of human brotherhood, we may calmly point to the monument we have this day erected to the memory of Abraham Lincoln.

Chapter V

The Judiciary

In *The Federalist* Hamilton argues that the Supreme Court's power of review follows from the concept of a limited constitution. Because there are limits to governmental activity, acts that exceed those limits are void, and therefore cannot be applied in particular cases by the Court. Judicial review signifies not judicial supremacy, but constitutional supremacy. The particular function of the court is thus to protect the rule of law.

Although the Constitution establishes the rule of law, there must be discretion for those who enact and administer the laws, or for the strictly political or elected branches of government. It is often difficult to draw the line between the discretion necessary for governing and the arbitrary exercise of power. In its job of defending the Constitution, the Court must often draw that line, deciding what matters are justiciable and what matters are political. In making that decision the Court itself exercises discretion. The possibility of arbitrary rule by the Judiciary parallels that of arbitrary rule by administrators, since neither the Court nor the administrator can avoid exercising discretion in particular cases before them. But although administrators are accountable to a political superior, the members of the Judiciary are relatively independent, holding office during good behavior. Hamilton argues that it is safe to give the Judiciary such independence, since it is the weakest of the three branches. Judges are able to declare laws unconstitutional only when a case is brought before them, and they depend on the Executive to enforce their decisions.

The Anti-Federalist writer Brutus is not persuaded by Hamilton's argument. He believes that the Court has the potential to become the most dangerous branch of government. If as in Britain the Court had no power to override the Acts of the legislature, there would be less danger from life tenure for judges. But life tenure combined with the power of judicial review holds the potential for the exercise of unrestrained arbitrary power.

Jefferson and Lincoln later expressed distrust of an arbitrary and powerful Court. Jefferson went so far as to deny that the Court possessed the power of judicial review. Each branch of government, Jefferson believed, must interpret the Constitution insofar as it applies to itself. He admits that "contradictory decisions" could arise under his scheme, but he relies on "the prudence of public functionaries, and the authority of public opinion" to "produce accommodation." In the absence of enlightened public opinion and statesmanship, Jefferson's version of separation of powers would lead to conflict between the branches and great confusion about the meaning of the law. Lincoln, like Jefferson, recognizes the danger of judicial review, but his position is more prudent. He emphasizes that while American citizens must abide by the *Dred Scott* decision, it applies only to the case at hand and cannot act as a precedent.

In *Marbury v. Madison* the Court declares a law of Congress unconstitutional. Marshall, speaking for the Court, explains why the Constitution implies that the Court has this power. Paradoxically, Congress went beyond its powers in enlarging those of the Court. In asserting the power of judicial review, Marshall also declared that the Court's own powers were limited by the Constitution. It was those limits that Congress had attempted to exceed in the Judiciary Act of 1789.

Marshall both affirms and limits judicial authority in another way as well. He distinguishes between acts of Executive officers that are and are not reviewable by the Court. An administrative officer is legally accountable for those acts that a law directs him to do, but not for those acts that the President directs him to do when exercising the discretionary political powers given him by the Constitution. *United States v. Nixon* goes beyond *Marbury* in restricting Executive discretion. There the issue is the discretion of the President himself rather than that of an administrative officer. Although the Court holds that "executive privilege" is implied in the office of the Presidency, it asserts that the Court itself is the judge of its applicability. The implications of the Court's opinion in *U.S. v. Nixon* entail a danger of judicial supremacy, not to Congress, but to the Presidency.

The question of the relation between the Court and the political branches is also raised by *Boerne v. Flores* and *U.S. v. Morrison*. At issue in *Boerne* are the power of Congress to elaborate the meaning of the Constitution through legislation and the role of the Court in providing authoritative interpretations of Constitutional provisions. Justice Kennedy, writing for the majority, claims that in the Religious Freedom Restoration Act (RFRA) Congress sought to overturn a judicial decision (*Oregon v. Smith*) regarding the meaning of the First Amendment through ordinary legislation. Kennedy contends that the Court's determination of Constitutional meaning can only be overturned by Constitutional amendment. Justice O'Connor in dissent argues that RFRA is in fact consistent with the free exercise clause and that *Oregon v. Smith* was incorrectly decided. The Court should now reconsider that opinion.

In *Morrison* a conservative majority defends the power of the Court to limit Congressional authority under the commerce clause, and it is the more liberal justices who call for judicial restraint. Thus the division between activists and restraintists does not fall neatly along ideological lines. Nonetheless, in the next two selections we find the classic liberal statement of activism in a speech by Justice William J. Brennan, Jr., and a classic conservative call for restraint put forth by Judge Robert Bork.

Justice Brennan claims that the Court must look beyond the text of the Constitution and the intention of its framers in order to deal with problems that arise in a modern world. He believes that the Constitution establishes a Court in order to protect the rights of minorities and the rights of individuals. The Court need not rely on any specific statutory or Constitutional language, but should instead look to these broader Constitutional goals.

Judge Robert Bork, however, argues that the doctrine of judicial activism is merely a convenient rationalization that allows judges to impose their own personal policy preferences on the Constitution and the nation. Bork believes that if the Constitution is to protect the rights of the people in the long-run, the text of the document and the intention of its framers must provide the boundaries within which judicial interpretation takes place. If the Constitution fails to settle an issue it is up to the more political branches of government to fill in the gaps through legislation or Constitutional amendment.

Like Brennan, Jefferson fears that the framers of a Constitution may not be able to anticipate the changing needs of the nation. But unlike Brennan Jefferson knows that his position ultimately calls into question an enduring Constitutional system. Jefferson does not think a Court can breathe life into an old Constitution. Men have no right to bind a future generation. Each generation must create its own Constitution. In response, Madison argued that generations are linked by the fact that later ones are beneficiaries of earlier ones, and to that extent obliged to follow their prescriptions. Since Madison was replying to Jefferson's objection to a "perpetual constitution," he must have had in mind his own generation's work of founding and the endurance of his own handiwork as the link among the individuals who were to live under the Constitution. Furthermore, a new government every generation, Madison argued, would not maintain the prejudice of the people in favor of the government "which is a salutary aid to the most rational government." Or, as he put it in Federalist 49, frequent appeals to the people about the fundamental principles of government would "deprive the government of that veneration that time bestows on everything."

In *California v. Bakke*, the judges reveal their different views of judicial review. As L. Peter Schultz points out, most of the Justices advocate that notion of a "living Constitution," which changes according to the problems and needs of the times. But although the majority of judges emphasize the necessity of a Constitution adaptable to the times, they differ in their understanding of how constitutional change should occur. Those judges who believe in an active Court hold that the Judiciary branch should reinterpret or adapt the Constitution from time to time. In *Bakke*, they uphold an expansion of the Equal Protection Clause of the Fourteenth Amendment so as to justify affirmative action. Their jurisprudence resembles that of the

Court in *Reynolds v. Sims*, where the Court's interpretation of Equal Protection overturned state apportionment schemes. The activists' position in *Bakke*, however was not endorsed by a majority of the Court. Another group of Justices, proponents of judicial self-restraint, refused to reach the Constitutional question of Equal Protection. They too advocate the "living Constitution," but they believe that it is the more political branches of government which should apply the changing standards of the age. These judges invalidated the affirmative action plan of the University of California on the ground that it violated the Civil Rights Act, which forbad state-funded institutions from making racial classifications. Whether the advocates of the "living Constitution" actively attempt to adapt the Constitution to their perception of the changing times, or restrain themselves in favor of the adaptations coming from the people and the more political branches, their understanding of the Constitution owes much to Jefferson's idea that one generation should not bind future generations and his hope for frequent constitutional conventions. The elaboration and protection of the permanent principles in the Constitution which Hamilton and Marshall thought was one of the Court's highest roles is found in the *Bakke* case, according to Schultz, only in the position of Justice Powell. Powell does join the "restraintists" to overturn affirmative action. But, unlike the restraintists, he reaches the constitutional issue. Nonetheless, he is "restrained" in deciding the case on the basis of enduring constitutional principles, refusing to expand those principles to suit the passing exigencies or even the latest prejudices of the times. It is only by such a combination of activism and restraint, Schultz argues, that judicial statesmanship can emerge.

Relying on Justice Powell's opinion in *Bakke*, Justice O'Connor upholds an affirmative action program at the University of Michigan School of Law in *Grutter v. Bollinger*. Although she defends the University's interest in diversity, she claims that her opinion looks forward to the day when such programs will no longer be necessary. The dissent argues, however, that her opinion ignores any Constitutional principles that might limit affirmative action in the present or future. The question we must ask is whether Powell and O'Connor illustrate the promise or the problems of judicial statemanship.

51

Alexander Hamilton

The Role of the Supreme Court (1788)

. . . As to the tenure by which the judges are to hold their places: this chiefly concerns their duration in office; the provisions for their support; the precautions for their responsibility.

According to the plan of the convention, all judges who may be appointed by the United States are to hold their offices *during good behavior*. The standard of good behavior for the continuance in office of the judicial magistracy, is certainly one of the most valuable of the modern improvements in the practice of government. In a monarchy it is an excellent barrier to the despotism of the prince; in a republic it is a no less excellent barrier to the encroachments and oppressions of the representative body. And it is the best expedient which can be devised in any government, to secure a steady, upright, and impartial administration of the laws.

Whoever attentively considers the different departments of power must perceive, that, in a government in which they are separated from each other, the judiciary, from the nature of its functions, will always be the least dangerous to the political rights of the Constitution; because it will be least in a capacity to annoy or injure them. The Executive not only dispenses the honors, but holds the sword of the community. The legislature not only commands the purse, but prescribes the rules by which the duties and rights of every citizen are to be regulated. The judiciary, on the contrary, has no influence over either the sword or the purse; no direction either of the strength or of the wealth of the society; and can take no active resolution whatever. It may truly be said to have neither FORCE nor WILL, but merely judgment; and must ultimately depend upon the aid of the executive arm even for the efficacy of its judgments.

This simple view of the matter suggests several important consequences. It proves incontestably, that the judiciary is beyond comparison the weakest of the three departments of power; that it can never attack with success either of the other two; and that all possible care is requisite to enable it to defend itself against their attacks. It equally proves, that though individual

From Federalist 78, in *The Federalist.*

oppression may now and then proceed from the courts of justice, the general liberty of the people can never be endangered from that quarter; I mean so long as the judiciary remains truly distinct from both the legislature and the Executive. For I agree, that "there is no liberty, if the power of judging be not separated from the legislative and executive powers." And it proves, in the last place, that as liberty can have nothing to fear from the judiciary alone, but would have every thing to fear from its union with either of the other departments; that as all the effects of such a union must ensue from a dependence of the former on the latter, notwithstanding a nominal and apparent separation; that as, from the natural feebleness of the judiciary, it is in continual jeopardy of being overpowered, awed, or influenced by its coordinate branches; and that as nothing can contribute so much to its firmness and independence as permanency in office, this quality may therefore be justly regarded as an indispensable ingredient in its constitution, and, in a great measure, as the citadel of the public justice and the public security.

The complete independence of the courts of justice is peculiarly essential in a limited Constitution. By a limited Constitution, I understand one which contains certain specified exceptions to the legislative authority; such, for instance, as that it shall pass no bills of attainder, no *ex-post-facto* laws, and the like. Limitations of this kind can be preserved in practice no other way than through the medium of courts of justice, whose duty it must be to declare all acts contrary to the manifest tenor of the Constitution void. Without this, all the reservations of particular rights or privileges would amount to nothing.

Some perplexity respecting the rights of the courts to pronounce legislative acts void, because contrary to the constitution, has arisen from an imagination that the doctrine would imply a superiority of the judiciary to the legislative power. It is urged that the authority which can declare the acts of another void, must necessarily be superior to the one whose acts may be declared void. As this doctrine is of great importance in all the American constitutions, a brief discussion of the ground on which it rests cannot be unacceptable.

There is no position which depends on clearer principles, than that every act of a delegated authority, contrary to the tenor of the commission under which it is exercised, is void. No legislative act, therefore, contrary to the Constitution, can be valid. To deny this, would be to affirm, that the deputy is greater than his principal; that the servant is above his master; that the representatives of the people are superior to the people themselves; that men acting by virtue of powers, may do not only what their powers do not authorize, but what they forbid.

If it be said that the legislative body are themselves the constitutional judges of their own powers, and that the construction they put upon them is conclusive upon the other departments, it may be answered, that this cannot be the natural presumption, where it is not to be collected from any particular provisions in the Constitution. It is not otherwise to be supposed, that the Constitution could intend to enable the representatives of the people to substitute their *will* to that of their constituents. It is far more rational to suppose, that the courts were designed to be an intermediate body between the people and the legislature, in order, among other things, to keep the latter within the limits assigned to their authority. The interpretation of the laws is the proper and peculiar province of the courts. A constitution is, in fact, and must be regarded by the judges, as a fundamental law. It therefore belongs to them to ascertain its meaning, as well as the meaning of any particular act proceeding from the legislative body. If there should happen to be an irreconcilable variance between the two, that which has the superior obligation and validity ought, of course, to be preferred; or, in other words, the Constitution ought to be preferred to the statute, the intention of the people to the intention of their agents.

Nor does this conclusion by any means suppose a superiority of the judicial to the legislative power. It only supposes that the power of the people is superior to both; and that where the will of the legislature, declared in its statutes, stands in opposition to that of the people, declared in the Constitution, the judges ought to be governed by the latter rather than the former. They ought to regulate their decisions by the fundamental laws, rather than by those which are not fundamental.

This exercise of judicial discretion, in determining between two contradictory laws, is exemplified in a familiar instance. It not uncommonly happens, that there are two statutes existing at one time, clashing in whole or in part with each other, and neither of them containing any repealing clause or expression. In such a case, it is the province of the courts to liquidate and fix their meaning and operation. So far as they can, by any fair construction, be reconciled to each other, reason and law conspire to dictate that this should be done; where this is impracticable, it becomes a matter of necessity to give effect to one, in exclusion of the other. The rule which has obtained in the courts for determining their relative validity is, that the last in order of time shall be preferred to the first. . . . [The Courts] thought it reasonable, that between the interfering acts of an *equal* authority, that which was the last indication of its will should have the preference.

But in regard to the interfering acts of a superior and subordinate authority, of an original and derivative power, the nature and reason of the thing indicate the converse of that rule as proper to be followed. They teach us that the prior act of a superior ought to be preferred to the subsequent act of an inferior and subordinate authority; and that accordingly, whenever a particular statute contravenes the Constitution, it will be the duty of the judicial tribunals to adhere to the latter and disregard the former.

It can be of no weight to say that the courts, on the pretence of a repugnancy, may substitute their own pleasure to the constitutional intentions of the legislature. This might as well happen in the case of two contradictory statutes; or it might as well happen in every adjudication upon any single statute. The courts must declare the sense of the law; and if they should be disposed to exercise WILL instead of JUDGMENT, the consequence would equally be the substitution of their pleasure to that of the legislative body. The observation, if it prove any thing, would prove that there ought to be no judges distinct from that body.

If, then, the courts of justice are to be considered as the bulwarks of a limited Constitution against legislative encroachments, this consideration will afford a strong argument for the permanent tenure of judicial offices since nothing will contribute so much as this to that independent spirit in the judges which must be essential to the faithful performance of so arduous a duty.

This independence of the judges is equally requisite to guard the Constitution and the rights of individuals from the effects of those ill humors, which the arts of designing men, or the influence of particular conjunctures, sometimes disseminate among the people themselves, and which, though they speedily give place to better information, and more deliberate reflection, have a tendency, in the meantime, to occasion dangerous innovations in the government, and serious oppressions of the minor party in the community. Though I trust the friends of the proposed Constitution will never concur with its enemies, in questioning that fundamental principle of republican government, which admits the right of the people to alter or abolish the established Constitution, whenever they find it inconsistent with their happiness, yet it is not to be inferred from this principle, that the representatives of the people, whenever a momentary inclination happens to lay hold of a majority of their constituents, incompatible with the provisions in the existing Constitution, would, on that account, be justifiable in a violation of those provisions; or that the courts would be under a greater obligation to connive at infractions in this shape, than when they had proceeded wholly from the cabals of the representative body. Until the people have, by some solemn and authoritative act, annulled or changed the established form, it is binding upon themselves collectively, as well as individually; and no presumption, or even knowledge, of their sentiments, can warrant their representatives in a departure from it, prior to such an act. But it is easy to see, that it would require an uncommon portion of fortitude in the judges to do their duty as faithful guardians of the Constitution, where legislative invasions of it had been instigated by the major voice of the community.

But it is not with a view to infractions of the Constitution only, that the independence of the judges may be an essential safeguard against the effects of occasional ill humors in the society. These sometimes extend no farther than to the injury of the private rights of particular classes of citizens, by unjust and partial laws. Here also the firmness of the judicial magistracy is of vast importance in mitigating the severity and confining the operation of such laws. It not only serves to moderate the immediate mischiefs of those which may have been passed but it operates as a check upon the legislative body in passing them; who, perceiving that obstacles to the success of iniquitous intention are to be expected from the scruples of the courts, are in a manner compelled, by the very motives of the injustice they meditate, to qualify their attempts. . . .

Periodical appointments, however regulated, or by whomsoever made, would, in some way or other, be fatal to [the judges'] necessary independence. . . .

There is yet a further and a weightier reason for the permanency of the judicial offices, which is deducible from the nature of the qualifications they require. It has been frequently remarked, with great propriety, that a voluminous code of laws is one of the inconveniences necessarily connected with the advantages of a free government. To avoid an arbitrary discretion in the courts, it is indispensable that they should be bound down by strict rules and precedents, which serve to define and point out their duty in every particular case that comes before them; and it will readily be conceived from the variety of controversies which grow out of the folly and wickedness of mankind, that the records of those precedents must unavoidably swell to a very considerable bulk, and must demand long and laborious study to acquire a competent knowledge of them. Hence it is, that there can be but few men in the society who will have sufficient skill in the laws to qualify them for the stations of judges. And making the proper deductions for the ordinary depravity of human nature, the number must be still smaller of those who unite the requisite integrity with the requisite knowledge. These considerations apprise us, that the government can have no great option between fit character; and that a temporary duration in office, which would naturally discourage such characters from quitting a lucrative line of practice to accept a seat on the bench, would have a tendency to throw the administration of justice into hands less able, and less well qualified, to conduct it with utility and dignity.

52

Brutus

The Problem of Judicial Review (1787)

. . . [T]he supreme court under this constitution [will] be exalted above all other power in the government, and subject to no controul. . . . I question whether the world ever saw, in any period of it, a court of justice invested with such immense powers, and yet placed in a situation so little responsible.

From Brutus XV, *New York Journal,* March 20, 1787.

Certain it is, that in England, and in the several states, where we have been taught to believe, the courts of law are put upon the most prudent establishment, they are on a very different footing.

The judges in England, it is true, hold their offices during their good behaviour, but then their determinations are subject to correction by the house of lords; and their power is by no means so extensive as that of the proposed supreme court of the union.—I believe they in no instance assume the authority to set aside an act of parliament under the idea that it is inconsistent with their constitution. They consider themselves bound to decide according to the existing laws of the land, and never undertake to controul them by adjudging that they are inconsistent with the constitution— much less are they vested with the power of giving an *equitable* construction to the constitution.

The judges in England are under the controul of the legislature, for they are bound to determine according to the laws passed by them. But the judges under this constitution will controul the legislature, for the supreme court are authorised in the last resort, to determine what is the extent of the powers of the Congress; they are to give the constitution an explanation, and there is no power above them to set aside their judgment. The framers of this constitution appear to have followed that of the British, in rendering the judges independent, by granting them their offices during good behaviour, without following the constitution of England, in instituting a tribunal in which their errors may be corrected; and without adverting to this, that the judicial under this system have a power which is above the legislative, and which indeed transcends any power before given to a judicial by any free government under heaven.

I do not object to the judges holding their commissions during good behaviour. I suppose it a proper provision provided they were made properly responsible. But I say, this system has followed the English government in this, while it has departed from almost every other principle of their jurisprudence, under the idea, of rendering the judges independent; which, in the British constitution, means no more than that they hold their places during good behaviour, and have fixed salaries, they have made the judges *independent*, in the fullest sense of the word. There is no power above them, to controul any of their decisions. There is no authority that can remove them, and they cannot be controuled by the laws of the legislature. In short, they are independent of the people, of the legislature, and of every power under heaven. Men placed in this situation will generally soon feel themselves independent of heaven itself. Before I proceed to illustrate the truth of these assertions, I beg liberty to make one remark—Though in my opinion the judges ought to hold their offices during good behaviour, yet I think it is clear, that the reasons in favour of this establishment of the judges in England, do by no means apply to this country.

The great reason assigned, why the judges in Britain ought to be commissioned during good behaviour, is this, that they may be placed in a situation, not to be influenced by the crown, to give such decisions, as would tend to increase its powers and prerogatives. While the judges held their places at the will and pleasure of the king, on whom they depended not only for their offices, but also for their salaries, they were subject to every undue influence. If the crown wished to carry a favorite point, to accomplish which the aid of the courts of law was necessary, the pleasure of the king would be signified to the judges. And it required the spirit of a martyr, for the judges to determine contrary to the king's will.—They were absolutely dependent upon him both for their offices and livings. The king, holding his office during life, and transmitting it to his posterity as an inheritance, has much stronger inducements to increase the prerogatives of his office than those who hold their offices for stated periods, or even for life. Hence the English nation gained a great point, in favour of liberty. When they obtained the appointment of the judges, during good behaviour, they got from the crown a concession, which deprived it of one of the most powerful engines with which it might enlarge the boundaries of the royal prerogative and encroach on the liberties of the people. But these reasons do not apply to this country, we have no hereditary monarch; those who appoint the judges do not hold their offices for life, nor do they descend to their children. The same arguments, therefore, which will conclude in favor of the tenor of the judge's offices for good behaviour, lose a considerable part of their weight when applied to the state and condition of America. But much less can it be shewn, that the nature of our government requires that the courts should be placed beyond all account more independent, so much so as to be above controul.

I have said that the judges under this system will be *independent* in the strict sense of the word: To prove this I will shew—That there is no power above them that can controul their decisions, or correct their errors. There is no authority that can remove them from office for any errors or want of capacity, or lower their salaries, and in many cases their power is superior to that of the legislature.

1st. There is no power above them that can correct their errors or controul their decisions—The adjudications of this court are final and irreversible, for there is no court above them to which appeals can lie, either in error or on the merits. In this respect it differs from the courts in England, for there the house of lords is the highest court, to whom appeals, in error, are carried from the highest of the courts of law.

2d. They cannot be removed from office or suffer a dimunition of their salaries, for any error in judgement or want of capacity.

It is expressly declared by the constitution,—"That they shall at stated times receive a compensation for their services which shall not be diminished during their continuance in office."

The only clause in the constitution which provides for the removal of the judges from office, is that which declares, that "the president, vice-president, and all civil officers of the United States, shall be removed from office, on impeachment for, and conviction of treason, bribery, or other high crimes and misdemeanors." By this paragraph, civil officers, in which the judges are included, are removable only for crimes. Treason and bribery are named, and the rest are included under the general terms of high crimes and misdemeanors.—Errors in judgement, or want of capacity to discharge the duties of the office, can never be supposed to be included in these words, *high crimes and misdemeanors*. A man may mistake a case in giving judgment, or manifest that he is incompetent to the discharge of the duties of a judge, and yet give no evidence of corruption or want of integrity. To support the charge, it will be necessary to give in evidence some facts that will shew, that the judges committed the error from wicked and corrupt motives.

3d. The power of this court is in many cases superior to that of the legislature. I have shewed, in a former paper, that this court will be authorised to decide upon the meaning of the constitution, and that, not only according to the natural and ob[vious] meaning of the words, but also according to the spirit and intention of it. In the exercise of this power they will not be subordinate to, but above the legislature. For all the departments of this government will receive their powers, so far as they are expressed in the constitution, from the people immediately, who are the source of power. The legislature can only exercise such powers as are given them by the constitution, they cannot assume any of the rights annexed to the judicial, for this plain reason, that the same authority which vested the legislature with their powers, vested the judicial with theirs—both are derived from the same source, both therefore are equally valid, and the judicial hold their powers independently of the legislature, as the legislature do of the judicial.—The supreme court then have a right, independent of the legislature, to give a construction to the constitution and every part of it, and there is no power provided in this system to correct their construction or do it away. If, therefore, the legislature pass any laws, inconsistent with the sense the judges put upon the constitution, they will declare it void; and therefore in this respect their power is superior to that of the legislature. . . .

53

Thomas Jefferson

Against Judicial Review (1815)

The . . . question, whether the judges are invested with exclusive authority to decide on the constitutionality of a law, has been heretofore a subject of consideration with me in the exercise of official duties. Certainly there is not a word in the constitution which has given that power to them more than to the executive or legislative branches. Questions of property, of character and of crime being ascribed to the judges, through a definite course of legal proceeding, laws involving such questions belong, of course, to them; and as they decide on them ultimately and without appeal, they of course decide *for themselves*. The constitutional validity of the law or laws again prescribing executive action, and to be administered by that branch ultimately and without appeal, the executive must decide for *themselves* also, whether, under the constitution, they are valid or not. So also as to laws governing the proceedings of the legislature, that body must judge *for itself* the constitutionality of the law, and equally without appeal or control from its coordinate branches. And, in general, that branch which is to act ultimately, and without appeal, on any law, is the rightful expositor of the validity of the law, uncontrolled by the opinions of the other co-ordinate authorities. It may be said that contradictory decisions may arise in such case, and produce inconvenience. This is possible, and is a necessary failing in all human proceedings. Yet the prudence of the public functionaries, and authority of public opinion, will generally produce accommodation. Such an instance of difference occurred between the judges of England (in the time of Lord Holt) and the House of Commons, but the prudence of those bodies prevented inconvenience from it. So in the cases of Duane and of William Smith of South Carolina, whose characters of citizenship stood precisely on the same ground, the judges in a question of meum and tuum which came before them, decided that Duane was not a citizen; and in a question of membership, the House of Representatives, under the same words of the same provision, adjudged William Smith

From *The Writings of Thomas Jefferson*, Vol. IX, G. P. Putnam's Sons, 1898.

to be a citizen. Yet no inconvenience has ensued from these contradictory decisions. This is what I believe myself to be sound. But there is another opinion entertained by some men of such judgment and information as to lessen my confidence in my own. That is, that the legislature alone is the exclusive expounder of the sense of the constitution, in every part of it whatever. And they allege in its support, that this branch has authority to impeach and punish a member of either of the others acting contrary to its declaration of the sense of the constitution. It may indeed be answered, that an act may still be valid although the party is punished for it, right or wrong. However, this opinion which ascribes exclusive exposition to the legislature, merits respect for its safety, there being in the body of the nation a control over them, which, if expressed by rejection on the subsequent exercise of their elective franchise, enlists public opinion against their exposition, and encourages a judge or executive on a future occasion to adhere to their former opinion. Between these two doctrines, every one has a right to choose, and I know of no third meriting any respect. . . .

54

Abraham Lincoln

The Authority of the Supreme Court (1857)

. . . And now as to the Dred Scott decision. That decision declares two propositions—first, that a negro cannot sue in the U.S. Courts; and secondly, that Congress cannot prohibit slavery in the Territories. It was made by a divided court—dividing differently on the different points. Judge Douglas does not discuss the merits of the decision; and, in that respect, I shall follow his example, believing I could no more improve on McLean and Curtis, than he could on Taney.

He denounces all who question the correctness of that decision, as offering violent resistance to it. But who resists it? Who has, in spite of the decision, declared Dred Scott free, and resisted the authority of his master over him?

From Speech at Springfield, Illinois, June 26, 1857, in *The Collected Works of Abraham Lincoln*, Vol. II, Rutgers University Press, 1953.

Judicial decisions have two uses—first, to absolutely determine the case decided, and secondly, to indicate to the public how other similar cases will be decided when they arise. For the latter use, they are called "precedents" and "authorities."

We believe, as much as Judge Douglas, (perhaps more) in obedience to, and respect for the judicial department of government. We think its decisions on Constitutional questions, when fully settled, should control, not only the particular cases decided, but the general policy of the country, subject to be disturbed only by amendments of the Constitution as provided in that instrument itself. More than this would be revolution. But we think the Dred Scott decision is erroneous. We know the court that made it, has often over-ruled its own decisions, and we shall do what we can to have it to overrule this. We offer no *resistance* to it.

Judicial decisions are of greater or less authority as precedents, according to circumstances. That this should be so, accords both with common sense, and the customary understanding of the legal profession.

If this important decision had been made by the unanimous concurrence of the judges, and without any apparent partisan bias, and in accordance with legal public expectation, and with the steady practice of the departments throughout our history, and had been in no part, based on assumed historical facts which are not really true; or, if wanting in some of these, it had been before the court more than once, and had there been affirmed and re-affirmed through a course of years, it then might be, perhaps would be, factious, nay, even revolutionary, to not acquiesce in it as a precedent.

But when, as it is true we find it wanting in all these claims to the public confidence, it is not resistance, it is not factious, it is not even disrespectful, to treat it as not having yet quite established a settled doctrine for the country— But Judge Douglas considers this view awful. Hear him:

"The courts are the tribunals prescribed by the Constitution and created by the authority of the people to determine, expound and enforce the law. Hence, whoever resists the final decision of the highest judicial tribunal, aims a deadly blow to our whole Republican system of government—a blow, which if successful would place all our rights and liberties at the mercy of passion, anarchy and violence. I repeat, therefore, that if resistance to the decisions of the Supreme Court of the United States, in a matter like the points decided in the Dred Scott case, clearly within their jurisdiction as defined by the Constitution, shall be forced upon the country as a political issue, it will become a distinct and naked issue between the friends and the enemies of the Constitution—the friends and the enemies of the supremacy of the laws."

Why this same Supreme court once decided a national bank to be constitutional; but Gen. Jackson, as President of the United States, disregarded the decision, and vetoed a bill for a re-charter, partly on constitutional ground, declaring that each public functionary must support the Constitution, *"as he understands it."* But hear the General's own words. Here they are, taken from his veto message:

"It is maintained by the advocates of the bank, that its constitutionality, in all its features, ought to be considered as settled by precedent, and by the decision of the Supreme Court. To this conclusion I cannot assent. Mere precedent is a dangerous source of authority, and should not be regarded as deciding questions of constitutional power, except where the acquiescence of the people and the States can be considered as well settled. So far from this being the case on this subject, an argument against the bank might be based on precedent. One Congress in 1791, decided in favor of a bank; another in 1811, decided against it. One Congress in 1815 decided against a bank; another in 1816 decided in its favor. Prior to the present Congress, therefore, the precedents drawn from that source were equal. If we resort to the States, the expressions of legislative, judicial and executive opinions against the bank have been probably to those in its favor as four to one. There is nothing in precedent, therefore, which if its authority were admitted, ought to weigh in favor of the act before me."

I drop the quotations merely to remark that all there ever was, in the way of precedent up to the Dred Scott decision, on the points therein decided, had been against that decision. But hear Gen. Jackson further—

"If the opinion of the Supreme court covered the whole ground of this act, it ought not to control the co-ordinate authorities of this Government. The Congress, the executive and the court, must each for itself be guided by its own opinion of the Constitution. Each public officer, who takes an oath to support the Constitution, swears that he will support it as he understands it, and not as it is understood by others." . . .

55

Marbury v. Madison (1803)

Chief Justice Marshall *delivered the opinion of the Court:*

At the last term on the affidavits then read and filed with the clerk, a rule was granted in this case, requiring the secretary of state to show cause

From *Marbury v. Madison*, 1 Cranch 137 (1803).

why a mandamus should not issue, directing him to deliver to William Marbury his commission as a justice of the peace for the county of Washington in the District of Columbia.

No cause has been shown, and the present motion is for a mandamus. The peculiar delicacy of this case, the novelty of some of its circumstances, and the real difficulty attending the points which occur in it, require a complete exposition of the principles on which the opinion to be given by the court is founded.

In the order in which the court has viewed this subject the following questions have been considered and decided.

1st. Has the applicant a right to the commission he demands?

2d. If he has a right, and that right has been violated, do the laws of his country afford him a remedy?

3d. If they do afford him a remedy, is it a mandamus issuing from this court?

The first object of inquiry is,

1st. Has the applicant a right to the commission he demands?

[The Court's discussion showing Marbury's right to the commission is omitted.]

Mr. Marbury, then, since his commission was signed by the President, and sealed by the Secretary of State, was appointed; and as the law creating the office, gave the officer a right to hold for five years, independent of the executive, the appointment was not revocable, but vested in the officer legal rights, which are protected by the laws of his country.

To withhold his commission, therefore, is an act deemed by the court not warranted by law, but violative of a vested legal right.

This brings us to the second inquiry; which is,

2d. If he has a right, and that right has been violated, do the laws of his country afford him a remedy? The very essence of civil liberty certainly consists in the right of every individual to claim the protection of the laws, whenever he receives an injury. One of the first duties of government is to afford that protection. In Great Britain the king himself is sued in the respectful form of a petition, and he never fails to comply with the judgment of his court. . . .

The government of the United States has been emphatically termed a government of laws, and not of men. It will certainly cease to deserve this high appellation, if the laws furnish no remedy for the violation of a vested legal right. . . .

[T]he question, whether the legality of an act of the head of a department be examinable in a court of justice or not, must always depend on the nature of that act.

If some acts be examinable, and others not, there must be some rule of law to guide the court in the exercise of its jurisdiction.

In some instances there may be difficulty in applying the rule to particular cases; but there cannot, it is believed, be much difficulty in laying down the rule.

By the constitution of the United States, the President is invested with certain important political powers, in the exercise of which he is to use his own discretion, and is accountable only to his country in his political character and to his own conscience. To aid him in the performance of these duties, he is authorized to appoint certain officers, who act by his authority, and in conformity with his orders.

In such cases, their acts are his acts; and whatever opinion may be entertained of the manner in which executive discretion may be used, still there exists, and can exist, no power to control that discretion. The subjects are political. They respect the nation, not individual rights, and being intrusted to the executive, the decision of the executive is conclusive. The application of this remark will be perceived by adverting to the act of congress for establishing the department of foreign affairs. This officer, as his duties were prescribed by that act, is to conform precisely to the will of the President. He is the mere organ by whom that will is communicated. The acts of such an officer, as an officer, can never be examinable by the courts.

But when the legislature proceeds to impose on that officer other duties; when he is directed peremptorily to perform certain acts; when the rights of individuals are dependent on the performance of those acts; he is so far the officer of the law; is amenable to the laws for his conduct; and cannot at his discretion sport away the vested rights of others.

The conclusion from this reasoning is, that where the heads of departments are the political or confidential agents of the executive, merely to execute the will of the President, or rather to act in cases in which the executive possesses a constitutional or legal discretion, nothing can be more perfectly clear than that their acts are only politically examinable. But where a specific duty is assigned by law, and individual rights depend upon the performance of that duty, it seems equally clear that the individual who considers himself injured, has a right to resort to the laws of his country for a remedy. . . .

It is, then, the opinion of the Court,

1st. That by signing the commission of Mr. Marbury, the President of the United States appointed him a justice of peace for the county of Washington, in the District of Columbia; and that the seal of the United States, affixed thereto by the Secretary of State, is conclusive testimony of the verity of the signature, and of the completion of the appointment; and that the appointment conferred on him a legal right to the office for the space of five years.

2d. That, having this legal title to the office, he has a consequent right to the commission; a refusal to deliver which is a plain violation of that right, for which the laws of his country afford him a remedy.

It remains to be inquired whether,

3d. He is entitled to the remedy for which he applies. This depends on, 1st. The nature of the writ applied for; and, 2d. The power of this court.

1st. The nature of the writ. . . .

This writ, if awarded, would be directed to an officer of government, and its mandate to him would be, to use the words of Blackstone, "to do a particular thing therein specified, which appertains to his office and duty, and which the court has previously determined, or at least supposes, to be consonant to right and justice." Or, in the words of Lord Mansfield, the applicant, in this case, has a right to execute an office of public concern, and is kept out of possession of that right.

These circumstances certainly concur in this case.

Still, to render the mandamus a proper remedy, the officer to whom it is to be directed, must be one to whom, on legal principles, such writ may be directed; and the person applying for it must be without any other specific and legal remedy.

1st. With respect to the officer to whom it would be directed. The intimate political relation subsisting between the President of the United States and the heads of departments, necessarily renders any legal investigation of the acts of one of those high officers peculiarly irksome, as well as delicate; and excites some hesitation with respect to the propriety of entering into such investigation. Impressions are often received without much reflection or examination, and it is not wonderful that in such a case as this the assertion, by an individual, of his legal claims in a court of justice, to which claims it is the duty of that court to attend, should at first view be considered by some, as an attempt to intrude into the cabinet, and to intermeddle with the prerogatives of the executive.

It is scarcely necessary for the court to disclaim all pretensions to such jurisdiction. An extravagance, so absurd and excessive, could not have been entertained for a moment. The province of the court is, solely, to decide on the rights of individuals, not to inquire how the executive, or executive officers, perform duties in which they have a discretion. Questions in their nature political, or which are, by the constitution and laws, submitted to the executive, can never be made in this court.

But, if this be not such a question; if, so far from being an intrusion into the secrets of the cabinet, it respects a paper which, according to law, is upon record, and to a copy of which the law gives a right, on the payment of ten cents; if it be no intermeddling with a subject over which the executive can be considered as having exercised any control; what is there in the exalted station of the officer, which shall bar a citizen from asserting, in a court of justice, his legal rights, or shall forbid a court to listen to the claim, or to issue a mandamus directing the performance of a duty, not depending on executive discretion, but on particular acts of congress, and the general principles of law?

If one of the heads of departments commits any illegal act, under colour of his office, by which an individual sustains an injury, it cannot be pretended that his office alone exempts him from being sued in the ordinary mode of proceeding, and being compelled to obey the judgment of the law. How, then, can his office exempt him from this particular mode of deciding on the legality of his conduct if the case be such a case as would, were any other individual the party complained of, authorize the process?

. . . [W]here he is directed by law to do a certain act affecting the absolute rights of individuals, in the performance of which he is not placed under the particular direction of the President, and the performance of which the President cannot lawfully forbid, and therefore is never presumed to have forbidden; as for example to record a commission, or a patent for land, which has received all the legal solemnities; or to give a copy of such record; in such cases, it is not perceived on what ground the courts of the country are further excused from the duty of giving judgment that right be done to an injured individual, than if the same services were to be performed by a person not the head of a department. . . .

This, then, is a plain case for a mandamus, either to deliver the commission, or a copy of it from the record; and it only remains to be inquired,

Whether it can issue from this court.

The act to establish the judicial courts of the United States authorizes the Supreme Court "to issue writs of mandamus in cases warranted by the principles and usages of law, to any courts appointed, or persons holding office, under the authority of the United States."

The Secretary of State, being a person holding an office under the authority of the United States, is precisely within the letter of the description, and if this court is not authorized to issue a writ of mandamus to such an officer, it must be because the law is unconstitutional, and therefore absolutely incapable of conferring the authority, and assigning the duties which its words purport to confer and assign.

The constitution vests the whole judicial power of the United States in one Supreme Court, and such inferior courts as congress shall, from time to time, ordain and establish. This power is expressly extended to all cases arising under the laws of the United States; and, consequently, in some form, may be exercised over the present case; because the right claimed is given by a law of the United States.

In the distribution of this power it is declared that "the Supreme Court shall have original jurisdiction in all cases affecting ambassadors, other public ministers and consuls, and those in which a state shall be a party. In all other cases, the Supreme Court shall have appellate jurisdiction."

It has been insisted, at the bar, that as the original grant of jurisdiction, to the Supreme and inferior courts, is general, and the clause, assigning original jurisdiction to the Supreme Court, contains no negative or restrictive words, the power remains to the legislature, to assign original jurisdiction to that court in other cases than those specified in the article which has been recited; provided those cases belong to the judicial power of the United States.

If it had been intended to leave it in the discretion of the legislature to apportion the judicial power between the supreme and inferior courts according to the will of that body, it would certainly have been useless to have proceeded further than to have defined the judicial power, and the tribunals in which it should be vested. The subsequent part of the section is mere surplusage, is entirely without meaning, if such is to be the construction. If congress remains at liberty to give this court appellate jurisdiction, where the constitution has declared their jurisdiction shall be original; and original jurisdiction where the constitution has declared it shall be appellate; the distribution of jurisdiction, made in the constitution, is form without substance. . . .

It is the essential criterion of appellate jurisdiction, that it revises and corrects the proceedings in a cause already instituted, and does not create that cause. Although, therefore, a mandamus may be directed to courts, yet to issue such a writ to an officer for the delivery of a paper, is in effect the same as to sustain an original action for that paper, and, therefore, seems not to belong to appellate but to original jurisdiction. Neither is it necessary in such a case as this, to enable the court to exercise its appellate jurisdiction.

The authority, therefore, given to the Supreme Court, by the act establishing the judicial courts of the United States, to issue writs of mandamus to public officers, appears not to be warranted by the constitution; and it becomes necessary to inquire whether a jurisdiction so conferred can be exercised.

The question, whether an act, repugnant to the constitution, can become the law of the land, is a question deeply interesting to the United States; but, happily, not of an intricacy proportioned to its interest. It seems only necessary to recognize certain principles, supposed to have been long and well established, to decide it.

That the people have an original right to establish, for their future government, such principles, as, in their opinion, shall most conduce to their own happiness is the basis on which the whole American fabric has been erected. The exercise of this original right is a very great exertion; nor can it, nor ought it, to be frequently repeated. The principles, therefore, so established, are deemed fundamental. And as the authority from which they proceed is supreme, and can seldom act, they are designed to be permanent.

This original and supreme will organizes the government, and assigns to different departments their respective powers. It may either stop here, or establish certain limits not to be transcended by those departments.

The government of the United States is of the latter description. The powers of the legislature are defined and limited; and that those limits may not be mistaken, or forgotten, the constitution is written. To what purpose are powers limited, and to what purpose is that limitation committed to writing, if these limits may, at any time, be passed by those intended to be restrained? The distinction between a government with limited and unlimited powers is abolished, if those limits do not confine the persons on whom they are imposed, and if acts prohibited and acts allowed, are of equal obligation. It is a proposition too plain to be contested, that the constitution controls any legislative act repugnant to it; or, that the legislature may alter the constitution by an ordinary act.

Between these alternatives there is no middle ground. The constitution is either a superior paramount law, unchangeable by ordinary means, or it is on a level with ordinary legislative acts, and, like other acts, is alterable when the legislature shall please to alter it.

If the former part of the alternative be true, then a legislative act contrary to the constitution is not law: if the latter part be true, then written constitutions are absurd attempts, on the part of the people, to limit a power in its own nature illimitable.

Certainly all those who have framed written constitutions contemplate them as forming the fundamental and paramount law of the nation, and, consequently, the theory of every such government must be, that an act of the legislature, repugnant to the constitution, is void.

This theory is essentially attached to a written constitution, and is, consequently, to be considered, by this court, as one of the fundamental principles of our society. It is not therefore to be lost sight of in the further consideration of this subject.

If an act of the legislature, repugnant to the constitution, is void, does it, notwithstanding its invalidity, bind the courts, and oblige them to give it effect? Or, in other words, though it be not law, does it constitute a rule as operative as if it was a law? This would be to overthrow in fact what was established in theory; and would seem, at first view, an absurdity too gross to be insisted on. It shall, however, receive a more attentive consideration.

It is emphatically the province and duty of the judicial department to say what the law is. Those who apply the rule to particular cases, must of necessity expound and interpret that rule. If two laws conflict with each other, the courts must decide on the operation of each.

So if a law be in opposition to the constitution; if both the law and the constitution apply to a particular case, so that the court must either decide that case conformably to the law, disregarding the constitution; or conformably to the constitution, disregarding the law; the court must determine which of these conflicting rules governs the case. This is of the very essence of judicial duty.

If, then, the courts are to regard the constitution, and the constitution is superior to any ordinary act of the legislature, the constitution, and not such ordinary act, must govern the case to which they both apply.

Those, then, who controvert the principle that the constitution is to be considered, in court, as a paramount law, are reduced to the necessity of maintaining that courts must close their eyes on the constitution, and see only the law.

This doctrine would subvert the very foundation of all written constitutions. It would declare that an act which, according to the principles and theory of our government, is entirely void, is yet, in practice, completely obligatory. It would declare that if the legislature shall do what is expressly forbidden, such act, notwithstanding the express prohibition, is in reality effectual. It would be giving to the legislature a practical and real omnipotence, with the same breath which professes to restrict their powers within narrow limits. It is prescribing limits, and declaring that those limits may be passed at pleasure.

That it thus reduces to nothing what we have deemed the greatest improvement on political institutions, a written constitution, would of itself be sufficient, in America, where written constitutions have been viewed with so much reverence, for rejecting the construction. But the peculiar expressions of the constitution of the United States furnish additional arguments in favour of its rejection.

The judicial power of the United States is extended to all cases arising under the constitution.

Could it be the intention of those who gave this power, to say that in using it the constitution should not be looked into? That a case arising under the constitution should be decided without examining the instrument under which it arises?

This is too extravagant to be maintained.

In some cases, then, the constitution must be looked into by the judges. And if they can open it at all, what part of it are they forbidden to read or to obey?

There are many other parts of the constitution which serve to illustrate this subject.

It is declared that "no tax or duty shall be laid on articles exported from any state." Suppose a duty on the export of cotton, of tobacco, or of flour; and a suit instituted to recover it. Ought judgment to be rendered in such a case? Ought the judges to close their eyes on the constitution, and only see the law?

The constitution declares "that no bill of attainder or ex post facto law shall be passed."

If, however, such a bill should be passed, and a person should be prosecuted under it; must the court condemn to death those victims whom the constitution endeavors to preserve?

"No person," says the constitution, "shall be convicted of treason unless on the testimony of two witnesses to the same overt act, or on confession in open court."

Here the language of the constitution is addressed especially to the courts. It prescribes, directly for them, a rule of evidence not to be departed from. If the legislature should change that rule, and declare one witness, or a confession out of court, sufficient for conviction, must the constitutional principle yield to the legislative act?

From these, and many other selections which might be made, it is apparent, that the framers of the constitution contemplated that instrument as a rule for the government of courts, as well as of the legislature.

Why otherwise does it direct the judges to take an oath to support it? This oath certainly applies in an especial manner, to their conduct in their official character. How immoral to impose it on them, if they were to be used as the instruments, and the knowing instruments, for violating what they swear to support! . . .

It is also not entirely unworthy of observation, that in declaring what shall be the supreme law of the land, the constitution itself is first mentioned; and not the laws of the United States generally, but those only which shall be made in pursuance of the constitution, have that rank.

Thus, the particular phraseology of the constitution of the United States confirms and strengthens the principle, supposed to be essential to all written constitutions, that a law repugnant to the constitution is void; and that courts, as well as other departments, are bound by that instrument. . . .

56

United States v. Nixon (1974)

Mr. Chief Justice Burger *delivered the opinion of the Court:*

On March 1, 1974, a grand jury of the United States District Court for the District of Columbia returned an indictment charging seven named individuals with various offenses, including conspiracy to defraud the United States and to obstruct justice. Although he was not designated as such in the indictment, the grand jury named the President, among others, as an unindicted coconspirator. On April 18, 1974, upon motion of the Special Prosecutor, see n. 8, *infra*, a subpoena *duces tecum* was issued pursuant to Rule 17(c) to the President by the United States District Court and made returnable on May 2, 1974. This subpoena required the production, in advance of the September 9 trial date, of certain tapes, memoranda, papers, transcripts or other writings relating to certain precisely identified meetings between the President and others. The Special Prosecutor was able to fix the time, place and persons present at these discussions because the White House daily

From *United States v. Nixon*, 418 U.S. 683 (1974).

logs and appointment records had been delivered to him. On April 30, the President publicly released edited transcripts of 43 conversations; portions of 20 conversations subject to subpoena in the present case were included. On May 1, 1974, the President's counsel filed a "special appearance" and a motion to quash the subpoena, under Rule 17(c). This motion was accompanied by a formal claim of privilege. . . .

In the District Court, the President's counsel argued that the court lacked jurisdiction to issue the subpoena because the matter was an intra-branch dispute between a subordinate and superior officer of the Executive Branch and hence not subject to judicial resolution. That argument has been renewed in this Court with emphasis on the contention that the dispute does not present a "case" or "controversy" which can be adjudicated in the federal courts. The President's counsel argues that the federal courts should not intrude into areas committed to the other branches of Government. He views the present dispute as essentially a "jurisdictional" dispute within the Executive Branch which he analogizes to a dispute between two congressional committees. Since the Executive Branch has exclusive authority and absolute discretion to decide whether to prosecute a case, it is contended that a President's decision is final in determining what evidence is to be used in a given criminal case. . . .

The mere assertion of a claim of an "intra-branch dispute," without more, has never operated to defeat federal jurisdiction; justiciability does not depend on such a surface inquiry. In *United States v. ICC*, the Court observed, "courts must look behind names that symbolize the parties to determine whether a justiciable case or controversy is presented."

Our starting point is the nature of the proceeding for which the evidence is sought—here a pending criminal prosecution. It is a judicial proceeding in a federal court alleging violation of federal laws and is brought in the name of the United States as sovereign. Under the authority of Article II, §2, Congress has vested in the Attorney General the power to conduct the criminal litigation of the United States Government. It has also vested in him the power to appoint subordinate officers to assist him in the discharge of his duties. Acting pursuant to those statutes, the Attorney General has delegated the authority to represent the United States in these particular matters to a Special Prosecutor with unique authority and tenure. The regulation gives the Special Prosecutor explicit power to contest the invocation of executive privilege in the process of seeking evidence deemed relevant to the performance of these specially delegated duties. . . .

So long as this regulation remains in force the Executive Branch is bound by it, and indeed the United States as the sovereign composed of the three branches is bound to respect and to enforce it. Moreover, the delegation of authority to the Special Prosecutor in this case is not an ordinary delegation by the Attorney General to a subordinate officer: with the authorization of the President, the Acting Attorney General provided in the regulation that the Special Prosecutor was not to be removed without the "consensus " of eight designated leaders of Congress. . . .

Here at issue is the production or nonproduction of specified evidence deemed by the Special Prosecutor to be relevant and admissible in a pending criminal case. It is sought by one official of the Government within the scope of his express authority; it is resisted by the Chief Executive on the ground of his duty to preserve the confidentiality of the communications of the President. Whatever the correct answer on the merits, these issues are "of a type which are traditionally justiciable." . . .

[W]e turn to the claim that the subpoena should be quashed because it demands "confidential conversations between a President and his close advisors that it would be inconsistent with the public interest to produce." The first contention is a broad claim that the separation of powers doctrine precludes judicial review of a President's claim of privilege. The second contention is that if he does not prevail on the claim of absolute privilege, the court should hold as a matter of constitutional law that the privilege prevails over the subpoena *duces tecum*.

In the performance of assigned constitutional duties each branch of the Government must initially interpret the Constitution, and the interpretation of its powers by any branch is due great respect from the others. The President's counsel, as we have noted, reads the Constitution as providing an absolute privilege of confidentiality for all presidential communications. Many decisions of this Court, however, have unequivocally reaffirmed the holding of *Marbury v. Madison*, that "it is emphatically the province and duty of the judicial department to say what the law is."

No holding of the Court has defined the scope of judicial power specifically relating to the enforcement of a subpoena for confidential presidential communications for use in a criminal prosecution, but other exercises of powers by the Executive Branch and the Legislative Branch have been found invalid as in conflict with the Constitution. *Powell v. McCormack, supra; Youngstown, supra*. In a series of cases, the Court interpreted the explicit immunity conferred by express provisions of the Constitution on Members of the House and Senate by the Speech or Debate Clause, U.S. Const. Art. 1, §6. Since this Court has consistently exercised the power to construe and delineate claims arising under express powers, it must follow that the Court has authority to interpret claims with respect to powers alleged to derive from enumerated powers.

Our system of government "requires that federal courts on occasion interpret the Constitution in a manner at variance with the construction given the document by another branch." *Powell v. McCormack*. And in *Baker v. Carr*, the Court stated:

> "[D]eciding whether a matter has in any measure been committed by the Constitution to another branch of government, or whether the action of that branch exceeds whatever

authority has been committed, is itself a delicate exercise in constitutional interpretation, and is a responsibility of this Court as ultimate interpreter of the Constitution."

Notwithstanding the deference each branch must accord the others, the "judicial power of the United States" vested in the federal courts by Art. III, § 1 of the Constitution can no more be shared with the Executive Branch than the Chief Executive, for example, can share with the Judiciary the veto power, or the Congress share with the Judiciary the power to override a presidential veto. Any other conclusion would be contrary to the basic concept of separation of powers and the checks and balances that flow from the scheme of a tripartite government. The Federalist, No. 47, p. 313. We therefore reaffirm that it is "emphatically the province and the duty" of this Court "to say what the law is" with respect to the claim of privilege presented in this case.

In support of his claim of absolute privilege, the President's counsel urges two grounds one of which is common to all governments and one of which is peculiar to our system of separation of powers. The first ground is the valid need for protection of communications between high government officials and those who advise and assist them in the performance of their manifold duties; the importance of this confidentiality is too plain to require further discussion. Human experience teaches that those who expect public dissemination of their remarks may well temper candor with a concern for appearances and for their own interests to the detriment of the decision-making process. Whatever the nature of the privilege of confidentiality of presidential communications in the exercise of Art. II powers the privilege can be said to derive from the supremacy of each branch within its own assigned area of constitutional duties. Certain powers and privileges flow from the nature of enumerated powers; the protection of the confidentiality of presidential communications has similar constitutional underpinnings.

The second ground asserted by the President's counsel in support of the claim of absolute privilege rests on the doctrine of separation of powers. Here it is argued that the independence of the Executive Branch within its own sphere, *Humphrey's Executor v. United States*, insulates a president from a judicial subpoena in an ongoing criminal prosecution, and thereby protects confidential presidential communications.

However, neither the doctrine of separation of powers, nor the need for confidentiality of high level communications, without more, can sustain an absolute, unqualified presidential privilege of immunity from judicial process under all circumstances. The President's need for complete candor and objectivity from advisers calls for great deference from the courts. However, when the privilege depends solely on the broad, undifferentiated claim of public interest in the confidentiality of such conversations, a confrontation with other values arises. Absent a claim of need to protect military, diplomatic or sensitive national security secrets, we find it difficult to accept the argument that even the very important interest in confidentiality of presidential communications is significantly diminished by production of such material for *in camera* inspection with all the protection that a district court will be obliged to provide.

The impediment that an absolute, unqualified privilege would place in the way of the primary constitutional duty of the Judicial Branch to do justice in criminal prosecutions would plainly conflict with the function of the courts under Art. III. In designing the structure of our Government and dividing and allocating the sovereign power among three coequal branches, the Framers of the Constitution sought to provide a comprehensive system, but the separate powers were not intended to operate with absolute independence. . . . To read the Art. II powers of the President as providing an absolute privilege as against a subpoena essential to enforcement of criminal statutes on no more than a generalized claim of the public interest in confidentiality of nonmilitary and nondiplomatic discussions would upset the constitutional balance of "a workable government" and gravely impair the role of the courts under Art. III.

Since we conclude that the legitimate needs of the judicial process may outweigh presidential privilege, it is necessary to resolve those competing interests in a manner that preserves the essential functions of each branch. The right and indeed the duty to resolve that question does not free the judiciary from according high respect to the representations made on behalf of the President.

The expectation of a President to the confidentiality of his conversations and correspondence, like the claim of confidentiality of judicial deliberations, for example, has all the values to which we accord deference for the privacy of all citizens and added to those values the necessity for protection of the public interest in candid, objective, and even blunt or harsh opinions in presidential decisionmaking. A President and those who assist him must be free to explore alternatives in the process of shaping policies and making decisions and to do so in a way many would be unwilling to express except privately. These are the considerations justifying a presumptive privilege for presidential communications. The privilege is fundamental to the operation of government and inextricably rooted in the separation of powers under the Constitution. In *Nixon v. Sirica*, the Court of Appeals held that such presidential communications are "presumptively privileged," and this position is accepted by both parties in the present litigation. We agree with Mr. Chief Justice Marshall's observation, therefore, that "in no case of this kind would a court be required to proceed against the President as against an ordinary individual." *United States v. Burr*.

But this presumptive privilege must be considered in light of our historic commitment to the rule of law. This is nowhere more profoundly manifest than in our view that "the twofold aim [of criminal justice] is that guilt shall not escape or innocence suffer." *Berger v. United States*. We have elected to employ an adversary system of criminal justice in which the parties contest all issues before a court of law. The need to develop all relevant facts in the adversary system is both fundamental and comprehensive. The ends of criminal justice would be defeated if judgments were to be founded on a partial or speculative presentation of the facts. The very integrity of the judicial system and public confidence in the system depend on full disclosure of all the facts, within the framework of the rules of evidence. To ensure that justice is done, it is imperative to the function of courts that compulsory process be available for the production of evidence needed either by the prosecution or by the defense.

Only recently the Court restated the ancient proposition of law, albeit in the context of a grand jury inquiry rather than a trial, " 'that the public . . . has a right to every man's evidence' except for those persons protected by a constitutional, common law, or statutory privilege." The privileges referred to by the Court are designed to protect weighty and legitimate competing interests. Thus, the Fifth Amendment to the Constitution provides that no man "shall be compelled in any criminal case to be a witness against himself." And, generally, an attorney or a priest may not be required to disclose what has been revealed in professional confidence. These and other interests are recognized in law by privileges against forced disclosure, established in the Constitution, by statute, or at common law. Whatever their origins, these exceptions to the demand for every man's evidence are not lightly created nor expansively construed, for they are in derogation of the search for truth.

In this case the President challenges a subpoena served on him as a third party requiring the production of materials for use in a criminal prosecution on the claim that he has a privilege against disclosure of confidential communications. He does not place his claim of privilege on the ground they are military or diplomatic secrets. As to these areas of Art. II duties the courts have traditionally shown the utmost deference to presidential responsibilities. . . . In *United States v. Reynolds*, dealing with a claimant's demand for evidence in a damage case against the Government the Court said:

> "It may be possible to satisfy the court, from all the circumstances of the case, that there is a reasonable danger that compulsion of the evidence will expose military matters which, in the interest of national security, should not be divulged. When this is the case, the occasion for the privilege is appropriate, and the court should not jeopardize the security which the privilege is meant to protect by insisting upon an examination of the evidence, even by the judge alone, in chambers."

No case of the Court, however, has extended this high degree of deference to a President's generalized interest in confidentiality. Nowhere in the Constitution, as we have noted earlier, is there any explicit reference to a privilege of confidentiality, yet to the extent this interest relates to the effective discharge of a President's powers, it is constitutionally based.

The right to the production of all evidence at a criminal trial similarly has constitutional dimensions. The Sixth Amendment explicitly confers upon every defendant in a criminal trial the right "to be confronted with the witnesses against him" and "to have compulsory process for obtaining witnesses in his favor." Moreover, the Fifth Amendment also guarantees that no person shall be deprived of liberty without due process of law. It is the manifest duty of the courts to vindicate those guarantees and to accomplish that it is essential that all relevant and admissible evidence be produced.

In this case we must weigh the importance of the general privilege of confidentiality of presidential communications in performance of his responsibilities against the inroads of such a privilege on the fair administration of criminal justice.* The interest in preserving confidentiality is weighty indeed and entitled to great respect. However we cannot conclude that advisers will be moved to temper the candor of their remarks by the infrequent occasions of disclosure because of the possibility that such conversations will be called for in the context of a criminal prosecution.

On the other hand, the allowance of the privilege to withhold evidence that is demonstrably relevant in a criminal trial would cut deeply into the guarantee of due process of law and gravely impair the basic function of the courts. A President's acknowledged need for confidentiality in the communications of his office is general in nature, whereas the constitutional need for production of relevant evidence in a criminal proceeding is specific and central to the fair adjudication of a particular criminal case in the administration of justice. Without access to specific facts a criminal prosecution may be totally frustrated. The President's broad interest in confidentiality of communications will not be vitiated by disclosure of a limited number of conversations preliminarily shown to have some bearing on the pending criminal cases.

We conclude that when the ground for asserting privilege as to subpoenaed materials sought for use in a criminal trial is based only on the generalized interest in confidentiality, it cannot prevail over the fundamental demands of due process of law in the fair administration of criminal justice. The generalized assertion of privilege must yield to the demonstrated, specific need for evidence in a pending criminal trial. . . .

---

*We are not here concerned with the balance between the President's generalized interest in confidentiality and the need for relevant evidence in civil litigation, nor with that between the confidentiality interest and congressional demands for information, nor with the President's interest in preserving state secrets. We address only the conflict between the President's assertion of a generalized privilege of confidentiality against the constitutional need for relevant evidence in criminal trials.

57

City of Boerne v. Flores (1997)

Justice Kennedy delivered the opinion of the Court.

A decision by local zoning authorities to deny a church a building permit was challenged under the Religious Freedom Restoration Act of 1993 (RFRA). The case calls into question the authority of Congress to enact RFRA. We conclude the statute exceeds Congress' power.

Situated on a hill in the city of Boerne, Texas, some 28 miles northwest of San Antonio, is St. Peter Catholic Church. Built in 1923, the church's structure replicates the mission style of the region's earlier history. The church seats about 230 worshippers, a number too small for its growing parish. Some 40 to 60 parishioners cannot be accommodated at some Sunday masses. In order to meet the needs of the congregation the Archbishop of San Antonio gave permission to the parish to plan alterations to enlarge the building.

A few months later, the Boerne City Council passed an ordinance authorizing the city's Historic Landmark Commission to prepare a preservation plan with proposed historic landmarks and districts. Under the ordinance, the Commission must preapprove construction affecting historic landmarks or buildings in a historic district.

Soon afterwards, the Archbishop applied for a building permit so construction to enlarge the church could proceed. City authorities, relying on the ordinance and the designation of a historic district (which, they argued, included the church), denied the application. The Archbishop brought this suit challenging the permit denial in the United States District Court for the Western District of Texas.

The complaint contained various claims, but to this point the litigation has centered on RFRA and the question of its constitutionality. The Archbishop relied upon RFRA as one basis for relief from the refusal to issue the permit. The District Court concluded that by enacting RFRA Congress exceeded the scope of its enforcement power under §5 of the Fourteenth Amendment. The court certified its order for interlocutory appeal and the Fifth Circuit reversed, finding RFRA to be constitutional. We granted certiorari, and now reverse.

From *City of Boerne v. Flores*, 521 U.S. 507 (1997).

Congress enacted RFRA in direct response to the Court's decision in *Employment Div., Dept. of Human Resources of Ore. v. Smith* (1990). There we considered a Free Exercise Clause claim brought by members of the Native American Church who were denied unemployment benefits when they lost their jobs because they had used peyote. Their practice was to ingest peyote for sacramental purposes, and they challenged an Oregon statute of general applicability which made use of the drug criminal. In evaluating the claim, we declined to apply the balancing test set forth in *Sherbert v. Verner* (1963), under which we would have asked whether Oregon's prohibition substantially burdened a religious practice and, if it did, whether the burden was justified by a compelling government interest. We stated:

> "[G]overnment's ability to enforce generally applicable prohibitions of socially harmful conduct . . . cannot depend on measuring the effects of a governmental action on a religious objector's spiritual development. To make an individual's obligation to obey such a law contingent upon the law's coincidence with his religious beliefs, except where the State's interest is 'compelling' . . . contradicts both constitutional tradition and common sense."

The application of the *Sherbert* test, the *Smith* decision explained, would have produced an anomaly in the law, a constitutional right to ignore neutral laws of general applicability. The anomaly would have been accentuated, the Court reasoned, by the difficulty of determining whether a particular practice was central to an individual's religion. We explained, moreover, that it "is not within the judicial ken to question the centrality of particular beliefs or practices to a faith, or the validity of particular litigants' interpretations of those creeds."

The only instances where a neutral, generally applicable law had failed to pass constitutional muster, the *Smith* Court noted, were cases in which other constitutional protections were at stake. In *Wisconsin v. Yoder* (1972), for example, we invalidated Wisconsin's mandatory school-attendance law as applied to Amish parents who refused on religious grounds to send their children to school. That case implicated not only the right to the free exercise of religion but also the right of parents to control their children's education.

The *Smith* decision acknowledged the Court had employed the *Sherbert* test in considering free exercise challenges to state unemployment compensation rules on three occasions where the balance had tipped in favor of the individual. Those cases, the Court explained, stand for "the proposition that where the State has in place a system of individual exemptions, it may not refuse to extend that system to cases of religious hardship without compelling reason." By contrast, where a general prohibition, such as Oregon's, is at issue, "the sounder approach, and the approach in accord with the vast majority of our precedents, is to hold the test inapplicable to [free exercise] challenges." *Smith* held that neutral, generally applicable laws may be applied to religious practices even when not supported by a compelling governmental interest.

Four Members of the Court disagreed. They argued the law placed a substantial burden on the Native American Church members so that it could be upheld only if the law served a compelling state interest and was narrowly tailored to achieve that end. Justice O'Connor concluded Oregon had satisfied the test, while Justice Blackmun, joined by Justice Brennan and Justice Marshall, could see no compelling interest justifying the law's application to the members.

These points of constitutional interpretation were debated by Members of Congress in hearings and floor debates. Many criticized the Court's reasoning, and this disagreement resulted in the passage of RFRA. Congress announced:

"(1)   [T]he framers of the Constitution, recognizing free exercise of religion as an unalienable right, secured its protection in the First Amendment to the Constitution;

"(2)   laws 'neutral' toward religion may burden religious exercise as surely as laws intended to interfere with religious exercise;

"(3)   governments should not substantially burden religious exercise without compelling justification;

"(4)   in *Employment Division v. Smith*, Supreme Court virtually eliminated the requirement that the government justify burdens on religious exercise imposed by laws neutral toward religion; and

"(5)   the compelling interest test as set forth in prior Federal court rulings is a workable test for striking sensible balances between religious liberty and competing prior governmental interests."

The Act's stated purposes are:

"(1)   to restore the compelling interest test as set forth in Sherbert v. Verner, and Wisconsin v. Yoder, and to guarantee its application in all cases where free exercise of religion is substantially burdened; and

"(2)   to provide a claim or defense to persons whose religious exercise is substantially burdened by government."

RFRA prohibits "[g]overnment" from "substantially burden[ing]" a person's exercise of religion even if the burden results from a rule of general applicability unless the government can demonstrate the burden "(1) is in furtherance of a compelling governmental interest; and (2) is the least restrictive means of furthering that compelling governmental interest." The Act's mandate applies to any "branch, department, agency, instrumentality, and official (or other person acting under color of law) of the United States," as well as to any "State, or . . . subdivision of a State." The Act's universal coverage is confirmed in §2000bb—3(a), under which RFRA "applies to all Federal and State law, and the implementation of that law, whether statutory or otherwise, and whether adopted before or after [RFRA's enactment]." In accordance with RFRA's usage of the term, we shall use "state law" to include local and municipal ordinances.

Under our Constitution, the Federal Government is one of enumerated powers. The judicial authority to determine the constitutionality of laws, in cases and controversies, is based on the premise that the "powers of the legislature are defined and limited; and that those limits may not be mistaken, or forgotten, the constitution is written."

Congress relied on its Fourteenth Amendment enforcement power in enacting the most far reaching and substantial of RFRA's provisions, those which impose its requirements on the States.

> "Section 1. . . . No State shall make or enforce any law which shall abridge the privileges or immunities of citizens of the United States; nor shall any State deprive any person of life, liberty, or property, without due process of law; nor deny to any person within its jurisdiction the equal protection of the laws.
>
> . . . . .
>
> "Section 5. The Congress shall have power to enforce, by appropriate legislation, the provisions of this article."

The parties disagree over whether RFRA is a proper exercise of Congress' §5 power "to enforce" by "appropriate legislation" the constitutional guarantee that no State shall deprive any person of "life, liberty, or property, without due process of law" nor deny any person "equal protection of the laws."

. . . In assessing the breadth of §5's enforcement power, we begin with its text. Congress has been given the power "to enforce" the "provisions of this article." . . .

Congress' power under §5, however, extends only to "enforc[ing]" the provisions of the Fourteenth Amendment. The Court has described this power as "remedial," The design of the Amendment and the text of §5 are inconsistent with the suggestion that Congress has the power to decree the substance of the Fourteenth Amendment's restrictions on the States. Legislation which alters the meaning of the Free Exercise Clause cannot be said to be enforcing the Clause. Congress does not enforce a constitutional right by changing what the right is. It has been given the power "to enforce," not the power to determine what constitutes a constitutional violation. Were it not so, what Congress would be enforcing would no longer be, in any meaningful sense, the "provisions of [the Fourteenth Amendment]."

While the line between measures that remedy or prevent unconstitutional actions and measures that make a substantive change in the governing law is not easy to discern, and Congress must have wide latitude in determining where it lies, the distinction exists and must be observed. There must be a congruence and proportionality between the injury to be prevented or remedied and the means adopted to that end. Lacking such a connection, legislation may become substantive in operation and effect. History and our case law support drawing the distinction, one apparent from the text of the Amendment. . . .

The remedial and preventive nature of Congress' enforcement power, and the limitation inherent in the power, were confirmed in our earliest cases on the Fourteenth Amendment. In the *Civil Rights Cases*, the Court invalidated sections of the Civil Rights Act of 1875 which prescribed criminal penalties for denying to any person "the full enjoyment of" public accommodations and conveyances, on the grounds that it exceeded Congress' power by seeking to regulate private conduct. The Enforcement Clause, the Court said, did not authorize Congress to pass "general legislation upon the rights of the citizen, but corrective legislation; that is, such as may be necessary and proper for counteracting such laws as the States may adopt or enforce, and which, by the amendment, they are prohibited from making or enforcing . . . ."

. . . If Congress could define its own powers by altering the Fourteenth Amendment's meaning, no longer would the Constitution be "superior paramount law, unchangeable by ordinary means." It would be "on a level with ordinary legislative acts, and, like other acts, . . . alterable when the legislature shall please to alter it." Under this approach, it is difficult to conceive of a principle that would limit congressional power. Shifting legislative majorities could change the Constitution and effectively circumvent the difficult and detailed amendment process contained in Article V.

We now turn to consider whether RFRA can be considered enforcement legislation under §5 of the Fourteenth Amendment.

Respondent contends that RFRA is a proper exercise of Congress' remedial or preventive power. . . .

While preventive rules are sometimes appropriate remedial measures, there must be a congruence between the means used and the ends to be achieved. The appropriateness of remedial measures must be considered in light of the evil presented. . . .

A comparison between RFRA and the Voting Rights Act is instructive. In contrast to the record which confronted Congress and the judiciary in the voting rights cases, RFRA's legislative record lacks examples of modern instances of generally applicable laws passed because of religious bigotry. The history of persecution in this country detailed in the hearings mentions no episodes occurring in the past 40 years.

. . . RFRA cannot be considered remedial, preventive legislation, if those terms are to have any meaning. RFRA is so out of proportion to a supposed remedial or preventive object that it cannot be understood as responsive to, or designed to prevent, unconstitutional behavior. It appears, instead, to attempt a substantive change in constitutional protections. Preventive measures prohibiting certain types of laws may be appropriate when there is reason to believe that many of the laws affected by the congressional enactment have a significant likelihood of being unconstitutional.

RFRA is not so confined. Sweeping coverage ensures its intrusion at every level of government, displacing laws and prohibiting official actions of almost every description and regardless of subject matter. RFRA's restrictions apply to every agency and official of the Federal, State, and local Governments. RFRA applies to all federal and state law, statutory or otherwise, whether adopted before or after its enactment. RFRA has no termination date or termination mechanism. Any law is subject to challenge at any time by any individual who alleges a substantial burden on his or her free exercise of religion. . . .

The stringent test RFRA demands of state laws reflects a lack of proportionality or congruence between the means adopted and the legitimate end to be achieved. If an objector can show a substantial burden on his free exercise, the State must demonstrate a compelling governmental interest and show that the law is the least restrictive means of furthering its interest. Claims that a law substantially burdens someone's exercise of religion will often be difficult to contest. Requiring a State to demonstrate a compelling interest and show that it has adopted the least restrictive means of achieving that interest is the most demanding test known to constitutional law. If " 'compelling interest' really means what it says . . . many laws will not meet the test. . . . [The test] would open the prospect of constitutionally required religious exemptions from civic obligations of almost every conceivable kind." Laws valid under *Smith* would fall under RFRA without regard to whether they had the object of stifling or punishing free exercise. We make these observations not to reargue the position of the majority in *Smith* but to illustrate the substantive alteration of its holding attempted by RFRA. Even assuming RFRA would be interpreted in effect to mandate some lesser test, say one equivalent to intermediate scrutiny, the statute nevertheless would require searching judicial scrutiny of state law with the attendant likelihood of invalidation. This is a considerable congressional intrusion into the States' traditional prerogatives and general authority to regulate for the health and welfare of their citizens.

The substantial costs RFRA exacts, both in practical terms of imposing a heavy litigation burden on the States and in terms of curtailing their traditional general regulatory power, far exceed any pattern or practice of unconstitutional conduct under the Free Exercise Clause as interpreted in *Smith*. . . . When Congress acts within its sphere of power and responsibilities, it has not just the right but the duty to make its own informed judgment on the meaning and force of the Constitution. . . .

Our national experience teaches that the Constitution is preserved best when each part of the government respects both the Constitution and the proper actions and determinations of the other branches. When the Court has interpreted the Constitution, it has acted within the province of the Judicial Branch, which embraces the duty to say what the law is. When the political branches of the Government act against the background of a judicial interpretation of the Constitution already issued, it must be understood that in later cases and controversies the Court will treat its precedents with the respect due them under settled principles, including *stare decisis,* and contrary expectations must be disappointed. RFRA was designed to control cases and controversies, such as the one before us; but as the provisions of the federal statute here invoked are beyond congressional authority, it is this Court's precedent, not RFRA, which must control.

Justice O'Connor, with whom Justice Breyer joins. . . . dissenting.

I dissent from the Court's disposition of this case. I agree with the Court that the issue before us is whether the Religious Freedom Restoration Act (RFRA) is a proper exercise of Congress' power to enforce §5 of the Fourteenth Amendment. But as a yardstick for measuring the constitutionality of RFRA, the Court uses its holding in *Employment Div., Dept. of Human Resources of Ore. v. Smith,* the decision that prompted Congress to enact RFRA as a means of more rigorously enforcing the Free Exercise Clause. I remain of the view that *Smith* was wrongly decided, and I would use this case to reexamine the Court's holding there. Therefore, I would direct the parties to brief the question whether *Smith* represents the correct understanding of the Free Exercise Clause and set the case for reargument. If the Court were to correct the misinterpretation of the Free Exercise Clause set forth in *Smith,* it would simultaneously put our First Amendment jurisprudence back on course and allay the legitimate concerns of a majority in Congress who believed that *Smith* improperly restricted religious liberty. We would then be in a position to review RFRA in light of a proper interpretation of the Free Exercise Clause. . . .

I continue to believe that *Smith* adopted an improper standard for deciding free exercise claims. In *Smith,* five Members of this Court–without briefing or argument on the issue–interpreted the Free Exercise Clause to permit the government to prohibit, without justification, conduct mandated by an individual's religious beliefs, so long as the prohibition is generally applicable. Contrary to the Court's holding in that case, however, the Free Exercise Clause is not simply an antidiscrimination principle that protects only against those laws that single out religious practice for unfavorable treatment. Rather, the Clause is best understood as an affirmative guarantee of the right to participate in religious practices and conduct without impermissible governmental interference, even when such conduct conflicts with a neutral, generally applicable law. Before *Smith,* our free exercise cases were generally in keeping with this idea: where a law substantially burdened religiously motivated conduct–regardless whether it was specifically targeted at religion or applied generally–we required government to justify that law with a compelling state interest and to use means narrowly tailored to achieve that interest. . . .

Accordingly, I believe that we should reexamine our holding in *Smith,* and do so in this very case. In its place, I would return to a rule that requires government to justify any substantial burden on religiously motivated conduct by a compelling state interest and to impose that burden only by means narrowly tailored to achieve that interest. . . .

The Religion Clauses of the Constitution represent a profound commitment to religious liberty. Our Nation's Founders conceived of a Republic receptive to voluntary religious expression, not of a secular society in which religious expression is tolerated only when it does not conflict with a generally applicable law. As the historical sources discussed above show, the Free Exercise Clause is properly understood as an affirmative guarantee of the right to participate in religious activities without impermissible governmental interference, even where a believer's conduct is in tension with a law of general application. Certainly, it is in no way anomalous to accord heightened protection to a right identified in the text of the First Amendment. For example, it has long been the Court's position that freedom of speech–a right enumerated only a few words after the right to free exercise–has special constitutional status. Given the centrality of freedom of speech and religion to the American concept of personal liberty, it is altogether reasonable to conclude that both should be treated with the highest degree of respect.

Although it may provide a bright line, the rule the Court declared in *Smith* does not faithfully serve the purpose of the Constitution. Accordingly, I believe that it is essential for the Court to reconsider its holding in *Smith*–and to do so in this very case. . . .

58

United States v. Morrison (2000)

Chief Justice Rehnquist delivered the opinion of the Court.

In these cases we consider the constitutionality of 42 U.S.C. § 13981 which provides a federal civil remedy for the victims of gender-motivated violence. The United States Court of Appeals for the Fourth Circuit, sitting en banc, struck down §13981 because it concluded that Congress lacked constitutional authority to enact the section's civil remedy. Believing that these cases are controlled by our decisions in *United States v. Lopez, United States v. Harris,* and the *Civil Rights Cases,* we affirm.

Petitioner Christy Brzonkala enrolled at Virginia Polytechnic Institute (Virginia Tech) in the fall of 1994. In September of that year, Brzonkala met

From *United States v. Morrison,* 529 U.S. 598 (2000).

respondents Antonio Morrison and James Crawford, who were both students at Virginia Tech and members of its varsity football team. Brzonkala alleges that, within 30 minutes of meeting Morrison and Crawford, they assaulted and repeatedly raped her. After the attack, Morrison allegedly told Brzonkala, "You better not have any . . . diseases." In the months following the rape, Morrison also allegedly announced in the dormitory's dining room that he "like[d] to get girls drunk and . . .

. . . In December 1995, Brzonkala sued Morrison, Crawford, and Virginia Tech in the United States District Court for the Western District of Virginia. Her complaint alleged that Morrison's and Crawford's attack violated §13981 and that Virginia Tech's handling of her complaint violated Title IX of the Education Amendments of 1972. Morrison and Crawford moved to dismiss this complaint on the grounds that it failed to state a claim and that §13981's civil remedy is unconstitutional. The United States intervened to defend §13981's constitutionality.

The District Court dismissed Brzonkala's Title IX claims against Virginia Tech for failure to state a claim upon which relief can be granted. It then held that Brzonkala's complaint stated a claim against Morrison and Crawford under §13981, but dismissed the complaint because it concluded that Congress lacked authority to enact the section under either the Commerce Clause or §5 of the Fourteenth Amendment.

A divided panel of the Court of Appeals reversed the District Court, reinstating Brzonkala's §13981 claim and her Title IX hostile environment claim. The full Court of Appeals vacated the panel's opinion and reheard the case en banc. The en banc court then issued an opinion affirming the District Court's conclusion that Brzonkala stated a claim under §13981 because her complaint alleged a crime of violence and the allegations of Morrison's crude and derogatory statements regarding his treatment of women sufficiently indicated that his crime was motivated by gender animus. Nevertheless, the court by a divided vote affirmed the District Court's conclusion that Congress lacked constitutional authority to enact §13981's civil remedy. Because the Court of Appeals invalidated a federal statute on constitutional grounds, we granted certiorari.

. . . Due respect for the decisions of a coordinate branch of Government demands that we invalidate a congressional enactment only upon a plain showing that Congress has exceeded its constitutional bounds. With this presumption of constitutionality in mind, we turn to the question whether §13981 falls within Congress' power under Article I, §8, of the Constitution.

. . . [O]ur interpretation of the Commerce Clause has changed as our Nation has developed. . . . [I]n the years since *NLRB v. Jones & Laughlin Steel Corp.*, Congress has had considerably greater latitude in regulating conduct and transactions under the Commerce Clause than our previous case law permitted. . . .

. . . "[E]ven [our] modern-era precedents which have expanded congressional power under the Commerce Clause confirm that this power is subject to outer limits. In *Jones & Laughlin Steel*, the Court warned that the scope of the interstate commerce power 'must be considered in the light of our dual system of government and may not be extended so as to embrace effects upon interstate commerce so indirect and remote that to embrace them, in view of our complex society, would effectually obliterate the distinction between what is national and what is local and create a completely centralized government.' "

. . . [M]odern Commerce clause jurisprudence has "identified three broad categories of activity that Congress may regulate under its commerce power." "First, Congress may regulate the use of the channels of interstate commerce." Second, Congress is empowered to regulate and protect the instrumentalities of interstate commerce, or persons or things in interstate commerce, even though the threat may come only from intrastate activities." "Finally, Congress' commerce authority includes the power to regulate those activities having a substantial relation to interstate commerce, . . . *i.e.*, those activities that substantially affect interstate commerce."

Petitioners do not contend that these cases fall within either of the first two of these categories of Commerce Clause regulation. They seek to sustain §13981 as a regulation of activity that substantially affects interstate commerce. Given §13981's focus on gender-motivated violence wherever it occurs (rather than violence directed at the instrumentalities of interstate commerce, interstate markets, or things or persons in interstate commerce), we agree that this is the proper inquiry.

Since [*U.S. v*] *Lopez* most recently canvassed and clarified our case law governing this third category of Commerce Clause regulation, it provides the proper framework for conducting the required analysis of §13981. In *Lopez*, we held that the Gun-Free School Zones Act of 1990, which made it a federal crime to knowingly possess a firearm in a school zone, exceeded Congress' authority under the Commerce Clause. Several significant considerations contributed to our decision.

First, we observed that [it] was "a criminal statute that by its terms has nothing to do with 'commerce' or any sort of economic enterprise, however broadly one might define those terms." Reviewing our case law, we noted that "we have upheld a wide variety of congressional Acts regulating intrastate economic activity where we have concluded that the activity substantially affected interstate commerce." . . . [W]e stated that the pattern of analysis is clear. "Where economic activity substantially affects interstate commerce, legislation regulating that activity will be sustained."

Both petitioners and Justice Souter's dissent downplay the role that the economic nature of the regulated activity plays in our Commerce Clause analysis. But a fair reading of *Lopez* shows that the noneconomic, criminal nature of the conduct at issue was central to our decision in that case. . . . ("Admittedly, a determination whether an intrastate activity is commercial or noncommercial may in some cases result in legal uncertainty. But, so long as Congress' authority is limited to those powers enumerated in the Constitution, and so long as those enumerated powers are interpreted as having judicially enforceable outer limits, congressional legislation under the Commerce Clause always will engender 'legal uncertainty' "). . . .

. . . *Lopez*'s review of Commerce Clause case law demonstrates that in those cases where we have sustained federal regulation of intrastate activity based upon the activity's substantial effects on interstate commerce, the activity in question has been some sort of economic endeavor.

Gender-motivated crimes of violence are not, in any sense of the phrase, economic activity. While we need not adopt a categorical rule against aggregating the effects of any noneconomic activity in order to decide these cases, thus far in our Nation's history our cases have upheld Commerce Clause regulation of intrastate activity only where that activity is economic in nature.

. . . [T]he concern that we expressed in *Lopez* that Congress might use the Commerce Clause to completely obliterate the Constitution's distinction between national and local authority seems well founded. The reasoning that petitioners advance seeks to follow the but-for causal chain from the initial occurrence of violent crime (the suppression of which has always been the prime object of the States' police power) to every attenuated effect upon interstate commerce. If accepted, petitioners' reasoning would allow Congress to regulate any crime as long as the nationwide, aggregated impact of that crime has substantial effects on employment, production, transit, or consumption. Indeed, if Congress may regulate gender-motivated violence, it would be able to regulate murder or any other type of violence since gender-motivated violence, as a subset of all violent crime, is certain to have lesser economic impacts than the larger class of which it is a part.

Petitioners' reasoning, moreover, will not limit Congress to regulating violence but may, as we suggested in *Lopez*, be applied equally as well to family law and other areas of traditional state regulation since the aggregate effect of marriage, divorce, and childrearing on the national economy is undoubtedly significant. Congress may have recognized this specter when it expressly precluded §13981 from being used in the family law context. Under our written Constitution, however, the limitation of congressional authority is not solely a matter of legislative grace.

We accordingly reject the argument that Congress may regulate noneconomic, violent criminal conduct based solely on that conduct's aggregate effect on interstate commerce. The Constitution requires a distinction between what is truly national and what is truly local. In recognizing this fact we preserve one of the few principles that has been consistent since the

Clause was adopted. The regulation and punishment of intrastate violence that is not directed at the instrumentalities, channels, or goods involved in interstate commerce has always been the province of the States. Indeed, we can think of no better example of the police power, which the Founders denied the National Government and reposed in the States, than the suppression of violent crime and vindication of its victims.

Petitioner Brzonkala's complaint alleges that she was the victim of a brutal assault. But Congress' effort in §13981 to provide a federal civil remedy can be sustained neither under the Commerce Clause nor under §5 of the Fourteenth Amendment. If the allegations here are true, no civilized system of justice could fail to provide her a remedy for the conduct of respondent Morrison. But under our federal system that remedy must be provided by the Commonwealth of Virginia, and not by the United States.

Justice Breyer, with whom Justice Stevens joins, and with whom Justice Souter and Justice Ginsburg join, dissenting.

No one denies the importance of the Constitution's federalist principles. Its state/federal division of authority protects liberty—both by restricting the burdens that government can impose from a distance and by facilitating citizen participation in government that is closer to home. The question is how the judiciary can best implement that original federalist understanding where the Commerce Clause is at issue.

The majority holds that the federal commerce power does not extend to such "noneconomic" activities as "noneconomic, violent criminal conduct" that significantly affects interstate commerce only if we "aggregate" the interstate "effect[s]" of individual instances. . . . [T]he majority's holding illustrates the difficulty of finding a workable judicial Commerce Clause touchstone—a set of comprehensible interpretive rules that courts might use to impose some meaningful limit, but not too great a limit, upon the scope of the legislative authority that the Commerce Clause delegates to Congress.

Consider the problems. The "economic/noneconomic" distinction is not easy to apply. Does the local street corner mugger engage in "economic" activity or "noneconomic" activity when he mugs for money? Would evidence that desire for economic domination underlies many brutal crimes against women save the present statute?

The line becomes yet harder to draw given the need for exceptions. The Court itself would permit Congress to aggregate, hence regulate, "noneconomic" activity taking place at economic establishments. And it would permit Congress to regulate where that regulation is "an essential part of a larger regulation of economic activity, in which the regulatory scheme could be undercut unless the intrastate activity were regulated." Given the former exception, can Congress simply rewrite the present law and limit its application to restaurants, hotels, perhaps universities, and other places of public accommodation? Given the latter exception, can Congress save the present law by including it, or much of it, in a broader "Safe Transport" or "Workplace Safety" act?

More important, why should we give critical constitutional importance to the economic, or noneconomic, nature of an interstate-commerce-affecting *cause?* If chemical emanations through indirect environmental change cause identical, severe commercial harm outside a State, why should it matter whether local factories or home fireplaces release them? The Constitution itself refers only to Congress' power to "regulate Commerce . . . among the several States," and to make laws "necessary and proper" to implement that power. Art.I, §8, cls.3, 18. The language says nothing about either the local nature, or the economic nature, of an interstate-commerce-affecting cause.

. . . [I]n a world where most everyday products or their component parts cross interstate boundaries, Congress will frequently find it possible to redraft a statute using language that ties the regulation to the interstate movement of some relevant object, thereby regulating local criminal activity or, for that matter, family affairs. Though this possibility does not give the Federal Government the power to regulate everything, it means that any substantive limitation will apply randomly in terms of the interests the majority seeks to protect. How much would be gained, for example, were Congress to reenact the present law in the form of "An Act Forbidding Violence Against Women Perpetrated at Public Accommodations or by Those Who Have Moved in, or through the Use of Items that Have Moved in, Interstate Commerce"? Complex Commerce Clause rules creating fine distinctions that achieve only random results do little to further the important federalist interests that called them into being. That is why modern (pre-*Lopez*) case law rejected them.

The majority, aware of these difficulties, is nonetheless concerned with what it sees as an important contrary consideration. To determine the lawfulness of statutes simply by asking whether Congress could reasonably have found that aggregated local instances significantly affect interstate commerce will allow Congress to regulate almost anything. Virtually all local activity, when instances are aggregated, can have "substantial effects on employment, production, transit, or consumption." Hence Congress could "regulate any crime," and perhaps "marriage, divorce, and childrearing" as well, obliterating the "Constitution's distinction between national and local authority."

This consideration, however, while serious, does not reflect a jurisprudential defect, so much as it reflects a practical reality. We live in a Nation knit together by two centuries of scientific, technological, commercial, and environmental change. Those changes, taken together, mean that virtually every kind of activity, no matter how local, genuinely can affect commerce, or its conditions, outside the State—at least when considered in the aggregate.

And that fact makes it close to impossible for courts to develop meaningful subject-matter categories that would exclude some kinds of local activities from ordinary Commerce Clause "aggregation" rules without, at the same time, depriving Congress of the power to regulate activities that have a genuine and important effect upon interstate commerce.

Since judges cannot change the world, the "defect" means that, within the bounds of the rational, Congress, not the courts, must remain primarily responsible for striking the appropriate state/federal balance. Congress is institutionally motivated to do so. Its Members represent state and local district interests. They consider the views of state and local officials when they legislate, and they have even developed formal procedures to ensure that such consideration takes place. Moreover, Congress often can better reflect state concerns for autonomy in the details of sophisticated statutory schemes than can the judiciary, which cannot easily gather the relevant facts and which must apply more general legal rules and categories. Not surprisingly, the bulk of American law is still state law, and overwhelmingly so.

. . . Moreover, as Justice Souter has pointed out, Congress compiled a "mountain of data" explicitly documenting the interstate commercial effects of gender-motivated crimes of violence. After considering alternatives, it focused the federal law upon documented deficiencies in state legal systems. And it tailored the law to prevent its use in certain areas of traditional state concern, such as divorce, alimony, or child custody. Consequently, the law before us seems to represent an instance, not of state/federal conflict, but of state/federal efforts to cooperate in order to help solve a mutually acknowledged national problem.

. . . I continue to agree with Justice Souter that the Court's traditional "rational basis" approach is sufficient. But I recognize that the law in this area is unstable and that time and experience may demonstrate both the unworkability of the majority's rules and the superiority of Congress' own procedural approach—in which case the law may evolve towards a rule that, in certain difficult Commerce Clause cases, takes account of the thoroughness with which Congress has considered the federalism issue.

59

William J. Brennan, Jr.

Constitutional Interpretation (1985)

. . . [T]he text I have chosen for exploration is the amended Constitution of the United States, which, of course, entrenches the Bill of Rights and the Civil War amendments, and draws sustenance from the bedrock principles of another great text, the Magna Carta. So fashioned, the Constitution embodies the aspiration to social justice, brotherhood, and human dignity that brought this nation into being. The Declaration of Independence, the Constitution and the Bill of Rights solemnly committed the United States to be a country where the dignity and rights of all persons were equal before all authority. In all candor we must concede that part of this egalitarianism in America has been more pretension than realized fact. But we are an aspiring people, a people with faith in progress. Our amended Constitution is the lodestar for our aspirations. Like every text worth reading, it is not crystalline. The phrasing is broad and the limitations of its provisions are not clearly marked. Its majestic generalities and ennobling pronouncements are both luminous and obscure. This ambiguity of course calls forth interpretation, the interaction of reader and text. The encounter with the constitutional text has been, in many senses, my life's work.

My approach to this text may differ from the approach of other participants in this symposium to their texts. Yet such differences may themselves stimulate reflection about what it is we do when we "interpret" a text. Thus I will attempt to elucidate my approach to the text as well as my substantive interpretation.

Perhaps the foremost difference is the fact that my encounters with the constitutional text are not purely or even primarily introspective; the Constitution cannot be for me simply a contemplative haven for private moral reflection. My relation to this great text is inescapably public. That is not to say that my reading of the text is not a personal reading, only that the personal

From "Address to the Text and Teaching Symposium," Georgetown University, October 12, 1985, Washington, D.C.

reading perforce occurs in a public context, and is open to critical scrutiny from all quarters.

The Constitution is fundamentally a public text—the monumental charter of a government and a people—and a Justice of the Supreme Court must apply it to resolve public controversies. For, from our beginning, a most important consequence of the constitutionally created separation of powers has been the American habit, extraordinary to other democracies, of casting social, economic, philosophical and political questions in the form of lawsuits, in an attempt to secure ultimate resolution by the Supreme Court. In this way, important aspects of the most fundamental issues confronting our democracy may finally arrive in the Supreme Court for judicial determination. Not infrequently, these are the issues upon which contemporary society is most deeply divided. They arouse our deepest emotions. The main burden of my twenty-nine terms on the Supreme Court has thus been to wrestle with the Constitution in this heightened public context, to draw meaning from the text in order to resolve public controversies.

Two other aspects of my relation to this text warrant mention. First, constitutional interpretation for a federal judge is, for the most part, obligatory. When litigants approach the bar of court to adjudicate a constitutional dispute, they may justifiably demand an answer. Judges cannot avoid a definitive interpretation because they feel unable to, or would prefer not to, penetrate to the full meaning of the Constitution's provisions. Unlike literary critics, judges cannot merely savor the tensions or revel in the ambiguities inhering in the text—judges must resolve them.

Second, consequences flow from a Justice's interpretation in a direct and immediate way. A judicial decision respecting the incompatibility of Jim Crow with a constitutional guarantee of equality is not simply a contemplative exercise in defining the shape of a just society. It is an order—supported by the full coercive power of the State—that the present society change in a fundamental aspect. Under such circumstances the process of deciding can be a lonely, troubling experience for fallible human beings conscious that their best may not be adequate to the challenge. We Justices are certainly aware that we are not final because we are infallible; we know that we are infallible only because we are final. One does not forget how much may depend on the decision. More than the litigants may be affected. The course of vital social, economic and political currents may be directed.

These three defining characteristics of my relation to the constitutional text—its public nature, obligatory character, and consequentialist aspect cannot help but influence the way I read that text. When Justices interpret the Constitution they speak for their community, not for themselves alone. The act of interpretation must be undertaken with full consciousness that it is, in a very real sense, the community's interpretation that is sought. Justices are not platonic guardians appointed to wield authority to their personal moral predilections. Precisely because coercive force must attend any judicial decision to countermand the will of a contemporary majority, the Justices must render constitutional interpretations that are received as legitimate. The source of legitimacy is, of course, a wellspring of controversy in legal and political circles. At the core of the debate is what the late Yale Law School Professor Alexander Bickel labeled "the counter-majoritarian difficulty." Our commitment to self-governance in a representative democracy must be reconciled with vesting in electorally unaccountable Justices the power to invalidate the expressed desires of representative bodies on the ground of inconsistency with higher law. Because judicial power resides in the authority to give meaning to the Constitution, the debate is really a debate about how to read the text, about constraints on what is legitimate interpretation.

There are those who find legitimacy in fidelity to what they call "the intentions of the Framers." In its most doctrinaire incarnation, this view demands that Justices discern exactly what the Framers thought about the question under consideration and simply follow that intention in resolving the case before them. It is a view that feigns self-effacing deference to the specific judgments of those who forged our original social compact. But in truth it is little more than arrogance cloaked as humility. It is arrogant to pretend that from our vantage we can gauge accurately the intent of the Framers on application of principle to specific, contemporary questions. All too often, sources of potential enlightenment such as records of the ratification debates provide sparse or ambiguous evidence of the original intention. Typically, all that can be gleaned is that the Framers themselves did not agree about the application or meaning of particular constitutional provisions, and hid their differences in cloaks of generality. Indeed, it is far from clear whose intention is relevant—that of the drafters, the congressional disputants, or the ratifiers in the states—or even whether the idea of an original intention is a coherent way of thinking about a jointly drafted document drawing its authority from a general assent of the states. And apart from the problematic nature of the sources, our distance of two centuries cannot but work as a prism refracting all we perceive. One cannot help but speculate that the chorus of lamentations calling for interpretation faithful to "original intention"—and proposing nullification of interpretations that fail this quick litmus test—must inevitably come from persons who have no familiarity with the historical record.

Perhaps most importantly, while proponents of this facile historicism justify it as a depoliticization of the judiciary, the political underpinnings of such a choice should not escape notice. A position that upholds constitutional claims only if they were within the specific contemplation of the Framers in effect establishes a presumption of resolving textual ambiguities against the claim of constitutional right. It is far from clear what justifies such a presumption against claims of right. Nothing intrinsic in the nature of interpretation—if there is such a thing as the "nature" of interpretation—commands such a passive approach to ambiguity. This is a choice no less political than any other; it expresses antipathy to claims of the minority rights against the majority. Those who would restrict claims of right to the values of 1789 specifically articulated in the Constitution turn a blind eye to social progress and eschew adaptation of overarching principles to changes of social circumstance.

Another, perhaps more sophisticated, response to the potential power of judicial interpretation stresses democratic theory: because ours is a government of the people's elected representatives, substantive value choices should by and large be left to them. This view emphasizes not the transcendant historical authority of the Framers but the predominant contemporary authority of the elected branches of government. Yet it has similar consequences for the nature of proper judicial interpretation. Faith in the majoritarian process counsels restraint. Even under more expansive formulations of this approach, judicial review is appropriate only to the extent of ensuring that our democratic process functions smoothly. Thus, for example, we would protect freedom of speech merely to ensure that the people are heard by their representatives, rather than as a separate, substantive value. When, by contrast, society tosses up to the Supreme Court a dispute that would require invalidation of a legislature's substantive policy choice, the Court generally would stay its hand because the Constitution was meant as a plan of government and not as an embodiment of fundamental substantive values.

The view that all matters of substantive policy should be resolved through the majoritarian process has appeal under some circumstances, but I think it ultimately will not do. Unabashed enshrinement of majority will would permit the imposition of a social caste system or wholesale confiscation of property so long as a majority of the authorized legislative body, fairly elected, approved. Our Constitution could not abide such a situation. It is the very purpose of a Constitution—and particularly of the Bill of Rights—to declare certain values transcendent, beyond the reach of temporary political majorities. The majoritarian process cannot be expected to rectify claims of minority right that arise as a response to the outcomes of that very majoritarian process. . . .

Faith in democracy is one thing, blind faith quite another. Those who drafted our Constitution understood the difference. One cannot read the text without admitting that it embodies substantive value choices; it places certain values beyond the power of any legislature. Obvious are the separation of powers; the privilege of the Writ of Habeas Corpus; prohibition of Bills of Attainder and *ex post facto* laws; prohibition of cruel and unusual punishments; the requirement of just compensation for official taking of property; the prohibition of laws tending to establish religion or enjoining the free exercise of religion; and, since the Civil War, the banishment of slavery and official race discrimination. With respect to at least such principles, we simply have not constituted ourselves as strict utilitarians. While the Constitution may be amended, such amendments require an immense effort by the People as a whole.

To remain faithful to the content of the Constitution, therefore, an approach to interpreting the text must account for the existence of these substantive value choices, and must accept the ambiguity inherent in the effort to apply them to modern circumstances. The Framers discerned fundamental principles through struggles against particular malefactions of the Crown; the struggle shapes the particular contours of the articulated principles. But our acceptance of the fundamental principles has not and should not bind us to those precise, at times anachronistic, contours. Successive generations of Americans have continued to respect these fundamental choices and adopt them as their own guide to evaluating quite different historical practices. Each generation has the choice to overrule or add to the fundamental principles enunciated by the Framers; the Constitution can be amended or it can be ignored. Yet with respect to its fundamental principles, the text has suffered neither fate. Thus, if I may borrow the words of an esteemed predecessor, Justice Robert Jackson, the burden of judicial interpretation is to translate "the majestic generalities of the Bill of Rights, conceived as part of the pattern of liberal government in the eighteenth century, into concrete restraints on officials dealing with the problems of the twentieth century." *Board of Education v. Barnette*, [319 U.S. 624, 639 (1943)].

We current justices read the Constitution in the only way that we can: as Twentieth Century Americans. We look to the history of the time of framing and to the intervening history of interpretation. But the ultimate question must be, what do the words of the text mean in our time? For the genius of the Constitution rests not in any static meaning it might have had in a world that is dead and gone, but in the adaptability of its great principles to cope with current problems and current needs. What the constitutional fundamentals meant to the wisdom of other times cannot be their measure to the vision of our time. Similarly, what those fundamentals mean for us, our descendants will learn, cannot be the measure to the vision of their time. This realization is not, I assure you, a novel one of my own creation. Permit me to quote from one of the opinions of our Court, *Weems v. United States*, [217 U.S. 349] written nearly a century ago:

> Time works changes, brings into existence new conditions and purposes. Therefore, a principle to be vital must be capable of wider application than the mischief which gave it birth. This is peculiarly true of constitutions. They are not ephemeral enactments, designed to meet passing occasions. They are, to use the words of Chief Justice John Marshall, 'designed to approach immortality as nearly as human institutions can approach it.' The future is their care and provision for events of good and bad tendencies of which no prophesy can be made. In the application of a constitution, therefore, our contemplation cannot be only of what has been, but of what may be.

Interpretation must account for the transformative purpose of the text. Our Constitution was not intended to preserve a preexisting society but to make a new one, to put in place new principles that the prior political community had not sufficiently recognized. Thus, for example, when we interpret the Civil War Amendments to the charter—abolishing slavery, guaranteeing blacks equality under law, and guaranteeing blacks the right to vote—we must remember that those who put them in place had no desire to enshrine the status quo. Their goal was to make over their world, to eliminate all vestige of slave caste.

Having discussed at some length how I, as a Supreme Court Justice, interact with this text, I think it time to turn to the fruits of this discourse. For the Constitution is a sublime oration on the dignity of man, a bold commitment by a people to the ideal of libertarian dignity protected through law. Some reflection is perhaps required before this can be seen.

The Constitution on its face is, in large measure, a structuring text, a blueprint for government. And when the text is not prescribing the form of government it is limiting the powers of that government. The original document, before addition of any of the amendments, does not speak primarily of the rights of man, but of the abilities and disabilities of government. When one reflects upon the text's preoccupation with the scope of government as well as its shape, however, one comes to understand that what this text is about is the relationship of the individual and the state. The text marks the metes and bounds of official authority and individual autonomy. When one studies the boundary that the text marks out, one gets a sense of the vision of the individual embodied in the Constitution.

As augmented by the Bill of Rights and the Civil War amendments, this text is a sparkling vision of the supremacy of the human dignity of every individual. This vision is reflected in the very choice of democratic self-governance: the supreme value of a democracy is the presumed worth of each individual. And this vision manifests itself most dramatically in the specific prohibitions of the Bill of Rights, a term which I henceforth will apply to describe not only the original first eight amendments, but the Civil War amendments as well. It is a vision that has guided us as a people throughout our history, although the precise rules by which we have protected fundamental human dignity have been transformed over time in response to both transformations of social condition and evolution of our concepts of human dignity.

Until the end of the nineteenth century, freedom and dignity in our country found meaningful protection in the institution of real property. In a society still largely agricultural, a piece of land provided men not just with sustenance but with the means of economic independence, a necessary precondition of political independence and expression. Not surprisingly, property relationships formed the heart of litigation and of legal practice, and lawyers and judges tended to think stable property relationships the highest aim of the law.

But the days when common law property relationships dominated litigation and legal practice are past. To a growing extent economic existence now depends on less certain relationships with government—licenses, employment, contracts, subsidies, unemployment benefits, tax exemptions, welfare and the like. Government participation in the economic existence of individuals is pervasive and deep. Administrative matters and other dealings with government are at the epicenter of the exploding law. We turn to government and to the law for controls which would never have been expected or tolerated before this century, when a man's answer to economic oppression or difficulty was to move two hundred miles west. Now hundreds of thousands of Americans live entire lives without any real prospect of the dignity and autonomy that ownership of real property could confer. Protection of the human dignity of such citizens requires a much modified view of the proper relationship of individual and state.

In general, problems of the relationship of the citizen with government have multiplied and thus have engendered some of the most important constitutional issues of the day. As government acts ever more deeply upon those areas of our lives once marked "private," there is an even greater need to see that individual rights are not curtailed or cheapened in the interest of what may temporarily appear to be the "public good." And as government continues in its role of provider for so many of our disadvantaged citizens, there is an even greater need to ensure that government act with integrity and consistency in its dealings with these citizens. To put this another way, the possibilities for collision between government activity and individual rights will increase as the power and authority of government itself expands, and this growth, in turn, heightens the need for constant vigilance at the collision points. If our free society is to endure, those who govern must recognize human dignity and accept the enforcement of constitutional limitations on their power conceived by the Framers to be necessary to preserve that dignity and the air of freedom which is our proudest heritage. Such recognition will not come from a technical understanding of the organs of government, or the new forms of wealth they administer. It requires something different, something deeper—a personal confrontation with the wellsprings of our society. . . .

I do not mean to suggest that we have in the last quarter century achieved a comprehensive definition of the constitutional ideal of human dignity. We are still striving toward that goal, and doubtless it will be an eternal quest. For if the interaction of this Justice and the constitutional text over the years confirms any single proposition, it is that the demands of human dignity will never cease to evolve. . . .

60

Robert H. Bork

Testimony Before the Senate Judiciary Committee (1987)

Judge Bork: I want to begin by thanking the President for placing my name in nomination for this most important position. . . .

As you have said, quite correctly, Mr. Chairman, and as others have said here today, this is in large measure a discussion of judicial philosophy, and I want to make a few remarks at the outset on that subject of central interest.

That is, my understanding of how a judge should go about his or her work. That may also be described as my philosophy of the role of a judge in a constitutional democracy.

The judge's authority derives entirely from the fact that he is applying the law and not his personal values. That is why the American public accepts the decisions of its courts, accepts even decisions that nullify the laws a majority of the electorate or of their representatives voted for.

The judge, to deserve that trust and that authority, must be every bit as governed by law as is the Congress, the President, the State Governors and legislatures, and the American people. No one, including a judge, can be above the law. Only in that way will justice be done and the freedom of Americans assured.

How should a judge go about finding the law? The only legitimate way, in my opinion, is by attempting to discern what those who made the law intended. The intentions of the lawmakers govern whether the lawmakers are the Congress of the United States enacting a statute or whether they are those who ratified our Constitution and its various Amendments.

Where the words are precise and the facts simple, that is a relatively easy task. Where the words are general, as is the case with some of the most profound protections of our liberties—in the Bill of Rights and in the Civil War Amendments—the task is far more complex. It is to find the principle or value that was intended to be protected and to see that it is protected.

As I wrote in an opinion for our court, the judge's responsibility "is to discern how the framers' values, defined in the context of the world they knew, apply in the world we know."

From Hearings Before the Committee on the Judiciary, United States Senate, 100th Congress First Session, Sept. 15, 1987, Senate No. J-100-4.

If a judge abandons intention as his guide, there is no law available to him and he begins to legislate a social agenda for the American people. That goes well beyond his legitimate power.

He or she then diminishes liberty instead of enhancing it. That is why I agree with Judge Learned Hand, one of the great jurists in our history, when he wrote that the judge's "authority and his immunity depend upon the assumption that he speaks with the mouths of others: the momentum of his utterances must be greater than any which his personal reputation and character can command if it is to do the work assigned to it—if it is to stand against the passionate resentments arising out of the interests he must frustrate." To state that another way, the judge must speak with the authority of the past and yet accommodate that past to the present.

The past, however, includes not only the intentions of those who first made the law, it also includes those past judges who interpreted it and applied it in prior cases. That is why a judge must have great respect for precedent. It is one thing as a legal theorist to criticize the reasoning of a prior decision, even to criticize it severely, as I have done. It is another and more serious thing altogether for a judge to ignore or overturn a prior decision. That requires much careful thought.

Times come, of course, when even a venerable precedent can and should be overruled. The primary example of a proper overruling is *Brown v. Board of Education*, the case which outlawed racial segregation accomplished by government action. *Brown* overturned the rule of separate but equal laid down 58 years before in *Plessy v. Ferguson*. Yet *Brown*, delivered with the authority of a unanimous Court, was clearly correct and represents perhaps the greatest moral achievement of our constitutional law.

Nevertheless, overruling should be done sparingly and cautiously. Respect for precedent is a part of the great tradition of our law, just as is fidelity to the intent of those who ratified the Constitution and enacted our statutes. That does not mean that constitutional law is static. It will evolve as judges modify doctrine to meet new circumstances and new technologies. Thus, today we apply the first amendment's guarantee of the freedom of the press to radio and television, and we apply to electronic surveillance the fourth amendment's guarantee of privacy for the individual against unreasonable searches of his or her home.

I can put the matter no better than I did in an opinion on my present court. Speaking of the judge's duty, I wrote: "The important thing, the ultimate consideration, is the constitutional freedom that is given into our keeping. A judge who refuses to see new threats to an established constitutional value and hence provides a crabbed interpretation that robs a provision of its full, fair and reasonable meaning, fails in his judicial duty. That duty, I repeat, is to ensure that the powers and freedoms the framers specified are made effective in today's circumstances."

But I should add to that passage that when a judge goes beyond this and reads entirely new values into the Constitution, values the framers and the ratifiers did not put there, he deprives the people of their liberty. That liberty, which the Constitution clearly envisions, is the liberty of the people to set their own social agenda through the processes of democracy.

Conservative judges frustrated that process in the mid-1930's by using the concept they had invented, the 14th amendment's supposed guarantee of a liberty of contract, to strike down laws designed to protect workers and labor unions. That was wrong then and it would be wrong now.

My philosophy of judging, Mr. Chairman, as you pointed out, is neither liberal nor conservative. It is simply a philosophy of judging which gives the Constitution a full and fair interpretation but, where the Constitution is silent, leaves the policy struggles to the Congress, the President, the legislatures and executives of the 50 States, and to the American people.

I welcome this opportunity to come before the committee and answer whatever questions the members may have. I am quite willing to discuss with you my judicial philosophy and the approach I take to deciding cases. I cannot, of course, commit myself as to how I might vote on any particular case and I know you would not wish me to do that. . . .

61

Thomas Jefferson and James Madison

Exchange on the Binding of Generations (1789–1790)

THOMAS JEFFERSON TO JAMES MADISON

Paris September 6, 1789.

Dear Sir

I sit down to write to you without knowing by what occasion I shall send my letter. I do it because a subject comes into my head which I would wish to develop a little more than is practicable in the hurry of the moment of making up general dispatches.

From *The Papers of Thomas Jefferson*, Vol. 15, Princeton University Press, 1969.

The question whether one generation of men has a right to bind another, seems never to have been stated either on this or our side of the water. Yet it is a question of such consequences as not only to merit decision, but place also, among the fundamental principles of every government. The course of reflection in which we are immersed here on the elementary principles of society has presented this question to my mind; and that no such obligation can be so transmitted I think very capable of proof.—I set out on this ground, which I suppose to be self evident, '*that the earth belongs in usufruct to the living*': that the dead have neither powers nor rights over it. The portion occupied by any individual ceases to be his when himself ceases to be, and reverts to the society. If the society has formed no rules for the appropriation of its lands in severalty, it will be taken by the first occupants. These will generally be the wife and children of the decedent. If they have formed rules of appropriation, those rules may give it to the wife and children, or to some one of them, or to the legatee of the deceased. So they may give it to his creditor. But the child, the legatee, or creditor takes it, not by any natural right, but by a law of the society of which they are members, and to which they are subject. Then no man can, by natural right, oblige the lands he occupied, or the persons who succeed him in that occupation, to the payment of debts contracted by him. For if he could, he might, during his own life, eat up the usufruct of the lands for several generations to come, and then the lands would belong to the dead, and not to the living, which would be the reverse of our principle.

What is true of every member of the society individually, is true of them all collectively, since the rights of the whole can be no more than the sum of the rights of the individuals.—To keep our ideas clear when applying them to a multitude, let us suppose a whole generation of men to be born on the same day, to attain mature age on the same day, and to die on the same day, leaving a succeeding generation in the moment of attaining their mature age all together. Let the ripe age be supposed of 21 years, and their period of life 34 years more, that being the average term given by the bills of mortality to persons who have already attained 21 years of age. Each successive generation would, in this way, come on, and go off the stage at a fixed moment, as individuals do now. Then I say the earth belongs to each of these generations, during its course, fully, and in their own right. The 2d. generation receives it clear of the debts and incumberances of the 1st. the 3d of the 2d. and so on. For if the 1st. could charge it with a debt, then the earth would belong to the dead and not the living generation. Then no generation can contract debts greater than may be paid during the course of its own existence. . . .— But a material difference must be noted between the succession of an individual, and that of a whole generation. Individuals are parts only of a society, subject to the laws of the whole. These laws may appropriate the portion of land occupied by a decendent to his creditor rather than to any other, or to his child on condition he satisfies the creditor. But when a whole generation, that is, the whole society dies, as in the case we have supposed, and another generation or society succeeds, this forms a whole, and there is no superior who can give their territory to a third society, who may have lent money to their predecessors beyond their faculties of paying.

What is true of a generation all arriving to self-government on the same day, and dying all on the same day, is true of those in a constant course of decay and renewal, with this only difference. A generation coming in and going out entire, as in the first case, would have a right in the 1st. year of their self-dominion to contract a debt for 33. years, in the 10th. for 24. in the 20th. for 14. in the 30th. for 4. whereas generations, changing daily by daily deaths and births, have one constant term, beginning at the date of their contract, and ending when a majority of those of full age at that date shall be dead. The length of that term may be estimated from the tables of mortality, corrected by the circumstances of climate, occupation &c. peculiar to the country of the contractors. Take, for instance, the table of M. de Buffon wherein he states 23,994 deaths, and the ages at which they happened. Suppose a society in which 23,994 persons are born every year, and live to the ages stated in this table. The conditions of that society will be as follows. 1st. It will consist constantly of 617,703. persons of all ages. 2ly. Of those living at any one instant of time, one half will be dead in 24 years 8 months. 3dly. 10,675 will arrive every year at the age of 21 years complete. 4ly. It will constantly have 348,417 persons of all ages above 21 years. 5ly. And the half of those of 21 years and upwards living at any one instant of time will be dead in 18 years 8 months, or say 19 years as the nearest integral number. Then 19 years is the term beyond which neither the representatives of a nation, nor even the whole nation itself assembled, can validly extend a debt. . . .

I suppose that the received opinion, that the public debts of one generation devolve on the next, has been suggested by our seeing habitually in private life that he who succeeds to lands is required to pay the debts of his ancestor or testator: without considering that this requisition is municipal only, not moral; flowing from the will of the society, which has found it convenient to appropriate lands, become vacant by the death of their occupant, on the condition of a payment of his debts: but that between society and society, or generation and generation, there is no municipal obligation, no umpire but the law of nature. We seem not to have perceived that, by the law of nature, one generation is to another as one independent nation to another.

The interest of the national debt of France being in fact but a two thousandth part of its rent roll, the payment of it is practicable enough: and so becomes a question merely of honor, or of expediency. But with respect to future debts, would it not be wise and just for that nation to declare, in the constitution they are forming, that neither the legislature, nor the nation itself, can validly contract more debt than they may pay within their own age, or within the term of 19 years? And that all future contracts will be deemed void as to what shall remain unpaid at the end of 19 years from their date? This would put the tenders, and the borrowers also, on their guard. By reducing too the faculty of borrowing within its natural limits, it would bridle the spirit of war, to which too free a course has been procured by the inattention of money-lenders to this law of nature, that succeeding generations are not responsible for the preceding.

On similar ground it may be proved that no society can make a perpetual constitution, or even a perpetual law. The earth belongs always to the living generation. They may manage it then, and what proceeds from it, as they please, during their usufruct. They are masters too of their own persons, and consequently may govern them as they please. But persons and property make the sum of the objects of government. The constitution and the laws of their predecessors extinguished then in their natural course with those who gave them being. This could preserve that being till it ceased to be itself, and no longer. Every constitution then, and every law, naturally expires at the end of 19 years. If it be enforced longer, it is an act of force, and not of right.—It may be said that the succeeding generation exercising in fact the power of repeal, this leaves them as free as if the constitution or law had been expressly limited to 19 years only. In the first place, this objection admits the right, in proposing an equivalent. But the power of repeal is not an equivalent. It might be indeed if every form of government were so perfectly contrived that the will of the majority could always be obtained fairly and without impediment. But this is true of no form. The people cannot assemble themselves. Their representation is unequal and vicious. Various checks are opposed to every legislative proposition. Factions get possession of the public councils. Bribery corrupts them. Personal interests lead them astray from the general interests of their constituents: and other impediments arise so as to prove to every practical man that a law of limited duration is much more manageable than one which needs a repeal. . . .

Turn this subject in your mind, my dear Sir, and particularly as to the power of contracting debts; and develop it with that perspicuity and cogent logic so peculiarly yours. Your station in the councils of our country gives you an opportunity of producing it to public consideration, of forcing it into discussion. At first blush it may be rallied, as a theoretical speculation: but examination will prove it to be solid and salutary. It would furnish matter for a fine preamble to our first law for appropriating the public revenue; and it will exclude at the threshold of our new government the contagious and ruinous errors of this quarter of the globe, which have armed despots with means, not sanctioned by nature, for binding in chains their fellow men. We have already given in example one effectual check to the Dog of war by transferring the power of letting him loose from the Executive to the Legislative body, from those who are to spend to those who are to pay. I should be pleased to see this second obstacle held out by us also in the first instance. No nation can make a declaration against the validity of long-contracted debts so disinterestedly as we, since we do not owe a shilling which may not be paid with ease, principal and interest, within the time of our own lives.—Establish the principle also in the new law to be passed for protecting copyrights and new inventions, by securing the exclusive right for 19 instead of 14 years. Besides familiarizing us to this term, it will be an instance the more of our taking reason for our guide, instead of English precedent, the habit of which fetters us with all the political heresies of a nation equally remarkable for its early excitement from some errors, and long slumbering under others. . . .

JAMES MADISON TO THOMAS JEFFERSON

New York Feb. 4, 1790

Dear Sir

Your favor of Jan. 9 enclosing one of Sept. last did not get to hand till a few days ago. The idea which the latter evolves is a great one; and suggests many interesting reflections to legislators; particularly when contracting and providing for public debts. Whether it can be received in the extent to which your reasonings carry it, is a question which I ought to turn more in my thoughts than I have yet been able to do, before I should be justified in making up a full opinion on it. My first thoughts lead me to view the doctrine as not in all respects, compatible with the course of human affairs. I will endeavor to sketch the grounds of my skepticism.

> "As the Earth belongs to the living, not to the dead, a living generation can bind itself only: in every Society the will of the majority binds the whole: according to the laws of mortality, a majority of those ripe for the exercise of their will do not live beyond the term of 19 years: to this term then is limited the validity of every act of the Society; nor can any act be continued beyond this term without an *express* declaration of the public will." This I understand to be the outline of the argument.

The acts of a political society may be divided into three classes.

1. The fundamental constitution of the government.
2. Laws involving some stipulation, which renders them irrevocable at the will of the legislature.
3. Laws involving no such irrevocable quality.

1. However applicable in theory the doctrine may be to a Constitution, it seems liable in practice to some weighty objections.

Would not a government ceasing of necessity at the end of a given term, unless prolonged by some constitutional act, previous to its expiration, be too subject to the casualty and consequences of an interregnum?

Would not a government so often revised become too mutable and novel to retain that share of prejudice in its favor which is a salutary aid to the most rational government?

Would not such a periodical revision engender pernicious factions that might not otherwise come into existence; and agitate the public mind more frequently and more violently than might be expedient?

2. In the second class of acts involving stipulations, must not exceptions at least to the doctrine, be admitted?

If the earth be the gift of *nature* to the living, their title can extend to the earth in its *natural* state only. The *improvements* made by the dead form a debt against the living who take the benefit of them. This debt cannot be otherwise discharged than by a proportionate obedience to the will of the authors of the improvements.

But a case less liable to be controverted may perhaps be stated. Debts may be incurred with a direct view to the interest of the unborn as well as of the living: Such are debts for repelling a conquest, the evils of which descend through many generations. Debts may even be incurred principally for the benefit of posterity: Such perhaps is the debt incurred by the U. States. In these instances the debts might not be dischargeable within the term of 19 years.

There seems then to be some foundation in the nature of things; in the relation which one generation bears to another, for the *descent* of obligations from one to another. Equity may require it. Mutual good may be promoted by it. And all that seems indispensable in stating the account between the dead and the living, is to see that the debits against the latter do not exceed the advances made by the former. Few of the incumbrances entailed on nations by their predecessors would bear a liquidation even on this principle.

3. Objections to the doctrine, as applied to the third class of acts must be merely practical. But in that view alone they appear to be material.

Unless such temporary laws should be kept in force by acts regularly anticipating their expiration, all the rights depending on positive laws, that is most of the rights of property would become absolutely defunct, and the most violent struggles ensue between the parties interested in reviving and those interested in reforming the antecedent state of property. Nor does it seem improbable that such an event might be suffered to take place. The checks and difficulties opposed to the passage of laws which render the power of repeal inferior to an opportunity to reject as a security against oppression, would here render the latter an insecure provision against anarchy. Add to this that the very possibility of an event so hazardous to the rights of property could not but depreciate its value; that the approach of the crisis would increase the effect; that the frequent return of periods superceding all the obligations depending on antecedent laws and usages, must by weakening the sense of them, co-operate with motives to licenciousness already too powerful; and that the general uncertainty and vicisitudes of such a state of things would, on one side, discourage every useful effort of steady industry pursued under the sanction of existing laws, and on the other, give an immediate advantage to the more sagacious over the less sagacious part of the society.

I can find no relief from such embarrassments, but in the received doctrine that a *tacit* assent may be given to established governments and laws, and that this assent is to be inferred from the omission of an express revocation. It seems more practicable to remedy by well constituted governments, the pestilent operation of this doctrine, in the unlimited sense in which it is at present received than it is to find a remedy for the evils necessarily springing from an unlimited admission of the contrary doctrine.

Is it not doubtful whether it be possible to exclude wholly the idea of an implied or tacit assent, without subverting the very foundation of civil society?

On what principle is it that the voice of the majority binds the minority? It does not result I conceive from a law of nature but from compact founded on utility. A greater proportion might be required by the fundamental constitution of society, if under any particular circumstances it were judged eligible. Prior therefore to the establishment of this principle, unanimity was necessary; and rigid theory, accordingly presupposes the assent of every individual to the rule, which subjects the minority to the will of the majority. If this assent cannot be given tacitly, or be not implied where no positive evidence forbids, no person born in society, could on attaining ripe age, be bound by any acts, of the majority, and either a unanimous renewal of every law would be necessary, as often as a new member should be added to the society, or the express consent of every new member be obtained to the rule by which the majority decides for the whole.

If these observations be not misapplied, it follows that a limitation of the validity of all acts to the computed life of the generation establishing them, is in some cases not required by theory, and in others not consistent with practice. They are not meant however to impeach either the utility of the principle as applied to the cases you have particularly in view, or the general importance of it in the eye of the philosophical legislator. On the contrary it would give me singular pleasure to see it first announced to the world in a law of the U. States, and always kept in view as a salutary restraint on living generations from unjust and unnecessary burdens on their successors. This is a pleasure however which I have no hope of enjoying. The spirit of philosophical legislation has not prevailed at all in some parts of America, and is by no means the fashion of this part, or of the present representative body. The evils suffered or feared from weakness in government and licenciousness in the people, have turned the attention more towards the means of strengthening the powers of the former, than of narrowing their extent in the minds of the latter. Besides this it is so much easier to descry the little difficulties immediately incident to every great plan, than to comprehend its general and remote benefits, that further light must be added to the councils of our country before many truths which are seen through the medium of philosophy, become visible to the naked eye of the ordinary politician.

62

James Madison

Federalist 49 (1788)

The author of the *Notes on the State of Virginia,* quoted in the last paper, has subjoined to that valuable work the draught of a constitution, which had been prepared in order to be laid before a convention expected to be called in 1783, by the legislature, for the establishment of a constitution for that commonwealth. . . . One of the precautions which he proposes, and on which he appears ultimately to rely as a palladium to the weaker departments of power against the invasions of the stronger, is perhaps altogether his own. . . .

His proposition is "that whenever any two of the three branches of government shall concur in opinion, each by the voices of two thirds of their whole number, that a convention is necessary for altering the Constitution, *or correcting breaches of it,* a convention shall be called for the purpose."

As the people are the only legitimate fountain of power, and it is from them that the constitutional charter, under which the several branches of government hold their power, is derived, it seems strictly consonant to the republican theory to recur to the same original authority, not only whenever it may be necessary to enlarge, diminish, or new-model the powers of government, but also whenever any one of the departments may commit encroachments on the chartered authorities of the others. The several departments being perfectly coordinate by the terms of their common commission, neither of them, it is evident, can pretend to an exclusive or superior right of settling the boundaries between their respective powers; and how are the encroachments of the stronger to be prevented, or the wrongs of the weaker to be redressed, without an appeal to the people themselves, who, as the grantors of the commission, can alone declare its true meaning, and enforce its observance? . . .

From *The Federalist.*

In the next place, it may be considered as an objection inherent in the principle that as every appeal to the people would carry an implication of some defect in the government, frequent appeals would, in great measure, deprive the government of that veneration which time bestows on everything, and without which perhaps the wisest and freest governments would not possess the requisite stability. If it be true that all governments rest on opinion, it is no less true that the strength of opinion in each individual, and its practical influence on his conduct, depend much on the number which he supposes to have entertained the same opinion. The reason of man, like man himself, is timid and cautious when left alone, and acquires firmness and confidence in proportion to the number with which it is associated. When the examples which fortify opinion are ancient as well as numerous, they are known to have a double effect. In a nation of philosophers, this consideration ought to be disregarded. A reverence for the laws would be sufficiently inculcated by the voice of an enlightened reason. But a nation of philosophers is as little to be expected as the philosophical race of kings wished for by Plato. And in every other nation, the most rational government will not find it a superfluous advantage to have the prejudices of the community on its side.

The danger of disturbing the public tranquillity by interesting too strongly the public passions is a still more serious objection against a frequent reference of constitutional questions to the decision of the whole society. Notwithstanding the success which has attended the revisions of our established forms of government and which does so much honor to the virtue and intelligence of the people of America, it must be confessed that the experiments are of too ticklish a nature to be unnecessarily multiplied. We are to recollect that all the existing constitutions were formed in the midst of a danger which repressed the passions most unfriendly to order and concord; of an enthusiastic confidence of the people in their patriotic leaders, which stifled the ordinary diversity of opinions on great national questions; of a universal ardor for new and opposite forms, produced by a universal resentment and indignation against the ancient government; and whilst no spirit of party connected with the changes to be made, or the abuses to be reformed, could mingle its leaven in the operation. The future situations in which we must expect to be usually placed do not present any equivalent security against the danger which is apprehended.

But the greatest objection of all is that the decisions which would probably result from such appeals would not answer the purpose of maintaining the constitutional equilibrium of the government. We have seen that the tendency of republican governments is to an aggrandizement of the legislative at the expense of the other departments. The appeals to the people, therefore, would usually be made by the executive and judiciary departments. But whether made by one side or the other, would each side enjoy equal advantages on the trial? Let us view their different situations. The members of the executive and judiciary departments are few in number, and can be personally known to a small part only of the people. The latter, by the mode of their appointment, as well as by the nature and permanency of it, are too far removed from the people to share much in their prepossessions. The former are generally the objects of jealousy and their administration is always liable to be discolored and rendered unpopular. The members of the legislative department, on the other hand, are numerous. They are distributed and dwell among the people at large. Their connections of blood, of friendship, and of acquaintance embrace a great proportion of the most influential part of the society. The nature of their public trust implies a personal influence among the people, and that they are more immediately the confidential guardians of the rights and liberties of the people. With these advantages it can hardly be supposed that the adverse party would have an equal chance for a favorable issue.

But the legislative party would not only be able to plead their cause most successfully with the people. They would probably be constituted themselves the judges. The same influence which had gained them an election into the legislature would gain them a seat in the convention. . . .

63

California v. Bakke (1978)

Justice POWELL announced the judgment of the Court.

This case presents a challenge to the special admissions program of the petitioner, the Medical School of the University of California at Davis, which is designed to assure the admission of a specified number of students from certain minority groups. The Superior Court of California sustained respondent's challenge, holding that petitioner's program violated the California Constitution, Title VI of the Civil Rights Act of 1964, and the Equal Protection Clause of the Fourteenth Amendment. The court enjoined petitioner from considering respondent's race or the race of any other applicant in making admissions decisions. It refused, however, to order respondent's admission to the Medical School, holding that he had not carried his burden of proving that he would have been admitted but for

From *Regents of the University of California v. Allan Bakke*, 438 U.S. 277 (1978).

the constitutional and statutory violations. The Supreme Court of California affirmed those portions of the trial court's judgment declaring the special admissions program unlawful and enjoining petitioner from considering the race of any applicant. It modified that portion of the judgment denying respondent's requested injunction and directed the trial court to order his admission.

For the reasons stated in the following opinion, I believe that so much of the judgment of the California court as holds petitioner's special admissions program unlawful and directs that respondent be admitted to the Medical School must be affirmed. . . .

I also conclude for the reasons stated in the following opinion that the portion of the court's judgment enjoining petitioner from according any consideration to race in its admissions process must be reversed. . . .

In this Court the parties neither briefed nor argued the applicability of Title VI of the Civil Rights Act of 1964. Rather, as had the California court, they focused exclusively upon the validity of the special admissions program under the Equal Protection Clause. Because it was possible, however, that a decision on Title VI might obviate resort to constitutional interpretation, we requested supplementary briefing on the statutory issue. . . .

The language of §601, 78 Stat. 252, like that of the Equal Protection Clause, is majestic in its sweep:

> "No person in the United States shall, on the ground of race, color, or national origin, be excluded from participation in, be denied the benefits of, or be subjected to discrimination under any program or activity receiving Federal financial assistance."

The concept of "discrimination," like the phrase "equal protection of the laws," is susceptible of varying interpretations, for as Mr. Justice Holmes declared, "[a] word is not a crystal, transparent and unchanged, it is the skin of a living thought and may vary greatly in color and content according to the circumstances and the time in which it is used." We must, therefore, seek whatever aid is available in determining the precise meaning of the statute before us. . . .

The problem confronting Congress was discrimination against Negro citizens at the hands of recipients of federal moneys. . . . Over and over again, proponents of the bill detailed the plight of Negroes seeking equal treatment in such programs. There simply was no reason for Congress to consider the validity of hypothetical preferences that might be accorded minority citizens. . . .

In addressing that problem, supporters of Title VI repeatedly declared that the bill enacted constitutional principles. . . . In the Senate, Senator Humphrey declared that the purpose of Title VI was "to insure that Federal funds are spent in accordance with the Constitution and the moral sense of the Nation." Senator Ribicoff agreed that Title VI embraced the constitutional standard: "Basically, there is a constitutional restriction against discrimination in the use of federal funds; and Title VI simply spells out the procedure to be used in enforcing that restriction." Other Senators expressed similar views. . . .

In view of the clear legislative intent, Title VI must be held to proscribe only those racial classifications that would violate the Equal Protection Clause or the Fifth Amendment. . . .

The parties do disagree as to the level of judicial scrutiny to be applied to the special admissions program. Petitioner argues that the court below erred in applying strict scrutiny. . . . That level of review, petitioner asserts, should be reserved for classifications that disadvantage "discrete and insular minorities." Respondent, on the other hand, contends that the California court correctly rejected the notion that the degree of judicial scrutiny accorded a particular racial or ethnic classification hinges upon membership in a discrete and insular minority and duly recognized that the "rights established [by the Fourteenth Amendment] are personal rights." . . .

The special admissions program is undeniably a classification based on race and ethnic background. To the extent that there existed a pool of at least minimally qualified minority applicants to fill the 16 special admissions seats, white applicants could compete only for 84 seats in the entering class, rather than the 100 open to minority applicants. . . .

The guarantees of the Fourteenth Amendment extend to all persons. . . . The guarantee of equal protection cannot mean one thing when applied to one individual and something else when applied to a person of another color. If both are not accorded the same protection, then it is not equal. . . . Racial and ethnic distinctions of any sort are inherently suspect and thus call for the most exacting judicial examination. . . .

Although many of the Framers of the Fourteenth Amendment conceived of its primary function as bridging the vast distance between members of the Negro race and the white "majority," the Amendment itself was framed in universal terms, without reference to color, ethnic origin, or condition of prior servitude. As this Court recently remarked in interpreting the 1866 Civil Rights Act to extend to claims of racial discrimination against white persons, "the 39th Congress was intent upon establishing in the federal law a broader principle than would have been necessary simply to meet the particular and immediate plight of the newly freed Negro slaves." . . .

Over the past 30 years, this Court has embarked upon the crucial mission of interpreting the Equal Protection Clause with the view of assuring to all persons "the protection of equal laws." . . .

Petitioner urges us to adopt for the first time a more restrictive view of the Equal Protection Clause and hold that discrimination against members of the white "majority" cannot be suspect if its purpose can be characterized as "benign." . . . It is far too late to argue that the guarantee of equal protection to *all* persons permits the recognition of special wards entitled to a degree of protection greater than that accorded others. . . .

[T]he difficulties entailed in varying the level of judicial review according to a perceived "preferred" status of a particular racial or ethnic minority are intractable. The concepts of "majority" and "minority" necessarily reflect temporary arrangements and political judgments. As observed above, the white "majority" itself is composed of various minority groups, most of which can lay claim to a history of prior discrimination at the hands of the State and private individuals. Not all of these groups can receive preferential treatment and corresponding judicial tolerance of distinctions drawn in terms of race and nationality, for then the only "majority" left would be a new minority of white Anglo-Saxon Protestants. There is no principled basis for deciding which groups would merit "heightened judicial solicitude" and which would not. Courts would be asked to evaluate the extent of the prejudice and consequent harm suffered by various minority groups. Those whose societal injury is thought to exceed some arbitrary level of tolerability then would be entitled to preferential classifications at the expense of individuals belonging to other groups. Those classifications would be free from exacting judicial scrutiny. As these preferences began to have their desired effect, and the consequences of past discrimination were undone, new judicial rankings would be necessary. The kind of variable sociological and political analysis necessary to produce such rankings simply does not lie within the judicial competence—even if they otherwise were politically feasible and socially desirable.

Moreover, there are serious problems of justice connected with the idea of preference itself. First, it may not always be clear that a so-called preference is in fact benign. . . . [P]referential programs may only reinforce common stereotypes holding that certain groups are unable to achieve success without special protection based on a factor having no relationship to individual worth. [Moreover,] there is a measure of inequity in forcing innocent persons in respondent's position to bear the burdens of redressing grievances not of their making.

By hitching the meaning of the Equal Protection Clause to these transitory considerations, we would be holding, as a constitutional principle, that judicial scrutiny of classifications touching on racial and ethnic background may vary with the ebb and flow of political forces. Disparate constitutional tolerance of such classifications well may serve to exacerbate racial and ethnic antagonisms rather than alleviate them. Also, the mutability of a constitutional principle, based upon shifting political and social judgments, undermines the chances for consistent application of the Constitution from one generation to the next, a critical feature of its coherent interpretation. In expounding the Constitution, the Court's role is to discern "principles sufficiently absolute to give them roots throughout the community and continuity over significant periods of time, and to lift them above the level of the pragmatic political judgments of a particular time and place." . . .

We have held that in "order to justify the use of a suspect classification, a State must show that its purpose or interest is both constitutionally permissible and substantial, and that its use of the classification is 'necessary . . . to the accomplishment' of its purpose or the safeguarding of its interest." The special admissions program purports to serve the purposes of: (i) "reducing the historic deficit of traditionally disfavored minorities in medical schools and in the medical profession," (ii) countering the effects of societal discrimination; (iii) increasing the number of physicians who will practice in communities currently underserved; and (iv) obtaining the educational benefits that flow from an ethnically diverse student body. It is necessary to decide which, if any, of these purposes is substantial enough to support the use of a suspect classification.

If petitioner's purpose is to assure within its student body some specified percentage of a particular group merely because of its race or ethnic origin, such a preferential purpose must be rejected not as insubstantial but as facially invalid. Preferring members of any one group for no reason other than race or ethnic origin is discrimination for its own sake. This the Constitution forbids. . . .

We have never approved a classification that aids persons perceived as members of relatively victimized groups at the expense of other innocent individuals in the absence of judicial, legislative, or administrative findings of constitutional or statutory violations. After such findings have been made, the governmental interest in preferring members of the injured groups at the expense of others is substantial, since the legal rights of the victims must be vindicated. In such a case, the extent of the injury and the consequent remedy will have been judicially, legislatively, or administratively defined. Also, the remedial action usually remains subject to continuing oversight to assure that it will work the least harm possible to other innocent persons competing for the benefit. Without such findings of constitutional or statutory violations, it cannot be said that the government has any greater interest in helping one individual than in refraining from harming another. Thus, the government has no compelling justification for inflicting such harm.

Petitioner does not purport to have made, and is in no position to make, such findings. Its broad mission is education, not the formulation of any legislative policy or the adjudication of particular claims of illegality. . . .

Petitioner identifies, as another purpose of its program, improving the delivery of health-care services to communities currently underserved. It may be assumed that in some situations a State's interest in facilitating the health care of its citizens is sufficiently compelling to support the use of a suspect classification. But there is virtually no evidence in the record indicating that petitioner's special admissions program is either needed or geared to promote that goal. . . . [T]here are more precise and reliable ways to identify applicants who are genuinely interested in the medical problems of minorities than by race. An applicant of whatever race who has demonstrated his concern for disadvantaged minorities in the past and who declares that practice in such a community is his primary professional goal would be more likely to contribute to alleviation of the medical shortage than one who is chosen entirely on the basis of race and disadvantage. . . .

The fourth goal asserted by petitioner is the attainment of a diverse student body. This clearly is a constitutionally permissible goal for an institution of higher education. Physicians serve a heterogeneous population. An otherwise qualified medical student with a particular background—whether it be ethnic, geographic, culturally advantaged or disadvantaged—may bring to a professional school of medicine experiences, outlooks, and ideas that enrich the training of its student body and better equip its graduates to render with understanding their vital service to humanity. . . .

It may be assumed that the reservation of a specified number of seats in each class for individuals from the preferred ethnic groups would contribute to the attainment of considerable ethnic diversity in the student body. But petitioner's argument that this is the only effective means of serving the interest of diversity is seriously flawed. . . . The diversity that furthers a compelling state interest encompasses a far broader array of qualifications and characteristics of which racial or ethnic origin is but a single though important element. . . .

The experience of other university admissions programs, which take race into account in achieving the educational diversity valued by the First Amendment, demonstrates that the assignment of a fixed number of places to a minority group is not a necessary means toward that end. An illuminating example is found in the Harvard College program. . . .

In such an admissions program, race or ethnic background may be deemed a "plus" in a particular applicant's file, yet it does not insulate the individual from comparison with all other candidates for the available seats. . . . This kind of program treats each applicant as an individual in the admissions process. The applicant who loses out on the last available scat to another candidate receiving a "plus" on the basis of ethnic background will not have been foreclosed from all consideration for that seat simply because he was not the right color or had the wrong surname. It would mean only that his combined qualifications, which may have included similar nonobjective factors, did not outweigh those of the other applicant. His qualifications would have been weighed fairly and competitively, and he would have no basis to complain of unequal treatment under the Fourteenth Amendment. . . .

In summary, it is evident that the Davis special admissions program involves the use of an explicit racial classification never before countenanced by this Court. It tells applicants who are not Negro, Asian, or Chicano that they are totally excluded from a specific percentage of the seats in an entering class. No matter how strong their qualifications, quantitative and extracurricular, including their own potential for contribution to educational diversity, they are never afforded the chance to compete with applicants from the preferred groups for the special admissions seats. At the same time, the preferred applicants have the opportunity to compete for every seat in the class.

The fatal flaw in petitioner's preferential program is its disregard of individual rights as guaranteed by the Fourteenth Amendment. Such rights are not absolute. But when a State's distribution of benefits or imposition of burdens hinges on ancestry or the color of a person's skin, that individual is entitled to a demonstration that the challenged classification is necessary to promote a substantial state interest. Petitioner has failed to carry this burden. For this reason, that portion of the California court's judgment holding petitioner's special admissions program invalid under the Fourteenth Amendment must be affirmed.

In enjoining petitioner from ever considering the race of any applicant, however, the courts below failed to recognize that the State has a substantial interest that legitimately may be served by a properly devised admissions program involving the competitive consideration of race and ethnic origin. For this reason, so much of the California court's judgment as enjoins petitioner from any consideration of the race of any applicant must be reversed. . . .

Opinion of Justice BRENNAN, Justice WHITE, Justice MARSHALL, and Justice BLACKMUN, concurring in the judgment in part and dissenting in part.

The threshold question we must decide is whether Title VI of the Civil Rights Act of 1964 bars recipients of federal funds from giving preferential consideration to disadvantaged members of racial minorities as part of a program designed to enable such individuals to surmount the obstacles imposed by racial discrimination. . . .

In our view, Title VI prohibits only those uses of racial criteria that would violate the Fourteenth Amendment if employed by a State or its agencies; it does not bar the preferential treatment of racial minorities as a means of remedying past societal discrimination to the extent that such action is consistent with the Fourteenth Amendment. . . .

The history of Title VI . . . reveals one fixed purpose: to give the Executive Branch of Government clear authority to terminate federal funding of private programs that use race as a means of disadvantaging minorities in a manner that would be prohibited by the Constitution if engaged in by government. . . . Congress' equating of Title VI's prohibition with the commands of the Fifth and Fourteenth Amendments, its refusal precisely to define that racial discrimination which it intended to prohibit, and its expectation that the statute would be administered in a flexible manner, compel the conclusion that Congress intended the meaning of the statute's prohibition to evolve with the interpretation of the commands of the Constitution. Thus, any claim that the use of racial criteria is barred by the plain language of the statute must fail in light of the remedial purpose of Title VI and its legislative history. . . . Section 602 of Title VI instructs federal agencies to promulgate regulations interpreting Title VI. These regulations, which, under the terms of the statute, require Presidential approval, are entitled to considerable deference in construing Title VI. Consequently, it is most significant that the Department of Health, Education, and Welfare (HEW), which provides much of the federal assistance to institutions of higher education, has adopted regulations *requiring* affirmative measures designed to enable racial minorities which have been previously discriminated against by a federally funded institution or program to overcome the effects of such actions and *authorizing* the voluntary undertaking of affirmative-action programs by federally funded institutions that have not been guilty of prior discrimination in order to overcome the effects of conditions which have adversely affected the degree of participation by persons of a particular race. . . . These regulations clearly establish that where there is a need to overcome the effects of past racially discriminatory or exclusionary practices engaged in by a federally funded institution, race-conscious action is not only permitted but required to accomplish the remedial objectives of Title VI. . . .

Finally, congressional action subsequent to the passage of Title VI eliminates any possible doubt about Congress' views concerning the permissibility of racial preferences for the purpose of assisting disadvantaged racial minorities. It confirms that Congress did not intend to prohibit and does not now believe that Title VI prohibits the consideration of race as part of a remedy for societal discrimination even where there is no showing that the institution extending the preference has been guilty of past discrimination nor any judicial finding that the particular beneficiaries of the racial preference have been adversely affected by societal discrimination. . . .

Our cases have always implied that an "overriding statutory purpose" could be found that would justify racial classifications. . . . And in *North Carolina Board of Education v. Swann* we held, again unanimously, that a statute mandating color-blind school-assignment plans could not stand "against the background of segregation," since such a limit on remedies would "render illusory the promise of Brown [I]."

We conclude, therefore, that racial classifications are not per se invalid under the Fourteenth Amendment. Accordingly, we turn to the problem of articulating what our role should be in reviewing state action that expressly classifies by race. . . .

Unquestionably we have held that a government practice or statute which restricts "fundamental rights" or which contains "suspect classifications" is to be subjected to "strict scrutiny" and can be justified only if it furthers a compelling government purpose and, even then, only if no less restrictive alternative is available. But no fundamental right is involved here. Nor do whites as a class have any of the "traditional indicia of suspectness: the class is not saddled with such disabilities, or subjected to such a history of purposeful unequal treatment, or relegated to such a position of political powerlessness as to command extraordinary protection from the majoritarian political process.". . .

[B]ecause of the significant risk that racial classifications established for ostensibly benign purposes can be misused, causing effects not unlike those created by invidious classifications, it is inappropriate to inquire only whether there is any conceivable basis that might sustain such a classification. Instead, to justify such a classification an important and articulated purpose for its use must be shown. In addition, any statute must be stricken that stigmatizes any group or that singles out those least well represented in the political process to bear the brunt of a benign program. . . .

Davis' articulated purpose of remedying the effects of past societal discrimination is, under our cases, sufficiently important to justify the use of race-conscious admissions programs where there is a sound basis for concluding that minority underrepresentation is substantial and chronic, and that the handicap of past discrimination is impeding access of minorities to the Medical School. . . .

Properly construed . . . our prior cases unequivocally show that a state government may adopt race-conscious programs if the purpose of such programs is to remove the disparate racial impact its actions might otherwise have and if there is reason to believe that the disparate impact is itself the product of past discrimination, whether its own or that of society at large. There is no question that Davis' program is valid under this test.

Certainly, on the basis of the undisputed factual submissions before this Court, Davis had a sound basis for believing that the problem of underrepresentation of minorities was substantial and chronic and that the problem was attributable to handicaps imposed on minority applicants by past and present racial discrimination. Until at least 1973, the practice of medicine in this country was, in fact, if not in law, largely the prerogative of whites. . . .

Davis clearly could conclude that the serious and persistent underrepresentation of minorities in medicine depicted by these statistics is the result of handicaps under which minority applicants labor as a consequence of a background of deliberate, purposeful discrimination against minorities in education and in society generally, as well as in the medical profession. From the inception of our national life, Negroes have been subjected to unique legal disabilities impairing access to equal educational opportunity. . . . The generation of minority students applying to Davis Medical School since it opened in 1968— most of whom were born before or about the time *Brown I* was decided— clearly have been victims of this discrimination. Judicial decrees recognizing discrimination in public education in California testify to the fact of widespread discrimination suffered by California-born minority applicants; many minority group members living in California, moreover, were born and reared in school districts in Southern States segregated by law. Since separation of school-children by race "generates a feeling of inferiority as to their status in the community that may affect their hearts and minds in a way unlikely ever to be undone," *Brown I,* the conclusion is inescapable that applicants to medical school must be few indeed who endured the effects of *de jure* segregation, the resistance to *Brown I,* or the equally debilitating pervasive private discrimination fostered by our long history of official discrimination, and yet come to the starting line with an education equal to whites. . . .

The second prong of our test—whether the Davis program stigmatizes any discrete group or individual and whether race is reasonably used in light of the program's objectives—is clearly satisfied by the Davis program.

It is not even claimed that Davis' program in any way operates to stigmatize or single out any discrete and insular, or even any identifiable, non-minority group. Nor will harm comparable to that imposed upon racial minorities by exclusion or separation on grounds of race be the likely result of the program. It does not, for example, establish an exclusive preserve for minority students apart from and exclusive of whites. Rather, its purpose is to overcome the effects of segregation by bringing the races together. True, whites are excluded from participation in the special admissions program, but this fact only operates to reduce the number of whites to be admitted in the regular admissions program in order to permit admission of a reasonable percentage—less than their proportion of the California population—of otherwise underrepresented qualified minority applicants.

Nor was Bakke in any sense stamped as inferior by the Medical School's rejection of him. Indeed, it is conceded by all that he satisfied those criteria regarded by the school as generally relevant to academic performance better than most of the minority members who were admitted. Moreover, there is absolutely no basis for concluding that Bakke's rejection as a result of Davis' use of racial preference will affect him throughout his life in the same way as the segregation of the Negro schoolchildren in *Brown I* would have affected them. Unlike discrimination against racial minorities, the use of racial preferences for remedial purposes does not inflict a pervasive injury upon individual whites in the sense that wherever they go or whatever they do there is a significant likelihood that they will be treated as second-class citizens because of their color. . . .

Accordingly, we would reverse the judgment of the Supreme Court of California holding the Medical School's special admissions program unconstitutional and directing respondent's admission, as well as that portion of the judgment enjoining the Medical School from according any consideration to race in the admissions process.

Justice BLACKMUN.

I participate fully, of course, in the opinion that bears the names of my Brothers BRENNAN, WHITE, MARSHALL, and myself. I add only some general observations that hold particular significance for me, and then a few comments on equal protection.

It is gratifying to know that the Court at least finds it constitutional for an academic institution to take race and ethnic background into consideration as one factor, among many, in the administration of its admissions program. I presume that that factor always has been there, though perhaps not conceded or even admitted. It is a fact of life, however, and a part of the real world of which we are all a part. The sooner we get down the road toward accepting and being a part of the real world, and not shutting it out and away from us, the sooner will these difficulties vanish from the scene.

I suspect that it would be impossible to arrange an affirmative-action program in a racially neutral way and have it successful. To ask that this be so is to demand the impossible. In order to get beyond racism, we must first take account of race. There is no other way. And in order to treat some persons equally, we must treat them differently. We cannot—we dare not—let the Equal Protection Clause perpetuate racial supremacy.

So the ultimate question, as it was at the beginning of this litigation, is: Among the qualified, how does one choose?

A long time ago, as time is measured for this Nation, a Chief Justice, both wise and farsighted, said:

"In considering this question, then, we must never forget, that it is a *constitution* we are expounding." McCulloch v. Maryland.

In the same opinion, the Great Chief Justice further observed:

"Let the end be legitimate, let it be within the scope of the constitution, and all means which are appropriate, which are plainly adapted to that end, which are not prohibited, but consist with the letter and spirit of the constitution, are constitutional."

More recently, one destined to become a Justice of this Court observed:

"The great generalities of the constitution have a content and a significance that vary from age to age." B. Cardozo.

And an educator who became a President of the United States said:

"But the Constitution of the United States is not a mere lawyer's document: it is a vehicle of life, and its spirit is always the spirit of the age." W. Wilson, Constitutional Government in the United States.

These precepts of breadth and flexibility and ever-present modernity are basic to our constitutional law. Today, again, we are expounding a *Constitution*. The same principles that governed *McCulloch's* case in 1819 govern *Bakke's* case in 1978. There can be no other answer.

Justice STEVENS, with whom THE CHIEF JUSTICE, Mr. Justice STEWART, and Mr. Justice REHNQUIST join, concurring in the judgment in part and dissenting in part.

. . . Both petitioner and respondent have asked us to determine the legality of the University's special admissions program by reference to the Constitution. Our settled practice, however, is to avoid the decision of a constitutional issue if a case can be fairly decided on a statutory ground. "If there is one doctrine more deeply rooted than any other in the process of constitutional adjudication, it is that we ought not to pass on questions of constitutionality . . . unless such adjudication is unavoidable." The more important the issue, the more force there is to this doctrine. In this case, we are presented with a constitutional question of undoubted and unusual importance. Since, however, a dispositive statutory claim was raised at the very inception of this case, and squarely decided in the portion of the trial court judgment affirmed by the California Supreme Court, it is our plain duty to confront it. Only if petitioner should prevail on the statutory issue would it be necessary to decide whether the University's admissions program violated the Equal Protection Clause of the Fourteenth Amendment.

Section 601 of the Civil Rights Act of 1964 provides:

> "No person in the United States shall, on the ground of race, color, or national origin, be excluded from participation in, be denied the benefits of, or be subjected to discrimination under any program or activity receiving Federal financial assistance."

The University, through its special admissions policy, excluded Bakke from participation in its program of medical education because of his race. The University also acknowledges that it was, and still is, receiving federal financial assistance. The plain language of the statute therefore requires affirmance of the judgment below. . . .

Title VI is an integral part of the far-reaching Civil Rights Act of 1964. No doubt, when this legislation was being debated, Congress was not directly concerned with the legality of "reverse discrimination" or "affirmative action" programs. Its attention was focused on the problem at hand, the "glaring . . . discrimination against Negroes which exists throughout our Nation," and, with respect to Title VI, the federal funding of segregated facilities. The genesis of the legislation, however, did not limit the breadth of the solution adopted. Just as Congress responded to the problem of employment discrimination by enacting a provision that protects all races, so, too, its answer to the problem of federal funding of segregated facilities stands as a broad prohibition against the exclusion of *any* individual from a federally funded program "on the ground of race." . . .

Petitioner contends, however, that exclusion of applicants on the basis of race does not violate Title VI if the exclusion carries with it no racial stigma. No such qualification or limitation of §601's categorical prohibition of "exclusion" is justified by the statute or its history. . . . The legislative history reinforces this reading. The only suggestion that §601 would allow exclusion of nonminority applicants came from opponents of the legislation. . . . In response, the proponents of the legislation gave repeated assurances that the Act would be "colorblind" in its application. . . .

As with other provisions of the Civil Rights Act, Congress' expression of its policy to end racial discrimination may independently proscribe conduct that the Constitution does not. However, we need not decide the congruence—or lack of congruence—of the controlling statute and the Constitution since the meaning of the Title VI ban on exclusion is crystal clear: Race cannot be the basis of excluding anyone from participation in a federally funded program. . . .

The University's special admissions program violated Title VI of the Civil Rights Act of 1964 by excluding Bakke from the medical school because of his race. It is therefore our duty to affirm the judgment ordering Bakke admitted to the University.

64

L. Peter Schultz

The Supreme Court, Affirmative Action, and the Judicial Function (1990)

The *Bakke* case presents a most interesting "alignment of forces" on the court. On the one hand, four Justices, viz., Berger, Rehnquist, Stevens and Stewart, voted to invalidate the Davis affirmative action program under the Civil Rights Act of 1964. For reasons to be discussed shortly, these four Justices may be labeled "restraintists." On the other hand, four Justices, viz., Blackmun,

By permission of the author.

Brennan, Marshall and White voted to uphold the Davis program under the 1964 Civil Rights Act and under the Constitution. These Justices may be called "activists." Finally, there is Justice Powell who unlike the restraintists reached the constitutional issue, but unlike the activists found the Davis program unconstitutional. The question arises then: What is Justice Powell, an activist, a restraintist, or something else altogether? This comment explores this question with an eye to illuminating the function of the Supreme Court.

We begin with the "restraintists" and their spokesman, Justice Stevens. At first, it may seem odd to label these Justices "restraintists" insofar as the doctrine of judicial restraint was born out of a concern with judicial activity that invalidated legislative or executive action, especially legislation deemed to be "progressive." However, applying this label to Justice Stevens, et. al., in *Bakke* is accurate for two reasons. First, Stevens stakes a claim to this label in his opinion:

> Our settled practice is to avoid the decision of a constitutional issue if a case can be fairly decided on a statutory ground. "If there is one doctrine more deeply rooted than any other in the process of constitutional adjudication, it is that we ought not pass on questions of constitutionality" unless such adjudication is unavoidable. The more important the issue, the more force there is to this doctrine.

And Justice Stevens argues that the doctrines should be applied even in cases such as *Bakke* which present "a constitutional question of undoubted and unusual importance."

There is little doubt then that Stevens wants to appear as a restraintist following a deeply rooted principle which commends judicial modesty vis-à-vis constitutional issues. Moreover, this stance is consistent with the doctrine of judicial restraint because, whatever the practical concerns that motivated the formulation of this doctrine, its assumptions point to the conclusion that the Court should not, except when absolutely necessary, decide constitutional questions. The doctrine's two basic assumptions are (1) the Court is not democratic and (2) the Constitution is or should be "alive." These assumptions are related in that "the living Constitution" puts a premium on adaptation in accordance with the wishes of the people. Restraintists do not dispute "the notion of a living Constitution," but they do dispute the legitimacy or ability of the Court to breathe life into that document. Primarily, bestowing life on the Constitution is the function of the more representative or political departments of the government, Congress and the executive or the same departments of state governments. This implies, however, that for the most part the court's judicial function does not comprehend deciding constitutional questions. As Stevens' opinion in *Bakke* illustrates, the Court should limit its concern to statutory interpretation whenever possible. Avoiding the constitutional aspect of "questions of undoubted and unusual importance" comports fully with the doctrine of judicial restraint, even if such avoidance results in invalidating "progressive" legislation.

While seemingly commendable for its modesty, such a stance is potentially injurious to the Constitution. Is the Constitution a clean slate upon which Congress and the states may write largely as they please? So the doctrine of judicial restraint implies, especially as this doctrine is expressed by Justice Stevens: "The more important the issue, the more force there is to this doctrine [of avoidance]." That is, for the most important issues, judicial silence is most appropriate. Now a few cases come to mind—e.g. *Dred Scott*—when avoidance of constitutional issues may have been commendable. But were judicial avoidance to become the rule in cases of such great import, the silence might be deafening and perhaps fatal to constitutional government.

Interestingly the Constitution fares little better with the activists, who agree with the restraintists that the Constitution is "alive". However, lacking the modesty of the restraintists, the activists are willing to supply this "defect" by helping to assure the "viability" of the Constitution through adaptation. Justice Blackmun, after quoting Chief Justice Marshall in *McCulloch* that "it is a constitution we are expounding," (2808) quotes first Cardozo and then Woodrow Wilson as follows:

> The great generalities of the Constitution have a content and significance that vary from age to age.
>   . . . the Constitution of the United States is not a mere lawyer's document, it is a vehicle of life, and its spirit is always the spirit of the ages.

Blackmun concludes by asserting that "These precepts of breadth and flexibility and *ever-present modernity* are basic to our constitutional law. Today, again, we are expounding a Constitution." (2808)

Now to say that the spirit of the Constitution "is *always* the spirit of the age" is to say that the Constitution has no abiding spirit of its own. Whatever else might be said of this assertion, it is not one that finds support in Marshall's opinion in *McCulloch*. There Marshall said: "Let the end be legitimate, let it be within the scope of the constitution, and all means which are appropriate, which are fairly adapted to that end, which are not prohibited, but consist with the letter and *spirit of the constitution*, are constitutional." For Marshall, the means employed toward legitimate ends should be judged by the Constitution, by its spirit. Also, the ends as well as the means should be judged by the Constitution. For Marshall, "the great generalities of the Constitution" are not distinguished by their "flexibility" or "ever-present modernity" but by their comprehensiveness. When Marshall admonishes us to remember that the Court is expounding a constitution, he admonishes us to remember not that the Constitution is infinitely "progressive" or adaptable to an ever-emerging "reality", but that its principles comprehend "the various crises of human affairs." Thus for Marshall, constitutional *interpretation*, saying what the law is, is the foremost function of the Court, whereas for the activists in *Bakke* the Court's foremost function is constitutional *adaptation*.

The activists are not aware, however, of the degree to which they "tinker" with the Constitution. For them, "the spirit of the age" is determined by history and necessity, past deeds and current needs. Past discrimination justifies race conscious policies today because, in the words of Justice Blackmun, "We cannot—we dare not—let the Equal Protection Clause perpetuate racial supremacy." (2807) These policies are temporary, their necessity ending where the results of past injustices are eradicated. The problem here is that "ideals" rather than needs determine the spirit of any age and the policies which arise therein. Affirmative action policies are no exception, resting on an ideal—simple egalitarianism—which is at odds with equal opportunity or the notion of life as a race among competing but unequally endowed individuals. Affirmative action programs cannot be temporary because that which they are said to modify, equal opportunity, does not and was not intended to result in the degree of equality sought by radical egalitarians. The activists in *Bakke* are not then the servants of "reality" or "progress" they pretend to be; rather, they are the vanguard of an egalitarian ideal in conflict with equal opportunity. As Woodrow Wilson knew, keeping the Constitution in touch with "the spirit of the age" sometimes requires radical reform or change.

Apparently aware of this, Justice Powell cautions against allowing the questions raised in *Bakke* to be settled either without reference to or by adaptation of constitutional principle. He rejects the restraintists' attempt to avoid the constitutional issue, arguing that given the purpose of the 1964 Civil Rights Act affirmative action programs need to be considered under the Fourteenth Amendment. Speaking to the activists, Powell argues that the Constitution's principles protect all individuals, thereby prohibiting almost all racial classifications or race conscious policies:

> The guarantee of the Fourteenth Amendment extends to all persons. Its language is explicit. . . . It is settled beyond question that the "rights created by . . . the Fourteenth Amendment are . . . guaranteed to the individual. The rights established are personal rights." The guarantee of equal protection cannot mean one thing when applied to one individual and something else when applied to a person of another color. (2747-8)

Moreover, Powell rejects the activists' position that the Fourteenth Amendment permits "benign" discrimination—drawing distinctions that favor rather than stigmatize a particular group. Such discrimination is not permissible, Powell maintains, because there is "no *principled* basis for deciding which groups would merit 'heightened judicial solicitude' and which would not. . . . By hitching the meaning of the Equal Protection clause to . . . transitory considerations, we would be holding, as a constitutional principle, that judicial scrutiny of classifications touching on racial and ethnic background may vary with the ebb and flow of political forces." (2751–2) Again, the activists have no principled way to determine which state-imposed racial classifications "stigmatize." All such classifications cause "resentment" and justifiably so: "One should not lightly dismiss *the inherent unfairness of . . .* a system of allocating benefits and privileges on the basis of color and ethnic origin." (2750, note 34). The activists "offer no principle for deciding whether preferential classifications reflect a benign remedial purpose or a malevolent stigmatic classification, since they . . . accept mere post hoc declarations by an isolated state entity . . . unadorned by particularized findings of past discrimination." *(ibid.)*

If the Constitution is color-blind, why then does Justice Powell not strike down all race-conscious policies? Powell's refusal to do this has left him open to the charge that his "judicial statesmanship" is merely a thinly-veiled policy of expediency. Not so much constitutional principle as compromise explains Powell's opinion in *Bakke*.

Powell's argument is that the color-blind principle or rule has never been absolute: "All legal restrictions which curtail the civil rights of a single racial group are immediately suspect . . . not to say . . . unconstitutional . . . [But] courts must subject them to the most rigid scrutiny." (2748) Subjecting the Davis program to such scrutiny, it is unconstitutional because it excludes some applicants from competing for some seats *solely* on grounds of race: "The fatal flaw in the petitioner's preferential program is its disregard of individual rights as guaranteed by the Fourteenth Amendment." (2763) Powell does find a constitutional justification for considering race as one factor in admissions, viz., the First Amendment and academic freedom asserted for the sake of diversity: "it is not too much to say that the 'nation's future depends upon leaders trained through wide exposure' to the ideas and mores of students as diverse as this Nation of many peoples." (2761) Viewed in this way, the Constitution does not require educational institutions to ignore race any more than it requires them to ignore religion, sex or place of residence. However, the Constitution does forbid such institutions excluding anyone solely on grounds of race.

Does Powell's opinion meet the standard of judicial statesmanship? If judicial statesmanship refers to enunciating absolute rules, then it cannot be said Powell rises to the challenge. But if judicial statesmanship refers to enunciating deeply-rooted or constitutionally nurtured principles, then Powell has risen to the occasion. Of course, Powell's interpretation of the strict scrutiny test will not satisfy all, but it does appear consistent with the Fourteenth Amendment in that race cannot be the determinative factor in allocating privileges. Race may be considered but it may not be considered decisive.

Although in *Bakke* Powell exercised judicial statesmanship in applying constitutional principle, the post-*Bakke* Court has not always followed this standard in dealing with affirmative action. In some instances, those in which the burdens implied by affirmative action are diffused, the Court has upheld state action that gives preferential treatment to minorities. This is the case in *Fulilove v. Klutznick* (1980), where the Court held a federal law constitutional although it required that ten per cent of all federal funds for local public works projects be allocated to minority-owned businesses. While such state action is inconsistent with *Bakke*'s holding that race cannot be the determinative or decisive factor in allocating privileges, the burden on non-minority businesses was diffused and indirect. In other cases, where the burden imposed by preferential policies is direct and burdensome, as when someone loses a job, the Court has not allowed race-conscious policies. In two 1980 cases (*Firefighters Local Union 1784 v. Stotts* and *Wygant v. Jackson Board of Education*), for example, where the Court upheld the claims of whites who had been laid off before blacks with less seniority, the burden was direct and heavy. In allowing diffused burdens, and in forbidding direct ones, the Court appears to be reacting against the infliction of pain rather than upholding constitutional principle. Without the kind of appeal to constitutional principle that we find in Powell's opinion in *Bakke*, the Court follows a policy of accommodation toward whatever wind seems strongest— or whatever pain seems greatest—in particular cases.

But why should we be concerned with whether the Court rose to the level of judicial statesmanship, i.e., of thinking through and applying fundamental constitutional principles? After all, the Court is a political institution, as are Congress and the presidency. Why should the Court be expected to recur to constitutional principle rather than solving political problems in the most timely way?

The answer, it must be admitted, is not perfectly clear. Timeliness is often of the essence in politics. As Publius knew, energy is one, and may even be the essential, ingredient of good government. But energy, according to Publius, belonged primarily to the Executive. Other institutions of government were intended to embody and foster other characteristics of good government. Publius also wrote that "veneration" of and "reverence" for the law are indispensable to stable and decent government. If time is to generate the requisite veneration for law, as Publius hoped, the fundamental law or the Constitution cannot be seen to change with the temporary needs of the age, as proponents of the "living Constitution" proclaim. Moreover, Publius may be incorrect in assuming that time always produces veneration, for in a democracy "old" is often treated as a suspect category. Judicial statesmanship— recurrence to the permanent principles of the Constitution—not only counteracts the notion of change implied in the doctrine of a "living Constitution," but in the best cases explains to citizens why the old is good. It is asking much of any institution, and especially a political institution, to reach so high, but such is the function constitutional government forces the Supreme Court to perform.

65

Grutter v. Bollinger (2003)

Justice O'Connor delivered the opinion of the Court.

This case requires us to decide whether the use of race as a factor in student admissions by the University of Michigan Law School is unlawful.

We last addressed the use of race in public higher education over 25 years ago. In the landmark *Bakke* case, we reviewed a racial set-aside program that reserved 16 out of 100 seats in a medical school class for members of certain minority groups. The decision produced six separate opinions, none of which commanded a majority of the Court. . . . The only holding for the Court in *Bakke* was that a "State has a substantial interest that legitimately may be served by a properly devised admissions program involving the competitive consideration of race and ethnic origin." Thus, we reversed that part of the lower court's judgment that enjoined the university "from any consideration of the race of any applicant."

Since this Court's splintered decision in *Bakke*, Justice Powell's opinion announcing the judgment of the Court has served as the touchstone for constitutional analysis of race-conscious admissions policies. Public and private universities across the Nation have modeled their own admissions programs on Justice Powell's views on permissible race-conscious policies.

Justice Powell began by stating that "[t]he guarantee of equal protection cannot mean one thing when applied to one individual and something else when applied to a person of another color. If both are not accorded the same protection, then it is not equal." In Justice Powell's view, when governmental decisions "touch upon an individual's race or ethnic background, he is entitled to a judicial determination that the burden he is asked to bear on that basis is precisely tailored to serve a compelling governmental interest." Under this exacting standard, only one of the interests asserted by the university survived Justice Powell's scrutiny.

First, Justice Powell rejected an interest in "reducing the historic deficit of traditionally disfavored minorities in medical schools and in the medical profession " as an unlawful interest in racial balancing. Second, Justice Powell rejected an interest in remedying societal discrimination because such measures would risk placing unnecessary burdens on innocent third parties

From *Grutter v. Bollinger*, 288 F.3d 732.

"who bear no responsibility for whatever harm the beneficiaries of the special admissions program are thought to have suffered." Third, Justice Powell rejected an interest in "increasing the number of physicians who will practice in communities currently underserved," concluding that even if such an interest could be compelling in some circumstances the program under review was not "geared to promote that goal."

Justice Powell approved the university's use of race to further only one interest: "the attainment of a diverse student body." . . .

We apply strict scrutiny to all racial classifications to "'smoke out' illegitimate uses of race by assuring that [government] is pursuing a goal important enough to warrant use of a highly suspect tool." [*Richmond*, 1989]

Strict scrutiny is not "strict in theory, but fatal in fact." [*Adarand Constructors*, 1995] Although all governmental uses of race are subject to strict scrutiny, not all are invalidated by it. As we have explained, "whenever the government treats any person unequally because of his or her race, that person has suffered an injury that falls squarely within the language and spirit of the Constitution's guarantee of equal protection." But that observation "says nothing about the ultimate validity of any particular law; that determination is the job of the court applying strict scrutiny." When race-based action is necessary to further a compelling governmental interest, such action does not violate the constitutional guarantee of equal protection so long as the narrow-tailoring requirement is also satisfied. . . .

The Law School's educational judgment that such diversity is essential to its educational mission is one to which we defer. The Law School's assessment that diversity will, in fact, yield educational benefits is substantiated by respondents and their *amici*. Our scrutiny of the interest asserted by the Law School is no less strict for taking into account complex educational judgments in an area that lies primarily within the expertise of the university. Our holding today is in keeping with our tradition of giving a degree of deference to a university's academic decisions, within constitutionally prescribed limits.

We have long recognized that, given the important purpose of public education and the expansive freedoms of speech and thought associated with the university environment, universities occupy a special niche in our constitutional tradition. In announcing the principle of student body diversity as a compelling state interest, Justice Powell invoked our cases recognizing a constitutional dimension, grounded in the First Amendment, of educational autonomy: "The freedom of a university to make its own judgment as to education includes the selection of its student body." From this premise, Justice Powell reasoned that by claiming "the right to select those students who will contribute the most to the 'robust exchange of ideas,' " a university "seek[s] to achieve a goal that is of paramount importance in the fulfillment of its mission." Our conclusion that the Law School has a compelling interest in a diverse student body is informed by our view that attaining a diverse student body is at the heart of the Law School's proper institutional mission, and that "good faith" on the part of a university is "presumed" absent "a showing to the contrary."

As part of its goal of "assembling a class that is both exceptionally academically qualified and broadly diverse," the Law School seeks to "enroll a 'critical mass' of minority students." The Law School's interest is not simply "to assure within its student body some specified percentage of a particular group merely because of its race or ethnic origin." That would amount to outright racial balancing, which is patently unconstitutional. Rather, the Law School's concept of critical mass is defined by reference to the educational benefits that diversity is designed to produce.

The Law School doe not premise its need for critical mass on "any belief that minority students always (or even consistently) express some characteristic minority viewpoint on any issue." To the contrary, diminishing the force of such stereotypes is both a crucial part of the Law School's mission, and one that it cannot accomplish with only token numbers of minority students. Just as growing up in a particular region or having particular professional experiences is likely to affect an individual's views, so too is one's own, unique experience of being a racial minority in a society, like our own, in which race unfortunately still matters. The Law School has determined, based on its experience and expertise, that a "critical mass" of underrepresented minorities is necessary to further its compelling interest in securing the educational benefits of a diverse student body.

Even in the limited circumstance when drawing racial distinctions is permissible to further a compelling state interest, government is still "constrained in how it may pursue that end: [T]he means chosen to accomplish the [government's] asserted purpose must be specifically and narrowly framed to accomplish that purpose." The purpose of the narrow tailoring requirement is to ensure that "the means chosen 'fit' . . . th[e] compelling goal so closely that there is little or no possibility that the motive for the classification was illegitimate racial prejudice or stereotype."

We find that the Law School's admissions program bears the hallmarks of a narrowly tailored plan. As Justice Powell made clear in *Bakke*, truly individualized consideration demands that race be used in a flexible, nonmechanical way. It follows from this mandate that universities cannot establish quotas for members of certain racial groups or put members of those groups on separate admissions tracks. Nor can universities insulate applicants who belong to certain racial or ethnic groups from the competition for admission. Universities can, however, consider race or ethnicity more flexibly as a "plus" factor in the context of individualized consideration of each and every applicant. . . .

Moreover, as Justice Kennedy concedes, between 1993 and 2000, the number of African-American, Latino, and Native-American students in each class at the Law School varied from 13.5 to 20.1 percent, a range inconsistent with a quota. . . .

That a race-conscious admissions program does not operate as a quota does not, by itself, satisfy the requirement of individualized consideration. When using race as a "plus" factor in university admissions, a university's admissions program must remain flexible enough to ensure that each applicant is evaluated as an individual and not in a way that makes an applicant's race or ethnicity the defining feature of his or her application.

What is more, the Law School actually gives substantial weight to diversity factors besides race. The Law School frequently accepts nonminority applicants with grades and test scores lower than underrepresented minority applicants (and other nonminority applicants) who are rejected. This shows that the Law School seriously weighs many other diversity factors besides race that can make a real and dispositive difference for nonminority applicants as well. By this flexible approach, the Law School sufficiently takes into account, in practice as well as in theory, a wide variety of characteristics besides race and ethnicity that contribute to a diverse student body. Justice Kennedy speculates that "race is likely outcome determinative for many members of minority groups" who do not fall within the upper range of LSAT scores and grades. But the same could be said of the Harvard plan discussed approvingly by Justice Powell in *Bakke,* and indeed of any plan that uses race as one of many factors.

We agree with the Court of Appeals that the Law School sufficiently considered workable race-neutral alternatives. The District Court took the Law School to task for failing to consider race-neutral alternatives such as "using a lottery system" or "decreasing the emphasis for all applicants on undergraduate GPA and LSAT scores." But these alternatives would require a dramatic sacrifice of diversity, the academic quality of all admitted students, or both.

We acknowledge that "there are serious problems of justice connected with the idea of preference itself." Narrow tailoring, therefore, requires that a race-conscious admissions program not unduly harm members of any racial group. Even remedial race-based governmental action generally "remains subject to continuing oversight to assure that it will work the least harm possible to other innocent persons competing for the benefit." To be narrowly tailored, a race-conscious admissions program must not "unduly burden individuals who are not members of the favored racial and ethnic groups."

We are mindful, however, that "[a] core purpose of the Fourteenth Amendment was to do away with all governmentally imposed discrimination based on race." Accordingly, race-conscious admissions policies must be limited in time. This requirement reflects that racial classifications, however compelling their goals, are potentially so dangerous that they may be employed no more broadly than the interest demands. Enshrining a permanent justification for racial preferences would offend this fundamental equal protection principle. We see no reason to exempt race-conscious admissions programs from the requirement that all governmental use of race must have a logical end point. The Law School, too, concedes that all "race-conscious programs must have reasonable durational limits."

In the context of higher education, the durational requirement can be met by sunset provisions in race-conscious admissions policies and periodic reviews to determine whether racial preferences are still necessary to achieve student body diversity. Universities in California, Florida, and Washington State, where racial preferences in admissions are prohibited by state law, are currently engaged in experimenting with a wide variety of alternative approaches. Universities in other States can and should draw on the most promising aspects of these race-neutral alternatives as they develop.

The requirement that all race-conscious admissions programs have a termination point "assure[s] all citizens that the deviation from the norm of equal treatment of all racial and ethnic groups is a temporary matter, a measure taken in the service of the goal of equality itself.". . . .

We take the Law School at its word that it would "like nothing better than to find a race-neutral admissions formula" and will terminate its race-conscious admissions program as soon as practicable. It has been 25 years since Justice Powell first approved the use of race to further an interest in student body diversity in the context of public higher education. Since that time, the number of minority applicants with high grades and test scores has indeed increased. We expect that 25 years from now, the use of racial preferences will no longer be necessary to further the interest approved today.

Chief Justice Rehnquist, with whom Justice Scalia, Justice Kennedy, and Justice Thomas join, dissenting.

I agree with the Court that, "in the limited circumstance when drawing racial distinctions is permissible," the government must ensure that its means are narrowly tailored to achieve a compelling state interest. I do not believe, however, that the University of Michigan Law School's means are narrowly tailored to the interest it asserts. The Law School claims it must take the steps it does to achieve a " 'critical mass' " of underrepresented minority students. But its actual program bears no relation to this asserted goal. Stripped of its "critical mass" veil, the Law School's program is revealed as a naked effort to achieve racial balancing.

Before the Court's decision today, we consistently applied the same strict scrutiny analysis regardless of the government's purported reason for using race and regardless of the setting in which race was being used. . . .

Although the Court recites the language of our strict scrutiny analysis, its application of that review is unprecedented in its deference.

In practice, the Law School's program bears little or no relation to its asserted goal of achieving "critical mass.". . . . From 1995 through 2000, the Law School admitted between 1,130 and 1,310 students. Of those, between 13 and 19 were Native American, between 91 and 108 were African-Americans, and between 47 and 56 were Hispanic. If the Law School is admitting between 91 and 108 African-Americans in order to achieve "critical mass," thereby preventing African-American students from feeling "isolated or like spokespersons for their race," one would think that a number of the same order of magnitude would be necessary to accomplish the same purpose for Hispanics and Native Americans. Similarly, even if all of the Native American applicants admitted in a given year matriculate, which the record demonstrates is not at all the case, how can this possibly constitute a "critical mass" of Native Americans in a class of over 350 students? In order for this pattern of admission to be consistent with the Law School's explanation of "critical mass," one would have to believe that the objectives of "critical mass" offered by respondents are achieved with only half the number of Hispanics and one-sixth the number of Native Americans as compared to African-Americans. But respondents offer no race-specific reasons for such disparities. Instead, they simply emphasize the importance of achieving "critical mass," without any explanation of why that concept is applied differently among the three under-represented minority groups. . . .

But the correlation between the percentage of the Law School's pool of applicants who are members of the three minority groups and the percentage of the admitted applicants who are members of these same groups is far too precise to be dismissed as merely the result of the school paying "some attention to [the] numbers." As the tables below show, from 1995 through 2000 the percentage of admitted applicants who were members of these minority groups closely tracked the percentage of individuals in the school's applicant pool who were from the same groups.

The tight correlation between the percentage of applicants and admittees of a given race, therefore, must result from careful race based planning by the Law School. It suggests a formula for admission based on the aspirational assumption that all applicants are equally qualified academically, and therefore that the proportion of each group admitted should be the same as the proportion of that group in the applicant pool. . . .

I do not believe that the Constitution gives the Law School such free rein in the use of race. The Law School has offered no explanation for its actual admissions practices and, unexplained, we are bound to conclude that the Law School has managed its admissions program, not to achieve a "critical mass," but to extend offers of admission to members of selected minority groups in proportion to their statistical representation in the applicant pool. But this is precisely the type of racial balancing that the Court itself calls "patently unconstitutional."

The Court suggests a possible 25-year limitation on the Law School's current program. Respondents, on the other hand, remain more ambiguous, explaining that "the Law School of course recognizes that race-conscious programs must have reasonable durational limits, and the Sixth Circuit properly found such a limit in the Law School's resolve to cease considering race when genuine race-neutral alternatives become available." These discussions of a time limit are the vaguest of assurances. In truth, they permit the Law School's use of racial preferences on a seemingly permanent basis. Thus, an important component of strict scrutiny—that a program be limited in time—is casually subverted.

The Court, in an unprecedented display of deference under our strict scrutiny analysis, upholds the Law School's program despite its obvious flaws. We have said that when it comes to the use of race, the connection between the ends and the means used to attain them must be precise. But here the flaw is deeper than that; it is not merely a question of "fit" between ends and means. Here the means actually used are forbidden by the Equal Protection Clause of the Constitution.

Chapter VI

Politics and Economics

How much government regulation of the economy is desirable? What is the proper relationship between politics and economics? Conservatives typically support some version of laissez-faire capitalism, while liberals advocate some version of the welfare state. Milton Friedman argues for minimal interference in the economy, on the ground that economic freedom is both itself an important component of freedom and the condition for political freedom. For Friedman, economic power should be independent of political power in order to check political power; socialism, by destroying economic liberty, destroys a protector of political freedom. Furthermore, a market economy can coordinate the activities of large numbers of individuals without resorting to coercion: each person pursues his own interest by voluntarily entering into relations with others. Government therefore should be primarily an umpire of economic activity.

Friedman's views stand in sharp contrast to the welfare state that Franklin D. Roosevelt established and defended. According to FDR, the rights of the Declaration of Independence must be redefined as social conditions change. By adding to the freedoms of religion and speech the new freedoms, the freedom from fear and the freedom from want, FDR gives to politics a new aim—making men happy by contenting them with their lot. Since a commercial society depends on the dynamism of individual acquisitiveness in a competitive market, FDR's new freedoms promote a distrust of such a society. Cooperation will replace competition in a future where the individual advances along a road on which thousands of others also advance, practicing "reciprocal self-denial" for the sake of the common advantage.

FDR says that the task has become one of distributing and administering rather than producing wealth. However, it is not entirely clear in his thought whether it is the success or the failure of the commercial republic that dictates the redefinition of political goals. He argues that we must end competition because the frontiers have closed and opportunity for advancement no longer exists. Yet he also speaks of the enjoyment of the fruits of scientific progress with an ever rising standard of living as one of the basic things we can expect government to provide in the welfare state.

Both the viability and the desirability of the welfare state are, however, open to question. Irving Kristol argues that the welfare state is premised on the belief that the government can "manage and manipulate" aggregate demand so as to maintain a healthy economy. But Kristol contends that such comprehensive centralized planning is impossible. Furthermore, he suggests that the attempt to "manage" the economy destroys the individual incentives that cause a productive economy. Kristol claims that supply-side economics seeks to correct the utopianism of centralized planning and to restore the incentives necessary for a sound economy.

In the early 19th century Alexis de Tocqueville expressed the fear that in democracies the people would gradually give up their independence in exchange for the security offered by a powerful national government. Such a state would be a "soft despotism" in which men become passive, their basic needs taken care of by a benevolent government on whom they would eventually become completely dependent. Equal prosperity might be attained at the price of dignity and freedom.

A consideration of earlier views on the relationship between government and economics helps to place the current debate in a broader perspective. As we see from his *Report on Manufacturers*, Hamilton favors government regulation of the economy. Congress is empowered to do so, he argues, by the general welfare clause of the Constitution. The constitutionality of much New Deal legislation is also derived from this clause. Although Hamilton thus shares with FDR a concept of active government, Hamilton is one of the greatest proponents of a commercial republic. He wants government to promote manufactures in order to increase productivity and therewith the wealth of the community. A prosperous nation, he argues, is a strong nation, subservient to no other country. FDR's emphasis on "the sufficiency of life" rather than Hamilton's "plethora of riches" seems to make him more like Jefferson than Hamilton, who thought that the United States should aspire "to a state of opulence." We cannot, however, conclude that FDR advocated Hamilton's means to Jefferson's ends. While both FDR and Jefferson decry the desire for excess, Jefferson speaks of the self-sufficiency of the farmer rather than the simple sufficiency of life. He opposes the promotion of manufactures because of the effect such work has on men—subservience, venality, and the stifling of virtue. Artisans are not fit citizens of a republic but the tools of a despot. In both Jefferson and Hamilton, we can see an emphasis on independence and pride that is missing in FDR's thought. For Jefferson, farming promotes the self-dependence of the individual; for Hamilton, manufactures promotes the self-dependence of the nation.

While Jefferson and Hamilton disagree about the character of the republic that economic policy should promote, they both consider the long-term political effects of economic policy on the kind of country the United States should be. Such considerations are absent in both FDR and Friedman. While Friedman does make freedom his end, he does not adequately consider the political conditions and ends of economic freedom. For both FDR and Friedman, politics is in the service of economics: for Friedman government regulates the acquisition of material benefits, and for FDR government itself is the dispenser of these benefits. The subordination of the public to the private stems from a denial that there are standards of right and wrong that a people can hold in common. Friedman, for example, argues that we should not coerce someone we see making a mistake, for, after all, he may be right and we wrong. Similarly, FDR cannot maintain that men have any rights in common, such as the natural rights referred to in the Declaration: since statesmen must redefine human rights as the social conditions change, there are at best only different rights for different social conditions.

In the 1990s the Supreme Court has called for a reconsideration of the constitutional constraints on the public regulation of private property. The majority opinion in *Lucas v. The South Carolina Coastal Commission* argues that while the state has a great deal of power to regulate private property in the public interest, that power is not without limits. If regulation goes so far as to deprive a person of the economic benefits of his or her property, the government must provide compensation for what in effect is a "taking." According to the 5th Amendment "private property [shall not] be taken for public use without just compensation." In *Kelo v. New London*, however, Justice Steven's majority opinion allows the government broad discretion in determining what constitutes a public purpose. He argues that the City of New London had every right to force homeowners to sell their property to the city so that it could in turn be sold to private developers who would increase the value of that property. Justice O'Connor, however, contends that the majority opinion undermines important Constitutional protections of private property. Under the majority's ruling, she argues, "public use" povisions of the Fifth Amendment cease to provide any restraint on the power of government.

Catherine H. Zuckert thinks that economic policy should be made to serve political ends. What economic policies, she asks, best enable a regime to guarantee to all the right to pursue happiness? She examines the rule of the middle-class majority to see whether it can be justified by its effects on the two economic extremes, the rich and the poor. The majority's claim that it secures the right of all to pursue happiness is supported because the majority both protects the wealth of the rich *and* gives welfare to the poor. Policies that include economic incentives are appropriate to such a regime because they foster habits in the citizens, such as individual effort, forethought, and self-control, that are necessary to maintain a free regime. Zuckert turns to Tocqueville as a model. Because private economic associations foster the habits conducive to political freedom, Tocqueville taught democratic statesmen that they should encourage the formation of such associations. Tocqueville thus offers some hope that we may avoid the soft despotism of the welfare state by means of carefully-framed policies. Zuckert both reminds us of this possibility and also shows us that welfare can be consistent with the premises of our regime and does not necessarily require a reformulation of them on egalitarian grounds.

66

Milton Friedman

Capitalism and Freedom (1962)

In a much quoted passage in his inaugural address, President Kennedy said, "Ask not what your country can do for you—ask what you can do for your country." It is a striking sign of the temper of our times that the controversy about this passage centered on its origin and not on its content. Neither half of the statement expresses a relation between the citizen and his government that is worthy of the ideals of free men in a free society. The paternalistic "what your country can do for you" implies that government is the patron, the citizen the ward, a view that is at odds with the free man's belief in his own responsibility for his own destiny. The organismic, "what you can do for your country" implies that government is the master or the deity, the citizen, the servant or the votary. To the free man, the country is the collection of individuals who compose it, not something over and above them. . . . He recognizes no national purpose except as it is the consensus of the purposes for which the citizens severally strive.

The free man will ask neither what his country can do for him nor what he can do for his country. He will ask rather "What can I and my compatriots do through government" to help us discharge our individual responsibilities, to achieve our several goals and purposes, and above all, to protect our freedom? . . . Government is necessary to preserve our freedom, it is an instrument through which we can exercise our freedom; yet by concentrating power in political hands, it is also a threat to freedom. . . .

How can we benefit from the promise of government while avoiding the threat to freedom? . . .

First, the scope of government must be limited. Its major function must be to protect our freedom both from the enemies outside our gates and from our fellow-citizens: to preserve law and order, to enforce private contracts, to foster competitive markets. Beyond this major function, government may enable us at times to accomplish jointly what we would find it more difficult

From Milton Friedman, *Capitalism and Freedom.* Copyright © 1962, 1982 by The University of Chicago. All rights reserved. Reprinted with the permission of The University of Chicago Press.

or expensive to accomplish severally. However, any such use of government is fraught with danger. We should not and cannot avoid using government in this way. But there should be a clear and large balance of advantages before we do. By relying primarily on voluntary co-operation and private enterprise, in both economic and other activities, we can insure that the private sector is a check on the powers of the governmental sector and an effective protection of freedom of speech, of religion, and of thought.

The second broad principle is that government power must be dispersed. If government is to exercise power, better in the county than in the state, better in the state than in Washington. If I do not like what my local community does, be it in sewage disposal, or zoning, or schools, I can move to another local community, and though few may take this step, the mere possibility acts as a check. If I do not like what my state does, I can move to another. If I do not like what Washington imposes, I have few alternatives in this world of jealous nations. . . .

The preservation of freedom is the protective reason for limiting and decentralizing governmental power. But there is also a constructive reason. The great advances of civilization, whether in architecture or painting, in science or literature, in industry or agriculture, have never come from centralized government. . . .

Government can never duplicate the variety and diversity of individual action. At any moment in time, by imposing uniform standards in housing, or nutrition, or clothing, government could undoubtedly improve the level of living of many individuals; by imposing uniform standards in schooling, road construction, or sanitation, central government could undoubtedly improve the level of performance in many local areas and perhaps even on the average of all communities. But in the process, government would replace progress by stagnation, it would substitute uniform mediocrity for the variety essential for that experimentation which can bring tomorrow's laggards above today's mean. . . .

As it developed in the late eighteenth and early nineteenth centuries, the intellectual movement that went under the name of liberalism emphasized freedom as the ultimate goal and the individual as the ultimate entity in the society. It supported laissez faire at home as a means of reducing the role of the state in economic affairs and thereby enlarging the role of the individual. . . .

Beginning in the late nineteenth century, and especially after 1930 in the United States, the term liberalism came to be associated with a very different emphasis, particularly in economic policy. It came to be associated with a readiness to rely primarily on the state rather than on private voluntary arrangements to achieve objectives regarded as desirable. The catchwords became welfare and equality rather than freedom. The nineteenth-century liberal regarded an extension of freedom as the most effective way to promote welfare and equality; the twentieth-century liberal regards welfare and equality as either prerequisites of or alternatives to freedom. In the name of welfare and equality, the twentieth-century liberal has come to favor a revival of the very policies of state intervention and paternalism against which classical liberalism fought. . . .

It is widely believed that politics and economics are separate and largely unconnected; that individual freedom is a political problem and material welfare an economic problem; and that any kind of political arrangements can be combined with any kind of economic arrangements. The chief contemporary manifestation of this idea is the advocacy of "democratic socialism" by many who condemn out of hand the restrictions on individual freedom imposed by "totalitarian socialism" in Russia, and who are persuaded that it is possible for a country to adopt the essential features of Russian economic arrangements and yet to ensure individual freedom through political arrangements. The thesis of this chapter is that such a view is a delusion. . . .

Economic arrangements play a dual role in the promotion of a free society. On the one hand, freedom in economic arrangements is itself a component of freedom broadly understood, so economic freedom is an end in itself. In the second place, economic freedom is also an indispensable means toward the achievement of political freedom.

The first of these roles of economic freedom needs special emphasis because intellectuals in particular have a strong bias against regarding this aspect of freedom as important. They tend to express contempt for what they regard as material aspects of life. . . .

A citizen of the United States who under the laws of various states is not free to follow the occupation of his own choosing unless he can get a license for it, is likewise being deprived of an essential part of his freedom. So is the man who would like to exchange some of his goods with, say, a Swiss for a watch but is prevented from doing so by a quota. So also is the Californian who was thrown into jail for selling Alka Seltzer at a price below that set by the manufacturer under so-called "fair trade" laws. So also is the farmer who cannot grow the amount of wheat he wants. And so on. Clearly, economic freedom, in and of itself, is an extremely important part of total freedom.

Viewed as a means to the end of political freedom, economic arrangements are important because of their effect on the concentration or dispersion of power. The kind of economic organization that provides economic freedom directly, namely, competitive capitalism, also promotes political freedom because it separates economic power from political power and in this way enables the one to offset the other. . . .

What are the logical links between economic and political freedom? In discussing these questions we shall consider first the market as a direct component of freedom, and then the indirect relation between market arrangements and political freedom. A by-product will be an outline of the ideal economic arrangements for a free society.

As liberals, we take freedom of the individual, or perhaps the family, as our ultimate goal in judging social arrangements. Freedom as a value in this sense has to do with the interrelations among people. . . . [I]n a society freedom has nothing to say about what an individual does with his freedom; it is not an all-embracing ethic. Indeed, a major aim of the liberal is to leave the ethical problem for the individual to wrestle with. The "really" important ethical problems are those that face an individual in a free society— what he should do with his freedom. . . .

The basic problem of social organization is how to co-ordinate the economic activities of large numbers of people. . . .

Literally millions of people are involved in providing one another with their daily bread, let alone with their yearly automobiles. The challenge to the believer in liberty is to reconcile this widespread interdependence with individual freedom.

Fundamentally, there are only two ways of coordinating the economic activities of millions. One is central direction involving the use of coercion— the technique of the army and of the modern totalitarian state. The other is voluntary co-operation of individuals—the technique of the market place.

The possibility of co-ordination through voluntary co-operation rests on the elementary—yet frequently denied—proposition that both parties to an economic transaction benefit from it, *provided the transaction is bilaterally voluntary and informed.*

Exchange can therefore bring about co-ordination without coercion. A working model of a society organized through voluntary exchange is a *free private enterprise exchange economy*—what we have been calling competitive capitalism. . . .

[I]n the complex enterprise and money-exchange economy, cooperation is strictly individual and voluntary *provided:* (a) that enterprises are private, so that the ultimate contracting parties are individuals and (b) that individuals are effectively free to enter or not to enter into any particular exchange, so that every transaction is strictly voluntary. . . .

So long as effective freedom of exchange is maintained, the central feature of the market organization of economic activity is that it prevents one person from interfering with another in respect of most of his activities. The consumer is protected from coercion by the seller because of the presence of other sellers with whom he can deal. The seller is protected from coercion by the consumer because of other consumers to whom he can sell. The employee is protected from coercion by the employer because of other employers for whom he can work, and so on. And the market does this impersonally and without centralized authority. . . .

The existence of a free market does not of course eliminate the need for government. On the contrary, government is essential both as a forum for determining the "rules of the game" and as an umpire to interpret and enforce the rules decided on. What the market does is to reduce greatly the range of issues that must be decided through political means, and thereby to minimize the extent to which government need participate directly in the game. The characteristic feature of action through political channels is that it tends to require or enforce substantial conformity. The great advantage of the market, on the other hand, is that it permits wide diversity. It is, in political terms, a system of proportional representation. Each man can vote, as it were, for the color of tie he wants and get it; he does not have to see what color the majority wants and then, if he is in the minority, submit.

It is this feature of the market that we refer to when we say that the market provides economic freedom. But this characteristic also has implications that go far beyond the narrowly economic. Political freedom means the absence of coercion of a man by his fellow men. . . . By removing the organization of economic activity from the control of political authority, the market eliminates this source of coercive power. It enables economic strength to be a check to political power rather than a reinforcement. . . .

One feature of a free society is surely the freedom of individuals to advocate and propagandize openly for a radical change in the structure of the society—so long as the advocacy is restricted to persuasion and does not include force or other forms of coercion. It is a mark of the political freedom of a capitalist society that men can openly advocate and work for socialism. Equally, political freedom in a socialist society would require that men be free to advocate the introduction of capitalism. How could the freedom to advocate capitalism be preserved and protected in a socialist society?

In order for men to advocate anything, they must in the first place be able to earn a living. This already raises a problem in a socialist society, since all jobs are under the direct control of political authorities. . . .

For advocacy of capitalism to mean anything, the proponents must be able to finance their cause—to hold public meetings, publish pamphlets, buy radio time, issue newspapers and magazines, and so on. How could they raise the funds? There might and probably would be men in the socialist society with large incomes, perhaps even large capital sums in the form of government bonds and the like, but these would of necessity be high public officials. . . .

The only recourse for funds would be to raise small amounts from a large number of minor officials. But this is no real answer. To tap these sources, many people would already have to be persuaded, and our whole problem is how to initiate and finance a campaign to do so. Radical movements in capitalist societies have never been financed this way. They have typically been supported by a few wealthy individuals who have become persuaded. . . .

This is a role of inequality of wealth in preserving political freedom that is seldom noted—the role of the patron. . . .

[I]ndeed, it is not even necessary to persuade people or financial institutions with available funds of the soundness of the ideas to be propagated. It is only necessary to persuade them that the propagation can be financially successful; that the newspaper or magazine or book or other venture will be profitable. . . .

But we are not yet through. In a free market society, it is enough to have the funds. The suppliers of paper are as willing to sell it to the *Daily Worker* as to the *Wall Street Journal*. In a socialist society, it would not be enough to have the funds. The hypothetical supporter of capitalism would have to persuade a government factory making paper to sell to him, the government printing press to print his pamphlets, a government post office to distribute them among the people, a government agency to rent him a hall in which to talk, and so on. . . .

By contrast, it is clear how a free market capitalist society fosters freedom.

A striking practical example of these abstract principles is the experience of Winston Churchill. From 1933 to the outbreak of World War II, Churchill was not permitted to talk over the British radio, which was, of course, a government monopoly administered by the British Broadcasting Corporation. Here was a leading citizen of his country, a Member of Parliament, a former cabinet minister, a man who was desperately trying by every device possible to persuade his countrymen to take steps to ward off the menace of Hitler's Germany. He was not permitted to talk over the radio to the British people because the BBC was a government monopoly and his position was too "controversial." . . .

Another example of the role of the market in preserving political freedom, was revealed in our experience with McCarthyism. Entirely aside from the substantive issues involved, and the merits of the charges made, what protection did individuals, and in particular government employees, have against irresponsible accusations and probings into matters that it went against their conscience to reveal? Their appeal to the Fifth Amendment would have been a hollow mockery without an alternative to government employment.

Their fundamental protection was the existence of a private-market economy in which they could earn a living. . . .

The "social security" program is one of those things on which the tyranny of the status quo is beginning to work its magic. Despite the controversy that surrounded its inception, it has come to be so much taken for granted that its desirability is hardly questioned any longer. Yet it involves a large-scale invasion into the personal lives of a large fraction of the nation without, so far as I can see, any justification that is at all persuasive, not only on liberal principles, but on almost any other. I propose to examine the biggest phase of it, that which involves payments to the aged.

As an operational matter, the program known as old age and survivor's insurance (OASI) consists of a special tax imposed on payrolls, plus payments to persons who have reached a specified age, of amounts determined by the age at which payments begin, family status, and prior earning record.

As an analytical matter, OASI consists of three separable elements:

1. The requirement that a wide class of persons must purchase specified annuities, i.e., compulsory provision for old age.
2. The requirement that the annuity must be purchased from the government; i.e., nationalization of the provision of these annuities.
3. A scheme for redistributing income, insofar as the value of the annuities to which people are entitled when they enter the system is not equal to the taxes they will pay.

Clearly, there is no necessity for these elements to be combined. . . .

Let us therefore consider each of these elements in turn to see how far, if at all, each can be justified. It will facilitate our analysis, I believe, if we consider them in reverse order.

1. Income redistribution. The present OASI program involves two major kinds of redistribution; from some OASI beneficiaries to others; from the general taxpayer to OASI beneficiaries.

The first kind of redistribution is primarily from those who entered the system relatively young, to those who entered it at an advanced age. The latter are receiving, and will for some time be receiving, a greater amount as benefits than the taxes they paid could have purchased. Under present tax and benefit schedules, on the other hand, those who entered the system at a young age will receive decidedly less.

I do not see any grounds—liberal or other—on which this particular redistribution can be defended. . . .

The second kind of redistribution arises because the system is not likely to be fully self-financing. During the period when many were covered and paying taxes, and few had qualified for benefits, the system appeared to be self-financing and indeed to be having a surplus. But this appearance depends on neglecting the obligation being accumulated with respect to the persons paying the tax. It is doubtful that the taxes paid have sufficed to finance the accumulated obligation. . . .

[Could] a subsidy from the general taxpayer . . . be justified if it is required[?] I see no grounds on which such a subsidy can be justified. We may wish to help poor people. Is there any justification for helping people whether they are poor or not because they happen to be a certain age? Is this not an entirely arbitrary redistribution?

The only argument I have ever come across to justify the redistribution involved in OASI is one that I regard as thoroughly immoral despite its wide use. This argument is that OASI redistribution on the average helps low-income people more than high-income people despite a large arbitrary element; that it would be better to do this redistribution more efficiently; but that the community will not vote for the redistribution directly though it will vote for it as part of a social security package. In essence, what this argument says is that the community can be fooled into voting for a measure that it opposes by presenting the measure in a false guise. . . .

2. *Nationalization of the provision of required annuities.* Suppose we avoid redistribution by requiring each person to pay for the annuity he gets, in the sense of course, that the premium suffices to cover the present value of the annuity, account being taken both of mortality and interest returns. What justification is there then for requiring him to purchase it from a governmental concern? If redistribution is to be accomplished, clearly the taxing power of the government must be used. But if redistribution is to be no part of the program . . . why not permit individuals who wish to do so to purchase their annuities from private concerns? . . .

Possible economies of scale are no argument for nationalizing the provision of annuities. If they are present, and the government sets up a concern to sell annuity contracts, it may be able to undersell competitors by virtue of its size. In that case, it will get the business without compulsion. If it cannot undersell them, then presumably economies of scale are not present or are not sufficient to overcome other diseconomies of governmental operation. . . .

3. *Compulsory Purchase of Annuities.* . . . One possible justification for such compulsion is strictly paternalistic. People could if they wished decide to do individually what the law requires them to do as a group. But they are separately short-sighted and improvident. "We" know better than "they" that it is in their own good to provide for their old age to a greater extent than they would voluntarily; we cannot persuade them individually; but we can persuade 51 per cent or more to compel all to do what is in their own good. This paternalism is for responsible people, hence does not even have the excuse of concern for children or madmen.

This position is internally consistent and logical. A thorough-going paternalist who holds it cannot be dissuaded by being shown that he is making a mistake in logic. He is our opponent on grounds of principle, not simply a well-meaning but misguided friend. Basically, he believes in dictatorship, benevolent and maybe majoritarian, but dictatorship none the less.

Those of us who believe in freedom must believe also in the freedom of individuals to make their own mistakes. If a man knowingly prefers to live for today, to use his resources for current enjoyment, deliberately choosing a penurious old age, by what right do we prevent him from doing so? We may argue with him, seek to persuade him that he is wrong, but are we entitled to use coercion to prevent him from doing what he chooses to do? Is there not always the possibility that he is right and that we are wrong? Humility is the distinguishing virtue of the believer in freedom; arrogance, of the paternalist. . . .

A possible justification on liberal principles for compulsory purchase of annuities is that the improvident will not suffer the consequence of their own action but will impose costs on others. We shall not, it is said, be willing to see the indigent aged suffer in dire poverty. We shall assist them by private and public charity. Hence the man who does not provide for his old age will become a public charge. Compelling him to buy an annuity is justified not for his own good but for the good of the rest of us. . . .

The belief that a large fraction of the community would become public charges if not compelled to purchase annuities owed its plausibility, at the time OASI was enacted, to the Great Depression. . . . This experience was unprecedented and has not been repeated since. It did not arise because people were improvident and failed to provide for their old age. . . .

Private arrangements for the care of the aged have altered greatly over time. Children were at one time the major means whereby people provided for their own old age. As the community became more affluent, the mores changed. The responsibilities imposed on children to care for their parents declined and more and more people came to make provision for old age in the form of accumulating property or acquiring private pension rights. More recently, the development of pension plans over and above OASI has accelerated. Indeed, some students believe that a continuation of present trends points to a society in which a large fraction of the public scrimps in their productive years to provide themselves with a higher standard of life in old age than they ever enjoyed in the prime of life. Some of us may think such a trend perverse, but if it reflects the tastes of the community, so be it.

Compulsory purchase of annuities has therefore imposed large costs for little gain. It has deprived all of us of control over a sizable fraction of our income, requiring us to devote it to a particular purpose, purchase of a retirement annuity, in a particular way, by buying it from a government concern. It has inhibited competition in the sale of annuities and the development of retirement arrangements. It has given birth to a large bureaucracy that shows tendencies of growing by what it feeds on, of extending its scope from one area of our life to another. And all this, to avoid the danger that a few people might become charges on the public. . . .

67

Franklin Delano Roosevelt

The New Goals of Politics (1932, 1935, 1941)

. . . The issue of Government has always been whether individual men and women will have to serve some system of Government or economics, or whether a system of Government and economics exists to serve individual men and women. . . .

A glance at the situation today only too clearly indicates that equality of opportunity as we have known it no longer exists. Our industrial plant is built; the problem just now is whether under existing conditions it is not overbuilt. Our last frontier has long since been reached, and there is practically no more free land. . . .

Just as freedom to farm has ceased, so also the opportunity in business has narrowed. It still is true that men can start small enterprises, trusting to native shrewdness and ability to keep abreast of competitors; but area after area has been preempted altogether by the great corporations, and even in the fields which still have no great concerns, the small man starts under a handicap. . . . If the process of concentration goes on at the same rate, at the end of another century we shall have all American industry controlled by a dozen corporations, and run by perhaps a hundred men. But plainly, we are steering a steady course toward economic oligarchy, if we are not there already.

Clearly, all this calls for a reappraisal of values. A mere builder of more industrial plants, a creator of more railroad systems, an organizer of more corporations, is as likely to be a danger as a help. The day of the great promoter or the financial Titan, to whom we granted anything if only he would build, or develop, is over. Our task now is not discovery or exploitation of natural

From Roosevelt, "The Commonwealth Club Address" (Sept., 1932), in *The Public Papers and Addresses of Franklin D. Roosevelt*, Vol. 1, Random House, 1938; "Address to the Young Democratic Clubs of America" (Aug., 1935), in *The Public Papers and Addresses of Franklin D. Roosevelt*, Vol. IV, 1938; "The Four Freedoms Speech" (1941), in *Development of United States Foreign Policy: Addresses and Messages of Franklin D. Roosevelt* (77th Cong., 2d sess.; Senate Doc. No. 188, Serial No. 10676 [Washington, 1942]).

resources, or necessarily producing more goods. It is the soberer, less dramatic business of administering resources and plants already in hand, of seeking to reestablish foreign markets for our surplus production, of meeting the problem of underconsumption, of adjusting production to consumption, of distributing wealth and products more equitably, of adapting existing economic organizations to the service of the people. The day of enlightened administration has come. . . .

As I see it, the task of Government in its relation to business is to assist the development of an economic declaration of rights, an economic constitutional order. This is the common task of statesman and business man. It is the minimum requirement of a more permanently safe order of things.

Happily, the times indicate that to create such an order not only is the proper policy of Government, but it is the only line of safety for our economic structures as well. We know, now, that these economic units cannot exist unless prosperity is uniform, that is, unless purchasing power is well distributed throughout every group in the nation. That is why even the most selfish of corporations for its own interest would be glad to see wages restored and unemployment ended and to bring the Western farmer back to his accustomed level of prosperity and to assure a permanent safety to both groups. That is why some enlightened industries themselves endeavor to limit the freedom of action of each man and business group within the industry in the common interest of all; why business men everywhere are asking a form of organization which will bring the scheme of things into balance, even though it may in some measure qualify the freedom of action of individual units within the business. . . .

We have now to apply the earlier concepts of American Government to the conditions of today.

The Declaration of Independence discusses the problem of Government in terms of a contract. Government is a relation of give and take, a contract, perforce, if we would follow the thinking out of which it grew. Under such a contract rulers were accorded power, and the people consented to that power on consideration that they be accorded certain rights. The task of statesmanship has always been the redefinition of these rights in terms of a changing and growing social order. New conditions impose new requirements upon Government and those who conduct Government.

I held, for example, in proceedings before me as Governor, the purpose of which was the removal of the Sheriff of New York, that under modern conditions it was not enough for a public official merely to evade the legal terms of official wrongdoing. He owed a positive duty as well. I said in substance that if he had acquired large sums of money, he was when accused required to explain the sources of such wealth. To that extent this wealth was colored with a public interest. I said that in financial matters, public servants should, even beyond private citizens, be held to a stern and uncompromising rectitude.

I feel that we are coming to a view through the drift of our legislation and our public thinking in the past quarter century that private economic power is, to enlarge an old phrase, a public trust as well. I hold that continued enjoyment of that power by any individual or group must depend upon the fulfillment of that trust. The men who have reached the summit of American business life know this best; happily, many of these urge the binding quality of this greater social contract.

The terms of that contract are as old as the Republic, and as new as the new economic order.

Every man has a right to life; and this means that he has also the right to make a comfortable living. He may by sloth or crime decline to exercise that right; but it may not be denied him. We have no actual famine or dearth; our industrial and agricultural mechanism can produce enough and to spare. Our Government formal and informal, political and economic, owes to everyone an avenue to possess himself of a portion of that plenty sufficient for his needs, through his own work.

Every man has a right to his own property; which means a right to be assured, to the fullest extent attainable, in the safety of his savings. By no other means can men carry the burdens of those parts of life which, in the nature of things, afford no chance of labor; childhood, sickness, old age. In all thought of property, this right is paramount; all other property rights must yield to it. If, in accord with this principle, we must restrict the operations of the speculator, the manipulator, even the financier, I believe we must accept the restriction as needful, not to hamper individualism but to protect it.

These two requirements must be satisfied, in the main, by individuals who claim and hold control of the great industrial and financial combinations which dominate so large a part of our industrial life. They have undertaken to be, not business men, but princes of property. I am not prepared to say that the system which produces them is wrong. I am very clear that they must fearlessly and competently assume the responsibility which goes with the power. . . .

[T]he responsible heads of finance and industry instead of acting each for himself, must work together to achieve the common end. They must, where necessary, sacrifice this or that private advantage; and in reciprocal self-denial must seek a general advantage. It is here that formal Government—political Government, if you choose—comes in. Whenever in the pursuit of this objective the lone wolf, the unethical competitor, the reckless promoter, the Ishmael or Insull whose hand is against every man's, declines to join in achieving an end recognized as being for the public welfare, and threatens to drag the industry back to a state of anarchy, the Government may properly be asked to apply restraint. . . .

I say from my heart that no man of my generation has any business to address youth unless he comes to that task not in a spirt of exultation, but in a spirit of humilty. I cannot expect you of a newer generation to believe me, of an older generation, if I do not frankly acknowledge that had the generation that brought you into the world been wiser and more provident and more unselfish, you would have been saved from needless difficult problems and needless pain and suffering. We may not have failed you in good intentions but we have certainly not been adequate in results. Your task, therefore, is not only to maintain the best in your heritage, but to labor to lift from the shoulders of the American people some of the burdens that the mistakes of a past generation have placed there. . . .

The severity of the recent depression, toward which we had been heading for a whole generation, has taught us that no economic or social class in the community is so richly endowed and so independent of the general community that it can safeguard its own security, let alone assure security for the general community.

The very objectives of young people have changed. In the older days a great financial fortune was too often the goal. To rule through wealth, or through the power of wealth, fired our imagination. This was the dream of the golden ladder—each individual for himself.

It is my firm belief that the newer generation of America has a different dream. You place emphasis on sufficiency of life, rather than on a plethora of riches. You think of the security for yourself and your family that will give you good health, good food, good education, good working conditions, and the opportunity for normal recreation and occasional travel. Your advancement, you hope, is along a broad highway on which thousands of your fellow men and women are advancing with you.

You and I know that this modern economic world of ours is governed by rules and regulations vastly more complex than those laid down in the days of Adam Smith or John Stuart Mill. They faced simpler mechanical processes and social needs. It is worth remembering, for example, that the business corporation, as we know it, did not exist in the days of Washington and Hamilton and Jefferson. Private businesses then were conducted solely by individuals or by partnerships in which every member was immediately and wholly responsible for success or failure. Facts are relentless. We must adjust our ideas to the facts of today. . . .

In 1911, twenty-four years ago, when I was first a member of the New York State Legislature, a number of the younger members of the Legislature worked against these old conditions and called for laws governing factory inspection, for workmen's compensation and for the limitation of work for women and children to fifty-four hours, with one day's rest in seven. Those of us who joined in this movement in the Legislature were called reformers, socialists, and wild men. We were opposed by many of the same organizations and the same individuals who are now crying aloud about the socialism involved in social security legislation, in bank deposit insurance, in farm credit, in the saving of homes, in the protection of investors and the regulation of public utilities. The reforms, however, for which we were condemned twenty-four years ago are taken today as a matter of course. And so, I believe, will be regarded the reforms that now cause such concern to the reactionaries of 1935. We come to an understanding of these new ways of protecting people because our knowledge enlarges and our capacity for organized action increases. People have learned that they can carry their burdens effectively only by cooperation. We have found out how to conquer the ravages of diseases that years ago were regarded as unavoidable and inevitable. We must learn that many other social ills can be cured.

Let me emphasize that serious as have been the errors of unrestrained individualism, I do not believe in abandoning the system of individual enterprise. The freedom and opportunity that have characterized American development in the past can be maintained if we recognize the fact that the individual system of our day calls for the collaboration of all of us to provide, at the least, security for all of us. Those words "freedom" and "opportunity" do not mean a license to climb upwards by pushing other people down.

Any paternalistic system which tries to provide for security for everyone from above only calls for an impossible task and a regimentation utterly uncongenial to the spirit of our people. But Government cooperation to help make the system of free enterprise work, to provide that minimum security without which the competitive system cannot function, to restrain the kind of individual action which in the past has been harmful to the community—that kind of governmental cooperation is entirely consistent with the best tradition of America. . . .

More than ever, we cherish the elective form of democratic government, but progress under it can easily be retarded by disagreements that relate to method and to detail rather than to the broad objectives upon which we are agreed. It is as if all of us were united in the pursuit of a common goal, but that each and every one of us were marching along a separate road of our own. If we insist on choosing different roads, most of us will not reach our common destination. . . .

Therefore, to the American youth of all parties I submit a message of confidence—Unite and Challenge! Rules are not necessarily sacred; principles are. The methods of the old order are not, as some would have you believe, above the challenge of youth. . . .

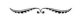

. . . [T]here is nothing mysterious about the foundations of a healthy and strong democracy. The basic things expected by our people of their political and economic systems are simple. They are:

Equality of opportunity for youth and for others.

Jobs for those who can work.

Security for those who need it.

The ending of special privilege for the few.

The preservation of civil liberties for all.

The enjoyment of the fruits of scientific progress in a wider and constantly rising standard of living.

These are the simple, basic things that must never be lost sight of in the turmoil and unbelievable complexity of our modern world. The inner and abiding strength of our economic and political systems is dependent upon the degree to which they fulfill these expectations.

Many subjects connected with our social economy call for immediate improvement.

As examples:

We should bring more citizens under the coverage of old-age pensions and unemployment insurance.

We should widen the opportunities for adequate medical care.

We should plan a better system by which persons deserving or needing gainful employment may obtain it.

I have called for personal sacrifice. I am assured of the willingness of almost all Americans to respond to that call.

A part of the sacrifice means the payment of more money in taxes. . . .

In the future days, which we seek to make secure, we look forward to a world founded upon four essential human freedoms.

The first is freedom of speech and expression—everywhere in the world.

The second is freedom of every person to worship God in his own way—everywhere in the world.

The third is freedom from want—which, translated into world terms, means economic understandings which will secure to every nation a healthy peacetime life for its inhabitants—everywhere in the world.

The fourth is freedom from fear—which, translated into world terms, means a world-wide reduction of armaments to such a point and in such a thorough fashion that no nation will be in a position to commit an act of physical aggression against any neighbor—anywhere in the world.

That is no vision of a distant millennium. It is a definite basis for a kind of world attainable in our own time and generation. That kind of world is the very antithesis of the so-called new order of tyranny which the dictators seek to create with the crash of a bomb.

To that new order we oppose the greater conception—the moral order. A good society is able to face schemes of world domination and foreign revolutions alike without fear.

Since the beginning of our American history, we have been engaged in change—in a perpetual peaceful revolution—a revolution which goes on steadily, quietly adjusting itself to changing conditions—without the concentration camp or the quick-lime in the ditch. The world order which we seek is the cooperation of free countries, working together in a friendly, civilized society.

This nation has placed its destiny in the hands and heads and hearts of its millions of free men and women; and its faith in freedom under the guidance of God. Freedom means the supremacy of human rights everywhere. Our support goes to those who struggle to gain those rights or keep them. Our strength is our unity of purpose.

To that high concept there can be no end save victory.

68

Irving Kristol

Ideology and Supply-Side Economics (1981)

The terms being applied—by the media, by politicians, by economists—to President Reagan's economic program, and most particularly to the tax-cutting aspect of this program, are "bold," "revolutionary," "a risky experiment," and so on. Clearly, a great many people are nervous about "supply-side" economics, and seem to have difficulty understanding its rationale. This is quite odd. For there is nothing really bold, or revolutionary, or experimental about this program. Nor is it at all difficult to understand. . . .

It must be said that the term itself, "supply-side economics," may be a source of initial confusion. It originates in deliberate contrast to the prevailing Keynesian approach, which emphasizes the need for government to manage and manipulate—through fiscal and monetary policies—aggregate demand so as to maintain full employment. Supply-side economists say government cannot really do this, no matter how many clever economists it hires, but that if business enterprise is permitted to function with a minimum of interference, it will invest and innovate, so as to *create* the requisite demand for the goods it produces.

There is certainly a difference in perspective here. Supply-side economists look at the economy from ground level, as it were—i.e., from the point

Reprinted from *Commentary*, Spring, 1981, by permission of the author.

426 POLITICS AND ECONOMICS

of view of the entrepreneurs and investors who are identified as the prime movers. Keynesian economists look at the economy from above—from the standpoint of a government that is a *deus ex machina,* and which, in its omniscience, intervenes discreetly to preserve a harmonious economic universe. But it is wrong to infer that we live in a Manichean world in which Supply and Demand are continually at odds, so that we always are having to declare allegiance to one as against the other. They are, rather, opposite sides of the same coin, coexisting of necessity, and there can be no question of *choosing* between them.

More precisely, it is absurd *economically* to think in terms of such a choice. Beyond a certain point, a tax on production becomes a tax on consumption—the goods become too expensive and demand falls. Similarly, beyond a certain point a tax on consumption becomes a tax on production— the decrease in demand inhibits supply. Shifting taxes from the one to the other may provide marginal benefits on occasion. But a tax on commercial transactions and economic activity is always a tax on *both* production and consumption.

When, however, one moves from a purely analytical-economic mode of thought to a political-ideological one—when, in short, one moves from economic analysis to economic policy—then the difference in perspective has significant implications. Supply-side economics naturally gives rise to an emphasis on growth, not redistribution. It aims at improving everyone's economic circumstances over time, but not necessarily in the same degree or in the same period of time. The aggregate demand created by economic activity, as seen from the supply-side, is indifferent to the issue of equality. Its bias is consequently in favor of a free market for economic activity, because this provides the most powerful economic incentives for investment, innovation, and growth. Those, on the other hand, for whom economic equality is at least as important as economic growth will always want to see government "restructure" this aggregate demand and will be indifferent to the issue of economic incentives.

However, there is another—incidental but important—source of controversy which has already been referred to, and that is the threat that supply-side economics represents to the economics profession as at present constituted. There can be little doubt that the nature of the controversy would be a lot clearer, and we would all be less befuddled, if it were not for the fact that so many distinguished economists are publicly accusing supply-side economics of being inconsistent with the principles of economic science as these are taught in graduate school and incarnated in, say, articles in the *American Economic Review.* To make matters worse, the accusation has a lot of truth in it, which is why so much of the writing in favor of supply-side economics originates outside the academic universe.

Thus one cannot understand the controversy over supply-side economics without paying some attention to the condition of the economics profession and to its vested interests, both intellectual and material. This condition is, at the moment, painfully ambiguous.

For more than three decades, we have all been looking to our best economists for guidance on economic policy. To that end we even established, after World War II, an extraordinary institution called the Council of Economic Advisers: three economists, with staff, who are supposed to provide the President and Congress with *authoritative* guidance on our economic problems, prospects, and policies. . . .

From what do their authority and expertise derive? They derive from the ambitious reconstruction of economic science after World War II in which the scheme of Keynesian macroeconomics was wedded to new, rigorous, analytical, largely mathematical techniques so as to provide, not a general, abstract model of the economic "system"—the 19th century gave us that—but a specific model of *our* economy at *this* particular time. Such a model consists of hundreds of complex correlations, spawned by econometric research, which relate one aspect of our national economic activity to another (or to many others), all fed into a computer which, having been properly programmed, can inform us as to where our economy has been coming from (to adopt a useful term from another part of the culture), where it is now, and whither it is drifting. . . . [T]his enterprise, . . . has come to be called "the neoclassical synthesis," or "neo-Keynesian" economics. . . .

It all went reasonably well for a couple of decades, though just what went reasonably well is itself one source of controversy. The neo-Keynesians will say that their sound analysis and good advice were at least partly responsible for our healthy economy from 1945 to 1970. Critics will argue that it was the existence of a healthy economy, created by businessmen and statesmen blissfully ignorant of sophisticated economic theories, that permitted economists to bask in a kind of reflected glory. (These critics point to the remarkable economic recoveries of Germany and Japan in a period when those nations had yet to learn of the neoclassical synthesis.)

But there can be no dispute over the fact that, beginning around 1970, it ceased going well and began to go badly. Not only were those annual forecasts too often very wide of the mark (especially with regard to inflation), but our economics establishment—for that is what it is, by now—could not explain the phenomenon of "stagflation," a combination of inflation and lagging economic growth that neo-Keynesian theory regards as an impossibility. . . .

Simultaneously, and inevitably, a great many people began to take a hard and critical look at the presuppositions of neo-Keynesian economics—and, above all, at the model of the economy upon which it relies. . . .

The new critique of the neo-Keynesian model . . . asserted that *this kind* of model, for all its complexity and sophistication—or one can even say because of its complexity and sophistication—reveals profound misconceptions about the nature of economic behavior, and especially about the kind of economic behavior that leads to economic growth.

It is important to realize that the conventional models are utterly blind to entrepreneurship and innovation (technological or otherwise). They can deal with quantifiable aggregates (like "investment") but what cannot be quantified they ignore. Basically, theirs is a kind of Newtonian model of an economic system, with all the "forces" balancing each other out—except sometimes, when (for reasons still unclear) there is a mismatch between overall supply and overall demand, on which occasions the government, like some benign deity, pumps in the missing quantity of demand and restores the system to equilibrium. All specifically human motivations, intentions, aspirations are ignored. It is the results of past human *behavior* that the model blandly reflects, and always after the fact. In a sense, the revolt against neo-Keynesian economics is part of a larger revulsion, visible in other social sciences as well, against behaviorism as an adequate guide to human reality.

Economists attuned to the theories incarnated in such models cannot explain the "whys" of economic phenomena. They cannot, for instance, explain why economies grow, and why some economies grow faster than others. . . .

Is that surprising? Only if we forget that economics is still a "social" science—the most methodologically rigorous of them all, to be sure, but still a social science—and not a "natural" science like physics or chemistry. We are hardly astonished, after all, if our political scientists fail to come up with a rigorous theory of political change, or if our sociologists fail to come up with a rigorous theory of social change, one which informs us precisely and authoritatively as to where our polity and society have been, where they are, where they are going. That is because we understand intuitively that any such theory, dealing with human beings, would require a degree of self-knowledge—of our present characters and personalities, from which we could make strong inferences as to our future motivations and actions—which is, by the nature of things, unavailable. (If we had any such complete self-knowledge we would be God—the Being in Whom thought and existence are one.) But economics, in striving to become an objective and positive science like physics, has promised us exactly this kind of self-knowledge, at least insofar as we are economic men and women. . . .

Supply-side economics may be viewed as a kind of "humanistic" rebellion against the mathematical-mechanical type of economic analysis in which economic aggregates, themselves dubious in nature, are related to one another so as to achieve a supposedly accurate series of snapshots of the economic universe we inhabit—something comparable to the universe we perceive when we go to a planetarium. Supply-side economics is uninterested in such a beautifully architected equilibrium because it believes this is the wrong paradigm for understanding an economy that consists of the *purposive* yet *inconstant* behavior of millions of individuals. Purposive, because economic behavior generally has as its goal the improvement of one's economic conditions. Inconstant, because only the individual himself can define "improvement" for us, and his behavior will be profoundly influenced by all sorts of contingent factors—religious heritage, family relations, and, not least, the actions of government. . . .

Nothing conveys more clearly the radically different perspectives on economic activity of supply-side and neo-Keynesian theory than the issue of incentives. . . .

Supply-side economics takes incentives—the innate human impulse to better one's condition, as Adam Smith would put it—as the *fons et origo* of economic activity and, most important, of economic growth. We do indeed know of primitive cultures where that impulse is either weak or missing— and where economic growth is, as a consequence, also weak or missing. We know, too, of historical societies where the impulse has been frustrated by religious or political authorities—and where economic growth has been sporadic and cyclical. It is only with the emergence of a modern, commercial civilization, in which self-interested transactions in the marketplace are morally vindicated and politically tolerated, that the impulse to better one's condition becomes translated into steady, progressive economic growth over decades and centuries.

Now, one way of frustrating that impulse, and economic growth as well, is to tax it. This accords with both common sense and common observation. As a matter of fact, it is a proposition that any economist, even the most devoted neo-Keynesian, will casually agree to. But when you suggest that one way of encouraging economic growth is to *decrease* the taxes on economic activity, many of these same economists will suddenly and inexplicably balk.

This balkiness is unquestionably ideological. These are people who are persuaded that the "collective goods" our taxes pay for—not only public works but also a more equal distribution of income—give us fair value, if not in purely economic terms. This is a perfectly sensible argument in defense of a tax system, but it is rarely made in the United States in 1981, presumably because it is not so evident that our taxes are actually getting us our "money's worth" in those collective goods. Instead, these economists engage in the most curious kind of research to refute the notion that anyone's incentive will be affected by a cut in taxes.

This research involves polling people, asking them whether they will work harder if their taxes are cut by 10 percent or 20 percent—or will they, perhaps, just consume more, by way of goods or leisure? Such studies often find that it makes little or no difference. . . .

Who on earth ever said that, in a commercial society such as ours, we achieve economic growth by having to work harder? On the contrary: the whole point of economic growth is that people should work *less hard*—but more productively. The human impulse to work less hard is just as strong as the human impulse to better one's condition—always has been, one suspects always will be. It is the genius of market capitalism to satisfy both of these impulses at once by encouraging entrepreneurship, the incentive to innovate, among that minority of human beings who are, unlike most of us, peculiarly "economic activists." The existence of such human beings—of entrepreneurs who, by innovating, make us all more productive without necessarily being less lazy—is simply ignored in the atomistic poll data or the aggregate statistics that economists so solemnly analyze.

It does not matter in the least whether you or I will respond to a tax cut by sharpening our economic incentives. Some of us will, some of us will not. What does matter is that there is out there, in the real business world as distinct from the academic world of the economists, a minority who will respond in this way—not necessarily the nicest people, not necessarily the smartest people, but the ones who, for whatever reason, relish economic success. For such people, the incentives to save and invest (and invest again) are extraordinarily powerful, and it is the incentives of these "economic activists" that are blunted and thwarted by a heavy tax burden. . . .

Still, taxes do have to be paid to acquire the necessary and desirable level of public services, and the question is immediately posed: how do we know, in fact, that taxes are *too* high? . . . This brings us to the so-called "Laffer curve" . . . .

All that the Laffer curve says is that, *after a certain point*, a tax—or the tax level as a whole—can become counterproductive. It is the point at which people experience taxes as an excessive and unfair burden—they are not getting their "money's worth" for the tax they pay—with the result that their incentives to economic activity are adversely affected. The tax, in effect, *represses* economic activity to such an extent that, if it were substantially reduced, the government would end up collecting more in tax revenues, since there would be a lot more economic activity contributing to these tax revenues. . . .

The question that academic critics of the Laffer curve raise is whether the American tax system has gone beyond the point of diminishing returns. "How do we know this?" they ask querulously. "Prove it," they demand. To judge by last November's election results, a clear majority of Americans are already convinced. But academic economists want *academic* proof—not, one suspects, because of their devotion to pure science, but because they would really prefer that government collect money and redistribute it more equally than see everyone improve his condition unequally through untrameled economic growth.

The academic question as to whether we are beyond the point of diminishing returns in our tax system is unanswereable in strictly academic terms.

It is a matter for *political* judgment, since it all depends on how people *feel* about the level of taxation. In wartime they feel one way; in peacetime, another. Yes, people always do grumble about taxes, at just about any level, but they don't always do something about it. They don't always make strenuous efforts to avoid or evade; they don't always regard overtime (at time-and-a-half pay) with indifference or hostility. . . .

Though one cannot provide the kind of elegant, mathematical proof economists wish, there are in fact some persuasive signs that the American economy has gone too far up on the Laffer curve. One is our flourishing (because untaxed) underground economy—just how large it is, no one knows. . . .

Another such sign is the tens of billions of dollars that seek and find legal tax shelters, investments that would not exist except for their relative tax advantage and which are therefore, by definition as it were, uneconomic. . . .

The real opposition to the Laffer curve has less to do with economics than with liberal egalitarianism. . . . Does anyone really think that, even if we could prove beyond the shadow of a doubt that reducing the tax rates on more affluent Americans would result in their actually paying more in taxes than they now do, the reductions would become less controversial? There are many people, including quite a few economists, for whom it is more important to have a symbolic tax rate of 70 percent on very high incomes even if very few of the rich actually pay it, than to have an effective tax rate of, say, 40 percent which many of the rich would pay instead of fooling around with (often problematic) tax shelters.

But there are some thoughtful people who, having little quarrel with the general tenor of supply-side economics, nevertheless wonder whether it is appropriate in today's inflationary economy. . . .

That classical tradition has its own policy for coping with inflation. And, in truth, it is a policy that has always worked. It involves slowing down the rate of growth of the money supply to bring it in line with the growth in productivity. It also involves reducing governmental expenditures and bringing the budget into balance. . . . Both of these measures, taken jointly, induce a recession, during which all of the distortions caused by inflation are "purged" from (or "wrung out of") the economic system. After the recession has achieved this effect, a normal economic recovery may be expected to set in, and noninflationary growth is once again possible. . . .

I have noted that these policies have in fact worked in the past. But would they work under the present, truly novel, circumstances? . . . One of the novel things about our present economic condition is not merely the endemic high inflation but the existence of a welfare state. This means that as the economy slows down, government expenditures actually increase, as the number of people who are now "in need" increases, and all sorts of welfare programs are triggered. The deficit, instead of going down, tends to go up—especially since tax revenues are also decreasing. As a result, whereas a relatively shallow and short-lived recession could do the trick in a pre-welfare state economy, what is now required is a deep and prolonged recession. (This is what Margaret Thatcher has discovered, to her dismay.) The economic costs of such a recession are so enormous as to make it a most questionable instrument of policy.

And the political costs are, to put it bluntly, intolerable. . . .

That is why the Reagan administration has added a cut in tax rates, for business firms and individuals, to the traditional dual strategy of fighting inflation by slowing down the growth of the money supply and of government spending. It is the only possible answer to our predicament—encouraging economic growth so as to annul or at least ameliorate the recessionary effects of other anti-inflationary policies. . . .

Will it work? There are plenty of good reasons for thinking it will. True, it might temporarily increase the deficit and the national debt—but if the predicted growth eventually occurs, both deficit and debt will be imposed on a larger and stronger economy which can easily support them.

Moreover, we do have some solid historical evidence that the "feedback" effects of cuts in tax rates, in terms of increased tax revenues, are always larger than our economists and Treasury officials—whose econometric models cannot cope with such "feedback" effects—expect to be the case. This is what happened with the Kennedy-Johnson tax cuts which were as large, in terms of the 1964 economy, as the Reagan tax cuts are in the 1981 economy. There is no reason why it should not happen again.

One final point, often overlooked. Because of the increase in social-security taxes that has taken effect this year, and because of automatic "bracket creep" in the income tax resulting from inflation, we shall in effect be experiencing something like a $40-billion tax *increase* in 1981. No economist of any persuasion, no politician of any persuasion, no commentator (liberal or conservative) has been heard to say that such a tax increase would be good for the economy in its present condition. Yet many of these same people are volubly disturbed by a tax cut that will, in 1981, at best keep our tax burden in a steady state, and in 1982 only alleviate it modestly.

Somehow, the current condition of economic theory, combined with existing ideological trends, has given us a level of public discourse on economic policy that is disgracefully inadequate to our economic and political realities. No one, critical though he may be, seems even to feel the need to offer a practicable alternative to Reagan's economic policy. One even suspects that many critics of supply-side economics want above all to see it fail, since its success would threaten their ideological investments.

69

Alexis de Tocqueville

Soft Despotism (1840)

The principle of equality, which makes men independent of each other, gives them a habit and a taste for following in their private actions no other guide but their own will. This complete independence, which they constantly enjoy toward their equals and in the intercourse of private life, tends to make them look upon all authority with a jealous eye and speedily suggests to them the notion and the love of political freedom. Men living at such times have a natural bias towards free institutions. Take any one of them at a venture and search if you can his most deep-seated instincts, and you will find that, of all governments, he will soonest conceive and most highly value that government whose head he has himself elected and whose administration he may control.

Of all the political effects produced by the equality of conditions, this love of independence is the first to strike the observing and to alarm the timid; nor can it be said that their alarm is wholly misplaced, for anarchy has a more formidable aspect in democratic countries than elsewhere. . . .

I am, however, persuaded that anarchy is not the principal evil that democratic ages have to fear, but the least. For the principle of equality begets two tendencies: the one leads men straight to independence and may suddenly drive them into anarchy; the other conducts them by a longer, more secret, but more certain road to servitude. Nations readily discern the former tendency and are prepared to resist it; they are led away by the latter, without perceiving its drift; hence it is peculiarly important to point it out.

For myself, I am so far from urging as a reproach to the principle of equality that it renders men intractable, that this very circumstance principally calls forth my approbation. I admire to see how it deposits in the mind and heart of man that dim conception and instinctive love of political independence, thus preparing the remedy for the ill which it engenders. It is on this very account that I am attached to it.

From *Democracy in America* by Alexis de Tocqueville, translated by Henry Reeve, 1862, with minor changes.

The notion of secondary powers placed between the sovereign and his subjects occurred naturally to the imagination of aristocratic nations, because those communities contained individuals or families raised above the common level and apparently destined to command by their birth, their education, and their wealth. This same notion is naturally wanting in the minds of men in democratic ages, for converse reasons; it can only be intro-duced artificially, it can only be kept there with difficulty. . . . Moreover, in politics as well as in philosophy and in religion the intellect of democratic nations is peculiarly open to simple and general notions. Complicated sys-tems are repugnant to it, and its favorite conception is that of a great nation composed of citizens all resembling the same pattern and all governed by a single power.

The very next notion to that of a sole and central power which presents itself to the minds of men in the ages of equality is the notion of uniformity of legislation. As every man sees that he differs but little from those about him, he cannot understand why a rule that is applicable to one man should not be equally applicable to all others. Hence the slightest privileges are repugnant to his reason; the faintest dissimilarities in the political institu-tions of the same people offend him, and uniformity of legislation appears to him to be the first condition of good government. . . .

As the conditions of men become equal among a people, individuals seem of less importance and society of greater dimensions; or rather every citizen, being assimilated to all the rest, is lost in the crowd, and nothing stands conspicuous but the great and imposing image of the people at large. . . .

As the men who inhabit democratic countries have no superiors, no inferiors, and no habitual or necessary partners in their undertakings, they readily fall back upon themselves and consider themselves as beings apart. I had occasion to point this out at considerable length in treating of individ-ualism. Hence such men can never, without an effort, tear themselves from their private affairs to engage in public business. . . .

I have also had occasion to show how the increasing love of well-being and the fluctuating character of property cause democratic nations to dread all violent disturbance. The love of public tranquillity is frequently the only passion which these nations retain. . . .

As in ages of equality no man is compelled to lend his assistance to his fellow men, and none has any right to expect much support from them, every-one is at once independent and powerless. These two conditions, which must never be either separately considered or confounded together, inspire the citizen of a democratic country with very contrary propensities. His independence fills him with self-reliance and pride among his equals; his debility makes him feel from time to time the want of some outward assistance, which he cannot expect from any of them, because they are all impotent and unsympathizing.

In this predicament he naturally turns his eyes to that imposing power which alone rises above the level of universal depression. . . .

My object is to remark that all these various rights which have been successively wrested, in our time, from classes, corporations, and individuals have not served to raise new secondary powers on a more democratic basis, but have uniformly been concentrated in the hands of the sovereign. Everywhere the state acquires more and more direct control over the humblest members of the community and a more exclusive power of governing each of them in his smallest concerns.

Almost all the charitable establishments of Europe were formerly in the hands of private persons or of corporations; they are now almost all dependent on the supreme government, and in many countries are actually administered by that power. The state almost exclusively undertakes to supply bread to the hungry, assistance and shelter to the sick, work to the idle, and to act as the sole reliever of all kinds of misery.

Education, as well as charity, has become in most countries at the present day a national concern. The state receives, and often takes, the child from the arms of the mother to hand it over to official agents; the state undertakes to train the heart and to instruct the mind of each generation. Uniformity prevails in the courses of public instruction as in everything else; diversity as well as freedom is disappearing day by day. . . .

There exists among the modern nations of Europe one great cause, independent of all those which have already been pointed out, which perpetually contributes to extend the agency or to strengthen the prerogative of the supreme power, though it has not been sufficiently attended to: I mean the growth of manufactures, which is fostered by the progress of social equality. Manufacturers generally collect a multitude of men on the same spot, among whom new and complex relations spring up. These men are exposed by their calling to great and sudden alternations of plenty and want, during which public tranquillity is endangered. It may also happen that these employments sacrifice the health and even the life of those who gain by them or of those who live by them. Thus the manufacturing classes require more regulation, superintendence, and restraint than the other classes of society, and it is natural that the powers of government should increase in the same proportion as those classes. . . .

As a nation becomes more engaged in manufactures, the want of roads, canals, harbors, and other works of a semi-public nature, which facilitate the acquisition of wealth, is more strongly felt; and as a nation becomes more democratic, private individuals are less able, and the state more able, to execute works of such magnitude. I do not hesitate to assert that the manifest tendency of all governments at the present time is to take upon themselves alone the execution of these undertakings, by which means they daily hold in closer dependence the population which they govern.

On the other hand, in proportion as the power of a state increases and its necessities are augmented, the state consumption of manufactured produce is always growing larger; and these commodities are generally made in the arsenals or establishments of the government. Thus in every kingdom the ruler becomes the principal manufacturer: he collects and retains in his service a vast number of engineers, architects, mechanics, and handicraftsmen.

Not only is he the principal manufacturer, but he tends more and more to become the chief, or rather the master, of all other manufacturers. As private persons become powerless by becoming more equal, they can effect nothing in manufactures without combination; but the government naturally seeks to place these combinations under its own control.

It must be admitted that these collective beings, which are called combinations, are stronger and more formidable than a private individual can ever be, and that they have less of the responsibility for their own actions; whence it seems reasonable that they should not be allowed to retain so great an independence of the supreme government as might be conceded to a private individual. . . .

[T]he incessant increase of the prerogative of the supreme government, [becomes] more centralized, more adventurous, more absolute, more extensive, the people perpetually falling under the control of the public administration, led insensibly to surrender to it some further portion of their individual independence, till the very men who from time to time upset a throne and trample on a race of kings bend more and more obsequiously to the slightest dictate of a clerk. . . .

I seek to trace the novel features under which despotism may appear in the world. The first thing that strikes the observation is an innumerable multitude of men, all equal and alike, incessantly endeavoring to procure the petty and paltry pleasures with which they glut their lives. Each of them, living apart, is as a stranger to the fate of all the rest; his children and his private friends constitute to him the whole of mankind. As for the rest of his fellow citizens, he is close to them, but he sees them not; he touches them, but he feels them not; he exists but in himself and for himself alone; and if his kindred still remain to him, he may be said at any rate to have lost his country.

Above this race of men stands an immense and tutelary power, which takes upon itself alone to secure their gratifications and to watch over their fate. That power is absolute, minute, regular, provident, and mild. It would be like the authority of a parent if, like that authority, its object was to prepare men for manhood; but it seeks, on the contrary, to keep them in perpetual childhood: it is well content that the people should rejoice, provided they think of nothing but rejoicing. For their happiness such a government willingly labors, but it chooses to be the sole agent and the only arbiter of that happiness; it provides for their security, foresees and supplies their necessities, facilitates their pleasures, manages their principal concerns, directs their industry, regulates the descent of property, and subdivides their inheritances: what remains, but to spare them all the care of thinking and all the trouble of living?

Thus it every day renders the exercise of the free agency of man less useful and less frequent; it circumscribes the will within a narrower range and gradually robs a man of all the uses of himself. The principle of equality has prepared men for these things; it has predisposed men to endure them and often to look on them as benefits.

After having thus successively taken each member of the community in its powerful grasp and fashioned him at will, the supreme power then extends its arm over the whole community. It covers the surface of society with a network of small complicated rules, minute and uniform, through which the most original minds and the most energetic characters cannot penetrate, to rise above the crowd. The will of man is not shattered, but softened, bent, and guided; men are seldom forced by it to act, but they are constantly restrained from acting. Such a power does not destroy, but it prevents existence; it does not tyrannize, but it compresses, enervates, extinguishes, and stupefies a people, till each nation is reduced to being nothing better than a flock of timid and industrious animals, of which the government is the shepherd.

I have always thought that servitude of the regular, quiet, and gentle kind which I have just described might be combined more easily than is commonly believed with some of the outward forms of freedom, and that it might even establish itself under the wing of the sovereignty of the people.

Our contemporaries are constantly excited by two conflicting passions: they want to be led. and they wish to remain free. As they cannot destroy either the one or the other of these contrary propensities, they strive to satisfy them both at once. They devise a sole, tutelary, and all-powerful form of government, but elected by the people. They combine the principle of centralization and that of popular sovereignty; this gives them a respite: they console themselves for being in tutelage by the reflection that they have chosen their own guardians. Every man allows himself to be put in leadingstrings, because he sees that it is not a person or a class of persons, but the people at large who hold the end of his chain.

By this system the people shake off their state of dependence just long enough to select their master and then relapse into it again. A great many persons at the present day are quite contented with this sort of compromise between administrative despotism and the sovereignty of the people; and they think they have done enough for the protection of individual freedom when they have surrendered it to the power of the nation at large. This does not satisfy me: the nature of him I am to obey signifies less to me than the fact of extorted obedience. . . .

It is in vain to summon a people who have been rendered so dependent on the central power to choose from time to time the representatives of that power; this rare and brief exercise of their free choice, however important it may be, will not prevent them from gradually losing the faculties of thinking, feeling, and acting for themselves, and thus gradually falling below the level of humanity. . . .

70

Thomas Jefferson

Against Manufacturing (1787)

. . . The political economists of Europe have established it as a principle, that every State should endeavor to manufacture for itself; and this principle, like many others, we transfer to America, without calculating the difference of circumstance which should often produce a difference of result. In Europe the lands are either cultivated, or locked up against the cultivator. Manufacture must therefore be resorted to of necessity not of choice, to support the surplus of their people. But we have an immensity of land courting the industry of the husbandman. Is it best then that all our citizens should be employed in its improvement, or that one half should be called off from that to exercise manufactures and handicraft arts for the other? Those who labor in the earth are the chosen people of God, if ever He had a chosen people, whose breasts He has made His peculiar deposit for substantial and genuine virtue. It is the focus in which he keeps alive that sacred fire, which otherwise might escape from the face of the earth. Corruption of morals in the mass of cultivators is a phenomenon of which no age nor nation has furnished an example. It is the mark set on those, who, not looking up to heaven, to their own soil and industry, as does the husbandman, for their subsistence, depend for it on casualties and caprice of customers. Dependence begets subservience and venality, suffocates the germ of virtue, and prepares fit tools for the designs of ambition. This, the natural progress and consequence of the arts, has sometimes perhaps been retarded by accidental circumstances; but, generally speaking, the proportion which the aggregate of the other classes of citizens bears in any State to that of its husbandmen, is

From Jefferson, "Query XIX," in *Notes on the State of Virginia*, London, 1787.

the proportion of its unsound to its healthy parts, and is a good enough barometer whereby to measure its degree of corruption. While we have land to labor then, let us never wish to see our citizens occupied at a workbench, or twirling a distaff. Carpenters, masons, smiths, are wanting in husbandry; but, for the general operations of manufacture, let our workshops remain in Europe. It is better to carry provisions and materials to workmen there, than bring them to the provisions and materials, and with them their manners and principles. The loss by the transportation of commodities across the Atlantic will be made up in happiness and permanence of government. The mobs of great cities add just so much to the support of pure government, as sores do to the strength of the human body. It is the manners and spirit of a people which preserve a republic in vigor. A degeneracy in these is a canker which soon eats to the heart of its laws and constitution.

71

Alexander Hamilton

Report on Manufactures (1791)

. . . It ought readily to be conceded that the cultivation of the earth—as the primary and most certain source of national supply—as the immediate and chief source of subsistence to man—as the principal source of those materials which constitute the nutriment of other kinds of labor—as including a state most favourable to the freedom and independence of the human mind—one, perhaps, most conducive to the multiplication of the human species—has *intrinsically a strong claim to pre-eminence over every other kind of industry.*

But, that it has a title to anything like an exclusive predilection, in any country, ought to be admitted with great caution. . . .

It has been maintained that agriculture is, not only, the most productive, but the only productive, species of industry. . . .

To this it has been answered. . . .

From Hamilton, *Report on Manufactures,* in *Reports of the Secretary of the Treasury of the United States,* Vol. I (Washington, 1837).

"That the annual produce of the land and labour of a country can only be increased in two ways—by some improvement in the *productive powers* of the useful labour, which actually exists within it, or by some increase in the quantity of such labour: That with regard to the first, the labor of artificers being capable of greater subdivision and simplicity of operation than that of cultivators, it is susceptible, in a proportionably greater degree, of improvement in its *productive powers*, whether to be derived from an accession of skill, or from the application of ingenious machinery; in which particular, therefore, the labor employed in the culture of land can pretend to no advantage over that engaged in manufactures. . . ."

. . . But while the *exclusive* productiveness of agricultural labour has been thus denied and refuted, the superiority of its productiveness has been conceded without hesitation. . . .

One of the arguments made use of in support of the idea may be pronounced both quaint and superficial—It amounts to this—That in the productions of the soil, nature co-operates with man; and that the effect of their joint labour must be greater than that of the labour of man alone.

This however, is far from being a necessary inference. It is very conceivable, that the labor of man alone, laid out upon a work requiring great skill and art to bring it to perfection, may be more productive, *in value*, than the labour of nature and man combined, when directed towards more simple operations and objects: And when it is recollected to what an extent the agency of nature, in the application of the mechanical powers, is made auxiliary to the prosecution of manufactures, the suggestion, which has been noticed, loses even the appearance of plausibility.

It might also be observed, with a contrary view, that the labor employed in agriculture is in a great measure periodical and occasional, depending on seasons, liable to various and long intermissions; while that occupied in many manufactures is constant and regular, extending through the year, embracing in some instances night as well as day. It is also probable, that there are among the cultivators of land, more examples of remissness, than among artificers. The farmer, from the peculiar fertility of his land, or some other favorable circumstance, may frequently obtain a livelihood, even with a considerable degree of carelessness in the mode of cultivation; but the artisan can with difficulty effect the same object, without exerting himself pretty equally with all those who are engaged in the same pursuit. And if it may likewise be assumed as a fact, that manufactures open a wider field to exertions of ingenuity than agriculture, it would not be a strained conjecture, that the labour employed in the former, being at once more *constant*, more uniform and more ingenious, than that which is employed in the latter, will be found, at the same time more productive. . . .

It is now proper to proceed a step further, and to enumerate the principal circumstances, from which it may be inferred—that manufacturing establishments not only occasion a positive augmentation of the produce and revenue of the society, but that they contribute essentially to rendering them greater than they could possibly be, without such establishments. These circumstances are—

1. The division of labour.
2. An extension of the use of machinery.
3. Additional employment to classes of the community not ordinarily engaged in the business.
4. The promoting of emigration from foreign countries.
5. The furnishing greater scope for the diversity of talents and dispositions which discriminate men from each other.
6. The affording a more ample and various field for enterprize.
7. The creating in some instances a new, and securing in all, a more certain and steady demand for the surplus produce of the soil.

Each of these circumstances has a considerable influence upon the total mass of industrious effort in a community: Together, they add to it a degree of energy and effect, which are not easily conceived. . . .

It has justly been observed, that there is a scarcely any thing of greater moment in the economy of a nation than the proper division of labour. The separation of occupations causes each to be carried to a much greater perfection, than it could possibly acquire, if they were blended. This arises principally from three circumstances—

1st. The greater skill and dexterity naturally resulting from a constant and undivided application to a single object. It is evident, that these properties must increase, in proportion to the separation and simplification of objects and the steadiness of the attention devoted to each; and must be less in proportion to the complication of objects, and the number among which the attention is distracted.

2nd. The economy of time, by avoiding the loss of it, incident to a frequent transition from one operation to another of a different nature. This depends on various circumstanes—the transition itself—the orderly disposition of the implements, machines and materials employed in the operation to be relinquished—the preparatory steps to the commencement of a new one—the interruption of the impulse, which the mind of the workman acquires, from being engaged in a particular operation—the distractions, hesitations and reluctances, which attend the passage from one kind of business to another.

3rd. An extension of the use of machinery. A man occupied on a single object will have it more in his power, and will be more naturally led to exert his imagination in devising methods to facilitate and abridge labour, than if he were perplexed by a variety of independent and dissimilar operations. . . .

The employment of Machinery forms an item of great importance in the general mass of national industry. 'Tis an artificial force brought in aid of the natural force of man; and, to all the purposes of labour, is an increase of hands; an accession of strength, *unencumbered too by the expense of maintaining the laborer*. May it not therefore be fairly inferred, that those occupations, which give greatest scope to the use of this auxiliary, contribute most to the general Stock of industrious effort, and, in consequence, to the general product of industry? . . .

For the purpose of this vent, a domestic market is greatly to be preferred to a foreign one; because it is the nature of things, far more to be relied upon. . . .

[T]he multiplication of manufactories not only furnishes a market for those articles which have been accustomed to be produced in abundance in a country, but it likewise creates a demand for such as were either unknown or produced in inconsiderable quantities. The bowels as well as the surface of the earth are ransacked for articles which were before neglected. Animals, plants and minerals acquire a utility and a value which were before unexplored. . . .

If the system of perfect liberty to industry and commerce were the prevailing system of nations, the arguments which dissuade a country, in the predicament of the United States, from the zealous pursuit of manufactures, would doubtless have great force. . . . In such a state of things, each country would have the full benefit of its peculiar advantages to compensate for its deficiencies or disadvantages. . . .

But the system which has been mentioned, is far from characterising the general policy of nations. The prevalent one has been regulated by an opposite spirit. The consequence of it is, that the United States are to a certain extent in the situation of a country precluded from foreign commerce. They can indeed, without difficulty obtain from abroad the manufactured supplies, of which they are in want; but they experience numerous and very injurious impediments to the emission and vent of their own commodities. . . .

In such a position of things, the United States cannot exchange with Europe on equal terms; and the want of reciprocity would render them the victim of a system which should induce them to confine their views to agriculture, and refrain from manufactures. A constant and increasing necessity, on their part, for the commodities of Europe, and only a partial and occasional demand for their own, in return, could not but expose them to a state of impoverishment, compared with the opulence to which their political and natural advantages authorise them to aspire. . . .

The conversion of their waste into cultivated lands is certainly a point of great moment in the political calculations of the United States. . . .

But it does, by no means, follow, that the progress of new settlements would be retarded by the extension of manufactures. The desire of being an independent proprietor of land is founded on such strong principles in the human breast, that where the opportunity of becoming so is as great as it is in the United States, the proportion will be small of those, whose situations would otherwise lead to it, who would be diverted from it towards manufactures. . . .

The remaining objections to a particular encouragement of manufacturers in the United States now require to be examined.

One of these turns on the proposition, that industry, if left to itself, will naturally find its way to the most useful and profitable employment: whence it is inferred that manufactures without the aid of government will grow up as soon and as fast, as the natural state of things and the interest of the community may require.

Against the solidity of this hypothesis, in the full latitude of the terms, very cogent reasons may be offered. These have relation to—the strong influence of habit and the spirit of imitation—the fear of want of success in untried enterprises—the intrinsic difficulties incident to first essays towards a competition with those who have previously attained to perfection in the business to be attempted—the bounties premiums and other artificial encouragements, with which foreign nations second the exertions of their own citizens in the branches, in which they are to be rivalled.

Experience teaches, that men are often so much governed by what they are accustomed to see and practise, that the simplest and most obvious improvements, in the most ordinary occupations, are adopted with hesitation, reluctance, and by slow gradations. The spontaneous transition to new pursuits, in a community long habituated to different ones, may be expected to be attended with proportionably greater difficulty. When former occupations ceased to yield a profit adequate to the subsistence of their followers, or when there was an absolute deficiency of employment in them, owing to the superabundance of hands, changes would ensue; but these changes would be likely to be more tardy than might consist with the interest either of individuals or of the society. In many cases they would not happen, while a bare support could be insured by an adherence to ancient courses; though a resort to a more profitable employment might be practicable. To produce the desirable changes as early as may be expedient, may therefore require the incitement and patronage of government. . . .

Not only the wealth, but the independence and security of a country, appear to be materially connected with the prosperity of manufactures. Every nation, with a view to those great objects, ought to endeavour to possess within itself all the essentials of national supply. These comprise the means of *subsistence, habitation, clothing,* and *defence.*

The possession of these is necessary to the perfection of the body politic; to the safety as well as to the welfare of the society; the want of either is the want of an important organ of political life and motion; and in the various crises which await a state, it must severely feel the effects of any such deficiency. The extreme embarrassments of the United States during the late war, from an incapacity of supplying themselves, are still matter of keen recollection: A future war might be expected again to exemplify the mischiefs and dangers of a situation to which that incapacity is still in too great a degree applicable, unless changed by timely and vigorous exertion. To effect this change, as fast as shall be prudent, merits all the attention and all the Zeal of our Public Councils; 'tis the next great work to be accomplished. . . .

Among the political means for promoting manufactures that Hamilton discusses are duties on foreign articles competing with domestic ones, prohibitions of competing articles, pecuniary bounties for new enterprises, premiums, exempting materials of manufacture from duties, encouraging new inventions and discoveries, and facilitating transportation of commodities. In discussing objections to bounties, Hamilton wrote:

It is a species of encouragement more positive and direct than any other, and for that very reason, has a more immediate tendency to stimulate and uphold new enterprises, increasing the chances of profit, and diminishing the risks of loss, in the first attempts. . . .

A question has been made concerning the constitutional right of the government of the United States to apply this species of encouragement, but there is certainly no good foundation for such a question. The National Legislature has express authority "To lay and collect taxes, duties, imposts, and excises, to pay the debts, and provide for the *common defence* and *general welfare*" with no other qualifications than that "all duties, imposts, and excises shall be *uniform* throughout the United States and that no capitation or other direct tax shall be laid unless in proportion to numbers ascertained by a census or enumeration taken on the principles prescribed in the Constitution," and that "no tax or duty shall be laid on articles exported from any State."

These three qualifications excepted the power to *raise money* is plenary and *indefinite*, and the objects to which it may be *appropriated* are no less comprehensive than the payment of the public debts, and the providing for the common defence and *general welfare*. The terms "*general welfare*" were doubtless intended to signify more than was expressed or imported in those which preceded; otherwise, numerous exigencies incident to the affairs of a nation would have been left without a provision. The phrase is as comprehensive as any that could have been used; because it was not fit that the constitutional authority of the Union to appropriate its revenues should have been restricted within narrower limits than the "General Welfare" and because this necessarily embraces a vast variety of particulars, which are susceptible neither of specification or of definition.

It is therefore of necessity left to the discretion of the National Legislature, to pronounce upon the objects, which concern the general welfare, and for which under that description, an appropriation of money is requisite and proper. And there seems to be no room for a doubt that whatever concerns the general interest of *learning*, of *agriculture*, of *manufactures*, and of *commerce*, are within the sphere of the national councils, *as far as regards an application of money*. . . .

72

Lucas v. South Carolina Coastal Council (1992)

Justice Scalia delivered the opinion of the Court.

. . . Lucas in 1986 purchased the two lots at issue in this litigation. . . . [A]t the time Lucas acquired these parcels, he was not legally obliged to obtain a permit from the Council in advance of any development activity. His intention with respect to the lots was to do what the owners of the immediately adjacent parcels had already done: erect single family residences. He commissioned architectural drawings for this purpose.

The Beachfront Management Act brought Lucas's plans to an abrupt end. Under that 1988 legislation, the Council was directed to establish a "baseline" connecting the landward most "point[s] of erosion . . . during the past forty years" in the region of the Isle of Palms that includes Lucas's lots. In action not challenged here, the Council fixed this baseline landward of Lucas's parcels. That was significant, for under the Act construction of occupable improvements was flatly prohibited seaward of a line drawn 20 feet landward of, and parallel to, the baseline. The Act provided no exceptions.

Lucas promptly filed suit in the South Carolina Court of Common Pleas, contending that the Beachfront Management Act's construction bar effected a taking of his property without just compensation. Lucas did not take issue with the validity of the Act as a lawful exercise of South Carolina's police power, but contended that the Act's complete extinguishment of his property's value entitled him to compensation regardless of whether the legislature had acted in furtherance of legitimate police power objectives. Following a bench trial, the court agreed. Among its factual determinations was the finding that "at the time Lucas purchased the two lots, both were zoned for single family residential construction and . . . there were no restrictions imposed upon such use of the property by either the State of South Carolina, the County of Charleston, or the Town of the Isle of Palms." The trial court further found that the Beachfront Management Act decreed a permanent ban on construction insofar as Lucas's lots were concerned, and that this prohibition "deprive[d] Lucas of any reasonable economic use of the lots, . . . eliminated the unrestricted right of use, and render[ed] them valueless." The court thus concluded that Lucas's properties had been "taken" by operation

From *Lucas v. South Carolina Coastal Council*, 505 U.S. 1003 (1992).

of the Act, and it ordered respondent to pay "just compensation" in the amount of $1,232,387.50.

The Supreme Court of South Carolina reversed. It found dispositive what it described as Lucas's concession "that the Beachfront Management Act [was] properly and validly designed to preserve . . . South Carolina's beaches." Failing an attack on the validity of the statute as such, the court believed itself bound to accept the "uncontested . . . findings" of the South Carolina legislature that new construction in the coastal zone—such as petitioner intended—threatened this public resource. The Court ruled that when a regulation respecting the use of property is designed "to prevent serious public harm," no compensation is owing under the Takings Clause regardless of the regulation's effect on the property's value.

. . . Prior to Justice Holmes' exposition in *Pennsylvania Coal Co. v. Mahon*, it was generally thought that the Takings Clause reached only a "direct appropriation" of property, or the functional equivalent of a "practical ouster of [the owner's] possession." Justice Holmes recognized in *Mahon*, however, that if the protection against physical appropriations of private property was to be meaningfully enforced, the government's power to redefine the range of interests included in the ownership of property was necessarily constrained by constitutional limits. If, instead, the uses of private property were subject to unbridled, uncompensated qualification under the police power, "the natural tendency of human nature [would be] to extend the qualification more and more until at last private property disappear[ed]." These considerations gave birth in that case to the oft cited maxim that, "while property may be regulated to a certain extent, if regulation goes too far it will be recognized as a taking."

Nevertheless, our decision in *Mahon* offered little insight into when, and under what circumstances, a given regulation would be seen as going "too far" for purposes of the Fifth Amendment. In 70 odd years of succeeding "regulatory takings" jurisprudence, we have generally eschewed any "set formula" for determining how far is too far, preferring to "engag[e] in . . . essentially ad hoc, factual inquiries," We have, however, described at least two discrete categories of regulatory action as compensable without case specific inquiry into the public interest advanced in support of the restraint. The first encompasses regulations that compel the property owner to suffer a physical "invasion" of his property. In general (at least with regard to permanent invasions), no matter how minute the intrusion, and no matter how weighty the public purpose behind it, we have required compensation. For example, in *Loretto v. Teleprompter Manhattan CATV Corp.*, we determined that New York's law requiring landlords to allow television cable companies to emplace cable facilities in their apartment buildings constituted a taking, even though the facilities occupied at most only 1 1/2 cubic feet of the landlords' property. . . .

The second situation in which we have found categorical treatment appropriate is where regulation denies all economically beneficial or productive use of land. As we have said on numerous occasions, the Fifth Amendment is violated when land use regulation "does not substantially advance legitimate state interests *or denies an owner economically viable use of his land.*" We have never set forth the justification for this rule. Perhaps it is simply, as Justice Brennan suggested, that total deprivation of beneficial use is, from the landowner's point of view, the equivalent of a physical appropriation. . . .

On the other side of the balance, affirmatively supporting a compensation requirement, is the fact that regulations that leave the owner of land without economically beneficial or productive options for its use—typically, as here, by requiring land to be left substantially in its natural state—carry with them a heightened risk that private property is being pressed into some form of public service under the guise of mitigating serious public harm. . . .

We think, in short, that there are good reasons for our frequently expressed belief that when the owner of real property has been called upon to sacrifice *all* economically beneficial uses in the name of the common good, that is, to leave his property economically idle, he has suffered a taking.

The trial court found Lucas's two beachfront lots to have been rendered valueless by respondent's enforcement of the coastal zone construction ban. Under Lucas's theory of the case, which rested upon our "no economically viable use" statements, that finding entitled him to compensation. Lucas believed it unnecessary to take issue with either the purposes behind the Beachfront Management Act, or the means chosen by the South Carolina Legislature to effectuate those purposes. The South Carolina Supreme Court, however, thought otherwise. In its view, the Beachfront Management Act was no ordinary enactment, but involved an exercise of South Carolina's "police powers" to mitigate the harm to the public interest that petitioner's use of his land might occasion. By neglecting to dispute the findings enumerated in the Act or otherwise to challenge the legislature's purposes, petitioner "concede[d] that the beach/dune area of South Carolina's shores is an extremely valuable public resource; that the erection of new construction, *inter alia*, contributes to the erosion and destruction of this public resource; and that discouraging new construction in close proximity to the beach/dune area is necessary to prevent a great public harm." In the court's view, these concessions brought petitioner's challenge within a long line of this Court's cases sustaining against Due Process and Takings Clause challenges the State's use of its "police powers" to enjoin a property owner from activities akin to public nuisances.

It is correct that many of our prior opinions have suggested that "harmful or noxious uses" of property may be proscribed by government regulation without the requirement of compensation. For a number of reasons, however, we think the South Carolina Supreme Court was too quick to conclude that that principle decides the present case. . . .

When it is understood that "prevention of harmful use" was merely our early formulation of the police power justification necessary to sustain (without compensation) *any* regulatory diminution in value; and that the distinction between regulation that "prevents harmful use" and that which "confers benefits" is difficult, if not impossible, to discern on an objective, value free basis; it becomes self evident that noxious use logic cannot serve as a touchstone to distinguish regulatory "takings"—which require compensation— from regulatory deprivations that do not require compensation. A *fortiori* the legislature's recitation of a noxious use justification cannot be the basis for departing from our categorical rule that total regulatory takings must be compensated. If it were, departure would virtually always be allowed. The South Carolina Supreme Court's approach would essentially nullify *Mahon*'s affirmation of limits to the noncompensable exercise of the police power. Our cases provide no support for this: None of them that employed the logic of "harmful use" prevention to sustain a regulation involved an allegation that the regulation wholly eliminated the value of the claimant's land.

Where the State seeks to sustain regulation that deprives land of all economically beneficial use, we think it may resist compensation only if the logically antecedent inquiry into the nature of the owner's estate shows that the proscribed use interests were not part of his title to begin with. This accords, we think, with our "takings" jurisprudence, which has traditionally been guided by the understandings of our citizens regarding the content of, and the State's power over, the "bundle of rights" that they acquire when they obtain title to property. It seems to us that the property owner necessarily expects the uses of his property to be restricted, from time to time, by various measures newly enacted by the State in legitimate exercise of its police powers; "[a]s long recognized, some values are enjoyed under an implied limitation and must yield to the police power." *Pennsylvania Coal Co. v. Mahon.* And in the case of personal property, by reason of the State's traditionally high degree of control over commercial dealings, he ought to be aware of the possibility that new regulation might even render his property economically worthless (at least if the property's only economically productive use is sale or manufacture for sale). In the case of land, however, we think the notion pressed by the Council that title is somehow held subject to the "implied limitation" that the State may subsequently eliminate all economically valuable use is inconsistent with the historical compact recorded in the Takings Clause that has become part of our constitutional culture.

Where "permanent physical occupation" of land is concerned, we have refused to allow the government to decree it anew (without compensation), no matter how weighty the asserted "public interests" involved—though we assuredly *would* permit the government to assert a permanent easement that was a pre-existing limitation upon the landowner's title. We believe similar treatment must be accorded confiscatory regulations, *i.e.*, regulations that prohibit all economically beneficial use of land: Any limitation so severe cannot be newly legislated or decreed (without compensation), but must inhere in the title itself, in the restrictions that background principles of the State's law of property and nuisance already place upon land ownership. A law or decree with such an effect must, in other words, do no more than duplicate the result that could have been achieved in the courts—by adjacent landowners (or other uniquely affected persons) under the State's law of private nuisance, or by the State under its complementary power to abate nuisances that affect the public generally, or otherwise.

On this analysis, the owner of a lake bed, for example, would not be entitled to compensation when he is denied the requisite permit to engage in a landfilling operation that would have the effect of flooding others' land. Nor the corporate owner of a nuclear generating plant, when it is directed to remove all improvements from its land upon discovery that the plant sits astride an earthquake fault. Such regulatory action may well have the effect of eliminating the land's only economically productive use, but it does not proscribe a productive use that was previously permissible under relevant property and nuisance principles. . . .

The "total taking" inquiry we require today will ordinarily entail (as the application of state nuisance law ordinarily entails) analysis of, among other things, the degree of harm to public lands and resources, or adjacent private property, posed by the claimant's proposed activities, the social value of the claimant's activities and their suitability to the locality in question, and the relative ease with which the alleged harm can be avoided through measures taken by the claimant and the government (or adjacent private landowners) alike. The fact that a particular use has long been engaged in by similarly situated owners ordinarily imports a lack of any common law prohibition (though changed circumstances or new knowledge may make what was previously permissible no longer so. . . .

It seems unlikely that common law principles would have prevented the erection of any habitable or productive improvements on petitioner's land; they rarely support prohibition of the "essential use" of land. The question, however, is one of state law to be dealt with on remand. We emphasize that to win its case South Carolina must do more than proffer the legislature's declaration that the uses Lucas desires are inconsistent with the public interest, or the conclusory assertion that they violate a common law maxim such as *sic utere tuo ut alienum non laedas*. As we have said, a "State, by *ipse dixit*, may not transform private property into public property without compensation. . . ." Instead, as it would be required to do if it sought to restrain Lucas in a common law action for public nuisance, South Carolina must identify background principles of nuisance and property law that prohibit the uses he now intends in the circumstances in which the property is presently found.

Only on this showing can the State fairly claim that, in proscribing all such beneficial uses, the Beachfront Management Act is taking nothing.

The judgment is reversed and the cause remanded for proceedings not inconsistent with this opinion.

73

Kelo v. New London (2005)

Justice Stevens delivered the opinion of the Court:

In 2000, the city of New London approved a development plan that, in the words of the Supreme Court of Connecticut, was "projected to create in excess of 1,000 jobs, to increase tax and other revenues, and to revitalize an economically distressed city, including its downtown and waterfront areas." In assembling the land needed for this project, the city's development agent has purchased property from willing sellers and proposes to use the power of eminent domain to acquire the remainder of the property from unwilling owners in exchange for just compensation. The question presented is whether the city's proposed disposition of this property qualifies as a "public use" within the meaning of the Takings Clause of the Fifth Amendment to the Constitution.

The city of New London (hereinafter City) sits at the junction of the Thames River and the Long Island Sound in southeastern Connecticut. Decades of economic decline led a state agency in 1990 to designate the City a "distressed municipality." In 1996, the Federal Government closed the Naval Undersea Warfare Center, which had been located in the Fort Trumbull area of the City and had employed over 1,500 people. In 1998, the City's unemployment rate was nearly double that of the State, and its population of just under 24,000 residents was at its lowest since 1920.

These conditions prompted state and local officials to target New London, and particularly its Fort Trumbull area, for economic revitalization. To this end, respondent New London Development Corporation (NLDC), a private nonprofit entity established some years earlier to assist the City in planning economic development, was reactivated. In January 1998, the State

From *Kelo v. New London*, 545 U.S. 469 (2005).

authorized a $5.35 million bond issue to support the NLDC's planning activities and a $10 million bond issue toward the creation of a Fort Trumbull State Park. In February, the pharmaceutical company Pfizer Inc. announced that it would build a $300 million research facility on a site immediately adjacent to Fort Trumbull; local planners hoped that Pfizer would draw new business to the area, thereby serving as a catalyst to the area's rejuvenation. After receiving initial approval from the city council, the NLDC continued its planning activities and held a series of neighborhood meetings to educate the public about the process. In May, the city council authorized the NLDC to formally submit its plans to the relevant state agencies for review. Upon obtaining state-level approval, the NLDC finalized an integrated development plan focused on 90 acres of the Fort Trumbull area. . . .

The NLDC intended the development plan to capitalize on the arrival of the Pfizer facility and the new commerce it was expected to attract. In addition to creating jobs, generating tax revenue, and helping to "build momentum for the revitalization of downtown New London," the plan was also designed to make the City more attractive and to create leisure and recreational opportunities on the waterfront and in the park.

The city council approved the plan in January 2000, and designated the NLDC as its development agent in charge of implementation. The city council also authorized the NLDC to purchase property or to acquire property by exercising eminent domain in the City's name. The NLDC successfully negotiated the purchase of most of the real estate in the 90-acre area, but its negotiations with petitioners failed. As a consequence, in November 2000, the NLDC initiated the condemnation proceedings that gave rise to this case.

Petitioner Susette Kelo has lived in the Fort Trumbull area since 1997. She has made extensive improvements to her house, which she prizes for its water view. Petitioner Wilhelmina Dery was born in her Fort Trumbull house in 1918 and has lived there her entire life. Her husband Charles (also a petitioner) has lived in the house since they married some 60 years ago. In all, the nine petitioners own 15 properties in Fort Trumbull. . . . Ten of the parcels are occupied by the owner or a family member; the other five are held as investment properties. There is no allegation that any of these properties is blighted or otherwise in poor condition; rather, they were condemned only because they happen to be located in the development area.

. . . [T]he Supreme Court of Connecticut . . . held, over a dissent, that all of the City's proposed takings were valid. It began by upholding the lower court's determination that the takings were authorized by chapter 132, the State's municipal development statute. That statute expresses a legislative determination that the taking of land, even developed land, as part of an economic development project is a "public use" and in the "public interest." Next, relying on cases such as *Hawaii Housing Authority v. Midkiff* (1984) and *Berman v. Parker* (1954), the court held that such economic development qualified as a valid public use under both the Federal and State Constitutions. . . .

We granted certiorari to determine whether a city's decision to take property for the purpose of economic development satisfies the "public use" requirement of the Fifth Amendment.

Two polar propositions are perfectly clear. On the one hand, it has long been accepted that the sovereign may not take the property of A for the sole purpose of transferring it to another private party B, even though A is paid just compensation. On the other hand, it is equally clear that a State may transfer property from one private party to another if future "use by the public" is the purpose of the taking; the condemnation of land for a railroad with common-carrier duties is a familiar example. Neither of these propositions, however, determines the disposition of this case.

As for the first proposition, the City would no doubt be forbidden from taking petitioners' land for the purpose of conferring a private benefit on a particular private party. Nor would the City be allowed to take property under the mere pretext of a public purpose, when its actual purpose was to bestow a private benefit. The takings before us, however, would be executed pursuant to a "carefully considered" development plan. The trial judge and all the members of the Supreme Court of Connecticut agreed that there was no evidence of an illegitimate purpose in this case. Therefore, as was true of the statute challenged in *Midkiff*, the City's development plan was not adopted "to benefit a particular class of identifiable individuals."

On the other hand, this is not a case in which the City is planning to open the condemned land—at least not in its entirety—to use by the general public. Nor will the private lessees of the land in any sense be required to operate like common carriers, making their services available to all comers. But although such a projected use would be sufficient to satisfy the public use requirement, this "Court long ago rejected any literal requirement that condemned property be put into use for the general public." Indeed, while many state courts in the mid-19th century endorsed "use by the public" as the proper definition of public use, that narrow view steadily eroded over time. Not only was the "use by the public" test difficult to administer (*e.g.*, what proportion of the public need have access to the property? at what price?), but it proved to be impractical given the diverse and always evolving needs of society. Accordingly, when this Court began applying the Fifth Amendment to the States at the close of the 19th century, it embraced the broader and more natural interpretation of public use as "public purpose." Thus, in a case upholding a mining company's use of an aerial bucket line to transport ore over property it did not own, Justice Holmes' opinion for the Court stressed "the inadequacy of use by the general public as a universal test." We have repeatedly and consistently rejected that narrow test ever since.

The disposition of this case therefore turns on the question whether the City's development plan serves a "public purpose." Without exception, our cases have defined that concept broadly, reflecting our longstanding policy of deference to legislative judgments in this field.

In *Berman v. Parker*, this Court upheld a redevelopment plan targeting a blighted area of Washington, D. C., in which most of the housing for the area's 5,000 inhabitants was beyond repair. Under the plan, the area would be condemned and part of it utilized for the construction of streets, schools, and other public facilities. The remainder of the land would be leased or sold to private parties for the purpose of redevelopment, including the construction of low-cost housing.

The owner of a department store located in the area challenged the condemnation, pointing out that his store was not itself blighted and arguing that the creation of a "better balanced, more attractive community" was not a valid public use. Writing for a unanimous Court, Justice Douglas refused to evaluate this claim in isolation, deferring instead to the legislative and agency judgment that the area "must be planned as a whole" for the plan to be successful. The Court explained that "community redevelopment programs need not, by force of the Constitution, be on a piecemeal basis–lot by lot, building by building." The public use underlying the taking was unequivocally affirmed:

> "We do not sit to determine whether a particular housing project is or is not desirable. The concept of the public welfare is broad and inclusive. . . . The values it represents are spiritual as well as physical, aesthetic as well as monetary. It is within the power of the legislature to determine that the community should be beautiful as well as healthy, spacious as well as clean, well-balanced as well as carefully patrolled. In the present case, the Congress and its authorized agencies have made determinations that take into account a wide variety of values. It is not for us to reappraise them. If those who govern the District of Columbia decide that the Nation's Capital should be beautiful as well as sanitary, there is nothing in the Fifth Amendment that stands in the way."

In *Hawaii Housing Authority v. Midkiff*, the Court considered a Hawaii statute whereby fee title was taken from lessors and transferred to lessees (for just compensation) in order to reduce the concentration of land ownership. We unanimously upheld the statute and rejected the Ninth Circuit's view that it was "a naked attempt on the part of the state of Hawaii to take the property of A and transfer it to B solely for B's private use and benefit." Reaffirming *Berman's* deferential approach to legislative judgments in this field, we concluded that the State's purpose of eliminating the "social and economic evils of a land oligopoly" qualified as a valid public use. Our opinion also rejected the contention that the mere fact that the State immediately transferred the properties to private individuals upon condemnation somehow diminished the public character of the taking. "[I]t is only the taking's purpose, and not its mechanics," we explained, that matters in determining public use. . . .

Viewed as a whole, our jurisprudence has recognized that the needs of society have varied between different parts of the Nation, just as they have evolved over time in response to changed circumstances. Our earliest cases in particular embodied a strong theme of federalism, emphasizing the "great respect" that we owe to state legislatures and state courts in discerning local public needs. For more than a century, our public use jurisprudence has wisely eschewed rigid formulas and intrusive scrutiny in favor of affording legislatures broad latitude in determining what public needs justify the use of the takings power.

Those who govern the City were not confronted with the need to remove blight in the Fort Trumbull area, but their determination that the area was sufficiently distressed to justify a program of economic rejuvenation is entitled to our deference. The City has carefully formulated an economic development plan that it believes will provide appreciable benefits to the community, including—but by no means limited to—new jobs and increased tax revenue. As with other exercises in urban planning and development, the City is endeavoring to coordinate a variety of commercial, residential, and recreational uses of land, with the hope that they will form a whole greater than the sum of its parts. To effectuate this plan, the City has invoked a state statute that specifically authorizes the use of eminent domain to promote economic development. Given the comprehensive character of the plan, the thorough deliberation that preceded its adoption, and the limited scope of our review, it is appropriate for us, as it was in *Berman*, to resolve the challenges of the individual owners, not on a piecemeal basis, but rather in light of the entire plan. Because that plan unquestionably serves a public purpose, the takings challenged here satisfy the public use requirement of the Fifth Amendment.

To avoid this result, petitioners urge us to adopt a new bright-line rule that economic development does not qualify as a public use. Putting aside the unpersuasive suggestion that the City's plan will provide only purely economic benefits, neither precedent nor logic supports petitioners' proposal. Promoting economic development is a traditional and long accepted function of government. There is, moreover, no principled way of distinguishing economic development from the other public purposes that we have recognized. In our cases upholding takings that facilitated agriculture and mining, for example, we emphasized the importance of those industries to the welfare of the States in question, in *Berman*, we endorsed the purpose of transforming a blighted area into a "well-balanced" community through redevelopment, in *Midkiff*, we upheld the interest in breaking up a land oligopoly that "created artificial deterrents to the normal functioning of the State's residential land market". . . . It would be incongruous to hold that the City's interest in the economic benefits to be derived from the development of the Fort Trumbull area has less of a public character than any of those other interests.

Clearly, there is no basis for exempting economic development from our tra-ditionally broad understanding of public purpose.

Petitioners contend that using eminent domain for economic develop-ment impermissibly blurs the boundary between public and private takings. Again, our cases foreclose this objection. Quite simply, the government's pursuit of a public purpose will often benefit individual private parties. For example, in *Midkiff*, the forced transfer of property conferred a direct and sig-nificant benefit on those lessees who were previously unable to purchase their homes. . . . We cannot say that public ownership is the sole method of promoting the public purposes of community redevelopment projects."

It is further argued that without a bright-line rule nothing would stop a city from transferring citizen A's property to citizen B for the sole reason that citizen B will put the property to a more productive use and thus pay more taxes. Such a one-to-one transfer of property, executed outside the confines of an integrated development plan, is not presented in this case. While such an unusual exercise of government power would certainly raise a suspicion that a private purpose was afoot, the hypothetical cases posited by petitioners can be confronted if and when they arise. They do not warrant the crafting of an artificial restriction on the concept of public use.

Alternatively, petitioners maintain that for takings of this kind we should require a "reasonable certainty" that the expected public benefits will actually accrue. Such a rule, however, would represent an even greater departure from our precedent. "When the legislature's purpose is legitimate and its means are not irrational, our cases make clear that empirical debates over the wisdom of takings–no less than debates over the wisdom of other kinds of socioeconomic legislation–are not to be carried out in the federal courts." *Midkiff* . . . . The disadvantages of a heightened form of review are especially pronounced in this type of case. Orderly implementation of a com-prehensive redevelopment plan obviously requires that the legal rights of all interested parties be established before new construction can be commenced. A constitutional rule that required postponement of the judicial approval of every condemnation until the likelihood of success of the plan had been assured would unquestionably impose a significant impediment to the suc-cessful consummation of many such plans. . . .

In affirming the City's authority to take petitioners' properties, we do not minimize the hardship that condemnations may entail, notwithstanding the payment of just compensation. We emphasize that nothing in our opin-ion precludes any State from placing further restrictions on its exercise of the takings power. Indeed, many States already impose "public use" requirements that are stricter than the federal baseline. Some of these requirements have been established as a matter of state constitutional law, while others are expressed in state eminent domain statutes that carefully limit the grounds upon which takings may be exercised. As the submissions of the parties and their *amici* make clear, the necessity and wisdom of using eminent domain to promote economic development are certainly matters of legitimate public debate. This Court's authority, however, extends only to determining whether the City's proposed condemnations are for a "public use" within the meaning of the Fifth Amendment to the Federal Constitution. Because over a century of our case law interpreting that provision dictates an affirmative answer to that question, we may not grant petitioners the relief that they seek.

The judgment of the Supreme Court of Connecticut is affirmed.

Justice O'Connor, with whom The Chief Justice, Justice Scalia, and Justice Thomas join, dissenting:

> Over two centuries ago, just after the Bill of Rights was ratified, Justice Chase wrote:
>
> "An act of the Legislature (for I cannot call it a law) contrary to the great first principles of the social compact, cannot be considered a rightful exercise of legislative authority. . . . A few instances will suffice to explain what I mean. . . . [A] law that takes property from A. and gives it to B: It is against all reason and justice, for a people to entrust a Legislature with such powers; and, therefore, it cannot be presumed that they have done it." *Calder v. Bull* (1798).

Today the Court abandons this long-held, basic limitation on government power. Under the banner of economic development, all private property is now vulnerable to being taken and transferred to another private owner, so long as it might be upgraded–*i.e.*, given to an owner who will use it in a way that the legislature deems more beneficial to the public–in the process. To reason, as the Court does, that the incidental public benefits resulting from the subsequent ordinary use of private property render economic development takings "for public use" is to wash out any distinction between private and public use of property–and thereby effectively to delete the words "for public use" from the Takings Clause of the Fifth Amendment. Accordingly I respectfully dissent.

Petitioners are nine resident or investment owners of 15 homes in the Fort Trumbull neighborhood of New London, Connecticut. Petitioner Wilhelmina Dery, for example, lives in a house on Walbach Street that has been in her family for over 100 years. She was born in the house in 1918; her husband, petitioner Charles Dery, moved into the house when they married in 1946. Their son lives next door with his family in the house he received as a wedding gift, and joins his parents in this suit. Two petitioners keep rental properties in the neighborhood. . . .

To save their homes, petitioners sued New London and the NLDC, to whom New London has delegated eminent domain power. Petitioners maintain that the Fifth Amendment prohibits the NLDC from condemning their properties for the sake of an economic development plan. Petitioners are not hold-outs; they do not seek increased compensation, and none is opposed to new development in the area. Theirs is an objection in principle: They claim that the NLDC's proposed use for their confiscated property is not a "public" one for purposes of the Fifth Amendment. While the government may take their homes to build a road or a railroad or to eliminate a property use that harms the public, say petitioners, it cannot take their property for the private use of other owners simply because the new owners may make more productive use of the property.

The Fifth Amendment to the Constitution, made applicable to the States by the Fourteenth Amendment, provides that "private property [shall not] be taken for public use, without just compensation." When interpreting the Constitution, we begin with the unremarkable presumption that every word in the document has independent meaning, "that no word was unnecessarily used, or needlessly added." In keeping with that presumption, we have read the Fifth Amendment's language to impose two distinct conditions on the exercise of eminent domain: "the taking must be for a 'public use' and 'just compensation' must be paid to the owner."

These two limitations serve to protect "the security of Property," which Alexander Hamilton described to the Philadelphia Convention as one of the "great obj[ects] of Gov[ernment]." Together they ensure stable property ownership by providing safeguards against excessive, unpredictable, or unfair use of the government's eminent domain power–particularly against those owners who, for whatever reasons, may be unable to protect themselves in the political process against the majority's will.

While the Takings Clause presupposes that government can take private property without the owner's consent, the just compensation requirement spreads the cost of condemnations and thus "prevents the public from loading upon one individual more than his just share of the burdens of government." The public use requirement, in turn, imposes a more basic limitation, circumscribing the very scope of the eminent domain power: Government may compel an individual to forfeit her property for the *public's* use, but not for the benefit of another private person. This requirement promotes fairness as well as security.

Where is the line between "public" and "private" property use? We give considerable deference to legislatures' determinations about what governmental activities will advantage the public. But were the political branches the sole arbiters of the public-private distinction, the Public Use Clause would amount to little more than hortatory fluff. An external, judicial check on how the public use requirement is interpreted, however limited, is necessary if this constraint on government power is to retain any meaning.

Our cases have generally identified three categories of takings that comply with the public use requirement, though it is in the nature of things that the boundaries between these categories are not always firm. Two are relatively straightforward and uncontroversial. First, the sovereign may transfer private property to public ownership–such as for a road, a hospital, or a military base. Second, the sovereign may transfer private property to private parties, often common carriers, who make the property available for the public's use–such as with a railroad, a public utility, or a stadium. But "public ownership" and "use-by-the-public" are sometimes too constricting and impractical ways to define the scope of the Public Use Clause. Thus we have allowed that, in certain circumstances and to meet certain exigencies, takings that serve a public purpose also satisfy the Constitution even if the property is destined for subsequent private use.

This case returns us for the first time in over 20 years to the hard question of when a purportedly "public purpose" taking meets the public use requirement. It presents an issue of first impression: Are economic development takings constitutional? I would hold that they are not. We are guided by two precedents about the taking of real property by eminent domain. In *Berman*, we upheld takings within a blighted neighborhood of Washington, D. C. The neighborhood had so deteriorated that, for example, 64.3% of its dwellings were beyond repair. It had become burdened with "overcrowding of dwellings," "lack of adequate streets and alleys," and "lack of light and air." Congress had determined that the neighborhood had become "injurious to the public health, safety, morals, and welfare" and that it was necessary to "eliminat[e] all such injurious conditions by employing all means necessary and appropriate for the purpose," including eminent domain. Mr. Berman's department store was not itself blighted. Having approved of Congress' decision to eliminate the harm to the public emanating from the blighted neighborhood, however, we did not second-guess its decision to treat the neighborhood as a whole rather than lot-by-lot.

In *Midkiff*, we upheld a land condemnation scheme in Hawaii whereby title in real property was taken from lessors and transferred to lessees. At that time, the State and Federal Governments owned nearly 49% of the State's land, and another 47% was in the hands of only 72 private landowners. Concentration of land ownership was so dramatic that on the State's most urbanized island, Oahu, 22 landowners owned 72.5% of the fee simple titles. The Hawaii Legislature had concluded that the oligopoly in land ownership was "skewing the State's residential fee simple market, inflating land prices, and injuring the public tranquility and welfare," and therefore enacted a condemnation scheme for redistributing title.

In those decisions, we emphasized the importance of deferring to legislative judgments about public purpose. Because courts are ill-equipped to evaluate the efficacy of proposed legislative initiatives, we rejected as unworkable the idea of courts' " 'deciding on what is and is not a governmental function and . . . invalidating legislation on the basis of their view on that question at the moment of decision, a practice which has proved impracticable in other fields.' " Likewise, we recognized our inability to evaluate whether, in a given case, eminent domain is a necessary means by which to pursue the legislature's ends.

Yet for all the emphasis on deference, *Berman and Midkiff* hewed to a bedrock principle without which our public use jurisprudence would collapse: "A purely private taking could not withstand the scrutiny of the public use requirement; it would serve no legitimate purpose of government and would thus be void." To protect that principle, those decisions reserved "a role for courts to play in reviewing a legislature's judgment of what constitutes a public use . . . [though] the Court in *Berman* made clear that it is 'an extremely narrow' one."

The Court's holdings in Berman and *Midkiff* were true to the principle underlying the Public Use Clause. In both those cases, the extraordinary, precondemnation use of the targeted property inflicted affirmative harm on society—in *Berman* through blight resulting from extreme poverty and in *Midkiff* through oligopoly resulting from extreme wealth. And in both cases, the relevant legislative body had found that eliminating the existing property use was necessary to remedy the harm. Thus a public purpose was realized when the harmful use was eliminated. Because each taking *directly* achieved a public benefit, it did not matter that the property was turned over to private use. Here, in contrast, New London does not claim that Susette Kelo's and Wilhelmina Dery's well-maintained homes are the source of any social harm. Indeed, it could not so claim without adopting the absurd argument that any single-family home that might be razed to make way for an apartment building, or any church that might be replaced with a retail store, or any small business that might be more lucrative if it were instead part of a national franchise, is inherently harmful to society and thus within the government's power to condemn.

In moving away from our decisions sanctioning the condemnation of harmful property use, the Court today significantly expands the meaning of public use. It holds that the sovereign may take private property currently put to ordinary private use, and give it over for new, ordinary private use, so long as the new use is predicted to generate some secondary benefit for the public—such as increased tax revenue, more jobs, maybe even aesthetic pleasure. But nearly any lawful use of real private property can be said to generate some incidental benefit to the public. Thus, if predicted (or even guaranteed) positive side-effects are enough to render transfer from one private party to another constitutional, then the words "for public use" do not realistically exclude any takings, and thus do not exert *any* constraint on the eminent domain power.

. . . [I]n a coda, the Court suggests that property owners should turn to the States, who may or may not choose to impose appropriate limits on economic development takings. This is an abdication of our responsibility. States play many important functions in our system of dual sovereignty, but compensating for our refusal to enforce properly the Federal Constitution (and a provision meant to curtail state action, no less) is not among them.

It was possible after *Berman and Midkiff* to imagine unconstitutional transfers from A to B. Those decisions endorsed government intervention when private property use had veered to such an extreme that the public was suffering as a consequence. Today nearly all real property is susceptible to condemnation on the Court's theory. . . . This is why economic development takings "seriously jeopardiz[e] the security of all private property ownership."

Any property may now be taken for the benefit of another private party, but the fallout from this decision will not be random. The beneficiaries are likely to be those citizens with disproportionate influence and power in the political process, including large corporations and development firms. As for the victims, the government now has license to transfer property from those with fewer resources to those with more. The Founders cannot have intended this perverse result. "[T]hat alone is a *just* government," wrote James Madison, "which *impartially* secures to every man, whatever is his *own*."

74

Catherine H. Zuckert

The Political Lessons of Economic Life (1977)

. . . The argument of this paper is that strictly economic analysis [of public policy] both abstracts from important politically determined conditions and distorts the alternatives by stating them in quantitative and commensurable terms. If the political conditions are clearly stated, however, economic incentives and interests do provide a particularly appropriate and effective means of achieving the ends of public policy. They are appropriate because the basic political institutions of the United States constitute just such an attempt to establish the conditions in which individuals seeking their own self-interest, largely economic, will in the process serve public interests as well. The principles of the institutions can, therefore, provide a model for the design of more specific public policies, if those principles

By permission of the author.

are understood as setting the conditions in which private interests work rather than mere processes of accommodation. . . .

I. THE ATTRACTIONS AND LIMITATIONS OF ECONOMIC ANALYSIS

If policy issues and questions of priority could be established merely by listing our collective and some special group desires-demands, determining what it would cost to satisfy each separately and in various combinations, and comparing them, then economic analysis would supply an adequate foundation for policy determination, though merely listing and calculating all the alternatives would itself constitute a tremendous task. . . .

[However,] economic analysis in itself cannot establish the priorities and thus it does not provide standards by which to choose among competing goals and methods of achieving them.

Economists themselves are the first to emphasize that the accuracy and predictability of economic analysis depends upon stringently defined assumptions about the desires and behavior of individuals or firms, the goods to be exchanged and the conditions of exchange. "All other things being equal," individuals (or firms) will "rationally" seek to maximize their gain and minimize their cost. . . . The explicit admission that individuals do not, in fact, always act "rationally" to maximize their gains and that all goods, especially political "goods" are not actually commensurable, makes the direct application of an economic framework of analysis to questions of public policy extremely problematic. . . .

Economic rationality does not and will not suffice to maintain a nation. It is never, for example, in the interest of an "economic man" to risk his life for his country. . . .

The conflict between the requirement that governmental programs constitute the most efficient use of economic resources and the need for consent, hence for some participation of the individuals or groups to be regulated, has long been noted. American laws often represent a compromise among several competing goals, so that a calculation of the suitability or efficiency of the means of administering the program becomes almost impossible. . . .

The desirability for voluntary compliance becomes [a] source of the attraction of economic frameworks of analysis, however, when those analyses proceed in terms of "incentives." Policies incorporating "incentives" have the advantage of making the outcome a product of individual choice and hence "free." They are thus both ideologically and politically attractive. And they are more likely to be effective. Such policies are designed to make it in the economic self-interest of individuals to serve the public end, so that there is eager cooperation rather than resistance, active or passive, to government regulations and their enforcement. Economic "incentives" do, therefore, constitute important means or "tools" of democratic government. The difficulty is that the tool does not prescribe the limitations or the goals of its use.

Economic methods of decision and allocations of resources look particularly attractive at a time when direct public regulation, in energy, schools, or welfare, for example, does not seem to work, at least not very well. And as skepticism about present governmental programs grows, so does interest in the suggestions Milton Friedman has made about ways to replace public with private decisions by utilizing the market. . . .

In the name of freedom, Friedman would like to minimize governmental regulation and to maximize individual choice. He seeks, therefore, to minimize politics and extend the sphere of economic decision. By sharpening the the public's understanding of the issues and requiring that one decision be made for everyone, Friedman argues, political debate serves to coalesce opposing sides and to intensify conflict. The resulting decision forces the minority to obey the majority. Since political action rests so much on the threat of force, it should be kept to a minimum. The market, on the other hand, operates as a voluntary system of proportional representation. The majority can buy most of the goods it prefers at the cheapest price through the economies of scale, yet the minority may still purchase the more expensive version. Neither is coerced. So long as there is a market, the goods will be produced. Indeed, since producers seek new markets, the choice and variety is apt to expand. Thus, in all possible cases, the economic process should replace the political process as a means of reaching agreement. . . .

Friedman's proposals [,however,] systematically substitute short-run preferences for long-run conditions or goals, because his goal is stated negatively, as minimizing government, and so the only positive measure becomes the expression of divergent individual preferences. He does not ask whether these choices undermine the conditions of choice in the long-run. . . .

Friedman admits that there are some "indivisible" goods such as national defense which can be provided only on an "either/or" basis and so require governmental support. But, he argues, the public should pay what the service is worth rather than coercing young men to provide it by conscripting them. Thus he suggested the institution of a "volunteer army." Salaries in the armed forces should be competitive with those in private industry. The result may be that Americans pay what they think that defense is worth; Congress spends more every year. Manpower, procurement, and research and development have all dropped, however, because so much of the total defense budget must now go to salaries and pensions, though, to put it kindly, the capabilities of the people employed has not much improved. So we pay more and get less; what an uneconomic result! Of course, the volunteer army was not in fact instituted for economic reasons; rather it served the political goal of substantially reducing the major source of opposition to the war in Vietnam. . . . The result is that we seem to have gained domestic peace in the short run at the cost of national defense over the long haul. . . .

Friedman's proposals are as attractive as they are, because they seem to maximize individual choice and efficiency at the same time. They fail because he does not take sufficient account of either the conditions necessary to present individuals with real choices or the long-run effects of the choices they make. Individuals do not have "real" choices unless (a) they know what the alternatives are and (b) they can choose without risking probable death or permanent damage. The man who "chooses" between starvation and "starvation wages" does not have much choice at all. Both education and income distribution are to a large extent subject to governmental action, however. . . . If we could specify the political conditions and institutions which set the context for the operation of economic incentives, we might then be able to be more specific about the desired and predictable political results. (We would then have defined the limitations of the operation of economic incentives as well.) But here we reach the central problem. Many agree that the economic approach is limited and that there is a broader political dimension. But no one seems able to say exactly what that political dimension is. The common sensical answer of "government" seems too restrictive; it puts too much emphasis on the external institutional framework and so detracts attention from the forces that actually make the institutions work. Yet the more inclusive definitions of politics as "power" or "authoritative allocation of values" are too broad to distinguish political from other activities and too abstract to provide much guidance for policymakers. . . .

II. The Close Relation of Politics and Economics in the Modern Liberal Regime

America remains basically a liberal regime. The national "creed" declares:

> We hold these truths to be self-evident; that all men are created equal, that they are endowed by their Creator with certain inalienable rights, and that among these are life, liberty, and the pursuit of happiness;—that to secure these rights, governments are instituted among men. . . .

American governmental institutions secure the rights to life and liberty by establishing a legal system that not only forbids "impairing the obligation of contract" but also requires "due process" and "equal protection of the laws." Thus they also establish the necessary conditions for the growth of an advanced economy, because a high degree of order (predictability and peace) is required to make economic investment rational and so to increase productivity. Governments provide the conditions for economic growth not for their own sake, however, but only in order to secure a more fundamental political end, to secure the "right" to the "pursuit of happiness." Both modern politics and modern economics ultimately serve the same political goal in attempting to establish the conditions under which each person can pursue his own vision of the good life. As a result, economic and political ends and means are easily fused and confused. It proves imperative to remember the priority of the political ends, however, if our policies are to be effective in the long run.

As Tocqueville also observed, instituting government on the basis of equal rights does not necessarily result in rule of or for all individuals. The need to secure equal conditions for all may justify the rule of a few with much force. Even with free institutions, securing the equal rights of all means, in practice, the rule of the majority for the interests of the majority.

> No one has yet found a political structure that equally favors the growth and prosperity of all the classes composing society. When the rich alone rule, the interests of the poor are always in danger; and when the poor make the law, the interests of the rich run great risks. . . . The real advantage of democracy is not, as some have said, to favor the prosperity of all, but only to serve the well-being of the greatest number.

The modern regime is still a regime, therefore; it is a democracy. The difference is that the majority now come from the middle class and use their power not to seize the goods of others (at home or abroad) but only to establish the conditions in which all individuals can pursue their own (largely economic) self-interest.

Though limited, even self-restrained in its ends, if not its power, and justified to itself only insofar as it secures the rights or opportunities of all, the modern regime constitutes a variety of majority rule. And that fact has several consequences. Recognition of the effective control of the majority creates fear at both the economic extremes. Second, although the modern majority does not explicitly require and directly reward living in a typically middle-class fashion or penalize those who do not, the laws which merely allow all individuals to follow their self-interest in effect require them to do so as well. They do not forbid aristocratic leisure or non-conformist rebellion; they merely make them economically impractical if not altogether unfeasible. If a person is actually forced to work to support himself he will have to do something for which there is a market; and it is a "mass market." The conformism and "middle-class morality" of America have been much criticized. I will, on the contrary, argue that these oft-derided characteristics are useful, perhaps even essential to maintaining decent, free political institutions.

First, we must look at the fate and prospects of the two threatened minorities, because in the fate of these minorities we will find the contradiction or affirmation of the majority's claim to rule for the benefit of everyone. Much early American political thought was concerned with the preservation of rights, especially the property rights of the minority (rich) from expropriation by the majority (previously poor). The chief protection consisted in the widespread participation in these rights; men with their own special interests and properties would not seek to have special interests prosecuted and property rights violated. . . . People have an interest in placing ceilings on wealth only if they are sure they themselves will never succeed in exceeding them. So long as they think they or their children may join the rich, they will protect the rights of wealth as they protect their own opportunities, especially if they see that the accumulation of wealth serves through investment to increase their opportunities to become rich as well. The preservation of the rights of the rich then depends upon maintaining conditions in which middle class people may hope to grow rich and seeing the rich contribute to the increase of these opportunities through demonstrating superior enterprise and inventive investment in the place of conspicuous consumption.

From this point of view, American income tax legislation makes much more sense than the surface contradictions indicate. As a result, perhaps, of the "closing of the frontier" and more surely expressing a sense of a growing and more rigid gap between the rich of Scott Fitzgerald and the ordinary man, the progressive income tax is enacted on the thought that those who benefit most from the system should pay more to support it, not just absolutely but relatively as well. Yet as soon as the progressive tax is enacted, the exceptions begin and grow precisely because the majority are willing, even anxious to have the wealth generated used to further general social and economic ends, especially those which create more opportunity for more people to join in the economic benefit. In effect, American tax laws allow the rich to retain some of their earnings to give others incentive to earn more; through deductions they allow the rich to keep control of even more of their income and property so long as they devote it to publicly desired uses and goals. The tax laws, thus, in effect, produce social responsibility in the rich, if not a social conscience.

The advantages of tax incentives have already been emphasized. What has not been sufficiently publicized, largely as a result of the incremental process whereby the tax law is drafted and amended over many years, is that the "exemptions," "loopholes," and deductions that have been exposed with so much ire of late, all serve as indirect means of executing public policy, and that they often work much better to achieve the desired ends than direct public regulations. . . .

If the concern of older defenders of the liberal regime was to make its claim to secure rights of all good against the ancient democratic proclivity to expropriate the rich, modern defenders have been more concerned to show not only that it allows each man to keep what he has gained but also that it enables all its citizens to gain. Even if the middle class extends the protection of life, liberty, and property it establishes in its own self-interest to the rich, its rule remains selfish and thus fundamentally unjust unless its rule also protects and benefits the poor minority. The modern middle-class majority does not, after all, justify its rule on the basis of its excellence of character, so much as on its ability to secure the rights of all. Securing the right to pursue happiness does not mean guaranteeing prosperity, much less happiness. That would be incompatible with individual freedom. It does mean in practice securing the option to participate in the economic system that provides the means for that broader pursuit. And securing that option becomes exceedingly complicated in a highly differentiated economy.

Some taxation is always justified, because the individual always owes part of his gain to the existence of an ordered society. His wealth is not simply, although it is surely in part, a product of his individual effort, ingenuity and foresight. For the same reason, an individual may come to grief through no personal fault of his own. He becomes a victim of the "system" from which he previously benefited. He may be highly trained in aerodynamics, for example, and still find himself unemployed. In order for the market to work, there must be shifts in labor as well as capital; yet the shifts in labor may result in grievous and undeserved suffering for significant numbers. Without assistance, displaced workers may fall into destitution and so create an enduring economic problem rather than a cyclical adjustment by moving into another area and/or trade. There are greater obstacles to the flow of resources than theory allows; so governmental action for relief (unemployment) and support for retraining becomes necessary not only on charitable but also on economic grounds. As any member of the middle-class can see, he, too, can become a victim. It is thus not surprising that the majority has passed legislation to help the victims of technological advance and shifts in supply and demand.

Much of the welfare system in the U.S. dispenses such temporary relief. The aged and handicapped constitute the second major category of recipients who are unable to participate in the economic system through no personal fault of their own. Though the legally instituted system could provide more incentive for family care of the aged and hiring the handicapped in order to reduce further weakening of family ties and personal (in contrast with "official") concern for human dignity, these programs are not very controversial. The controversy and the failure of the welfare system to help the poor occurs when the system does not serve merely to relieve suffering caused by economic dislocation but rather to perpetuate and even extend the need for support. This failure becomes even more problematic when a large number of the individuals involved visibly belong to a group that has previously suffered both legal and informal discrimination and oppression. *Prima facie* the regime does not secure the rights of all its citizens; and its legitimacy is thus brought into question. . . .

If the dominant groups in society were merely interested in maintaining their economy, they would use force to suppress any disruptive or potentially disruptive group. So long as the propertyless, so long as those who see no ground to hope that effort on their part will result in an improvement of their situation remain a minority—and they must begin as such—, force is a more economic and more efficient means of dealing with the problem than a complicated system of welfare payments. The reason why liberal societies attempt to institute the welfare state is not to maintain their wealth, but to maintain the grounds upon which they believe their wealth, both individual and social, is justified. And that justification for both the wealth and its necessarily unequal distribution is only that it is the way and, indeed, the only way of producing means sufficient to allow individuals to pursue their different visions of happiness. . . .

III. Economic Incentives as Means of Public Education

The reason economic incentives tend to be more legitimate and effective [than direct governmental regulation] is that they are peculiarly consonant with the principles of this regime. They work on the basis of choice and are, to that extent, free. Economic considerations can, to be sure, have coercive power. In incentives, that power operates indirectly and is designed to operate to the advantage of both individual and public. The choice offered is not between two indifferent alternatives; an incentive means that one alternative will be clearly economically advantageous. But the difference between such a choice and direct command or conditioning to the point that the individual no longer sees that there is an alternative remains considerable. Incentives work, moreover, because they do not serve merely as means to unrelated ends. Rather, by using incentives, one encourages the development and so one teaches the economic rationality necessary to make both the liberal economy and the liberal polity go. Economic rationality involves not only the weighing of alternatives in terms of their respective costs and benefits. It also entails the ability to identify long-run interests and to calculate the means necessary to secure those interests (forethought) as well as the discipline to carry out the plan. Economic analysis assumes, of course, economic rationality; and the analysis describes reality only insofar as that rationality exists. Public policies incorporating the use of economic incentives thus support general economic interests, not only by augmenting investment and labor resources but, more importantly, by establishing the conditions in which economic operations work. The habits of thought we call economic rationality are desirable not only for their strictly economic results but even more for their political effects.

American public policy should be designed to encourage individual effort, forethought and self-control, rather than supporting individuals only after they fail, as at present, because it is only through the development of such skills and habits that an individual can participate in the political community in a meaningful way or take real control of his own life. These skills and habits are the absolutely necessary conditions for the maintenance of a free regime. People are not born with these abilities; they learn them, and government can have a role in this broad form of education. Self-control is a very old-fashioned virtue that has been brought into question repeatedly in recent years by being renamed repression. Yet it is quite clear upon reflection that choice has no practical meaning whatsoever if one is not able to pause long enough to identify the alternatives or lacks the ability to identify the means necessary to achieve his desired end and the discipline to execute them. Quite simply, if one does not control oneself, one will be controlled by external forces or by others. The benefits of incentive structures in policy do not thus inhere solely or even primarily in their economic results. They lie rather in the kind of training they provide. . . .

IV. The Place of Economic Incentives and Interests in the American Political System

American political institutions are often thought to be founded on distrust. Madison's words in *Federalist* 51 to this effect are among his most famous.

> Ambition must be made to counteract ambition. The interest of the man must be connected with the constitutional rights of the place.

. . . Yet it is only partly true that the foundation is distrust. In *Federalist* 10 [Madison] explicitly recognizes that a direct conflict of interest, especially economic interest, produces tyranny—in direct democracies, tyranny of the majority. The point of encouraging and celebrating the multiplicity of interests in the extended sphere is not that the conflict of contending groups in itself necessarily produces the best outcome. Rather, the advantage of developing a multiplicity of interests is that, given representative institutions, the only way to form a majority and so to act at all is then through compromise and cooperation. Both require not only the qualification of particular interests, but the assertion of some common interest as well. If no group itself constitutes a majority and cannot get its narrow interest directly through political action, the political interest it will hold in common with other groups will always include the preservation of the rights of minorities. The majorities form, moreover, not to act directly but only to elect representatives. These representatives are directly responsible to the people through elections, but there is a "cushion" inserted by means of these elections, held in large districts incorporating many interests, between the actual process by which policy is decided in the legislature and direct economic pressures.

The system is intended to keep elected representatives "in line," however, and there is more attention paid to problems of corruption in the form of bribery in the *Federalist Papers* than in most recent treatises in political science, with the possible exception of those directed explicitly at "Watergate." Neither the "checks" nor elections would in themselves suffice. Rather, one had to tie the interest of the man to the office, so that it would be more in his interest to remain in office than to gouge the public treasury. Hamilton makes an explicit argument to this effect in support of an open-ended series of four year Presidential terms in #72. The institutions of the federal government are intentionally designed to produce public trust by "engineering" private interest. . . .

This paper concludes with a consideration of Tocqueville, because the French observer is the only writer thus far to have applied the concept of regime directly to American politics. And he shows the importance of economic behavior, not primarily for productivity, but as a kind of civil training which maintains the opinions and habits necessary for the operation of a liberal polity. . . .

[Tocqueville] does [not] believe . . . groups arise "spontaneously." On the contrary, he states

> The common interests of civil life seldom naturally induce great numbers to act together. A great deal of artifice is required to produce such a result.

If a citizen merely defines his interest solely in economic terms, he is not apt to join associations. "One cannot take part in most civil associations without risking some of one's property." By concentrating on short-run, monetary gain, citizens will lose the political abilities and so destroy the conditions under which they will be able to live free or satisfying lives, to enjoy even their economic gains in the long run.

> Intent only on getting rich, they do not notice the close connection between private fortunes and general prosperity. They find it a tiresome inconvenience to exercise political rights which distract them from industry. When required to elect representatives, to support authority by personal service, or to discuss public business together, they find they have no time. They cannot waste their precious time in unrewarding work. . . . Such folk think they are following the doctrine of self-interest, but they have a very crude idea thereof, and the better to guard their interests, they neglect the chief of them, that is, to remain their own masters.

Tocqueville's interest in the formation of private associations is that individuals attain the organizational skills and the experience of having some effect on what happens. He praises the decentralized and thus more participatory political institutions of the United States chiefly because political life accustoms people to the idea and formation of associations that break down the isolation and feeling of powerlessness of isolated individuals. . . . Tocqueville admits that federal institutions are complicated and may result in some inefficiency in administration. But the political advantages far outweigh the costs. By involving people in making the decisions that determine the conditions in which they live, decentralized political institutions (local governments) make the connection between the individual's fate and the community very clear. They give individuals confidence that they can have an effect, so these institutions encourage all sorts of new enterprises, private even more than public. . . .

Thus Tocqueville argues, governments and governmental programs can be designed to induce rather than depress individual enterprise. Designing programs with this end becomes most important because the dominant forces in modern civil societies push in the other direction. Governments cannot make their citizens independent or enterprising—directly. They can create conditions which encourage the development of the attitudes, habits and abilities which enable individuals to act on their own behalf. . . .

Chapter VII

Foreign Policy and the American Regime

Should morality enter into our deliberation about foreign policy? If it should, what does morality demand? Cropsey presents the arguments for two predominant foreign policy perspectives: one states that we have a duty to other nations, while the other advocates a crude and calculating self-interest. Finding that both the morality of selfless duty and a self-interest that abstracts from virtue are inadequate guides to action, Cropsey offers a synthesis of these two positions that meets the demands of both morality and survival. This synthesis is a self-regarding morality based on nobility and honor rather than on altruism. Unfortunately, the American regime, Cropsey argues, vacillates between the two extremes that he criticizes, and is therefore not likely to adopt a self-regarding morality of honor.

Morgenthau's account of the history of American foreign policy substantiates Cropsey's claim that the American regime alternates between the extremes of self-interest and selfless duty. For Morgenthau there are three periods in American history: that of the Founding generation, which advocated a policy of national interest in abstraction from moral considerations; a period where national interests were pursued but couched in moralistic terms; and the period since Woodrow Wilson, in which, contemptuous of calculating self-interest, the United States pursues moral goals in its dealings with other nations. Morgenthau calls for a return to the interest-oriented politics of Hamilton and Washington. Neglect of national interest, he argues, will lead to the death of the nation, and there is no morality except in the context of national communities. Morgenthau's argument for national survival, however, does not answer the question of why our nation is worth preserving. His argument for national self-preservation addresses all nations, whereas Cropsey argues that it is the character of the nation that makes the nation worth preserving.

Furthermore, we may question whether Hamilton and Washington did in fact ignore moral considerations in their foreign policy. Although Washington and Hamilton advocate national self-preservation, they conceive of the nation as having a certain character or excellence, and think that the preservation of that character is necessary to the nation's preservation. In Hamilton's Pacificus papers as well as in Washington's Farewell Address, foreign policy deliberations involve both national interest and morality, if morality is conceived of as self-dependence or self-respect rather than altruism. Although Hamilton argues that, given the circumstances, we should not go to war in aid of France, he tells us that we must be ready to defend our rights and to vindicate our honor. He does condemn "self-denying gratitude" toward other nations and "moral" considerations that harm the nation. But when Hamilton asks whether, by aiding France, our usefulness to the cause of liberty would outweigh the harm to ourselves, he assumes that there *are* circumstances in which we should assist others in a fight for liberty. Indeed, for Hamilton the cause of liberty, pursued with justice and good faith, appears to be the nation's highest purpose.

It is unclear that either self-interest or morality will provide an adequate guide for U.S. foreign policy in the future. As James Pontuso explains, the Cold War presented a situation in which the United States could pursue a foreign policy that was both self-interested and moral. Communism was a threat both to our interests and anathema to our principles. But the end of the Cold War appears to eliminate the major threat to our national survival and the major opponent to our democratic principles. Some commentators have even gone so far as to say that it signals the end of history. Democracy has triumphed and foreign policy, understood as the clash of great powers or great principles, is no longer necessary.

Pontuso claims, however, that even if the optimism regarding Communism's demise proves to be well founded, the fundamental causes of international conflict have not been banished. Bosnia, Kosovo, 9/11 and its aftermath all suggest that Pontuso is correct. International conflict continues and with that conflict the question of the relation between our morality and self interest continues to arise. President Barack Obama argues that we must broaden our conception of self interest to include the protection of our values as well as the achievement of victory, whereas former Vice President Cheney contends that our concept of morality must be broad enough to allow for measures necessary for our self defense. According to Cheney, "no moral value held dear by the American people obliges public servants ever to sacrifice innocent lives to spare a captured terrorist from unpleasant things."

75

Joseph Cropsey

The Moral Basis of International Action (1961)

The power of nations to inflict pain, destruction, and death in warfare has been brought to such a peak that men feel themselves compelled as never before to find means for preventing that power from being used. The instruments of mutilation and devastation are tremendous and their action comprehensive to such a degree that their employment would produce effects that shock the mind, for they reach perhaps to the impairment of the human race as a whole. It is by no means easy to obtain agreement as to the essence of moral offense in general; but it is transcendently easy to obtain agreement that it would be monstrous, and if monstrous then immoral, for men to burn up the moiety of mankind and to denature the loins of those who survive. . . .

It therefore appears that each nation is by duty bound to practice a voluntary restraint, to limit its own action and power of action in the interest of some good which is not its obvious, immediate self-benefit. For the sake of fulfilling a duty to the rest of mankind, each nation should to some extent deprive itself of the means to supremacy or even of defense. As we reflect on this duty, we notice how well it corresponds with what appears as the notion of morality at large. Morality is a standard of conduct which guides men to recognize and show concern for others, and to act out of some larger motive than the convenience, safety and well-being of themselves.

The demand of morality may be said to be in the direction of deliberate self-incapacitation. So far as this is true, morality is in apparent conflict with policy, or in other words with calculation in the interest of the actor. This is admitted both by the friends of morality, who see it as moderating the brutal egotism of life, and by the cynics, who see it as the delusion by which the strong are seduced to abstain from benefiting from their strength. . . .

From Cropsey, "The Moral Basis of International Action," in *America Armed*, ed. Robert A. Goldwin, Rand McNally College Publishing Company, 1961. Reprinted by permission of the Public Affairs Conference Center, Kenyon College, Gambier, Ohio.

[T]he two moral extremes, the one of absolute duty to all men as men and the other of simple calculation in the interest of the agent, [present] these difficulties: either the moral action of the one party exposes him to ruin at the hands of an immoral antagonist (with the consequence that morality leads invariably to the triumph of evil); or the possibility of moral discrimination disappears entirely, leaving as the only criterion of action the submoral criterion of success in survival. In either case, what begins as morality ends as immorality.

With this behind us, we can set down the requirements of a moral ground for international action, military and other. And if it turns out that no moral system can without self-contradiction meet these requirements, then we may conclude that morality is irrelevant to the conduct of nations, and all is just in hate and lust. The requirements for such a moral order are these: (1) That a nation be able to abide by the rules of right conduct without harm to itself even if every other nation in the world ignore or violate them. (2) That notwithstanding the full compatibility of the moral order with survival and victory, the rule of morality not simply dissolve into the right of the stronger, that is, the criterion of success.

Beginning again, we recur to the simplest and most generally admitted notion as to the meaning of morality: morality is self-restraint. Hitherto, we have taken self-restraint to mean a voluntary holding back either from violating an abstract precept of duty or from injuring others. The implicit supposition has been that the overriding problem to which morality addresses itself is how to define the duties or rights of men, the extreme solutions to the problem being either duty apart from calculation or calculation apart from duty. But there is no need for morality to mean either the one or the other so exclusively. This becomes clear to us when we consult the normal human understanding of what conduct deserves blame and what deserves praise. We blame people who deceive, defraud, plunder, attack, and murder; but curiously we also blame those who are vacillating, miserly, gluttonous, lewd, or craven, although it is not possible to say, for example, "gluttonous toward others." These latter defects are not primarily the sources of injury to other men. They are rather flaws of weakness, for example, the weakness of being unrestrainedly fond of some external good, or of being incapable of exercising that amount of self-control that enables a man to come to a conclusion or to suppress cruel, effete, or otherwise disgusting passions. We might note at the same time that a man overcome with the sense of duty, who plunged incontinently, that is, unrestrainedly into every situation where good needed to be done, would come under deserved censure as a dangerous meddler, especially if the only good accomplished was the salving of his conscience. There is a path between morality in the service of preservation and morality in the service of duty, abstractly considered; and that path is the one indicated by the general understanding of mankind. It follows the rule that self-restraint is not confined to the agent's acts against others but touches his character more comprehensively. . . .

Morality . . . is not intelligible as an abstract or formal principle but only as the sum of concrete characteristics, the possession of which enables the agent to deserve praise and respect. Morality without virtues is vanity.

What are those praiseworthy characteristics, and what does any of this have to do with the international action of the United States? The answer to the first will be tantamount to the answer to the second. Neither a nation nor a man can avoid shame if it is craven, heedless, self-indulgent, wanton in ease, irresolute in deliberation, wastrel in pleasure, squeamish in contest, faint in adversity. Virtue is etymologically related to manliness; but the relation is evidently more than etymological. . . .

I believe that if we test this rule of morality, which rises more or less directly out of common human experience, we will find that it meets the two conditions laid down earlier as being indispensable if the moral criterion is to be applicable to the nation's action. We are at no disadvantage if all the world but us behave brutally, foolishly, aggressively, deceitfully, and in every other way immorally. Prudence and decency demand of us that we make every effort to withstand every attempt that can be made against us; to do less would be contemptible and thus immoral. To do as much would be to work toward safety through morality. It goes without saying that morality so conceived utterly excludes those avoidable deeds of massive violence that can be defended only on the premise that success justifies everything. Certainly success is not the touchstone of morality as naturally understood, and it is not sensible to infer righteousness from survival, nor vice from failure. It is indeed possible to be respectable in defeat and contemptible in victory; but it is not possible to be respectable in defeat if defeat is the result of sloth, decadence, or a failure of nerve.

By this view, war and therefore the preparation for war are, in themselves, neither morally good nor morally bad, any more than homicide is morally good or bad. The homicide of a police officer upon a fleeing criminal is morally good, the homicide of a fleeing criminal upon a police officer morally bad. War is dreadful, and the preparation for it painful; but a theory that defines the painful as the immoral is nothing but hedonism or an encouragement to hedonism, no matter what appeals it may make to sentiment, conscience, or a show of rights. War is bad but it is not bad in the way that a supine indifference to disgrace and slavery are bad, for the latter comes from moral corruption and the former only from a fearful necessity that some men cannot, because of the vice of others, avoid.

War is bad because pain and death are bad, and death worse than pain. But we must reflect on the order of things, and recognize the difference between the death of men and the death of nations. Individuals die, but those remaining make up the loss. Cities are reduced to material chaos, but in an amazingly short time the destruction is repaired. The resurrection of a regime, however, is a thing rarely seen. The Constitution subverted, liberty disappears, and the human flotsam remaining suffer the ultimate demoralization, which is not death but subjection to the unlimited will of a master. Those who would investigate war and peace as part of the moral problem may never stray out of sight of the fact that the necessary condition for all morality is freedom, and the condition for freedom is the absolute integrity of the body politic—guaranteed by the power and willingness to make war.

It is evident that morality can retain its connection with self-restraint without collapsing into self-incapacitation. On the contrary, the demands of morality, seen in their relation to freedom and honor, are more energizing than they are paralyzing. Then the question arises whether there is anything at all that could contribute to the greatness and safety of the nation for which a justification could not be found by appealing to honor. The answer to this is surely No if the appeal to honor is a specious pretext, and as surely Yes if the appeal to honor is itself honorable. But assuming for the moment that the appeal to honor is not hypocritical, what sort of act would a nation be compelled to deny itself for purely moral reasons, contrary to its urgent interest? Is there something dishonorable, for example, in espionage? In deceitful counterintelligence? In the apprehension of a rebel by means of a ruse? In the subversion of a foreign government with which we are not at war? Not one of these questions can be answered except with knowledge of concrete circumstances. The most relevant circumstance is the character of the nation doing the deed in question, and the character of the men or nation to which it is done. . . .

Those who raise the question, Who shall judge? do so, very often, in the belief that it is self-evidently absurd for us to be judge of our own morality. In truth it is no less, and perhaps far more absurd to hope that a reliable judgment on our morality will be brought by a poll of the nations, many of which are moved by animosity and envy, and more by ignorance. . . . The teaching of morality may be reduced to this: we must do everything that needs to be done to insure the survival of ourselves, our friends, and our free principles, indulging neither ourselves nor others, avoiding sentimentality no less than brutality, and mindful that if we weakly hang back, we will ignominiously hang alone. Those who desire to see this wisdom reduced to a punched-tape program must await their translation to another, better universe; likewise those who wish to see it purged of all severity.

It will surely be objected that to imperil the human race on the point of honor is to inflate Quixotism from an eccentricity to a calamity. We must therefore try to keep separate in our minds these two principles of action: the one, that it is wrong and dishonorable weakly to submit to domination; and the second, quite different, that what deserves to be defended should be defended, and what deserves to be resisted should be resisted, but that it is not sober to make a virtue out of defense and resistance regardless of the worth of things to be defended and resisted. In other words, the appeal to honor alone is defective, and must be perfected by a showing that honor is aroused in a good cause; otherwise it is suspected of being a euphemism for truculence or ferocious obstinacy. Do we have any reason for believing that the sovietization of the world is an evil commensurate with the peril created by opposing it? that it is the menace to dignity and freedom it was earlier said to be? To answer this question fully would require a full statement of the character of communism; here we can provide only the barest intimation.

Marxism begins with materialism and ends with the homogeneity of mankind. Marxist materialism differs from traditional materialism in attaching fundamental importance to the process of production, that is, to self-preservation by means of "technology," primitive or complex. The problem of preservation is primarily a technological, not a political problem for Marx. Indeed the complete solution of the problem of preservation is radically non-political: when the means of production are commonly owned and production is made a wholly social process, politics, or ruling and being ruled, will cease among men. The aspiration of communism is a total solution of the economic problem by means that would reduce all mankind to a single class-less, that is, homogeneous mass: a huge herd of sheep safely grazing. Human distinction is the source of the human problem, and therefore distinction must be terminated. The "heroes" will be "heroes of the shovel" and "heros of the loom": heroes of social production. This could be called the ultimate vul-garization of humanity, or the final indignity. We see it foreshadowed in the substitution of the shoe for the gavel in council, and the hairy chest for the clean collar in diplomacy. Because dignity is inseparable from distinction, the resistance to sovietization was said to be in the interest of human dignity.

What of freedom? Communism aims at life without the state, or without formal government. . . . The formlessness of the herd without distinction exposes it perpetually to the highest concentration of irresponsible author-ity—wielded for the noble end of administration, all other problems having vanished. More simply, a flock demands a shepherd.

The bias of Marxism toward matter and in opposition to form bears fruit in an unprecedented threat to human dignity and freedom. Honorable resis-tance to sovietization is thus more than merely honorable.

Readers may be pardoned for failing to see in the Soviet Union now a pop-ulation of grazing sheep. Far from a fat and torpid flock, they are an active, patriotic, spirited community, exhilarated by their hard-won achievements, conscious of greatness and lusting for its gratifications. That they are all these things is a vindication, not a contradiction of what was said above: finding their revolution confronted by hindrances, they compel themselves to rise to formidable heights of exertion. They are in the irrational condition of hero-ically laboring to destroy the possibility of any future heroic labor, while congratulating themselves on their own heroism. It is not the self-contradiction but the menace in their doings that is our present concern, and how we must respond to it.

We are in the position of respecting and praising the sense of honor, and of discerning it well-developed in our enemy. We will prove his right to rule us if we do not prevent him from exercising it; and we can maintain our right to be free only by being in a position to exercise it. In plain language, to his irresistible force we must oppose an immovable obstacle. . . .

There is not one iota of preponderance on the side of the view that the activator of the great force will choose to dash it against an absolute resistance. But if he entertains any reasonable doubt that our response will be absolute and remorseless, he will have less reason to keep the peace. This means that at a certain moment we must harden ourselves to look at the beauties of peace and prepare to see in their stead a contaminated chaos peopled with human carrion. If we cannot stand this thought, we are not ready to fight and will therefore be compelled to do so—or to truckle and prostrate ourselves.

On one condition would the sacrifice of ruin not be excessive: if we triumphed and the enemy were in the end destroyed. It is absurd to say that there are no victors in war. The one who survives in freedom is the victor; the one who must humble himself and surrender his ways and institutions at the dictate of his enemy is vanquished. . . .

Perhaps it will be said that there can be no victory where there are no survivors. . . . Then there must not be a next war. To argue so is plausible, but . . . inconclusive, for the argument tells us nothing about the form in which the cost of avoiding war must be paid. It might be that we pay for peace by abject surrender. That is unthinkable. It is unthinkable because the argument in favor of doing so is based upon the premise that, morally and politically, nothing matters—nothing, that is, except survival. The proper name for this position is not philanthropic morality but nihilism without intestines. The fortified species of nihilism also argues that nothing matters—except success. We have lost contact with the human spirit if we can no longer sense the repulsiveness of nihilism and the depravity of it in its emasculated form. If nothing matters, then human life does not matter. (Who would mourn it?) If anything matters, it is the decency of life and the possible self-respect of men. Still, where there is life there is hope for some amendment of any evil. We agree, and recommend the thought to our enemy; it deserves his consideration no less than ours. In brief, there is one cost of avoiding war which is more than we can afford: subhuman self-abasement.

Then we must pay for peace by making such a preparation for war that apprehensions for the safety of mankind will for once begin to influence the calculations of the enemy. If he is beyond or beneath a care for man's preservation, he is the manifest enemy of the race, fit to be hedged in or destroyed, certainly requiring to be diligently guarded against. If he is capable of such a care, then we need not, as truly we ought not assume the whole burden of providence. . . .

We seem to have concluded that the dictate of morality coincides with the interest of men and nations whose purposes are compatible with freedom and high-mindedness. This conclusion was the one intended.

In the course of our attempt to clarify the moral basis of international action, we have been led to take up two extreme but not unrepresentative examples of moral doctrine and a third which avoids the extremes. To simplify, the three could be said to turn, respectively, on Duty, Rights, and Honor. The conclusion has been that the first two are, for the purposes of guiding international action, imperfect, and the third is to be preferred. Supposing this for the moment to be true, of what practical value is the conclusion? Is it possible for a nation simply to adopt the moral principle of its choice for application to its international business? There is reason to doubt that this can be done with complete ease or freedom. The reason is that each nation is given its character by the elaborate set of moral judgments already embodied in its system of laws and practices. Implicit in the laws and customs is a notion of what action is just, what is proper and decent, what is worthy of esteem—in brief, of morality. . . . If all our notions of tolerable conduct are fashioned by one system of judgments, can we act externally on another?

The problem is made especially severe by the kinship that exists between our general moral outlook as a community and the two moral dispensations described above as the "extremes." When we go back to the Declaration of Independence, for example, we read of man's inalienable rights—which are the same natural rights that we noticed earlier in the discussion—all derivative from the natural right of all men to self-preservation. The Declaration enumerates the inalienable rights to life, liberty, and the pursuit of happiness; the Constitution speaks of life, liberty, and property. The replacement made by the Constitution is not of the nature of a revision but a clarification: the rights to life, liberty, and property are inseparably connected with happiness, in our moral and political understanding as a nation. It is only when each man is guaranteed in his person that his property is secure, and only when he is safeguarded in his property that his person is inviolate. Our political system makes provision for translating those natural rights into a meaningful ground of civil life by wedding the institutions of capitalism to those of constitutional government. Political freedom is possible on various bases; in the Western world it exists on the foundation of certain economic institutions, and the concurrence of capitalism and modern democracy is by no means a coincidence. Liberty and prosperity, the aims of our order, are provided for at one and the same time by a principle that authorizes the individuals to act in their own behalf under the protection of a government to whose rule they give their consent so long as it defends them in their freedom to act in their own behalf. The essence of acting in one's own behalf is calculation. This is the basis for the remark made at the head of this paragraph, to the effect that deep in our own moral and political foundations there is a kinship with the extreme moral principle named after "Rights," leading to undiluted calculation.

But the assertion was also made that as a nation we have an affinity for the opposite moral extreme as well, the one called by the name of "absolute Duty." Long ago, the reduction of morality to the rules of calculation was seen to be open to various objections. One line of objection was to the effect that when morality collapses into mere calculation, patriotism or love of the common good tends to languish or to disappear. This view when broadened or exaggerated becomes the criticism that, under the reign of private calculation or institutionalized egotism, care for the absolute worth or dignity of man as man vanishes, and life deteriorates accordingly in the moral respect. Those who hold this view feel a need to oppose "human rights" to "property rights." The objection on behalf of patriotism or civic virtue found a certain expression in the yearning for republican, agrarian simplicity often voiced in our earlier history. The criticism on behalf of man as man is more characteristic of the reforming or Liberal tendency as it now is among us. What began as solicitude for a sort of virtue that can become patriotism has been replaced by a solicitude for humanity or Society, a care that need not eventuate in patriotism.

Thus our moral life as a nation vibrates between the poles of calculation and a radicalized alternative to it, the former polarizing on Property, the latter on hostility to it and on radical, undiscriminating Equality. The former is at the heart of our national conservatism, the latter epitomizes contemporary Liberalism. Neither . . . pays heed above all to honor, the sober mean somewhere between calculation and duty.

There is indeed a lack of perfect congruity between our ruling moral predilections and the preferred moral basis of international action. But if we must act on the strength of what we are rather than what we might wish to be, there is little doubt as to the course we ought to follow. One of the two poles of our moral world stands as an encouragement to men to love their theory of homogeneous mankind more than they love their country and their countrymen, where the demands of the two come in competition. The other pole, grounded on the perhaps low but surely solid principle of calculation, is not out of contact with the intermediate moral ground of decent self-regard or honor. Husbanding our strength, gathering our allies, and preparing to avoid the supreme disaster of servility and disgrace, we at least avoid the imprudence of opposing armed brutality with impotent dogma. . . . Under the circumstances, we may allow ourselves to be led by calculation where perhaps we cannot be taught to soar by honor.

We began by thinking of man's duty to mankind. Reflecting on morality in its connection with the deeds of nations, we could not avoid the themes of honor and nobility, or more largely of human excellence. Human excellence, as it finds its expression among the masses of men ranked in their nations, is called civilization. Whatever reminds us of civilization reminds us at the same time of our duty to civilization, which means in practice to civilized men. What begins as a reflection on duty to man ends, under the influence of a glimpse at human superiority, as a reflection on duty to civilized man and to civilized nations. The way to discharge our duty to civilization is to sustain it where it exists before trying to inspire it where it never has been. Upon this point, remote from doctrinairism, the morality of calculation and the morality of honor come within sight of one another. The resulting gain in strategic competence brings them within earshot of one another. We must not despair if they never join hands.

76

Hans J. Morgenthau

The Mainsprings of American Foreign Policy (1950)

. . . [T]his generation of Americans must shed the illusions of their fathers and grandfathers and relearn the great principles of statecraft which guided the path of the republic in its first decade and—in moralistic disguise—in the first century of its existence. . . .

This classic age of American statecraft comes to an end with the physical disappearance of that generation of American statesmen. . . . Until very recently the American people seemed to be content to live in a political desert. . . . What in that period, stretching over more than a century, went under the name of foreign policy was either improvisation in the face of an urgent problem which had to be dealt with somehow, or—and especially in our century—the invocation of some abstract moral principle in the image of which the world was to be made over. Improvisation as a substitute for foreign policy was largely successful, for in the past the margin of American and allied power to spare generally exceeded the degree to which American

From Morgenthau, "The Mainsprings of American Foreign Policy," *American Political Science Review*, December 1950. Reprinted by permission of the American Political Science Association.

improvidence fell short of the demands of the hour. The invocation of abstract moral principles was in part hardly more than an innocuous pastime; for embracing everything it came to grips with nothing. In part, however, it was a magnificent instrument for marshalling public opinion in support of war and warlike policies—and for losing the peace to follow. The intoxication with moral abstractions which as a mass phenomenon started with the Spanish-American War, and which in our time has become the prevailing substitute for political thought, is indeed one of the great sources of weakness and failure in American foreign policy. . . .

In the Western Hemisphere we have always endeavored to preserve the unique position of the United States as a predominant power without rival. We have not been slow in recognizing that this predominance was not likely to be effectively threatened by any one American nation or combination of them, acting without support from outside the Western Hemisphere. It was, then, imperative for the United States to isolate the Western Hemisphere from the political and military policies of non-American nations. . . .

Since a threat to the national interest of the United States in the Western Hemisphere can come only from outside it, that is, historically from Europe, the United States has always striven to prevent the development of conditions in Europe which would be conducive to a European nation's interference in the affairs of the Western Hemisphere or to a direct attack upon the United States. Such conditions would be most likely to arise if a European nation had gained such predominance that it could afford to look across the sea for conquest without fear of being menaced at the center of its power, that is, in Europe itself. It is for this reason that the United States has consistently—the War of 1812 is the sole major exception—pursued policies aiming at the maintenance of the balance of power in Europe. . . . It is by virtue of this concern that the United States has intervened in both World Wars on the side of the initially weaker coalition and that its European policies have so largely paralleled those of Great Britain; for from Henry VIII to this day Great Britain has invariably pursued one single objective in Europe: the maintenance of the balance of power.

With Asia the United States has been vitally concerned only since the turn of the century, and the relation of Asia to the national interest of the United States has never been obvious or clearly defined. . . . Yet beneath the confusions, reversals of policy, and moralistic generalities, which have made up the surface of our Asiatic policy since McKinley, one can detect an underlying consistency which, however vaguely, reflects the permanent interest of the United States in Asia. . . .

However unsure of itself the Asiatic policy of the United States has been, it has always assumed that the domination of China by another nation would create so great an accumulation of power as to threaten the security of the United States.

Not only with regard to Asia, however, but wherever American foreign policy has operated, political thought has been divorced from political action. . . . We have acted on the international scene, as all nations must, in power-political terms; we have tended to conceive of our actions in nonpolitical, moralistic terms. This aversion to seeing problems of international politics as they are and the inclination to viewing them instead in nonpolitical, moralistic terms can be attributed both to certain misunderstood peculiarities of the American experience in foreign affairs and to the general climate of opinion prevailing in the Western world during the better part of the nineteenth and the first decade of the twentieth centuries. . . .

The expansion of the United States up to the Spanish-American War seemed to provide conclusive proof both for the distinctiveness and moral superiority of American foreign policy. The settlement of the better part of a continent by the thirteen original states seemed to be an act of civilization rather than of conquest and as such essentially different from, and morally superior to, the imperialistic ventures, wars of conquest, and colonial acquisitions with which the history of other nations is replete. Yet it was not so much political virtue as the contiguity of the sparsely settled object of conquest with the original territory of departure, which put the mark of uniqueness upon American expansion. . . . Furthermore, the utter political, military, and numerical inferiority of the Indian opponent tended to obscure the element of power, which was less obtrusive in, but no more absent from, the continental expansion of the United States than the expansionist movements of other nations. . . .

American isolation was an established political fact until the end of the nineteenth century. . . .

From the shores of the North American continent, the citizens of the new world watched the strange spectacle of the struggle for power unfolding on the distant scenes of Europe, Africa, and Asia. Since for the better part of the nineteenth century their foreign policy enabled them to retain the role of spectators, what was actually the result of a passing historic constellation appeared to Americans as a permanent condition, self-chosen as well as naturally ordained. At worst they would continue to watch the game of power politics played by others. At best the time was close at hand when, with democracy established everywhere, the final curtain would fall and the game of power politics would no longer be played.

To aid in the achievement of this goal was conceived to be part of America's mission. . . .

To understand the American mission in such selfless, humanitarian terms was the easier as the United States—in contrast to the other great powers—was generally not interested, at least outside the Western Hemisphere, in a particular advantage to be defined in terms of power or of territorial gain. Its national interest was exhausted by the preservation of its predominance in the Western Hemisphere and of the balance of power in Europe and Asia. . . .

In one sense, this ideal of a free, peaceful, and prosperous world, from which popular government had banished power politics forever, was a natural outgrowth of the American experience. In another sense, this ideal expressed in a particularly eloquent and consistent fashion the general philosophy which during the better part of the nineteenth century dominated the Western world. This philosophy contains two basic propositions: that the struggle for power on the international scene is a mere accident of history, naturally associated with non-democratic government and, hence, destined to disappear with the triumph of democracy throughout the world; and that, in consequence, conflicts between democratic and non-democratic nations must be conceived not as struggles for mutual advantage in terms of power but primarily as a contest between good and evil, which can only end with the complete triumph of good and with evil being wiped off the face of the earth. . . .

The illusion that a nation can escape, if it only wants to, from power politics into a realm where action is guided by moral principles rather than by considerations of power, not only is deeply rooted in the American mind; it also took more than a century for this illusion to crowd out the older notion that international politics is an unending struggle for power in which the interests of individual nations must necessarily be defined in terms of power. Out of the struggle between these two opposing conceptions three types of American statesmen emerge: the realist, thinking in terms of power and represented by Alexander Hamilton; the ideological, acting in terms of power, thinking in terms of moral principles, and represented by Thomas Jefferson and John Quincy Adams; the moralist, thinking and acting in terms of moral principles and represented by Woodrow Wilson. To these three types, three periods of American foreign policy roughly correspond: the first covering the first decade of the history of the United States as an independent nation, the second covering the nineteenth century to the Spanish-American War, the third covering the half century after that war. . . .

On April 22, 1793, Washington issued a proclamation of neutrality, and it was in defense of that proclamation that Hamilton wrote the "Pacificus" and "Americanus" articles. Among the arguments directed against the proclamation were three derived from moral principles. Faithfulness to treaty obligations, gratitude toward a country which had lent its assistance to the colonies in their struggle for independence, and the affinity of republican institutions were cited to prove that the United States must side with France. Against these moral principles, Hamilton invoked the national interest of the United States. . . .

Must a nation subordinate its security, its happiness, nay, its very existence to the respect for treaty obligations, to the sentiment of gratitude, to sympathy with a kindred political system? This was the question which

Hamilton proposed to answer, and his answer was an unequivocal "no." Hamilton unswervingly applied one standard to the issues raised by the opposition to Washington's proclamation of neutrality: the national interest of the United States. He put the legalistic and moralistic arguments of the opposition . . . into the context of the concrete power situation in which the United States found itself on the international scene. . . .

Considerations such as these, recognized for what they are, have guided American foreign policy but for a short period, that is, as long as the Federalists were in power. *The Federalist* and Washington's Farewell Address are their classic expression. . . . During the century following their brief flowering, they have by and large continued to influence policies as well, under the cover, as it were, of those moral principles with which from Jefferson onward American statesmen have liked to justify their moves on the international scene. . . . [W]hat the moral law demanded was by a felicitous coincidence always identical with what the national interest seemed to require. Political thought and political action moved on different planes, which, however, were so inclined as to merge in the end. . . .

The Monroe Doctrine's moral postulates of anti-imperialism and mutual non-intervention were the negative conditions for the safety and enduring greatness of the United States. . . .

This period initiated by McKinley, in which moral principles no longer justify the enduring national interest as in the second, but replace it as a guide for action, finds its fulfillment in the political thought of Woodrow Wilson. Wilson's thought not only disregards the national interest, but is explicitly opposed to it on moral grounds. "It is a very perilous thing," he said in his address at Mobile on October 27, 1913,

> to determine the foreign policy of a nation in the terms of material interest. It not only is unfair to those with whom you are dealing, but it is degrading as regards your own actions. . . . We dare not turn from the principle that morality and not expediency is the thing that must guide us, and that we will never condone iniquity because it is most convenient to do so.

. . . Not only did the crusading fervor of moral reformation obliterate the awareness of the United States' traditional interest in the maintenance of the European balance of power, to be accomplished through the defeat of Germany. Wilson's moral fervor also had politically disastrous effects, for which there is no precedent in the history of the United States. Wilson's moral objective required the destruction of the Kaiser's autocracy, and this happened also to be required by the political interests of the United States. The political interests of the United States required, beyond this immediate objective of total victory, the restoration of the European balance of power, traditional guarantor of American security. Yet it was in indignation at the moral deficiencies of that very balance of power, "forever discredited," as he thought, that Wilson had asked the American people to take up arms against the Central Powers! Once military victory had put an end to the immediate threat to American security, the very logic of his moral position—let us remember that consistency is the moralist's supreme virtue—drove him toward substituting for the concrete national interest of the United States the general postulate of a brave new world where the national interest of the United States, as that of all nations, would disappear in a community of interests comprising mankind.

Consequently, Wilson considered it to be the purpose of victory not to restore a new, viable balance of power, but to make an end to it once and forever. . . .

Faced with the national interests of the great allied powers, Wilson had nothing to oppose or support them with but his moral principles, with the result that the neglect of the American national interest was not compensated for by the triumph of political morality. In the end Wilson had to consent to a series of uneasy compromises which were a betrayal of his moral principles—for principles can, by their very nature, not be made the object of compromise—and which satisfied nobody's national aspirations. . . .

Yet Wilson returned to the United States, unaware of his failure. He offered the American people what he had offered the allied nations at Paris: moral principles divorced from political reality. "The day we have left behind us," he proclaimed at Los Angeles on September 20, 1919,

> was a day of balances of power. It was a day of "every nation take care of itself or make a partnership with some other nation or group of nations to hold the peace of the world steady or to dominate the weaker portions of the world." Those were the days of alliances. This project of the League of Nations is a great process of disentanglement. . . .

[W]hat is significant for the course which American foreign policy was to take in the interwar years is not so much that the American people rejected Wilsonianism, but that they rejected it by ratifying the denial of the American tradition of foreign policy which was implicit in the political thought of Wilson. . . . The isolationism of the interwar period could delude itself into believing that it was but the restorer of the early realist tradition of American foreign policy. . . . The isolationists of the twenties and thirties did not see what was the very essence of the policies of the Founding Fathers—that both the isolated and the preponderant position of the United States in the Western Hemisphere was not a fact of nature, and that the freedom from entanglements in European conflicts was not the result of mere abstention on the part of the United States. Both benefits were the result of political conditions outside the Western Hemisphere and of policies carefully contrived and purposefully executed in their support. For the realists of the first period, isolation was an objective of policy, which had to be striven for to be attained. For the isolationists of the interwar period, isolation was, as it were, a natural state, which only needed to be left undisturbed in order to continue forever. Conceived in such terms, it was the very negation of foreign policy. . . .

In a profound sense [isolationism and Wilsonianism] are brothers under the skin. Both are one in maintaining that the United States has no interest in any particular political and military constellation outside the Western Hemisphere. While isolationism stops here, Wilsonianism asserts that the American national interest is nowhere in particular but everywhere, being identical with the interests of mankind itself. The political awareness of both refuses to concern itself with the concrete issues with regards to which the national interest must be asserted. . . .

When internationalism triumphed in the late thirties, it did so in the moral terms of Wilsonianism. . . .

The practical results of this philosophy of international affairs, as applied to the political war and post-war problems, were, then, bound to be quite similar to those which had made the allied victory in the First World War politically meaningless. . . .

The thought that the war might be waged in view of a new balance of power to be established after the war, occured in the West only to Winston Churchill—and, of course, to Joseph Stalin. . . .

The equation of political moralism with morality and of political realism with immorality is itself untenable. . . . The basic fact of international politics is the absence of a society able to protect the existence, and to promote the interest, of the individual nations. For the individual nations to take care of their own national interests is, then, a political necessity. There can be no moral duty to neglect them; for as the international society is at present constituted, the consistent neglect of the national interest can only lead to national suicide. Yet it can be shown that there exists even a positive moral duty for the individual nation to take care of its national interests.

Self-preservation for the individual as well as for societies is not only a biological and psychological necessity, but in the absence of an overriding moral obligation a moral duty as well. In the absence of an integrated international society, in particular, the attainment of a modicum of order and the realization of a minimum of moral values are predicated upon the existence of national communities capable of preserving order and realizing moral values within the limits of their power. It is obvious that such a state of affairs falls far short of that order and realized morality to which we are accustomed in national societies. The only relevant question is, however, what the practical alternative is to these imperfections of an international society based upon the national interests of its component parts. The attainable alternative is not a higher morality realized through the application of universal moral principles, but moral deterioration through either political failure or the fanaticism of political crusades. . . .

77

Alexander Hamilton

On Neutrality Toward France (1793–1794)

. . . [The] objection to the Proclamation [of Neutrality] namely that it is inconsistent with the Treaties between the United States and France will now be examined. . . .

The Alliance between the United States and France is a Defensive *Alliance*. In the Caption of it it is denominated a "Treaty of Alliance eventual and *defensive*." . . .

[I]n determining the *legal* and *positive* obligations of the UStates the only point of inquiry is—whether the War was *in fact* begun by France or by her enemies. . . . [I]n a *defensive* alliance, when *war is made upon* one of the allies, the other is bound to fulfil the conditions stipulated on its part, without inquiry whether the war is rightfully begun or not—as on the other hand when war is begun by one of the allies the other is exempted from the obligation of assisting; however just the commencement of it may have been. . . .

[T]hough the manifest injustice of the war has been affirmed by some, to be a good cause for not executing the formal obligations of a treaty, I have no where found it maintained, that the justice of a war is a consideration, which can *oblige* a nation to do what its formal obligations do not require; as in the case of a *defensive* alliance, to furnish the succours stipulated, though the formal obligation did not exist, by reason of the ally having begun the war, instead of being the party attacked.

But if this were not the true doctrine, an impartial examination would prove, that with respect to some of the powers, France is not blameless in the circumstances, which preceded and led to the war with those powers; that if she received, she also gave cause of offense, and that the justice of the War on her side is, in those cases, not a little problematical. . . .

[France] gave a general and just cause of alarm to Nations, by that Decree of the 19th. of November 1792 whereby the Convention, in the name

From Hamilton, "Pacificus II–IV" and "Americanus I–II," *The Papers of Alexander Hamilton*, Vol. XV and XVI, Columbia University Press, 1969.

of the French Nation, declare that they will grant *fraternity* and *assistance* to every People who *wish* to recover their liberty and charge the Executive Power to send the necessary orders to *the Generals* to give assistance to such people, and to *defend those citizens who may have been or who may be vexed for the cause of liberty*; which decree was ordered to be printed *in all languages*.

When a Nation has actually come to a resolution to throw off a yoke, under which it may have groaned, and to assert its liberties—it is justifiable and meritorious in another nation to afford assistance to the one which has been oppressed & is *in the act* of liberating itself; but it is not warrantable for any Nation *beforehand* to hold out a general invitation to insurrection and revolution, by promising to assist *every people* who may *wish* to recover their liberty and to defend *those citizens*, of every country, *who may have been or who may be vexed for the cause of liberty*; still less to commit to the *Generals* of its armies the discretionary power of judging when the Citizens of a foreign Country have been vexed for the cause of Liberty by their own government. . . .

Such a conduct as that indicated by this Decree has a natural tendency to disturb the tranquillity of nations, to excite fermentation and revolt every where; and therefore justified neutral powers, who were in a situation to be affected by it in taking measures to repress the spirit by which it had been dictated.

But the principle of this Decree received a more particular application to Great Britain by some subsequent circumstances.

Among the proofs of this are two answers, which were given by the President of the National Convention at a public sitting on the 28th. of November. . . .

"Nature and *principles* draw *towards us* England Scotland and Ireland. Let the cries of friendship resound through the two *REPUBLICS*." "Principles are waging war against Tyranny, which will fall under the blows of philosophy. *Royalty in Europe is either destroyed or on the point of perishing*, on the ruins of feudality; and the *Declaration of Rights placed by the side of thrones is a devouring fire which will consume them. WORTHY Republicans*."

Declarations of this sort cannot but be considered as a direct application of the principle of the Decree to Great Britain; as an open patronage of a Revolution in that Country; a conduct which proceeding from the head of the body that governed France in the presence and on behalf of that body was unquestionably an offense and injury to the Nation to which it related.

The decree of the 15 of November is another cause of offence to all the Governments of Europe. By That Decree "*The French Nation declares*, that it will *treat as enemies the people*, who *refusing* or *renouncing* liberty and equality *are desirous* of preserving their *Prince* and *privileged castes*—or of *entering into an accomodation* with them &c." This decree was little short of a declaration of War against all Nations, having *princes* and *privileged classes*. . . .

Whatever partiality may be entertained for the general object of the French Revolution, it is impossible for any well informed or soberminded man not to condemn the proceedings which have been stated; as repugnant to the general rights of Nations, to the true principles of liberty, to the freedom of opinion of mankind; & not to acknowledge as a consequence of this, that the justice of the war on the part of France, with regard to some of the powers with which she is engaged, is from those causes questionable enough to free the UStates from all embarrassment on that score; if it be at all incumbent upon them to go into the inquiry.

The policy of a defensive alliance is so essentially distinct from that of an offensive one, that it is every way important not to confound their effects. The first kind has in view the prudent object of mutual defence, when either of the allies is involuntarily forced into a war by the attack by some third power. The latter kind subjects the peace of each ally to the will of the other, and obliges each to partake in the wars of policy & interest, as well as in those of safety and defence, of the other. To preserve their boundaries distinct it is necessary that each kind should be governed by plain and obvious rules. This would not be the case, if instead of taking the simple fact of who begun the war as a guide, it was necessary to travel into metaphysical niceties about the justice or injustice of the cause which led to it. . . .

France at the time of issuing the proclamation was engaged & likely to be engaged in war, with all or almost all Europe; without a single ally in that quarter of the Globe.

In such a state of things, it is evident, that however she may be able to defend herself at home (a thing probably still practicable if her factions can be appeased, and system and order introduced) she cannot make any *external* efforts, in any degree proportioned to those which can be made against her.

By this situation of things alone, the United States would be dispensed from an obligation to embark in her quarrel.

It is known that we are wholly destitute of naval force. France, with all the great maritime Powers united against her, is unable to supply this deficiency. She can not afford us that species of cooperation, which is necessary to render our efforts useful to her and to prevent our experiencing the entire destruction of our Trade and the most calamitous inconveniences in other respects.

Our guarantee does not respect France herself. It does not relate to her own immediate defence or preservation. It relates merely to the defence & preservation of her American colonies; objects of which (though of considerable importance) she might be deprived and yet remain a great and powerful and a happy Nation. . . .

There would be no proportion between the mischiefs and perils, to which the UStates would expose themselves by embarking in the War, and the benefit *which the nature of their stipulation aims at securing* to France, or that, which it would be in their power actually to render her, by becoming a party.

This disproportion would be a valid reason for not executing the Guarantee. All contracts are to receive a reasonable construction. Self preservation is the first duty of a Nation; and though in the performance of stipulations relating to war, good faith requires that the *ordinary hazards* of war should be fairly encountered, because they are directly contemplated by such stipulations, yet it does not require that *extraordinary* and *extreme* hazards should be run; especially where the object, for which they are to be run, is only a *partial* and *particular* interest of the ally, for whom they are to to be run.

As in the present instance good faith does not require, that the UStates should put in jeopardy their essential interests, perhaps their very existence, in one of the most unequal contests, in which a nation could be engaged—to secure to France what?—her West India Islands and other less important possessions in America. . . .

[Another] objection to the Proclamation is, that it is inconsistent with the gratitude due to France, for the services rendered us in our own Revolution. . . .

[I]t may not be without use to indulge some reflections on this very favourite topic of gratitude to France; since it is at this shrine we are continually invited to sacrifice the true interests of the Country; as if "*All for love and the world well lost*" were a fundamental maxim in politics.

Faith and Justice between nations are virtues of a nature sacred and unequivocal. They cannot be too strongly inculcated nor too highly respected. Their obligations are definite and positive their utility unquestionable. . . .

But the same cannot be said of gratitude. . . .

The basis of gratitude, is a benefit received or intended, which there was no right to claim, originating in a regard to the interest or advantage of the party, on whom the benefit is or is meant to be conferred. If a service is rendered from views *chiefly* relative to the immediate interest of the party, who renders it, and is productive of reciprocal advantages, there seems scarcely in such a case to be an adequate basis for a sentiment like that of gratitude. . . .

Between individuals, occasion is not unfrequently given to the exercise of gratitude. Instances of conferring benefits, from kind and benevolent dispositions or feelings towards the person benefitted, without any other interest on the part of the person, who confers the benefit, than the pleasure of doing a good action, occur every day among individuals. But among nations they perhaps never occur. It may be affirmed as a general principle, that the predominant motive of good offices from one nation to another is the interest or advantage of the Nations, which performs them.

Indeed the rule of morality is in this respect not exactly the same between Nations as between individuals. The duty of making its own welfare the guide of its actions is much stronger upon the former than upon the latter; in proportion to the greater magnitude and importance of national compared with individual happiness, to the greater permanency of the effects of national than of individual conduct. Existing Millions and for the most part future generations are concerned in the present measures of a government: While the consequences of the private actions of an individual, for the most part, terminate with himself or are circumscribed within a narrow compass.

Whence it follows, that an individual may on numerous occasions meritoriously indulge the emotions of generosity and benevolence; not only without an eye to, but even at the expence of his own interest. But a Nation can rarely be justified in pursuing a similar course; and when it does so ought to confine itself within much stricter bounds. Good offices, which are indifferent to the Interest of a Nation performing them, or which are compensated by the existence or expectation of some reasonable equivalent or which produce an essential good to the nation, to which they are rendered, without real detriment to the affairs of the nation rendering them, prescribe the limits of national generosity or benevolence.

It is not meant here to advocate a policy absolutely selfish or interested in nations; but to show that a policy regulated by their own interest, as far as justice and good faith permit, is, and ought to be their prevailing policy: and that either to ascribe to them a different principle of action, or to deduce from the supposition of it arguments for a self-denying and self-sacrificing gratitude on the part of a Nation, which may have received from another good offices, is to misconceive or mistake what usually are and ought to be the springs of National Conduct. . . .

An examination into the question how far *regard to the cause of Liberty* ought to induce the United States to take part with France in the present war, is rendered necessary by the efforts which [some] are making to establish an opinion that it ought to have that effect. In order to make a right judgment on the point, it is requisite to consider the question under two aspects.

I. Whether the cause of France be truly the cause of Liberty, pursued with justice and humanity, and in a manner likely to crown it with honorable success.

II. Whether the degree of service we could render, by participating in the conflict, was likely to compensate, by its utility to the cause, the evils which would probably flow from it to ourselves.

If either of these questions can be answered in the negative, it will result, that the consideration which has been stated ought not to embark us in the war. . . .

All who are not wilfully blind must see and acknowlege that this Country at present enjoys an unexampled state of prosperity. That war would interrupt it need not be affirmed. We should then by war lose the advantage of that astonishing progress in strength wealth and improvement, which we are now making, and which if continued for a few years will place our national rights and interests upon immoveable foundations. This loss alone would be of infinite moment: it is such a one as no prudent or good man would encounter but for some clear necessity or some positive duty.

If while Europe is exhausting herself in a destructive war, this country can maintain its peace, the issue will open to us a wide field of advantages, which even imagination can with difficulty compass.

But a check to the *progress* of our prosperity is not the greatest evil to be anticipated. Considering the naval superiority of the enemies of France we cannot doubt that our commerce would be in a great degree annihilated by a war. Our Agriculture would of course with our commerce receive a deep wound. The exportations which now contribute to animate it could not fail to be essentially diminished. Our mechanics would experience their full share of the common calamity. That lively and profitable industry which now spreads a smile over all our cities and Towns would feel an instantaneous and rapid decay. . . .

The certain evils of our joining France in the war are sufficient dissuasives from so intemperate a measure. . . .

To defend its own rights, to vindicate its own honor, there are occasions when a Nation ought to hazard even its existence. Should such an occasion occur, I trust those who are now most averse to commit the peace of the country will not be the last to face the danger, nor the first to turn their backs upon it.

But let us at least have the consolation of not having rashly courted misfortune. Let us have to act under the animating reflection of being engaged in repelling wrongs which we neither sought nor merited, in vindicating our rights, invaded without provocation, in defending our honor violated without cause. Let us not have to reproach ourselves with having voluntarily bartered blessings for calamities.

But we are told that our own Liberty is at stake upon the event of the war against France—that if she falls we shall be the next victim. The combined powers, it is said, will never forgive in us the origination of those principles which were the germs of the French Revolution. They will endeavour to eradicate them from the world.

If this suggestion were ever so well founded, it would perhaps be a sufficient answer to it to say, that our interference is not likely to alter the case—that it could only serve prematurely to exhaust our strength.

But other answers more conclusive present themselves.

The war against France requires on the part of her enemies efforts unusually violent. They are obliged to strain every nerve, to exert every resource. However it may terminate, they must find themselves spent in an extreme degree; a situation not very favourable to the undertaking a new, and even to Europe combined, an immense enterprize.

To subvert by force republican Liberty in this Country, nothing short of entire conquest would suffice. This conquest, with our present increased population; greatly distant as we are from Europe, would either be impracticable or would demand such exertions, as following immediately upon those which will have been requisite to the subversion of the French Revolution, would be absolutely ruinous to the undertakers. . . .

There are too great errors in our reasoning upon this subject. One is that the combined Powers will certainly attribute to us the same principles which they deem so exceptionable in France; the other, that our principles are in fact the same.

If left to themselves, they will all except one naturally see in us a people who originally resorted to a Revolution in Government as a refuge from encroachment on rights and privileges *antecedently* enjoyed—not as a people who from choice have sought a radical and entire change in the established Government, in pursuit of new privileges and rights carried to an extreme, not reconciliable perhaps with any form of regular Government. They will see in us a people who have a due respect for property and personal security—who in the midst of our revolution abstained with exemplary moderation from everything violent or sanguinary instituting governments adequate to the protection of persons and property; who since the completion of our rev-olution have in a very short period, from mere reasoning and reflection, with-out tumult or bloodshed adopted a form of general Government calculated as well as the nature of things would permit—to remedy antecedent defects—to give strength and security to the Nation—to rest the foundations of Liberty on the basis of Justice Order and Law—who at all times have been content to govern ourselves; unmeddling in the Governments or Affairs of other Nations: in fine, they will see in us sincere Republicans but decided enemies to licentiousness and anarchy—sincere republicans but decided friends to the freedom of opinion, to the order and tranquility of all Mankind. They will not see in us a people whose best passions have been misled and whose best qualities have been perverted from their true aim by headlong fanatical or designing leaders to the perpetration of acts from which humanity shrinks—to the commission of outrages, over which the eye of reason weeps—to the profession and practice of principles which tend to shake the foundations of morality—to dissolve the social bands—to disturb the peace of mankind—to substitute confusion [for] order, anarchy [for] Government.

Such at least is the light in which the Reason or the passions of the Powers confederated against France lead them to view her principles and conduct. And it is to be lamented that so much cause has been given for their opinions. If on our part, we give no incitement to their passions, facts too prominent and too decisive to be combated will forbid their reason to bestow the same character upon us.

It is therefore matter of real regret that there should be an effort on our part to level the distinctions, which discriminate our case from that of France—to confound the two cases in the view of foreign powers—and to hazard our own principles, by persuading ourselves of a similitude which does not exist. . . .

But let us not corrupt ourselves by false comparisons or glosses—nor shut our eyes to the true nature of transactions which ought to grieve and warn us—not rashly mingle our destiny in the consequences of the errors and extravagances of another nation.

78

James Madison

First Inaugural Address (1809)

. . . Indulging no passions which trespass on the rights or the repose of other nations, it has been the true glory of the United States to cultivate peace by observing justice, and to entitle themselves to the respect of the nations at war by fulfilling their neutral obligations with the most scrupulous impartiality. . . .

This unexceptionable course could not avail against the injustice and violence of the belligerent powers. In their rage against each other, or impelled by more direct motives, principles of retaliation have been introduced equally contrary to universal reason and acknowledged law. How long their arbitrary edicts will be continued in spite of the demonstrations that not even a pretext for them has been given by the United States, and of the fair and liberal attempt to induce a revocation of them, can not be anticipated. Assuring myself that under every vicissitude the determined spirit and united councils of the nation will be safeguards to its honor and its essential interests, I repair to the post assigned me with no other discouragement than what springs from my own inadequacy to its high duties. If I do not sink under the weight of this deep conviction it is because I find some support in a consciousness of the purposes and a confidence in the principles which I bring with me into this arduous service.

To cherish peace and friendly intercourse with all nations having correspondent dispositions; to maintain sincere neutrality toward belligerent nations; to prefer in all cases amicable discussion and reasonable accommodation of differences to a decision of them by an appeal to arms; to

From *Inaugural Addresses of the Presidents of the United States*, United States Government Printing Office, 1969.

exclude foreign intrigues and foreign partialities, so degrading to all countries and so baneful to free ones; to foster a spirit of independence too just
to invade the rights of others, too proud to surrender our own, too liberal
to indulge unworthy prejudices ourselves and too elevated not to look
down upon them in others; to hold the union of the States as the basis of
their peace and happiness; to support the Constitution, which is the
cement of the Union, as well in its limitations as in its authorities; to
respect the rights and authorities reserved to the States and to the people
as equally incorporated with and essential to the success of the general system;to promote by authorized means improvements friendly to agriculture,
to manufactures, and to external as well as internal commerce; to favor in
like manner the advancement of science and the diffusion of information
as the best aliment to true liberty; to carry on the benevolent plans which
have been so meritoriously applied to the conversion of our aboriginal
neighbors from the degradation and wretchedness of savage life to a participation [in] the improvements of which the human mind and manners are
susceptible in a civilized state—as far as sentiments and intentions such as
these can aid the fulfillment of my duty, they will be a resource which can
not fail me. . . .

79

James F. Pontuso

American Foreign Policy and the Victory of Liberal Democracy (2001)

In 1989 one of my students cut class, left school, and boarded an airplane to
take part in one of the most momentous events of the twentieth century.
When he returned a few days later, he brought back a present to make up for
taking his unexcused road trip. It is not much to look at, just a three inch
chunk of cement painted on one side with iridescent blue paint. Yet this little
hunk of rubble is a symbol of a global struggle during which the future of the

Printed by permission of the author. This article was originally prepared with a grant
from the Earhart Foundation.

human race hung in the balance. It represents the defeat of a mighty enemy, the triumph of our way of life, and the beginning of American's unchallenged supremacy as a world power. My gift was a piece of the Berlin Wall.

For almost fifty years the struggle between the Communist nations of the East and the liberal democracies (governments that protect individual rights and decide issues by consent of the governed) of the West was fought out on a world stage. The conflict was dubbed the Cold War since neither side wanted a direct military confrontation for fear of beginning a nuclear exchange. The Berlin Wall was a emblem of that contest. Ostensibly it was built to keep Western trouble-makers out of East Germany, but in actuality it was constructed to prohibit the people of East Berlin from fleeing their tyrannical system of government. When the Wall was torn down, it marked the end of the contest between East and West. Not only was East Berlin liberated but all Europeans broke free from the yoke of Communism.

What was at the root of the conflict during the Cold War? What could have caused nations to risk nuclear annihilation? The Cold War began at the conclusion of World War II when the Soviet Union used its military might to install Communist governments in the nations of Central Europe. During World War II the United States, Great Britain, and the Soviet Union had fought as allies against the Nazis. As the war neared its end, the leaders of those nations—Franklin Roosevelt, Winston Churchill, and Joseph Stalin—met to map out an arrangement that would bring stability to Europe and peace to the world. It was decided that each of the Great Powers would have a sphere of influence. Since the Soviet army occupied Central Europe there was little doubt that the Soviets would dominate that region. The Soviet Union also wanted to have a buffer between itself and the Western powers, especially Germany, to avoid the catastrophic losses (estimated at 20 million people) that it had suffered during the war. But the agreement between the Great Powers was faulty. It promised that the governments of Central Europe would be freely elected and that they would be congenial toward the Soviet Union. However, if the people of that area had been given a choice, they would never have elected leaders sympathetic to the Soviet Union. There were long-standing hostilities toward Russia that were only made worse by the fear of Communist domination.

Stalin enforced his part of the deal. He brutally crushed all independent political movements in Central Europe and installed Communist leaders who mimicked the Soviet line. Harry Truman, who had become President after Roosevelt's death, pressed Stalin to comply with the other half of the agreement—democratic elections—but to no avail. Truman also worried that the Soviets were supporting Communist insurgencies in Turkey, Greece and Iran. He feared that Stalin might use his typically fierce tactics to establish Communist governments in those nations as well. To counter Soviet moves, the United States began to rearm and re-deploy its military forces, so recently withdrawn from Europe at the end of the war against Nazism. The idea was to encircle the Soviet Union with a group of alliances and to prohibit it from further expansion. That principle became the cornerstone of Western policy toward the Soviets, and remained so for nearly fifty years. Although there were a number of conflicts during that era, such as Korea, Vietnam, and Afghanistan, direct confrontation between the superpowers was avoided.

Such were the origins of the Cold War. But it is important to remember that there were deeper motivations for the discord. The most fundamental was ideology. Karl Marx, on whose ideas the Communists claimed to base their system, argued that the bourgeois way of life, that is the political and social system of a liberal democracy such as the United States, was the source of great suffering and injustice. He claimed that the natural rights Americans so cherish were nothing more than a mechanism of class oppression. In order to perform tasks more efficiently, Marx reasoned, every society employs a division of labor. Over time, these divisions evolve into social classes. Some people benefit more from this economic arrangement than do others. In bourgeois societies the class differences become particularly acute, since the owners of businesses, or capitalists, use their wealth and position to amass great fortunes. The political rights guaranteed in capitalist states (for example in the United States, by such documents as the Declaration of Independence and the Bill of Rights) insure that no one will interfere with the owners' liberty to acquire more, always more.

Marx maintained that although the workers are "free" to vote and to sell their labor to the highest bidder, they are reduced to subsistence wages. This "iron law," as he called it, is true because of the intense competition inherent in capitalism. In order to keep up with their rivals, corporations are compelled to produce goods rapidly and efficiently, and at the same time to lower the cost of production. To attain these goals the owners must introduce evermore complex machines and simultaneously reduce wages. Thus, the laborers, the most numerous class, become alienated from their toil and, indeed, their very existence. They are made to work at tedious jobs, the result of assembly line techniques and advanced machinery, for meager wages, the absolute minimum expenditure needed to maintain them as functioning units of production. All fulfillment is lost in such labor since the workers have control over neither the finished product nor the means by which those products are created. For the workers, political freedom results in slavery and degradation.

Marx theorized that capitalism's very efficiency would eventually cause its downfall. It would produce such a glut of goods that consumption would fall behind production, resulting in massive layoffs and finally economic collapse. The inequity of a system in which the owners enjoy all the luxuries of life but do not labor and the workers labor but live in poverty would become so apparent that the workers would seize the means of production and transform the social arrangement so that all would share equally in its bounty. The inexorable movement of history made it inevitable that a new era would be born in which there would be real equality, full liberty, and universal brotherhood.

Because Marx's vision was so appealing, some in the West came to agree with his goals of equality, liberation and community. Yet most Westerners believed that no matter how humane the aim, his principles were impractical. Human beings are not equal in ability or determination. The attempt to make all people equal necessitates denying liberty to some, normally the talented. Furthermore, Marx's promise to make people equal, in fact, results in denying equality of opportunity to everyone. Critics of Marx also maintained that total liberation was not feasible. Human beings need some form of government to restrain their baser instincts. By its very nature, government implies that there will be restrictions on people's liberty. Even universal community is unrealistic; for in all of recorded history people have found it normal to live in distinct political communities.

Even more worrisome than the principles of Communist countries were their practices. Marx's philosophy led people to believe that society could be thoroughly reformed. Thus, Communist rulers worked tirelessly to usher in a transformation of the human condition. But most people could not measure up to this perfect image; they were more often concerned with their own interests than with the triumph of Communism. In an effort to make reality conform to theory, Communist rulers employed the most uncompromising forms of control. When people still failed to meet expectations, Communists became vicious. Despite the tightly controlled media in Communist countries, stories of ruthlessness and savagery filtered into the West from émigrés who had escaped. The most important account of Soviet Terror was given by the Russian dissident Alexander Solzhenitsyn in his massive work *The Gulag Archipelago*. The tales were almost too fantastic to believe. Millions of people were executed for political offenses. Even more were sent to forced labor camps where many died from overwork. The crimes of these people consisted of being born into the wrong social class (bourgeois), or of opposing the government in any way. Under Stalin a person could be jailed for, among other things, "anti-Soviet thought" or for being a "wife or child of an enemy of the people." For many years Communist rulers denied these allegations, and the people of the West, although wary, thought them exaggerated. Secret police files made public since the collapse of Communism show that many of the most far-fetched anecdotes were true.

Not only did Marxism make Communists cruel to their own citizens, it made them hostile to the West. A variety of methods were employed with the purpose of overthrowing Western democracies. For instance, disclosures from once secret files indicate that for many years sanctuary and aid were given to a number of terrorists groups intent on undermining the fabric of Western society. It is probably true that the Soviet Secret Police (KGB) ordered the assassination of the fiercely anti-Communist Pope John Paul II.

It is not exactly clear why Communism failed. Some say that Soviet leader Mikhail Gorbachev caused Communism's demise, although Gorbachev himself claimed that he wanted to reform and strengthen the system, not kill it. Others hold that the centralized and bureaucratic Soviet-style economies were so inefficient that ruin was inevitable. The computer may have also led to Communism's ruin. To compete militarily and economically, the Soviets needed to keep up with the information made possible in the West by the widespread use of computers. But, it is impossible to control the flow of information and maintain a tyranny once people have access to computers. Many former Soviet military leaders maintain that Ronald Reagan was responsible for the fall of the Soviet Union. President Reagan predicted that Communism would be thrown on the trash heap of history and labeled the Soviet Union an evil empire. He implemented a massive military build-up, including the so-called Star Wars defense against ballistic missiles. Reagan's rhetoric and the expansion of America's defense frightened Soviet policy-makers. They responded by attempting to spend more on military preparedness. But the Soviet economy was stretched to the limit. Already allotting seventy percent of governmental expenditures to the military, the whole system toppled in an effort to meet Reagan's challenge.

The Cold War is over and the West won. The threat of war and global destruction is diminished. The tyrannical system of politics and economics that challenged our way of life is no longer a threat. The peoples held captive in Soviet Empire are free. Could there be anything bad about the end of the Cold War?

One thesis put forward by Francis Fukuyama contends that with the cessation of the Cold War history has come to an end. Fukuyama does not maintain that time is about to stop. Rather, he argues that the West won the Cold War and that its principles predominate throughout the world. Turning Marx's historical analysis around, Fukuyama claims that over the past two hundred years, liberal democracy has triumphed over all its enemies; monarchy and autocracy during World War I, Fascism during World War II, and Communism during the Cold War. The ideas of liberal democracy are now almost universally accepted as the proper way to organize political communities. Those nations that have not yet adopted the institutions of liberal democracy will eventually do so because behavior follows theory, practices follow ideas. What Fukuyama means by the end of history, then, is that there will no longer be revolutionary movements based on new philosophic doctrines to challenge the status quo. No seminal events or epoch-changing upheavals, as occurred during the American, French and Russian Revolutions, will mark the future.

For the most part Fukuyama believes that the victory of liberal democracy is a good thing, except that life might become boring. After all, public-spirited people who seek a place in history—such as those who spent their careers defending the West against communism—will have to discover other outlets for their energies. For instance in a 1990 commencement address former secretary of defense James Schlesinger reminisced wistfully about his experiences as a cold warrior. Although he was delighted that his efforts had brought about success, he wondered out loud about what could replace the "excitement, challenge, and fun" of protecting the United States from totalitarianism.

Critics have attacked Fukuyama's announcement that history has ended as premature. Yet an honest assessment of the current international situation indicates that Fukuyama's views may have validity. America is now the unchallenged power in the world. Perhaps no country has enjoyed such incontestable strength since the Roman Empire. As exhibited in the wars with Iraq in 1990 and Serbia in 1999, American weapons are vastly superior to any of its potential enemies and the technology gap is widening. Moreover, it is almost inconceivable that any nation or group of nations could defeat the united force of the liberal democracies, nations that have never had a war among themselves.

The dominance of America has created new difficulties for its policymakers. The United States is so powerful that it is often blamed for its behavior whether it acts or not. For instance, when President Bush (the elder) refused to intervene in Haiti to restore the elected government, the United States was accused of supporting a military dictatorship, but when President Clinton sent in the marines it was argued that the United States was meddling in the affairs of a weaker neighbor. President Clinton was criticized for not acting to end the bloodshed in the civil wars in Rwanda and Bosnia, but when he sent American peace-keeping forces into the Balkans, he was accused of making America the "policeman of the world."

Despite its strength, America has little real interest in using military force to subjugate other nations. Yet the United States' influence is paramount nonetheless, primarily because its popular culture is so widely dispersed and so extensively accepted. Who needs the Roman Legions to conquer the world when America has MTV, Mickey Mouse, McDonalds, Pepsi, and other seductive creations of the popular imagination. Indeed, it is the very simplicity and universality of America's popular culture that has led people worldwide to emulate its concepts.

Fukuyama also states that the triumph of America's way of life is likely to bring about a stable and peaceful world. This is surely a fine thing, but he wonders what people will do with themselves during an era of universal peace and prosperity. Perhaps, shopping malls will suddenly be filled with browsers, the demand for on-line video games will skyrocket, and the popularity of professional wrestling, already America's most lucrative "sport," will reach an all-time high. People will pursue only material, i.e. bodily pleasures, or expend themselves in mindless distractions. There will be nothing to inspire people; no excitement, no desire for distinction, no need for noble sacrifice, no cause to spur courageous acts, and not even an impulse toward beauty. The serious question that Fukuyama raises is whether life will be satisfying if those magnificent endeavors people have so honored in the past are no longer required. Yet, the enduring fascination with World War II, as visible almost every evening on cable television's various "documentary" channels, suggests that there is something in the human soul that is stirred by the sight of stalwart people in a desperate situation acting gallantly for the sake of a righteous cause.

Although Fukuyama makes some interesting claims, there are difficulties with his analysis of the international situation. In particular, it is unlikely that life will be tranquil as the result of the end of the Cold War. Although liberal democracies have fulfilled their promise of producing a better material life for most people, they has been less successful at explaining the meaning of life. Liberal democracies are founded on the truth discovered by the scientific method, not on the precepts understood through faith. They are secular and have, for the most part, scrupulously avoided spiritual issues. However, since human beings are finite creatures who can imagine the infinite, they want answers to questions involving life and death and the purpose of existence. Because of the lingering doubts about our lives that liberal democracies have left unresolved, religious movements, which do offer answers to spiritual perplexities, continue to flourish. Most especially Islamic fundamentalism challenges the scientific mode of thought and secular way of life of the West.

Another source of discord in the world, as Fukuyama mentions in passing, will be nationalism. We can see evidence of national rivalries disrupting the peace in the brutal civil wars in Yugoslavia and the violent quarrel between Russia and Chechnya, just to name two. Even in the West national disharmony is evident. Quebec and the English-speaking provinces of Canada are having difficulty reconciling their cultural differences.

Why will nationalism likely remain a disruptive force in international relations? "There are certain social principles in human nature," Alexander Hamilton stated at the New York convention to ratifying the Constitution, "from which we may draw the most solid conclusions with respect to the conduct of individuals, and of communities. We love our families, more than we love our neighbors: We love our neighbors, more than our countrymen in general. The human affections, like solar heat, lose their intensity, as they depart the center." This "love of one's own," as it might be called, is more than mere narrow-minded bigotry. In fact, it counteracts personal selfishness and attracts people into political communities. As such, it can be the source of civic responsibility and dedication to one's friends and fellow countrymen. By caring for one's own, however, one must exclude outsiders since the range which human affections can be stretched does not seem to be indefinite. (This process explains why sporting events are more fun to watch when one has a home team to root for.) Other people, too, form themselves into communities, and because the interests of these communities are sometimes at odds, there are bound to be clashes.

It is exactly because of these conflicts that some citizens are able to show their commitment to the community. They seek "recognition" from their fellow citizens and are even willing to risk their own safety in order to protect their family, country, or way of life, and, of course, to attain prestige for themselves in the process. Indeed, there seems to an element of the human soul that longs to transcend the physical part of our being. It is this urge that makes us discipline and suppress our bodily desires in hopes of achieving something extraordinary. This impulse motivates people to imperil themselves in order to attain honor. There is also a darker side to this passion. Those under its influence are sometimes not constrained by laws or morality. They strike out at others either from the pleasure of defeating a rival or from the sheer exhilaration of breaking the norms of society.

During the years of the Cold War ethnic and national rivalries were kept at bay by the intense ideological struggle that gripped the world and by the discipline that the superpowers enforced on their allies. People on both sides of the Iron Curtain put aside their parochial distrust of each other in order to combat a more threatening enemy. As Abraham Lincoln argued, a common opponent can be a powerful source of unity. During the first fifty years of our nationhood, he explained, "the jealousy, envy, and avarice, incident to our nature, and so common to a state of peace, prosperity and conscious strength, were, for the time, in a great measure smothered and rendered inactive; while the deep rooted principle of hate, and the powerful motive of revenge, instead of being turned against each other, were directed exclusively against the British nation." Now that the Cold War is over and the fear of the common enemy is gone, the spirit of "hatred" and "revenge" within the former political blocs is likely to predominate. Fukuyama is correct to assert that the foreseeable future will lack the titanic struggles for the hearts and minds of the human race that have occurred in the last two centuries. Yet he seems to have underestimated how petty wars between nationalities and factional strife among ethnic groups within nations would become the occasion for international disharmony.

Fukuyama states that in the contemporary world people will want to improve their material condition. The key to economic progress is free trade, open communication, and the unfettered flow of information and technology. Societies that seek to maintain closed, inward-looking policies cannot satisfy the material aspirations of their citizens. The superior material conditions of nations more open to freedom will become apparent and any government not dedicated to protecting the liberty to advance economically will eventually be replaced. Moreover, since liberal democracies are founded on the consent of the governed, citizens in those societies are "recognized" as full and equal members of the community, and their views must be sought out by political leaders before policies can be adopted.

Yet, Fukuyama may have been too optimistic about the ability of all people to rationally and harmoniously pursue their goals. Some nations have resisted progress and it has become the duty of the United States and its liberal democratic allies in Western Europe to oppose leaders, such as Serbia's former President Slobodan Milosevic, who pursue parochial nationalistic policies that thwart natural rights and threaten their less powerful neighbors.

It is good that the Cold War is over and that the United States dominates the world. But it has become the burdensome responsibility of the United States to enforce the ideals of human rights and democratic government throughout the world. If we are successful in this goal, there is no surety that the human race will embrace such a peaceful but uninspiring future. Observers of politics ought to recall Hamilton's statement that, "Tis the portion of man assigned to him by the eternal allotment of Providence that every good he enjoys, shall be alloyed with ills."

80

Barack Obama

Remarks on National Security (2009)

. . . . These are extraordinary times for our country. We're confronting a historic economic crisis. We're fighting two wars. We face a range of challenges that will define the way that Americans will live in the 21st century. So there's no shortage of work to be done, or responsibilities to bear. . . .

In the midst of all these challenges, however, my single most important responsibility as President is to keep the American people safe. It's the first thing that I think about when I wake up in the morning. It's the last thing that I think about when I go to sleep at night.

The full text of this speech, delivered by President Barack Obama to the nation on May 21, 2009, can be found at http://www.whitehouse.gov/the_press_office/Remarks-by-the-President-On-National-Security-5-21-09/.

And this responsibility is only magnified in an era when an extremist ideology threatens our people, and technology gives a handful of terrorists the potential to do us great harm. We are less than eight years removed from the deadliest attack on American soil in our history. We know that al Qaeda is actively planning to attack us again. We know that this threat will be with us for a long time, and that we must use all elements of our power to defeat it.

Already, we've taken several steps to achieve that goal. For the first time since 2002, we're providing the necessary resources and strategic direction to take the fight to the extremists who attacked us on 9/11 in Afghanistan and Pakistan. We're investing in the 21st century military and intelligence capabilities that will allow us to stay one step ahead of a nimble enemy. We have re-energized a global non-proliferation regime to deny the world's most dangerous people access to the world's deadliest weapons. And we've launched an effort to secure all loose nuclear materials within four years. We're better protecting our border, and increasing our preparedness for any future attack or natural disaster. We're building new partnerships around the world to disrupt, dismantle, and defeat al Qaeda and its affiliates. And we have renewed American diplomacy so that we once again have the strength and standing to truly lead the world.

These steps are all critical to keeping America secure. But I believe with every fiber of my being that in the long run we also cannot keep this country safe unless we enlist the power of our most fundamental values. The documents that we hold in this very hall—the Declaration of Independence, the Constitution, the Bill of Rights—these are not simply words written into aging parchment. They are the foundation of liberty and justice in this country, and a light that shines for all who seek freedom, fairness, equality, and dignity around the world.

I stand here today as someone whose own life was made possible by these documents. My father came to these shores in search of the promise that they offered. My mother made me rise before dawn to learn their truths when I lived as a child in a foreign land. My own American journey was paved by generations of citizens who gave meaning to those simple words—"to form a more perfect union." I've studied the Constitution as a student, I've taught it as a teacher, I've been bound by it as a lawyer and a legislator. I took an oath to preserve, protect, and defend the Constitution as Commander-in-Chief, and as a citizen, I know that we must never, ever, turn our back on its enduring principles for expedience sake.

I make this claim not simply as a matter of idealism. We uphold our most cherished values not only because doing so is right, but because it strengthens our country and it keeps us safe. Time and again, our values have been our best national security asset—in war and peace; in times of ease and in eras of upheaval.

Fidelity to our values is the reason why the United States of America grew from a small string of colonies under the writ of an empire to the strongest nation in the world.

It's the reason why enemy soldiers have surrendered to us in battle, knowing they'd receive better treatment from America's Armed Forces than from their own government.

It's the reason why America has benefitted from strong alliances that amplified our power, and drawn a sharp, moral contrast with our adversaries.

It's the reason why we've been able to overpower the iron fist of fascism and outlast the iron curtain of communism, and enlist free nations and free peoples everywhere in the common cause and common effort of liberty.

From Europe to the Pacific, we've been the nation that has shut down torture chambers and replaced tyranny with the rule of law. That is who we are. And where terrorists offer only the injustice of disorder and destruction, America must demonstrate that our values and our institutions are more resilient than a hateful ideology.

After 9/11, we knew that we had entered a new era—that enemies who did not abide by any law of war would present new challenges to our application of the law; that our government would need new tools to protect the American people, and that these tools would have to allow us to prevent attacks instead of simply prosecuting those who try to carry them out.

Unfortunately, faced with an uncertain threat, our government made a series of hasty decisions. I believe that many of these decisions were motivated by a sincere desire to protect the American people. But I also believe that all too often our government made decisions based on fear rather than foresight; that all too often our government trimmed facts and evidence to fit ideological predispositions. Instead of strategically applying our power and our principles, too often we set those principles aside as luxuries that we could no longer afford. And during this season of fear, too many of us—Democrats and Republicans, politicians, journalists, and citizens—fell silent.

In other words, we went off course. And this is not my assessment alone. It was an assessment that was shared by the American people who nominated candidates for President from both major parties who, despite our many differences, called for a new approach—one that rejected torture and one that recognized the imperative of closing the prison at Guantanamo Bay.

Now let me be clear: We are indeed at war with al Qaeda and its affiliates. We do need to update our institutions to deal with this threat. But we must do so with an abiding confidence in the rule of law and due process; in checks and balances and accountability. For reasons that I will explain, the decisions that were made over the last eight years established an ad hoc legal approach for fighting terrorism that was neither effective nor sustainable—a framework that failed to rely on our legal traditions and time-tested institutions, and that failed to use our values as a compass. And that's why I took several steps upon taking office to better protect the American people.

First, I banned the use of so-called enhanced interrogation techniques by the United States of America.

I know some have argued that brutal methods like waterboarding were necessary to keep us safe. I could not disagree more. As Commander-in-Chief, I see the intelligence. I bear the responsibility for keeping this country safe. And I categorically reject the assertion that these are the most effective means of interrogation. What's more, they undermine the rule of law. They alienate us in the world. They serve as a recruitment tool for terrorists, and increase the will of our enemies to fight us, while decreasing the will of others to work with America. They risk the lives of our troops by making it less likely that others will surrender to them in battle, and more likely that Americans will be mistreated if they are captured. In short, they did not advance our war and counterterrorism efforts—they undermined them, and that is why I ended them once and for all. . . .

The second decision that I made was to order the closing of the prison camp at Guantanamo Bay.

For over seven years, we have detained hundreds of people at Guantanamo. During that time, the system of military commissions that were in place at Guantanamo succeeded in convicting a grand total of three suspected terrorists. Let me repeat that: three convictions in over seven years. Instead of bringing terrorists to justice, efforts at prosecution met setback after setback, cases lingered on, and in 2006 the Supreme Court invalidated the entire system. Meanwhile, over 525 detainees were released from Guantanamo under not my administration, under the previous administration. Let me repeat that: Two-thirds of the detainees were released before I took office and ordered the closure of Guantanamo.

There is also no question that Guantanamo set back the moral authority that is America's strongest currency in the world. Instead of building a durable framework for the struggle against al Qaeda that drew upon our deeply held values and traditions, our government was defending positions that undermined the rule of law. In fact, part of the rationale for establishing Guantanamo in the first place was the misplaced notion that a prison there would be beyond the law—a proposition that the Supreme Court soundly rejected. Meanwhile, instead of serving as a tool to counter terrorism, Guantanamo became a symbol that helped al Qaeda recruit terrorists to its cause. Indeed, the existence of Guantanamo likely created more terrorists around the world than it ever detained.

So the record is clear: Rather than keeping us safer, the prison at Guantanamo has weakened American national security. It is a rallying cry for our enemies. It sets back the willingness of our allies to work with us in fighting an enemy that operates in scores of countries. By any measure, the costs of keeping it open far exceed the complications involved in closing it. That's why I argued that it should be closed throughout my campaign, and that is why I ordered it closed within one year.

The third decision that I made was to order a review of all pending cases at Guantanamo. I knew when I ordered Guantanamo closed that it would be difficult and complex. There are 240 people there who have now spent years in legal limbo. In dealing with this situation, we don't have the luxury of starting from scratch. We're cleaning up something that is, quite simply, a mess—a misguided experiment that has left in its wake a flood of legal challenges that my administration is forced to deal with on a constant, almost daily basis, and it consumes the time of government officials whose time should be spent on better protecting our country. . . .

Now let me be blunt. There are no neat or easy answers here. I wish there were. But I can tell you that the wrong answer is to pretend like this problem will go away if we maintain an unsustainable status quo. As President, I refuse to allow this problem to fester. I refuse to pass it on to somebody else. It is my responsibility to solve the problem. Our security interests will not permit us to delay. Our courts won't allow it. And neither should our conscience. . . .

Now, let me begin by disposing of one argument as plainly as I can: We are not going to release anyone if it would endanger our national security, nor will we release detainees within the United States who endanger the American people. Where demanded by justice and national security, we will seek to transfer some detainees to the same type of facilities in which we hold all manner of dangerous and violent criminals within our borders—namely, highly secure prisons that ensure the public safety.

As we make these decisions, bear in mind the following fact: Nobody has ever escaped from one of our federal, supermax prisons, which hold hundreds of convicted terrorists. As Republican Lindsey Graham said, the idea that we cannot find a place to securely house 250-plus detainees within the United States is not rational.

We are currently in the process of reviewing each of the detainee cases at Guantanamo to determine the appropriate policy for dealing with them. And as we do so, we are acutely aware that under the last administration, detainees were released and, in some cases, returned to the battlefield. That's why we are doing away with the poorly planned, haphazard approach that let those detainees go in the past. Instead we are treating these cases with the care and attention that the law requires and that our security demands. . . .

In 2006, I did strongly oppose legislation proposed by the Bush administration and passed by the Congress because it failed to establish a legitimate legal framework, with the kind of meaningful due process rights for the accused that could stand up on appeal.

I said at that time, however, that I supported the use of military commissions to try detainees, provided there were several reforms, and in fact there were some bipartisan efforts to achieve those reforms. Those are the reforms that we are now making. Instead of using the flawed commissions of the last seven years, my administration is bringing our commissions in line with the rule of law. We will no longer permit the use . . . as evidence statements that have been obtained using cruel, inhuman, or degrading interrogation methods. We will no longer place the burden to prove that hearsay is unreliable on the opponent of the hearsay. And we will give detainees greater latitude in selecting their own counsel, and more protections if they refuse to testify. These reforms, among others, will make our military commissions a more credible and effective means of administering justice, and I will work with Congress and members of both parties, as well as legal authorities across the political spectrum, on legislation to ensure that these commissions are fair, legitimate, and effective. . . .

Now, finally, there remains the question of detainees at Guantanamo who cannot be prosecuted yet who pose a clear danger to the American people. And I have to be honest here—this is the toughest single issue that we will face. We're going to exhaust every avenue that we have to prosecute those at Guantanamo who pose a danger to our country. But even when this process is complete, there may be a number of people who cannot be prosecuted for past crimes, in some cases because evidence may be tainted, but who nonetheless pose a threat to the security of the United States. Examples of that threat include people who've received extensive explosives training at al Qaeda training camps, or commanded Taliban troops in battle, or expressed their allegiance to Osama bin Laden, or otherwise made it clear that they want to kill Americans. These are people who, in effect, remain at war with the United States.

Let me repeat: I am not going to release individuals who endanger the American people. Al Qaeda terrorists and their affiliates are at war with the United States, and those that we capture—like other prisoners of war—must be prevented from attacking us again. Having said that, we must recognize that these detention policies cannot be unbounded. They can't be based simply on what I or the executive branch decide alone. That's why my administration has begun to reshape the standards that apply to ensure that they are in line with the rule of law. We must have clear, defensible, and lawful standards for those who fall into this category. We must have fair procedures so that we don't make mistakes. We must have a thorough process of periodic review, so that any prolonged detention is carefully evaluated and justified.

I know that creating such a system poses unique challenges. And other countries have grappled with this question; now, so must we. But I want to be very clear that our goal is to construct a legitimate legal framework for the remaining Guantanamo detainees that cannot be transferred. Our goal is not to avoid a legitimate legal framework. In our constitutional system, prolonged detention should not be the decision of any one man. If and when we determine that the United States must hold individuals to keep them from carrying out an act of war, we will do so within a system that involves judicial and congressional oversight. And so, going forward, my administration will work with Congress to develop an appropriate legal regime so that our efforts are consistent with our values and our Constitution. . . .

I have confidence that the American people are more interested in doing what is right to protect this country than in political posturing. I am not the only person in this city who swore an oath to uphold the Constitution—so did each and every member of Congress. And together we have a responsibility to enlist our values in the effort to secure our people, and to leave behind the legacy that makes it easier for future Presidents to keep this country safe.

Now, let me touch on a second set of issues that relate to security and transparency.

National security requires a delicate balance. One the one hand, our democracy depends on transparency. On the other hand, some information must be protected from public disclosure for the sake of our security—for instance, the movement of our troops, our intelligence-gathering, or the information we have about a terrorist organization and its affiliates. In these and other cases, lives are at stake.

Now, several weeks ago, as part of an ongoing court case, I released memos issued by the previous administration's Office of Legal Counsel. I did not do this because I disagreed with the enhanced interrogation techniques that those memos authorized, and I didn't release the documents because I rejected their legal rationales—although I do on both counts. I released the memos because the existence of that approach to interrogation was already widely known, the Bush administration had acknowledged its existence, and I had already banned those methods. The argument that somehow by releasing those memos we are providing terrorists with information about how they will be interrogated makes no sense. We will not be interrogating terrorists using that approach. That approach is now prohibited.

In short, I released these memos because there was no overriding reason to protect them. And the ensuing debate has helped the American people better understand how these interrogation methods came to be authorized and used.

On the other hand, I recently opposed the release of certain photographs that were taken of detainees by U.S. personnel between 2002 and 2004. Individuals who violated standards of behavior in these photos have been investigated and they have been held accountable. There was and is no debate as to whether what is reflected in those photos is wrong. Nothing has been concealed to absolve perpetrators of crimes. However, it was my judgment—informed by my national security team—that releasing these photos would inflame anti-American opinion and allow our enemies to paint U.S. troops with a broad, damning, and inaccurate brush, thereby endangering them in theaters of war.

In short, there is a clear and compelling reason to not release these par-ticular photos. There are nearly 200,000 Americans who are serving in harm's way, and I have a solemn responsibility for their safety as Commander-in-Chief. Nothing would be gained by the release of these photos that matters more than the lives of our young men and women serving in harm's way.

Now, in the press's mind and in some of the public's mind, these two cases are contradictory. They are not to me. In each of these cases, I had to strike the right balance between transparency and national security. And this balance brings with it a precious responsibility. There's no doubt that the American people have seen this balance tested over the last several years. In the images from Abu Ghraib and the brutal interrogation tech-niques made public long before I was President, the American people learned of actions taken in their name that bear no resemblance to the ideals that generations of Americans have fought for. And whether it was the run-up to the Iraq war or the revelation of secret programs, Americans often felt like part of the story had been unnecessarily withheld from them. And that caused suspicion to build up. And that leads to a thirst for accountability.

I understand that. I ran for President promising transparency, and I meant what I said. And that's why, whenever possible, my administration will make all information available to the American people so that they can make informed judgments and hold us accountable. But I have never argued—and I never will—that our most sensitive national security matters should simply be an open book. I will never abandon—and will vigorously defend—the neces-sity of classification to defend our troops at war, to protect sources and meth-ods, and to safeguard confidential actions that keep the American people safe. Here's the difference though: Whenever we cannot release certain informa-tion to the public for valid national security reasons, I will insist that there is oversight of my actions—by Congress or by the courts.

We're currently launching a review of current policies by all those agen-cies responsible for the classification of documents to determine where reforms are possible, and to assure that the other branches of government will be in a position to review executive branch decisions on these matters. Because in our system of checks and balances, someone must always watch over the watchers—especially when it comes to sensitive administration—information.

Now, along these same lines, my administration is also confronting chal-lenges to what is known as the "state secrets" privilege. This is a doctrine that allows the government to challenge legal cases involving secret pro-grams. It's been used by many past Presidents—Republican and Democrat—for many decades. And while this principle is absolutely necessary in some circumstances to protect national security, I am concerned that it has been over-used. It is also currently the subject of a wide range of lawsuits. So let me lay out some principles here. We must not protect information merely because it reveals the violation of a law or embarrassment to the government. And that's why my administration is nearing completion of a thorough review of this practice. . . .

Now, in all the areas that I've discussed today, the policies that I've proposed represent a new direction from the last eight years. To protect the American people and our values, we've banned enhanced interrogation techniques. We are closing the prison at Guantanamo. We are reforming military commissions, and we will pursue a new legal regime to detain terrorists. We are declassifying more information and embracing more oversight of our actions, and we're narrowing our use of the state secrets privilege. These are dramatic changes that will put our approach to national security on a surer, safer, and more sustainable footing. Their implementation will take time, but they will get done. . . .

Now, this is what I mean when I say that we need to focus on the future. I recognize that many still have a strong desire to focus on the past. When it comes to actions of the last eight years, passions are high. Some Americans are angry; others want to re-fight debates that have been settled, in some cases debates that they have lost. I know that these debates lead directly, in some cases, to a call for a fuller accounting, perhaps through an independent commission.

I've opposed the creation of such a commission because I believe that our existing democratic institutions are strong enough to deliver accountability. The Congress can review abuses of our values, and there are ongoing inquiries by the Congress into matters like enhanced interrogation techniques. The Department of Justice and our courts can work through and punish any violations of our laws or miscarriages of justice. . . .

We see that, above all, in the recent debate—how the recent debate has obscured the truth and sends people into opposite and absolutist ends. On the one side of the spectrum, there are those who make little allowance for the unique challenges posed by terrorism, and would almost never put national security over transparency. And on the other end of the spectrum, there are those who embrace a view that can be summarized in two words: "Anything goes." Their arguments suggest that the ends of fighting terrorism can be used to justify any means, and that the President should have blanket authority to do whatever he wants—provided it is a President with whom they agree.

Both sides may be sincere in their views, but neither side is right. The American people are not absolutist, and they don't elect us to impose a rigid ideology on our problems. They know that we need not sacrifice our security for our values, nor sacrifice our values for our security, so long as we approach difficult questions with honesty and care and a dose of common sense. That, after all, is the unique genius of America. That's the challenge laid down by our Constitution. That has been the source of our strength through the ages. That's what makes the United States of America different as a nation. . . .

The Framers who drafted the Constitution could not have foreseen the challenges that have unfolded over the last 222 years. But our Constitution has endured through secession and civil rights, through World War and Cold War, because it provides a foundation of principles that can be applied pragmatically; it provides a compass that can help us find our way. It hasn't always been easy. We are an imperfect people. Every now and then, there are those who think that America's safety and success requires us to walk away from the sacred principles enshrined in this building. And we hear such voices today. But over the long haul the American people have resisted that temptation. And though we've made our share of mistakes, required some course corrections, ultimately we have held fast to the principles that have been the source of our strength and a beacon to the world.

Now this generation faces a great test in the specter of terrorism. And unlike the Civil War or World War II, we can't count on a surrender ceremony to bring this journey to an end. Right now, in distant training camps and in crowded cities, there are people plotting to take American lives. That will be the case a year from now, five years from now, and—in all probability—10 years from now. Neither I nor anyone can stand here today and say that there will not be another terrorist attack that takes American lives. But I can say with certainty that my administration—along with our extraordinary troops and the patriotic men and women who defend our national security—will do everything in our power to keep the American people safe. And I do know with certainty that we can defeat al Qaeda. Because the terrorists can only succeed if they swell their ranks and alienate America from our allies, and they will never be able to do that if we stay true to who we are, if we forge tough and durable approaches to fighting terrorism that are anchored in our timeless ideals. This must be our common purpose.

I ran for President because I believe that we cannot solve the challenges of our time unless we solve them together. We will not be safe if we see national security as a wedge that divides America—it can and must be a cause that unites us as one people and as one nation. We've done so before in times that were more perilous than ours. We will do so once again.

Thank you, God bless you, and God bless the United States of America.

81

Richard B. Cheney

Remarks on National Security (2009)

. . . . Right now there is considerable debate in this city about the measures our administration took to defend the American people. Today I want to set forth the strategic thinking behind our policies. I do so as one who was there every day of the Bush administration who supported the policies when they were made, and without hesitation would do so again in the same circumstances.

When President Obama makes wise decisions, as I believe he has done in some respects on Afghanistan, and in reversing his plan to release incendiary photos, he deserves our support. And when he faults or mischaracterizes the national security decisions we made in the Bush years, he deserves an answer. The point is not to look backward. Now and for years to come, a lot rides on our President's understanding of the security policies that preceded him. And whatever choices he makes concerning the defense of this country, those choices should not be based on slogans and campaign rhetoric, but on a truthful telling of history.

Our administration always faced its share of criticism, and from some quarters it was always intense. That was especially so in the later years of our term, when the dangers were as serious as ever, but the sense of general alarm after September 11, 2001 was a fading memory. Part of our responsibility, as we saw it, was not to forget the terrible harm that had been done to America . . . and not to let 9/11 become the prelude to something much bigger and far worse.

That attack itself was, of course, the most devastating strike in a series of terrorist plots carried out against Americans at home and abroad. In 1993, terrorists bombed the World Trade Center, hoping to bring down the towers with a blast from below. The attacks continued in 1995, with the bombing of U.S. facilities in Riyadh, Saudi Arabia; the killing of servicemen at Khobar Towers in 1996; the attack on our embassies in East Africa in 1998; the

Richard B. Cheney, former vice president of the United States and now a member of the Board of Trustees of the American Enterprise Institute, spoke on May 21, 2009 at AEI. The full text of his speech can be found at http://aei.org/speech/100050.

murder of American sailors on the USS Cole in 2000; and then the hijackings of 9/11, and all the grief and loss we suffered on that day.

9/11 caused everyone to take a serious second look at threats that had been gathering for a while, and enemies whose plans were getting bolder and more sophisticated. Throughout the 90s, America had responded to these attacks, if at all, on an ad hoc basis. The first attack on the World Trade Center was treated as a law enforcement problem, with everything handled after the fact—crime scene, arrests, indictments, convictions, prison sentences, case closed.

That's how it seemed from a law enforcement perspective, at least—but for the terrorists the case was not closed. For them, it was another offensive strike in their ongoing war against the United States. And it turned their minds to even harder strikes with higher casualties. Nine-eleven made necessary a shift of policy, aimed at a clear strategic threat—what the Congress called "an unusual and extraordinary threat to the national security and foreign policy of the United States." From that moment forward, instead of merely preparing to round up the suspects and count up the victims after the next attack, we were determined to prevent attacks in the first place.

We could count on almost universal support back then, because everyone understood the environment we were in. We'd just been hit by a foreign enemy—leaving 3,000 Americans dead, more than we lost at Pearl Harbor. In Manhattan, we were staring at 16 acres of ashes. The Pentagon took a direct hit, and the Capitol or the White House were spared only by the Americans on Flight 93, who died bravely and defiantly.

Everyone expected a follow-on attack, and our job was to stop it. We didn't know what was coming next, but everything we did know in that autumn of 2001 looked bad. This was the world in which al-Qaeda was seeking nuclear technology, and A. Q. Khan was selling nuclear technology on the black market. We had the anthrax attack from an unknown source. We had the training camps of Afghanistan, and dictators like Saddam Hussein with known ties to Mideast terrorists.

These are just a few of the problems we had on our hands. And foremost on our minds was the prospect of the very worst coming to pass—a 9/11 with nuclear weapons.

For me, one of the defining experiences was the morning of 9/11 itself. As you might recall, I was in my office in that first hour, when radar caught sight of an airliner heading toward the White House at 500 miles an hour. That was Flight 77, the one that ended up hitting the Pentagon. With the plane still inbound, Secret Service agents came into my office and said we had to leave, now. A few moments later I found myself in a fortified White House command post somewhere down below.

There in the bunker came the reports and images that so many Americans remember from that day—word of the crash in Pennsylvania, the final phone calls from hijacked planes, the final horror for those who jumped to their death to escape burning alive. In the years since, I've heard occasional speculation that I'm a different man after 9/11. I wouldn't say that. But I'll freely admit that watching a coordinated, devastating attack on our country from an underground bunker at the White House can affect how you view your responsibilities.

To make certain our nation is never again faced such a day of horror, we developed a comprehensive strategy, beginning with far greater homeland security to make the United States a harder target. But since wars cannot be won on the defensive, we moved decisively against the terrorists in their hideouts and sanctuaries, and committed to using every asset to take down their networks. We decided, as well, to confront the regimes that sponsored terrorists, and to go after those who provide sanctuary, funding, and weapons to enemies of the United States. We turned special attention to regimes that had the capacity to build weapons of mass destruction, and might transfer such weapons to terrorists.

We did all of these things, and with bipartisan support put all these policies in place. It has resulted in serious blows against enemy operations: the take-down of the A.Q. Khan network and the dismantling of Libya's nuclear program. It's required the commitment of many thousands of troops in two theaters of war, with high points and some low points in both Iraq and Afghanistan—and at every turn, the people of our military carried the heaviest burden. Well over seven years into the effort, one thing we know is that the enemy has spent most of this time on the defensive—and every attempt to strike inside the United States has failed.

So we're left to draw one of two conclusions—and here is the great dividing line in our current debate over national security. You can look at the facts and conclude that the comprehensive strategy has worked, and therefore needs to be continued as vigilantly as ever. Or you can look at the same set of facts and conclude that 9/11 was a one-off event—coordinated, devastating, but also unique and not sufficient to justify a sustained wartime effort. Whichever conclusion you arrive at, it will shape your entire view of the last seven years, and of the policies necessary to protect America for years to come.

The key to any strategy is accurate intelligence, and skilled professionals to get that information in time to use it. In seeking to guard this nation against the threat of catastrophic violence, our Administration gave intelligence officers the tools and lawful authority they needed to gain vital information. We didn't invent that authority. It is drawn from Article Two of the Constitution. And it was given specificity by the Congress after 9/11, in a Joint Resolution authorizing "all necessary and appropriate force" to protect the American people.

Our government prevented attacks and saved lives through the Terrorist Surveillance Program, which let us intercept calls and track contacts between al-Qaeda operatives and persons inside the United States. The program was top secret, and for good reason, until the editors of the *New York Times* got it and put it on the front page. After 9/11, the Times had spent months publishing the pictures and the stories of everyone killed by al-Qaeda on 9/11. Now here was that same newspaper publishing secrets in a way that could only help al-Qaeda. It impressed the Pulitzer committee, but it damn sure didn't serve the interests of our country, or the safety of our people.

In the years after 9/11, our government also understood that the safety of the country required collecting information known only to the worst of the terrorists. And in a few cases, that information could be gained only through tough interrogations.

In top secret meetings about enhanced interrogations, I made my own beliefs clear. I was and remain a strong proponent of our enhanced interrogation program. The interrogations were used on hardened terrorists after other efforts failed. They were legal, essential, justified, successful, and the right thing to do. The intelligence officers who questioned the terrorists can be proud of their work and proud of the results, because they prevented the violent death of thousands, if not hundreds of thousands, of innocent people.

Our successors in office have their own views on all of these matters.

By presidential decision, last month we saw the selective release of documents relating to enhanced interrogations. This is held up as a bold exercise in open government, honoring the public's right to know. We're informed, as well, that there was much agonizing over this decision.

Yet somehow, when the soul-searching was done and the veil was lifted on the policies of the Bush administration, the public was given less than half the truth. The released memos were carefully redacted to leave out references to what our government learned through the methods in question. Other memos, laying out specific terrorist plots that were averted, apparently were not even considered for release. For reasons the administration has yet to explain, they believe the public has a right to know the method of the questions, but not the content of the answers.

Over on the left wing of the president's party, there appears to be little curiosity in finding out what was learned from the terrorists. The kind of answers they're after would be heard before a so-called "Truth Commission." Some are even demanding that those who recommended and approved the interrogations be prosecuted, in effect treating political disagreements as a punishable offense, and political opponents as criminals. It's hard to imagine a worse precedent, filled with more possibilities for trouble and abuse, than to have an incoming administration criminalize the policy decisions of its predecessors....

One person who by all accounts objected to the release of the interrogation memos was the Director of Central Intelligence, Leon Panetta. He was joined in that view by at least four of his predecessors. I assume they felt this way because they understand the importance of protecting intelligence sources, methods, and personnel. But now that this once top-secret information is out for all to see—including the enemy—let me draw your attention to some points that are routinely overlooked.

It is a fact that only detainees of the highest intelligence value were ever subjected to enhanced interrogation. You've heard endlessly about waterboarding. It happened to three terrorists. One of them was Khalid Sheikh Muhammed—the mastermind of 9/11, who has also boasted about beheading Daniel Pearl.

We had a lot of blind spots after the attacks on our country. We didn't know about al-Qaeda's plans, but Khalid Sheikh Muhammed and a few others did know. And with many thousands of innocent lives potentially in the balance, we didn't think it made sense to let the terrorists answer questions in their own good time, if they answered them at all. . . .

In public discussion of these matters, there has been a strange and sometimes willful attempt to conflate what happened at Abu Ghraib prison with the top secret program of enhanced interrogations. At Abu Ghraib, a few sadistic prison guards abused inmates in violation of American law, military regulations, and simple decency. For the harm they did, to Iraqi prisoners and to America's cause, they deserved and received Army justice. And it takes a deeply unfair cast of mind to equate the disgraces of Abu Ghraib with the lawful, skillful, and entirely honorable work of CIA personnel trained to deal with a few malevolent men.

Even before the interrogation program began, and throughout its operation, it was closely reviewed to ensure that every method used was in full compliance with the Constitution, statutes, and treaty obligations. On numerous occasions, leading members of Congress, including the current speaker of the House, were briefed on the program and on the methods.

Yet for all these exacting efforts to do a hard and necessary job and to do it right, we hear from some quarters nothing but feigned outrage based on a false narrative. In my long experience in Washington, few matters have inspired so much contrived indignation and phony moralizing as the interrogation methods applied to a few captured terrorists.

I might add that people who consistently distort the truth in this way are in no position to lecture anyone about "values." Intelligence officers of the United States were not trying to rough up some terrorists simply to avenge the dead of 9/11. We know the difference in this country between justice and vengeance. Intelligence officers were not trying to get terrorists to confess to past killings; they were trying to prevent future killings. From the beginning of the program, there was only one focused and all-important purpose. We sought, and we in fact obtained, specific information on terrorist plans.

Those are the basic facts on enhanced interrogations. And to call this a program of torture is to libel the dedicated professionals who have saved American lives, and to cast terrorists and murderers as innocent victims. What's more, to completely rule out enhanced interrogation methods in the future is unwise in the extreme. It is recklessness cloaked in righteousness, and would make the American people less safe.

The administration seems to pride itself on searching for some kind of middle ground in policies addressing terrorism. They may take comfort in hearing disagreement from opposite ends of the spectrum. If liberals are unhappy about some decisions, and conservatives are unhappy about other decisions, then it may seem to them that the President is on the path of sensible compromise. But in the fight against terrorism, there is no middle ground, and half-measures keep you half exposed. You cannot keep just some nuclear-armed terrorists out of the United States, you must keep every nuclear-armed terrorist out of the United States. Triangulation is a political strategy, not a national security strategy. When just a single clue that goes unlearned, one lead that goes unpursued, can bring on catastrophe—it's no time for splitting differences. There is never a good time to compromise when the lives and safety of the American people are in the balance.

Behind the overwrought reaction to enhanced interrogations is a broader misconception about the threats that still face our country. You can sense the problem in the emergence of euphemisms that strive to put an imaginary distance between the American people and the terrorist enemy. Apparently using the term "war" where terrorists are concerned is starting to feel a bit dated. So henceforth we're advised by the administration to think of the fight against terrorists as, quote, "Overseas contingency operations." In the event of another terrorist attack on America, the Homeland Security Department assures us it will be ready for this, quote, "man-made disaster"— never mind that the whole Department was created for the purpose of protecting Americans from terrorist attack.

And when you hear that there are no more, quote, "enemy combatants," as there were back in the days of that scary war on terror, at first that sounds like progress. The only problem is that the phrase is gone, but the same assortment of killers and would-be mass murderers are still there. And finding some less judgmental or more pleasant-sounding name for terrorists doesn't change what they are—or what they would do if we let them loose.

On his second day in office, President Obama announced that he was closing the detention facility at Guantanamo. This step came with little deliberation and no plan. Now the President says some of these terrorists should be brought to American soil for trial in our court system. Others, he says, will be shipped to third countries. But so far, the United States has had little luck getting other countries to take hardened terrorists. So what happens then? Attorney General Holder and others have admitted that the

United States will be compelled to accept a number of the terrorists here, in the homeland, and it has even been suggested US taxpayer dollars will be used to support them. On this one, I find myself in complete agreement with many in the President's own party. Unsure how to explain to their constituents why terrorists might soon be relocating into their states, these Democrats chose instead to strip funding for such a move out of the most recent war supplemental.

The administration has found that it's easy to receive applause in Europe for closing Guantanamo. But it's tricky to come up with an alternative that will serve the interests of justice and America's national security. Keep in mind that these are hardened terrorists picked up overseas since 9/11. The ones that were considered low-risk were released a long time ago. And among these, we learned yesterday, many were treated too leniently, because 1 in 7 cut a straight path back to their prior line of work and have conducted murderous attacks in the Middle East. I think the President will find, upon reflection, that to bring the worst of the worst terrorists inside the United States would be cause for great danger and regret in the years to come.

In the category of euphemism, the prizewinning entry would be a recent editorial in a familiar newspaper that referred to terrorists we've captured as, quote, "abducted." Here we have ruthless enemies of this country, stopped in their tracks by brave operatives in the service of America, and a major editorial page makes them sound like they were kidnap victims, picked up at random on their way to the movies.

It's one thing to adopt the euphemisms that suggest we're no longer engaged in a war. These are just words, and in the end it's the policies that matter most. You don't want to call them enemy combatants? Fine. Call them what you want—just don't bring them into the United States. Tired of calling it a war? Use any term you prefer. Just remember it is a serious step to begin unraveling some of the very policies that have kept our people safe since 9/11.

Another term out there that slipped into the discussion is the notion that American interrogation practices were a "recruitment tool" for the enemy. On this theory, by the tough questioning of killers, we have supposedly fallen short of our own values. This recruitment-tool theory has become something of a mantra lately, including from the President himself. And after a familiar fashion, it excuses the violent and blames America for the evil that others do. It's another version of that same old refrain from the Left, "We brought it on ourselves."

It is much closer to the truth that terrorists hate this country precisely because of the values we profess and seek to live by, not by some alleged failure to do so. Nor are terrorists or those who see them as victims exactly the best judges of America's moral standards, one way or the other.

Critics of our policies are given to lecturing on the theme of being consistent with American values. But no moral value held dear by the American people obliges public servants ever to sacrifice innocent lives to spare a captured terrorist from unpleasant things. And when an entire population is targeted by a terror network, nothing is more consistent with American values than to stop them.

As a practical matter, too, terrorists may lack much, but they have never lacked for grievances against the United States. Our belief in freedom of speech and religion, our belief in equal rights for women, our support for Israel, our cultural and political influence in the world—these are the true sources of resentment, all mixed in with the lies and conspiracy theories of the radical clerics. These recruitment tools were in vigorous use throughout the 1990s, and they were sufficient to motivate the nineteen recruits who boarded those planes on September 11, 2001.

The United States of America was a good country before 9/11, just as we are today. List all the things that make us a force for good in the world—for liberty, for human rights, for the rational, peaceful resolution of differences—and what you end up with is a list of the reasons why the terrorists hate America. If fine speech-making, appeals to reason, or pleas for compassion had the power to move them, the terrorists would long ago have abandoned the field. And when they see the American government caught up in arguments about interrogations, or whether foreign terrorists have constitutional rights, they don't stand back in awe of our legal system and wonder whether they had misjudged us all along. Instead the terrorists see just what they were hoping for—our unity gone, our resolve shaken, our leaders distracted. In short, they see weakness and opportunity.

What is equally certain is this: The broad-based strategy set in motion by President Bush obviously had nothing to do with causing the events of 9/11. But the serious way we dealt with terrorists from then on, and all the intelligence we gathered in that time, had everything to do with preventing another 9/11 on our watch. The enhanced interrogations of high-value detainees and the terrorist surveillance program have without question made our country safer. Every senior official who has been briefed on these classified matters knows of specific attacks that were in the planning stages and were stopped by the programs we put in place.

This might explain why President Obama has reserved unto himself the right to order the use of enhanced interrogation should he deem it appropriate. What value remains to that authority is debatable, given that the enemy now knows exactly what interrogation methods to train against, and which ones not to worry about. Yet having reserved for himself the authority to order enhanced interrogation after an emergency, you would think that President Obama would be less disdainful of what his predecessor authorized after 9/11. It's almost gone unnoticed that the president has retained the power to order the same methods in the same circumstances. When they talk about interrogations, he and his administration speak as if they have resolved some great moral dilemma in how to extract critical information from terrorists. Instead they have put the decision off, while assigning a presumption of moral superiority to any decision they make in the future.

Releasing the interrogation memos was flatly contrary to the national security interest of the United States. The harm done only begins with top secret information now in the hands of the terrorists, who have just received a lengthy insert for their training manual. Across the world, governments that have helped us capture terrorists will fear that sensitive joint operations will be compromised. And at the CIA, operatives are left to wonder if they can depend on the White House or Congress to back them up when the going gets tough. Why should any agency employee take on a difficult assignment when, even though they act lawfully and in good faith, years down the road the press and Congress will treat everything they do with suspicion, outright hostility, and second-guessing? Some members of Congress are notorious for demanding they be briefed into the most sensitive intelligence programs. They support them in private, and then head for the hills at the first sign of controversy.

As far as the interrogations are concerned, all that remains an official secret is the information we gained as a result. Some of his defenders say the unseen memos are inconclusive, which only raises the question why they won't let the American people decide that for themselves. I saw that information as vice president, and I reviewed some of it again at the National Archives last month. I've formally asked that it be declassified so the American people can see the intelligence we obtained, the things we learned, and the consequences for national security. And as you may have heard, last week that request was formally rejected. It's worth recalling that ultimate power of declassification belongs to the President himself. President Obama has used his declassification power to reveal what happened in the interrogation of terrorists. Now let him use that same power to show Americans what did not happen, thanks to the good work of our intelligence officials.

I believe this information will confirm the value of interrogations—and I am not alone. President Obama's own Director of National Intelligence, Admiral Blair, has put it this way: "High value information came from interrogations in which those methods were used and provided a deeper understanding of the al-Qaeda organization that was attacking this country." End quote. Admiral Blair put that conclusion in writing, only to see it mysteriously deleted in a later version released by the administration—the missing twenty-six words that tell an inconvenient truth. But they couldn't change the words of George Tenet, the CIA Director under Presidents Clinton and Bush, who bluntly said: "I know that this program has saved lives. I know we've disrupted plots. I know this program alone is worth more than the FBI, the Central Intelligence Agency, and the National Security Agency put together have been able to tell us."

If Americans do get the chance to learn what our country was spared, it'll do more than clarify the urgency and the rightness of enhanced interrogations in the years after 9/11. It may help us to stay focused on dangers that have not gone away. Instead of idly debating which political opponents to prosecute and punish, our attention will return to where it belongs—on the continuing threat of terrorist violence, and on stopping the men who are planning it.

For all the partisan anger that still lingers, our administration will stand up well in history—not despite our actions after 9/11, but because of them. . . .

To the very end of our administration, we kept al-Qaeda terrorists busy with other problems. We focused on getting their secrets, instead of sharing ours with them. And on our watch, they never hit this country again. After the most lethal and devastating terrorist attack ever, seven and a half years without a repeat is not a record to be rebuked and scorned, much less criminalized. It is a record to be continued until the danger has passed.

Along the way there were some hard calls. No decision of national security was ever made lightly, and certainly never made in haste. As in all warfare, there have been costs—none higher than the sacrifices of those killed and wounded in our country's service. And even the most decisive victories can never take away the sorrow of losing so many of our own—all those innocent victims of 9/11, and the heroic souls who died trying to save them.

For all that we've lost in this conflict, the United States has never lost its moral bearings. And when the moral reckoning turns to the men known as high-value terrorists, I can assure you they were neither innocent nor victims. As for those who asked them questions and got answers: they did the right thing, they made our country safer, and a lot of Americans are alive today because of them.

Like so many others who serve America, they are not the kind to insist on a thank-you. But I will always be grateful to each one of them, and proud to have served with them for a time in the same cause. They, and so many others, have given honorable service to our country through all the difficulties and all the dangers. I will always admire them and wish them well. And I am confident that this nation will never take their work, their dedication, or their achievements, for granted.

Thank you very much.

Chapter VIII

Liberty and Equality

The two dominant principles of the American Regime are liberty and equality. But what do they mean? Are they unqualified goods or do they require limitation? Are they mutually reinforcing, or are they at odds with one another? When the Supreme Court interprets and applies the Bill of Rights and the Fourteenth Amendment, it explores the meaning of these two principles.

Communities, in order to govern themselves, require citizens who are capable of governing themselves and sufficiently informed to make sound judgments about community affairs. Freedom of speech is necessary for self-government. Anastaplo argues that the First Amendment absolutely prohibits Congress from abridging political speech, that is, speech about the duties and concerns of self-governing citizens. Any governmental censorship of the press, he argues, will undermine our regime as a self-governing community. Ironically, Anastaplo argues that one of our culture's most pervasive forms of speech, television, is in need of restraint. Television, he claims, is making Americans less able to govern themselves. As a nationalizing force, television breaks down smaller communities and neighborhoods—isolating individuals and producing a conformity of tastes and desires reduced to the lowest common denominator. Anastaplo therefore proposes that we abolish television. Such a move is not forbidden, he says, because the First Amendment extends absolute protection only to political speech; indeed, we must abolish television in order to protect the self-governing community the First Amendment was meant to serve.

Although few Supreme Court justices would be willing to permit a limitation of speech as radical as that proposed by Anastaplo, most judges agree that the First Amendment does not protect all kinds of expression. In *Miller v. California*, the Court affirmed its earlier holdings that obscenity is not protected by the First Amendment. Moreover, under the Court's ruling, obscenity should be judged by the local standards of the various states rather than by a uniform national standard. This decision supports federalism by permitting each state to perpetuate its own standards of decency. The Court's opinion assumes that it is appropriate for states to do this. Perhaps a self-governing community is possible only when citizens have a certain moral character and share standards of decency.

Douglas dissents in *Miller* on the ground that the First Amendment forbids the government to ban publications merely because some people are offended by them. What shocks one man "may be sustenance for [his] neighbor." Government should not favor any standard of decency, according to Douglas, because such standards are merely matters of taste. Freedom is made necessary by the equality of all opinions and desires. Douglas' taking freedom as an absolute ironically undermines community, which is supported by common standards, and promotes national uniformity.

Perhaps the most controversial issue concerning the definition and limits of liberty in recent years has been the issue of abortion. Both the "pro life" and the "pro choice" camps consider themselves to be the defenders of individual rights. Pro lifers appeal to the rights of the unborn child while pro choice advocates appeal to the right of a woman to control her own body. By making either the rights of the fetus or the rights of the mother paramount, each side seeks to decide the conflict by recourse to an unqualified definition of rights. It is precisely these absolutist perspectives that make resolution of the issue next to impossible.

The Court, however, has not spoken in absolutist terms. In *Roe v. Wade* even Justice Blackmun speaks of the need to take into account not only the rights of the mother but also the state's interest in protecting potential life and in establishing standards of medical safety. But Justice Blackmun's majority opinion also divides pregnancy into three parts: the first trimester of which neither the concerns of medical safety nor the state's interest in potential life justify interference with a woman's "right to privacy;" the second trimester of which concerns for medical safety may allow for state regulation; and the third of which both the concern for safety and the state interest in potential life allow for regulation. This division is based upon Blackmun's understanding of the point in pregnancy when an abortion becomes more dangerous than child birth and the point in pregnancy when the fetus may be viable outside of the mother's body.

The opinion of the Court in *Roe* has led to confusion and controversy over the extent of state regulation of abortion that is permissable. The case of *Pennsylvania v. Casey* provides a good example of the various interpretations that are possible. The liberal wing of the Court, including Blackmun, argues that any restrictions on abortion must be subject to strict scrutiny. On the other side, Rehnquist, Scalia, Thomas, and White believe that *Roe* was wrongly decided and should be overturned. Justices O'Connor, Kennedy and Souter reaffirm the ruling in *Roe*, but unlike the more liberal wing, they take seriously the need for balancing the rights of the mother with other legitimate state interests. They are not willing to judge particular cases on the basis of an unqualified right of the mother or unquestioned deference to legislative concerns. They see a need for the Court to define the extent and limits of rights. For them, the doctrine of individual rights does not require or even allow an absolutist interpretation.

Although abortion cases such as Casey have adopted a balancing test, in the 2003 case of *Lawrence v. Texas*, which declared a Texas statue banning homosexual sodomy unconstitutional, Justice Kennedy argues that "[t]he Texas statute furthers no legitimate state interest which can justify its intrusion into the personal and private life of the individual." There is no legitimate state interest that may moderate or restrict individual autonomy in these matters. Homosexual sodomy, according to Kennedy "involves liberty of the person both in its spatial and more transcendent dimensions." Therefore the Court's 1986 decision upholding an anti-sodomy statue, *Bowers v. Hardwick* was overturned. Justice O'Connor, however argues in a concurring opinion that Bowers need not be overturned. Instead of basing its decision on the grounds of a constitutional right to privacy, Justice O'Connor argues that the Texas statute is void under the equal protection clause of the Fourteenth Amendment. It outlaws behavior for homosexual couples, but allows the same conduct for heterosexual couples. Does it matter whether the Court relies on privacy rights or equal protection rights in these cases? Which have the more solid Constitutional foundation and how are they related under the Constitution?

Racial discrimination cases have been understood almost exclusively in terms of the equal protection clause of the Fourteenth Amendment. In *Plessy v. Ferguson* the Court ruled that equality had a very limited meaning. The Constitutional standard of "the equal protection of the laws" in no way prevented state legislatures from instituting legal segregation. The only requirement was that separate accommodations be equal. In practice, even this limited nod toward equality was largely ignored for many years. It was not until 1954 and the decision of *Brown v. Board of Education* that the separate but equal doctrine was overturned. But the *Brown* decision raised new questions about the meaning of equality. Not only did the Court say that the state could not impose distinctions based on race, the Court also called into question the legitimacy of any policy that resulted in inequalities between the races. Segregation was wrong, according to the Court, because it produced feelings of inferiority and did irremedial damage to the hearts and minds of black children. But can the elimination of feelings of inferiority be the goal of the Court, or should the Court limit itself to preventing legally sanctioned inequalities? Or, in more familiar terms, is the goal of the Constitution equal opportunity or equal outcome?

In his dissent in *Plessy v. Ferguson* Justice Harlan argues that equal opportunity should be the standard. According to Harlan, the Constitution and the laws should be color blind. He would permit neither a color consciousness that justifies legal segregation or a color consciousness that guarantees equality of result by instituting "benign discrimination."

Another argument against racial discrimination is found in *Bolling v Sharpe*, a companion case to *Brown v. Board of Education*. Because the

District of Columbia is not a state, the equal protection clause of the Fourteenth Amendment do not apply. Instead the Court relies on the due process clause of the Fifth Amendment. Chief Justice Burger argues that policies based on racial discrimination are arbitrary and therefore an infringement of the liberty of individuals. Arbitrary government action is inconsistent with the Constitutional guarantee that liberty cannot be denied without due process of law. Are the arguments of *Brown* and *Bolling* consistent with each other? Could the Court have relied solely on the principles of *Bolling* in deciding both cases?

Eugene McCarthy argues that the goal of many current reforms is not equality of opportunity but equality itself. The limitations on campaign contributions, for example, are "attempts to equalize the non-voting influence on candidates." Further results of the emphasis on equality, he argues, include such guarantees as a college diploma to all. He finds this "security of equalization" degrading to the human personality. Kurt Vonnegut depicts the horrors of an egalitarian society where outstanding individuals are handicapped in order that they be made equal to everybody else. The radical egalitarianism McCarthy and Vonnegut criticize has its counterpart in the belief in absolute freedom—both stem from a leveling of distinctions between higher and lower. Jefferson, on the other hand, defends equality as the condition for the emergence of a natural aristocracy. In free elections citizens will elevate men of uncommon virtue and ability to public office. But a system of public education is necessary to prepare people to select the natural aristocracy and to prepare the natural aristocracy for its tasks. From the free schools in each community, the best students would be selected for further education at district schools, and the best selected from these to attend a university. Public education, like free election, would separate the wheat from the chaff.

Tocqueville suggests reasons why Jefferson's scheme for education is not likely to be actualized in America. Equality, he says, produces men who envy excellence rather than men wishing to elevate it. Moreover, in equal social conditions, there is a universal competition for the goods of life; consequently, there is much ambition to rise without any hope of rising very far. But is the emergence of a natural aristocracy likely in such a situation? The greatest danger for America, Tocqueville believes, is the mediocrity rather than the boldness of desires. Therefore it would be beneficial, he concludes, if the community were from time to time exposed to matters of difficulty and danger "in order to raise ambition and give it a field of action."

82

George Anastaplo

Self-Government and the Mass Media:
A Practical Man's Guide (1974)

Delenda est Carthago.
—Cato the Elder

It should be instructive, in considering the significance among us of the mass media, to consider how we deal today with the press and the television industry. . . .

There is considerable effort made by some theorists to have us treat these two means of communication the same way. To treat them the same way not only would overlook vital differences between them, but would also threaten the integrity of our regime even more than it may already be. We must, above all, be practical about these matters.

We should take care, whatever we may say or do, not to undermine the privileges and hence the usefulness of a press that has traditionally had a vital part to play in our constitutional system. . . .

Although the prohibition in the First Amendment is absolute (we see here a restraint upon Congress which is unqualified, among other Bill of Rights restraints which *are* qualified) the absolute prohibition does not relate to all forms of expression, but only to that which the term "freedom of speech, or of the press" was then taken to encompass: political speech, that

From Anastaplo, "Self-Government and the Mass Media: A Practical Man's Guide," in *The Mass Media and Modern Democracy*, ed. Harry M. Clor, Rand McNally College Publishing Company, 1974. Reprinted by permission of the Public Affairs Conference Center, Kenyon College, Gambier, Ohio. Corrections were made by the author. This article is republished in Anastaplo, *The American Moralist: On Law, Ethics, and Government* (Athens, Ohio: Ohio University Press/Swallow Press, 1991).

The author has developed further his discussion of these matters in Anastaplo, *Human Being and Citizen: Essays on Virtue, Freedom, and the Common Good*, (Chicago: Swallow Press, 1975). He is also the author of *The Constitution of 1787: A Commentary* (Baltimore: Johns Hopkins University Press, 1989).

is, speech having to do with the duties and concerns of self-governing citizens. Thus, for example, this constitutional provision is not primarily or directly concerned with what we now call artistic expression or with the problem of obscenity. Rather, the First Amendment acknowledges that the sovereign citizen body has the right freely to discuss public business, a privilege theretofore claimed only for members of legislative bodies. . . .

I am prepared to defend the propositions that, for the sake of our way of life, there cannot be in ordinary constitutional circumstances *any* previous restraints of publications and that there should be even more "previous restraint" than we now have of the television industry. . . .

The right of the people to know, of which we hear much today, includes the duty to think. This has, as a precondition, the opportunity to learn as well as the ability to discern what it is necessary to learn. Information and opinions about vital matters of public concern are needed among us on a day-to-day basis.

Even more important than day-to-day concerns, however, and indeed central to this paper, are several perennial questions: what kind of people is presupposed by institutions that include the absolute prohibition, at least in practice, of previous restraints on the press? What produces and preserves such a people? Is not a people of a certain character, rather than merely a with certain information, political opinions and morale, presupposed by our institutions? . . .

Vital to a people's self-governance are its experience and ability in forming and choosing its leaders and policies. This means that the character of our people cannot be left only to chance, to private influences, or to the vagaries of a "free trade in ideas." We should be concerned to preserve in our people a character that permits it to use responsibly the extensive freedom of speech and of the press traditionally and constitutionally available to it. . . . .

The modern mass media tend more toward centralization of power, while the old-fashioned press tended to be more localizing in its efforts and effects. The local is apt to be both more provincial and healthier; certainly, it is to be encouraged in this day and age. When we go "national" today, whether in the media or in politics, everything tends to become somewhat more gross and less discriminating. A facile simplification is rewarded and hence promoted. Is there then a tendency toward homogeneity of tastes and opinions as well as a general lowering of effective moral, political, and intellectual standards?

Industrialization with its marvels-laden technology can be said to be responsible for such developments. With such developments comes also the sense of helplessness and of rootlessness to which modern man is peculiarly subject. In modern circumstances one has less the impression of being "one's own man'" of being able to do things for oneself. One is forced into a passive role, not the role of the alert observer but that of the pampered slave. . . . .

The press continues to provide us with the serious searching out and recording of the news of the day, whereas television is in this respect for the most part parasitic. I believe it significant that the newscaster on television is rarely the man who has investigated the story being broadcast. Rather, he is usually part of a "show" that draws primarily on what newspapermen have gathered and put on the wire. Thus there is no necessary connection between the influence or "image" of television "personalities" and their competence. These television personalities wield tremendous influence, but such influence is both ephemeral and beyond their comprehension and hence their control. . . .

To speak as I have of "public opinion" is to recognize in *public* a body that acts and is somehow keyed to political concerns; it is also to recognize in *opinion* something that does depend ultimately upon notions of right and wrong and hence upon reason. This is quite different from the passive audiences upon which television depends and which it creates.

The television industry, in its distinctive modernity, is representative of the mass media and their infatuation with appearances. The term *mass media* aptly records what happens when modern electronic technology is applied to communications. The decisive factor becomes the necessarily "mass" character of passive and pacified audiences made up of countless private or isolated parties. The emphasis in the term *media* is upon the industry as little more than a conduit. Does not a people lose its moral and hence political sense when it becomes the "masses"? One may even be obliged to consider whether some previous restraint of the press might not become necessary if the people should, because of the debilitating effects of the mass media, become so childish as to be unable to govern itself. . . .

The effects of television are pervasive and are felt both directly and indirectly: directly through what almost six hours a day of *exposure* (not necessarily of viewing) do to the souls of our people; indirectly through the adjustments the press and others consider themselves obliged to make to compete with the television industry in capturing people's attention and thus being able to stay in business.

It should be noticed that much of the time devoted to television must be taken from other activities, such as reading, writing, conversation or courting or playing. What had been the effect on us heretofore of such activities? What is the effect of their radical curtailment? It is unrealistic to assume that such revolutionary changes as we have undergone have no significant effect on the souls of people.

Commercial considerations are obviously much more important for television than for the press, whatever may be said about the influence of advertisers upon publishers. Television was invented during a more commercial age than was printing; the press developed more naturally as an extension of thinking and writing rather than as an agency for advertising and selling.

The commercial aspects of the press simply cannot assert themselves as much as the commercial aspects of television do. For example, one can easily ignore the advertisements in a newspaper. No one doubts the considerable effect that sponsors have in the United States upon the content of television programs and upon audiences. The commercial aspects of television, however important they may be in so many critiques of the industry, are not our primary concern. Nor does the specific content of television broadcasting concern us here, insofar as this can be corrected by a people determined to do so, but rather the very form of it and the consequent effects of the displacement by television of the other means by which souls have been engaged heretofore. . . .

[A]re not the good things on television always an incidental part of the whole? Are not even the good uses to which television has been put due in large part to chance? The issues that capture public attention and get considerable "play" are all too often contrived or accidental. However adept television may be at exposing some public figures, the professional television personalities are themselves litte more than animated masks so far as the viewing audience is concerned. Why this should be so depends on the very nature of the medium. Distortion and superficiality are among the inevitable effects of television, including effects of the technology itself that are accentuated by the expense of television and its consequent need for large audiences. Television cannot help but cater to the worst in us, even when it is trying to do its best. Certain things are made to appear easier than they really are. Shallow illusions are promoted, including the illusion that the viewer can learn enough from capsule presentations (a kind of discourse by headline) to get a serious notion of what is going on in the world and to be able to make sensible judgments and responsible choices. Television seems to liberate even while it really cripples, and it does this in so enticing a manner as to drive its competitors either out of the "market" or into suicidal imitation.

Thus, television helps create the illusion that it has informed us and that we have "participated" in something we have witnessed "close up." It emphasizes that one must "get it" at once; one can't tarry to look at what has been broadcast, to take one's time studying what one may not understand. One must get it all now, for something else is coming soon. One is discouraged from looking back: everything is before us; recollection and reflection are discouraged or at least made difficult. Is not all this more appropriate for entertainment than for serious discourse? . . .

The electronic media are very voracious and insatiable. Consequently, they promote novelty which seems to fit in better with youthfulness, with those who are by nature always changing and experimenting. A "culture" keyed to or shaped by the mass media is bound to be youth-oriented, an unnatural state of affairs for a community. There is constant change, with a consequent profound dissatisfaction and rootlessness. Fashions become more important and character less. Since the visual is necessarily emphasized, the length of discourse that can be presented on television is much shorter than serious issues require, much less than what would be possible in a meeting hall. Yet most viewers are given the impression that television presents enough. . . .

It is sometimes said that the young, and some of the old, know today much more about the world—how big and diverse it is, for example—than people did a generation ago. The mass media no doubt contribute to this sense of liberation: they do "open up" the world. But because of the inefficiency of television (consider the amount of material that can be spoken as against what can be read in a given time) one simply cannot get much detail beyond the immediately visible. Even the "educated" young probably know less than any generation heretofore about what has gone before or about the serious questions to which men have always addressed themselves. The young spread themselves over much more than did their predecessors, but much more thinly. Hence they cannot begin to know themselves. Yet they readily believe themselves to be more enlightened than their predecessors. . . . Children, as well as adults, are discouraged by television from becoming practiced in reading. Once television becomes available, reading appears to most people laborious and even less attractive; the attention span is likely to be shortened for activities requiring deliberate effort; discipline is not encouraged for serious work, and this suggests that everyday passions are even more likely to make themselves felt than they have always been. The general deterioration of serious reading ability will eventually lead to deterioration of the ability to write. Does not this entail for us the impairment of the ability to think seriously? Despite what is said about television's ability to "take the clothes off a man," his television "image" is likely to be quite different from what he is truly like. In fact, it may be virtually impossible for anyone to be more than an image before the camera. But one's written statements may be very much what one is. In fact, they may be essentially what one is, insofar as one is a thinking being. . . .

Serious association with one another, whether for purposes of entertainment, education, worship, politics, or sports, is undermined by television, especially since viewers and performers (or, as they once were, people and leaders) can make no serious contact with one another. For example, politicians tailor what they say and eventually believe to what can be "put across" on the television screen. The screen depends upon and encourages the wrong kind of simplification. No matter how complicated the subject presented may be, it is all too often pretended if not sincerely believed that it can be adequately dealt with, as if magically, in a few minutes. . . .

Yet it is also felt that something like television is needed for an aggregate as large as the United States has become. It is, some might even say, a necessary evil to cure an even worse one, the divisiveness of bigness.

Television does bring us all together, in a way, but too many at a time and at too low a level. In the process it breaks down smaller communities that until its coming had still been viable despite the onslaughts of the automobile and of the Second World War. The isolation of people, whether the elderly or the infirm or the housewife, that is intensified if not induced by the disruption of our towns and urban neighborhoods, seems to lead to a "need" for television. . . .

The easy intrusion of television into our lives undermines what friendship and influence should mean. Appearance becomes even more important than it had been. It is my impression that television fits better with an emphasis upon presidential rather than congressional or state politics. Rule by television plebiscite seems to be developing among us, a kind of rule that is peculiarly responsive to the volatile mass taste that television promotes and serves. The constitutional tendency of television—of the way of life that permits and is in turn shaped by television—is to unleash desires and arouse expectations that undermine among us the moderation of tradition, the restraints both of diversity and of a genuine respect of quality, and the requirements and advantages of federalism.

This social indictment of television can be summed up thus: Each of us is constantly addressed by television apart from the others, and yet none of us is ever really spoken to. The ability to read, and hence to think and to join in serious common discourse, suffers. Every kind of association is filtered through the camera and stripped of its humanity. The community is depreciated while a hollow privacy is emphasized; communal tastes are reduced to the lowest common denominator and then shamelessly catered to. Spectacle replaces theater; feeling replaces thought; image replaces character. The world shaped by television is an empty one, starved and frenetic, dreamlike and debilitating. It can be expected to culminate eventually in a crippling mediocrity and perhaps even in tyranny. . . .

It has long seemed obvious to me that the television industry should be abolished completely in this country and that nothing short of this can purge its crippling influence from American life. If this is indeed a society open to experimentation, then let us deliberately experiment for at least a decade with the remedy of complete suppression of television.

If television should be abolished, we should be obliged to go out again into our streets, if only to attend more movies. Local entertainment, local gatherings (religious as well as secular), and even genuine popular culture might become important again. Even more importantly, the intrinsically harmful influences of television would no longer have to be contended with.

Is it not revealing that something so harmful as television should have become so entrenched so soon? It is like noxious weeds that happen to be blown in by the wind. Its abolition today is, of course, virtually unthinkable; yet we did not have it a generation ago, however natural it may now seem to most of us.

If we move against television, we reassert ourselves as a community even as we act together on behalf of communal interests. We would show we care about what affects us, thereby again becoming a community. We would show as well that we recognize that mere desires should not govern our lives, that temperance is vital to enduring happiness. . . .

I see in the abolition of television no serious First Amendment problem. Rather than abridge the "freedom of speech" guaranteed by the First Amendment, the abolition of television, and hence a radical reform of the mass media, would enlarge freedom of speech among us. Television interferes, I have argued, with serious general education in a country such as ours: it affects the ability to read and hence the ability to think and the very status of thought among us, playing up to the passions as it does. The abolition of television would probably contribute *among us* to the preservation of self-government and hence genuine freedom. . . .

We are, of course, [not] likely to abolish television. . . .

What *can* be done about television, short of the total abolition I have advocated? Various reforms, which reflect some of the criticisms I have made in this paper, can be attempted. I collect here, as illustrative of how one may begin to think about reforms, a half-dozen suggestions:

1. There should be a curtailment in the amount of television available daily. It would be good *not* to have continuous television, but only a couple of hours of transmission at a time, followed by extended intermissions during which there is no local transmission at all. It would also be good to have certain evenings of the week, and perhaps most, if not all, of Sunday, completely free from television as well as from most other commerical activity. . . .

2. The commercial influence upon television in this country should be reduced. It would be good to experiment with the means by which British commercial television has ensured that there be no identification of advertisers with particular programs.

3. What is the relation between television's pervasive commercialism and its national programming? Whatever it may be, there is much to be said for encouraging local programming, thereby emphasizing the importance of the local community. We should expect with more local programming a decline in the professional quality of programs, at least until local talent begins to assert itself.

4. The immediate effect of television on our political life should be eliminated if we are to be left free and equipped to assess such things as television upon that way of life. Should not television be explicitly reserved for entertainment, leaving the discussion of politics to more appropriate forums? . . .

5. If there is to be politics on television, the emphasis should be on lengthy talks and extended civic proceedings. It would probably be prudent to reconsider the "fairness doctrine," for that may provide an overly zealous administration in Washington too great an opportunity to control the

political discourse of the country. Insofar as television is permitted to provide a forum for political discourse, it is good for us that it should be able to rely on First Amendment privileges.

6. The nonpolitical content of television, with a view to the effects on viewers of such things as portrayals of violence and legitimation of greed, should be periodically assessed by civic-minded people who recognize that the virtues, vices, and accomplishments of human beings are not without causes. . . .

7. It should go without saying that any family or neighborhood which "deprives" itself of television is likely to be better off than those families or neighborhoods addicted to it. It may become generally apparent someday, perhaps even in time to make a difference, that the many who are saddled with television are being exploited by the few who profit from it, and that the exploited are so deluded as to "choose" this form of self-enslavement. This is like the relationship between cigarette manufacturers and their victims. It may then become generally apparent that any community respectful of its integrity or concerned about the under-privileged should abolish television root and branch. . . .

It *is* instructive that we do not (perhaps, by now, cannot) see the risks we are running, and that we will not do anything serious, partly because of immediate pleasures and profits, partly because of profound confusion about causes and effects, and about the nature itself of cause and effect, in moral and political matters. An attempt to return ourselves to a more austere and healthier way of life, a life more conducive to a republican form of government and to the full development of the human soul is virtually unthinkable. It would also be instructive if the reader, in attempting to assess the argument I have presented here, should be induced to investigate and to make explicit what we take for granted as to *how* a particular way of life is established and perpetuated. . . .

83

Miller v. California (1973)

Mr. Chief Justice Burger *delivered the opinion of the Court.*

This is one of a group of "obscenity-pornography" cases being reviewed by the Court in a re-examination of standards enunciated in earlier cases involving what Mr. Justice Harlan called "the intractable obscenity problem."

From *Miller v. California*, 413 U.S. 15 (1973).

Appellant conducted a mass mailing campaign to advertise the sale of illustrated books, euphemistically called "adult" material. After a jury trial, he was convicted of violating California Penal Code §311.2(a), a misdemeanor, by knowingly distributing obscene matter, and the Appellate Department, Superior Court of California, County of Orange, summarily affirmed the judgment without opinion. Appellant's conviction was specifically based on his conduct in causing five unsolicited advertising brochures to be sent through the mail in an envelope addressed to a restaurant in Newport Beach, California. The envelope was opened by the manager of the restaurant and his mother. They had not requested the brochures; they complained to the police. . . .

This case involves the application of a State's criminal obscenity statute to a situation in which sexually explicit materials have been thrust by aggressive sales action upon unwilling recipients who had in no way indicated any desire to receive such materials. . . .

[S]ince the Court now undertakes to formulate standards more concrete than those in the past, it is useful for us to focus on two of the landmark cases in the somewhat tortured history of the Court's obscenity decisions. In *Roth v. United States*, the Court sustained a conviction under a federal statute punishing the mailing of "obscene, lewd, lascivious or filthy . . ." materials. The key to that holding was the Court's rejection of the claim that obscene materials were protected by the First Amendment. Five Justices joined in the opinion stating:

> "All ideas having even the slightest redeeming social importance—unorthodox ideas, controversial ideas, even ideas hateful to the prevailing climate of opinion—have the full protection of the [First Amendment] guaranties, unless excludable because they encroach upon the limited area of more important interest. But implicit in the history of the First Amendment is the rejection of obscenity as utterly without redeeming social importance. . . . This is the same judgment expressed by this Court in *Chaplinsky v. New Hampshire:*
>
> "'. . . There are certain well-defined and narrowly limited classes of speech, the prevention and punishment of which have never been thought to raise any Constitutional problem. *These include the lewd and obscene. . . . It has been well observed that such utterances are no essential part of any exposition of ideas, and are of such slight social value as a step to truth that any benefit that may be derived from them is clearly outweighed by the social interest in order and morality. . . .*' [Emphasis by Court in *Roth* opinion.]
>
> "We hold that obscenity is not within the area of constitutionally protected speech or press."

Nine years later, in *Memoirs v. Massachusetts*, the Court veered sharply away from the *Roth* concept and, with only three Justices in the plurality opinion, articulated a new test of obscenity. The plurality held that under the *Roth* definition

> "as elaborated in subsequent cases, three elements must coalesce: it must be established that (a) the dominant theme of the material taken as a whole appeals to a prurient interest in sex; (b) the material is patently offensive because it affronts contemporary community

standards relating to the description or representation of sexual matters; and (c) the material is utterly without redeeming social value."

. . . While *Roth* presumed "obscenity" to be "utterly without redeeming social importance," *Memoirs* required that to prove obscenity it must be affirmatively established that the material is "utterly without redeeming social value." Thus, even as they repeated the words of *Roth*, the *Memoirs* plurality produced a drastically altered test that called on the prosecution to prove a negative, i.e., that the material was "utterly without redeeming social value"—a burden virtually impossible to discharge under our criminal standards of proof. . . .

This much has been categorically settled by the Court, that obscene material is unprotected by the First Amendment. . . . We acknowledge, however, the inherent dangers of undertaking to regulate any form of expression. State statutes designed to regulate obscene materials must be carefully limited. See *Interstate Circuit, Inc. v. Dallas.* As a result, we now confine the permissible scope of such regulation to works which depict or describe sexual conduct. That conduct must be specifically defined by the applicable state law, as written or authoritatively construed. A state offense must also be limited to works which, taken as a whole, appeal to the prurient interest in sex, which portray sexual conduct in a patently offensive way, and which, taken as a whole, do not have serious literary, artistic, political, or scientific value.

The basic guidelines for the trier of fact must be: (a) whether "the average person, applying contemporary community standards" would find that the work, taken as a whole, appeals to the prurient interest, (b) whether the work depicts or describes, in a patently offensive way, sexual conduct specifically defined by the applicable state law; and (c) whether the work, taken as a whole, lacks serious literary, artistic, political, or scientific value. We do not adopt as a constitutional standard the "*utterly* without redeeming social value" test of *Memoirs v. Massachusetts;* that concept has never commanded the adherence of more than three Justices at one time.[1] . . .

At a minimum, prurient, patently offensive depiction or description of sexual conduct must have serious literary, artistic, political, or scientific value to merit First Amendment protection. For example, medical books for the education of physicians and related personnel necessarily use graphic illustrations and descriptions of human anatomy. In resolving the inevitably sensitive questions of fact and law, we must continue to rely on the jury system, accompanied by the safeguards that judges, rules of evidence, presumption of innocence, and other protective features provide, as we do with rape, murder, and a host of other offenses against society and its individual members.[2] . . .

Under a National Constitution, fundamental First Amendment limitations on the powers of the States do not vary from community to community, but this does not mean that there are, or should or can be, fixed,

uniform national standards of precisely what appeals to the "prurient interest" or is "patently offensive." These are essentially questions of fact, and our
Nation is simply too big and too diverse for this Court to reasonably expect
that such standards could be articulated for all 50 States in a single formulation, even assuming the prerequisite consensus exists. When triers of fact are
asked to decide whether "the average person, applying contemporary community standards" would consider certain materials "prurient," it would be
unrealistic to require that the answer be based on some abstract formulation.
The adversary system, with lay jurors as the usual ultimate fact-finders in
criminal prosecutions, has historically permitted triers of fact to draw on the
standards of their community, guided always by limiting instructions on the
law. To require a State to structure obscenity proceedings around evidence of
a *national* "community standard" would be an exercise in futility. . . .

During the trial, both the prosecution and the defense assumed that the
relevant "community standards" in making the factual determination of
obscenity were those of the State of California, not some hypothetical standard of the entire United States of America. Defense counsel at trial never
objected to the testimony of the State's expert on community standards or to
the instructions of the trial judge on "statewide" standards. . . .

We conclude that neither the State's alleged failure to offer evidence of
"national standards," nor the trial court's charge that the jury consider state
community standards, were constitutional errors. Nothing in the First
Amendment requires that a jury must consider hypothetical and unascertain-
able "national standards" when attempting to determine whether certain
materials are obscene as a matter of fact. . . .

It is neither realistic nor constitutionally sound to read the First Amendment as requiring that the people of Maine or Mississippi accept public
depiction of conduct found tolerable in Las Vegas, or New York City.[3] . . .

People in different States vary in their tastes and attitudes, and this diversity is not to be strangled by the absolutism of imposed uniformity. As the Court
made clear in *Mishkin v. New York*, the primary concern with requiring a jury to
apply the standard of "the average person, applying contemporary community
standards" is to be certain that, so far as material is not aimed at a deviant
group, it will be judged by its impact on an average person, rather than a particularly susceptible or sensitive person—or indeed a totally insensitive one. . . .

The dissenting Justices sound the alarm of repression. But, in our view,
to equate the free and robust exchange of ideas and political debate with
commercial exploitation of obscene material demeans the grand conception
of the First Amendment and its high purposes in the historic struggle for
freedom. It is a "misuse of the great guarantees of free speech and free
press. . . ." The First Amendment protects works which, taken as a whole,
have serious literary, artistic, political, or scientific value, regardless of
whether the government or a majority of the people approve of the *ideas*

these works represent. "The protection given speech and press was fashioned to assure unfettered interchange of ideas for the bringing about of political and social changes desired by the people," *Roth v. United States*. But the public portrayal of hard-core sexual conduct for its own sake, and for the ensuing commercial gain, is a different matter. . . .

Mr. Justice Douglas, dissenting.

. . . The difficulty is that we do not deal with constitutional terms, since "obscenity" is not mentioned in the Constitution or Bill of Rights. And the First Amendment makes no such exception from "the press" which it undertakes to protect. . . . So there are no constitutional guidelines for deciding what is and what is not "obscene." The Court is at large because we deal with tastes and standards of literature. What shocks me may be sustenance for my neighbor. What causes one person to boil up in rage over one pamphlet or movie may reflect only his neurosis, not shared by others. . . .

The idea that the First Amendment permits government to ban publications that are "offensive" to some people puts an ominous gloss on freedom of the press. That test would make it possible to ban any paper or any journal or magazine in some benighted place. The First Amendment was designed "to invite dispute," to induce "a condition of unrest," to "create dissatisfaction with conditions as they are," and even to stir "people to anger." *Terminiello v. Chicago*. The idea that the First Amendment permits punishment for ideas that are "offensive" to the particular judge or jury sitting in judgment is astounding. No greater leveler of speech or literature has ever been designed. To give the power to the censor, as we do today, is to make a sharp and radical break with the traditions of a free society. The First Amendment was not fashioned as a vehicle for dispensing tranquilizers to the people. Its prime function was to keep debate open to "offensive" as well as to "staid" people. The tendency throughout history has been to subdue the individual and to exalt the power of government. The use of the standard "offensive" gives authority to government that cuts the very vitals out of the First Amendment. As is intimated by the Court's opinion, the materials before us may be garbage. But so is much of what is said in political campaigns, in the daily press, on TV, or over the radio. By reason of the First Amendment—and solely because of it—speakers and publishers have not been threatened or subdued because their thoughts and ideas may be "offensive" to some. . . .

We deal with highly emotional, not rational, questions. To many the Song of Solomon is obscene. I do not think we, the judges, were ever given the constitutional power to make definitions of obscenity. If it is to be defined, let the people debate and decide by a constitutional amendment what they want to ban as obscene and what standards they want the legislatures and the courts to apply. Perhaps the people will decide that the path towards a mature, integrated society requires that all ideas competing for acceptance must have no censor. Perhaps they will decide otherwise.

Whatever the choice, the courts will have some guidelines. Now we have none except our own predilections.

Notes

1. "A quotation from Voltaire in the flyleaf of a book will not constitutionally redeem an otherwise obscene publication. . . ." We also reject, as a constitutional standard, the ambiguous concept of "social importance."

2. The mere fact juries may reach different conclusions as to the same material does not mean that constitutional rights are abridged. As this Court observed in *Roth v. United States,* "it is common experience that different juries may reach different results under any criminal statute. That is one of the consequences we accept under our jury system. . . ."

3. In *Jacobellis v. Ohio,* two Justices argued that application of "local" community standards would run the risk of preventing dissemination of materials in some places because sellers would be unwilling to risk criminal conviction by testing variations in standards from place to place. The use of "national" standards, however, necessarily implies that materials found tolerable in some places, but not under the "national" criteria, will nevertheless be unavailable where they are acceptable. Thus, in terms of danger to free expression, the potential for suppression seems at least as great in the application of a single nationwide standard as in allowing distribution in accordance with local tastes, a point which Mr. Justice Harlan often emphasized.

    Appellant also argues that adherence to a "national standard" is necessary "in order to avoid unconscionable burdens on the free flow of interstate commerce." . . . Obscene material may be validly regulated by a State in the exercise of its traditional local power to protect the general welfare of its population despite some possible incidental effect on the flow of such materials across state lines.

84

Roe v. Wade (1973)

Mr. Justice Blackmun delivered the opinion of the Court:

   . . . Three reasons have been advanced to explain historically the enactment of criminal abortion laws in the 19th century and to justify their continued existence.

From *Roe v. Wade,* 410 U.S. 113 (1973).

It has been argued occasionally that these laws were the product of a Victorian social concern to discourage illicit sexual conduct. Texas, however, does not advance this justification in the present case, and it appears that no court or commentator has taken the argument seriously. The appellants and amici contend, moreover, that this is not a proper state purpose at all and suggest that, if it were, the Texas statutes are overbroad in protecting it since the law fails to distinguish between married and unwed mothers.

A second reason is concerned with abortion as a medical procedure. When most criminal abortion laws were first enacted, the procedure was a hazardous one for the woman. . . .

Modern medical techniques have altered this situation. Appellants and various amici refer to medical data indicating that abortion in early pregnancy, this is, prior to the end of the first trimester, although not without its risk, is now relatively safe. Mortality rates for women undergoing early abortions, where the procedure is legal, appear to be as low as or lower than the rates for normal childbirth. Consequently, any interest of the State in protecting the woman from an inherently hazardous procedure, except when it would be equally dangerous for her to forgo it, has largely disappeared. Of course, important state interests in the area of health and medical standards do remain.

The State has a legitimate interest in seeing to it that abortion, like any other medical procedure, is performed under circumstances that insure maximum safety for the patient. This interest obviously extends at least to the performing physician and his staff, to the facilities involved, to the availability of aftercare, and to adequate provision for any complication or emergency that might arise. The prevalence of high mortality rates at illegal "abortion mills" strengthens, rather than weakens, the State's interest in regulating the conditions under which abortions are performed. Moreover, the risk to the woman increases as her pregnancy continues. Thus, the State retains a definite interest in protecting the woman's own health and safety when an abortion is proposed at a late stage of pregnancy.

The third reason is the State's interest—some phrase it in terms of duty—in protecting prenatal life. Some of the argument for this justification rests on the theory that a new human life is present from the moment of conception. The State's interest and general obligation to protect life then extends, it is argued, to prenatal life. Only when the life of the pregnant mother herself is at stake, balanced against the life she carries within her, should the interest of the embryo or fetus not prevail. Logically, of course, a legitimate state interest in this area need not stand or fall on acceptance of the belief that life begins at conception or at some other point prior to live birth. In assessing the State's interest, recognition may be given to the less rigid claim that as long as at least potential life is involved, the State may assert interests beyond the protection of the pregnant woman alone. . . .

The Constitution does not explicitly mention any right of privacy. In a line of decisions, however, going back perhaps as far as *Union Pacific R. Co. v. Botsford* (1891), the Court has recognized that a right of personal privacy, or a guarantee of certain areas or zones of privacy, does exist under the Constitution. In varying contexts, the Court or individual Justices have, indeed, found at least the roots of that right in the First Amendment, *Stanley v. Georgia* (1969); in the Fourth and Fifth Amendments, *Terry v. Ohio* (1968), *Katz v. United States* (1967), in the penumbras of the Bill of Rights, *Griswold v. Connecticut* (1965) . . .; in the Ninth Amendment, id., at 486 (Goldberg, J., concurring); or in the concept of liberty guaranteed by the first section of the Fourteenth Amendment, see *Meyer v. Nebraska* (1923). These decisions make it clear that only personal rights that can be deemed "fundamental" or "implicit in the concept of ordered liberty," *Palko v. Connecticut* (1937), are included in this guarantee of personal privacy. They also make it clear that the right has some extension to activities relating to marriage, *Loving v. Virginia* (1967); procreation, *Skinner v. Oklahoma* (1942); contraception, *Eisenstadt v. Baird* (1972) (White, J., concurring in result); family relationships, *Prince v. Massachusetts* (1944); and child rearing and education, *Pierce v. Society of Sisters* (1925). . . .

This right of privacy, whether it be founded in the Fourteenth Amendment's concept of personal liberty and restrictions upon state action, as we feel it is, or, as the District Court determined, in the Ninth Amendment's reservation of rights to the people, is broad enough to encompass a woman's decision whether or not to terminate her pregnancy. The detriment that the State would impose upon the pregnant woman by denying this choice altogether is apparent. Specific and direct harm medically diagnosable even in early pregnancy may be involved. Maternity, or additional offspring, may force upon the woman a distressful life and future. Psychological harm may be imminent. Mental and physical health may be taxed by child care. There is also the distress, for all concerned, associated with the unwanted child, and there is the problem of bringing a child into a family already unable, psychologically and otherwise, to care for it. In other cases, as in this one, the additional difficulties and continuing stigma of unwed motherhood may be involved. All these are factors the woman and her responsible physician necessarily will consider in consultation.

On the basis of elements such as these, appellant and some amici argue that the woman's right is absolute and that she is entitled to terminate her pregnancy at whatever time, in whatever way, and for whatever reason she alone chooses. With this we do not agree. Appellant's arguments that Texas either has no valid interest at all in regulating the abortion decision, or no interest strong enough to support any limitation upon the woman's sole determination, is unpersuasive. The Court's decisions recognizing a right of privacy also acknowledge that some state regulation in areas protected by that right is appropriate. As noted above, a State may properly assert important interests in safeguarding health, in maintaining medical standards, and in protecting potential life. At some point in pregnancy, these respective interests become sufficiently compelling to sustain regulation of the factors that govern the abortion decision. The privacy right involved, therefore, cannot be said to be absolute. In fact, it is not clear to us that the claim asserted by some amici that one has an unlimited right to do with one's body as one pleases bears a close relationship to the right of privacy previously articulated in the Court's decisions. The Court has refused to recognize an unlimited right of this kind in the past. *Jacobson v. Massachusetts* (1905) . . . (vaccination); *Buck v. Bell* (1927) . . . (sterilization).

We, therefore, conclude that the right of personal privacy includes the abortion decision, but that this right is not unqualified and must be considered against important state interests in regulation.

Where certain "fundamental rights" are involved, the Court has held that regulation limiting these rights may be justified only by a "compelling state interest," . . . and that legislative enactments must be narrowly drawn to express only the legitimate state interests at stake. . . .

The District Court held that the appellee failed to meet his burden of demonstrating that the Texas statute's infringement upon Roe's rights was necessary to support a compelling state interest. . . . Appellee argues that the State's determination to recognize and protect prenatal life from and after conception constitutes a compelling state interest. As noted above, we do not agree fully with either formulation.

A. The appellee and certain amici argue that the fetus is a "person" within the language and meaning of the Fourteenth Amendment. In support of this, they outline at length and in detail the well-known facts of fetal development. If this suggestion of personhood is established, the appellant's case, of course, collapses, for the fetus' right to life is then guaranteed specifically by the Amendment. The appellant conceded as much on reargument. On the other hand, the appellee conceded on reargument that no case could be cited that holds that a fetus is a person within the meaning of the Fourteenth Amendment.

The Constitution does not define "person" in so many words. Section 1 of the Fourteenth Amendment contains three references to "person." The first, in defining "citizens," speaks of "persons born or naturalized in the United States." The word also appears both in the Due Process Clause and in the Equal Protection Clause. "Person" is used in other places in the Constitution. . . . But in nearly all these instances, the use of the word is such that it has application only postnatally. None indicates, with any assurance, that it has any possible prenatal application.

All this, together with our observation, supra, that throughout the major portion of the 19th century prevailing legal abortion practices were far freer than they are today, persuades us that the word "person," as used in the Fourteenth Amendment, does not include the unborn. . . .

B. The pregnant woman cannot be isolated in her privacy. She carries an embryo and, later, a fetus, if one accepts the medical definitions of the developing young in the human uterus. . . . The situation therefore is inherently different from marital intimacy, or bedroom possession of obscene material, or marriage, or procreation, or education, with which *Eisenstadt, Griswold, Stanley, Loving, Skinner, Pierce,* and *Meyer* were respectively concerned. As we have intimated above, it is reasonable and appropriate for a State to decide that at some point in time another interest, that of health of the mother or that of potential human life, becomes significantly involved. The woman's privacy is no longer sole and any right of privacy she possesses must be measured accordingly.

Texas urges that, apart from the Fourteenth Amendment, life begins at conception and is present throughout pregnancy, and that, therefore, the State has a compelling interest in protecting that life from and after conception. We need not resolve the difficult question of when life begins. When those trained in the respective disciplines of medicine, philosophy, and theology are unable to arrive at any consensus, the judiciary, at this point in the development of man's knowledge, is not in a position to speculate as to the answer.

It should be sufficient to note briefly the wide divergence of thinking on this most sensitive and difficult question. . . .

In view of all this, we do not agree that, by adopting one theory of life, Texas may override the rights of the pregnant woman that are at stake. We repeat, however, that the State does have an important and legitimate interest in preserving and protecting the health of the pregnant woman, whether she be a resident of the State or a nonresident who seeks medical consultation and treatment there, and that it has still another important and legitimate interest in protecting the potentiality of human life. These interests are separate and distinct. Each grows in substantiality as the woman approaches term and, at a point during pregnancy, each becomes "compelling."

With respect to the State's important and legitimate interest in the health of the mother, the "compelling" point, in the light of present medical knowledge, is at approximately the end of the first trimester. This is so because of the now-established medical fact, referred to above . . . that until the end of the first trimester mortality in abortion may be less than mortality in normal childbirth. It follows that, from and after this point, a State may regulate the abortion procedure to the extent that the regulation reasonably relates to the preservation and protection of maternal health. Examples of permissible state regulation in this area are requirements as to the qualifications of the person who is to perform the abortion; as to the licensure of that person; as to the facility in which the procedure is to be performed, that is, whether it must be a hospital or may be a clinic or some other place of less-than-hospital status; as to the licensing of the facility; and the like.

This means, on the other hand, that, for the period of pregnancy prior to this "compelling" point, the attending physician, in consultation with his patient, is free to determine, without regulation by the State, that, in his medical judgment, the patient's pregnancy should be terminated. If that decision is reached, the judgment may be effectuated by an abortion free of interference by the State.

With respect to the State's important and legitimate interest in potential life, the "compelling" point is at viability. This is so because the fetus then presumably has the capability of meaningful life outside the mother's womb. State regulation protective of fetal life after viability thus has both logical and biological justifications. If the State is interested in protecting fetal life after viability, it may go so far as to proscribe abortion during that period, except when it is necessary to preserve the life or health of the mother.

Measured against these standards, Art. 1196 of the Texas Penal Code, in restricting legal abortions to those "procured or attempted by medical advice for the purpose of saving the life of the mother," sweeps too broadly. The statute makes no distinction between abortions performed early in pregnancy and those performed later, and it limits to a single reason, "saving" the mother's life, the legal justification for the procedure. The statute, therefore, cannot survive the constitutional attack made upon it here. . . .

85

Planned Parenthood of Southeastern Pa. v. Casey (1992)

Justice O'Connor, Justice Kennedy, and Justice Souter announced the judgment of the Court and delivered the opinion of the Court.

Liberty finds no refuge in a jurisprudence of doubt. Yet 19 years after our holding that the Constitution protects a woman's right to terminate her pregnancy in its early stages, *Roe v. Wade*, that definition of liberty is still questioned. Joining the respondents as *amicus curiae*, the United States, as it has done in five other cases in the last decade, again asks us to overrule *Roe*.

At issue in these cases are five provisions of the Pennsylvania Abortion Control Act of 1982 as amended in 1988 and 1989. The Act requires that a woman seeking an abortion give her informed consent prior to the abortion

From *Planned Parenthood of Southeastern Pa. v. Casey*, 505 U.S. 833 (1992).

procedure, and specifies that she be provided with certain information at least 24 hours before the abortion is performed. For a minor to obtain an abortion, the Act requires the informed consent of one of her parents, but provides for a judicial bypass option if the minor does not wish to or cannot obtain a parent's consent. Another provision of the Act requires that, unless certain exceptions apply, a married woman seeking an abortion must sign a statement indicating that she has notified her husband of her intended abortion. The Act exempts compliance with these three requirements in the event of a "medical emergency," which is defined in § 3203 of the Act. In addition to the above provisions regulating the performance of abortions, the Act imposes certain reporting requirements on facilities that provide abortion services.

. . . After considering the fundamental constitutional questions resolved by *Roe*, principles of institutional integrity, and the rule of *stare decisis*, we are led to conclude this: the essential holding of *Roe v. Wade* should be retained and once again reaffirmed.

It must be stated at the outset and with clarity that *Roe*'s essential holding, the holding we reaffirm, has three parts. First is a recognition of the right of the woman to choose to have an abortion before viability and to obtain it without undue interference from the State. Before viability, the State's interests are not strong enough to support a prohibition of abortion or the imposition of a substantial obstacle to the woman's effective right to elect the procedure. Second is a confirmation of the State's power to restrict abortions after fetal viability, if the law contains exceptions for pregnancies which endanger a woman's life or health. And third is the principle that the State has legitimate interests from the outset of the pregnancy in protecting the health of the woman and the life of the fetus that may become a child. These principles do not contradict one another; and we adhere to each.

. . . Men and women of good conscience can disagree, and we suppose some always shall disagree, about the profound moral and spiritual implications of terminating a pregnancy, even in its earliest stage. Some of us as individuals find abortion offensive to our most basic principles of morality, but that cannot control our decision. Our obligation is to define the liberty of all, not to mandate our own moral code. The underlying constitutional issue is whether the State can resolve these philosophic questions in such a definitive way that a woman lacks all choice in the matter, except perhaps in those rare circumstances in which the pregnancy is itself a danger to her own life or health, or is the result of rape or incest.

It is conventional constitutional doctrine that where reasonable people disagree the government can adopt one position or the other. That theorem, however, assumes a state of affairs in which the choice does not intrude upon a protected liberty. Thus, while some people might disagree about whether or not the flag should be saluted, or disagree about the proposition that it may not be defiled, we have ruled that a State may not compel or enforce one view or the other.

Our law affords constitutional protection to personal decisions relating to marriage, procreation, contraception, family relationships, child rearing, and education. Our cases recognize "the right of the *individual*, married or single, to be free from unwarranted governmental intrusion into matters so fundamentally affecting a person as the decision whether to bear or beget a child." Our precedents "have respected the private realm of family life which the state cannot enter." These matters, involving the most intimate and personal choices a person may make in a lifetime, choices central to personal dignity and autonomy, are central to the liberty protected by the Fourteenth Amendment. At the heart of liberty is the right to define one's own concept of existence, of meaning, of the universe, and of the mystery of human life. Beliefs about these matters could not define the attributes of personhood were they formed under compulsion of the State.

. . . While we appreciate the weight of the arguments made on behalf of the State in the case before us, arguments which in their ultimate formulation conclude that *Roe* should be overruled, the reservations any of us may have in reaffirming the central holding of *Roe* are outweighed by the explication of individual liberty we have given combined with the force of *stare decisis*. . . .

. . . While *Roe* has, of course, required judicial assessment of state laws affecting the exercise of the choice guaranteed against government infringement, and although the need for such review will remain as a consequence of today's decision, the required determinations fall within judicial competence.

. . . We have seen how time has overtaken some of *Roe's* factual assumptions: advances in maternal health care allow for abortions safe to the mother later in pregnancy than was true in 1973, and advances in neonatal care have advanced viability to a point somewhat earlier. But these facts go only to the scheme of time limits on the realization of competing interests, and the divergences from the factual premises of 1973 have no bearing on the validity of *Roe's* central holding, that viability marks the earliest point at which the State's interest in fetal life is constitutionally adequate to justify a legislative ban on nontherapeutic abortions. The soundness or unsoundness of that constitutional judgment in no sense turns on whether viability occurs at approximately 28 weeks, as was usual at the time of *Roe*, at 23 to 24 weeks, as it sometimes does today, or at some moment even slightly earlier in pregnancy, as it may if fetal respiratory capacity can somehow be enhanced in the future. Whenever it may occur, the attainment of viability may continue to serve as the critical fact, just as it has done since *Roe* was decided; which is to say that no change in *Roe's* factual underpinning has left its central holding obsolete, and none supports an argument for overruling it.

. . . The Court's duty in the present case is clear. In 1973, it confronted the already divisive issue of governmental power to limit personal choice to undergo abortion, for which it provided a new resolution based on the due process guaranteed by the Fourteenth Amendment. Whether or not a new social consensus is developing on that issue, its divisiveness is no less today than in 1973, and pressure to overrule the decision, like pressure to retain it, has grown only more intense. A decision to overrule *Roe*'s essential holding under the existing circumstances would address error, if error there was, at the cost of both profound and unnecessary damage to the Court's legitimacy, and to the Nation's commitment to the rule of law. It is therefore imperative to adhere to the essence of *Roe*'s original decision, and we do so today.

From what we have said so far it follows that it is a constitutional liberty of the woman to have some freedom to terminate her pregnancy. We conclude that the basic decision in *Roe* was based on a constitutional analysis which we cannot now repudiate. The woman's liberty is not so unlimited, however, that from the outset the State cannot show its concern for the life of the unborn, and at a later point in fetal development the State's interest in life has sufficient force so that the right of the woman to terminate the pregnancy can be restricted.

. . . We conclude the line should be drawn at viability, so that before that time the woman has a right to choose to terminate her pregnancy. We adhere to this principle for two reasons. First, as we have said, is the doctrine of *stare decisis*. Any judicial act of line drawing may seem somewhat arbitrary, but *Roe* was a reasoned statement, elaborated with great care. . . .

The second reason is that the concept of viability, as we noted in *Roe*, is the time at which there is a realistic possibility of maintaining and nourishing a life outside the womb, so that the independent existence of the second life can in reason and all fairness be the object of state protection that now overrides the rights of the woman. Consistent with other constitutional norms, legislatures may draw lines which appear arbitrary without the necessity of offering a justification. But courts may not. We must justify the lines we draw. And there is no line other than viability which is more workable. . . .

The woman's right to terminate her pregnancy before viability is the most central principle of *Roe v. Wade*. It is a rule of law and a component of liberty we cannot renounce. . . .

Yet it must be remembered that *Roe v. Wade* speaks with clarity in establishing not only the woman's liberty but also the State's "important and legitimate interest in potential life." That portion of the decision in *Roe* has been given too little acknowledgement and implementation by the Court in its subsequent cases. Those cases decided that any regulation touching upon the abortion decision must survive strict scrutiny, to be sustained only if drawn in narrow terms to further a compelling state interest. Not all of the cases decided under that formulation can be reconciled with the holding in *Roe* itself that the State has legitimate interests in the health of the woman and in protecting the potential life within her. In resolving this tension, we choose to rely upon *Roe*, as against the later cases.

Roe established a trimester framework to govern abortion regulations. Under this elaborate but rigid construct, almost no regulation at all is permitted during the first trimester of pregnancy; regulations designed to protect the woman's health, but not to further the State's interest in potential life, are permitted during the second trimester; and during the third trimester, when the fetus is viable, prohibitions are permitted provided the life or health of the mother is not at stake. Most of our cases since *Roe* have involved the application of rules derived from the trimester framework.

The trimester framework no doubt was erected to ensure that the woman's right to choose not become so subordinate to the State's interest in promoting fetal life that her choice exists in theory but not in fact. We do not agree, however, that the trimester approach is necessary to accomplish this objective. A framework of this rigidity was unnecessary and in its later interpretation sometimes contradicted the State's permissible exercise of its powers.

Though the woman has a right to choose to terminate or continue her pregnancy before viability, it does not at all follow that the State is prohibited from taking steps to ensure that this choice is thoughtful and informed. Even in the earliest stages of pregnancy, the State may enact rules and regulations designed to encourage her to know that there are philosophic and social arguments of great weight that can be brought to bear in favor of continuing the pregnancy to full term and that there are procedures and institutions to allow adoption of unwanted children as well as a certain degree of state assistance if the mother chooses to raise the child herself. "[T]he Constitution does not forbid a State or city, pursuant to democratic processes, from expressing a preference for normal childbirth." It follows that States are free to enact laws to provide a reasonable framework for a woman to make a decision that has such profound and lasting meaning. This, too, we find consistent with *Roe*'s central premises, and indeed the inevitable consequence of our holding that the State has an interest in protecting the life of the unborn.

We reject the trimester framework, which we do not consider to be part of the essential holding of *Roe*. Measures aimed at ensuring that a woman's choice contemplates the consequences for the fetus do not necessarily interfere with the right recognized in *Roe*, although those measures have been found to be inconsistent with the rigid trimester framework announced in that case. A logical reading of the central holding in *Roe* itself, and a necessary reconciliation of the liberty of the woman and the interest of the State in promoting prenatal life, require, in our view, that we abandon the trimester framework as a rigid prohibition on all previability regulation aimed at the protection of fetal life. The trimester framework suffers from these basic flaws: in its formulation it misconceives the nature of the pregnant woman's interest; and in practice it undervalues the State's interest in potential life, as recognized in *Roe*. As our jurisprudence relating to all liberties save perhaps abortion has recognized, not every law which makes a right more difficult to exercise is, *ipso facto*, an infringement of that right. An example clarifies the point. We have held that not every ballot access limitation amounts to an infringement of the right to vote. Rather, the States are granted substantial flexibility in establishing the framework within which voters choose the candidates for whom they wish to vote. The abortion right is similar. Numerous forms of state regulation might have the incidental effect of increasing the cost or decreasing the availability of medical care, whether for abortion or any other medical procedure. The fact that a law which serves a valid purpose, one not designed to strike at the right itself, has the incidental effect of making it more difficult or more expensive to procure an abortion cannot be enough to invalidate it. Only where state regulation imposes an undue burden on a woman's ability to make this decision does the power of the State reach into the heart of the liberty protected by the Due Process Clause.

For the most part, the Court's early abortion cases adhered to this view. In *Maher v. Roe*, the Court explained: "*Roe* did not declare an unqualified 'constitutional right to an abortion,' as the District Court seemed to think. Rather, the right protects the woman from unduly burdensome interference with her freedom to decide whether to terminate her pregnancy."

. . . All abortion regulations interfere to some degree with a woman's ability to decide whether to terminate her pregnancy. It is, as a consequence, not surprising that despite the protestations contained in the original *Roe* opinion to the effect that the Court was not recognizing an absolute right, the Court's experience applying the trimester framework has led to the striking down of some abortion regulations which in no real sense deprived women of the ultimate decision. Those decisions went too far because the right recognized by *Roe* is a right "to be free from unwarranted governmental intrusion into matters so fundamentally affecting a person as the decision whether to bear or beget a child." Not all governmental intrusion is of necessity unwarranted; and that brings us to the other basic flaw in the trimester framework: even in *Roe*'s terms, in practice it undervalues the State's interest in the potential life within the woman.

Roe v. Wade was express in its recognition of the State's "important and legitimate interest[s] in preserving and protecting the health of the pregnant woman [and] in protecting the potentiality of human life." The trimester framework, however, does not fulfill *Roe*'s own promise that the State has an interest in protecting fetal life or potential life. *Roe* began the contradiction by using the trimester framework to forbid any regulation of abortion designed to advance that interest before viability. Before viability, *Roe* and subsequent cases treat all governmental attempts to influence a woman's decision on behalf of the potential life within her as unwarranted. This treatment is, in our judgment, incompatible with the recognition that there is a substantial state interest in potential life throughout pregnancy.

The very notion that the State has a substantial interest in potential life leads to the conclusion that not all regulations must be deemed unwarranted. Not all burdens on the right to decide whether to terminate a pregnancy will be undue. In our view, the undue burden standard is the appropriate means of reconciling the State's interest with the woman's constitutionally protected liberty.

The concept of an undue burden has been utilized by the Court as well as individual members of the Court, including two of us, in ways that could be considered inconsistent. Because we set forth a standard of general application to which we intend to adhere, it is important to clarify what is meant by an undue burden.

A finding of an undue burden is a shorthand for the conclusion that a state regulation has the purpose or effect of placing a substantial obstacle in the path of a woman seeking an abortion of a nonviable fetus. A statute with this purpose is invalid because the means chosen by the State to further the interest in potential life must be calculated to inform the woman's free choice, not hinder it. And a statute which, while furthering the interest in potential life or some other valid state interest, has the effect of placing a substantial obstacle in the path of a woman's choice cannot be considered a permissible means of serving its legitimate ends. To the extent that the opinions of the Court or of individual Justices use the undue burden standard in a manner that is inconsistent with this analysis, we set out what in our view should be the controlling standard. In our considered judgment, an undue burden is an unconstitutional burden. Understood another way, we answer the question, left open in previous opinions discussing the undue burden formulation, whether a law designed to further the State's interest in fetal life which imposes an undue burden on the woman's decision before fetal viability could be constitutional. The answer is no.

Some guiding principles should emerge. What is at stake is the woman's right to make the ultimate decision, not a right to be insulated from all others in doing so. Regulations which do no more than create a structural mechanism by which the State, or the parent or guardian of a minor, may express profound respect for the life of the unborn are permitted, if they are not a substantial obstacle to the woman's exercise of the right to choose. Unless it has that effect on her right of choice, a state measure designed to persuade her to choose childbirth over abortion will be upheld if reasonably related to that goal. Regulations designed to foster the health of a woman seeking an abortion are valid if they do not constitute an undue burden.

Even when jurists reason from shared premises, some disagreement is inevitable. That is to be expected in the application of any legal standard which must accommodate life's complexity. We do not expect it to be otherwise with respect to the undue burden standard.

. . . The Court of Appeals applied what it believed to be the undue burden standard and upheld each of the provisions except for the husband notification requirement. We agree generally with this conclusion, but refine the undue burden analysis in accordance with the principles articulated above. We now consider the separate statutory sections at issue.

. . . Except in a medical emergency, the statute requires that at least 24 hours before performing an abortion a physician inform the woman of the nature of the procedure, the health risks of the abortion and of childbirth, and the "probable gestational age of the unborn child." The physician or a qualified nonphysician must inform the woman of the availability of printed materials published by the State describing the fetus and providing information about medical assistance for childbirth, information about child support from the father, and a list of agencies which provide adoption and other services as alternatives to abortion. An abortion may not be performed unless the woman certifies in writing that she has been informed of the availability of these printed materials and has been provided them if she chooses to view them.

Our prior decisions establish that as with any medical procedure, the State may require a woman to give her written informed consent to an abortion. In this respect, the statute is unexceptional. Petitioners challenge the statute's definition of informed consent because it includes the provision of specific information by the doctor and the mandatory 24-hour waiting period. The conclusions reached by a majority of the Justices in the separate opinions filed today and the undue burden standard adopted in this opinion require us to overrule in part some of the Court's past decisions, decisions driven by the trimester framework's prohibition of all previability regulations designed to further the State's interest in fetal life.

. . . To the extent *Akron I* and *Thornburgh* find a constitutional violation when the government requires, as it does here, the giving of truthful, nonmisleading information about the nature of the procedure, the attendant health risks and those of childbirth, and the "probable gestational age" of the fetus, those cases go too far, are inconsistent with *Roe's* acknowledgment of an important interest in potential life, and are overruled. This is clear even on the very terms of *Akron I* and *Thornburgh*. Those decisions, along with *Danforth*, recognize a substantial government interest justifying a requirement that a woman be apprised of the health risks of abortion and childbirth. It cannot be questioned that psychological well being is a facet of health. Nor can it be doubted that most women considering an abortion would deem the impact on the fetus relevant, if not dispositive, to the decision. In attempting to ensure that a woman apprehend the full consequences of her decision, the State furthers the legitimate purpose of reducing the risk that a woman may elect an abortion, only to discover later, with devastating psychological consequences, that her decision was not fully informed. If the information the State requires to be made available to the woman is truthful and not misleading, the requirement may be permissible.

. . . Whether the mandatory 24-hour waiting period is nonetheless invalid because in practice it is a substantial obstacle to a woman's choice to terminate her pregnancy is a closer question. The findings of fact by the District Court indicate that because of the distances many women must travel to reach an abortion provider, the practical effect will often be a delay of much more than a day because the waiting period requires that a woman seeking an abortion make at least two visits to the doctor. The District Court also found that in many instances this will increase the exposure of women seeking abortions to "the harassment and hostility of anti-abortion protestors demonstrating outside a clinic." As a result, the District Court found that for those women who have the fewest financial resources, those who must travel long distances, and those who have difficulty explaining their whereabouts to husbands, employers, or others, the 24-hour waiting period will be "particularly burdensome."

These findings are troubling in some respects, but they do not demonstrate that the waiting period constitutes an undue burden. We do not doubt that, as the District Court held, the waiting period has the effect of "increasing the cost and risk of delay of abortions," but the District Court did not conclude that the increased costs and potential delays amount to substantial obstacles. Rather, applying the trimester framework's strict prohibition of all regulation designed to promote the State's interest in potential life before viability, the District Court concluded that the waiting period does not further the state "interest in maternal health" and "infringes the physician's discretion to exercise sound medical judgment." Yet, as we have stated, under the undue burden standard a State is permitted to enact persuasive measures which favor childbirth over abortion, even if those measures do not further a health interest. And while the waiting period does limit a physician's discretion, that is not, standing alone, a reason to invalidate it. In light of the construction given the statute's definition of medical emergency by the Court of Appeals, and the District Court's findings, we cannot say that the waiting period imposes a real health risk. . . .

Section 3209 of Pennsylvania's abortion law provides, except in cases of medical emergency, that no physician shall perform an abortion on a married woman without receiving a signed statement from the woman that she has notified her spouse that she is about to undergo an abortion. The woman has the option of providing an alternative signed statement certifying that her husband is not the man who impregnated her; that her husband could not be located; that the pregnancy is the result of spousal sexual assault which she has reported; or that the woman believes that notifying her husband will cause him or someone else to inflict bodily injury upon her. A physician who performs an abortion on a married woman without receiving the appropriate signed statement will have his or her license revoked, and is liable to the husband for damages. The District Court heard the testimony of numerous expert witnesses, and made detailed findings of fact regarding the effect of this statute. . . .

. . . The American Medical Association (AMA) has published a summary of the recent research in this field, which indicates that in an average 12-month period in this country, approximately two million women are the victims of severe assaults by their male partners. In a 1985 survey, women reported that nearly one of every eight husbands had assaulted their wives during the past year. The AMA views these figures as "marked underestimates," because the nature of these incidents discourages women from reporting them, and because surveys typically exclude the very poor, those who do not speak English well, and women who are homeless or in institutions or hospitals when the survey is conducted. According to the AMA, "[r]esearchers on family violence agree that the true incidence of partner violence is probably *double* the above estimates; or four million severely assaulted women per year. Studies suggest that from one fifth to one third of all women will be physically assaulted by a partner or ex partner during their lifetime." Thus on an average day in the United States, nearly 11,000 women are severely assaulted by their male partners. Many of these incidents involve sexual assault. In families where wife beating takes place, moreover, child abuse is often present as well . . .

. . . This information and the District Court's findings reinforce what common sense would suggest. In well functioning marriages, spouses discuss important intimate decisions such as whether to bear a child. But there are millions of women in this country who are the victims of regular physical and psychological abuse at the hands of their husbands. Should these women become pregnant, they may have very good reasons for not wishing to inform their husbands of their decision to obtain an abortion. Many may have justifiable fears of physical abuse, but may be no less fearful of the consequences of reporting prior abuse to the Commonwealth of Pennsylvania. Many may have a reasonable fear that notifying their husbands will provoke further instances of child abuse; these women are not exempt from § 3209's notification requirement. Many may fear devastating forms of psychological abuse from their husbands, including verbal harassment, threats of future violence, the destruction of possessions, physical confinement to the home, the withdrawal of financial support, or the disclosure of the abortion to family and friends. . . .

The spousal notification requirement is thus likely to prevent a significant number of women from obtaining an abortion. It does not merely make abortions a little more difficult or expensive to obtain; for many women, it will impose a substantial obstacle. . . .

. . . The unfortunate yet persisting conditions we document above will mean that in a large fraction of the cases in which § 3209 is relevant, it will operate as a substantial obstacle to a woman's choice to undergo an abortion. It is an undue burden, and therefore invalid.

. . . The husband's interest in the life of the child his wife is carrying does not permit the State to empower him with this troubling degree of authority over his wife. The contrary view leads to consequences reminiscent of the common law. A husband has no enforceable right to require a wife to advise him before she exercises her personal choices. . . .

. . . We next consider the parental consent provision. Except in a medical emergency, an unemancipated young woman under 18 may not obtain an abortion unless she and one of her parents (or guardian) provide informed consent as defined above. If neither a parent nor a guardian provides consent, a court may authorize the performance of an abortion upon a determination that the young woman is mature and capable of giving informed consent and has in fact given her informed consent, or that an abortion would be in her best interests. We have been over most of this ground before. Our cases establish, and we reaffirm today, that a State may require a minor seeking an abortion to obtain the consent of a parent or guardian, provided that there is an adequate judicial bypass procedure. Under these precedents, in our view, the one parent consent requirement and judicial bypass procedure are constitutional.

. . . Under the recordkeeping and reporting requirements of the statute, every facility which performs abortions is required to file a report stating its name and address as well as the name and address of any related entity, such as a controlling or subsidiary organization. In the case of state funded institutions, the information becomes public.

For each abortion performed, a report must be filed identifying: the physician (and the second physician where required); the facility; the referring physician or agency; the woman's age; the number of prior pregnancies and prior abortions she has had; gestational age; the type of abortion procedure; the date of the abortion; whether there were any pre-existing medical conditions which would complicate pregnancy; medical complications with the abortion; where applicable, the basis for the determination that the abortion was medically necessary; the weight of the aborted fetus; and whether the woman was married, and if so, whether notice was provided or the basis for the failure to give notice. Every abortion facility must also file quarterly reports showing the number of abortions performed broken down by trimester. In all events, the identity of each woman who has had an abortion remains confidential.

In *Danforth*, we held that recordkeeping and reporting provisions "that are reasonably directed to the preservation of maternal health and that properly respect a patient's confidentiality and privacy are permissible." We think that under this standard, all the provisions at issue here except that relating to spousal notice are constitutional. Although they do not relate to the State's interest in informing the woman's choice, they do relate to health. The collection of information with respect to actual patients is a vital element of medical research, and so it cannot be said that the requirements serve no purpose other than to make abortions more difficult. Nor do we find that the requirements impose a substantial obstacle to a woman's choice. . . .

The Constitution is a covenant running from the first generation of Americans to us and then to future generations. It is a coherent succession. Each generation must learn anew that the Constitution's written terms embody ideas and aspirations that must survive more ages than one. We accept our responsibility not to retreat from interpreting the full meaning of the covenant in light of all of our precedents. We invoke it once again to define the freedom guaranteed by the Constitution's own promise, the promise of liberty.

Justice Blackmun, concurring in part, concurring in the judgment in part, and dissenting in part.

. . . Today, no less than yesterday, the Constitution and decisions of this Court require that a State's abortion restrictions be subjected to the strictest of judicial scrutiny. Our precedents and the joint opinion's principles require us to subject all non *de minimis* abortion regulations to strict scrutiny. Under this standard, the Pennsylvania statute's provisions requiring content based counseling, a 24-hour delay, informed parental consent, and reporting of abortion related information must be invalidated. . . .

. . . Strict scrutiny of state limitations on reproductive choice still offers the most secure protection of the woman's right to make her own reproductive decisions, free from state coercion. No majority of this Court has ever agreed upon an alternative approach. The factual premises of the trimester framework have not been undermined, and the *Roe* framework is far more administrable, and far less manipulable, than the "undue burden" standard adopted by the joint opinion. . . .

In sum, *Roe's* requirement of strict scrutiny as implemented through a trimester framework should not be disturbed. No other approach has gained a majority, and no other is more protective of the woman's fundamental right. Lastly, no other approach properly accommodates the woman's constitutional right with the State's legitimate interests.

If there is much reason to applaud the advances made by the joint opinion today, there is far more to fear from The Chief Justice's opinion. The Chief Justice's criticism of *Roe* follows from his stunted conception of individual liberty. While recognizing that the Due Process Clause protects more than simple physical liberty, he then goes on to construe this Court's personal liberty cases as establishing only a laundry list of particular rights, rather than a principled account of how these particular rights are grounded in a more general right of privacy. This constricted view is reinforced by The Chief Justice's exclusive reliance on tradition as a source of fundamental rights. . . .

In one sense, the Court's approach is worlds apart from that of The Chief Justice and Justice Scalia. And yet, in another sense, the distance between the two approaches is short—the distance is but a single vote.

I am 83 years old. I cannot remain on this Court forever, and when I do step down, the confirmation process for my successor well may focus on the issue before us today. That, I regret, may be exactly where the choice between the two worlds will be made.

Chief Justice Rehnquist, with whom Justice White, Justice Scalia, and Justice Thomas join, concurring in the judgment in part and dissenting in part.

The joint opinion, following its newly minted variation on *stare decisis*, retains the outer shell of *Roe v. Wade*, but beats a wholesale retreat from the substance of that case. We believe that *Roe* was wrongly decided, and that it can and should be overruled consistently with our traditional approach to *stare decisis* in constitutional cases. We would adopt the approach of the plurality in *Webster v. Reproductive Health Services*, and uphold the challenged provisions of the Pennsylvania statute in their entirety.

. . . The joint opinion of Justices O'Connor, Kennedy, and Souter cannot bring itself to say that *Roe* was correct as an original matter, but the authors are of the view that "the immediate question is not the soundness of *Roe*'s resolution of the issue, but the precedential force that must be accorded to its holding." Instead of claiming that *Roe* was correct as a matter of original constitutional interpretation, the opinion therefore contains an elaborate discussion of *stare decisis*. This discussion of the principle of *stare decisis* appears to be almost entirely dicta, because the joint opinion does not apply that principle in dealing with *Roe*. *Roe* decided that a woman had a fundamental right to an abortion. The joint opinion rejects that view. *Roe* decided that abortion regulations were to be subjected to "strict scrutiny" and could be justified only in the light of "compelling state interests." The joint opinion rejects that view. *Roe* analyzed abortion regulation under a rigid trimester framework, a framework which has guided this Court's decisionmaking for 19 years. The joint opinion rejects that framework.

Stare decisis is defined in Black's Law Dictionary as meaning "to abide by, or adhere to, decided cases." Whatever the "central holding" of *Roe* that is left after the joint opinion finishes dissecting it is surely not the result of that principle. While purporting to adhere to precedent, the joint opinion instead revises it. *Roe* continues to exist, but only in the way a storefront on a western movie set exists: a mere facade to give the illusion of reality. . . .

. . . Apparently realizing that conventional *stare decisis* principles do not support its position, the joint opinion advances a belief that retaining a portion of *Roe* is necessary to protect the "legitimacy" of this Court. Because the Court must take care to render decisions "grounded truly in principle," and not simply as political and social compromises, the joint opinion properly declares it to be this Court's duty to ignore the public criticism and protest that may arise as a result of a decision. Few would quarrel with this statement, although it may be doubted that Members of this Court, holding their tenure as they do during constitutional "good behavior," are at all likely to be intimidated by such public protests.

But the joint opinion goes on to state that when the Court "resolve[s] the sort of intensely divisive controversy reflected in *Roe* and those rare, comparable cases," its decision is exempt from reconsideration under established principles of *stare decisis* in constitutional cases. This is so, the joint opinion contends, because in those "intensely divisive" cases the Court has "call[ed] the contending sides of a national controversy to end their national division by accepting a common mandate rooted in the Constitution," and must therefore take special care not to be perceived as "surrender[ing] to political pressure" and continued opposition. This is a truly novel principle, one which is contrary to both the Court's historical practice and to the Court's traditional willingness to tolerate criticism of its opinions. Under this principle, when the Court has ruled on a divisive issue, it is apparently prevented from overruling that decision for the sole reason that it was incorrect, *unless opposition to the original decision has died away.*

. . . We have stated above our belief that the Constitution does not subject state abortion regulations to heightened scrutiny. Accordingly, we think that the correct analysis is that set forth by the plurality opinion in *Webster.* A woman's interest in having an abortion is a form of liberty protected by the Due Process Clause, but States may regulate abortion procedures in ways rationally related to a legitimate state interest. . . .

86

Lawrence v. Texas (2003)

Justice Kennedy delivered the opinion of the Court:

Liberty protects the person from unwarranted government intrusions into a dwelling or other private places. In our tradition the State is not omnipresent in the home. And there are other spheres of our lives and existence, outside the home, where the State should not be a dominant presence. Freedom extends beyond spatial bounds. Liberty presumes an autonomy of self that includes freedom of thought, belief, expression, and certain intimate conduct. The instant case involves liberty of the person both in its spatial and more transcendent dimensions.

The question before the Court is the validity of a Texas statute making it a crime for two persons of the same sex to engage in certain intimate sexual conduct.

In Houston, Texas, officers of the Harris County Police Department were dispatched to a private residence in response to a reported weapons disturbance. They entered an apartment where one of the petitioners, John Geddes Lawrence, resided. The right of the police to enter does not seem to have been questioned. The officers observed Lawrence and another man, Tyron Garner, engaging in a sexual act. The two petitioners were arrested, held in custody over night, and charged and convicted before a Justice of the Peace.

The complaints described their crime as "deviate sexual intercourse, namely anal sex, with a member of the same sex (man)." . . .

The Court of Appeals for the Texas Fourteenth District considered the petitioners' federal constitutional arguments under both the Equal Protection and Due Process Clauses of the Fourteenth Amendment. After hearing the case en banc the court, in a divided opinion, rejected the constitutional arguments and affirmed the convictions. The majority opinion indicates that the Court of Appeals considered our decision in *Bowers v. Hardwick* (1986), to be controlling on the federal due process aspect of the case. *Bowers* then being authoritative, this was proper.

From *Lawrence v. Texas*, 539 U.S. 558 (2003).

We granted certiorari to consider three questions:

"1. Whether Petitioners' criminal convictions under the Texas "Homosexual Conduct" law–which criminalizes sexual intimacy by same-sex couples, but not identical behavior by different-sex couples–violate the Fourteenth Amendment guarantee of equal protection of laws?

"2. Whether Petitioners' criminal convictions for adult consensual sexual intimacy in the home violate their vital interests in liberty and privacy protected by the Due Process Clause of the Fourteenth Amendment?

"3. Whether *Bowers v. Hardwick* should be overruled?"

The petitioners were adults at the time of the alleged offense. Their conduct was in private and consensual.

We conclude the case should be resolved by determining whether the petitioners were free as adults to engage in the private conduct in the exercise of their liberty under the Due Process Clause of the Fourteenth Amendment to the Constitution. For this inquiry we deem it necessary to reconsider the Court's holding in *Bowers*. . . .

In *Griswold* [*v. Connecticut* (1965)] the Court invalidated a state law prohibiting the use of drugs or devices of contraception and counseling or aiding and abetting the use of contraceptives. The Court described the protected interest as a right to privacy and placed emphasis on the marriage relation and the protected space of the marital bedroom.

After *Griswold* it was established that the right to make certain decisions regarding sexual conduct extends beyond the marital relationship. In *Eisenstadt v. Baird* (1972), the Court invalidated a law prohibiting the distribution of contraceptives to unmarried persons. The case was decided under the Equal Protection Clause, but with respect to unmarried persons, the Court went on to state the fundamental proposition that the law impaired the exercise of their personal rights. It quoted from the statement of the Court of Appeals finding the law to be in conflict with fundamental human rights, and it followed with this statement of its own:

"It is true that in *Griswold* the right of privacy in question inhered in the marital relationship. . . . If the right of privacy means anything, it is the right of the individual, married or single, to be free from unwarranted governmental intrusion into matters so fundamentally affecting a person as the decision whether to bear or beget a child."

The opinions in *Griswold* and *Eisenstadt* were part of the background for the decision in *Roe v. Wade* (1973). As is well known, the case involved a challenge to the Texas law prohibiting abortions, but the laws of other States were affected as well. Although the Court held the woman's rights were not absolute, her right to elect an abortion did have real and substantial protection as an exercise of her liberty under the Due Process Clause. The Court cited cases that protect spatial freedom and cases that go well beyond it. *Roe* recognized the right of a woman to make certain fundamental decisions affecting her destiny and confirmed once more that the protection of liberty under the Due Process Clause has a substantive dimension of fundamental significance in defining the rights of the person. . . .

The facts in *Bowers* had some similarities to the instant case. A police officer, whose right to enter seems not to have been in question, observed Hardwick, in his own bedroom, engaging in intimate sexual conduct with another adult male. The conduct was in violation of a Georgia statute making it a criminal offense to engage in sodomy. One difference between the two cases is that the Georgia statute prohibited the conduct whether or not the participants were of the same sex, while the Texas statute, as we have seen, applies only to participants of the same sex. Hardwick was not prosecuted, but he brought an action in federal court to declare the state statute invalid. He alleged he was a practicing homosexual and that the criminal prohibition violated rights guaranteed to him by the Constitution. The Court, in an opinion by Justice White, sustained the Georgia law. . . .

The Court began its substantive discussion in *Bowers* as follows: "The issue presented is whether the Federal Constitution confers a fundamental right upon homosexuals to engage in sodomy and hence invalidates the laws of the many States that still make such conduct illegal and have done so for a very long time." That statement, we now conclude, discloses the Court's own failure to appreciate the extent of the liberty at stake. To say that the issue in *Bowers* was simply the right to engage in certain sexual conduct demeans the claim the individual put forward, just as it would demean a married couple were it to be said marriage is simply about the right to have sexual intercourse. The laws involved in *Bowers* and here are, to be sure, statutes that purport to do no more than prohibit a particular sexual act. Their penalties and purposes, though, have more far-reaching consequences, touching upon the most private human conduct, sexual behavior, and in the most private of places, the home. The statutes do seek to control a personal relationship that, whether or not entitled to formal recognition in the law, is within the liberty of persons to choose without being punished as criminals.

This, as a general rule, should counsel against attempts by the State, or a court, to define the meaning of the relationship or to set its boundaries absent injury to a person or abuse of an institution the law protects. It suffices for us to acknowledge that adults may choose to enter upon this relationship in the confines of their homes and their own private lives and still retain their dignity as free persons. When sexuality finds overt expression in intimate conduct with another person, the conduct can be but one element in a personal bond that is more enduring. The liberty protected by the Constitution allows homosexual persons the right to make this choice.

Having misapprehended the claim of liberty there presented to it, and thus stating the claim to be whether there is a fundamental right to engage in consensual sodomy, the *Bowers* Court said: "Proscriptions against that conduct have ancient roots." . . .

At the outset it should be noted that there is no longstanding history in this country of laws directed at homosexual conduct as a distinct matter. Beginning in colonial times there were prohibitions of sodomy derived from the English criminal laws passed in the first instance by the Reformation Parliament of 1533. The English prohibition was understood to include relations between men and women as well as relations between men and men. . . . Thus early American sodomy laws were not directed at homosexuals as such but instead sought to prohibit nonprocreative sexual activity more generally. This does not suggest approval of homosexual conduct. It does tend to show that this particular form of conduct was not thought of as a separate category from like conduct between heterosexual persons.

Laws prohibiting sodomy do not seem to have been enforced against consenting adults acting in private. A substantial number of sodomy prosecutions and convictions for which there are surviving records were for predatory acts against those who could not or did not consent, as in the case of a minor or the victim of an assault. As to these, one purpose for the prohibitions was to ensure there would be no lack of coverage if a predator committed a sexual assault that did not constitute rape as defined by the criminal law. Thus the model sodomy indictments presented in a 19th-century treatise, addressed the predatory acts of an adult man against a minor girl or minor boy. Instead of targeting relations between consenting adults in private, 19th-century sodomy prosecutions typically involved relations between men and minor girls or minor boys, relations between adults involving force, relations between adults implicating disparity in status, or relations between men and animals.

. . . [T]he historical grounds relied upon in *Bowers* are more complex than the majority opinion and the concurring opinion by Chief Justice Burger indicate. Their historical premises are not without doubt and, at the very least, are overstated.

It must be acknowledged, of course, that the Court in *Bowers* was making the broader point that for centuries there have been powerful voices to condemn homosexual conduct as immoral. The condemnation has been shaped by religious beliefs, conceptions of right and acceptable behavior, and respect for the traditional family. For many persons these are not trivial concerns but profound and deep convictions accepted as ethical and moral principles to which they aspire and which thus determine the course of their lives. These considerations do not answer the question before us, however. The issue is whether the majority may use the power of the State to enforce these views on the whole society through operation of the criminal law. "Our obligation is to define the liberty of all, not to mandate our own moral code."

Chief Justice Burger joined the opinion for the Court in *Bowers* and further explained his views as follows: "Decisions of individuals relating to homosexual conduct have been subject to state intervention throughout the history of Western civilization. Condemnation of those practices is firmly rooted in Judeo-Christian moral and ethical standards." As with Justice White's assumptions about history, scholarship casts some doubt on the sweeping nature of the statement by Chief Justice Burger as it pertains to private homosexual conduct between consenting adults. In all events we think that our laws and traditions in the past half century are of most relevance here. These references show an emerging awareness that liberty gives substantial protection to adult persons in deciding how to conduct their private lives in matters pertaining to sex. "[H]istory and tradition are the starting point but not in all cases the ending point of the substantive due process inquiry." *County of Sacramento v. Lewis* (1998).

This emerging recognition should have been apparent when *Bowers* was decided. In 1955 the American Law Institute promulgated the Model Penal Code and made clear that it did not recommend or provide for "criminal penalties for consensual sexual relations conducted in private." It justified its decision on three grounds: (1) The prohibitions undermined respect for the law by penalizing conduct many people engaged in; (2) the statutes regulated private conduct not harmful to others; and (3) the laws were arbitrarily enforced and thus invited the danger of blackmail. In 1961 Illinois changed its laws to conform to the Model Penal Code. Other States soon followed.

In *Bowers* the Court referred to the fact that before 1961 all 50 States had outlawed sodomy, and that at the time of the Court's decision 24 States and the District of Columbia had sodomy laws. Justice Powell pointed out that these prohibitions often were being ignored, however. Georgia, for instance, had not sought to enforce its law for decades.

The sweeping references by Chief Justice Burger to the history of Western civilization and to Judeo-Christian moral and ethical standards did not take account of other authorities pointing in an opposite direction. A committee advising the British Parliament recommended in 1957 repeal of laws punishing homosexual conduct. Parliament enacted the substance of those recommendations 10 years later.

Of even more importance, almost five years before *Bowers* was decided the European Court of Human Rights considered a case with parallels to *Bowers* and to today's case. An adult male resident in Northern Ireland alleged he was a practicing homosexual who desired to engage in consensual homosexual conduct. . . . The court held that the laws proscribing the conduct were invalid under the European Convention on Human Rights. Authoritative in all countries that are members of the Council of Europe (21 nations then, 45 nations now), the decision is at odds with the premise in *Bowers* that the claim put forward was insubstantial in our Western civilization.

In our own constitutional system the deficiencies in *Bowers* became even more apparent in the years following its announcement. The 25 States with laws prohibiting the relevant conduct referenced in the *Bowers* decision are reduced now to 13, of which 4 enforce their laws only against homosexual conduct. In those States where sodomy is still proscribed, whether for same-sex or heterosexual conduct, there is a pattern of nonenforcement with respect to consenting adults acting in private. The State of Texas admitted in 1994 that as of that date it had not prosecuted anyone under those circumstances.

Two principal cases decided after *Bowers* cast its holding into even more doubt. In *Planned Parenthood of Southeastern Pa. v. Casey*, the Court reaffirmed the substantive force of the liberty protected by the Due Process Clause. The *Casey* decision again confirmed that our laws and tradition afford constitutional protection to personal decisions relating to marriage, procreation, contraception, family relationships, child rearing, and education. In explaining the respect the Constitution demands for the autonomy of the person in making these choices, we stated as follows:

> "These matters, involving the most intimate and personal choices a person may make in a lifetime, choices central to personal dignity and autonomy, are central to the liberty protected by the Fourteenth Amendment. At the heart of liberty is the right to define one's own concept of existence, of meaning, of the universe, and of the mystery of human life. Beliefs about these matters could not define the attributes of personhood were they formed under compulsion of the State."

Persons in a homosexual relationship may seek autonomy for these purposes, just as heterosexual persons do. The decision in *Bowers* would deny them this right.

The second post-*Bowers* case of principal relevance is *Romer v. Evans* (1996). There the Court struck down class-based legislation directed at homosexuals as a violation of the Equal Protection Clause. *Romer* invalidated an amendment to Colorado's constitution which named as a solitary class persons who were homosexuals, lesbians, or bisexual either by "orientation, conduct, practices or relationships," and deprived them of protection under state antidiscrimination laws. We concluded that the provision was "born of animosity toward the class of persons affected" and further that it had no rational relation to a legitimate governmental purpose.

As an alternative argument in this case, counsel for the petitioners and some amici contend that *Romer* provides the basis for declaring the Texas statute invalid under the Equal Protection Clause. That is a tenable argument, but we conclude the instant case requires us to address whether *Bowers* itself has continuing validity. Were we to hold the statute invalid under the Equal Protection Clause some might question whether a prohibition would be valid if drawn differently, say, to prohibit the conduct both between same-sex and different-sex participants.

Equality of treatment and the due process right to demand respect for conduct protected by the substantive guarantee of liberty are linked in important respects, and a decision on the latter point advances both interests. If protected conduct is made criminal and the law which does so remains unexamined for its substantive validity, its stigma might remain even if it were not enforceable as drawn for equal protection reasons. When homosexual conduct is made criminal by the law of the State, that declaration in and of itself is an invitation to subject homosexual persons to discrimination both in the public and in the private spheres. The central holding of *Bowers* has been brought in question by this case, and it should be addressed. Its continuance as precedent demeans the lives of homosexual persons.

The stigma this criminal statute imposes, moreover, is not trivial. . . .

The foundations of *Bowers* have sustained serious erosion from our recent decisions in *Casey* and *Romer*. When our precedent has been thus weakened, criticism from other sources is of greater significance. In the United States criticism of *Bowers* has been substantial and continuing, disapproving of its reasoning in all respects, not just as to its historical assumptions. . . .

The right the petitioners seek in this case has been accepted as an integral part of human freedom in many other countries. There has been no showing that in this country the governmental interest in circumscribing personal choice is somehow more legitimate or urgent.

The doctrine of stare decisis is essential to the respect accorded to the judgments of the Court and to the stability of the law. It is not, however, an inexorable command. In Casey we noted that when a Court is asked to overrule a precedent recognizing a constitutional liberty interest, individual or societal reliance on the existence of that liberty cautions with particular strength against reversing course. The holding in *Bowers*, however, has not induced detrimental reliance comparable to some instances where recognized individual rights are involved. Indeed, there has been no individual or societal reliance on *Bowers* of the sort that could counsel against overturning its holding once there are compelling reasons to do so. *Bowers* itself causes uncertainty, for the precedents before and after its issuance contradict its central holding.

The rationale of *Bowers* does not withstand careful analysis. In his dissenting opinion in *Bowers* Justice Stevens came to these conclusions:

> "Our prior cases make two propositions abundantly clear. First, the fact that the governing majority in a State has traditionally viewed a particular practice as immoral is not a sufficient reason for upholding a law prohibiting the practice; neither history nor tradition could save a law prohibiting miscegenation from constitutional attack. Second, individual decisions by married persons, concerning the intimacies of their physical relationship, even when not intended to produce offspring, are a form of "liberty" protected by the Due Process Clause of the Fourteenth Amendment. Moreover, this protection extends to intimate choices by unmarried as well as married persons."

Justice Stevens' analysis, in our view, should have been controlling in *Bowers* and should control here.

Bowers was not correct when it was decided, and it is not correct today. It ought not to remain binding precedent. *Bowers v. Hardwick* should be and now is overruled.

The present case does not involve minors. It does not involve persons who might be injured or coerced or who are situated in relationships where consent might not easily be refused. It does not involve public conduct or prostitution. It does not involve whether the government must give formal recognition to any relationship that homosexual persons seek to enter. The case does involve two adults who, with full and mutual consent from each other, engaged in sexual practices common to a homosexual lifestyle. The petitioners are entitled to respect for their private lives. The State cannot demean their existence or control their destiny by making their private sexual conduct a crime. Their right to liberty under the Due Process Clause gives them the full right to engage in their conduct without intervention of the government. "It is a promise of the Constitution that there is a realm of personal liberty which the government may not enter." *Casey.* The Texas statute furthers no legitimate state interest which can justify its intrusion into the personal and private life of the individual.

Had those who drew and ratified the Due Process Clauses of the Fifth Amendment or the Fourteenth Amendment known the components of liberty in its manifold possibilities, they might have been more specific. They did not presume to have this insight. They knew times can blind us to certain truths and later generations can see that laws once thought necessary and proper in fact serve only to oppress. As the Constitution endures, persons in every generation can invoke its principles in their own search for greater freedom.

The judgment of the Court of Appeals for the Texas Fourteenth District is reversed, and the case is remanded for further proceedings not inconsistent with this opinion.

Justice O'Connor, concurring in the judgment:

The Court today overrules *Bowers v. Hardwick.* I joined *Bowers,* and do not join the Court in overruling it. Nevertheless, I agree with the Court that Texas' statute banning same-sex sodomy is unconstitutional. Rather than relying on the substantive component of the Fourteenth Amendment's Due Process Clause, as the Court does, I base my conclusion on the Fourteenth Amendment's Equal Protection Clause.

The Equal Protection Clause of the Fourteenth Amendment "is essentially a direction that all persons similarly situated should be treated alike." Under our rational basis standard of review, "legislation is presumed to be valid and will be sustained if the classification drawn by the statute is rationally related to a legitimate state interest" *Cleburne v. Cleburne Living Center* (1985). . . .

We have been most likely to apply rational basis review to hold a law unconstitutional under the Equal Protection Clause where, as here, the challenged legislation inhibits personal relationships. . . . In Eisenstadt v. Baird, we refused to sanction a law that discriminated between married and unmarried persons by prohibiting the distribution of contraceptives to single persons. Likewise, in *Cleburne v. Cleburne Living Center,* we held that it was irrational for a State to require a home for the mentally disabled to obtain a special use permit when other residences–like fraternity houses and apartment buildings–did not have to obtain such a permit. And in *Romer v. Evans,* we disallowed a state statute that "impos[ed] a broad and undifferentiated disability on a single named group"–specifically, homosexuals. The dissent apparently agrees that if these cases have stare decisis effect, Texas' sodomy law would not pass scrutiny under the Equal Protection Clause, regardless of the type of rational basis review that we apply. . . .

The statute at issue here makes sodomy a crime only if a person "engages in deviate sexual intercourse with another individual of the same sex." Sodomy between opposite-sex partners, however, is not a crime in Texas. That is, Texas treats the same conduct differently based solely on the participants. Those harmed by this law are people who have a same-sex sexual orientation and thus are more likely to engage in behavior prohibited by §21.06.

The Texas statute makes homosexuals unequal in the eyes of the law by making particular conduct–and only that conduct–subject to criminal sanction. It appears that prosecutions under Texas' sodomy law are rare. This case shows, however, that prosecutions under §21.06 do occur. And while the penalty imposed on petitioners in this case was relatively minor, the consequences of conviction are not. . . .

And the effect of Texas' sodomy law is not just limited to the threat of prosecution or consequence of conviction. Texas' sodomy law brands all homosexuals as criminals, thereby making it more difficult for homosexuals to be treated in the same manner as everyone else. Indeed, Texas itself has previously acknowledged the collateral effects of the law, stipulating in a prior challenge to this action that the law "legally sanctions discrimination against [homosexuals] in a variety of ways unrelated to the criminal law," including in the areas of "employment, family issues, and housing."

Texas attempts to justify its law, and the effects of the law, by arguing that the statute satisfies rational basis review because it furthers the legitimate governmental interest of the promotion of morality. In *Bowers,* we held that a state law criminalizing sodomy as applied to homosexual couples did not violate substantive due process. We rejected the argument that no rational basis existed to justify the law, pointing to the government's interest in promoting morality. The only question in front of the Court in *Bowers* was whether the substantive component of the Due Process Clause protected a right to engage in homosexual sodomy. *Bowers* did not hold that moral disapproval of a group is a rational basis under the Equal Protection Clause to criminalize homosexual sodomy when heterosexual sodomy is not punished.

This case raises a different issue than *Bowers*: whether, under the Equal Protection Clause, moral disapproval is a legitimate state interest to justify by itself a statute that bans homosexual sodomy, but not heterosexual sodomy. It is not. Moral disapproval of this group, like a bare desire to harm the group, is an interest that is insufficient to satisfy rational basis review under the Equal Protection Clause. Indeed, we have never held that moral disapproval, without any other asserted state interest, is a sufficient rationale under the Equal Protection Clause to justify a law that discriminates among groups of persons.

Moral disapproval of a group cannot be a legitimate governmental interest under the Equal Protection Clause because legal classifications must not be "drawn for the purpose of disadvantaging the group burdened by the law." Texas' invocation of moral disapproval as a legitimate state interest proves nothing more than Texas' desire to criminalize homosexual sodomy. But the Equal Protection Clause prevents a State from creating "a classification of persons undertaken for its own sake." And because Texas so rarely enforces its sodomy law as applied to private, consensual acts, the law serves more as a statement of dislike and disapproval against homosexuals than as a tool to stop criminal behavior. The Texas sodomy law "raise[s] the inevitable inference that the disadvantage imposed is born of animosity toward the class of persons affected."

Texas argues, however, that the sodomy law does not discriminate against homosexual persons. Instead, the State maintains that the law discriminates only against homosexual conduct. While it is true that the law applies only to conduct, the conduct targeted by this law is conduct that is closely correlated with being homosexual. Under such circumstances, Texas' sodomy law is targeted at more than conduct. It is instead directed toward gay persons as a class. "After all, there can hardly be more palpable discrimination against a class than making the conduct that defines the class criminal." When a State makes homosexual conduct criminal, and not "deviate sexual intercourse" committed by persons of different sexes, "that declaration in and of itself is an invitation to subject homosexual persons to discrimination both in the public and in the private spheres." . . .

Whether a sodomy law that is neutral both in effect and application would violate the substantive component of the Due Process Clause is an issue that need not be decided today. I am confident, however, that so long as the Equal Protection Clause requires a sodomy law to apply equally to the private consensual conduct of homosexuals and heterosexuals alike, such a law would not long stand in our democratic society. In the words of Justice Jackson:

> "The framers of the Constitution knew, and we should not forget today, that there is no more effective practical guaranty against arbitrary and unreasonable government than to require that the principles of law which officials would impose upon a minority be imposed generally. Conversely, nothing opens the door to arbitrary action so effectively as to allow those officials to pick and choose only a few to whom they will apply legislation and thus to escape the political retribution that might be visited upon them if larger numbers were affected." (*Railway Express Agency, Inc. v. New York* (1949) (concurring opinion).

That this law as applied to private, consensual conduct is unconstitutional under the Equal Protection Clause does not mean that other laws distinguishing between heterosexuals and homosexuals would similarly fail under rational basis review. Texas cannot assert any legitimate state interest here, such as national security or preserving the traditional institution of marriage. Unlike the moral disapproval of same-sex relations–the asserted state interest in this case–other reasons exist to promote the institution of marriage beyond mere moral disapproval of an excluded group.

A law branding one class of persons as criminal solely based on the State's moral disapproval of that class and the conduct associated with that class runs contrary to the values of the Constitution and the Equal Protection Clause, under any standard of review. I therefore concur in the Court's judgment that Texas' sodomy law banning "deviate sexual intercourse" between consenting adults of the same sex, but not between consenting adults of different sexes, is unconstitutional.

Justice Scalia, with whom The Chief Justice and Justice Thomas join, dissenting:

"Liberty finds no refuge in a jurisprudence of doubt." That was the Court's sententious response, barely more than a decade ago, to those seeking to overrule *Roe v. Wade*. The Court's response today, to those who have engaged in a 17-year crusade to overrule *Bowers v. Hardwick* is very different. The need for stability and certainty presents no barrier. . . .

I begin with the Court's surprising readiness to reconsider a decision rendered a mere 17 years ago in *Bowers v. Hardwick*. I do not myself believe in rigid adherence to stare decisis in constitutional cases; but I do believe that we should be consistent rather than manipulative in invoking the doctrine. . . .

Today's approach to stare decisis invites us to overrule an erroneously decided precedent (including an "intensely divisive" decision) if: (1) its foundations have been "eroded" by subsequent decisions; (2) it has been subject to "substantial and continuing" criticism; and (3) it has not induced "individual or societal reliance" that counsels against overturning. The problem is that *Roe* itself–which today's majority surely has no disposition to overrule–satisfies these conditions to at least the same degree as *Bowers*. . . .

Having decided that it need not adhere to stare decisis, the Court still must establish that *Bowers* was wrongly decided and that the Texas statute, as applied to petitioners, is unconstitutional.

Texas Penal Code Ann. §21.06 undoubtedly imposes constraints on liberty. So do laws prohibiting prostitution, recreational use of heroin, and, for that matter, working more than 60 hours per week in a bakery. But there is no right to "liberty" under the Due Process Clause, though today's opinion repeatedly makes that claim. The Fourteenth Amendment expressly allows States to deprive their citizens of "liberty," so long as "due process of law" is provided:

> "No state shall . . . deprive any person of life, liberty, or property, without due process of law." Our opinions applying the doctrine known as "substantive due process" hold that the Due Process Clause prohibits States from infringing fundamental liberty interests, unless the infringement is narrowly tailored to serve a compelling state interest.

The Court's description of "the state of the law" at the time of *Bowers* only confirms that *Bowers* was right. But that case expressly disclaimed any reliance on the doctrine of "substantive due process," and grounded the so-called "right to privacy" in penumbras of constitutional provisions other than the Due Process Clause. *Eisenstadt v. Baird* likewise had nothing to do with "substantive due process"; it invalidated a Massachusetts law prohibiting the distribution of contraceptives to unmarried persons solely on the basis of the Equal Protection Clause. Of course *Eisenstadt* contains well known dictum relating to the "right to privacy," but this referred to the right recognized in *Griswold*–a right penumbral to the specific guarantees in the Bill of Rights, and not a "substantive due process" right.

Roe v. Wade recognized that the right to abort an unborn child was a "fundamental right" protected by the Due Process Clause. The Roe Court, however, made no attempt to establish that this right was " 'deeply rooted in this Nation's history and tradition' "; instead, it based its conclusion that "the Fourteenth Amendment's concept of personal liberty . . . is broad enough to encompass a woman's decision whether or not to terminate her pregnancy" on its own normative judgment that anti-abortion laws were undesirable. . . .

It is (as *Bowers* recognized) entirely irrelevant whether the laws in our long national tradition criminalizing homosexual sodomy were "directed at homosexual conduct as a distinct matter." Whether homosexual sodomy was prohibited by a law targeted at same-sex sexual relations or by a more general law prohibiting both homosexual and heterosexual sodomy, the only relevant point is that it was criminalized–which suffices to establish that homosexual sodomy is not a right "deeply rooted in our Nation's history and tradition."

The Court today agrees that homosexual sodomy was criminalized and thus does not dispute the facts on which *Bowers* actually relied. . . . *Bowers'* conclusion that homosexual sodomy is not a fundamental right "deeply rooted in this Nation's history and tradition" is utterly unassailable. . . .

I turn now to the ground on which the Court squarely rests its holding: the contention that there is no rational basis for the law here under attack. . . . If, as the Court asserts, the promotion of majoritarian sexual morality is not even a legitimate state interest, none of the above-mentioned laws can survive rational-basis review.

Justice O'Connor argues that the discrimination in this law which must be justified is not its discrimination with regard to the sex of the partner but its discrimination with regard to the sexual proclivity of the principal actor.

"While it is true that the law applies only to conduct, the conduct targeted by this law is conduct that is closely correlated with being homosexual. Under such circumstances, Texas' sodomy law is targeted at more than conduct. It is instead directed toward gay persons as a class." Of course the same could be said of any law. A law against public nudity targets "the conduct that is closely correlated with being a nudist," and hence "is targeted at more than conduct"; it is "directed toward nudists as a class." But be that as it may. Even if the Texas law does deny equal protection to "homosexuals as a class," that denial still does not need to be justified by anything more than a rational basis, which our cases show is satisfied by the enforcement of traditional notions of sexual morality.

Let me be clear that I have nothing against homosexuals, or any other group, promoting their agenda through normal democratic means. Social perceptions of sexual and other morality change over time, and every group has the right to persuade its fellow citizens that its view of such matters is the best. That homosexuals have achieved some success in that enterprise is attested to by the fact that Texas is one of the few remaining States that criminalize private, consensual homosexual acts. But persuading one's fellow citizens is one thing, and imposing one's views in absence of democratic majority will is something else. . . .

At the end of its opinion—after having laid waste the foundations of our rational-basis jurisprudence—the Court says that the present case "does not involve whether the government must give formal recognition to any relationship that homosexual persons seek to enter." Do not believe it. More illuminating than this bald, unreasoned disclaimer is the progression of thought displayed by an earlier passage in the Court's opinion, which notes the constitutional protections afforded to "personal decisions relating to marriage, procreation, contraception, family relationships, child rearing, and education," and then declares that "[p]ersons in a homosexual relationship may seek autonomy for these purposes, just as heterosexual persons do." Today's opinion dismantles the structure of constitutional law that has permitted a distinction to be made between heterosexual and homosexual unions, insofar as formal recognition in marriage is concerned. If moral disapprobation of homosexual conduct is "no legitimate state interest" for purposes of proscribing that conduct; and if, as the Court coos (casting aside all pretense of neutrality), "[w]hen sexuality finds overt expression in intimate conduct with another person, the conduct can be but one element in a personal bond that is more enduring,"; what justification could there possibly be for denying the benefits of marriage to homosexual couples exercising "[t]he liberty protected by the Constitution"? Surely not the encouragement of procreation, since the sterile and the elderly are allowed to marry. This case "does not involve" the issue of homosexual marriage only if one entertains the belief that principle and logic have nothing to do with the decisions of this Court. Many will hope that, as the Court comfortingly assures us, this is so.

The matters appropriate for this Court's resolution are only three: Texas's prohibition of sodomy neither infringes a "fundamental right" (which the Court does not dispute), nor is unsupported by a rational relation to what the Constitution considers a legitimate state interest, nor denies the equal protection of the laws.

87

Plessy v. Ferguson (1896)

Mr. Justice Brown *delivered the opinion of the Court:*

This case turns upon the constitutionality of an act of the General Assembly of the State of Louisiana, passed in 1890, providing for separate railway carriages for the white and colored races.

The first section of the statute enacts "that all railway companies carrying passengers in their coaches in this State, shall provide equal but separate accommodations for the white, and colored races, by providing two or more passenger coaches for each passenger train, or by dividing the passenger coaches by a partition so as to secure separate accommodations: *Provided,* That this section shall not be construed to apply to street railroads. No person or persons shall be permitted to occupy seats in coaches other than the ones assigned to them, on account of the race they belong to." . . .

From *Plessy v. Ferguson,* 163 U.S. 537 (1896).

The information filed in the criminal district court charged in substance that Plessy, being a passenger between two stations within the state of Louisiana, was assigned by officers of the company to the coach used by the race to which he belonged, but he insisted upon going into a coach used by the race to which he did not belong. Neither in the information nor plea was his particular race or color averred. . . .

[Justice Brown summarized the provisions of the first section of the Fourteenth Amendment.]

The object of the amendment was undoubtedly to enforce the absolute equality of the two races before the law, but in the nature of things it could not have been intended to abolish distinctions based upon color, or to enforce social as distinguished from political equality, or a commingling of the two races upon terms unsatisfactory to either. Laws permitting, and even requiring, their separation in places where they are liable to be brought into contact do not necessarily imply the inferiority of either race to the other, and have been generally, if not universally, recognized as within the competency of the state legislatures in the exercise of their police power. The most common instance of this is connected with the establishment of separate schools for white and colored children, which has been held to be a valid exercise of the legislative power even by courts of States where the political rights of the colored race have been longest and most earnestly enforced. . . .

The distinction between laws interfering with the political equality of the negro and those requiring the separation of the two races in schools, theaters, and railway carriages, has been frequently drawn by this court. Thus, in *Strauder v. West Virginia*, it was held that a law of West Virginia limiting to white male persons, twenty-one years of age and citizens of the state, the right to sit upon juries, was a discrimination which implied a legal inferiority in civil society. . . . [The further discussion of the distinction between laws denying political equality and laws denying social equality is omitted.]

So far, then, as a conflict with the 14th Amendment is concerned, the case reduces itself to the question whether the statute of Louisiana is a reasonable regulation, and with respect to this there must necessarily be a large discretion on the part of the legislature. In determining the question of reasonableness it is at liberty to act with reference to the established usages, customs and traditions of the people, and with a view to the promotion of their comfort, and preservation of the public peace and good order. Gauged by this standard, we cannot say that a law which authorizes or even requires the separation of the two races in public conveyances is unreasonable, or more obnoxious to the 14th Amendment than the acts of Congress requiring separate schools for colored children in the District of Columbia, the constitutionality of which does not seem to have been questioned, or the corresponding acts of state legislatures.

We consider the underlying fallacy of the plaintiff's argument to consist in the assumption that the enforced separation of the two races stamps the colored race with a badge of inferiority. If this be so, it is not by reason of anything found in the act, but solely because the colored race chooses to put that construction upon it. The argument necessarily assumes that if as has been more than once the case, and is not unlikely to be so again, the colored race should become the dominant power in the state legislature, and should enact a law in precisely similar terms, it would thereby relegate the white race to an inferior position. We imagine that the white race, at least, would not acquiesce in this assumption. The argument also assumes that social prejudices may be overcome by legislation, and that equal rights cannot be secured to the negro except by an enforced commingling of the two races. We cannot accept this proposition. If the two races are to meet upon terms of social equality, it must be the result of natural affinities, a mutual appreciation of each other's merits and voluntary consent of individuals. As was said by the court of appeals of New York in *People v. Gallagher,* "this end can neither be accomplished nor promoted by laws which conflict with the general sentiment of the community upon whom they are designed to operate. When the government, therefore, has secured to each of its citizens equal rights before the law and equal opportunities for improvement and progress, it has accomplished the end for which it was organized and performed all of the functions respecting social advantages with which it is endowed." Legislation is powerless to eradicate racial instincts or to abolish distinctions based upon physical differences, and the attempt to do so can only result in accentuating the difficulties of the present situation. If the civil and political rights of both races be equal, one cannot be inferior to the other civilly or politically. If one race be inferior to the other socially, the Constitution of the United States cannot put them upon the same plane. . . .

Mr. Justice Harlan, dissenting.

. . . It was said in argument that the statute of Louisiana does not discriminate against either race, but prescribes a rule applicable alike to white and colored citizens. But this argument does not meet the difficulty. Every one knows that the statute in question had its origin in the purpose, not so much to exclude white persons from railroad cars occupied by blacks, as to exclude colored people from coaches occupied by or assigned to white persons. Railroad corporations of Louisiana did not make discrimination among whites in the matter of accommodation for travelers. The thing to accomplish was, under the guise of giving equal accommodation for whites and blacks, to compel the latter to keep to themselves while traveling in railroad passenger coaches. No one would be so wanting in candor as to assert the contrary. The fundamental objection, therefore, to the statute, is that it interferes with the personal freedom of citizens. . . .

The white race deems itself to be the dominant race in this country. And so it is, in prestige, in achievements, in education, in wealth, and in power. So, I doubt not, it will continue to be for all time, if it remains true to its great heritage, and holds fast to the principles of constitutional liberty. But in view of the constitution, in the eye of the law, there is in this country no superior, dominant, ruling class of citizens. There is no caste here. Our constitution is color-blind, and neither knows nor tolerates classes among citizens. In respect of civil rights, all citizens are equal before the law. The humblest is the peer of the most powerful. The law regards man as man, and takes no account of his surroundings or of his color when his civil rights as guaranteed by the supreme law of the land are involved. It is therefore to be regretted that this high tribunal, the final expositor of the fundamental law of the land, has reached the conclusion that it is competent for a state to regulate the enjoyment by citizens of their civil rights solely upon the basis of race. . . .

The arbitrary separation of citizens, on the basis of race, while they are on a public highway, is a badge of servitude wholly inconsistent with the civil freedom and the equality before the law established by the constitution. It cannot be justified upon any legal grounds.

If evils will result from the commingling of the two races upon public highways established for the benefit of all, they will be infinitely less than those that will surely come from state legislation regulating the enjoyment of civil rights upon the basis of race. We boast of the freedom enjoyed by our people above all other peoples. But it is difficult to reconcile that boast with a state of the law which, practically, puts the brand of servitude and degradation upon a large class of our fellow citizens,—our equals before the law. The thin disguise of "equal" accommodations for passengers in railroad coaches will not mislead anyone, nor atone for the wrong this day done. . . .

88

Brown v. Board of Education (1954)

Mr. Chief Justice Warren *delivered the opinion of the Court:*

These cases come to us from the States of Kansas, South Carolina, Virginia, and Delaware. They are premised on different facts and different local conditions, but a common legal question justifies their consideration together in this consolidated opinion.

From *Brown v. Board of Education* 347 U.S. 483 (1954).

In each of the cases, minors of the Negro race, through their legal representatives, seek the aid of the courts in obtaining admission to the public schools of their community on a nonsegregated basis. In each instance, they have been denied admission to schools attended by white children under laws requiring or permitting segregation according to race. This segregation was alleged to deprive the plaintiffs of the equal protection of the laws under the Fourteenth Amendment. . . .

In the first cases in this Court construing the Fourteenth Amendment, decided shortly after its adoption, the Court interpreted it as proscribing all state-imposed discriminations against the Negro race. The doctrine of "separate but equal" did not make its appearance in this Court until 1896 in the case of *Plessy v. Ferguson, supra,* involving not education but transportation. American courts have since labored with the doctrine for over half a century. In this Court, there have been six cases involving the "separate but equal" doctrine in the field of public education. In *Cumming v. Board of Education of Richmond County,* and *Gong Lum v. Rice,* the validity of the doctrine itself was not challenged. In more recent cases, all on the graduate school level, inequality was found in that specific benefits enjoyed by white students were denied to Negro students of the same educational qualifications. In none of these cases was it necessary to reexamine the doctrine to grant relief to the Negro plaintiff. And in *Sweatt v. Painter* the Court expressly reserved decision on the question whether *Plessy v. Ferguson* should be held inapplicable to public education.

In approaching this problem, we cannot turn the clock back to 1868 when the Amendment was adopted, or even to 1896 when *Plessy v. Ferguson* was written. We must consider public education in the light of its full development and its present place in American life throughout the Nation. Only in this way can it be determined if segregation in public schools deprives these plaintiffs of the equal protection of the laws.

Today, education is perhaps the most important function of state and local governments. Compulsory school attendance laws and the great expenditures for education both demonstrate our recognition of the importance of education to our democratic society. It is required in the performance of our most basic public responsibilities, even service in the armed forces. It is the very foundation of good citizenship. Today it is a principal instrument in awakening the child to cultural values, in preparing him for later professional training, and in helping him to adjust normally to his environment. In these days, it is doubtful that any child may reasonably be expected to succeed in life if he is denied the opportunity of an education. Such an opportunity, where the state has undertaken to provide it, is a right which must be made available to all on equal terms.

We come then to the question presented: Does segregation of children in public schools solely on the basis of race, even though the physical facilities and other "tangible" factors may be equal, deprive the children of the minority group of equal educational opportunities? We believe that it does.

In *Sweatt v. Painter*, in finding that a segregated law school for Negroes could not provide them equal educational opportunities, this Court relied in large part on "those qualities which are incapable of objective measurement but which make for greatness in a law school." In *McLaurin v. Oklahoma State Regents*, the Court, in requiring that a Negro admitted to a white graduate school be treated like all other students, again resorted to intangible considerations: ". . . his ability to study, to engage in discussions and exchange views with other students, and, in general, to learn his profession." Such considerations apply with added force to children in grade and high schools. To separate them from others of similar age and qualifications solely because of their race generates a feeling of inferiority as to their status in the community that may affect their hearts and minds in a way unlikely ever to be undone. The effect of this separation on their educational opportunities was well stated by a finding in the Kansas case by a court which nevertheless felt compelled to rule against the Negro plaintiffs:

> "Segregation of white and colored children in public schools has a detrimental effect upon the colored children. The impact is greater when it has the sanction of the law; for the policy of separating the races is usually interpreted as denoting the inferiority of the negro group. A sense of inferiority affects the motivation of a child to learn. Segregation with the sanction of law, therefore, has a tendency to [retard] the educational and mental development of Negro children and to deprive them of some of the benefits they would receive in a racial[ly] integrated school system."

Whatever may have been the extent of psychological knowledge at the time of *Plessy v. Ferguson*, this finding is amply supported by modern authority.* Any language in *Plessy v. Ferguson* contrary to this finding is rejected.

We conclude that in the field of public education the doctrine of "separate but equal" has no place. Separate educational facilities are inherently unequal. Therefore, we hold that the plaintiffs and others similarly situated for whom the actions have been brought are, by reason of the segregation

---

*K. B. Clark, Effect of Prejudice and Discrimination on Personality Development (Mid-century White House Conference on Children and Youth, 1950); Witmer and Kotinsky, Personality in the Making (1952), c. VI; Deutscher and Chen, The Psychological Effects of Enforced Segregation: A Survey of Social Science Opinion, 26 J. Psychol. 259 (1948); Chein, What are the Psychological Effects of Segregation Under Conditions of Equal Facilities?, 3 Int. J. Opinion and Attitude Res. 229 (1949); Brameld, Educational Costs, in Discrimination and National Welfare (MacIver, ed. 1949), 44–48; Frazier, the Negro in the United States (1949), 674–681. And see generally Myrdal, An American Dilemma (1944).

complained of, deprived of the equal protection of the laws guaranteed by the Fourteenth Amendment. . . .

89

Bolling v. Sharpe (1954)

Chief Justice Warren delivered the opinion of the Court:

This case challenges the validity of segregation in the public schools of the District of Columbia. The petitioners, minors of the Negro race, allege that such segregation deprives them of due process of law under the Fifth Amendment. They were refused admission to a public school attended by white children solely because of their race. They sought the aid of the District Court for the District of Columbia in obtaining admission. That court dismissed their complaint. The Court granted a writ of certiorari before judgment in the Court of Appeals because of the importance of the constitutional question presented.

We have this day held that the Equal Protection Clause of the Fourteenth Amendment prohibits the states from maintaining racially segregated public schools. The legal problem in the District of Columbia is somewhat different, however. The Fifth Amendment, which is applicable in the District of Columbia, does not contain an equal protection clause, as does the Fourteenth Amendment, which applies only to the states. But the concepts of equal protection and due process, both stemming from our American ideal of fairness, are not mutually exclusive. The "equal protection of the laws" is a more explicit safeguard of prohibited unfairness than "due process of law," and therefore we do not imply that the two are always interchangeable phrases. But, as this Court has recognized, discrimination may be so unjustifiable as to be violative of due process.

Classifications based solely upon race must be scrutinized with particular care, since they are contrary to our traditions, and hence constitutionally suspect. . . .

From *Billing v. Sharpe*, 347 v.s. 497 (1954).

[I]n *Buchanan v. Warley* (1917), the Court held that a statute which limited the right of a property owner to convey his property to a person of another race was, as an unreasonable discrimination, a denial of due process of law.

Although the Court has not assumed to define "liberty" with any great precision, that term is not confined to mere freedom from bodily restraint. Liberty under law extends to the full range of conduct which the individual is free to pursue, and it cannot be restricted except for a proper governmental objective. Segregation in public education is not reasonably related to any proper governmental objective, and thus it imposes on Negro children of the District of Columbia a burden that constitutes an arbitrary deprivation of their liberty in violation of the Due Process Clause.

In view of our decision that the Constitution prohibits the states from maintaining racially segregated public schools, it would be unthinkable that the same Constitution would impose a lesser duty on the Federal Government. We hold that racial segregation in the public schools of the District of Columbia is a denial of the due process of law guaranteed by the Fifth Amendment to the Constitution.

90

Eugene J. McCarthy

A Note on the New Equality (1977)

. . . Alexis de Tocqueville, in *Democracy in America,* wrote of the powerful appeal and danger of the idea of equality in a democratic society. He wrote also of its potential for demagoguery. I would be less concerned about the rise to popularity of the word, and the idea, if I thought it the result of conscious intention to elicit political support—that is, if those who made the appeal knew that they were being demagogic. I fear, however, that the use of the word is not intentionally demagogic. It seems to approach the automatic "It is good" justification that George Orwell described as characterizing the world order of 1984.

In his inaugural address President Carter said: "We have already found a high degree of personal liberty, and we are now struggling to enhance equality of opportunity." One may well question the President's language. Liberty was a goal of the American Revolution. We have it in this country not because we "found" it but rather as a result of our having declared it a political and social goal and then achieving it in some measure. As to the President's second point, that "we are now struggling to enhance equality of opportunity," such language does not clearly describe the concept of "equality" as it is applied today. Economic, educational, political, and cultural equality—and not equality of opportunity, "enhanced" or otherwise—is the goal in the new application.

Economic equality is in this new conception to be achieved primarily through equalizing income. Equalization of wealth—that is, of wealth already accumulated—may come later. Economic equality is not conceived as a base upon which differences may then build, but as an average. One state governor occasionally asks if it might be better if people doing unpleasant work were paid as much as or more than those whose work is culturally and physically preferable.

Political economists have developed the notion of a negative income tax as the basis for tax reform. Essentially the idea is this: that everyone should have enough income to pay taxes at the beginning or threshold rate, and that if one does not have enough income to reach that level, something should be done to make up for the deficiency. Where the idea came from, or how the taxable level of income was chosen as the absolute standard for relative judgments and adjustments, is not clear. It seems that the tax base is to be accepted as a first principle upon which we are to build. It is an axiom, rather like "I think, therefore I am." One could as well arbitrarily assert that everyone should, for the good of the commonwealth, pay $100 in income taxes, and then proceed through measures of redistribution to raise all incomes to the level at which everyone would have to pay $100 in taxes. . . .

The second area in which the new concept of equality is being applied is in politics and government. The principle of one-person-one-vote was formally recognized in a Supreme Court ruling affecting defined political jurisdictions. The court did not in its ruling extend the principle to relationships among jurisdictions. The ruling simply said that, within given units of government, each vote should be equal to every other vote. Thus, since the Constitution provides for direct election of the House of Representatives on the basis of population, the rule requires that each congressional district have roughly the same number of persons.

The Constitution also provides that each state, no matter what its size, shall have two Senators. Thus the citizen of a small state gets proportionally more of a vote than the resident of a large state. The Constitution further provides that the President shall be elected through the Electoral College, on a state-by-state basis, thus weighting the votes of smaller states favorably as against those cast in larger states. The drive now is to eliminate that weighting by abolishing the Electoral College and instituting direct popular election of the President. No proposal has yet been made to reduce senatorial representation to a strict population base.

The principle of equality is also applied through the Federal Election Campaign Act, which attempts to equalize the non-voting influence of citizens on candidates for political office. The present law limits the size of contributions to a political candidate in any one campaign to $1,000 per contributor. This is considered a transitional phase to a time when all campaigns will be publicly financed. The argument for the limitation is that the larger the contribution, the greater the influence a contributor has on the officeholder and the more time he gets to spend with the officeholder. Theoretically, with public financing, every taxpayer will have made an equal contribution and will be entitled to as much time with the officeholder as any other taxpayer. What time non-taxpayers will get has not yet been determined by the reformers. Despite the $1,000 limit on contributions in the last national elections, and the fact that the presidential campaigns were financed principally through federal grants, within a few days of the election President-elect Carter flew to St. Simon's Island, the domain of the Reynolds family, and President Ford went to Palm Springs—presumably to speak to the average citizens who dwell in those precincts.

It does not take much imagination to foresee a time when citizens might go to court, charging that they were discriminated against because their calls were not taken in presidential telethons and transmitted to the President for his attention. A full practical application of this principle would argue for an equal right to speak or otherwise communicate with all officeholders, even removing the personal screening of Walter Cronkite.

The objective of equalizing communications and influence on office-holders is also sought in efforts to control lobbyists. Proposals generally recommend more thorough regulation of lobbyists, limits on their expenditures, and public disclosure not only of expenditures but also of meetings and communications with officeholders.

It will not be surprising if someone suggests having lobbyists provided at government expense, so as to insulate them from the undue influence of their principals, in somewhat the same way that officeholders are to be insulated from their constituencies. Under this arrangement, anyone who had a case to make to the government would apply for a lobbyist who would be assigned from a pool in the way that public defenders are assigned by the courts. . . .

The new concept of equality is also applied in government and government-influenced employment practices, in what has been labeled the "quota system." The rationale of the quota system is that, since not every person can be hired, we should have within each employed group a representation or sampling of the total employable work force. Selection currently is on the basis of physiological characteristics of age, sex, and race. There are some obvious historical reasons as to why these standards are being tried. There are also some obvious difficulties in their application, especially if one attempts to extend the principle—as will surely be done—to other racial and ethnic groups, or to groups less easily defined in terms of psychological and cultural differences.

A similar drive to realize the new idea of equality has marked educational development in recent years. The standardized curriculum, quota admissions, open admissions, and free college education are all manifestations of this drive. Full application of the principle could lead to compulsory college education, with the level of education so reduced that all who enter do so with assurance of successful graduation. With no possible abandonment of hope at any point, they could look forward to something like the judgment of the Dodo after the caucus race in Alice in Wonderland. "*Everybody* has won, and *all* must have prizes."

What are the dangers in this drive to a newly conceived equality? I see a danger first in the inevitable weakening of those institutions that are expected to give form and direction to society, such as professional and educational institutions, and which have traditionally been treated as having an identity separate from politically-controlled areas of society.

I see it also as significantly affecting the individual's conception of his place in society. Most persons cannot stand either physical or cultural isolation, and will seek a base of some certainty in a community of persons and in a cultural complex. The cultural security of Americans traditionally has been found in a society of some tension, but a society in which a balance between individual freedom and liberty on the one side and the social good on the other could be achieved. The alternative now offered, the security of equalization, is depersonalizing. It is a deceptively angelistic conception of man in society. It is one which cannot be sustained. It will in all likelihood move persons in search of security, if not identity, to accept greater and greater socialization in politics, in economics, and in culture.

91

Kurt Vonnegut, Jr.

Harrison Bergeron (1961)

The year was 2081, and everybody was finally equal. They weren't only equal before God and the law. They were equal every which way. Nobody was smarter than anybody else. Nobody was better looking than anybody else. Nobody was stronger or quicker than anybody else. All this equality was due to the 211th, 212th, and 213th Amendments to the Constitution, and to the unceasing vigilance of agents of the United States Handicapper General.

Some things about living still weren't quite right, though. April, for instance, still drove people crazy by not being springtime. And it was in that clammy month that the H-G men took George and Hazel Bergeron's fourteen-year-old son, Harrison, away.

It was tragic, all right, but George and Hazel couldn't think about it very hard. Hazel had a perfectly average intelligence, which meant she couldn't think about anything except in short bursts. And George, while his intelligence was way above normal, had a little mental handicap radio in his ear. He was required by law to wear it at all times. It was tuned to a government transmitter. Every twenty seconds or so, the transmitter would send out some sharp noise to keep people like George from taking unfair advantage of their brains.

George and Hazel were watching television. There were tears on Hazel's cheeks, but she'd forgotten for the moment what they were about.

On the television screen were ballerinas.

A buzzer sounded in George's head. His thoughts fled in panic, like bandits from a burglar alarm.

"That was a real pretty dance, that dance they just did," said Hazel.

"Huh?" said George.

"That dance—it was nice," said Hazel.

"Yup," said George. He tried to think a little about the ballerinas. They weren't really very good—no better than anybody else would have been, anyway. They were burdened with sashweights and bags of birdshot, and their faces were masked, so that no one, seeing a free and graceful gesture or a pretty face, would feel like something the cat drug in. George was toying with the vague notion that maybe dancers shouldn't be handicapped. But he didn't get very far with it before another noise in his ear radio scattered his thoughts.

George winced. So did two out of the eight ballerinas.

Hazel saw him wince. Having no mental handicap herself, she had to ask George what the latest sound had been.

"Sounded like somebody hitting a milk bottle with a ball peen hammer," said George.

"I'd think it would be real interesting, hearing all the different sounds," said Hazel, a little envious. "All the things they think up."

"Um," said George.

"Only, if I was Handicapper General, you know what I would do?" said Hazel. Hazel, as a matter of fact, bore a strong resemblance to the Handicapper General, a woman named Diana Moon Glampers. "If I was Diana Moon Glampers," said Hazel, "I'd have chimes on Sunday—just chimes. Kind of in honor of religion."

"I could think, if it was just chimes," said George.

"Well—maybe make 'em real loud," said Hazel. "I think I'd make a good Handicapper General."

"Good as anybody else," said George.

"Who knows bett'n I do what normal is?" said Hazel.

"Right," said George. He began to think glimmeringly about his abnormal son who was now in jail, about Harrison, but a twenty-one-gun salute in his head stopped that.

"Boy!" said Hazel, "that was a doozy, wasn't it?"

It was such a doozy that George was white and trembling, and tears stood on the rims of his red eyes. Two of the eight ballerinas had collapsed to the studio floor, were holding their temples.

"All of a sudden you look so tired," said Hazel. "Why don't you stretch out on the sofa, so's you can rest your handicap bag on the pillows, honey-bunch." She was referring to the forty-seven pounds of birdshot in a canvas bag, which was padlocked around George's neck. "Go on and rest the bag for a little while," she said. "I don't care if your're not equal to me for a while."

George weighed the bag with his hands. "I don't mind it," he said. "I don't notice it any more. It's just a part of me."

"You been so tired lately—kind of wore out," said Hazel. "If there was just some way we could make a little hole in the bottom of the bag, and just take out a few of them lead balls. Just a few."

"Two years in prison and two thousand dollars fine for every ball I took out, " said George. "I don't call that a bargain."

"If you could just take a few out when you came home from work," said Hazel. "I mean—you don't compete with anybody around here. You just set around."

"If I tried to get away with it," said George, "then other people'd get away with it—and pretty soon we'd be right back to the dark ages again, with everybody competing against everybody else. You wouldn't like that, would you?"

"I'd hate it," said Hazel.

"There you are," said George. "The minute people start cheating on laws, what do you think happens to society?"

If Hazel hadn't been able to come up with an answer to this question, George couldn't have supplied one. A siren was going off in his head. "Reckon it'd fall all apart," said Hazel.

"What would?" said George blankly.

"Society," said Hazel uncertainly. "Wasn't that what you just said?"

"Who knows?" said George.

The television program was suddenly interrupted for a news bulletin. It wasn't clear at first as to what the bulletin was about, since the announcer, like all announcers, had a serious speech impediment. For about half a minute, and in a state of high excitement, the announcer tried to say, "Ladies and gentlemen—"

He finally gave up, handed the bulletin to a ballerina to read.

"That's all right—" Hazel said of the announcer, "he tried. That's the big thing. He tried to do the best he could with what God gave him. He should get a nice raise for trying so hard. "

"Ladies and gentlemen—" said the ballerina, reading the bulletin. She must have been extraordinarily beautiful, because the mask she wore was hideous. And it was easy to see that she was the strongest and most graceful of all the dancers, for her handicap bags were as big as those worn by two-hundred-pound men.

And she had to apologize at once for her voice, which was a very unfair voice for a woman to use. Her voice was a warm, luminous, timeless melody. "Excuse me—" she said, and she began again, making her voice absolutely uncompetitive.

"Harrison Bergeron, age fourteen," she said in a grackle squawk, "has just escaped from jail, where he was held on suspicion of plotting to overthrow the government. He is a genius and an athlete, is underhandicapped, and should be regarded as extremely dangerous."

A police photograph of Harrison Bergeron was flashed on the screen upside down, then sideways, upside down again, then right side up. The picture showed the full length of Harrison against a background calibrated in feet and inches. He was exactly seven feet tall.

The rest of Harrison's appearance was Halloween and hardware. Nobody had ever born heavier handicaps. He had outgrown hindrances faster than the H-G men could think them up. Instead of a little ear radio for a mental handicap, he wore a tremendous pair of earphones, and spectacles with thick wavy lenses. The spectacles were intended to make him not only half blind, but to give him whanging headaches besides.

Scrap metal was hung all over him. Ordinarily, there was a certain symmetry, a military neatness to the handicaps issued to strong people, but Harrison looked like a walking junkyard. In the race of life, Harrison carried three hundred pounds.

And to offset his good looks, the H-G men required that he wear at all times a red rubber ball for a nose, keep his eyebrows shaved off, and cover his even white teeth with black caps at snaggle-tooth random.

"If you see this boy," said the ballerina, "do not—I repeat, do not—try to reason with him."

There was the shriek of a door being torn from its hinges.

Screams and barking cries of consternation came from the television set. The photograph of Harrison Bergeron on the screen jumped again and again, as though dancing to the tune of an earthquake.

George Bergeron correctly identified the earthquake, and well he might have—for many was the time his own home had danced to the same crashing tune. "My God—" said George, "that must be Harrison!"

The realization was blasted from his mind instantly by the sound of an automobile collision in his head.

When George could open his eyes again, the photograph of Harrison was gone. A living, breathing Harrison filled the screen.

Clanking, clownish, and huge, Harrison stood in the center of the studio. The knob of the uprooted studio door was still in his hand. Ballerinas, technicians, musicians, and announcers cowered on their knees before him, expecting to die.

"I am the Emperor!" cried Harrison. "Do you hear? I am the Emperor! Everybody must do what I say at once!" He stamped his foot and the studio shook.

"Even as I stand here—" he bellowed, "crippled, hobbled, sickened—I am a greater ruler than any man who ever lived! Now watch me become what I *can* become!"

Harrison tore the straps of his handicap harness like wet tissue paper, tore straps guaranteed to support five thousand pounds.

Harrison's scrap-iron handicaps crashed to the floor.

Harrison thrust his thumbs under the bar of the padlock that secured his head harness. The bar snapped like celery. Harrison smashed his headphones and spectacles against the wall.

He flung away his rubber-ball nose, revealed a man that would have awed Thor, the god of thunder.

"I shall now select my Empress!" he said, looking down on the cowering people. "Let the first woman who dares rise to her feet claim her mate and her throne!"

A moment passed, and then a ballerina arose, swaying like a willow.

Harrison plucked the mental handicap from her ear, snapped off her physical handicaps with marvelous delicacy. Last of all, he removed her mask.

She was blindingly beautiful.

"Now—" said Harrison, taking her hand, "shall we show the people the meaning of the word dance? Music!" he commanded.

The musicians scrambled back into their chairs, and Harrison stripped them of their handicaps, too. "Play your best," he told them, "and I'll make you barons and dukes and earls."

The music began. It was normal at first—cheap, silly, false. But Harrison snatched two musicians from their chairs, waved them like batons as he sang the music as he wanted it played. He slammed them back into their chairs.

The music began again and was much improved.

Harrison and his Empress merely listened to the music for a while listened gravely, as though synchronizing their heartbeats with it.

They shifted their weights to their toes.

Harrison placed his big hands on the girl's tiny waist, letting her sense the weightlessness that would soon be hers.

And then, in an explosion of joy and grace, into the air they sprang!

Not only were the laws of the land abandoned, but the law of gravity and the laws of motion as well.

They reeled, whirled, swiveled, flounced, capered, gamboled, and spun.

They leaped like deer on the moon.

The studio ceiling was thirty feet high, but each leap brought the dancers nearer to it.

It became their obvious intention to kiss the ceiling.

They kissed it.

And then, neutralizing gravity with love and pure will, they remained suspended in air inches below the ceiling, and they kissed each other for a long, long time.

It was then that Diana Moon Glampers, the Handicapper General, came into the studio with a double-barreled ten-gauge shotgun. She fired twice, and the Emperor and the Empress were dead before they hit the floor.

Diana Moon Glampers loaded the gun again. She aimed it at the musicians and told them they had ten seconds to get their handicaps back on.

It was then that the Bergerons' television tube burned out.

Hazel turned to comment about the blackout to George. But George had gone out into the kitchen for a can of beer.

George came back in with the beer, paused while a handicap signal shook him up. And then he sat down again. "You been crying?" he said to Hazel.

"Yup," she said.

"What about?" he said.

"I forget," she said. "Something real sad on television."

"What was it?" he said.

"It's all kind of mixed up in my mind," said Hazel.

"Forget sad things," said George.

"I always do," said Hazel.

"That's my girl," said George. He winced. There was the sound of a riveting gun in his head.

"Gee—I could tell that one was a doozy," said Hazel.

"You can say that again," said George.

"Gee—" said Hazel, "I could tell that one was a doozy."

92

Thomas Jefferson

The Natural Aristocracy (1813)

JEFFERSON TO ADAMS

. . . For I agree with you that there is a natural aristocracy among men. The grounds of this are virtue and talents. Formerly bodily powers gave place among the aristoi. But since the invention of gunpowder has armed the weak as well as the strong with missile death, bodily strength, like beauty, good humor, politeness and other accomplishments, has become but an auxiliary ground of distinction. There is also an artificial aristocracy founded on wealth and birth, without either virtue or talents; for with these it would belong to the first class. The natural aristocracy I consider as the most precious gift of nature for the instruction, the trusts, and government of society. And indeed it would have been inconsistent in creation to have formed man for the social state, and not to have provided virtue and wisdom enough to manage the concerns of the society. May we not even say that that form of government is the best which provides the most effectually for a pure selection of these natural aristoi into the offices of government?

From *The Adams-Jefferson Letters*. Vol. 11, Lester J. Cappon, ed., University of North Carolina Press, 1959.

The artificial aristocracy is a mischievous ingredient in government, and provision should be made to prevent it's ascendancy. On the question, What is the best provision, you and I differ; but we differ as rational friends, using the free exercise of our own reason, and mutually indulging its errors. *You* think it best to put the Pseudo-aristoi into a separate chamber of legislation where they may be hindered from doing mischief by their coordinate branches, and where also they may be a protection to wealth against the Agrarian and plundering enterprises of the Majority of the people. I think that to give them power in order to prevent them from doing mischief, is arming them for it, and increasing instead of remedying the evil. For if the coordinate branches can arrest their action, so may they that of the coordinates. Mischief may be done negatively as well as positively. Of this a cabal in the Senate of the U.S. has furnished many proofs. Nor do I believe them necessary to protect the wealthy; because enough of these will find their way into every branch of the legislation to protect themselves. From 15 to 20 legislatures of our own, in action for 30 years past, have proved that no fears of an equalisation of property are to be apprehended from them.

I think the best remedy is exactly that provided by all our constitutions, to leave to the citizens the free election and separation of the aristoi from the pseudo-aristoi, of the wheat from the chaff. In general they will elect the real good and wise. In some instances, wealth may corrupt, and birth blind them; but not in sufficient degree to endanger the society.

It is probable that our difference of opinion may in some measure be produced by a difference of character in those among whom we live. From what I have seen of Massachusetts and Connecticut myself, and still more from what I have heard and the character given of the former by yourself, who know them so much better, there seems to be in these two states a traditionary reverence for certain families, which has rendered the offices of the government nearly hereditary in those families. I presume that from an early period of your history, members of these families happening to possess virtue and talents, have honestly exercised them for the good of the people, and by their services have endeared their names to them. . . .

At the first session of our legislature after the Declaration of Independence, we passed a law abolishing entails. And this was followed by one abolishing the privilege of Primogeniture, and dividing the lands of intestates equally among all their children, or other representatives. These laws, drawn by myself, laid the axe to the root of Pseudo-aristocracy. And had another which I prepared been adopted by the legislature, our work would have been complete. It was a Bill for more general diffusion of learning. This proposed to divide every county into wards of 5 or 6 miles square, like your townships; to establish in each ward a free school for reading, writing and common arithmetic; to provide for the annual selection of the best subjects from these schools who might receive at the public expense a higher degree of education at a district school; and from these district schools to select a certain number of the most promising subjects to be completed at an University, where all the useful sciences should be taught. Worth and genius would thus have been sought out from every condition of life, and completely prepared by education for defeating the competition of wealth and birth for public trusts.

My proposition had for a further object to impart to these wards those portions of self-government for which they are best qualified, by confiding to them the care of their poor, their roads, police, elections, the nomination of jurors, administration of justice in small cases, elementary exercises of militia, in short, to have made them little republics, with a Warden at the head of each, for all those concerns which, being under their eye, they would better manage than the larger republics of the county or state. A general call of ward-meetings by their Wardens on the same day thro' the state would at any time produce the genuine sense of the people on any required point, and would enable the state to act in mass, as your people have so often done, and with so much effect, by their town meetings. The law for religious freedom, which made a part of this system, having put down the aristocracy of the clergy, and restored to the citizen the freedom of the mind, and those of entails and descents nurturing an equality of condition among them, this on Education would have raised the mass of the people to the high ground of moral respectability necessary to their own safety, and to orderly government; and would have completed the great object of qualifying them to select the veritable aristoi, for the trusts of government, to the exclusion of the Pseudalists: and the same Theognis who has furnished the epigraphs of your two letters assures us that 'ουδεμιαν' πω Κυρν' αγαθοι πολιν ωλεσαν ανδρεσ ["Curnis, good men have never harmed any city"]'. Altho' this law has not yet been acted on but in a small and inefficient degree, it is still considered as before the legislature, with other bills of the revised code, not yet taken up, and I have great hope that some patriotic spirit will, at a favorable moment, call it up, and make it the key-stone of the arch of our government.

With respect to Aristocracy, we should further consider that, before the establishment of the American states, nothing was known to History but the Man of the old world, crowded within limits either small or overcharged, and steeped in the vices which that situation generates. A government adapted to such men would be one thing; but a very different one than for the Man of these states. Here every one may have land to labor for himself if he chuses; or, preferring the exercise of any other industry, may exact for it such compensation as not only to afford a comfortable subsistence, but wherewith to provide for a cessation from labor in old age. Every one, by his property, or by his satisfactory situation, is interested in the support of law and order. And such men may safely and advantageously reserve to themselves a wholesome control over their public affairs, and a degree of freedom, which in the hands of the Canaille of the cities of

Europe, would be instantly perverted to the demolition and destruction of every thing public and private. The history of the last 25 years of France, and of the last 40 years in America, nay of it's last 200 years, proves the truth of both parts of this observation.

But even in Europe a change has sensibly taken place in the mind of Man. Science had liberated the ideas of those who read and reflect, and the American example had kindled feelings of right in the people. An insurrection has consequently begun, of science, talents and courage against rank and birth, which have fallen into contempt. It has failed in it's first effort, because the mobs of the cities, the instrument used for it's accomplishment, debased by ignorance, poverty and vice, could not be restrained to rational action. But the world will recover from the panic of this first catastrophe. Science is progressive, and talents and enterprize on the alert. Resort may be had to the people of the country, a more governable power from their principles and subordination; and rank, and birth, and tinsel-aristocracy will finally shrink into insignificance, even there. This however we have no right to meddle with. It suffices for us, if the moral and physical condition of our own citizens qualifies them to select the able and good for the direction of their government, with a recurrence of elections at such short periods as will enable them to displace an unfaithful servant before the mischief he meditates may be irremediable. . . .

93

Alexis de Tocqueville

Why So Many Ambitious Men and So Little Lofty Ambition Are to Be Found in the United States (1840)

The first thing that strikes a traveler in the United States is the innumerable multitude of those who seek to emerge from their original condition; and the second is the rarity of lofty ambition to be observed in the midst of the universally ambitious stir of society. No Americans are devoid of a yearning desire to rise, but hardly any appear to entertain hopes of great magnitude or to drive at

From *Democracy in America* by Alexis de Tocqueville, translated by Henry Reeve, 1862, with minor changes.

very lofty aims. All are constantly seeking to acquire property, power, and reputation; few contemplate these things upon a great scale; and this is the more surprising as nothing is to be discerned in the manners or laws of America to limit desire or to prevent it from spreading its impulses in every direction. . . .

What chiefly diverts the men of democracies from lofty ambition is not the scantiness of their fortunes, but the vehemence of the exertions they daily make to improve them. They strain their faculties to the utmost to achieve paltry results, and this cannot fail speedily to limit their discernment and to circumscribe their powers. They might be much poorer and still be greater.

The small number of opulent citizens who are to be found amidst a democracy do not constitute an exception to this rule. A man who raises himself by degrees to wealth and power contracts, in the course of this protracted labor, habits of prudence and restraint which he cannot afterwards shake off. A man cannot enlarge his mind as he does his house. . . .

In a democratic society, as well as elsewhere, there is only a certain number of great fortunes to be made; and as the paths that lead to them are indiscriminately open to all, the progress of all must necessarily be slackened. As the candidates appear to be nearly alike, and as it is difficult to make a selection without infringing the principle of equality, which is the supreme law of democratic societies, the first idea which suggests itself is to make them all advance at the same rate and submit to the same probation. . . . From hatred of privilege and from the embarrassment of choosing, all men are at last constrained, whatever may be their standard, to pass the same ordeal; all are indiscriminately subjected to a multitude of petty preliminary exercises, in which their youth is wasted and their imagination quenched, so that they despair of ever fully attaining what is held out to them; and when at length they are in a condition to perform any extraordinary acts, the taste for such things has forsaken them.

In China, where the equality of conditions is exceedingly great and very ancient, no man passes from one public office to another without undergoing a probationary trial. This probation occurs afresh at every stage of his career; and the notion is now so rooted in the manners of the people that I remember to have read a Chinese novel in which the hero, after numberless crosses, succeeds at length in touching the heart of his mistress by taking honors. A lofty ambition breathes with difficulty in such an atmosphere.

I confess that I apprehend much less for democratic society from the boldness that from the mediocrity of desires. What appears to me most to be dreaded is that in the midst of the small, incessant occupations of private life, ambition should lose its vigor and its greatness; that the passions of man should abate, but at the same time be lowered; so that the march of society should every day become more tranquil and less aspiring.

I think, then, that the leaders of modern society would be wrong to seek to lull the community by a state of too uniform and too peaceful happiness, and that it is well to expose it from time to time to matters of difficulty and danger in order to raise ambition and to give it a field of action.

Moralists are constantly complaining that the ruling vice of the present time is pride. This is true in one sense, for indeed everyone thinks that he is better than his neighbor or refuses to obey his superior; but it is extremely false in another, for the same man who cannot endure subordination or equality has so contemptible an opinion of himself that he thinks he is born only to indulge in vulgar pleasures. He willingly takes up with low desires without daring to embark on lofty enterprises, of which he scarcely dreams.

Thus, far from thinking that humility ought to be preached to our contemporaries, I would have endeavors made to give them a more enlarged idea of themselves and of their kind. Humility is unwholesome to them; what they most want is, in my opinion, pride. I would willingly exchange several of our small virtues for this one vice.

Appendix

The Constitution of the United States of America

We the People of the United States, in Order to form a more perfect Union, establish Justice, insure domestic Tranquillity, provide for the common defence, promote the general Welfare, and secure the Blessings of Liberty to ourselves and our Posterity, do ordain and establish this Constitution for the United States of America.

ARTICLE. I.

Section. 1. All legislative Powers herein granted shall be vested in a Congress of the United States, which shall consist of a Senate and House of Representatives.

Section. 2. The House of Representatives shall be composed of Members chosen every second Year by the People of the several States, and the Electors in each State shall have the Qualifications requisite for Electors of the most numerous Branch of the State Legislature.

No Person shall be a Representative who shall not have attained to the age of twenty-five Years, and been seven Years a Citizen of the United States, and who shall not, when elected, be an Inhabitant of that State in which he shall be chosen.

Representatives and direct Taxes shall be apportioned among the several States which may be included within this Union, according to their respective Numbers, which shall be determined by adding to the whole Number of free Persons, including those bound to Service for a Term of Years, and excluding Indians not taxed, three-fifths of all other Persons. The actual Enumeration shall be made within three Years after the first Meeting of the Congress of the United States, and within every subsequent Term of ten Years, in such Manner as they shall by Law direct. The Number of Representatives shall not exceed one for every thirty Thousand, but each State shall have at Least one Representative; and until such enumeration shall be made, the State of New Hampshire shall be entitled to chuse three, Massachusetts eight, Rhode-Island and Providence Plantations one, Connecticut five,

New York six, New Jersey four, Pennsylvania eight, Delaware one, Maryland six, Virginia ten, North Carolina five, South Carolina five, and Georgia three.

When vacancies happen in the Representation from any State, the Executive Authority thereof shall issue Writs of Election to fill such Vacancies.

The House of Representatives shall chuse their Speaker and other Officers; and shall have the sole Power of Impeachment.

Section. 3. The Senate of the United States shall be composed of two Senators from each State, chosen by the Legislature thereof, for six Years; and each Senator shall have one Vote.

Immediately after they shall be assembled in Consequence of the first Election, they shall be divided as equally as may be into three Classes. The Seats of the Senators of the first Class shall be vacated at the Expiration of the second Year, of the second Class at the Expiration of the fourth Year, and of the third Class at the Expiration of the sixth Year, so that one third may be chosen every second Year; and if Vacancies happen by Resignation, or otherwise, during the Recess of the Legislature of any State, the Executive thereof may make temporary Appointments until the next Meeting of the Legislature, which shall then fill such Vacancies.

No Person shall be a Senator who shall not have attained to the Age of thirty Years, and been nine Years a Citizen of the United States, and who shall not, when elected, be an Inhabitant of that State for which he shall be chosen.

The Vice President of the United States shall be President of the Senate, but shall have no Vote, unless they be equally divided.

The Senate shall chuse their other Officers, and also a President pro tempore, in the Absence of the Vice President, or when he shall exercise the Office of President of the United States.

The Senate shall have the sole Power to try all Impeachments. When sitting for that Purpose, they shall be on Oath or Affirmation. When the President of the United States is tried the Chief Justice shall preside: And no Person shall be convicted without the Concurrence of two thirds of the Members present.

Judgment in Cases of Impeachment shall not extend further than to removal from Office, and disqualification to hold and enjoy any Office of honor, Trust or Profit under the United States: but the Party convicted shall nevertheless be liable and subject to Indictment, Trial, Judgment and Punishment, according to Law.

Section. 4. The Times, Places and Manner of holding Elections for Senators and Representatives, shall be prescribed in each State by the Legislature thereof; but the Congress may at any time by Law make or alter such Regulations, except as to the Places of chusing Senators.

The Congress shall assemble at least once in every Year, and such Meeting shall be on the first Monday in December, unless they shall by Law appoint a different Day.

Section. 5. Each House shall be the Judge of the Elections, Returns and Qualifications of its own Members, and a Majority of each shall constitute a Quorum to do Business; but a smaller Number may adjourn from day to day, and may be authorized to compel the Attendance of absent Members, in such Manner, and under such Penalties as each House may provide.

Each House may determine the Rules of its Proceedings, punish its Members for disorderly Behaviour, and, with the Concurrence of two-thirds, expel a Member.

Each House shall keep a Journal of its Proceedings, and from time to time publish the same, excepting such Parts as may in their Judgment require Secrecy; and the Yeas and Nays of the Members of either House on any question shall, at the Desire of one-fifth of those Present, be entered on the Journal.

Neither House, during the Session of Congress, shall, without the Consent of the other, adjourn for more than three days, nor to any other Place than that in which the two Houses shall be sitting.

Section. 6. The Senators and Representatives shall receive a Compensation for their Services, to be ascertained by Law, and paid out of the Treasury of the United States. They shall in all Cases, except Treason, Felony and Breach of the Peace, be privileged from Arrest during their Attendance at the Session of their respective Houses, and in going to and returning from the same; and for any Speech or Debate in either House, they shall not be questioned in any other Place.

No Senator or Representative shall, during the Time for which he was elected, be appointed to any civil Office under the Authority of the United States, which shall have been created, or the Emoluments whereof shall have been encreased during such time; and no Person holding any Office under the United States, shall be a Member of either House during his Continuance in Office.

Section. 7. All Bills for raising Revenue shall originate in the House of Representatives; but the Senate may propose or concur with amendments as on other Bills.

Every Bill which shall have passed the House of Representatives and the Senate, shall, before it become a Law, be presented to the President of the United States; If he approve he shall sign it, but if not he shall return it, with his Objections to that House in which it shall have originated, who shall enter the Objections at large on their Journal, and proceed to reconsider it. If after such Reconsideration two thirds of that House shall agree to pass the Bill, it shall be sent, together with the Objections, to the other House, by which it shall likewise be reconsidered, and if approved by two thirds of that House, it shall become a Law. But in all such Cases the Votes of both Houses shall be determined by yeas and Nays, and the Names of the Persons voting for and against the Bill shall be entered on the Journal of each House respectively. If any Bill shall not be returned by the President within ten Days (Sunday excepted) after it shall have been presented to him, the Same shall be a Law, in like Manner as if he had signed it, unless the Congress by their Adjournment prevent its Return, in which Case it shall not be a Law.

Every Order, Resolution, or Vote to which the Concurrence of the Senate and House of Representatives may be necessary (except on a question of Adjournment) shall be presented to the President of the United States; and before the Same shall take Effect, shall be approved by him, or being disapproved by him, shall be repassed by two thirds of the Senate and House of Representatives, according to the Rules and Limitations prescribed in the Case of a Bill.

Section. 8. The Congress shall have Power To lay and collect Taxes, Duties, Imposts, and Excises, to pay the Debts and provide for the common Defence and general Welfare of the United States; but all Duties, Imposts and Excises shall be uniform throughout the United States;

To borrow Money on the credit of the United States;

To regulate Commerce with foreign Nations, and among the several States, and with the Indian Tribes;

To establish an uniform Rule of Naturalization, and uniform Laws on the subject of Bankruptcies throughout the United States;

To coin Money, regulate the Value thereof, and of foreign Coin, and fix the Standard of Weights and Measures;

To provide for the Punishment of counterfeiting the Securities and current Coin of the United States; To establish Post Offices and Post Roads;

To promote the Progress of Science and useful Arts, by securing for limited Times to Authors and Inventors the exclusive Right to their respective Writings and Discoveries;

To constitute Tribunals inferior to the supreme Court;

To define and punish Piracies and Felonies committed on the high Seas, and Offences against the Law of Nations;

To declare War, grant Letters of Marque and Reprisal, and make Rules concerning Captures on Land and Water;

To raise and support Armies, but no Appropriation of Money to that Use shall be for a longer Term than two Years;

To provide and maintain a Navy;

To make Rules for the Government and Regulation of the land and naval Forces;

To provide for calling forth the Militia to execute the Laws of the Union, suppress Insurrections and repel Invasions;

To provide for organizing, arming, and disciplining, the Militia, and for governing such Part of them as may be employed in the Service of the United States, reserving to the States respectively, the Appointment of the Officers, and the Authority of training the Militia according to the discipline prescribed by Congress;

To exercise exclusive Legislation in all Cases whatsoever, over such District (not exceeding ten Miles square) as may, by Cession of Particular States, and the Acceptance of Congress, become the Seat of the Government of the United States, and to exercise like Authority over all Places purchased by the Consent of the Legislature of the State in which the Same shall be, for the Erection of Forts, Magazines, Arsenals, dock-Yards, and other needful Buildings;—And

To make all Laws which shall be necessary and proper for carrying into Execution the foregoing Powers, and all other Powers vested by this Constitution in the Government of the United States, or in any Department or Officer thereof.

Section. 9. The Migration or Importation of such Persons as any of the States now existing shall think proper to admit, shall not be prohibited by the Congress prior to the Year one thousand eight hundred and eight, but a Tax or duty may be imposed on such Importation, not exceeding ten dollars for each Person.

The Privilege of the Writ of Habeas Corpus shall not be suspended, unless when in Cases of Rebellion or Invasion the public Safety may require it.

No Bill of Attainder or ex post facto Law shall be passed.

No Capitation, or other direct, Tax shall be laid, unless in Proportion to the Census of Enumeration herein before directed to be taken.

No Tax or Duty shall be laid on Articles exported from any State.

No Preference shall be given by any Regulation of Commerce or Revenue to the Ports of one State over those of another; nor shall Vessels bound to, or from, one State, be obliged to enter, clear or pay Duties in another.

No Money shall be drawn from the Treasury, but in Consequence of Appropriations made by Law; and a regular Statement and Account of the Receipts and Expenditures of all public Money shall be published from time to time.

No Title of Nobility shall be granted by the United States; And no Person holding any Office of Profit or Trust under them, shall, without the Consent of the Congress, accept of any present, Emolument, Office, or Title, of any kind whatever, from any King, Prince, or foreign State.

Section. 10. No State shall enter into any Treaty, Alliance, or Confederation; grant Letters of Marque and Reprisal; coin Money; emit Bills of Credit; make any Thing but gold and silver Coin a Tender in Payment of Debts; pass any Bill of Attainder, ex post facto Law, or Law impairing the Obligation of Contracts, or grant any Title of Nobility.

No State shall, without the Consent of the Congress, lay any Imposts or Duties on Imports or Exports, except what may be absolutely necessary for executing its inspection Laws; and the net Produce of all Duties and Imposts, laid by any State on Imports or Exports, shall be for the Use of the Treasury of the United States; and all such Laws shall be subject to the Revision and Controul of the Congress.

No State shall, without the Consent of Congress, lay any Duty of Tonnage, keep Troops, or Ships of War in time of Peace, enter into any Agreement or Compact with another State, or with a foreign Power, or engage in War, unless actually invaded, or in such imminent Danger as will not admit of delay.

Article. II.

Section. 1. The executive Power shall be vested in a President of the United States of America. He shall hold his Office during the Term of four Years, and, together with the Vice President, chosen for the same Term, be elected, as follows

Each State shall appoint, in such Manner as the Legislature thereof may direct, a Number of Electors, equal to the whole Number of Senators and Representatives to which the State may be entitled in the Congress: but no Senator or Representative, or Person holding an Office of Trust or Profit under the United States, shall be appointed an Elector.

The Electors shall meet in their respective States, and vote by Ballot for two Persons, of whom one at least shall not be an Inhabitant of the same State with themselves. And they shall make a List of all the Persons voted for, and of the Number of Votes for each; which List they shall sign and certify, and transmit sealed to the Seat of the Government of the United States, directed to the President of the Senate. The President of the Senate shall, in the Presence of the Senate and House of Representatives, open all the Certificates, and the Votes shall then be counted. The Person having the greatest Number of Votes shall be the President, if such Number be a Majority of the whole Number of Electors appointed; and if there be more than one who have such Majority, and have an equal Number of Votes, then the House of Representatives shall immediately chuse by Ballot one of them for President; and if no Person have a Majority, then from the five highest on the List the said House shall in like Manner chuse the President. But in chusing the President, the Votes shall be taken by States, the Representation from each State having one Vote; a quorum for this Purpose shall consist of a Member or Members from two thirds of the States, and a Majority of all the States shall be necessary to a Choice. In every Case, after the Choice of the President, the Person having the greatest Number of Votes of the Electors shall be the Vice President. But if there should remain two or more who have equal Votes, the Senate shall chose from them by Ballot the Vice President.

The Congress may determine the Time of chusing the Electors, and the Day on which they shall give their votes; which Day shall be the same throughout the United States.

No Person except a natural born Citizen, or a Citizen of the United States, at the time of the Adoption of this Constitution, shall be eligible to the Office of President; neither shall any person be eligible to that Office who shall not have attained to the Age of thirty five Years, and been fourteen Years a Resident within the United States.

In Case of the Removal of the President from Office, or of his Death, Resignation, or Inability to discharge the Powers and Duties of the said Office, the Same shall devolve on the Vice President, and the Congress may by Law provide for the Case of Removal, Death, Resignation or Inability, both of the President and Vice President, declaring what Officer shall then act as President, and such Officer shall act accordingly, until the Disability be removed, or a President shall be elected.

The President shall, at stated Times, receive for his Services, a Compensation, which shall neither be encreased nor diminished during the Period for which he shall have been elected, and he shall not receive within that Period any other Emolument from the United States, or any of them.

Before he enter on the Execution of his Office, he shall take the following Oath or Affirmation:—"I do solemnly swear (or affirm) that I will faithfully execute the Office of President of the United States, and will to the best of my Ability, preserve, protect and defend the Constitution of the United States."

Section. 2. The President shall be Commander in Chief of the Army and Navy of the United States, and of the Militia of the several States, when called into the actual Service of the United States; he may require the Opinion, in writing, of the principal Officer in each of the executive Departments, upon any Subject relating to the Duties of their respective Offices, and he shall have Power to grant Reprieves and Pardons for Offenses against the United States, except in Cases of Impeachment.

He shall have Power, by and with the Advice and Consent of the Senate, to make Treaties, provided two thirds of the Senators present concur; and he shall nominate, and by and with the Advice and Consent of the Senate, shall appoint Ambassadors, other public Ministers and Consuls, Judges of the supreme Court, and all other Officers of the United States, whose Appointments are not herein otherwise provided for, and which shall be established by Law; but the Congress may by Law vest the Appointment of such inferior Officers, as they think proper, in the President alone, in the Courts of Law, or in the Heads of Departments.

The President shall have Power to fill up all Vacancies that may happen during the Recess of the Senate, by granting Commissions which shall expire at the End of their next Session.

Section. 3. He shall from time to time give to the Congress Information of the State of the Union, and recommend to their Consideration such Measures as he shall judge necessary and expedient; he may, on extraordinary Occasions, convene both Houses, or either of them, and in Case of Disagreement between them, with Respect to the Time of Adjournment, he may adjourn them to such Time as he shall think proper; he shall receive Ambassadors and other public Ministers; he shall take Care that the Laws be faithfully executed, and shall Commission all the Officers of the United States.

Section. 4. The President, Vice President and all Civil Officers of the United States, shall be removed from Office on Impeachment for, and Conviction of, Treason, Bribery, or other high Crimes and Misdemeanors.

Article. III.

Section. 1. The judicial Power of the United States, shall be vested in one supreme Court, and in such inferior Courts as the Congress may from time to time ordain and establish. The Judges, both of the supreme and inferior Courts, shall hold their Offices during good Behaviour, and shall, at stated Times, receive for their Services, a Compensation, which shall not be diminished during their Continuance in Office.

Section. 2. The judicial Power shall extend to all Cases, in Law and Equity, arising under this Constitution, the Laws of the United States, and Treaties made, or which shall be made, under their Authority;—to all Cases affecting Ambassadors, other public Ministers and Consuls;—to all Cases of admiralty and maritime Jurisdiction;—to Controversies to which the United States shall be a Party;—to Controversies between two or more States;—between a State and Citizens of another State;—between Citizens of different States;—between Citizens of the same State claiming Lands under Grants of different States, and between a State, or the Citizens thereof, and foreign States, Citizens or Subjects.

In all Cases affecting Ambassadors, other public Ministers and Consuls, and those in which a State shall be Party, the supreme Court shall have original Jurisdiction. In all the other Cases before mentioned, the supreme Court shall have appellate Jurisdiction, both as to Law and Fact, with such Exceptions, and under such Regulations as the Congress shall make.

The Trial of all Crimes, except in Cases of Impeachment, shall be by Jury; and such Trial shall be held in the State where the said Crimes shall have been committed; but when not committed within any State, the Trial shall be at such Place or Places as the Congress may by Law have directed.

Section. 3. Treason against the United States, shall consist only in levying War against them, or in adhering to their Enemies, giving them Aid and Comfort. No Person shall be convicted of Treason unless on the Testimony of two Witnesses to the same overt Act, or on Confession in open Court. The Congress shall have Power to declare the Punishment of Treason, but no Attainder of Treason shall work Corruption of Blood, or Forfeiture except during the Life of the Person attainted.

Article. IV.

Section. 1. Full Faith and Credit shall be given in each State to the public Acts, Records, and judicial Proceedings of every other State. And the Congress may by general Laws prescribe the Manner in which such Acts, Records and Proceedings shall be proved, and the Effect thereof.

Section. 2. The Citizens of each State shall be entitled to all Privileges and Immunities of Citizens in the several States.

A Person charged in any State with Treason, Felony, or other Crime, who shall flee from Justice, and be found in another State, shall on Demand of the executive Authority of the State from which he fled, be delivered up, to be removed to the State having Jurisdiction of the Crime.

No Person held to Service or Labour in one State, under the Laws thereof, escaping into another, shall, in Consequence of any Law or Regulation therein, be discharged from such Service or Labour, but shall be delivered up on Claim of the Party to whom such Service or Labour may be due.

Section. 3. New States may be admitted by the Congress into this Union; but no new State shall be formed or erected within the Jurisdiction of any other State; nor any State be formed by the Junction of two or more States, or Parts of States, without the Consent of the Legislatures of the States concerned as well as of the Congress.

The Congress shall have Power to dispose of and make all needful Rules and Regulations respecting the Territory or other Property belonging to the United States; and nothing in this Constitution shall be so construed as to Prejudice any Claims of the United States, or of any particular State.

Section. 4. The United States shall guarantee to every State in this Union a Republican Form of Government, and shall protect each of them against Invasion; and on Application of the Legislature, or of the Executive (when the Legislature cannot be convened) against domestic Violence.

ARTICLE. V.

The Congress, whenever two thirds of both Houses shall deem it necessary, shall propose Amendments to this Constitution, or, on the Application of the Legislatures of two thirds of the several States, shall call a Convention for proposing Amendments, which, in either Case, shall be valid to all Intents and Purposes, as Part of this Constitution, when ratified by the Legislatures of three fourths of the several States, or by Conventions in three fourths thereof, as the one or the other Mode of Ratification may be proposed by the Congress; Provided that no Amendment which may be made prior to the Year One thousand eight hundred and eight shall in any Manner affect the first and fourth Clauses in the Ninth Section of the first Article; and that no State, without its Consent, shall be deprived of its equal Suffrage in the Senate.

ARTICLE. VI.

All Debts contracted and Engagements entered into, before the Adoption of this Constitution, shall be as valid against the United States under this Constitution, as under the Confederation.

This Constitution, and the Laws of the United States which shall be made in Pursuance thereof; and all Treaties made, or which shall be made, under the Authority of the United States, shall be the supreme Law of the Land; and the Judges in every State shall be bound thereby, any Thing in the Constitution or Laws of any State to the Contrary notwithstanding.

The Senators and Representatives before mentioned, and the Members of the several State Legislatures, and all executive and judicial Officers, both of the United States and of the several States, shall be bound by Oath or Affirmation, to support this Constitution; but no religious Test shall ever be required as a Qualification to any Office or public Trust under the United States.

ARTICLE. VII.

The Ratification of the Conventions of nine States, shall be sufficient for the Establishment of this Constitution between the States so ratifying the Same.

done in Convention by the Unanimous Consent of the States present the Seventeenth Day of September in the Year of our Lord one thousand seven hundred and Eighty seven and of the Independence of the United States of America the Twelfth In witness where of We have hereunto subscribed our Names, Go. Washington—President. and deputy from Virginia

AMENDMENTS TO THE CONSTITUTION

Amendment [I]*

Congress shall make no law respecting an establishment of religion, or prohibiting the free exercise thereof; or abridging the freedom of speech, or of the press; or the right of the People peaceably to assemble, and to petition the Government for a redress of grievances.
[Ratified December 15, 1791]

Amendment [II]

A well regulated Militia, being necessary to the security of a free State, the right of the people to keep and bear Arms, shall not be infringed.
[Ratified December 15, 1791]

Amendment [III]

No Soldier shall, in time of peace be quartered in any house, without the consent of the Owner, nor in time of war, but in a manner to be prescribed by law.
[Ratified December 15, 1791]

---

* Brackets enclosing an amendment number indicate that the number was not specifically assigned in the resolution proposing the amendment.

Amendment [IV]

The right of the people to be secure in their persons, houses, papers, and effects, against unreasonable searches and seizures, shall not be violated, and no Warrants shall issue, but upon probable cause, supported by Oath or affirmation, and particularly describing the place to be searched, and the persons or things to be seized.
[Ratified December 15, 1791]

Amendment [V]

No person shall be held to answer for a capital, or otherwise infamous crime, unless on a presentment or indictment of a Grand Jury, except in cases arising in the land or naval forces, or in the Militia, when in actual service in time of War or public danger; nor shall any person be subject for the same offence to be twice put in jeopardy of life or limb; nor shall be compelled in any criminal case to be a witness against himself, nor be deprived of life, liberty, or property, without due process of law; nor shall private property be taken for public use, without just compensation.
[Ratified December 15, 1791]

Amendment [VI]

In all criminal prosecutions, the accused shall enjoy the right to a speedy and public trial, by an impartial jury of the State and district wherein the crime shall have been committed, which district shall have been previously ascertained by law, and to be informed of the nature and cause of the accusation; to be confronted with the witnesses against him; to have compulsory process for obtaining witnesses in his favor, and to have the Assistance of Counsel for his defence.
[Ratified December 15, 1791]

Amendment [VII]

In Suits at common law, where the value in controversy shall exceed twenty dollars, the right of trial by jury shall be preserved, and no fact tried by a jury, shall be otherwise re-examined in any Court of the United States, than according to the rules of the common law.
[Ratified December 15, 1791]

Amendment [VIII]

Excessive bail shall not be required, nor excessive fines imposed, nor cruel and unusual punishments inflicted.
[Ratified December 15, 1791]

Amendment [IX]

The enumeration in the Constitution, of certain rights, shall not be construed to deny or disparage others retained by the people.
[Ratified December 15, 1791]

Amendment [X]

The powers not delegated to the United States by the Constitution, nor prohibited by it to the States, are reserved to the States respectively, or to the people.
[Ratified December 15, 1791]

Amendment [XI]

The Judicial power of the United States shall not be construed to extend to any suit in law or equity, commenced or prosecuted against one of the United States by Citizens of another State, or by Citizens or Subjects of any Foreign State.
[Ratified January 23, 1798]

Amendment [XII]

The Electors shall meet in their respective states and vote by ballot for President and Vice-President, one of whom, at least, shall not be an inhabitant of the same state with themselves; they shall name in their ballots the person voted for as President, and in distinct ballots the person voted for as Vice-President, and they shall make distinct lists of all persons voted for as President, and of all persons voted for as Vice-President, and of the number of votes for each, which lists they shall sign and certify, and transmit sealed to the seat of the government of the United States, directed to the President of the Senate;—The President of the Senate shall, in the presence of the Senate and House of Representatives, open all the certificates and the votes shall then be counted;—The person having the greatest number of votes for President, shall be the President, if such number be a majority of the whole number of Electors appointed; and if no person have such majority, then from the persons having the highest numbers not exceeding three on the list of those voted for as President, the House of Representatives shall choose immediately by ballot, the President. But in choosing the President, the votes shall be taken by states, the representation from each state having one vote; a quorum for this purpose shall consist of a member or members from two-thirds of the states, and a majority of all the states shall be necessary to a choice. And if the House of Representatives shall not choose a President whenever the right of choice shall devolve upon them, before the fourth day of March next following, then the Vice-President shall act as President, as in the case of the death or other constitutional disability of the President.—The

person having the greatest number of votes as Vice-President, shall be the Vice-President, if such number be a majority of the whole number of Electors appointed, and if no person have a majority, then from the two highest numbers on the list, the Senate shall choose the Vice-President; a quorum for the purpose shall consist of two-thirds of the whole number of Senators, and a majority of the whole number shall be necessary to a choice. But no person constitutionally ineligible to the office of President shall be eligible to that of Vice-President of the United States.
[Ratified June 15, 1804]

Amendment [XIII]

Section 1. Neither slavery nor involuntary servitude, except as a punishment for crime whereof the party shall have been duly convicted, shall exist within the United States, or any place subject to their jurisdiction.

Section 2. Congress shall have power to enforce this article by appropriate legislation.
[Ratified December 6, 1865]

Amendment [XIV]

Section 1. All persons born or naturalized in the United States and subject to the jurisdiction thereof, are citizens of the United States and of the State wherein they reside. No State shall make or enforce any law which shall abridge the privileges or immunities of citizens of the United States; nor shall any State deprive any person of life, liberty, or property, without due process of law; nor deny to any person within its jurisdiction the equal protection of the laws.

Section 2. Representatives shall be apportioned among the several States according to their respective numbers, counting the whole number of persons in each State, excluding Indians not taxed. But when the right to vote at any election for the choice of electors for President and Vice President of the United States, Representatives in Congress, the Executive and Judicial officers of a State, or the members of the Legislature thereof, is denied to any of the male inhabitants of such State, being twenty-one years of age, and citizens of the United States, or in any way abridged, except for participation in rebellion, or other crime, the basis of representation therein shall be reduced in the proportion which the number of such male citizens shall bear to the whole number of male citizens twenty-one years of age in such State.

Section 3. No person shall be a Senator or Representative in Congress, or elector of President and Vice President, or hold any office, civil or military, under the United States, or under any State, who, having previously taken an oath, as a member of Congress, or as an officer of the United States, or as a member of any State legislature, or as an executive or judicial officer of any State, to support the Constitution of the United States, shall have engaged in insurrection or rebellion against the same, or given aid or comfort to the enemies thereof. But Congress may by a vote of two-thirds of each House, remove such disability.

Section 4. The validity of the public debt of the United States, authorized by law, including debts incurred for payment of pensions and bounties for services in suppressing insurrection or rebellion, shall not be questioned. But neither the United States nor any State shall assume or pay any debt or obligation incurred in aid of insurrection or rebellion against the United States, or any claim for the loss or emancipation of any slave; but all such debts, obligations and claims shall be held illegal and void.

Section 5. The Congress shall have power to enforce, by appropriate legislation, the provisions of this article.
[Ratified July 9, 1868]

Amendment [XV]

Section 1. The right of citizens of the United States to vote shall not be denied or abridged by the United States or by any State on account of race, color, or previous condition of servitude.

Section 2. The Congress shall have power to enforce this article by appropriate legislation.
[Ratified February 2, 1870]

Amendment [XVI]

The Congress shall have power to lay and collect taxes on incomes, from whatever source derived, without apportionment among the several States, and without regard to any census or enumeration.
[Ratified February 3, 1913]

Amendment [XVII]

The Senate of the United States shall be composed of two Senators from each State, elected by the people thereof, for six years; and each Senator shall have one vote. The electors in each State shall have the qualifications requisite for electors of the most numerous branch of the State legislatures.

When vacancies happen in the representation of any State in the Senate, the executive authority of such State shall issue writs of election to fill such vacancies; *Provided,* That the legislature of any State may empower the executive thereof to make temporary appointments until the people fill the vacancies by election as the legislature may direct.

This amendment shall not be so construed as to affect the election or term of any Senator chosen before it becomes valid as part of the Constitution. [Ratified April 8, 1913]

Amendment [XVIII]

Section 1. After one year from the ratification of this article the manufacture, sale, or transportation of intoxicating liquors within, the importation thereof into, or the exportation thereof from the United States and all territory subject to the jurisdiction thereof for beverage purposes is hereby prohibited.

Section 2. The Congress and the several States shall have concurrent power to enforce this article by appropriate legislation.

Section 3. This article shall be inoperative unless it shall have been ratified as an amendment to the Constitution by the legislatures of the several States, as provided in the Constitution, within seven years from the date of the submission hereof to the States by the Congress. [Ratified January 16, 1919]

Amendment [XIX]

The right of citizens of the United States to vote shall not be denied or abridged by the United States or by any State on account of sex.

Congress shall have power to enforce this article by appropriate legislation. [Ratified August 18, 1920]

Amendment [XX]

Section 1. The terms of the President and Vice President shall end at noon on the 20th day of January, and the terms of Senators and Representatives at noon on the 3d day of January, of the years in which such terms would have ended if this article had not been ratified; and the terms of their successors shall then begin.

Section 2. The Congress shall assemble at least once in every year, and such meeting shall begin at noon on the 3d day of January, unless they shall by law appoint a different day.

Section 3. If, at the time fixed for the beginning of the term of the President, the President elect shall have died, the Vice President elect shall become President. If a President shall not have been chosen before the time fixed for the beginning of his term, or if the President elect shall have failed to qualify, then the Vice President elect shall act as President until a President shall have qualified; and the Congress may by law provide for the case wherein neither a President elect nor a Vice President elect shall have qualified, declaring who shall then act as President, or the manner in which one who is to act shall be selected, and such person shall act accordingly until a President or Vice President shall have qualified.

Section 4. The Congress may by law provide for the case of the death of any of the persons for whom the House of Representatives may choose a President whenever the right of choice shall have devolved upon them, and for the case of the death of any of the persons from whom the Senate may choose a Vice President whenever the right of choice shall have devolved upon them.

Section 5. Sections 1 and 2 shall take effect on the 15th day of October following the ratification of this article.

Section 6. This article shall be inoperative unless it shall have been ratified as an amendment to the Constitution by the legislatures of three-fourths of the several States within seven years from the date of its submission. [Ratified January 23, 1933]

Amendment [XXI]

Section 1. The eighteenth article of amendment to the Constitution of the United States is hereby repealed.

Section 2. The transportation or importation into any State, Territory or possession of the United States for delivery or use therein of intoxicating liquors, in violation of the laws thereof, is hereby prohibited.

Section 3. This article shall be inoperative unless it shall have been ratified as an amendment to the Constitution by conventions in the several States, as provided in the Constitution, within seven years from the date of the submission thereof to the States by the Congress. [Ratified December 5, 1933]

Amendment [XXII]

Section 1. No person shall be elected to the office of the President more than twice, and no person who has held the office of President, or acted as President, for more than two years of a term to which some other person was elected President shall be elected to the office of the President more than once. But this Article shall not apply to any person holding the office of President when this Article was proposed by the Congress, and shall not prevent any person who may be holding the office of President, or acting as President, during the term within which this Article becomes operative from holding the office of President or acting as President during the remainder of such term.

Section 2. This Article shall be inoperative unless it shall have been ratified as an amendment to the Constitution by the legislatures of three-fourths of the several States within seven years from the date of its submission to the States by the Congress. [Ratified March 1, 1951]

Amendment [XXIII]

Section 1. The District constituting the seat of Government of the United States shall appoint in such manner as the Congress may direct:

A number of electors of President and Vice President equal to the whole number of Senators and Representatives in Congress to which the District would be entitled if it were a State, but in no event more than the least populous State; they shall be in addition to those appointed by the States, but they shall be considered, for the purposes of the election of President and Vice President, to be electors appointed by a State; and they shall meet in the District and perform such duties as provided by the twelfth article of amendment.

Section 2. The Congress shall have power to enforce this article by appropriate legislation.
[Ratified April 3, 1961]

Amendment [XXIV]

Section. 1. The right of citizens of the United States to vote in any primary or other election for President or Vice President, for electors for President or Vice President, or for Senator or Representative in Congress, shall not be denied or abridged by the United States or any State by reason of failure to pay any poll tax or other tax.

Section 2. The Congress shall have power to enforce this article by appropriate legislation.
[Ratified January 23, 1964]

Amendment [XXV]

Section 1. In case of the removal of the President from office or his death or resignation, the Vice President shall become President.

Section 2. Whenever there is a vacancy in the office of the Vice President, the President shall nominate a Vice President who shall take office upon confirmation by a majority vote of both houses of Congress.

Section 3. Whenever the President transmits to the President pro tempore of the Senate and the Speaker of the House of Representatives his written declaration that he is unable to discharge the powers and duties of his office, and until he transmits to them a written declaration to the contrary, such powers and duties shall be discharged by the Vice President as Acting President.

Section 4. Whenever the Vice President and a majority of either the principal officers of the executive department or of such other body as Congress may by law provide, transmit to the President pro tempore of the Senate and the Speaker of the House of Representatives their written declaration that the President is unable to discharge the powers and duties of his office, the

Vice President shall immediately assume the powers and duties of the office as Acting President.

Thereafter, when the President transmits to the President pro tempore of the Senate and the Speaker of the House of Representatives his written declaration that no inability exists, he shall resume the powers and duties of his office unless the Vice President and a majority of either the principal officers of the executive department or of such other body as Congress may by law provide, transmit within four days to the President pro tempore of the Senate and the Speaker of the House of Representatives their written declaration that the President is unable to discharge the powers and duties of his office. Thereupon Congress shall decide the issue, assembling within 48 hours for that purpose if not in session. If the Congress, within 21 days after receipt of the latter written declaration, or, if Congress is not in session, within 21 days after Congress is required to assemble, determines that the President is unable to discharge the powers and duties of his office, the Vice President shall continue to discharge the same as Acting President; otherwise, the President shall resume the powers and duties of his office.
[Ratified February 11, 1967]

Amendment [XXVI]

Section 1. The right of citizens of the United States, who are 18 years of age or older, to vote shall not be denied or abridged by the United States or any state on account of age.

Section 2. The Congress shall have the power to enforce this article by appropriate legislation.
[Ratified July 5, 1971]

Amendment [XXVII]

No law, varying the compensation for the services of the Senators and Representatives, shall take effect, until an election of Representatives shall have intervened.
[Ratified May 5, 1992]